Timeline

	1500	1600	1700
Africa	Portugal dominates East Africa, ca. 1500–1650 Height of Kanem-Bornu, 1571–1603	Dutch West India Co. supplants Portuguese in West Africa, ca. 1630 Dutch settle Cape Town, 1651	Rise of Ashanti Empire, ca. 1700
The Americas	Mesoamerican and South American holocaust, ca. 1500–1600 First African slaves brought to Americas, ca. 1510 Cortés arrives in Mexico, 1519; Aztec Empire falls, 1521 Pizarro reaches Peru, conquers Incas, 1531	British settle Jamestown, 1607; first plantations established Champlain founds Quebec, 1608 Dutch found New Amsterdam, 1624	Silver production quadruples in Mexico and Peru, ca. 1700–1800 Spain's defeat in War of the Spanish Succession results in colonial dependence on Spanish goods, ca. 1700–1800
Asia and Oceania	Babur defeats Delhi sultanate, 1526–1527; founds Mughal Empire Christian missionaries active in China and Japan, ca. 1550–1650 Akbar expands Mughal Empire, 1556–1605 Unification of Japan, 1568–1600 Spain conquers Philippines, 1571	Tokugawa Shogunate, 1600–1867 Height of Mughal Empire, 1628–1658 Japan expels all Europeans, 1637 Manchus establish Qing Dynasty, 1644–1911 British found Calcutta, 1690	Height of Edo urban culture in Japan, ca. 1700 Decline of Mughal Empire, ca. 1700–1800 Persian invaders loot Delhi, 1739 French and British fight for control of India, 1740–1763
Europe	Luther's Ninety-five Theses, 1517 Charles V elected Holy Roman emperor, 1519 English Reformation begins, 1532 Council of Trent, 1545–1563 Dutch declare independence, 1581 Spanish Armada, 1588	Thirty Years' War, 1618–1648 English civil war, 1642–1649 Growth of absolutism in central and eastern Europe, ca. 1680–1790 The Enlightenment, ca. 1680–1800 Ottomans besiege Vienna, 1683 Revocation of Edict of Nantes, 1685 Glorious Revolution in England, 1688	War of the Spanish Succession, 1701–1713 Peace of Utrecht, 1713 Cabinet system develops in England, 1714–1742
Middle East	Safavid Empire in Persia, 1501–1722 Peak of Ottoman power under Suleiman, 1520–1566 Battle of Lepanto, 1571 Height of Safavid Empire under Shah Abbas, 1587–1629		Decline of Safavid Empire under Nadir Shah, 1737–1747

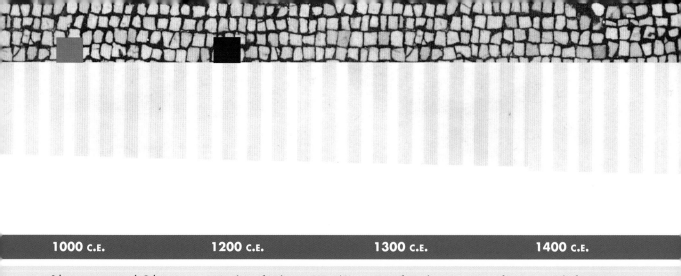

1000 C.E.	1200 C.E.	1300 C.E.	1400 C.E.
Islam penetrates sub-Saharan Africa, ca. 1000–1100	Kingdom of Mali, ca. 1200–1450	Rise of Yoruba states, West Africa, ca. 1300	Arrival of Portuguese in Benin, ca. 1440
Great Zimbabwe built, flourishes, ca. 1100–1400	Mongols conquer Baghdad, 1258; fall of Abbasid Dynasty	Height of Swahili (East African) city-states, ca. 1300–1500	Songhay Empire, ca. 1450–1591
Kingdom of Benin, ca. 1100–1897		Mansa Musa rules Mali, 1312–1337	Atlantic slave trade, ca. 1450–1850
			Da Gama reaches East Africa, 1498

Great Mosque at Kilwa: Karen Samson Photography

Manco Capac, first Inca king, ca. 1200

Inca civilization in South America, ca. 1000–1500		Aztecs arrive in Valley of Mexico, found Tenochtitlán (Mexico City), ca. 1325	Height of Inca Empire, 1438–1493
Toltec state collapses, 1174			Reign of Montezuma I, 1440–1468; height of Aztec culture
			Columbus reaches Americas, 1492

Vietnam gains independence from China, ca. 1000	Peak of Khmer Empire, ca. 1200	Ashikaga Shogunate, 1336–1408	Ming policy encourages foreign trade, ca. 1400–1500
Construction of Angkor Wat, ca. 1100–1150	Turkish sultanate at Delhi, 1206–1526	Hong Wu defeats Mongols, 1368; founds Ming Dynasty, 1368–1644	Ming maritime expeditions to India, Middle East, Africa, 1405–1433
China divided into Song, Jin empires, 1127	Mongols invade China, 1215	Tamerlane conquers the Punjab, 1398	Sultan Mehmed II, 1451–1481
Kamakura Shogunate, 1185–1333	Yuan (Mongol) Dynasty, 1271–1368		Da Gama reaches India, 1498
Muslim conquerors end Buddhism in India, 1192	Mongols invade Japan, 1274, 1281		
	Marco Polo arrives at Kublai Khan's court, ca. 1275		

Mongol horse and groom
National Palace Museum, Taipei, Taiwan

Yaroslav the Wise, 1019–1054; peak of Kievan Russia	Magna Carta, 1215	Babylonian Captivity of papacy, 1307–1377	Italian Renaissance, ca. 1400–1530
Latin, Greek churches split, 1054	Nevsky recognizes Mongol overlordship of Moscow, 1252	Tver revolt in Russia, 1327–1328	Voyagers of discovery, ca. 1450–1600
Norman Conquest of England, 1066	Aquinas, *Summa Theologica*, 1253	Hundred Years' War, 1337–1453	Ottomans capture Constantinople, 1453; end of Byzantine Empire
Investiture struggle, 1073–1122		Bubonic plague, 1347–1700	Wars of the Roses in England, 1453–1471
Crusades, 1096–1270		Beginnings of representative government, ca. 1350–1500	Unification of Spain completed, 1492
Growth of trade and towns, ca. 1100–1400			
Barbarossa invades Italy, 1154–1158			

Seljuk Turks take Baghdad, 1055	Mongol invasion of Middle East, ca. 1220	Ottomans invade Europe, 1356	Ottoman Empire, 1453–1918

1750	1800	1850	1900
British seize Cape Town, 1795 Napoleon's campaign in Egypt, 1798	Muhammad Ali founds dynasty in Egypt, 1805–1848 Slavery abolished in British Empire, 1807 Peak year of African transatlantic slave trade, 1820	Suez Canal opens, 1869 European "scramble for Africa," 1880–1900 Battle of Omdurman, 1898 South African War, 1899–1902	Union of South Africa formed, 1910 French annex Morocco, 1912 Ottoman Empire dissolved, 1919; Kemal's nationalist struggle in Turkey
"French and Indian Wars," 1756–1763 Quebec Act, 1774 American Revolution, 1775–1783 Comunero revolution, New Granada, 1781	Latin American wars of independence, 1806–1825 Brazil wins independence, 1822 Monroe Doctrine, 1823 Political instability in most Latin American countries, 1825–1870 U.S.-Mexican War, 1846–1848	U.S. Civil War, 1861–1865 British North America Act, 1867, for Canada Diaz controls Mexico, 1876–1911 Immigration from Europe and Asia to the Americas, 1880–1914 U.S. practices "dollar diplomacy" in Latin America, 1890–1920s Spanish-American War, 1898	Mexican Revolution, 1910 Panama Canal opens, 1914 Mexico adopts constitution, 1917
Height of Qing Empire, 1759 Treaty of Paris gives French colonies in India to Britain, 1763 Cook in Australia, 1768–1771 East India Act, 1784 First British convict-settlers arrive in Australia, 1788	British found Singapore, 1819 Java War, 1825–1830 Opium War, 1839–1842 Treaty of Nanjing, 1842: Manchus surrender Hong Kong to British British defeat last independent native state in India, 1848	Taiping Rebellion, 1850–1864 Perry opens Japan to trade, 1853 Great Rebellion in India, 1857–1858 Meiji Restoration in Japan, 1867 Indian National Congress, 1885 Japanese constitution, 1890 French acquire Indochina, 1893 Sino-Japanese War, 1894–1895 U.S. gains Philippines, 1898	Commonwealth of Australia, 1900 Boxer Rebellion, 1900–1903 Russo-Japanese War, 1904–1905 Muslim League formed, 1906 First calls for Indian independence, 1907 Chinese revolution; fall of Qing Dynasty, 1911 Chinese Republic, 1912–1949
Watt produces first steam engine, 1769 Outbreak of French Revolution, 1789 National Convention declares France a republic, 1792	Napoleonic Empire, 1804–1814 Congress of Vienna, 1814–1815 European economic penetration of non-Western countries, ca. 1816–1880 Greece wins independence, 1830 Revolution of 1848	Second Empire and Third Republic in France, 1852–1914 Unification of Italy, 1859–1870 Bismarck controls Germany, 1862–1890 Second Reform Bill, Great Britain, 1867 Franco-Prussian War, 1870–1871; foundation of the German Empire	Revolution in Russia; Tsar Nicholas II issues October Manifesto, 1905 Triple Entente (Britain, Russia, France), 1914–1918 World War I, 1914–1918 Treaty of Versailles, 1919
Selim III introduces administrative and military reforms, 1761–1808	Ottoman Empire launches Tanzimat reforms, 1839	Crimean War, 1853–1856	

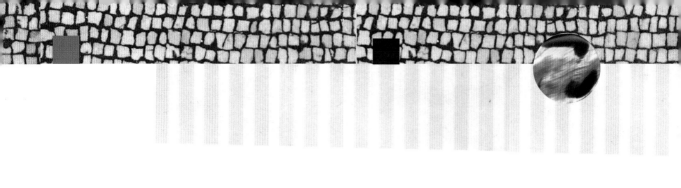

200 C.E.	**300** C.E.	**500** C.E.	**700** C.E.
Camel first used for trans-Saharan transport, ca. 200 Axum (Ethiopia) controls Red Sea trade, ca. 250	Axum accepts Christianity, ca. 300–400	Political and commercial ascendancy of Axum, ca. 500–700 African Mediterranean slave trade, ca. 600–1900	Berbers control trans-Saharan trade, ca. 700–900 Decline of Ethiopia, ca. 800–900 Kingdom of Ghana, ca. 900–1300

Maya palace doorway lintel.
© Justin Kerr 1985

	Maya civilization in Central America, ca. 300–1500 Classic period of Teotihuacán civilization in Mexico, ca. 300–900	Maya civilization reaches peak, ca. 600–900 Tiahuanaco civilization in South America, ca. 600–1000	Teotihuacán, Monte Alban destroyed, ca. 700 "Time of Troubles" in Mesoamerica, 800–1000 Toltec hegemony, ca. 980–1000

Creation of Yamato state in Japan, ca. 200–300 Buddhism gains popularity in China and Japan, ca. 220–590 Fall of Han Dynasty, 220; Period of Division, 220–589 Fall of the Parthian empire, rise of the Sasanids, ca. 225	Three Kingdoms Period in Korea, 313–668 China divides into northern, southern regimes, 316 Chandragupta I founds Gupta Dynasty in India, ca. 320–480 Gupta expansion, trade with Middle East and China, ca. 400 Huns invade India, ca. 450	Sui Dynasty restores order in China, 581–618 Sanskrit drama, ca. 600–1000 Shotoku's "Constitution" in Japan, 604 Tang Dynasty, 618–907; cultural flowering Taika Reforms in Japan, 646 Korea unified, 668	Nara era, creation of Japan's first capital, 710–794 Islam reaches India, 713 Heian era in Japan, 794–1185 Khmer Empire (Kampuchea) founded, 802 Era of the Five Dynasties in China, 907–960 Song Dynasty, 960–1279

Reforms by Diocletian, 284–305	Constantine, 306–337; Edict of Milan, 313; founding of Constantinople, 324; Council of Nicaea, 325 Christianity official state religion of Roman Empire, 380 Germanic raids on western Europe, 400s Clovis rules Gauls, 481–511	*Rule* of Saint Benedict, 529 *Code* of Justinian, 529 Synod of Whitby, 664	Charles Martel defeats Muslims at Tours, 732 Charlemagne rules, 768–814 Viking, Magyar invasions, 845–90• Treaty of Verdun divides Carolingian Empire, 843 Cluny monastery founded, 909

Benedict
Biblioteca Apostolica Vaticana

Sassanid Empire in Persia, 226–650		Muhammad, 570–632; the *hijra,* 622 Umayyad Dynasty, 661–750; continued expansion of Islam	Abbasid Dynasty, 750–1258; Islamic capital moved to Baghdad Golden age of Muslim learning, ca. 900–1100

1920	1940	1950	1960

Cultural nationalism in Africa, 1920s

African farmers organize first "cocoa holdups," 1930–1931

Apartheid system in South Africa, 1948–1991

Egypt declared a republic; Nasser named premier, 1954

Morocco, Tunisia, Sudan, and Ghana gain independence, 1956–1957

French-British Suez invasion, 1956

Mali, Nigeria, and the Congo gain independence, 1960

Biafra declares independence from Nigeria, 1967

U.S. "consumer revolution," 1920s

Stock market crash in U.S.; Great Depression begins, 1929

Revolutions in six South American countries, 1930

New Deal begins in United States, 1933

Surprise attack by Japan on Pearl Harbor, 1941

United Nations established, 1945

Perón rules Argentina, 1946–1953

Castro takes power in Cuba, 1959

Cuban missile crisis, 1962

Military dictatorship in Brazil, 1964–1985

United States escalates war in Vietnam, 1964

Kita Ikki advocates ultranationalism in Japan, 1923

Jiang Jieshi unites China, 1928

Gandhi's Salt March, 1930

Japan invades China, 1931

Mao Zedong's Long March, 1934

Sino-Japanese War, 1937–1945

Japan conquers Southeast Asia, 1939–1942

United States drops atomic bombs on Hiroshima and Nagasaki, 1945

Chinese civil war, 1945–1949; Communists win

Philippines gain independence, 1946

India (Hindu) and Pakistan (Muslim) gain independence, 1947

Japan begins long period of rapid economic growth, 1950

Korean War, 1950–1953

Vietnamese Nationalists defeat French; Vietnam divided, 1954

Islamic Republic of Pakistan declared, 1956

Mao Zedong announces Great Leap Forward, 1958

Sino-Soviet split becomes apparent, 1960

Great Proletarian Cultural Revolution in China, 1965–1969

Indira Gandhi prime minister of India, 1966–1977, 1980–1984

Mussolini seizes power in Italy, 1922

Stalin takes power in U.S.S.R., 1927

Great Depression, 1929–1933

Hitler gains power, 1933

Civil war in Spain, 1936–1939

World War II, 1939–1945

Marshall Plan, 1947

NATO formed, 1949

Soviet Union and Communist China sign 30-year alliance, 1949

Death of Stalin, 1953

Warsaw Pact, 1955

Revolution in Hungary, 1956

Common Market formed, 1957

Student revolution in France, 1968

Soviet invasion of Czechoslovakia, 1968

Brandt's Ostpolitik, 1969–1973

Yalta: F.D.R. Library

Czechs protest Soviet invasion: Bettmann/Corbis

Turkish Republic recognized, 1923

Reza Shah leads Iran, 1925–1941

Iraq gains independence, 1932

Suez crisis, 1956

Arabs and Jews at war in Palestine; Israel created, 1948

OPEC founded, 1960

Arab-Israeli Six-Day War, 1967

OF WORLD SOCIETIES:

McKay • Hill • Buckler • Ebrey • Beck • Crowston • Wiesner-Hanks

1000 B.C.E.	500 B.C.E.	250 B.C.E.	1 C.E.
Political fragmentation of Egypt; rise of small kingdoms, ca. 1100–700 Ironworking spreads throughout Africa, ca. 1000 B.C.E.–300 C.E. Persians conquer Egypt, 525	Death of Alexander, 323; Ptolemy conquers Egypt, Seleucus rules Asia	Scipio Africanus defeats Hannibal at Zama, 202 Meroë becomes iron-smelting center, 1st century B.C.E.	Expansion of Bantu-speaking peoples, ca. 100–900
Chavin civilization in Andes, ca. 1000–200 Olmec center at San Lorenzo destroyed, ca. 900; power passes to La Venta		Andean peoples intensify agriculture, ca. 200	Moche civilization flourishes in Peru, ca. 100–800

Fall of La Venta, 300; Tres Zapotes becomes leading Olmec site

Nok woman. National Museum, Lagos, Nigeria/Werner Forman Archive, Art Resource, NY

1000 B.C.E.	500 B.C.E.	250 B.C.E.	1 C.E.
Zhou Dynasty, ca. 1027–256 Later Vedic Age, solidification of caste system, ca. 1000–500 Upanishads; foundation of Hinduism, 700–500 Confucius, 551–479 Siddhartha Gautama (Buddha), 528–461 Persians conquer parts of India, 513	Warring States Period in China, 403–221 Zhuangzi and development of Daoism, 369–268 Alexander invades India, 327–326 Chandragupta founds Mauryan Dynasty, 322–ca. 185 Ashoka, 269–232	Qin Dynasty unifies China; Great Wall begun, 221–210 Han Dynasty, 206 B.C.E.–220 C.E. Greeks invade India, ca. 183–145 Silk Road opens to Parthia, Rome; Buddhism enters China, ca. 104 Bhagavad Gita, ca. 100 B.C.E.–100 C.E.	First (Chinese) written reference to Japan, 45 C.E. Shakas and Kushans invade eastern Parthia and India, 1st century C.E. Kushan rule in northwestern India, ca. 100–300 Chinese invent paper, 105 Roman attacks on Parthian empire, 115–211
Greek Lyric Age; rise of Sparta and Athens, 800–500 Origin of Greek polis, ca. 700 Roman Republic founded, 509	Persian Wars, 499–479 Athenian Empire, flowering of art and philosophy, 5th century Peloponnesian War, 431–404 Roman expansion, 390–146 Conquests of Alexander the Great, 334–323 Punic Wars, destruction of Carthage, 264–146	Late Roman Republic, 133–27 Julius Caesar killed, 44 Octavian seizes power, rules imperial Rome as Augustus, 27 B.C.E.–14 C.E.	Roman Empire at greatest extent 117 Breakdown of pax Romana, ca. 180–284
Assyrian Empire, 900–612 Zoroaster, ca. 600 Babylonian captivity of Hebrews, 586–539 Cyrus the Great founds Persian Empire, 550 Darius and Xerxes complete Persian conquest of Middle East, 521–464	Alexander the Great extends empire, 334–331	Arsaces of Parthia begins conquest of Persia, ca. 250–137 Pompey conquers Syria and Palestine, 63	Jesus Christ, ca. 4 B.C.E.–30 C.E. Jews revolt; Romans destroy temple in Jerusalem: end of Hebrew state, 70

National Museum, inari/Art Resource, NY

A HISTORY O
A BRIEF OVERVIEW

	10,000 B.C.E.	2500 B.C.E.	1500 B.C.E.
Africa	New Stone Age culture, ca. 10,000–3500 Farming begins in Nile River Valley, ca. 6000 Unification of Egypt, 3100–2660	Bantu migrations throughout western Africa, ca. 2000–500 Egypt's Old Kingdom, 2660–2180 Egypt's Middle Kingdom, 2080–1640 Hyksos "invade" Egypt, 1640–1570	Egypt's New Kingdom; Egyptian empire, ca. 1570–1075 Akhenaten institutes worship of Aton, ca. 1360
The Americas	Migration into Americas begins, ca. 20,000 Maize domesticated in Mexico, ca. 5000 First pottery in Americas, Ecuador, ca. 3000	First metalworking in Peru, ca. 2000	Olmec civilization, Mexico, ca. 1500 B.C.E.–300 C.E.
Asia and Oceania	Farming begins in Yellow River Valley, ca. 4000 Indus River Valley civilization, ca. 2800–1800; capitals at Mohenjo-daro and Harappa	Horse domesticated in China, ca. 2500	Shang Dynasty, first writing in China, ca. 1500–ca. 1050 Aryans arrive in India; Early Vedic Age, ca. 1500–1000 Vedas, oldest Hindu sacred texts, ca. 1500–500
Europe	New Stone Age culture, ca. 10,000–3500	Greek Bronze Age, 2000–1100 Height of Minoan culture, 1700–1450 Arrival of Greeks in peninsular Greece, ca. 1650	Mycenaeans conquer Minoan Crete, ca. 1450 Mycenaean Age, 1450–1200 Trojan War, ca. 1180 Greek Dark Age, ca. 1100–800
Middle East	Farming begins in Tigris-Euphrates River Valley, ca. 6000 First writing in Sumeria; city-states emerge, ca. 3500	Akkadian empire, ca. 2331–2200 Hammurabi, 1792–1750 Hebrew monotheism, ca. 1700	Hittite Empire, ca. 1475–1200 Moses leads Hebrews out of Egypt, ca. 1300–1200 United Hebrew kingdom, 1020–922

Neolithic jade plaque: Zhejiang Provincial Institute of Archaeology/ Cultural Relics Publishing House

1970	1980	1990	2000

Nelson Mandela Mohamed Lounes/Gamma

South African president Frederik de Klerk legalizes African National Congress, 1989

Nelson Mandela freed, 1990

Growth of Islamic fundamentalism, 1990 to present

Nelson Mandela elected president of South Africa, 1994

Rwandan genocide, 1994

AIDS epidemic, 2000 to present

Civil war and genocide in Darfur, 2003 to present

Zimbabwean President Robert Mugabe increases violence against opponents after losing election, 2008

Military coup in Chile, 1973

U.S. Watergate scandal, 1974

Revolutions in Nicaragua and El Salvador, 1979

U.S. military buildup, 1980–1988

Argentina restores civilian rule, 1983

Canada, Mexico, and United States form free-trade area (NAFTA), 1994

Haiti establishes democratic government, 1994

Permanent extension of Treaty on the Non-Proliferation of Nuclear Weapons, 1995

Terrorist attack on United States, September 11, 2001

Space shuttle *Columbia* explodes, 2003

Hurricanes Katrina and Rita ravage Gulf Coast of U.S., 2005

Raúl Castro succeeds his ailing brother Fidel as president of Cuba, 2008

India-Pakistan war, 1971

Communist victory in Vietnam War, 1975

China pursues modernization, 1976 to present

Chinese invade Vietnam, 1979

Japanese foreign investment surge, 1980–1992

Sikh nationalism in India, 1984 to present

China crushes democracy movement, 1989

Chinese students in 1989 Erika Lansner/Stockphoto.com

Economic growth and political repression in China, 1990 to present

Vietnam embraces foreign investment, 1990 to present

U.S. military bases closed in Philippines, 1991

Hong Kong returns to Chinese rule, 1997

China joins WTO, 2001

India and Pakistan come close to all-out war, 2002

Tsunami in Southeast Asia, 2004

North Korea dismantles nuclear facilities, 2007

Cyclone Nargis in Myanmar (Burma), 2008

8.0 magnitude earthquake in Sichuan Province, China, 2008

Helsinki Accord on human rights, 1975

Soviet invasion of Afghanistan, 1979

Soviet reform under Gorbachev, 1985–1991

Communism falls in eastern Europe, 1989–1990

Maastricht treaty proposes monetary union, 1990

Conservative economic policies, 1990s

End of Soviet Union, 1991

Civil war in Bosnia, 1991–1995

Creation of European Union, 1993

Euro note enters circulation, 2002

Madrid train bombing, 2004

Chechen terrorists take Russian schoolchildren hostage, 2004

London subway and bus bombing, 2005

"Yom Kippur War," 1973

Islamic revolution in Iran, 1979

Camp David Accords, 1979

Iran-Iraq War, 1980–1988

Growth of Islamic fundamentalism, 1990 to present

Iraq driven from Kuwait by United States and allies, 1991

Israel and Palestinians sign peace agreement, 1993

Assassination of Israeli prime minister Yitzak Rabin, 1995

Israel begins construction of West Bank barrier, 2003

Wars in Iraq and Afghanistan, 2003 to present

Iran advances nuclear energy program, 2004 to present

Benazir Bhutto assassinated, 2007

A HISTORY OF
WORLD SOCIETIES

A HISTORY OF WORLD SOCIETIES

Volume A
From Antiquity to 1500

eighth
edition

John P. McKay
University of Illinois at Urbana-Champaign

Bennett D. Hill
Late of Georgetown University

John Buckler
University of Illinois at Urbana-Champaign

Patricia Buckley Ebrey
University of Washington

Roger B. Beck
Eastern Illinois University

Clare Haru Crowston
University of Illinois at Urbana-Champaign

Merry E. Wiesner-Hanks
University of Wisconsin–Milwaukee

BEDFORD / ST. MARTIN'S
Boston · New York

FOR BEDFORD/ST. MARTIN'S

Publisher for History: Mary Dougherty
Executive Editor for History: Traci Mueller
Director of Development for History: Jane Knetzger
Executive Marketing Manager: Jenna Bookin Barry
Copyeditor: Sybil Sosin
Proofreader: Angela Hoover Morrison
Text Design and Page Layout: Janet Theurer
Photo Research: Carole Frohlich
Indexer: Leoni McVey
Cover Design: Donna Lee Dennison
Cover Art: Ay performing the opening of the mouth ceremony on the mummy of Tutankhamun
   (ca. 1370–1352 B.C.E.), from the Tomb of Tutankhamun, Valley of the Kings, Thebes, Egypt.
   New Kingdom (wall painting). © The Bridgeman Art Library.
Cartography: Charlotte Miller/GeoNova
Composition: NK Graphics
Printing and Binding: R.R. Donnelley & Sons Company

President: Joan E. Feinberg
Editorial Director: Denise B. Wydra
Director of Marketing: Karen R. Soeltz
Director of Editing, Design, and Production: Marcia Cohen
Assistant Director of Editing, Design, and Production: Elise S. Kaiser
Managing Editor: Elizabeth M. Schaaf

Library of Congress Control Number: 2008933879

Manufactured in the United States of America.

3   2   1   0
f   e   d   c   b

For information, write: Bedford/St. Martin's, 75 Arlington Street, Boston, MA 02116 (617-399-4000)

ISBN-10: 0–312–68293–X   ISBN-13: 978–0–312–68293–4   (combined edition)
ISBN-10: 0–312–68294–8   ISBN-13: 978–0–312–68294–1   (Vol. I)
ISBN-10: 0–312–68295–6   ISBN-13: 978–0–312–68295–8   (Vol. II)
ISBN-10: 0–312–68296–4   ISBN-13: 978–0–312–68296–5   (Vol. A)
ISBN-10: 0–312–68297–2   ISBN-13: 978–0–312–68297–2   (Vol. B)
ISBN-10: 0–312–68298–0   ISBN-13: 978–0–312–68298–9   (Vol. C)

Preface

In this age of a global environment and global warming, of a global economy and global banking, of global migration and rapid global travel, of global sports and global popular culture, the study of world history becomes more urgent. Surely, an appreciation of other, and earlier, societies helps us to understand better our own and to cope more effectively in pluralistic cultures worldwide. The large numbers of Turks living in Germany, of Italians, Hungarians, and Slavic peoples living in Australia, of Japanese living in Peru and Argentina, and of Arabs, Mexicans, Chinese, and Filipinos living in the United States—to mention just a few obvious examples—represent diversity on a global scale. The movement of large numbers of peoples from one continent to another goes back thousands of years, at least as far back as the time when peoples migrated from Asia into the Americas. Swift air travel and the Internet have accelerated these movements, and they testify to the incredible technological changes the world has experienced in the last half of the twentieth century and beginning of the twenty-first.

For most peoples, the study of history has traditionally meant the study of their own national, regional, and ethnic pasts. Fully appreciating the great differences among various societies and the complexity of the historical problems surrounding these cultures, we have wondered if the study of local or national history is sufficient for people who will spend their lives in the twenty-first century on one small interconnected planet. The authors of this book believe the study of world history in a broad and comparative context is an exciting, important, and highly practical pursuit. It is our conviction, based on considerable experience in introducing large numbers of students to the broad sweep of world history, that a book reflecting current trends can excite readers and inspire an enduring interest in the long human experience. Our strategy has been twofold.

First, we have made social history the core element of our work. We not only incorporate recent research by social historians but also seek to re-create the life of ordinary people in appealing human terms. A strong social element seems especially appropriate in a world history text, for identification with ordinary men and women of the past allows today's reader to reach an empathetic understanding of different cultures. At the same time we have been mindful of the need to give great economic, political, intellectual, and cultural developments the attention they deserve. We want to give individual students and instructors a balanced, integrated perspective so that they can pursue on their own or in the classroom those themes and questions that they find particularly exciting and significant.

Second, we have made every effort to strike an effective global balance. We are acutely aware of the great drama of our times—the passing of the era of Western dominance and the increasing complexity in lines of political, economic, and cultural power and influence. Today the whole world interacts, and to understand that interaction and what it means for today's citizens, we must study the whole world's history. Thus we have adopted a comprehensive yet manageable global perspective. We study all geographical areas, conscious of the separate histories of many parts of the world, particularly in the earliest millennia of human development. We also stress the links among cultures, political units, and economic systems, for it is these connections and interactions that have made the world what it is today.

Changes in the Eighth Edition

In preparing the Eighth Edition of this book, we have worked hard to keep our book up-to-date and to strengthen our distinctive yet balanced approach.

Organizational Changes

Responding to the wishes of many of the faculty who use this book, we have shortened the text significantly. The narrative has been tightened in each chapter, and the consolidations improve the overall global balance of our work.

In addition, several chapters have been extensively reorganized. Merry Wiesner-Hanks from the University of Wisconsin-Milwaukee and Clare Crowston from the University of Illinois joined the author team with this edition, taking responsibility for Chapters 7, 10, 13, and 14 and Chapters 15–17 and 21, respectively. Chapter 7, "Europe and Western Asia, ca. 350–850," has a broader geographic focus, with more material on the Byzantine Empire and the various migrating peoples. Former Chapter 13 on the Americas has been brought into the story earlier as new Chapter 10, and the chapter has been rewritten to reflect the newest scholarship on early cultures of North America, Mesoamerica, and South America. Discussion of the Thirty Years' War has been integrated into Chapter 16, allowing a better assessment of its impact on state-building, along with broader coverage of economic and demographic trends. Other chapters have been restructured as well. Chapter 19, "The Islamic World Powers, ca. 1400–1800," has been completely reorganized to highlight parallels among the Ottoman, Safavid, and Mughal Empires in terms of political, cultural, and economic developments. Reflecting current understandings of the connections around the Atlantic world, Chapter 21 includes extensive discussion of the Haitian Revolution along with the American and French Revolutions. Chapter 26, "Nation Building in the Western Hemisphere and Australia," contains a new section that places the nations in comparative perspective. In addition, former chapters 33 and 34 are now combined as a new and streamlined Chapter 33, "A New Era in World History." The new chapter focuses on global political and economic issues (such as the United Nations, terrorism, globalization and its consequences, and vital resources), plus global issues that affect individuals (such as poverty, disease, urbanization, and education), and shows how they evolved over the course of the twentieth century. "The Middle East in Today's World," a supplement to later printings of the seventh edition, has been updated to reflect recent developments in the Middle East, and is now the Epilogue.

Geographical and Gender Issues

In previous editions we added significantly more discussion of groups and regions that are often shortchanged in the general histories of world civilizations, and we have continued to do so in this new revision. This expanded scope reflects the renewed awareness within the historical profession of the enormous diversity of the world's peoples. Examples include more material on the Etruscans in Chapter 5, the Huns in Chapter 7, and the Turks in Chapter 8. Chapter 10 includes increased discussion of the Hohokam, Hopewell, and Mississippian peoples in North America and of pre-Inca cultures in Peru. Study of the Mongols and other peoples of Central Asia has exploded in the past several years, which has shaped the changes in Chapter 11. Chapter 17 includes a new discussion of new ideas about race during the Enlightenment. Chapter 21 has considerable new material on the Haitian Revolution. Overall, an expanded treatment of non-European societies and cultures has been achieved.

In addition, we have continued to include updated and expanded material relating to gender in nearly every chapter, incorporating insights from women's history, the history of sexuality, the history of the family, and the new history of masculinities. Chapter 4 includes revised coverage of Greek sexuality and the family, with new focus in Chapter 7 on the role of women in barbarian society, Chapter 8 on women in classical Islamic society, Chapter 12 on women's lives in Song China, Chapter 14 on gender hierarchies in Renaissance Europe and on the Reformation and marriage, Chapter 18 on women, marriage, and work in early modern Africa, Chapter 22 on the sexual division of labor in the Industrial Revolution, and Chapter 33 on women's rights and feminist movements. In addition to "Individuals in Society" features from previous editions that focus on the lives of specific women, several new ones have been added: the feature in Chapter 1 focuses on the Egyptian monarch Nefertiti, in Chapter 7 on Empress Theodora of Constantinople, in Chapter 13 on the Christian abbess Hildegard of Bingen, and in Chapter 16 on the Jewish merchant and diarist Glückel of Hameln. Chapter 8 includes a new "Listening to the Past" feature on the etiquette of marriage in the Islamic world.

Cross-Cultural Comparisons and Connections

In this edition we have continued to expand our comparative coverage to help students see and understand the cross-cultural connections of world history. Chapter 2 offers expanded discussion of trading networks in early India, and both Chapters 5 and 6 provide enhanced discussion of the Silk Road. Chapter 7 includes a reframed discussion of the barbarian migrations into Europe. Chapter 8 addresses new questions such as "How were the Muslim lands governed and what new challenges did they face?" and "What social distinctions were important in Muslim society?" Updated treatment of the trans-Saharan trade appears in Chapter 9, and Chapter 10 now discusses trade along the rivers and lakes of North America. Chapter 15 has been extensively rewritten, with a new section on global economies, forced migrations, and cultural encounters. Chapter 24 addresses the important question "What were the global consequences of European industrialization between 1800 and 1914?"

Incorporation of Recent Scholarship

As in previous revisions we have made a serious effort to keep our book fresh and up-to-date by incorporating new and important scholarship throughout the Eighth Edition. Chapter 4 includes new findings about the role of women in religious movements in the ancient world, including Christianity. Chapter 7 highlights the continuing significance of the Byzantines and the transformations brought through barbarian migrations. Chapter 10 features innovative research on agricultural communities in the Americas and the connections among them. New sections on popular religion and social hierarchies appear in Chapters 13 and 14. Chapters 14 and 17 include sections derived from the new scholarship on changing conceptions of race. Chapter 17 also draws upon new work about the emergence of the public sphere in Enlightenment Europe to discuss the political and social implications of intellectual change. Chapter 20 features new treatment of maritime East Asia. Chapter 26 includes a new comparative discussion of the incorporation of the nations of the Americas into the world economy. Material in the final three chapters and the Epilogue has been updated to ensure a clear account of contemporary world history. Thus, the text includes discussion of such events as the unfolding war in Iraq, the worsening crisis in Afghanistan, Hezbollah's revival in Lebanon, moves toward peace in Israel, elections in Zimbabwe, charges of genocide against the Sudanese president, China and Tibet and the 2008 Olympics, and North Korea's dismantling of its nuclear facilities. In sum, we have tried hard to bring new research and interpretation into our global history, believing it essential to keep our book stimulating, accurate, and current for students and instructors.

Revised Full-Color Art and Map Program

Finally, the illustrative component of our work has been carefully revised. We have added many new illustrations to our extensive art program, which includes over three hundred color reproductions, thus highlighting the connections among art, material culture, events, and social changes. Illustrations have been selected to support and complement the text, and, wherever possible, illustrations are contemporaneous with the textual material discussed. Considerable research went into many of the captions in order to make them as informative as possible. We have reflected on the observation that "there are more valid facts and details in works of art than there are in history books," and we would modify it to say that art is "a history book." Artwork remains an integral part of our book; the past can speak in pictures as well as in words. The maps have been completely redesigned and revised in this edition to be more dynamic, engaging, and relevant than ever before. The use of full color serves to clarify the maps and graphs and to enrich the textual material. The maps and map captions have been updated to correlate directly to the text.

Distinctive Features

Distinctive features from earlier editions guide the reader in the process of historical understanding. Many of these features also show how historians sift through and evaluate evidence. Our goal is to suggest how historians actually work and think. We want the reader to think critically and to realize that history is neither a list of cut-and-dried facts nor a senseless jumble of conflicting opinions.

"Individuals in Society" Feature

The Eighth Edition presents eight new short studies of a fascinating woman or man, which are carefully integrated into the main discussion of the text. This "Individuals in Society" feature grew out of our long-standing focus on people's lives and the varieties of historical experience, and we believe that readers will empathize with these flesh-and-blood human beings as they themselves seek to define their own identities today. The spotlighting of individuals, both famous and obscure, carries forward the greater attention to cultural and intellectual developments that we have used to invigorate our social history, and it reflects changing interests within the historical profession as well as the development of "micro history."

The men and women included in the Eighth Edition represent a wide range of careers and personalities. Several are renowned historical or present-day figures, such as Plutarch, the Greek historian and biographer (Chapter 5); Amda Siyon, probably the most important ruler of Ethiopia's Solomonic dynasty (Chapter 9); Giuseppe Garibaldi, the flamboyant, incorruptible popular hero of Italy's national unification (Chapter 23); and the Dalai Lama, exiled spiritual leader of a captive nation (Chapter 33). Two individuals were brilliant writers who testified to tragedy and calamitous destruction: Vera Brittain, an English nurse on the frontlines in World War I (Chapter 27); and Primo Levi, an Italian Jewish chemist who survived the Holocaust and probed the horrors of the death camps (Chapter 30). Others are lesser-known individuals, yet highly accomplished in their own societies and time, such as the Ban family from China, who were influential in the military, government, and literary fields (Chapter 6); Bhaskara, the Indian astronomer and mathematician who published many books in those fields (Chapter 11); Tan Yunxian, a Chinese female doctor who devoted her practice to the treatment of women (Chapter 20); and José Rizal, a Philippine nationalist and author (Chapter 25).

"Listening to the Past" Feature

A two-page excerpt from a primary source concludes each chapter. This signature feature, entitled "Listening to the Past," extends and illuminates a major historical issue considered in the chapter. Each primary source opens with a problem-setting introduction and closes with "Questions for Analysis" that invite students to evaluate the evidence as historians would. Drawn from a range of writings addressing a variety of social, cultural, political, and intellectual issues, these sources promote active involvement and critical interpretation. Selected for their interest and importance and carefully fitted into their historical context, these sources do indeed allow the student to "listen to the past" and to observe how history has been shaped by individual men and women, some of them great aristocrats, others ordinary folk.

"Global Trade" Feature

In the form of two-page essays that focus on a particular commodity, this popular feature explores the world trade, social and economic impact, and cultural influence of that commodity. Each essay is accompanied by a detailed map showing the trade routes of the commodity. Retaining the seven essays of the previous edition on pottery, silk, tea, slaves, indigo, oil, and arms, we added one on spices in Chapter 11. We believe that careful attention to all of these essays will enable the student to appreciate the complex ways in which trade has connected and influenced the various parts of the world.

Improved Pedagogy

To help make the narrative accessible to students, we have put a number of pedagogical features in the text. At the start of each chapter, an outline of the major section titles provides students with a brief preview of the chapter coverage. Also at the beginning of each chapter, we pose specific historical questions to help guide the reader toward understanding. These questions are then answered in the course of the chapter, and each chapter concludes with a concise summary of its findings. All of the questions and summaries have been re-examined and frequently revised in order to maximize their usefulness.

Throughout the chapter we have highlighted in boldface the major terms with which a student should become familiar. These Key Terms are then listed at the conclusion of the chapter. The student may use these terms to test his or her understanding of the chapter's material. A complete list of the Key Terms and definitions is also provided on the student website, along with electronic flashcards that allow students to quiz themselves on their mastery of the terms.

In addition to posing chapter-opening questions and presenting more problems in historical interpretation, we have quoted extensively from a wide variety of primary sources in the narrative, demonstrating in our use of these quotations how historians evaluate evidence. Thus primary sources are examined as an integral part of the narrative as well as presented in extended form in the "Listening to the Past" chapter feature. We believe that such an extensive program of both integrated and separate primary source excerpts will help readers learn to interpret and think critically.

Each chapter concludes with a Summary section and carefully selected suggestions for further reading. These suggestions are briefly described to help readers know where to turn to continue thinking and learning about the world. Also, chapter bibliographies have been thoroughly revised and updated to keep them current with the vast amount of new work being done in many fields.

Revised Timelines

To better present the flow of critical developments, the comparative timelines of earlier editions have been converted into chapter chronologies in each chapter. The extended comparative timeline has been moved to the front of the book and is now a perforated foldout poster. Comprehensive and easy to locate, this useful timeline poster allows students to compare simultaneous political, economic, social, cultural, intellectual, and scientific developments over the centuries.

Flexible Format

World history courses differ widely in chronological structure from one campus to another. To accommodate the various divisions of historical time into intervals that fit a two-quarter, three-quarter, or two-semester period, *A History of World Societies* is published in three versions that embrace the complete work:

- One-volume hardcover edition: *A History of World Societies* (Chapters 1–33 and Epilogue)
- Two-volume paperback edition: *Volume I: To 1715* (Chapters 1–16); and *Volume II: Since 1500* (Chapters 15–33 and Epilogue)
- Three-volume paperback edition: *Volume A: From Antiquity to 1500* (Chapters 1–13); *Volume B: From 800 to 1815* (Chapters 10–21); and *Volume C: From 1775 to the Present* (Chapters 21–33 and Epilogue)

Overlapping chapters in two-volume and three-volume editions facilitate matching the appropriate volume with the opening and closing dates of a specific course. In addition, this title is available as an e-Book.

Ancillaries

We are pleased to introduce a full ancillary package that will help students in learning and instructors in teaching:

*A **History of World Societies** e-Book,* an electronic version of the eighth edition, presents the complete text of the print book, with easy-to-use highlighting, searching, and note-taking tools, at a significantly reduced price.

The new print reader, *Sources of World Societies,* provides a broad selection of over 140 primary source documents as well as editorial apparatus to facilitate student analysis. Available free when packaged with the text.

The free **Online Study Guide at bedfordstmartins .com/mckayworld** features a wide array of review materials that include audio chapter summaries, learning objectives, chapter outlines, pre-class quizzes, and other self-testing material such as interactive flashcards and chronological ordering exercises. Students can also find an online glossary and many of the primary sources printed in the accompanying reader.

The **Instructor's Resource Manual** at bedfordstmartins.com/mckayworld/catalog contains advice on teaching the world history course, instructional objectives, chapter outlines, lecture suggestions, paper and class activity topics, primary source and map activities, and suggestions for cooperative learning.

The **Instructor's Resource CD-ROM** features *PowerPoint* maps and images from the text for use in classroom presentations as well as questions and answers for use with personal response system software and blank outline maps.

The **Computerized Test Bank** offers over 80 exercises per chapter, including multiple-choice, map, and short and long essay questions. The answer key includes model essay responses. Instructors can customize quizzes, add or edit both questions and answers, and export questions to a variety of formats, including WebCT and Blackboard.

Make History at bedfordstmartins.com/mckayworld provides one-stop access to relevant digital content including maps, images, documents, and Web links. Students and instructors can browse this free database by topic, date, or resource type, download content, and create collections.

A variety of the student and instructor resources developed for this textbook are ready for use in **course management systems** such as WebCT and Blackboard.

Packaging Opportunities

In addition, instructors have numerous options for packaging Bedford/St. Martin's titles with *A History of World Societies* for free or at a discount.

The primary source reader **Sources of World History** described above, the **Rand McNally Historical Atlas of the World,** and the **Bedford Glossary for World History** are free when packaged with the text, as is **World History Matters: A Student Guide to World History Online,** which is based on the popular "World History Matters" websites produced by the Center for History and New Media at George Mason University.

Over 100 titles in the **Bedford Series in History and Culture** combine first-rate scholarship, historical narrative, and important primary documents for undergraduate courses. Each book is brief, inexpensive, and focused on a specific topic or period. Package discounts are available.

Trade books published by Farrar, Straus and Giroux; Henry Holt and Company; Hill and Wang; Picador;

St. Martin's Press; and Palgrave Macmillan are available at a 50 percent discount when packaged with Bedford/St. Martin's textbooks. For more information, visit **bedfordstmartins.com/tradeup**.

Acknowledgments

It is a pleasure to thank the many instructors who have read and critiqued the manuscript throughout its development:

Wayne Ackerson
Salisbury University

Edward M. Anson
University of Arkansas at Little Rock

Beau Bowers
Central Piedmont Community College

Eric Dorn Brose
Drexel University

Erwin F. Erhardt III
Thomas More College

Dolores Grapsas
New River Community College

Candace Gregory-Abbott
California State University, Sacramento

Roger Hall
Allan Hancock College

John Jovan Markovic
Andrews University

Christopher E. Mauriello
Salem State College

Michael G. Murdock
Brigham Young University

Phyllis E. Pobst
Arkansas State University

Thomas Saylor
Concordia University

Jason M. Stratton
Bakersfield College

Ruth Smith Truss
University of Montevallo

Claude Welch
State University of New York at Buffalo

It is also a pleasure to thank our editors for their efforts over many years. To Christina Horn, who guided production, and to Tonya Lobato, our development editor, we express our admiration and special appreciation. And we thank Carole Frohlich for her contributions in photo research and selection.

Many of our colleagues at the University of Illinois, University of Washington, Eastern Illinois University, and the University of Wisconsin–Milwaukee continue to provide information and stimulation, often without even knowing it. We thank them for it.

Each of us has benefited from the criticism of his or her coauthors, although each of us assumes responsibility for what he or she has written. John Buckler has written Chapters 1, 4, and 5. Patricia Buckley Ebrey has written or updated Chapters 2–3, 6, 8, 11–12, 19–20, and 25–26. Bennett Hill originally conceived the narrative for Chapters 7–9, 12–15, 18–20, and 26; since his untimely death his coauthors have taken on his chapters. In this edition new coauthor Merry Wiesner-Hanks handled Chapters 7, 10, 13, and 14; and new coauthor Clare Crowston handled Chapters 15–17 and 21. Roger Beck contributed to Chapters 9 and 18 and handled Chapters 27–33 in this edition. Roger Beck also wrote the Epilogue. John McKay originally wrote the narrative for Chapters 16–17, 21–24, and 27–30, and he continues to take responsibility for Chapters 22–24 in this edition. Finally, we continue to welcome the many comments and suggestions that have come from our readers, for they have helped us greatly in this ongoing endeavor.

J.P.M.

J.B.

P.B.E.

R.B.B.

C.H.C.

M.W-H.

Brief Contents

Contents

Maps

Listening to the Past

Individuals in Society

About the Authors

JOHN P. MᶜKAY Born in St. Louis, John P. McKay received his B.A. from Wesleyan University (1961), his M.A. from the Fletcher School of Law and Diplomacy (1962), and his Ph.D. from the University of California, Berkeley (1968). He began teaching history at the University of Illinois in 1966 and became a Professor there in 1976. John won the Herbert Baxter Adams Prize for his book *Pioneers for Profit: Foreign Entrepreneurship and Russian Industrialization, 1885–1913* (1970). He has also written *Tramways and Trolleys: The Rise of Urban Mass Transport in Europe* (1976) and has translated Jules Michelet's *The People* (1973). His research has been supported by fellowships from the Ford Foundation, the Guggenheim Foundation, the National Endowment for the Humanities, and IREX. He has written well over a hundred articles, book chapters, and reviews, which have appeared in numerous publications, including *The American Historical Review, Business History Review, The Journal of Economic History,* and *Slavic Review.* He contributed extensively to C. Stewart and P. Fritzsche, eds., *Imagining the Twentieth Century* (1997).

BENNETT D. HILL A native of Philadelphia, Bennett D. Hill earned an A.B. from Princeton (1956) and advanced degrees from Harvard (A.M., 1958) and Princeton (Ph.D., 1963). He taught history at the University of Illinois, where he was department chair from 1978 to 1981. He published *English Cistercian Monasteries and Their Patrons in the Twelfth Century* (1968), *Church and State in the Middle Ages* (1970), and articles in *Analecta Cisterciensia, The New Catholic Encyclopaedia, The American Benedictine Review,* and *The Dictionary of the Middle Ages.* His reviews appeared in *The American Historical Review, Speculum, The Historian,* the *Journal of World History,* and *Library Journal.* He was one of the contributing editors to *The Encyclopedia of World History* (2001). He was a Fellow of the American Council of Learned Societies and served on the editorial board of *The American Benedictine Review,* on committees of the National Endowment for the Humanities, and as vice president of the American Catholic Historical Association (1995–1996). A Benedictine monk of St. Anselm's Abbey in Washington, D.C., he was also a Visiting Professor at Georgetown University.

JOHN BUᶜKLER Born in Louisville, Kentucky, John Buckler received his Ph.D. from Harvard University in 1973. In 1980 Harvard University Press published his *Theban Hegemony, 371–362 B.C.* He published *Philip II and the Sacred War* (Leiden 1989) and also edited *BOIOTIKA: Vorträge vom 5. Internationalen Böotien-Kolloquium* (Munich 1989). In 2003 he published *Aegean Greece in the Fourth Century B.C.* In the following year appeared his editions of W. M. Leake, *Travels in the Morea* (three volumes), and Leake's *Peloponnesiaca.* Cambridge University Press published his *Central Greece and the Politics of Power in the Fourth Century BC,* edited by Hans Beck, in 2008.

PATRIᶜIA BUᶜKLEY EBREY Born in Hasbrouck Heights, New Jersey, Patricia Ebrey received her A.B. from the University of Chicago in 1968 and her Ph.D. from Columbia University in 1975. She taught Asian history and culture at the University of Illinois for twenty years before moving to the University of Washington in 1997. Her research has been supported by fellowships from the American Council of Learned Societies, the National Endowment for the Humanities, the Guggenheim Foundation, and the Chiang Ching-Kuo Foundation. Probably the best known of her many books are *Chinese Civilization: A Sourcebook* (1981, 1993), *The Inner Quarters: Marriage and the Lives of Chinese Women in the Sung Period* (1993) (which won the Levenson Prize of the Association for Asian Studies), and *The Cambridge Illustrated History of China* (1996). *East Asia: A Cultural, Social, and Political History,* coauthored with Anne Walthall and James Palais, is now in its second edition.

ROGER B. BEᶜK An Indiana native, Roger B. Beck received his B.A. from the University of Evansville (1969), and an M.S. in social studies education (1977), M.A. in history (1979), and Ph.D. in African history (1987) from Indiana University. He taught history at international schools in Paris, Tokyo, and London for six years and was a visiting lecturer at the University of Cape Town in 1981. He has taught at Eastern Illinois University since 1987, where he is Distinguished Professor of African, World, and Twentieth-century World History. His publications include *The History of South Africa* (2000), a translation of P. J. van der Merwe's *The Migrant Farmer in the History of the Cape Colony, 1657–1842,* and more than seventy-five articles, book chapters, and reviews. He is a senior consultant to McDougal Littell's widely used high school text *World History: Patterns of Interaction,* now in its third edition. He is the recipient of two Fulbright fellowships. He has been an active member of the World Hisvtory Association for nearly twenty years, including serving a term on the executive council and as treasurer for six years.

CLARE HARU CROWSTON Born in Cambridge, Massachusetts, and raised in Toronto, Clare Haru Crowston received her B.A. in 1985 from McGill University and her Ph.D. in 1996 from Cornell University. Since 1996, she has taught at the University of Illinois, where she has served as associate chair and Director of Graduate Studies, and is currently Associate Professor of history. She is the author of *Fabricating Women: The Seamstresses of Old Regime France, 1675–1791* (Duke University Press, 2001), which won two awards, the Berkshire Prize and the Hagley Prize. She edited two special issues of the *Journal of Women's History* (vol. 18, nos. 3 and 4) and has published numerous articles and reviews in journals such as *Annales: Histoire, Sciences Sociales, French Historical Studies, Gender and History,* and the *Journal of Economic History.* Her research has been supported with grants from the National Endowment for the Humanities, the Mellon Foundation, and the Bourse Châteaubriand of the French government. She is a past president of the Society for French Historical Studies and a former chair of the Pinkney Prize Committee.

MERRY E. WIESNER-HANKS Having grown up in Minneapolis, Merry E. Wiesner-Hanks received her B.A. from Grinnell College in 1973 (as well as an honorary doctorate some years later), and her Ph.D. from the University of Wisconsin–Madison in 1979. She taught first at Augustana College in Illinois, and since 1985 at the University of Wisconsin–Milwaukee, where she is currently UWM Distinguished Professor in the department of history. She is the co-editor of the *Sixteenth Century Journal* and the author or editor of nineteen books and many articles that have appeared in English, German, Italian, Spanish, and Chinese. These include *Early Modern Europe, 1450–1789* (Cambridge, 2006), *Women and Gender in Early Modern Europe* (Cambridge, 3d ed., 2008), and *Gender in History* (Blackwell, 2001). She currently serves as the Chief Reader for Advanced Placement World History and has also written a number of source books for use in the college classroom, including *Discovering the Western Past* (Houghton Mifflin, 6th ed, 2007) and *Discovering the Global Past* (Houghton Mifflin, 3d. ed., 2006), and a book for young adults, *An Age of Voyages, 1350–1600* (Oxford 2005).

ARCTIC OCEAN

ALASKA RANGE

ROCKY MOUNTAINS

CANADIAN SHIELD

**NORTH
AMERICA**

APPALACHIAN MTS.

Mississippi R.

Rio Grande

NORTH PACIFIC OCEAN

NORTH
ATLANTIC
OCEAN

Tropic of Cancer

Arctic Cir

Equator

Amazon R.

**SOUTH
AMERICA**

ANDES MOUNTAINS

Tropic of Capricorn

SOUTH PACIFIC OCEAN

SOUTH
ATLANTIC
OCEAN

Cape Horn

Antarctic Circle

80°N

60°N

40°N

20°N

0°

20°S

40°S

60°S

80°S

180° 160°W 140°W 120°W 100°W 80°W 60°W 40°W 20°W

180°

Sea ice
Ice cap
Tundra
Forest
Grassland
Desert
Mountains

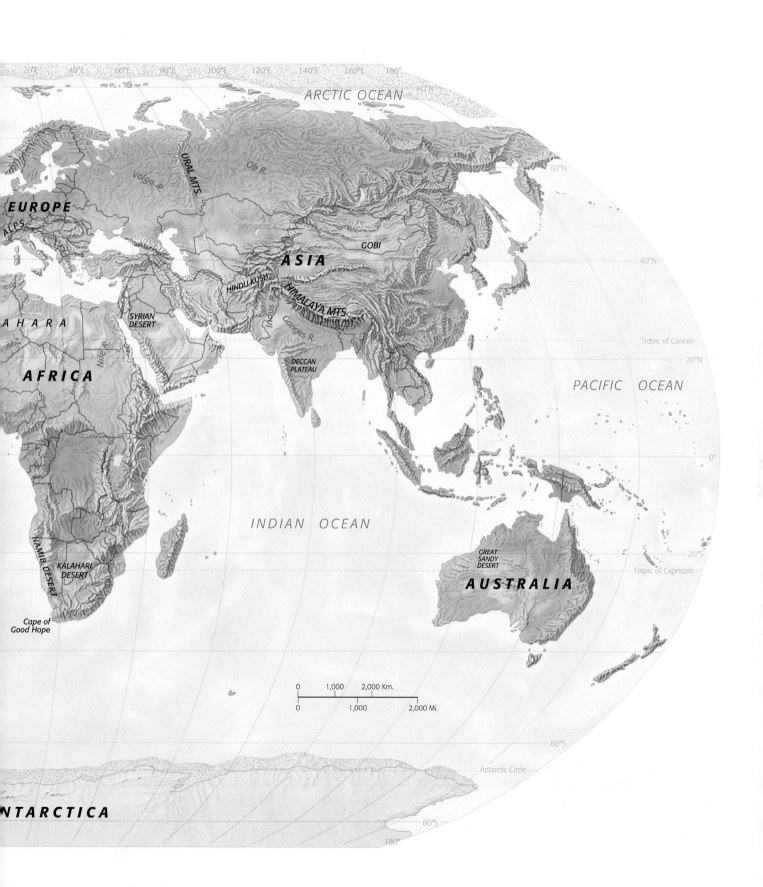

ARCTIC OCEAN

80°N

20°E 40°E 60°E 80°N 100°E 120°E 140°E 160°E 180°

60°N

URAL MTS.

Volga R.

Ob R.

EUROPE

ALPS

GOBI

ASIA

40°N

HINDU KUSH

HIMALAYA MTS.

SAHARA

SYRIAN
DESERT

Nile R.

Indus R.

Ganges R.

Tropic of Cancer

20°N

AFRICA

DECCAN
PLATEAU

PACIFIC OCEAN

INDIAN OCEAN

0°

NAMIB DESERT

GREAT
SANDY
DESERT

20°S

KALAHARI
DESERT

Tropic of Capricorn

AUSTRALIA

Cape of
Good Hope

60°S

Antarctic Circle

0   1,000   2,000 Km.

0   1,000   2,000 Mi.

NTARCTICA

80°S

180°

GREENLAND
(DENMARK)

80°N

ICELAND

ALASKA
(U.S.)

60°N

CANADA

UNI
KING

IRELAND

40°N

SP

PORTUGAL

Azores
(Port.)

UNITED STATES

Bermuda
(U.K.)

ATLANTIC OCEAN

MOROC

Midway Is.
(U.S.)

WESTERN
SAHARA
(MOROCCO)

BAHAMAS

MEXICO

Hawaiian Is.
(U.S.)

DOMINICAN REP.
Virgin Is.
(U.S.)

CUBA

20°N

MAURITANIA

HAITI

JAMAICA

CAPE
VERDE

ST. KITTS AND NEVIS
ANTIGUA AND BARBUDA
DOMINICA

SENEGAL

BELIZE
HONDURAS

Puerto Rico
(U.S.)

B

BARBADOS

GAMBIA

GUATEMALA
EL SALVADOR

ST. LUCIA
GRENADA

ST. VINCENT AND
THE GRENADINES

GUINEA-BISSAU

GUINEA

NICARAGUA

PACIFIC OCEAN

SIERRA
LEONE

IVORY
COAST

COSTA RICA

TRINIDAD AND TOBAGO

VENEZUELA

GUYANA

LIBERIA

GHA

PANAMA

EQUATO

FR. GUIANA
(FRANCE)

COLOMBIA

SÃO TOMÉ AN

Equator

0°

Galapagos Is.
(Ecuador)

ECUADOR

SURINAM

SAMOA

PERU

BRAZIL

French Polynesia
(France)

BOLIVIA

20°S

TONGA

PARAGUAY

Easter Is.
(Chile)

CHILE

URUGUAY

ARGENTINA

40°S

| 0 | 1,000 | 2,000 Km. |
| 0 | 1,000 | 2,000 Mi. |

Falkland Is.
(U.K.)

160°W   140°W   120°W   100°W   80°W   60°W   40°W   20°W   60°S

80°S

ATLANTIC OCEAN

PACIFIC OCEAN

INDIAN OCEAN

NORWAY
FINLAND
SWEDEN
ESTONIA
DEN.
NTH.
LATVIA
LITHUANIA
BELARUS
GERMANY POLAND
CZ.
SLK.
UKRAINE
AUS.
HUNG.
MOLDOVA
SLN. CR.
ROMANIA
ITALY
B. H. SE.
MO. K.
BULGARIA
ALBANIA MAC.
GREECE
TURKEY
CYPRUS
ARMENIA
TUNISIA
MALTA
LEBANON
ISRAEL
SYRIA
IRAQ
AZERBAIJAN
JORDAN
IRAN
LIBYA
EGYPT
KUWAIT
SAUDI
ARABIA
BAHRAIN
QATAR
UNITED
ARAB EMIRATES
OMAN

RUSSIA

KAZAKHSTAN

MONGOLIA

GEORGIA
UZBEKISTAN
KYRGYZSTAN
TURKMENISTAN
TAJIKISTAN
AFGHANISTAN
PAKISTAN

PEOPLE'S REPUBLIC OF CHINA

N. KOREA
S. KOREA
JAPAN

BHUTAN
NEPAL
BANGLADESH
INDIA
MYANMAR
(BURMA)
TAIWAN

LAOS
VIETNAM

NIGER
CHAD
ERITREA
YEMEN
BENIN
SUDAN
DJIBOUTI
NIGERIA
ETHIOPIA
CENTRAL
AFRICAN REP.
CAMEROON
SOMALIA
NEA
UGANDA
KENYA
GABON
RWANDA
DEM. REP.
OF CONGO
F CONGO
BURUNDI
TANZANIA

THAILAND
CAMBODIA
(KAMPUCHEA)
PHILIPPINES

SRI LANKA

MALDIVES

BRUNEI
DARUSSALAM
MALAYSIA
SINGAPORE

PALAU

Mariana
Islands
(U.S.)
Guam
(U.S.)

Wake I.
(U.S.)

MARSHALL
ISLANDS

FEDERATED STATES
OF MICRONESIA

KIRIBATI

NAURU

SEYCHELLES

ANGOLA
ZAMBIA
MALAWI
COMOROS
NAMIBIA
ZIMBABWE
MADAGASCAR
BOTSWANA
MAURITIUS
MOZAMBIQUE
SWAZILAND
SOUTH
AFRICA
LESOTHO

INDONESIA
TIMOR LESTE

PAPUA
NEW
GUINEA

SOLOMON IS.

TUVALU

VANUATU

FIJI

New Caledonia
(France)

AUSTRALIA

NEW
ZEALAND

ABBREVIATIONS

AUS.	AUSTRIA
BEL.	BELGIUM
B. H.	BOSNIA AND HERZEGOVINA
CR.	CROATIA
CZ.	CZECH REPUBLIC
DEN.	DENMARK
HUNG.	HUNGARY
K.	KOSOVO
LUX.	LUXEMBOURG
MAC.	MACEDONIA
MO.	MONTENEGRO
NETH.	NETHERLANDS
SE.	SERBIA
SLK.	SLOVAKIA
SLN.	SLOVENIA
SWITZ.	SWITZERLAND

20°E 40°E 60°E 80°E 100°E 120°E 140°E 160°E

A·HISTORY·OF
WORLD·SOCIETIES

Peace Panel, Standard of Ur. This scene depicts the royal family on the upper band, and various conquered peoples bringing the king tribute on the lower bands. *(Courtesy of the Trustees of the British Museum)*

1 EARLY CIVILIZATION IN AFROEURASIA, TO 450 B.C.E.

Human beings began the long road from their origins to the contemporary world in numerous places and under various circumstances. Although conditions were sometimes similar in all of them, their paths were unique. None fits into a tidy pattern. This chapter begins with the events that shaped the history of one of those places, the ancient **Near East,** or what is today often called the Middle East. Chapter 2 traces the origins of civilization in India, and Chapter 3 in China.

The ancient Near East includes parts of northeastern Africa, western Asia, and Mesopotamia, modern Iraq. It thus forms part of the larger Eurasia, the area from modern England in the west to Japan in the east. Within a small part of Eurasia, ancient Mesopotamian people invented writing, which allowed them to preserve knowledge of their achievements. They recorded their past and spread their learning, lore, and literature to posterity. Their innovations and those of the Egyptians laid the foundations of civilization in the region.

MESOPOTAMIAN CIVILIZATION FROM SUMER TO BABYLON (CA. 3000–1595 B.C.E.)

How did the Sumerians lay the foundations of a flourishing civilization in the hard land of Mesopotamia?

A good place from which to see the long path from nomadic hunters to urban folk is Mesopotamia, the Greek name for the land between the Euphrates and Tigris Rivers. Settled life in this region began only between 7000 and 3000 B.C.E., an era known as the Neolithic period. The term *Neolithic,* which means "neio stone age," comes from the new stone tools that people used to create a life of farming and animal husbandry. By ca. 3000 B.C.E. they had invented the wheel. Sustained agriculture resulted in a more stable life. Larger populations made possible the division of labor. These developments led to the evolution of towns and a new way of life (see Map 1.1). The growth and

3

● **Stonehenge** Seen in regal isolation, Stonehenge sits among the stars and in April 1997 along the path of the comet Hale-Bopp. Long before Druids existed, a Neolithic society laboriously built this circle to mark the passing of the seasons. *(Jim Burgess)*

Near East *The region between the eastern coast of the Mediterranean Sea and the Tigris and Euphrates Rivers.*

Neolithic period *The period between 7000 and 3000 B.C.E. that serves as the dividing line between anthropology and history. The term itself refers to the new stone tools that came into use at this time.*

● FIGURE 1.1 **Sumerian Writing** *(Source: Excerpted from S. N. Kramer,* The Sumerians, *University of Chicago Press, Chicago, 1963, pp. 302–306. Reprinted by permission of the publisher.)*

	MEANING	PICTOGRAPH	IDEOGRAM	PHONETIC SIGN
A	Star			
B	Woman			
C	Mountain			
D	Slave woman			
E	Water In			

diversity of the population created the need for the earliest governments that transcended families. Towns functioned and prospered through a recognized central authority governed by laws. Stable, strong populations organized themselves for peace and war, with the result that towns became the most successful feature of the **Neolithic period**.

The Invention of Writing and Intellectual Advances (ca. 3000–2331 B.C.E.)

By ca. 3000 B.C.E. the Sumerians, whose origins are mysterious, had established a number of towns in the southernmost part of Mesopotamia, which became known as Sumer. Towns grew into cities, and one of the Sumerian's many advances was the invention of writing. This momentous innovation helped unify Sumerian society by making communications much easier and opening Sumerian society to a broader world.

The Sumerians started by drawing pictures of objects, pictographs, from which they developed the style of writing known as cuneiform. The name comes from the Latin term for "wedge-shaped" used to describe the strokes making up the signs. The next step was to simplify the system. Instead of drawing pictures, the scribe made *ideograms:* conventionalized signs that were generally understood to represent ideas. The sign for star could also be used to indicate heaven, sky, or even god. (See line A in Figure 1.1.) The real breakthrough came when the scribe learned to use signs to represent sounds. For instance, the scribe drew two parallel wavy lines to indicate the word *a* or "water" (line E). Besides water, the word *a* in Sumerian also meant "in." The word *in* expresses a relationship that is very difficult to represent pictorially. Instead of trying to invent a sign to mean "in," some clever scribe used the sign for water because the two words sounded alike. This phonetic use of signs made possible the combining of signs to convey abstract ideas.

The Sumerian system of writing was so complicated that only professional scribes mastered it after many years of study. By 2500 B.C.E. scribal schools flourished throughout Sumer. Most students came from wealthy families and were male. Each school had a master, a teacher, and monitors. Discipline was strict, and students were caned for sloppy work and misbehavior. One graduate of a scribal school had few fond memories of the joy of learning:

My headmaster read my tablet, said:
"There is something missing," caned me.
. . . .
The fellow in charge of silence said:
"Why did you talk without permission," caned me.
The fellow in charge of the assembly said:
"Why did you stand at ease without permission," caned me.[1]

Although Sumerian education was primarily intended to produce scribes for administrative work, schools were also centers of culture and scholarship.

Sumerian Thought and Religion

The building of cities, palaces, temples, and canals demanded practical knowledge of geometry and trigonometry. The Sumerians and later Mesopotamians made significant advances in mathematics using a numerical system based on units of sixty, ten, and six. They also developed the concept of place value—that the value of a number depends on where it stands in relation to other numbers.

Sumerian medicine was a combination of magic, prescriptions, and surgery. Sumerians believed that demons and evil spirits caused sickness and that magic spells and prescriptions could drive them out. Over time some prescriptions worked, and in this slow but empirical fashion medical understanding grew.

The Sumerians originated many religious beliefs, and their successors added to them. The Mesopotamians were polytheists—that is, they believed that many gods run the world. They did not, however, consider all gods and goddesses equal. Some deities had very important jobs taking care of music, victory, law, and sex, while others had lesser tasks, overseeing leatherworking and basketweaving. Mesopotamian gods were powerful and immortal and could make themselves invisible. Otherwise, they were very human: they celebrated with food and drink and they raised families. They enjoyed their own "Garden of Eden," a green and fertile paradise. They could be irritable, vindictive, and irresponsible. Nor were the motives of the gods always clear. In times of affliction one could only pray and offer sacrifices to appease them. Encouraged and directed by the traditional priesthood, which was dedicated to understanding the ways of the gods, the people erected shrines in the center of each city around which they built their houses. The best way to honor the gods was to make the shrine as grand and as impressive as possible, for gods who had a splendid temple might think twice about sending floods to destroy the city.

Chronology

ca. 7000–3000 B.C.E.	Neolithic period
ca. 3000–2331 B.C.E.	Sumerian and Akkadian domination
ca. 3000 B.C.E.	Invention of cuneiform writing
ca. 3100–2180 B.C.E.	Rise of Egypt
1792–ca. 717 B.C.E.	Babylonian rule in Mesopotamia
ca. 1790 B.C.E.	*Epic of Gilgamesh* and Hammurabi's law code
ca. 1650–ca. 1200 B.C.E.	Hittite rule in Anatolia
ca. 1570–1075 B.C.E.	New Kingdom in Egypt
1367–1350 B.C.E.	Reign of Akhenaten in Egypt
1100–653 B.C.E.	Third Intermediate Period in Egypt
ca. 1000–587 B.C.E.	Development of Hebrew kingdom
ca. 950–500 B.C.E.	Beginning of Hebrew Bible
ca. 800–612 B.C.E.	Period of Assyrian Empire
550–464 B.C.E.	Creation of Persian Empire
ca. 600–500 B.C.E.	Spread of Zoroastrianism

The Sumerians had many myths to account for the creation of the universe. According to one (echoed in Genesis, the first book of the Hebrew Bible), only the primeval sea existed at first. The sea produced heaven and earth, which were united. Heaven and earth gave birth to Enlil, who separated them and made possible the creation of the other gods. Myths are the earliest known attempts to answer the question "How did it all begin?"

In addition to myths, the Sumerians produced the first epic poem, the *Epic of Gilgamesh*. An epic poem is a narration of the achievements, the labors, and sometimes the failures of heroes that embodies a people's or a nation's conception of its own past. The Sumerian epic recounts the wanderings of Gilgamesh, the semihistorical king of Uruk, and his search for eternal life. He learns that life after death is so dreary that he returns to Uruk, where he ends his life. The *Epic of Gilgamesh* shows the Sumerians grappling with such enduring questions as life and death, people and deity, and immortality. (See the feature "Listening to the Past: A Quest for Immortality on pages 26–27.)

Primary Source: *From* The Epic of Gilgamesh

Sumerian Society

nobles *The top level of Sumerian society: the king and his family, the chief priests, and high palace officials.*

Sumerian society was a complex arrangement of freedom and dependence, and its members were divided into four categories: nobles, clients, commoners, and slaves. **Nobles** consisted of the king and his family, the chief priests, and high palace officials. The king generally rose to power as a war leader, elected by the citizenry, who established a regular army, trained it, and led it into battle. The might of the king and the

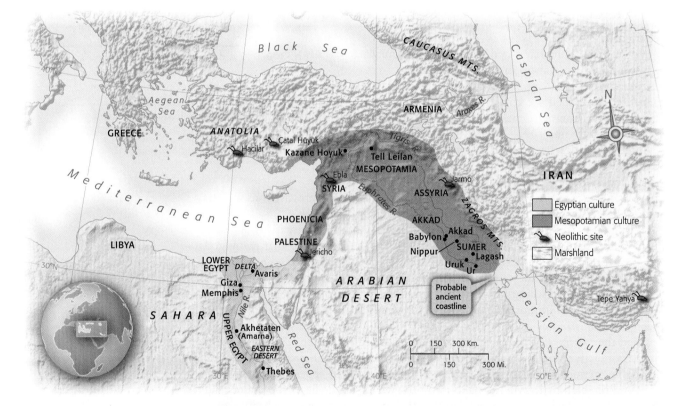

MAP 1.1 **Spread of Cultures in the Ancient Near East** This map illustrates the spread of the Mesopotamian and Egyptian cultures through a semicircular stretch of land often called the Fertile Crescent. From this area, knowledge and use of agriculture spread throughout western Asia.

frequency of warfare quickly made him the supreme figure in the city, and kingship soon became hereditary. The symbol of royal status was the palace, which rivaled the temple in its grandeur.

The king and the lesser nobility held extensive tracts of land that were, like the estates of the temple, worked by clients and slaves. Slaves were prisoners of war, convicts, and debtors. While they were subject to any treatment their owners might mete out, they could engage in trade, make profits, and even buy their freedom. **Clients** were free people who were dependent on the nobility. In return for their labor, they received small plots of land to work for themselves. Although this arrangement assured the clients of a livelihood, the land they worked remained the possession of the nobility or the temple. Commoners were free and could own land in their own right. Male commoners had a voice in the political affairs of the city and full protection under the law. Each of these social categories included both men and women, but Sumerian society also made clear distinctions based on gender. Sumerian society was *patriarchal,* that is, most power was held by older adult men.

● **Ziggurat** The ziggurat is a stepped tower that dominated the landscape of the Sumerian city. Surrounded by a walled enclosure, it stood as a monument to the gods. Monumental stairs led to the top, where sacrifices were offered for the welfare of the community. *(Charles & Josette Lenars/Corbis)*

clients *Free men and women who were dependent on the nobility; in return for their labor, they received small plots of land to work for themselves.*

The Triumph of Babylon and the Spread of Mesopotamian Civilization (2331–ca. 1595 B.C.E.)

Although the Sumerians established the basic social, economic, and intellectual patterns of Mesopotamia, the Semites played a large part in spreading Sumerian culture far beyond the boundaries of Mesopotamia. Semites are people related by the Semitic language spoken by Jews, Arabs, Phoenicians, Assyrians, and others. In 2331 B.C.E. the Semitic chieftain Sargon conquered Sumer and created a new empire. The symbol of his triumph was a new capital, the city of Akkad. Sargon led his armies to the Mediterranean Sea, spreading Mesopotamian culture throughout the Fertile Crescent (see Map 1.1). Though extensive, Sargon's empire soon fell to the Babylonians, who united Mesopotamia politically and culturally.

Hammurabi (r. 1792–1750 B.C.E.), king of the Amorites, another Semitic people, won control of the region and established his capital at Babylon. He accomplished three things: he made his kingdom secure, unified Mesopotamia, and joined together the Sumerian idea of urban kingship and the Semitic concept of tribal chieftain. He succeeded culturally in making Marduk, the god of Babylon, the sovereign of all other Mesopotamian deities. Hammurabi's most memorable achievement was the code that

Primary Source: Hammurabi, *Hammurabi's Code: The State Regulates Health Care*

established the law of the land. Hammurabi claimed that divine authority stood behind the laws that promoted the welfare of the people. The code differentiates people in terms of laws and punishments according to social status and gender.

Because of farming's fundamental importance, Hammurabi's code dealt extensively with agriculture. It governed the duties and rights of tenant farmers, who were expected carefully to cultivate the land. They were also responsible for keeping canals and ditches in good repair. Negligence in either case could ruin or damage crops. Tenants who were negligent either bore the cost of losses or were sold into slavery.

Hammurabi gave careful attention to marriage and the family. The fathers of the prospective bride and groom legally arranged the marriage, with the bride receiving from her father a dowry that remained hers for the rest of her life. The groom's father gave a bridal gift to the bride's father. The wife was expected to be rigorously faithful, primarily to ensure the legitimacy of the children. Only then could they legally inherit their father's property. In cases of adultery, the guilty wife was put to death. But an accused wife could clear herself before the city council. If the investigation found her innocent, she could take her dowry and leave her husband.

The husband technically had absolute power over his household. He could sell his wife and children into slavery for debt and disinherit his son, although the law made it very difficult for him to go to these extremes. Evidence other than the law code indicates that family life was not so grim. Countless wills and testaments show that husbands habitually left their estates to their wives, who in turn willed the property to their children. Though supposedly banned from commercial pursuits, many women engaged in business without hindrance. Though marriage was primarily an arrangement between families, a few poems speak of romantic love.

● **Law Code of Hammurabi**
Hammurabi ordered his code to be inscribed on a stone pillar and set up in public. At the top of the pillar Hammurabi is depicted receiving the scepter of authority from the god Shamash. *(Hirmer Verlag München)*

EGYPT, THE LAND OF THE PHARAOHS (3100–1200 B.C.E.)

How did geography enable the Egyptians easily to form a cohesive, prosperous society?

The Greek historian and traveler Herodotus in the fifth century B.C.E. called Egypt the "gift of the Nile." No other single geographical factor had such a fundamental and profound impact on the shaping of Egyptian life, society, and history as the Nile (see Map 1.2). The Egyptians praised the Nile primarily as a creative and comforting force:

Hail to thee, O Nile, that issues from the earth and comes to keep Egypt alive! . . .
He that waters the meadows which Ra created,
He that makes to drink the desert . . .
He who makes barley and brings emmer [wheat] into being . . .
He who brings grass into being for the cattle . . .
He who makes every beloved tree to grow . . .
O Nile, verdant art thou, who makest man and cattle to live.[2]

Primary Source:
Hymn to the Nile

To the Egyptians, the Nile was the source of life.

Egypt was also nearly self-sufficient. Besides the fertility of its soil, Egypt possessed enormous quantities of stone, which served as the raw material of architecture and sculpture. Abundant clay was available for pottery, as was gold for jewelry and ornaments. The raw materials that Egypt lacked were close at hand. The Egyptians obtained copper from Sinai and timber from Lebanon. They had little cause to look to the outside world for their necessities, a fact that helps to explain the insular quality of Egyptian life.

The God-King of Egypt

Geographical unity quickly gave rise to political unification of the country under the authority of a king whom the Egyptians called **"pharaoh."** The precise details of this process have been lost. The Egyptians themselves told of a great king, Menes, who united Upper and Lower Egypt into a single kingdom around 3100 B.C.E. Thereafter, they divided their history into dynasties, or families, of kings. For modern historical purposes, however, it is useful to divide Egyptian history into periods (see page 10). The political unification of Egypt ushered in the period known as the Old Kingdom (2660–2180 B.C.E.), an era remarkable for prosperity, artistic flowering, and the evolution of religious beliefs.

In religion, the Egyptians developed complex, often contradictory, ideas of their gods. They were polytheistic in that they worshiped many gods, some mightier than others. Their beliefs were rooted in the environment and human ecology. The most powerful of the gods were Amon, a primeval sky-god, and Ra, the sun-god. Amon created the entire cosmos by his thoughts. He brought life to the land and its people, and he sustained both. The Egyptians cherished Amon because he championed fairness and honesty, especially for the common people. The Egyptians considered Ra the creator of life. He commanded the sky, earth, and the underworld. Ra was associated with the falcon-god Horus, the "lord of the sky," who served as the symbol of divine kingship. Horus united Egypt and bestowed divinity on the pharaoh. The obvious similarities between Amon and Ra eventually led the Egyptians to combine them into one god, **Amon-Ra.** Yet the Egyptians never fashioned a formal theology to resolve the differences. Instead, they worshiped these gods as different aspects of the same celestial phenomena.

The Egyptians likewise developed views of an afterlife that reflected the world around them. The dry air of Egypt preserves much that would decay in other climates. The dependable rhythm of the seasons also shaped the fate of the dead. According to the Egyptians, Osiris, a fertility god associated with the Nile, died each year, and each year his wife, Isis, brought him back to life. Osiris eventually became king of the dead, and he weighed human beings' hearts to determine whether they had lived justly enough to deserve everlasting life. Osiris's care of the dead was shared

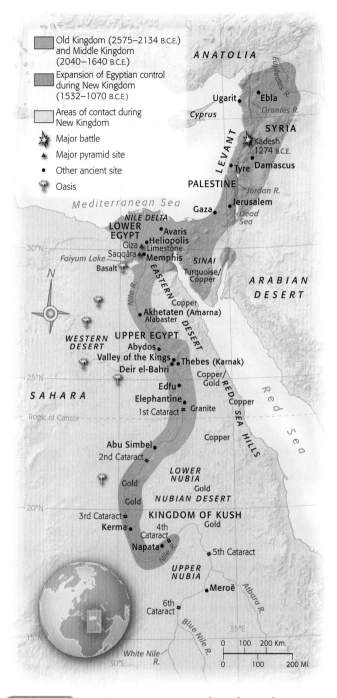

MAP 1.2   Ancient Egypt   Geography and natural resources provided Egypt with centuries of peace and abundance.

pharaoh   *The leader of religious and political life in the Old Kingdom, he commanded the wealth, the resources, and the people of Egypt.*

Amon-Ra   *An Egyptian god, consisting of Amon, a primeval sky-god, and Ra, the sun-god.*

Periods of Egyptian History

PERIOD	DATES	SIGNIFICANT EVENTS
Archaic	3100–2660 B.C.E.	Unification of Egypt
Old Kingdom	2660–2180 B.C.E.	Construction of the pyramids
First Intermediate	2180–2080 B.C.E.	Political chaos
Middle Kingdom	2080–1640 B.C.E.	Recovery and political stability
Second Intermediate	1640–1570 B.C.E.	Hyksos "invasion"
New Kingdom	1570–1075 B.C.E.	Creation of an Egyptian empire Akhenaten's religious policy
Third Intermediate	1100–653 B.C.E.	Political fragmentation

Primary Source:
The Egyptian Book of the Dead: The Declaration of Innocence

Book of the Dead *An Egyptian book that preserved their ideas about death and the afterlife; it explains that after death, the soul leaves the body to become part of the divine.*

pyramid *The burial place of a pharaoh; a massive tomb that contained all things needed for the afterlife. It also symbolized the king's power and his connection with the sun-god.*

by Anubis, the jackal-headed god who annually helped Isis resuscitate Osiris. Anubis was the god of mummification, essential to Egyptian funerary rites. The Egyptians preserved these ideas in the *Book of the Dead*, which explained that after death the soul and the body became part of the divine. They entered gladly through the gate of heaven where they remained in the presence of Aton (a sun-god) and the stars. Thus for the Egyptians life did not end with death.

The focal point of religious and political life in the Old Kingdom was the pharaoh, who commanded the wealth, resources, and people of all Egypt. The Egyptians considered him to be Horus in human form. In Egyptian religion Horus was the son of Isis and Osiris, which meant that the pharaoh, a living god on earth, became one with Osiris after death. The pharaoh was the power that achieved the integration between gods and human beings, a pledge that the gods of Egypt (strikingly unlike those of Mesopotamia) cared for their people.

The king's surroundings had to be worthy of a god. Only a magnificent palace was suitable for his home. In fact, the very word *pharaoh* means "great house." Just as the pharaoh occupied a great house in life, so he reposed in a great **pyramid** after death. The massive tomb contained everything the pharaoh needed in his afterlife. The walls of the burial chamber were inscribed with religious texts and spells relating to the king's journeys after death. The pyramid also symbolized the king's power and his connection with the sun-god. To this day the great pyramids at Giza near Cairo bear silent but magnificent testimony to the god-kings of Egypt.

The Pharaoh's People

Because the common folk stood at the bottom of the social and economic scale, they were always at the mercy of grasping officials. Taxes might amount to 20 percent of the harvest, and tax collection could be brutal.

The regularity of the climate meant that the agricultural year was routine and dependable, so farmers seldom suffered from foul weather and damaged crops. Farmers sowed wheat and nurtured a large variety of trees, vegetables, and vines. They tended cattle and poultry, and when time permitted they hunted and fished in the marshlands of the Nile.

Egyptian society seems to have been a curious mixture of freedom and constraint. Slavery did not become widespread until the New Kingdom (1570–1075 B.C.E.). There was neither a caste system nor a color bar, and humble people could rise to the highest positions if they possessed talent. On the other hand, most ordinary folk were probably little more than serfs who could not easily leave the land of their own free will. Peasants were also subject to forced labor, including work on the pyramids and canals. Young men were drafted into the pharaoh's army, which served both as a fighting force and as a labor corps.

To ancient Egyptians the pharaoh embodied justice and order—harmony among people, nature, and the divine. If the pharaoh was weak or allowed anyone to challenge his unique position, he opened the way to chaos. Twice in Egyptian history the pharaoh failed to maintain rigid centralization. During those two eras, known as the First and Second Intermediate Periods, Egypt was exposed to civil war and invasion. Yet the monarchy survived, and in each period a strong pharaoh arose to crush the rebels or expel the invaders and restore order.

Primary Source: Nebmare-nakht, *Advice to Ambitious Young Egyptians from a Royal Scribe*

The Hyksos in Egypt (1640–1570 B.C.E.)

While Egyptian civilization flourished behind its bulwark of sand and sea, momentous changes were taking place around it that would leave their mark even on rich, insular Egypt. These changes involved vast and remarkable movements, especially of peoples who spoke Semitic tongues.

The original home of the Semites was perhaps the Arabian peninsula. Some tribes moved into northern Mesopotamia, others into Syria and Palestine, and still others into Egypt. Shortly after 1800 B.C.E., people whom the Egyptians called **Hyksos,** which means "rulers of the uplands," began to settle in the Nile Delta. The movements of the Hyksos were part of a larger pattern of migration of peoples during this period. Such nomads normally settled in and accommodated themselves with the native cultures. The process was mutual, for each group had something to give and to learn from the other.

Hyksos *Called "rulers of the uplands" by the Egyptians, these people began to settle in the Nile Delta shortly after 1800 B.C.E.*

● **Pyramids of Giza** Giza was the burial place of the pharaohs of the Old Kingdom and of their aristocracy, whose smaller rectangular tombs surround the two foremost pyramids. The small pyramid probably belonged to a pharaoh's wife. *(Jose Fuste Raga/Corbis)*

● **Egyptian Harvest Scene** This cheerful wall painting depicts two aspects of the harvest. Workers at the top right pick bunches of ripe grapes for winemaking. Their colleagues in the center stamp the grapes, and the large pottery jars store the wine. *(Louvre/Réunion des Musées Nationaux/Art Resource, NY)*

So too in Egypt, where bands of Hyksos entered the delta looking for good land. Their success led them to settle and to establish a capital city at Avaris in the northeastern Nile Delta. They probably exercised direct control no farther south. The Hyksos brought with them the method of making bronze and casting it into tools and weapons that became standard in Egypt. They thereby brought Egypt fully into the **Bronze Age** culture of the Mediterranean world. Bronze tools made farming more efficient than ever before because they were sharper and more durable than the copper tools they replaced. The Hyksos's use of bronze armor and weapons as well as horse-drawn chariots and the composite bow revolutionized Egyptian warfare. Yet the newcomers also absorbed Egyptian culture. The Hyksos came to worship Egyptian gods and modeled their monarchy on the pharaonic system.

Bronze Age *The period in which the production and use of bronze implements became basic to society; bronze made farming more efficient and revolutionized warfare.*

The New Kingdom: Revival and Empire (1570–1075 B.C.E.)

The pharaohs of the Eighteenth Dynasty arose to challenge the Hyksos. These pharaohs pushed the Hyksos out of the delta, subdued Nubia in the south, and conquered Palestine and parts of Syria in the northeast. Egyptian warrior-pharaohs thereby inaugurated the New Kingdom—a period characterized by enormous wealth and conscious imperialism. They created the first Egyptian empire, which they celebrated with monuments on a scale unparalleled since the pyramids of the Old Kingdom. Also during this period, probably for the first time, widespread slavery became a feature of Egyptian life. The pharaoh's armies returned home leading hordes of slaves who constituted a new labor force for imperial building projects.

One pharaoh of this period, Akhenaten (r. 1367–1350 B.C.E.), was more concerned with religion than with conquest. Nefertiti, his wife and queen, encouraged his religious bent (see the feature "Individuals in Society: Nefertiti, the 'Perfect Woman'"). They worshiped the sun-god Aton as universal, the only god, whereas the Egyptian people were polytheistic—they believed in many gods. Akhenaten considered all these and other deities frauds and so suppressed their worship. Although the precise nature of Akhenaten's religious beliefs remain debatable, most historians agree that the royal pair were monotheists: they believed in only one god. Yet this **monotheism,** imposed from above and enforced by intolerance, failed to find a place among the people. Akhenaten's religion died with him.

monotheism *The belief in one god; when applied to Egypt, it means that only Aton among the traditional Egyptian deities was god.*

Nefertiti, the "Perfect Woman"

Egyptians understood the pharaoh to be the living embodiment of the god Horus, the source of law and morality, and the mediator between gods and humans. His connection with the divine stretched to members of his family, so that his siblings and children were also viewed as in some ways divine. Because of this, a pharaoh often took his sister or half-sister as one of his wives. This concentrated divine blood set the pharaonic family apart from other Egyptians (who did not marry close relatives) and allowed the pharaohs to imitate the gods, who in Egyptian mythology often married their siblings. A pharaoh chose one of his wives to be the "Great Royal Wife," or principal queen. Often this was a relative, though sometimes it was one of the foreign princesses who married pharaohs to establish political alliances.

The familial connection with the divine allowed a handful of women to rule in their own right in Egypt's long history. We know the names of four female pharaohs, of whom the most famous was Hatshepsut (r. 1479–1458 B.C.). She was the sister and wife of Thutmose II and, after he died, served as regent for her young stepson Thutmose III, who was actually the son of another woman. Hatshepsut sent trading expeditions and sponsored artists and architects, ushering in a period of artistic creativity and economic prosperity. She built one of the world's great buildings, an elaborate terraced temple at Deir el Bahri, which eventually served as her tomb. Hatshepsut's status as a powerful female ruler was difficult for Egyptians to conceptualize, and she is often depicted in male dress or with a false beard, thus looking more like the male rulers who were the norm. After her death, Thutmose III tried to destroy all evidence that she had ever ruled, smashing statues and scratching her name off inscriptions, perhaps because of personal animosity and perhaps because he wanted to erase the fact that a woman had once been pharaoh. Only within the last decades have historians and archaeologists begun to (literally) piece together her story.

Though female pharaohs were very rare, many royal women had power through their position as "Great Royal Wives." The most famous of these was Nefertiti, the wife of Akhenaten. Her name means "the perfect (or beautiful) woman has come," and inscriptions also give her many other titles. Nefertiti used her position to spread the new religion of the sun-god Aton.

Nefertiti, queen of Egypt. *(Bildarchiv Preussischer Kulturbesitz/ Art Resource, NY)*

Together she and Akhenaten built a new palace at Akhetaten, the present Amarna, away from the old centers of power. There they developed the cult of Aton to the exclusion of the traditional deities. Nearly the only literary survival of their religious belief is the "Hymn to Aton," which declares Aton to be the only god. It describes Nefertiti as "the great royal consort whom he! Akhenaten! Loves, the mistress of the Two Lands! Upper and Lower Egypt!"

Nefertiti is often shown the same size as her husband, and in some inscriptions she is performing religious rituals that would normally have been done only by the pharaoh. The exact details of her power are hard to determine, however. An older theory held that her husband removed her from power, though there is also speculation that she may have ruled secretly in her own right after his death. Her tomb has long since disappeared, though in 2003 an enormous controversy developed over her possible remains. There is no controversy that the bust shown above, now in a Berlin museum, represents Nefertiti, nor that it has become an icon of female beauty since it was first discovered in the early twentieth century.

Questions for Analysis

1. Why might it have been difficult for Egyptians to accept a female ruler?

2. What opportunities do hereditary monarchies such as that of ancient Egypt provide for women? How does this fit with gender hierarchies in which men are understood as superior?

THE RISE OF THE HITTITES
(CA. 1650–CA. 1200 B.C.E.)

How did the Hittites affect the life of the ancient Near East?

Indo-European *Refers to a large family of languages that includes English, most of the languages of modern Europe, Greek, Latin, Persian, and Sanskrit, the sacred tongue of ancient India.*

Around 1650 B.C.E. the Hittites, who had long been settled in Anatolia (modern Turkey), became a major power in that region and began to expand east and south (see Map 1.3). The Hittites were an Indo-European people. The term **Indo-European** refers to a large family of languages that includes English, most of the languages of modern Europe, Greek, Latin, Persian, and Sanskrit, the sacred tongue of ancient India. The Hittite king Hattusilis I built a hill citadel at Hattusas, the modern Boghazköy, from which he led his people against neighboring kingdoms. His grandson and successor, Mursilis I (r. ca. 1595 B.C.E.), extended the Hittite conquests as far as Babylon. Upon his return home, the victorious Mursilis was assassinated by members of his own family, which opened the door to foreign invasion. Only when the Hittites were united behind a strong king were they a power to be reckoned with. Unshaken, the Hittites produced an energetic line of kings who built a powerful empire. Their major technological contribution was the introduction of iron into war and agriculture in the form of weapons and tools.

Around 1300 B.C.E. the Hittites stopped the Egyptian army of Rameses II (r. ca. 1290–1224 B.C.E.) at the Battle of Kadesh in Syria. Having fought each other to a standstill, the Hittites and Egyptians first made peace and then an alliance. The two greatest powers of the Near East thus tried to make war between them impossible.

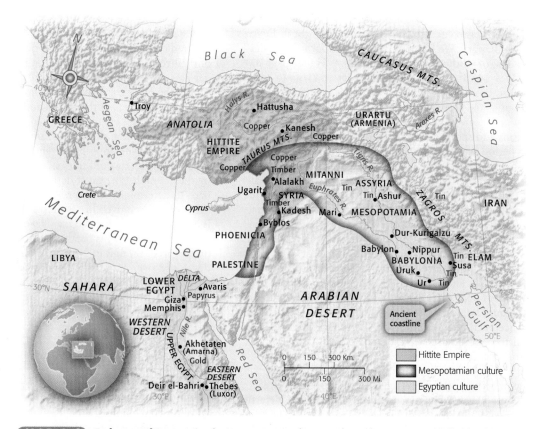

MAP 1.3 **Balance of Power in the Near East** This map shows the regions controlled by the Hittites and Egyptians at the height of their power. The Hittites conquered part of Mesopotamia during their expansion eastward.

● **Hittite Solar Disk** This cult standard represents Hittite concepts of fertility and prosperity. The circle surrounding the animals is the sun, beneath which stands a stag flanked by two bulls. Stylized bull's horns spread from the base of the disk. The symbol is also one of might and protection from outside harm. *(Museum of Anatolian Civilizations, Ankara)*

The Hittites and Egyptians next included the Babylonians in their diplomacy. They all made alliance for offensive and defensive protection, and swore to uphold one another's authority. These contacts facilitated the exchange of ideas throughout western Asia. The Hittites also passed much knowledge from the east to the newly arrived Greeks in Europe. Like the Hittite kings, Rameses II used the peace after the Battle of Kadesh to promote prosperity and concentrate the income from the natural wealth and the foreign trade of Egypt on internal affairs. In many ways, he was the last great pharaoh of Egypt.

This peaceful situation lasted until the late thirteenth century B.C.E., when both the Hittite and Egyptian empires fell to invaders. The most famous of these marauders, the **Sea Peoples,** remain one of the puzzles of ancient history. The Sea Peoples were a collection of peoples who went their own individual ways after their attacks on the Hittites and Egyptians. They dealt both the Hittites and the Egyptians hard blows, making the Hittites vulnerable to overland invasion from the north and driving the Egyptians back to the Nile Delta. The Hittites fell under these attacks, but the battered Egyptians managed to retreat to the delta and hold on.

Sea Peoples *Invaders who destroyed the Egyptian empire in the late thirteenth century; they are otherwise unidentifiable because they went their own ways after their attacks on Egypt.*

A Shattered Egypt and a Rising Phoenicia

The invasions of the Sea Peoples brought the great days of Egyptian power to an end. The long wars against invaders weakened and impoverished Egypt, causing political upheaval and economic chaos. Egypt suffered a four-hundred-year period of political fragmentation, a new dark age known to Egyptian specialists as the Third Intermediate Period (ca. 1100–653 B.C.E.).

In southern Egypt, meanwhile, the pharaoh's decline opened the way for the energetic Nubians to extend their authority northward throughout the Nile Valley. Since the imperial days of the Eighteenth Dynasty, the Nubians, too, had adopted many features of Egyptian culture. Now they embraced Egyptian culture wholesale.

The reunification of Egypt occurred late and unexpectedly. With Egypt disorganized, an independent African state, the kingdom of Kush, grew up in the region of

● FIGURE 1.2 **Origins of the Alphabet** List of hiero-glyphic, Ugaritic, Phoenician, Greek, and Roman sign forms. *(Source: A. B. Knapp, The History and Culture of Ancient Western Asia and Egypt. © 1988 Wadsworth, a part of Cengage Learning, Inc. Reproduced by permission, www.cengage.com/permissions)*

HIEROGLYPHIC	REPRESENTS	UGARITIC	PHOENICIAN	GREEK	ROMAN
)	Throw stick	T	⌐	Γ	G
𓀠	Man with raised arms	E	ⅎ	E	E
⌐	Basket with handle	▷	↓	K	K
∧∧∧	Water	⊢	𝍳	M	M
⌐	Snake	⋙⊢	\	N	N
⊘	Eye	◁	O	O	O
⌒	Mouth	⊨	?	Π	P
☌	Head	⊞	9	P	R
𓊖	Pool with lotus flowers	◁⅄	W	Σ	S
⊏⊐	House	皿	9	B	B
𓃾	Ox-head	⊢	K	A	A

modern Sudan with its capital at Nepata. Like the Libyans, the Kushites worshiped Egyptian gods and used Egyptian hieroglyphs. In the eighth century B.C.E., their king Piankhy swept through the entire Nile Valley from Nepata in the south to the delta in the north. United once again, Egypt enjoyed a brief period of peace during which the Egyptians continued to assimilate their conquerors. Nonetheless, reunification of Egypt did not lead to a new empire.

Yet Egypt's legacy to its African neighbors remained rich. By trading and exploring southward along the coast of the Red Sea, the Egyptians introduced their goods and ideas as far south as the land of Punt, probably a region on the Somali coast. Egypt was the primary civilizing force in Nubia, which became another version of the pha-raoh's realm, complete with royal pyramids and Egyptian deities. Egyptian religion penetrated as far south as Ethiopia.

Among the sturdy peoples who rose to prominence were the Phoenicians, a Semitic-speaking people who had long inhabited several cities along the coast of mod-ern Lebanon. Phoenicians took to the sea to become outstanding explorers and mer-chants. They played a predominant role in international trade, in which they exported their manufactured goods. Their most valued products were purple and blue textiles, from which originated their Greek name, Phoenicians, meaning **"Purple People."** They also worked metals, which they shipped processed or as ore. They imported rare goods and materials from Persia in the east and from their neighbors to the south. Their exported wares went to Egypt, as far as North Africa and Spain, and even into the Atlantic. The variety and quality of their exports generally made them welcome visitors. Although their goal was trade, not colonization, they nevertheless founded Carthage in 813 B.C.E., a city that would one day struggle with Rome for domination of the western Mediterranean. Their voyages naturally brought them into contact with the Greeks, to whom they introduced the older cultures of the Near East. In-deed, their enduring significance lay in their spreading the experiences of the Near East throughout the western Mediterranean.

Phoenician culture was urban, based on the prosperous commercial centers of Tyre, Sidon, and Byblos. The Phoenicians' overwhelming cultural legacy was the develop-

Purple People *The Greek name for the Phoenicians, a culture that inhabited the eastern coast of the Mediterranean Sea, so called because of the remarkable purple dye they produced from certain sea snails.*

ment of an alphabet (see Figure 1.2). Unlike other literate peoples, they used one letter to designate one sound, a system that vastly simplified writing and reading. The Greeks modified this alphabet and then used it to write their own language. We still use it today.

THE CHILDREN OF ISRAEL (CA. 950–538 B.C.E.)

How did the Hebrews form a small kingdom after the fall of larger neighboring empires?

The fall of the Hittite Empire and Egypt's collapse allowed the rise of numerous small states. South of Phoenicia arose a small kingdom, the land of the ancient Jews or Hebrews. It is difficult to say precisely who the Hebrews were because virtually the only source for much of their history is the Hebrew Bible, a religious document that contains many myths and legends as well as historical material. Like the earlier Hyksos, they probably migrated into the Nile Delta seeking good land. There, according to the Bible, the Egyptians enslaved them. The Hebrews followed their leader Moses out of Egypt, and in the thirteenth century B.C.E. they settled in Palestine. There they encountered the Philistines; the Amorites, relatives of Hammurabi's Babylonians; and the Semitic-speaking Canaanites. Despite numerous wars, contact between the Hebrews and their new neighbors was not always hostile. They freely mingled with the Canaanites, and some went so far as to worship Baal, an ancient Semitic fertility-god represented as a golden calf. Only later did the Hebrews consider Yahweh the only god. Despite the anger expressed in the Bible over Hebrew worship of **Baal,** there is nothing surprising about the phenomenon. Once again, newcomers adapted themselves to the culture of an older, well-established people.

The greatest danger to the Hebrews came from the Philistines, whose superior technology and military organization at first made them invincible. The Hebrew leader Saul (ca. 1000 B.C.E.), while keeping the Philistines at bay, established a monarchy over the twelve Hebrew tribes. David of Bethlehem continued Saul's work and captured the city of Jerusalem, which he enlarged and made the religious center of the realm. His work is consolidating the monarchy and enlarging the kingdom paved the way for his son Solomon (ca. 965–925 B.C.E.). Solomon created a nation by dividing it into twelve territorial districts cutting across the old tribal borders. He also launched a building program that included cities, palaces, fortresses, and roads. The most symbolic of these projects was the Temple of Jerusalem, which became the home of the Ark of the Covenant, the chest that contained the holiest of Hebrew religious articles. The temple in Jerusalem was intended to be the religious heart of the kingdom and the symbol of Hebrew unity.

At Solomon's death his kingdom broke into political halves. The northern part became Israel, with its capital at Samaria. The southern half was Judah, and Jerusalem remained its center. With political division went religious rift: Israel established rival sanctuaries for gods other than Yahweh. Although the Assyrians later wiped out the northern kingdom of Israel, Judah survived numerous calamities until the Babylonians crushed it in 587 B.C.E. The survivors were sent into exile in Babylonia, a period commonly known as the **Babylonian Captivity.** In 538 B.C.E. the Persian king Cyrus the Great permitted some forty thousand exiles to

Baal   *An ancient Semitic fertility god represented as a golden calf.*

Babylonian Captivity   *The period of Jewish history between 586 and 537 B.C.E. during which the political and spiritual leaders of the kingdom of Judah were deported to Babylon following the defeat of Judah by Nebuchadnezzer.*

● **The Golden Calf**   According to the Bible, Moses descended from Mount Sinai, where he had received the Ten Commandments, to find the Hebrews worshiping a golden calf, which was against Yahweh's laws. In July 1990 an American archaeological team found this model of a gilded calf inside a pot. The figurine, which dates to about 1550 B.C.E., is strong evidence for the existence of the cult represented by the calf in Palestine. *(Courtesy of the Leon Levy Expedition to Ashkelon. Photo: Carl Andrews)*

Primary Source:
*Book of Exodus:
Moses Descends
Mount Sinai with the
Ten Commandments*

return to Jerusalem. During and especially after the Babylonian Captivity, the exiles redefined their beliefs and practices, thereby establishing what they believed was the law of Yahweh. Those who lived by these precepts came to be called Jews.

Daily Life in Israel

Marriage and the nuclear family were fundamentally important in Jewish life; celibacy was frowned upon and almost all major Jewish thinkers and priests were married. With parents making all the arrangements, boys and girls were often married while little more than children. They were expected to begin their own families at once. Sons were especially desired because they maintained the family bloodline, while keeping ancestral property in the family. A firstborn son became the head of the household at his father's death. Daughters were less highly valued because they would eventually leave the family after marriage. Unlike other cultures, Jews forbade infanticide because Yahweh prohibited it.

Mothers oversaw the early education of the children, but as boys grew older, their fathers gave them more of their education. The most important task for observant Jews was studying religious texts, an activity limited to men until the twentieth century. Women were obliged to provide for men's physical needs while they were studying, so Jewish women were often more active economically than their contemporaries of other religions.

The Hebrews were originally nomadic, but they adopted settled agriculture in Palestine. The development of urban life among Jews created new economic opportunities, especially in crafts and trade. Jewish merchants began to participate in maritime and caravan trade, and in the process entered the mainstream of Near Eastern life. Yet they always faithfully retained their unique religion and culture.

MAP 1.4 **The Assyrian and Persian Empires** The Assyrian Empire at its height (ca. 650 B.C.E.) included almost all of the old centers of power in the ancient Near East. By 513 B.C.E., however, the Persian Empire not only included more of that area but also extended as far east as western India. With the rise of the Medes and Persians, the balance of power in the Near East shifted east of Mesopotamia for the first time.

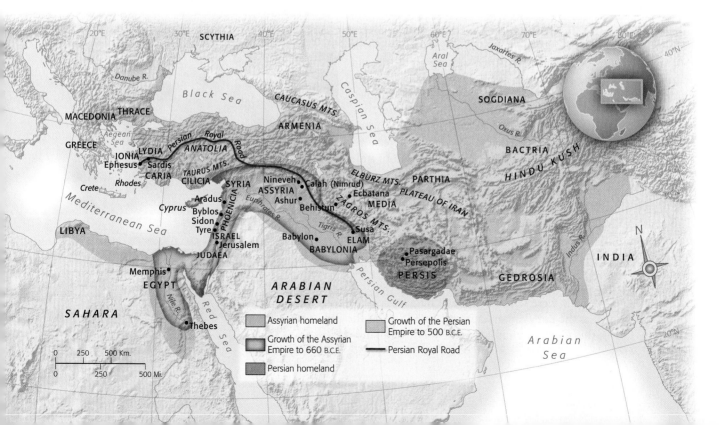

Siege of a City Art here serves to glorify horror. The Assyrian king Tiglath-pileser III launches an assault on a fortified city. The impaled bodies shown at center demonstrate the cruelty of Assyrian warfare. Also noticeable are the various weapons and means of attack used against the city. *(Courtesy of the Trustees of the British Museum)*

ASSYRIA, THE MILITARY MONARCHY (859–612 B.C.E.)

What enabled the Assyrians to conquer their neighbors, and how did they doom themselves by their cruelty?

Small kingdoms like those of the Phoenicians and the Jews could exist only in the absence of a major power. The beginning of the ninth century B.C.E. saw the rise of such a power in Assyria. The Assyrians dominated northern Mesopotamia with their chief capital at Nineveh on the Tigris River. The Assyrians were a Semitic people heavily influenced by the Babylonian culture to the south. They were also one of the most warlike people in history, and for over two hundred years they fought to dominate the Near East. The Assyrian kings Tiglath-pileser III (r. 774–727 B.C.E.) and Sargon II (r. 721–705 B.C.E.) conquered Syria, Palestine, and the two Jewish kingdoms, and in ca. 717 B.C.E. Sargon defeated the Egyptians before turning against Babylon. By almost constant warfare the two kings carved out an empire that stretched from east and north of the Tigris River to central Egypt (see Map 1.4).

Although atrocity and terrorism struck unspeakable fear into Assyria's subjects, Assyria's success was also due to sophisticated, farsighted, and effective military organization. Assyrian military genius was remarkable for the development of a wide variety of siege machinery and techniques, including excavations to undermine city walls and battering rams to knock down walls and gates. Never before in the Near East had anyone applied such technical knowledge to warfare. The Assyrians even invented the concept of a corps of engineers who bridged rivers with pontoons or provided soldiers with inflatable skins for swimming. The Assyrians also knew how to coordinate their efforts both in open battle and in siege warfare.

Not only did the Assyrians know how to win battles, but they also knew how to use their victories. As early as the reign of Tiglath-pileser III, the Assyrian kings began to organize their conquered territories into an empire. The lands closest to Assyria became provinces governed by Assyrian officials. Kingdoms beyond the provinces were not annexed but became dependent states that followed Assyria's lead. The Assyrian king chose their rulers either by regulating the succession of native kings or by supporting native kings who appealed to him. Against more distant states the Assyrian

Primary Source: Ashur-Nasir-Pal II, *An Assyrian Emperor's Resumé*

kings waged frequent war in order to conquer them outright or make the dependent states secure.

In the seventh century B.C.E. Assyrian power seemed firmly established. Yet the downfall of Assyria was swift and complete. Babylon finally won its independence in 626 B.C.E. and joined forces with a new people, the Medes, an Indo-European-speaking folk from Iran. Together the Babylonians and the Medes destroyed the Assyrian Empire in 612 B.C.E., paving the way for the rise of the Persians. The Hebrew prophet Nahum spoke for many when he asked: "Nineveh is laid waste: who will bemoan her?"[3] Their cities destroyed and their power shattered, the Assyrians disappeared from history, remembered only as a cruel people of the Bible. Two hundred years later, when the Greek adventurer and historian Xenophon passed by the ruins of Nineveh, he marveled at the extent of the former city but knew nothing of the Assyrians. The glory of their empire was forgotten.

● ●

THE EMPIRE OF THE PERSIAN KINGS (CA. 1000–464 B.C.E.)

How did Iranian nomads create the Persian Empire that ultimately embraced all of these earlier peoples?

The Iranians were Indo-Europeans from central Europe and southern Russia. They migrated into the land to which they have given their name, the area between the Caspian Sea and the Persian Gulf. They then fell under the spell of the more sophisticated cultures of their Mesopotamian neighbors. The Persians, the most important of the Iranian peoples, went on to create one of the greatest empires of the ancient Near East. Though as conquerors they willingly used force to accomplish their ends, they normally preferred to depend on diplomacy to rule. They usually respected their sub-

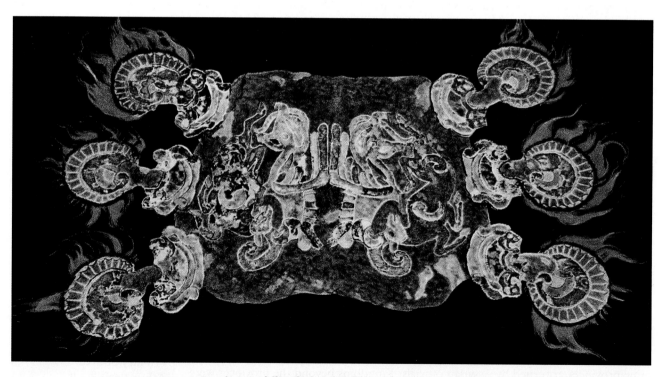

● **Persian Saddle-Cloth** This elaborately painted piece of leather, dating from the fourth or third centuries B.C.E., served a ceremonial rather than a practical function. (*© The State Hermitage Museum, St. Petersburg*)

jects and allowed them to practice their native customs and religions. Thus the Persians gave the Near East both political unity and cultural diversity.

Persia, modern Iran, is a stark land of towering mountains and flaming deserts, with a broad central plateau in the heart of the country (see Map 1.4). Between the Tigris-Euphrates Valley in the west and the Indus Valley in the east rises an immense plateau surrounded on all sides by lofty mountains that cut off the interior from the sea.

Iran's geographical position and topography explain its traditional role as the highway between western and eastern Asia. Throughout history wild nomadic peoples migrating from the broad steppes of Russia and Central Asia have streamed into Iran. Confronting the uncrossable salt deserts, most have turned either westward or eastward, moving on until they reached the advanced and wealthy urban centers of Mesopotamia and India. When cities emerged along the natural lines of east-west communication, Iran became the area where nomads met urban dwellers, a meeting ground of unique significance for the civilizations of both east and west.

The Coming of the Medes and Persians

The Iranians entered this land around 1000 B.C.E. as nomads who migrated with their flocks and herds. Like their kinsmen the Aryans, who moved into India, they were also horse breeders, and the horse gave them a decisive military advantage over the prehistoric peoples of Iran. The Iranians rode into battle in horse-drawn chariots or on horseback and easily swept the natives before them. Yet, because the influx of Iranians went on for centuries, there continued to be constant cultural interchange between conquering newcomers and conquered natives.

Gradually two groups of Iranians began coalescing into larger units. The Persians had settled in Persia, the modern region of Fars, in southern Iran. Their kinsmen the Medes occupied Media in the north, with their capital at Ecbatana, the modern Hamadan. Even though distracted by grave pressures from their neighbors, the Medes united under one king around 710 B.C.E. and extended their control over the Persians in the south. In 612 B.C.E. the Medes joined the Babylonians in overthrowing the Assyrian Empire. With the rise of the Medes, the balance of power in western Asia shifted for the first time east of Mesopotamia.

The Creation of the Persian Empire (550–464 B.C.E.)

In 550 B.C.E. Cyrus the Great (r. 559–530 B.C.E.), king of the Persians and one of the most remarkable statesmen of antiquity, conquered the Medes. His conquest resulted not in slavery and slaughter but in the union of the Iranian peoples. Having united Iran, Cyrus set out to achieve two goals. First, he wanted to win control of the west and thus of the terminal ports of the great trade routes that crossed Iran and Anatolia (modern western Turkey). Second, he strove to secure eastern Iran from the pressure of nomadic invaders. In a series of major campaigns Cyrus achieved both goals. He swept into Anatolia, easily overthrowing the young kingdom of Lydia. His generals subdued the Greek cities along the coast of Anatolia, thus gaining him flourishing ports on the Mediterranean. From Lydia Cyrus, marching to the far eastern corners of Iran, conquered

● **Funeral Pyre of Croesus** This scene, an excellent example of the precision and charm of ancient Greek vase painting, depicts the Lydian king Croesus on his funeral pyre. He pours a libation to the gods while his slave lights the fire. Herodotus has a happier ending, when he says that Cyrus the Great set fire to the pyre, but that Apollo sent rain to put it out. *(Louvre/ Réunion de Musées Nationaux/Art Resource, NY)*

● **The Impact of Zoroastrianism**   The Persian kings embraced Zoroastrianism as the religion of the realm. This rock carving at Behistun records the bond. King Darius I is seen trampling on one rebel with others behind him. Above is the sign of Ahuramazda, the god of truth and guardian of the Persian king. *(Robert Harding World Imagery)*

the regions of Parthia and Bactria. The Babylonians welcomed him as a liberator when his soldiers moved into their kingdom.

With these victories Cyrus demonstrated to the world his benevolence as well as his military might. He spared the life of Croesus, the conquered king of Lydia, to serve him as friend and adviser. He allowed the Greeks to live according to their customs, thus making possible the spread of Greek culture farther east. Cyrus's humanity likewise extended to the Jews, whom he found enslaved in Babylonia. He restored their sacred objects to them and returned them to Jerusalem, where he helped them rebuild their temple.

The Religion of Zoroaster

Around 600 B.C.E. Zoroaster, a religious thinker and preacher, introduced new spiritual concepts to the Iranian people. He taught that life is a constant battleground for the two opposing forces of good and evil. The Iranian god **Ahuramazda** embodied good and truth but was opposed by Ahriman, a hateful spirit who stood for evil and lies. Ahuramazda and Ahriman were locked together in a cosmic battle for the human race, a battle that stretched over thousands of years.

Zoroaster emphasized the individual's responsibility to choose between good and evil. He taught that people possessed the free will to decide between Ahuramazda and Ahriman and that they must rely on their own conscience to guide them through life. Their decisions were crucial, Zoroaster warned, for there would come a time of reckoning. The victorious Ahuramazda, like the Egyptian god Osiris, would preside over a last judgment to determine each person's eternal fate.

Zoroaster's teachings converted Darius, who did not, however, impose it on others. Under the protection of the Persian kings, **Zoroastrianism** won converts throughout Iran. It survived the fall of the Persian Empire to influence Judaism, Christianity, and early Islam. Good behavior in the world, even though unrecognized at the time, would receive ample reward in the hereafter. Evil, no matter how powerful in life,

Ahuramazda *The chief Iranian god, who was the creator and benefactor of all living creatures; unlike Yahweh, he was not a lone god.*

Zoroastrianism *The religion based on the teachings of Zoroaster, who emphasized the individual's responsibility to choose between good and evil. Though Zoroaster's teachings often met with opposition, the Persian ruler Darius was a convert.*

would be punished after death. In some form or another, Zoroastrian concepts still pervade many modern religions.

The Span of the Persian Empire

Cyrus's successors rounded out the Persian conquest of the ancient Near East. In 525 B.C.E. his son Cambyses (r. 530–522 B.C.E.) subdued Egypt. Darius (r. 521–486 B.C.E.) and his son Xerxes (r. 486–464 B.C.E.) unsuccessfully invaded Greece, but Darius in about 513 B.C.E. conquered western India. He created the Persian satrapy of Hindush, which included the valley of the Indus River. Thus, within thirty-seven years (550–513 B.C.E.) the Persians transformed themselves from a subject people to the rulers of an empire that included Asia Minor, Mesopotamia, Iran, and western India. They had created a vast empire encompassing all of the oldest and most honored kingdoms and peoples of these regions (see Map 1.4).

The Persians also knew how to preserve the peace they had won on the battlefield. Unlike the Assyrians, they did not resort to royal terrorism to maintain order. The Persians instead built an efficient administrative system to govern the empire based in their capital city of Persepolis near modern Schiras, Iran. From Persepolis they sent directions to the provinces and received reports back from their officials. To do so they built and maintained a sophisticated system of roads linking the empire. The main highway, the famous **Royal Road,** spanned some 1,677 miles (see Map 1.4). Other roads branched out to link all parts of the empire from the coast of Asia Minor to the valley of the Indus River. These highways meant that the king was usually in close touch with officials and subjects. The roads simplified the defense of the empire by making it easier to move Persian armies. The system also allowed the easy flow of trade. In all, these roads enabled the Persian kings to translate the concepts of right, justice, and good government into a practical reality.

Royal Road *The main highway created by the Persians; it spanned 1,677 miles from western Turkey to Iran.*

● **The Royal Palace at Persepolis** King Darius began and King Xerxes finished building a grand palace worthy of the glory of the Persian Empire. Pictured here is the monumental audience hall, where the king dealt with ministers of state and foreign envoys. *(George Holton/Photo Researchers)*

Chapter Summary

To assess your mastery of this chapter and read the primary sources listed in the margins, visit bedfordstmartins.com/mckayworld or see *Sources of World Societies*.

Key Terms

Near East
Neolithic period
nobles
clients
pharaoh
Amon-Ra
Book of the Dead
pyramid
Hyksos
Bronze Age
monotheism
Indo-European
Sea Peoples
Purple People
Baal
Babylonian Captivity
Ahuramazda
Zoroastrianism
Royal Road

• How did the Sumerians lay the foundations of a flourishing civilization in the hard land of Mesopotamia?

During the Neolithic period peoples used their new stone tools to create lives centered on towns. In Mesopotamia the Sumerians established the basic social, economic, and intellectual patterns that defined civilized life. These developments brought order and prosperity and led to the unification of Mesopotamia by Hammurabi and the Babylonians. They in turn nurtured and encouraged the spread of this rich life beyond Mesopotamia.

• How did geography enable the Egyptians easily to form a cohesive, prosperous society?

In Egypt, meanwhile, other peoples turned the fertile Nile Valley into the home of a rich, sophisticated society that lived harmoniously under the rule of kings, the pharaohs. This era saw the building of the pyramids, political stability, and long years of prosperity. During a period of internal weakness the Hyksos, a nomadic people, introduced Bronze Age technology into Egypt when they settled in the Nile Delta. Egyptian pharaohs, however, rallied to drive out the Hyksos and establish the rich period of the New Kingdom. A complex polytheistic mythology underlay Egyptian culture, and the pharaoh Akhenaten failed in his attempt to introduce Aton as the only true god.

• How did the Hittites affect the life of the ancient Near East?

From the northern fringes of this sphere came the Hittites, an Indo-European people who introduced iron tools and weapons. After establishing their own empire, they promoted a general alliance with the Egyptians and Babylonians that led to an era of peace.

• How did the Hebrews form a small kingdom after the fall of larger neighboring empires?

In the thirteenth century B.C.E. hostile invaders, the Sea Peoples, disrupted this stable world, which also allowed lesser native folk to become prominent. The Nubians of Africa adopted and preserved the old Egyptian civilization. The Phoenicians built small trading kingdoms that linked the Near East to the broader Mediterranean world. The Hebrews benefited from the absence of major powers to create a minor kingdom. They developed religious beliefs and a code of life that still flourish today.

• What enabled the Assyrians to conquer their neighbors, and how did they doom themselves by their cruelty?

In this world rose the Assyrians, another Semitic people who had lived on its periphery. Through effective military techniques and brutal aggression, they conquered the entire region, until a coalition of peoples utterly destroyed them.

• *How did Iranian nomads create the Persian Empire that ultimately embraced all of these earlier peoples?*

The Persians, one of the peoples instrumental in overthrowing the Assyrians, were also Indo-Europeans—Iranians from the north. They too created an empire, one that stretched from the eastern Mediterranean to western India. They introduced law, justice, and toleration into their imperial rule. They encouraged political unity and cultural diversity. Through their religion Zoroastrianism they fostered the concept of life as a battleground between good and evil.

Suggested Reading

Brosius, M. *The Persians: An Introduction.* 2006. Covers all of Persian history.

Edwards, D. N. *The Nubian Past.* 2004. Examines the history of Nubia and Sudan.

Hawass, Z. *Silent Images: Women in Pharaonic Egypt.* 2000. Blends texts and pictures to depict the history of Egyptian women.

Herzfeld, E. *Iran in the Ancient Near East.* 1987. Puts Persian history in a broad context.

Kuhrt, A. *The Ancient Near East,* 2 vols. 1995. Covers the region from the earliest times to Alexander's conquest.

Leick, G. *The Babylonians.* 2002. Introduces all aspects of Babylonian life and culture.

Marokoe, G. *The Phoenicians.* 2000. Presents these seafarers at home and abroad in the Mediterranean.

Oren, E. D. *The Hyksos.* 1997. Concentrates on the archaeological evidence for the Hyksos.

Rice, M. *Egypt's Early Making: The Origins of Ancient Egypt.* 2004. Treats the earliest periods of Egyptian history.

Visicato, C. *The Power of Writing.* 2000. Studies the practical importance of early Mesopotamian scribes.

Notes

1. Quoted in S. N. Kramer, *The Sumerians* (Chicago: University of Chicago Press, 1963), p. 238.
2. J.B. Pritchard, ed., *Ancient Near Eastern Texts,* 3d ed., p. 372. Copyright © 1969 by Princeton University Press. Reprinted by permission of Princeton University Press.
3. Nahum 3:7.

Listening to the
PAST

A Quest for Immortality

The human desire to escape the grip of death, to achieve immortality, is one of the oldest wishes of all peoples. The Sumerian Epic of Gilgamesh is the earliest recorded treatment of this topic. The oldest elements of the epic go back at least to the third millennium B.C.E. According to tradition, Gilgamesh was a king of Uruk whom the Sumerians, Babylonians, and Assyrians considered a hero-king and a god. In the story Gilgamesh and his friend Enkidu set out to attain immortality and join the ranks of the gods. They attempt to do so by performing wondrous feats against fearsome agents of the gods, who are determined to thwart them.

During their quest Enkidu dies. Gilgamesh, more determined than ever to become immortal, begins seeking anyone who might tell him how to do so. His journey involves the effort not only to escape from death but also to reach an understanding of the meaning of life.

The passage begins with Enkidu speaking of a dream that foretells his own death.

Listen, my friend [Gilgamesh], this is the dream I dreamed last night. The heavens roared, and earth rumbled back an answer; between them I stood before an awful being, the sombre-faced man-bird; he had directed on me his purpose. His was a vampire face, his foot was a lion's foot, his hand was an eagle's talon. He fell on me and his claws were in my hair, he held me fast and I smothered; then he transformed me so that my arms became wings covered with feathers. He turned his stare towards me, and he led me away to the palace of Irkalla, the Queen of Darkness [the goddess of the underworld; in other words, an agent of death], to the house from which none who enters ever returns, down the road from which there is no coming back.

At this point Enkidu dies, whereupon Gilgamesh sets off on his quest for the secret of immortality. During his travels he meets with Siduri, the wise and good-natured goddess of wine, who gives him the following advice.

Gilgamesh, where are you hurrying to? You will never find that life for which you are looking. When the gods created man they allotted to him death, but

life they retained in their own keeping. As for you, Gilgamesh, fill your belly with good things; day and night, night and day, dance and be merry, feast and rejoice. Let your clothes be fresh, bathe yourself in water, cherish the little child that holds your hand, and make your wife happy in your embrace; for this too is the lot of man.

Ignoring Siduri's advice, Gilgamesh continues his journey, until he finds Utnapishtim. Meeting Utnapishtim is especially important because, like Gilgamesh, he was once a mortal, but the gods so favored him that they put him in an eternal paradise. Gilgamesh puts to Utnapishtim the question that is the reason for his quest.

Oh, father Utnapishtim, you who have entered the assembly of the gods, I wish to question you concerning the living and the dead, how shall I find the life for which I am searching?

Utnapishtim said, "There is no permanence. Do we build a house to stand forever, do we seal a contract to hold for all time? Do brothers divide an inheritance to keep forever, does the flood-time of rivers endure? . . . What is there between the master and the servant when both have fulfilled their doom? When the Anunnaki [the gods of the underworld], the judges, come together, and Mammetun [the goddess of fate] the mother of destinies, together they decree the fates of men. Life and death they allot but the day of death they do not disclose.

Then Gilgamesh said to Utnapishtim the Faraway, "I look at you now, Utnapishtim, and your appearance is no different from mine; there is nothing strange in your features. I thought I should find you like a hero prepared for battle, but you lie here taking your ease on your back. Tell me truly, how was it that you came to enter the company of the gods and to possess everlasting life?" Utnapishtim said to Gilgamesh, "I shall reveal to you a mystery, I shall tell you a secret of the gods."

Utnapishtim then tells Gilgamesh of a time when the great god Enlil had become angered with the Sumerians and encouraged the other gods to wipe out humanity. The god

Gilgamesh, from decorative panel of a lyre unearthed at Ur. *(The University Museum, University of Pennsylvania, neg. T4-108)*

Ea, however, warned Utnapishtim about the gods' decision to send a great flood to destroy the Sumerians. He commanded Utnapishtim to build a boat big enough to hold his family, various artisans, and all animals in order to survive the flood that was to come. Although Enlil was infuriated by the Sumerians' survival, Ea rebuked him. Then Enlil relented and blessed Utnapishtim with eternal paradise. After telling the story, Utnapishtim foretells Gilgamesh's fate.

Utnapishtim said, ". . . The destiny was fulfilled which the father of the gods, Enlil of the mountain, had decreed for Gilgamesh: In nether-earth the darkness will show him a light: of mankind, all that are known, none will leave a monument for generations to compare with his. The heroes, the wise men, like the new moon have their waxing and waning. Men will say, Who has ever ruled with might and power like his? As in the dark month, the month of shadows, so without him there is no light. O Gilgamesh, this was the meaning of your dream [of immortality]. You were given the kingship, such was your destiny, everlasting life was not your destiny. Because of this do not be sad at heart, do not be grieved or oppressed; he [Enlil] has given you power to bind and to loose, to be the darkness and the light of mankind. He has given unexampled supremacy over the people, victory in battle from which no fugitive returns, in forays and assaults from which there is no going back. But do not abuse this power, deal justly with your servants in the palace, deal justly before the face of the Sun."

Questions for Analysis

1. What does the *Epic of Gilgamesh* reveal about Sumerian attitudes toward the gods and human beings?

2. At the end of his quest, did Gilgamesh achieve immortality? If so, what was the nature of that immortality?

3. What does the epic tell us about Sumerian views of the nature of human life? Where do human beings fit into the cosmic world?

Source: The Epic of Gilgamesh, translated by N. K. Sanders. Penguin Classics 1960, Second revised edition, 1972, pp. 91–119. Copyright © N. K. Sanders, 1960, 1964, 1972. Reproduced by permission of Penguin Books Ltd.

The North Gate at Sanchi, Madhya Pradesh. One of four ornately carved gates guarding this Buddhist memorial shrine, second century B.C.E. *(Jean-Louis Nou/akg-images)*

2 THE FOUNDATION OF INDIAN SOCIETY, TO 300 C.E.

Chapter Preview

The Land and Its First Settlers (ca. 3000–1500 B.C.E.)
• What does archaeology tell us about the earliest civilization in India?

The Aryans and the Vedic Age (ca. 1500–500 B.C.E.)
• What kind of society and culture did the Indo-European Aryans create?

India's Great Religions
• What ideas and practices were taught by the founders of Jainism, Buddhism, and Hinduism?

India and the West (ca. 513–298 B.C.E.)
• How did India respond to the expansion of the Persian and Greek empires?

The Mauryan Empire (ca. 322–185 B.C.E.)
• What were the consequences of the unification of much of India by Chandragupta and Ashoka?

Small States and Trading Networks (200 B.C.E.–300 C.E.)
• How was India shaped by political disunity and contacts with other cultures?

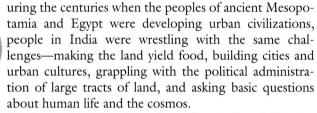

During the centuries when the peoples of ancient Mesopotamia and Egypt were developing urban civilizations, people in India were wrestling with the same challenges—making the land yield food, building cities and urban cultures, grappling with the political administration of large tracts of land, and asking basic questions about human life and the cosmos.

Like the civilizations of the Near East, the earliest Indian civilization centered on a great river, the Indus. From about 2800 to 1800 B.C.E., this Indus Valley, or Harappan, culture thrived, and numerous cities were built over a huge area. A very different Indian society emerged after the decline of this civilization. It was dominated by the Aryans, warriors who spoke an early version of Sanskrit. The Indian caste system and the Hindu religion, key features of Indian society into modern times, had their origins in early Aryan society. The earliest Indian literature consists of the epics and religious texts of these Aryan tribes.

By the middle of the first millennium B.C.E., the Aryans had set up numerous small kingdoms throughout north India. This was the great age of Indian religious creativity, when Buddhism and Jainism were founded and the early Brahmanic religion of the Aryans developed into Hinduism. Alexander the Great invaded north India in 326 B.C.E., and after his army withdrew, the first major Indian empire was created by the Mauryan dynasty (ca. 322–ca. 185 B.C.E.), which unified most of north India. This dynasty reached its peak under the great king Ashoka (r. ca. 269–232 B.C.E.), who actively promoted Buddhism both within his realm and beyond it. Not long afterward, however, the empire broke up, and for several centuries India was politically divided.

Although India never had a single language and only periodically had a centralized government, cultural elements dating back to the ancient period—the core ideas of Brahmanism, the caste system, and the early epics—gave India cultural identity. These cultural elements spread through trade and other contact, even when the subcontinent was divided into hostile kingdoms.

THE LAND AND ITS FIRST SETTLERS (CA. 3000–1500 B.C.E.)

What does archaeology tell us about the earliest civilization in India?

The subcontinent of India, a landmass as large as western Europe, juts southward into the warm waters of the Indian Ocean. Today this region is divided into the separate countries of Pakistan, Nepal, India, Bangladesh, and Sri Lanka, but these divisions are recent, and for premodern times the entire subcontinent will be called India here.

In India, as elsewhere, the possibilities for both agriculture and communication have always been strongly shaped by geography (see Map 2.1). Some regions are among the wettest on earth; others are arid deserts and scrubland. Most areas in India are warm all year, with temperatures over 100°F common. Average temperatures range from 79°F in the north to 85°F in the south. Monsoon rains sweep northward from the Indian Ocean each summer. The lower reaches of the Himalaya Mountains in the northeast are covered by dense forests, sustained by heavy rainfall. Immediately to the south are the fertile valleys of the Indus and Ganges Rivers. These lowland plains, which stretch all the way across the subcontinent, over time were tamed for agriculture, and India's great empires were centered there. To their west are the great deserts of Rajasthan and southeastern Pakistan, historically important in part because their flat terrain enabled invaders to sweep into India from the northwest. South of the great river valleys rise the jungle-clad Vindhya Mountains and the dry, hilly Deccan Plateau. In this part of India, only along the coasts do the hills give way to narrow plains where crop agriculture flourished. India's long coastlines and predictable winds fostered maritime trade with other countries bordering the Indian Ocean.

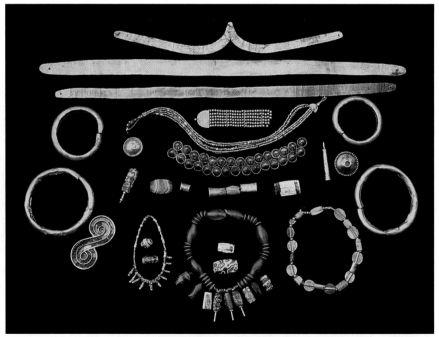

● **Harappan Artifacts** Small objects like seals and jewelry found at Harappan sites provide glimpses of early Indian religious imagination and daily life. The molded tablet shown on the left depicts a female deity battling two tigers. She stands above an elephant. The jewelry found at these sites, such as those pieces shown on the right, makes much use of gold and precious stones. *(J. M. Kenoyer/Courtesy Department of Archaeology and Museums, Government of Pakistan)*

Neolithic settlement of the Indian subcontinent occurred somewhat later than in the Middle East, but agriculture was well established by about 7000 B.C.E. Wheat and barley were the early crops, probably having spread in their domesticated form from the Middle East. Farmers also domesticated cattle, sheep, and goats and learned to make pottery.

The story of the first civilization in India is one of the most dramatic in the ancient world. From the Bible, Europeans knew about ancient Egypt and Ur, but no one knew about the ancient cities of the Indus Valley until 1921, when archaeologists found astonishing evidence of a thriving and sophisticated Bronze Age urban culture dating to about 2500 B.C.E. at Mohenjo-daro in what is now Pakistan.

This civilization is known today as the Indus Valley or the **Harappan** civilization, from the modern names of the river and a major city, respectively. Archaeologists have discovered some three hundred Harappan cities and many more towns and villages in both Pakistan and India, making it possible to see both the vast regional extent of the Harappan civilization and its evolution over a period of nearly a millennium. It was a literate civilization, like those of Egypt and Mesopotamia, but no one has been able to decipher the more than four hundred symbols inscribed on stone seals and copper tablets. Its most flourishing period was 2500 to 2000 B.C.E.

The Indus civilization extended over nearly five hundred thousand square miles in the Indus Valley, making it more than twice as large as the territories of the ancient Egyptian and Sumerian civilizations. Yet Harappan civilization was marked by a striking uniformity. Throughout the region, for instance, even in small villages, bricks were made to standard proportions of 4:2:1. Figurines of pregnant women have been found throughout the area, suggesting common religious ideas and practices.

Like Mesopotamian cities, Harappan cities were centers for crafts and trade surrounded by extensive farmland. Fine ceramics were made on the potter's wheel and decorated with geometric designs. Cotton was used to make cloth (the earliest anywhere) and was so abundant that goods were wrapped in it for shipment. Trade was extensive. As early as the reign of Sargon of Akkad in the third millennium B.C.E., trade between India and Mesopotamia carried goods and ideas between the two cultures, probably by way of the Persian Gulf. The port of Lothal had a stone dock seven hundred feet long, next to which were massive granaries and bead-making factories. Hundreds of seals were found there, some of Persian Gulf origin, indicating that Lothal was a major port of exit and entry.

Both Mohenjo-daro, in southern Pakistan, and Harappa, some four hundred miles to the north, were huge, more than three miles in circumference, and housed populations estimated at thirty-five thousand to forty thousand. They were both defended by great citadels that towered forty to fifty feet above the surrounding plain. Both cities had obviously been planned and built before being settled; they were not the

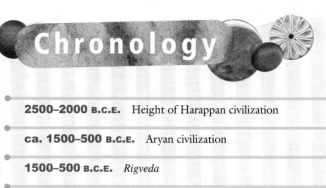

Chronology

2500–2000 B.C.E.	Height of Harappan civilization
ca. 1500–500 B.C.E.	Aryan civilization
1500–500 B.C.E.	*Rigveda*
ca. 1000 B.C.E.	Introduction of iron
750–500 B.C.E.	*Upanishads*
fl. ca. 520 B.C.E.	Vardhamana Mahavira, founder of Jainism
ca. 513 B.C.E.	Darius conquers Indus Valley
fl. ca. 500 B.C.E.	Siddhartha Gautama, the Buddha
ca. 400 B.C.E.–200 C.E.	Brahmanic religion evolves into Hinduism
326 B.C.E.	Alexander the Great enters Indus Valley
ca. 322–185 B.C.E.	Mauryan Empire
ca. 300 B.C.E.	Jain religion splits into two sects
ca. 269–232 B.C.E.	Reign of Ashoka
ca. 200 B.C.E.–200 C.E.	Classical period of Tamil culture
fl. ca. 100 C.E.	Nagarjuna, theorist of Mahayana Buddhism
ca. 200 C.E.	Code of Manu

Harappan   *The first Indian civilization; it is also known as the Indus Valley civilization.*

outcomes of villages that grew and sprawled haphazardly. Streets were straight and varied from nine to thirty-four feet in width. The houses were substantial, many two stories tall, some perhaps three. The focal point of a house was a central courtyard onto which the rooms opened, much like many houses today in both rural and urban India.

Perhaps the most surprising aspect of the elaborate planning of these cities is their complex system of drainage, well preserved at Mohenjo-daro. Each house had a bathroom with a drain connected to brick-lined sewers located under the major streets. Openings allowed the refuse to be collected, probably to be used as fertilizer on nearby fields. No other ancient city had such an advanced sanitation system.

Both cities also contained numerous large structures, which excavators think were public buildings. One of the most important was the large ventilated storehouse for the community's grain. Mohenjo-daro also had a marketplace or place of assembly, a palace, and a huge pool some thirty-nine feet long by twenty-three feet wide and eight feet deep. Like the later Roman baths, it had spacious dressing rooms for the bathers. Because the Great Bath at Mohenjo-daro resembles the ritual purification pools of later India, some scholars have speculated that power was in the hands of a priest-king and that the Great Bath played a role in the religious rituals of the city.

The prosperity of the Indus civilization depended on constant and intensive cultivation of the rich river valley. Although rainfall seems to have been greater then than in recent times, the Indus, like the Nile, flowed through a relatively dry region made fertile by annual floods and irrigation. And as in Egypt, agriculture was aided by a long, hot growing season and near constant sunshine.

Because the written language of the Harappan people has not been deciphered, their political, intellectual, and religious life is largely unknown. There clearly was a political structure with the authority to organize city planning and facilitate trade, but we do not even know whether there were hereditary kings. There are clear connections between Harappan and Sumerian civilization, but just as clear differences. For instance, the Harappan script, like the Sumerian, was incised on clay tablets and seals, but it has no connection to Sumerian cuneiform, and the artistic style of the Harappan seals also is distinct. There are many signs of continuity with later Indian civilization, ranging from the sorts of pottery ovens used to some of the images of gods. Some scholars think that the people of Harappa were the ancestors of the Dravidian-speaking peoples of modern south India. Analysis of skeletons, however, indicates that the population of the Indus Valley in ancient times was very similar to the modern population of the same region.

The decline of Harappan civilization, which began soon after 2000 B.C.E., cannot be attributed to the arrival of powerful invaders, as was once thought. Rather the decline was internally generated. The port of Lothal was abandoned by about 1900 B.C.E., and other major centers came to house only a fraction of their earlier populations. Scholars have offered many explanations for the mystery of the abandonment of these cities. Perhaps an earthquake led to a shift in the

● **Mohenjo-daro** Mohenjo-daro was a planned city built of fired mud brick. Its streets were straight, and covered drain-pipes were installed to carry away waste. From sites like this, we know that the early Indian political elite had the power and technical expertise to organize large, coordinated building projects. *(Josephine Powell)*

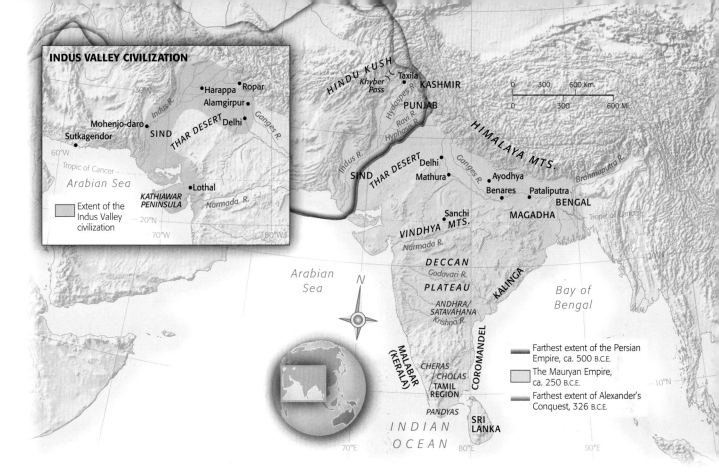

INDUS VALLEY CIVILIZATION

Extent of the Indus Valley civilization

Farthest extent of the Persian Empire, ca. 500 B.C.E.

The Mauryan Empire, ca. 250 B.C.E.

Farthest extent of Alexander's Conquest, 326 B.C.E.

MAP 2.1 **India from ca. 2500 B.C.E. to 300 C.E.** The earliest civilization in India developed in the Indus River valley in the west of the subcontinent. The Ganges River valley was the heart of the later Mauryan Empire. Although India is protected from the cold by mountains in the north, mountain passes in the northwest allowed both migration and invasion.

course of the river, or perhaps rainfall and snowmelt decreased and the rivers dried up. Perhaps the long-term practice of irrigation led to the buildup of salts and alkalines in the soil until they reached levels toxic to plants. Perhaps long-distance commerce collapsed, leading to an economic depression. Perhaps the population fell prey to diseases, such as malaria, that led people to flee the cities. Even though the Harappan people apparently lived on after scattering to villages, they were not able to retain key features of the high culture of the Indus civilization. For the next thousand years, India had no large cities, no kiln-fired bricks, and no written language.

THE ARYANS AND THE VEDIC AGE (CA. 1500–500 B.C.E.)

What kind of society and culture did the Indo-European Aryans create?

After the decline of the Indus Valley civilization, a people who called themselves **Aryans** became dominant in north India. They were speakers of an early form of Sanskrit, which was an Indo-European language closely related to ancient Persian and more distantly related to Latin, Greek, Celtic, and their modern descendants, such as English. The Sanskrit *nava,* "ship," is related to the English word *naval; deva,* "god," to *divine; raja,* "ruler," to *regal;* and so on. The word *Aryan* itself comes from *Arya,* "noble" or "pure" in Sanskrit, and has the same root as *Iran* and *Ireland.*

Until relatively recently, the dominant theory was that the Aryans came into India from outside, perhaps as part of the same movements of people that led to the Hittites

Aryans *The dominant people in North India after the decline of the Indus Valley civilization; they spoke an early form of Sanskrit.*

occupying parts of Anatolia, the Achaeans entering Greece, and the Kassites conquering Sumer—all in the period from about 1900 to 1750 B.C.E. Some scholars, however, have proposed that the Indo-European languages spread to this area much earlier; to them it seems possible that the Harappan people were speakers of an early Indo-European language. If that was the case, the Aryans would be one of the groups descended from this early population.

Modern politics complicates analysis of the appearance of the Aryans and their role in India's history. It was Europeans in the eighteenth and nineteenth centuries who developed the concept of Indo-European languages, and they did so in an age both highly conscious of race and in the habit of identifying races with languages. The racist potential of the concept was fully exploited by the Nazis, with their glorification of the Aryans as a superior race. But even in less politicized contexts, the notion of a group of people who entered India from outside and made themselves its rulers is troubling to many. Does it mean that the non-Aryans are the true Indians? Or, to the contrary, does it add legitimacy to those who in later times conquered India from outside? Does it justify or undermine the caste system? One of the difficulties faced by scholars who wish to take a dispassionate view of these issues is that the evidence for the earlier Harappan culture is entirely archaeological and the evidence for the Aryans is almost entirely based on linguistic analysis of modern languages and orally transmitted texts of uncertain date.

The central source for the early Aryans is the **Rigveda,** the earliest of the Vedas, a collection of hymns, ritual texts, and philosophical treatises composed between 1500 and 500 B.C.E. in Sanskrit. Like Homer's epics in Greece, these texts were transmitted orally and are in verse. The *Rigveda* portrays the Aryans as warrior tribes who glorified military skill and heroism; loved to drink, hunt, race, and dance; and counted their wealth in cattle. The Aryans did not sweep across India in a quick campaign, nor were they a disciplined army led by one conqueror. Rather they were a collection of tribes who frequently fought with each other and only over the course of several centuries came to dominate north India.

Those the Aryans fought often lived in fortified towns and put up a strong defense against them. The key to the Aryans' success probably lay in their superior military technology: they had fast two-wheeled chariots, horses, and bronze swords and spears. Their epics, however, present the struggle in religious terms: their chiefs were godlike heroes, and their opponents irreligious savages who did not perform the proper sacrifices. In time, however, the Aryans clearly absorbed much from those they conquered.

At the head of each Aryan tribe was a chief, or **raja,** who led his followers in battle and ruled them in peacetime. The warriors in the tribe elected the chief for his military skills. Next in importance to the chief was the priest. In time, priests evolved into a distinct class possessing precise knowledge of the complex rituals and of the invocations and formulas that accompanied them, rather like the priest classes in ancient Egypt, Mesopotamia, and Persia. The warrior nobility rode into battle in chariots and perhaps on horseback; they met at assemblies to reach decisions and advise the raja. The common tribesmen tended herds and in time worked the land. To the conquered non-Aryans fell the drudgery of menial tasks. It is difficult to define precisely their social status. Though probably not slaves, they were certainly subordinate to the Aryans and worked for them in return for protection.

Over the course of several centuries, the Aryans pushed farther east into the valley of the Ganges River, at that time a land of thick jungle populated by aboriginal forest peoples. The tremendous challenge of clearing the jungle was made somewhat easier by the introduction of iron around 1000 B.C.E. Iron made it possible to produce strong axes and knives relatively cheaply.

The Aryans did not gain dominance over the entire Indian subcontinent. South of the Vindhya range, people speaking Dravidian languages maintained their control. In the great Aryan epics the *Ramayana* and *Mahabharata,* the people of the south and Sri

● Bronze Sword A striking example of the quality of Aryan arms is this bronze sword, with its rib in the middle of the blade for strength. Superior weapons gave the Aryans military advantage. *(Courtesy of the Trustees of the British Museum)*

Rigveda *The earliest collection of hymns, ritual texts, and philosophical treatises, it is the central source of information on early Aryans.*

raja *From an ancient Indo-European word meaning "to rule," and related to the modern English "royal," raja refers to an Aryan tribal chieftain who led his people into battle and governed them during peacetime.*

Primary Source:
From **Rigveda**

Lanka are spoken of as dark-skinned savages and demons who resisted the Aryans' conquests. Still, in time these epics became part of the common cultural heritage of all of India.

Early Indian Society (1000–500 B.C.E.)

As Aryan rulers came to dominate large settled populations, the style of political organization changed from tribal chieftainship to territorial kingship. In other words, the ruler controlled an area whose people might change, not a nomadic tribe that moved as a group. Moreover, kings no longer needed to be elected by the tribe; it was enough to be invested by priests and to perform the splendid royal ceremonies they designed. The priests, or **Brahmans,** supported the growth of royal power in return for royal confirmation of their own power and status. The Brahmans also served as advisers to the kings. In the face of this royal-priestly alliance, the old tribal assemblies of warriors withered away. By the time Persian armies reached the Indus around 513 B.C.E., there were sixteen major kingdoms in north India.

Early Aryan society had distinguished among the warrior elite, the priests, ordinary tribesmen, and conquered subjects. These distinctions gradually evolved into the **caste system.** Society was conceived in terms of four hierarchical strata whose members do not eat with or marry each other. These strata (called **varna**) are *Brahman* (priests), *Kshatriya* (warriors and officials), *Vaishya* (merchants and artisans), and *Shudra* (peasants and laborers). The lowest level probably evolved out of the efforts of the numerically outnumbered Aryans to maintain their dominance over their subjects and not be absorbed by them. The three upper varnas probably accounted for no more than 30 percent of the population. Social and religious attitudes entered into these distinctions as well. Aryans considered the work of artisans impure. They left all such work to the local people, who were probably superior to them in these arts anyway. Trade, by contrast, was not viewed as demeaning. Brahmanic texts of the period refer to trade as equal in value to farming, serving the king, or serving as a priest.

Those without places in this tidy social division—that is, those who entered it later than the others or who had lost their caste status through violations of ritual—were **outcastes.** That simply meant that they belonged to no caste. In time, some of these people became "untouchables," because they were "impure." They were scorned because they earned their living by performing such "polluting" jobs as slaughtering animals and dressing skins.

Slavery was a feature of early social life in India, as it was in Egypt, Mesopotamia, and elsewhere in antiquity. Those captured in battle often became slaves, but captives could also be ransomed by their families. Later, slavery was less connected with warfare and became more of an economic and social institution. As in ancient Mesopotamia, a free man might sell himself and his family into slavery because he could not pay his debts. And, as in Hammurabi's Mesopotamia, he could, if clever, hard-working, or fortunate, buy his and his family's way out of slavery. At birth, slave children automatically became the slaves of their parents' masters. Indian slaves could be bought, used as collateral, or given away.

Women's lives in early India varied according to their social status, much as men's did. Like most nomadic tribes, the Aryans were patrilineal and patriarchal (tracing descent through males and placing power over family members in the senior men of the family). Thus women in Aryan society probably had more subordinate roles than did women among local Dravidian groups, many of whom were matrilineal. But even in Aryan society, women were treated somewhat more favorably than in later Indian society. They were not yet given in child-marriage, and widows had the right to remarry. In the epics such as the *Ramayana,* women are often portrayed as forceful personalities, able to achieve their goals both by feminine ploys of cajoling men and by more direct action. (See the feature "Listening to the Past: Rama and Sita" on pages 50–51.)

Brahmans *Priests of the Aryans. They supported the growth of royal power in return for royal confirmation of their own religious rights, power, and status.*

caste system *The Indian system of dividing society into hereditary groups that limited interaction with each other, especially marriage to each other.*

varna *The four strata into which Indian society was divided under the caste system.*

outcastes *People not belonging to a caste; they were often scorned and sometimes deemed "untouchables."*

Brahmanism

The gods of the Aryans shared some features with the gods of other early Indo-European societies such as the Persians and Greeks. Some of them were great brawling figures, such as Agni, the god of fire; Indra, wielder of the thunderbolt and god of war, who each year slew a dragon to release the monsoon rains; and Rudra, the divine archer who spread disaster and disease by firing his arrows at people. Varuna, the god of order in the universe, was a hard god, quick to punish those who sinned and thus upset the balance of nature. Ushas, the goddess of dawn, was a gentle deity who welcomed the birds, gave delight to human beings, and warded off evil spirits.

The core of the Aryans' religion was its focus on sacrifice. By giving valued things to the gods, people strengthened them and established relationships with them. Gradually, under the priestly monopoly of the Brahmans, correct sacrifice and proper ritual became so important that most Brahmans believed that a properly performed ritual would force a god to grant a worshiper's wish.

The *Upanishads,* composed between 750 and 500 B.C.E., record speculations about the mystical meaning of sacrificial rites and about cosmological questions of man's relationship to the universe. They document a gradual shift from the mythical world-view of the early Vedic age to a deeply philosophical one. Associated with this shift was a movement toward *asceticism*—severe self-discipline and self-denial. In search of wisdom, some men retreated to the forests. These ascetics concluded that disciplined meditation on the ritual sacrifice could produce the same results as the physical ritual itself. Thus they reinterpreted ritual sacrifices as symbolic gestures with mystical meanings.

samsara *The transmigration of souls by a continual process of rebirth.*

Ancient Indian cosmology focused not on a creator who made the universe out of nothing, but rather on endlessly repeating cycles. Key ideas were **samsara,** the transmigration of souls by a continual process of rebirth, and **karma,** the tally of good and bad deeds that determined the status of an individual's next life. Good deeds led to better future lives, evil deeds to worse future lives—even to reincarnation as an animal. Thus gradually arose the concept of a wheel of life that included human beings, animals, and even gods. Reward and punishment worked automatically; there was no all-knowing god who judged people and could be petitioned to forgive a sin, and each individual was responsible for his or her own destiny in a just and impartial world.

karma *The tally of good and bad deeds that determines the status of an individual's next life.*

To most people, especially those on the low end of the economic and social scale, these ideas were attractive. By living righteously and doing good deeds, people could improve their lot in the next life. Yet there was another side to these ideas: the wheel of life could be seen as a treadmill, giving rise to a yearning for release from the relentless cycle of birth and death. One solution offered in the *Upanishads* was **moksha,** or release from the wheel of life. Brahmanic mystics claimed that life in the world was actually an illusion and that the only way to escape the wheel of life was to realize that ultimate reality was unchanging.

moksha *Release from the wheel of life.*

This unchanging, ultimate reality was called **brahman.** The multitude of things in the world is fleeting; the only true reality is brahman. Even the individual soul or self is ultimately the same substance as the universal brahman, in the same way that each spark is in substance the same as a large fire. Equating the individual self with the ultimate reality suggested that the apparent duality in the world is in some sense unreal. At the same time it conveyed that all people had in themselves an eternal truth that corresponded to an identical but greater all-encompassing reality.

brahman *The unchanging, ultimate reality, according to the Upanishads.*

The *Upanishads* gave the Brahmans a high status to which the poor and lowly could aspire in a future life. Consequently, the Brahmans greeted the concepts presented in these works and those who taught them with tolerance and understanding and made a place for them in traditional religious practice. The rulers of Indian society also encouraged the new trends, since the doctrines of samsara and karma encouraged the poor and oppressed to labor peacefully and dutifully. In other words, although the new doctrines were intellectually revolutionary, in social and political terms they supported the existing power structure.

INDIA'S GREAT RELIGIONS

What ideas and practices were taught by the founders of Jainism, Buddhism, and Hinduism?

By the sixth and fifth centuries B.C.E., cities had reappeared in India, and merchants and trade were thriving. Bricks were again baked in kilns and used to build ramparts around cities. One particular kingdom, Magadha, had become much more powerful than any of the other states in the Ganges plain, defeating its enemies by using war elephants and catapults for hurling stones. Written language had by this point reappeared.

This was a period of intellectual ferment throughout Eurasia—the period of the early Greek philosophers, the Hebrew prophets, Zoroaster in Persia, and Confucius and the early Daoists in China. In India it led to numerous sects that rejected various elements of Brahmanic teachings. (See the feature "Individuals in Society: Gosala.") The two most important in world-historical terms were Jainism and Buddhism. Their founders were contemporaries living in east India in minor states of the Ganges plain. Hinduism emerged in response to these new religions but at the same time was the most direct descendant of the old Brahmanic religion.

Jainism

The key figure of Jainism, Vardhamana Mahavira (fl. ca. 520 B.C.E.), was the son of the chief of a petty state. Like many ascetics of the period, he left home to become a wandering holy man. For twelve years, from ages thirty to forty-two, he traveled through the Ganges Valley until he found enlightenment and became a "completed soul." Mahavira taught his doctrines for about thirty years, founding a disciplined order of monks and gaining the support of many lay followers, male and female.

Mahavira accepted the doctrines of karma and rebirth but developed these ideas in new directions. He argued that human beings, animals, plants, and even inanimate objects all have living souls enmeshed in matter, accumulated through the workings of karma. Even a rock has a soul locked inside it, enchained by matter but capable of suffering if someone kicks it. The souls conceived by the Jains have finite dimensions. They float or sink depending on the amount of matter with which they are enmeshed. The ascetic, who willingly undertakes suffering, can dissipate some of the accumulated karma and make progress toward liberation. If a soul at last escapes from all the matter weighing it down, it becomes lighter than ordinary objects and floats to the top of the universe, where it remains forever in inactive bliss.

Mahavira's followers pursued such liberation by living ascetic lives and avoiding evil thoughts and actions. The Jains considered all life sacred and tried to live without

● **Jain Ascetic** The most extreme of Jain ascetics not only endured the elements without the help of clothes but were also generally indifferent to bodily comfort. The Jain saint depicted in this eighth-century cave temple has maintained his yogic posture for so long that vines have grown up around him. *(Courtesy, Robert Fisher)*

destroying other life. Some early Jains went to the extreme of starving themselves to death, since it is impossible to eat without destroying at least plants, but most took the less extreme step of distinguishing between different levels of life. The most sacred life forms were human beings, followed by animals, plants, and inanimate objects. A Jain who wished to avoid violence to life became a vegetarian and took pains not to kill any creature, even tiny insects in the air and soil. Farming was impossible for Jains, who tended instead to take up trade. Among the most conservative, priests practiced nudity, for clinging to clothes, even a loincloth, was a form of attachment. Lay Jains could pursue Jain teachings by practicing nonviolence and not eating meat. The Jains' radical nonviolence was motivated by a desire to escape the karmic consequences of causing harm to a life. In other words, violence had to be avoided above all because it harms the person who commits it.

For the first century after Mahavira's death, the Jains were a comparatively small and unimportant sect. Jainism began to flourish under the Mauryan dynasty (ca. 322–185 B.C.E.; see pages 44–46), and Jain tradition claims the Mauryan Empire's founder, Chandragupta, as a major patron. About 300 B.C.E. the Jain scriptures were recorded, and the religion split into two sects, one maintaining the tradition of total nudity, the other choosing to wear white robes on the grounds that clothes were an insignificant external sign, unrelated to true liberation. Over the next few centuries, Jain monks were particularly important in spreading northern culture into the Deccan and Tamil regions of south India.

Although Jainism never took hold as widely as Hinduism and Buddhism, it has been an influential strand in Indian thought and has several million adherents in India today. Fasting and nonviolence as spiritual practices in India owe much to Jain teachings. Mahatma Gandhi was influenced by these ideas through his mother, and Dr. Martin Luther King, Jr., was influenced by Gandhi.

Siddhartha Gautama and Buddhism

> **Primary Source:**
> **The Buddha, *Setting in Motion the Wheel of Law***

Siddhartha Gautama (fl. ca. 500 B.C.E.), also called Shakyamuni ("sage of the Shakya tribe"), is best known as the Buddha ("enlightened one"). He was a contemporary of Mahavira and came from the same social class (that is, warrior, not Brahman). He was born the son of a chief of one of the tribes in the Himalayan foothills in what is now Nepal. At age twenty-nine, unsatisfied with his life of comfort and troubled by the suffering he saw around him, he left home to become a wandering ascetic. He traveled south to the kingdom of Magadha, where he studied with yoga masters but later took up extreme asceticism. According to tradition, while meditating under a bo tree at Bodh Gaya, he reached enlightenment—that is, he gained perfect insight into the processes of the universe. After several weeks of meditation, he preached his first sermon, urging a "middle way" between asceticism and worldly life. For the next forty-five years, the Buddha traveled through the Ganges Valley, propounding his ideas, refuting his adversaries, and attracting followers. To reach as wide an audience as possible, the Buddha preached in the local language, Magadhi, rather than in Sanskrit, which was already becoming a priestly language. Probably because he refused to recognize the divine authority of the Vedas and dismissed sacrifices, he attracted followers mostly from among merchants, artisans, and farmers, rather than Brahmans.

Four Noble Truths *The Buddha's message that pain and suffering are inescapable parts of life; suffering and anxiety are caused by human desires and attachments; people can understand and triumph over these weaknesses; and the triumph is made possible by following a simple code of conduct.*

In his first sermon, the Buddha outlined his main message, summed up in the **Four Noble Truths** and the **Eightfold Path.** The truths are as follows: (1) pain and suffering, frustration and anxiety, are ugly but inescapable parts of human life; (2) suffering and anxiety are caused by human desires and attachments; (3) people can understand these weaknesses and triumph over them; and (4) this triumph is made possible by following a simple code of conduct, the Eightfold Path. The basic insight of Buddhism is thus psychological. The deepest human longings can never be satisfied, and even those things that seem to give pleasure cause anxiety because we are afraid of losing them. Attachment to people and things causes sorrow at their loss.

Eightfold Path *The code of conduct, set forth by the Buddha in his first sermon, which began with "right conduct" and eventually reached "right contemplation."*

Gosala

Texts that survive from early India are rich in religious and philosophical speculation and in tales of gods and heroes but not in history of the sort written by the early Chinese and Greeks. Because Indian writers and thinkers of antiquity had little interest in recording the actions of rulers or accounting for the rise and decline of different states, few people's lives are known in any detail.

Religious literature, however, does sometimes include details of the lives of followers and adversaries. The life of Gosala, for instance, is known primarily from early Buddhist and Jain scriptures. He was a contemporary of both Mahavira, the founder of the Jains, and Gautama, the Buddha, and both of them saw him as one of their most pernicious rivals.

According to the Jain account, Gosala was born in the north Indian kingdom of Magadha, the son of a professional mendicant. The name Gosala, which means "cowshed," alluded to the fact that he was born in a cowshed where his parents had taken refuge during the rainy season. The Buddhist account adds that he became a naked wandering ascetic when he fled from his enraged master after breaking an oil jar. As a mendicant, he soon fell in with Mahavira, who had recently commenced his life as an ascetic. After accompanying Mahavira on his travels for at least six years, Gosala came to feel that he was spiritually more advanced than his master and left to undertake the practice of austerities on his own. After he gained magical powers, he challenged his master and gathered his own disciples.

Both Jain and Buddhist sources agree that Gosala taught a form of fatalism that they saw as dangerously wrong. A Buddhist source says that he taught that people are good or bad not because of their own efforts but because of fate. "Just as a ball of string, when it is cast forth, will spread out just as far and no farther than it can unwind, so both fools and wise alike, wandering in transmigration exactly for the allotted term, shall then, and only then, make an end of pain."* Some people reach perfection, but not by their own efforts; rather they are individuals who through the course of numerous rebirths over hundreds of thousands of years have rid themselves of bad karma.

The Jains claimed that Gosala lived with a potter woman, violating the celibacy expected of ascetics and moreover teaching that sexual relations were not sinful. The followers of Gosala, a Buddhist source stated, wore no clothing and were very particular about the food they accepted, refusing food specially prepared

The Jain founder in seated meditation.
(Philadelphia Museum of Art: Acquired from the National Museum, New Delhi, India [by exchange] with funds contributed by Mr. and Mrs. Roland L. Taylor [1969-30-1])

for them, food in a cooking pan, and food from couples or women with children. Like other ascetics, Gosala's followers owned no property, carrying the principle further than the Jains, who allowed the possession of a food bowl. They made a bowl from the palms of their hands, giving them the name "hand lickers."

Jain sources report that after sixteen years of separation, Mahavira happened to come to the town where Gosala lived. When Gosala heard that Mahavira spoke contemptuously of him, he and his followers went to Mahavira's lodgings, and the two sides came to blows. Soon thereafter Gosala became unhinged, gave up all ascetic restraint and, after six months of singing, dancing, drinking, and other riotous living, died, though not before telling his disciples, the Jains report, that Mahavira was right. Doubt is cast on this version of his end by the fact that for centuries to come, Gosala's followers, called the Ajivikas, were an important sect in several parts of India. Ashoka honored them among other sects and dedicated some caves to them.

Questions for Analysis

1. How would Gosala's own followers have described his life? What sorts of distortions are likely in a life known primarily from the writings of rivals?

2. How would the early Indian economy have been affected by the presence of ascetic mendicants?

*A.F.R. Hoernle, "Ajivikas," in *Encyclopedia of Religion and Ethics*, vol. 1, ed. James Hastings (Edinburgh: T. & T. Clark, 1908), p. 262.

● **Gandharan Frieze**   This carved stone (ca. 200 C.E.) portrays scenes from the life of the Buddha. The Buddha is seated below the Bodhi tree, where he was first enlightened. The soldiers and animals surrounding him are trying to distract him. Note the camel, elephant, horse, and monkey. *(Freer Gallery of Art, Smithsonian Institution, Washington, D.C., Purchase, F1949.9b)*

The Buddha offered an optimistic message, however, because all people can set out on the Eightfold Path toward liberation. All they have to do is take steps such as recognizing the universality of suffering, deciding to free themselves from it, and choosing "right conduct," "right speech," "right livelihood," and "right endeavor." For instance, they should abstain from taking life. The seventh step is "right awareness," constant contemplation of one's deeds and words, giving full thought to their importance and whether they lead to enlightenment. "Right contemplation," the last step, entails deep meditation on the impermanence of everything in the world. Those who achieve liberation are freed from the cycle of birth and death and enter the state called **nirvana,** a kind of blissful nothingness and freedom from reincarnation.

Although he accepted the Indian idea of reincarnation, the Buddha denied the integrity of the individual self or soul. He saw human beings as a collection of parts, physical and mental. As long as the parts remain combined, that combination can be called "I." When that combination changes, as at death, the various parts remain in existence, ready to become the building blocks of different combinations. According to Buddhist teaching, life is passed from person to person as a flame is passed from candle to candle.

Buddhism differed from Brahmanism and later Hinduism in that it ignored the caste system. Everyone, noble and peasant, educated and ignorant, male and female, could follow the Eightfold Path. Moreover, the Buddha was extraordinarily undogmatic. Convinced that each person must achieve enlightenment on his or her own, he emphasized that the path was important only because it led the traveler to enlightenment, not for its own sake. He compared it to a raft, essential to cross a river but useless once the traveler reached the far shore. There was no harm in honoring local gods or observing traditional ceremonies, as long as one remembered the goal of enlightenment and did not let sacrifices become snares or attachments.

Like Mahavira, the Buddha formed a circle of disciples, primarily men but including some women as well. He continually reminded them that each person must reach ultimate fulfillment by individual effort, but he also recognized the value of a group of people striving together for the same goal.

The Buddha's followers transmitted his teachings orally until they were written down in the second or first century B.C.E. These scriptures are called **sutras.** The form of monasticism that developed among the Buddhists was less strict than that of the Jains. Buddhist monks moved about for eight months of the year (except the rainy season), consuming only one meal a day obtained by begging, but they could bathe and wear clothes. Within a few centuries, Buddhist monks began to overlook the rule that they should travel. They set up permanent monasteries, generally on land donated by kings or other patrons. Orders of nuns also appeared, giving women the opportunity to seek truth in ways men had traditionally used. The main ritual that monks and nuns performed in their monastic establishments was the communal recitation of

nirvana   *A state of blissful nothingness and freedom from reincarnation.*

sutras   *The written teachings of the Buddha, first transcribed in the second or first century B.C.E.*

the sutras. Lay Buddhists could aid the spread of the Buddhist teachings by providing food for monks and support for their monasteries, and they could pursue their own spiritual progress by adopting practices such as abstaining from meat and alcohol.

Because there was no ecclesiastical authority like that developed by early Christian communities, early Buddhist communities developed several divergent traditions and came to stress different sutras. One of the most important of these, associated with the monk-philosopher Nagarjuna (fl. ca. 100 C.E.), is called **Mahayana,** or "Great Vehicle," because it is a more inclusive form of the religion. It drew on a set of discourses allegedly given by the Buddha and kept hidden by his followers for centuries. One branch of Mahayana taught that reality is empty (that is, nothing exists independently, of itself). Another branch held that ultimate reality is consciousness, that everything is produced by the mind.

Mahayana *The "Great Vehicle," a tradition of Buddhism that aspires to be more inclusive.*

Just as important as the metaphysical literature of Mahayana Buddhism was its devotional side, influenced by the religions then prevalent in Central Asia. The Buddha became deified and placed at the head of an expanding pantheon of other Buddhas and **bodhisattvas.** Bodhisattvas were Buddhas-to-be who had stayed in the world after enlightenment to help others on the path to salvation. These Buddhas and bodhisattvas became objects of veneration, especially the Buddha Amitabha and the bodhisattva Avalokitesvara. With the growth of Mahayana, Buddhism attracted more and more laypeople.

bodhisattvas *Buddhas-to-be who stayed in the world after enlightenment to help others on the path to salvation.*

Buddhism remained an important religion in India until about 1200 C.E. By that time, it had spread widely through East, Central, and Southeast Asia. After 1200 Buddhism declined in India, and the number of Buddhists in India today is small. In Sri Lanka and Nepal, however, Buddhism never lost its hold, and today it is also a major religion in Southeast Asia, Tibet, China, Korea, and Japan.

Hinduism

Both Buddhism and Jainism were direct challenges to the old Brahmanic religion. Both rejected animal sacrifice, which by then was a central element in Brahmanic power. Even more important, both religions tacitly rejected the caste system, accepting people of any caste into their ranks. In response to this challenge, over the next several centuries (ca. 400 B.C.E.–200 C.E.) the Brahmanic religion evolved in a more devotional direction, today commonly called Hinduism. In Hinduism Brahmans retained their high social status, but it became possible for individual worshipers to have more direct contact with the gods, showing their devotion to them without the aid of priests as intermediaries.

The bedrock of Hinduism is the belief that the Vedas are sacred revelations and that a specific caste system is implicitly prescribed in them. Hinduism is a guide to life, the goal of which is to reach union with brahman, the ground of all being. There are four steps in this search, progressing from study of the Vedas in youth to complete asceticism in old age. In their

● **Shiva** One of the three most important Vedic gods, Shiva represented both destruction and procreation. Here Shiva, mounted on a bull and carrying a spear, attacks the demon Andhaka. Shiva is seen as a fierce and bloodthirsty warrior. *(C. M. Dixon/Ancient Art & Architecture Collection)*

dharma *The moral law that Hindus observe in their quest for brahman.*

quest for brahman, people are to observe **dharma,** the moral law. Dharma stipulates the legitimate pursuits of Hindus: material gain, as long as it is honestly and honorably achieved; pleasure and love, for the perpetuation of the family; and moksha, release from the wheel of life and unity with brahman. Because it recognizes the need for material gain and pleasure, Hinduism allows a joyful embracing of life.

Hinduism assumes that there are innumerable legitimate ways of worshiping the supreme principle of life. Consequently, it readily incorporates new sects, doctrines, beliefs, rites, and deities. After the third century B.C.E., Hinduism began to emphasize the roles and personalities of thousands of powerful gods. Brahma, the creator; Shiva, the cosmic dancer who both creates and destroys; and Vishnu, the preserver and sustainer of creation, are three main male deities. Female deities included Lakshmi, goddess of wealth, and Saraswati, goddess of learning and music. People could reach brahman by devotion to personal gods, usually represented by images. A worshiper's devotion to one god did not entail denial of other deities; ultimately all were manifestations of the divine force that pervades the universe.

A central ethical text of Hinduism is the *Bhagavad Gita,* a part of the world's longest ancient epic, the *Mahabharata.* The *Bhagavad Gita* offers guidance on the most serious problem facing a Hindu—how to live in the world and yet honor dharma and thus achieve release. The heart of the *Bhagavad Gita* is the spiritual conflict confronting Arjuna, a human hero about to ride into battle against his kinsmen. As he surveys the battlefield, struggling with the grim notion of killing his relatives, Arjuna voices his doubts to his charioteer, none other than the god Krishna. When at last Arjuna refuses to spill his family's blood, Krishna instructs him on the true meaning of Hinduism:

> **Primary Source:**
> *From* Mahabharata:
> *An Account of the Gods and the Creation of the World*

You grieve for those beyond grief,
and you speak words of insight;
but learned men do not grieve
for the dead or the living.

Never have I not existed,
nor you, nor these kings;
and never in the future
shall we cease to exist.

Just as the embodied self
enters childhood, youth, and old age,
so does it enter another body;
this does not confound a steadfast man.

Contacts with matter make us feel
heat and cold, pleasure and pain.
Arjuna, you must learn to endure
fleeting things—they come and go!

When these cannot torment a man,
when suffering and joy are equal
for him and he has courage,
he is fit for immortality.

Nothing of nonbeing comes to be,
nor does being cease to exist;
the boundary between these two
is seen by men who see reality.

Indestructible is the presence
that pervades all this;
no one can destroy
this unchanging reality.

Our bodies are known to end,
but the embodied self is enduring,
indestructible, and immeasurable;
therefore, Arjuna, fight the battle!

He who thinks this self a killer
and he who thinks it killed,
both fail to understand;
it does not kill, nor is it killed.

It is not born,
it does not die;
having been,
it will never not be;
unborn, enduring,
constant, and primordial,
it is not killed
when the body is killed.[1]

Krishna then clarifies the relationship between human reality and the eternal spirit. He explains compassionately to Arjuna the duty to act—to live in the world and carry out his duties as a warrior. Indeed, the *Bhagavad Gita* emphasizes the necessity of action, which is essential for the welfare of the world. Arjuna makes it the warrior's duty to wage war in compliance with his dharma. Only those who live within the divine law without complaint will be released from rebirth. One person's dharma may be different from another's, but both individuals must follow their own dharmas.

Besides providing a religion of enormous emotional appeal, Hinduism also inspired the preservation, in Sanskrit and the major regional languages of India, of literary masterpieces. Among these are the *Puranas,* which are stories of the gods and great warrior clans, and the *Mahabharata* and *Ramayana,* which are verse epics of India's early kings. Hinduism also validated the caste system, adding to the stability of everyday village life, since people all knew where they stood in society.

• •

INDIA AND THE WEST (CA. 513–298 B.C.E.)

How did India respond to the expansion of the Persian and Greek empires?

In the late sixth century B.C.E., west India was swept up in events that were changing the face of the ancient Middle East. During this period the Persians were creating an empire that stretched from the west coast of Anatolia to the Indus River (see pages 20–22). India became involved in these events when the Persian emperor Darius conquered the Indus Valley and Kashmir about 513 B.C.E.

Persian control did not reach eastward beyond the Punjab. Even so, it fostered increased contact between India and the Middle East and led to the introduction of new ideas, techniques, and materials into India. From Persian administrators Indians learned more about how to rule large tracts of land and huge numbers of people. They also learned the technique of minting silver coins, and they adopted the Persian monetary standard to facilitate trade with other parts of the empire. Even states in the Ganges Valley, which were never part of the Persian Empire, adopted the use of coinage.

Another result of contact with Persia was introduction of the Aramaic script, used to write the official language of the Persian Empire. To keep records and publish proclamations just as the Persians did, Indians in northwest India adapted the Aramaic script for writing several local languages (elsewhere, Indians developed the Brahmi script, the ancestor of the script used for modern Hindi). In time the sacred texts of the Buddhists and the Jains, as well as the epics and other literary works, all came to be recorded.

The Persian Empire in turn succumbed to Alexander the Great, and in 326 B.C.E. Alexander led his Macedonian and Greek troops through the Khyber Pass into the Indus Valley (see page 89). The India that Alexander encountered was composed of many rival states. He defeated some of these states in the northwest and heard reports of others. Porus, king of west Punjab, fought Alexander with a battalion of two thousand war elephants. After being defeated, he agreed to become a subordinate king under Alexander.

Alexander had heard of the sophistication of Indian philosophers and summoned some to instruct him or debate with him. The Greeks were impressed with Taxila, a major center of trade in the Punjab (see Map 2.1), and described it as "a city great and prosperous, the biggest of those between the Indus River and the Hydaspes [the modern Jhelum River]—a region not inferior to Egypt in size, with especially good pastures and rich in fine fruits."[2] From Taxila, Alexander followed the Indus River south, hoping to find the end of the world. His men, however, mutinied and refused to continue. When Alexander turned back, he left his general Seleucus in charge of his easternmost region.

THE MAURYAN EMPIRE (CA. 322–185 B.C.E.)

What were the consequences of the unification of much of India by Chandragupta and Ashoka?

The one to benefit most from Alexander's invasion was Chandragupta, the ruler of a growing state in the Ganges Valley. He took advantage of the crisis caused by Alexander's invasion to expand his territories, and by 322 B.C.E. he had made himself sole master of north India. In 304 B.C.E. he defeated the forces of Seleucus.

With stunning effectiveness, Chandragupta applied the lessons learned from Persian rule. He adopted the Persian practice of dividing the area into provinces. Each province was assigned a governor, usually drawn from Chandragupta's own family. He established a complex bureaucracy to see to the operation of the state and a bureaucratic taxation system that financed public services through taxes on agriculture. He also built a regular army, complete with departments for everything from naval matters to the collection of supplies.

From his capital at Pataliputra in the Ganges Valley (now Patna in Bihar), Chandragupta sent agents to the provinces to oversee the workings of government and to keep him informed of conditions in his realm. For the first time in Indian history, one man governed most of the subcontinent, exercising control through delegated power. In designing his bureaucratic system, Chandragupta enjoyed the able assistance of his great minister Kautilya, who wrote a treatise on how a king should seize, hold, and manipulate power, rather like the Legalist treatises produced in China later that century (see pages 70–71). Kautilya urged the king to use propaganda to gain support—for instance, to disguise secret agents to look like gods so that people would be awed when they saw him in their company. The king was also alerted to the fact that all his immediate neighbors were his enemies but the princes directly beyond them were his natural friends. When a neighboring prince was in trouble, that was the perfect time to attack him. Interstate relations were likened to the law of the fish: the large swallow the small.

Megasthenes, a Greek ambassador sent by Seleucus to Chandragupta's court, left a lively description of life there. He described the city as square and surrounded by wooden walls, twenty-two miles on each side, with 570 towers and 64 gates. It had a university, a library, and magnificent palaces, temples, gardens, and parks. The king personally presided over court sessions where legal cases were heard and petitions received. The king claimed for the state all mines and forests, and there were large state farms, granaries, shipyards, and spinning and weaving factories. Even prostitution was controlled by the state.

Megasthenes described Chandragupta as afraid of treachery and attempts at assassination:

Attendance on the king's person is the duty of women, who indeed are bought from their fathers. Outside the gates of the palace stand the bodyguards and the rest of the soldiers. . . . Nor does the king sleep during the day, and at night he is forced at various hours to change his bed because of those plotting against him. Of his non-military departures from the palace one is to the courts, in which he passes the day hearing cases to the end, even if the hour arrives for attendance on his person. . . . When he leaves to hunt, he is thickly surrounded by a circle of women, and on the outside by spear-carrying bodyguards. The road is fenced off with ropes, and to anyone who passes within the ropes as far as the women death is the penalty.[3]

Those measures apparently worked, as Chandragupta lived a long life. According to Jain tradition, Chandragupta became a Jain ascetic and died a peaceful death in 298 B.C.E. Although he personally adopted a nonviolent philosophy, he left behind a kingdom with the military might to maintain order and defend India from invasion.

The Reign of Ashoka (ca. 269–232 B.C.E.)

The years after Chandragupta's death were an epoch of political greatness, thanks largely to his grandson Ashoka, one of India's most remarkable figures. The era of Ashoka was enormously important in the religious history of the world, because Ashoka embraced Buddhism and promoted its spread beyond India.

As a young prince, Ashoka served as governor of two prosperous provinces where Buddhism flourished. At the death of his father about 274 B.C.E., Ashoka rebelled against his older brother, who had succeeded to the throne, and after four years of fighting won his bid for the throne. Crowned king, Ashoka ruled intelligently and energetically. He was equally serious about his pleasures, especially those of the banquet hall and harem.

In the ninth year of his reign, 261 B.C.E., Ashoka conquered Kalinga, on the east coast of India. In a grim and savage campaign, Ashoka reduced Kalinga by wholesale slaughter. As Ashoka himself admitted, "One hundred and fifty thousand were forcibly abducted from their homes, 100,000 were killed in battle, and many more died later on."[4] Instead of exulting like a conqueror, however, Ashoka was consumed with remorse and revulsion at the horror of war. He embraced Buddhism and used the machinery of his empire to spread Buddhist teachings throughout India. He supported the doctrine of not hurting humans or animals, then spreading among religious people of all sects. He banned animal sacrifices, and in place of hunting expeditions, he took pilgrimages. Two years after his conversion, he undertook a 256-day pilgrimage to all the holy sites of Buddhism, and on his return he sent missionaries to all known countries. Buddhist tradition also credits him with erecting eighty-four thousand stupas (Buddhist reliquary mounds) throughout India, among which the ashes or other bodily remains of the Buddha were distributed, beginning the association of Buddhism with monumental art and architecture.

Ashoka's remarkable crisis of conscience, like the later conversion to Christianity of the Roman emperor Constantine (see pages 126–127), affected the way he ruled. He emphasized compassion, nonviolence, and adherence to dharma. He appointed officials to oversee the moral welfare of the realm and required local officials to govern humanely. He may have perceived dharma as a kind of civic virtue, a universal ethical model capable of uniting the diverse peoples of his extensive empire. Ashoka erected stone pillars, on the Persian model, with inscriptions to inform the people of his policies. He also had long inscriptions carved into large rock surfaces near trade routes. In one inscription he spoke to his people like a father:

Whatever good I have done has indeed been accomplished for the progress and welfare of the world. By these shall grow virtues namely: proper support of mother and father, regard for preceptors and elders, proper treatment of Brahmans and ascetics, of the poor and the destitute, slaves and servants.[5]

These inscriptions are the earliest fully dated Indian texts. (Until the script in which they were written was deciphered in 1837, nothing was known of Ashoka's achievements.) The pillars on which they are inscribed are also the first examples of Indian art to survive since the end of the Indus civilization.

Ashoka felt the need to protect his new religion and to keep it pure. He warned Buddhist monks that he would not tolerate *schism*—divisions based on differences of opinion about doctrine or ritual. According to Buddhist tradition, a great council of Buddhist monks was held at Pataliputra, where the earliest canon of Buddhist texts was codified. At the same time, Ashoka honored India's other religions, even building

● **Ashokan Pillar** The best preserved of the pillars that King Ashoka erected in about 240 B.C.E. is this one in the Bihar region, near Nepal. The solid shaft of polished sandstone rises 32 feet in the air. It weighs about 50 tons, making its erection a remarkable feat of engineering. Like other Ashokan pillars, it is inscribed with accounts of Ashoka's political achievements and instructions to his subjects on proper behavior. These pillars are the earliest extant examples of Indian writing and a major historical source for the Mauryan period. *(Borromeo/ Art Resource, NY)*

shrines for Hindu and Jain worshipers. In one edict he banned rowdy popular fairs, allowing only religious gatherings.

Despite his devotion to Buddhism, Ashoka never neglected his duties as emperor. He tightened the central government of the empire and kept a close check on local officials. He also built roads and rest spots to improve communication within the realm. Ashoka himself described this work: "On the highways Banyan trees have been planted so that they may afford shade to men and animals; mango-groves have been planted; watering-places have been established for the benefit of animals and men."[6] These measures also facilitated the march of armies and the armed enforcement of Ashoka's authority.

Ashoka's inscriptions indirectly tell us much about the Mauryan Empire. He directly administered the central part of the empire, focusing on Magadha. Beyond it were four large provinces, under princes who served as viceroys, each with its own sets of smaller districts and officials. The interior of south India was described as inhabited by undefeated forest tribes. Farther south, along the coasts, were peoples that Ashoka maintained friendly relations with but did not rule, such as the Cholas and Pandyas. Relations with Sri Lanka were especially close under Ashoka, and the king sent a branch of the tree under which the Buddha gained enlightenment to the Sri Lankan king. According to Buddhist legend, Ashoka's son Mahinda traveled to Sri Lanka to convert the people there.

Ashoka ruled for thirty-seven years. After he died in about 232 B.C.E., the Mauryan dynasty went into decline, and India broke up into smaller units, much like those in existence before Alexander's invasion. Even though Chandragupta had instituted bureaucratic methods of centralized political control and Ashoka had vigorously pursued the political and cultural integration of the empire, the institutions they created were not entrenched enough to survive periods with weaker kings.

• •

SMALL STATES AND TRADING NETWORKS (200 B.C.E.–300 C.E.)

How was India shaped by political disunity and contacts with other cultures?

After the Mauryan dynasty collapsed in 185 B.C.E., and for much of subsequent Indian history, political unity would be the exception rather than the rule. By this time, however, key elements of Indian culture—the caste system; the religious traditions of Hinduism, Buddhism, and Jainism; and the great epics and legends—had given India a cultural unity strong enough to endure even without political unity.

In the years after the fall of the Mauryan dynasty, a series of foreign powers dominated the Indus Valley and adjoining regions. The first were hybrid Indo-Greek states ruled by the inheritors of Alexander's defunct empire stationed in what is now Afghanistan. The city of Taxila became a major center of trade, culture, and education, fusing elements of Greek and Indian culture.

The great, slow movement of nomadic peoples out of East Asia that brought the Scythians to the Middle East brought the Shakas to northwest India. They controlled the region from about 94 to 20 B.C.E., when they were displaced by a new nomadic invader, the Kushans, who ruled the region of today's Afghanistan, Pakistan, and west India as far south as Gujarat. Their king Kanishka (r. ca. 78–ca. 103 C.E.) is known from Buddhist sources. The famous silk trade from China to Rome (see pages 140–141) passed through his territory.

During the Kushan period, Greek culture had a considerable impact on Indian art. Indo-Greek artists and sculptors working in India adorned Buddhist shrines, modeling the earliest representation of the Buddha on Hellenistic statues of Apollo.

Another contribution from the Indo-Greek states was coins cast with images of the king, which came to be widely adopted by Indian rulers, aiding commerce and adding evidence to the historical record. Cultural exchange also went in the other direction. Old Indian animal folktales were translated into Syriac and Greek and from that source eventually made their way to Europe. South India in this period was also the center of active seaborne trade, with networks reaching all the way to Rome. Indian sailing technology was highly advanced, and much of this trade was in the hands of Indian merchants. Roman traders based in Egypt followed the routes already used by Arab traders, sailing with the monsoon from the Red Sea to the west coast of India in about two weeks, returning about six months later when the direction of the winds reversed. In the first century C.E. a Greek merchant involved in this trade reported that the traders sold coins, topaz, coral, crude glass, copper, tin, and lead and bought pearls, ivory, silk (probably originally from China), jewels of many sorts (probably many from Southeast Asia), and above all cinnamon and pepper. More Roman gold coins of the first and second centuries C.E. have been found near the southern tip of India than in any other area. The local rulers had slits made across the image of the Roman emperor to show that his sovereignty was not recognized, but they had no objection to the coins' circulating. (By contrast, the Kushan rulers in the north had Roman coins melted down to use to make coins with their own images on them.)

Even after the fall of Rome, many of the traders on the southwest coast of India remained. These diasporic communities of Christians and Jews lived in the coastal cities into modern times. When Vasco da Gama, the Portuguese explorer, reached Calicut in 1498, he found a local Jewish merchant who was able to interpret for him.

During these centuries there were significant advances in science, mathematics, and philosophy. This was also the period when Indian law was codified. The **Code of Manu,** which lays down family, caste, and commercial law, was compiled in the second or third century C.E.

Regional cultures tend to flourish when there is no dominant unifying state. In south India the third century B.C.E. to the third century C.E. is considered the classical period of Tamil culture, when many great works of literature were written under the patronage of the regional kings. Some of the poems take a hard look at war:

Harvest of War

Great king
you shield your men from ruin,
so your victories, your greatness
are bywords.

Loose chariot wheels
lie about the battleground
with the long white tusks
of bull-elephants.

Flocks of male eagles
eat carrion
with their mates.

Headless bodies
dance about
before they fall
to the ground.

Blood glows,
like the sky before nightfall,
in the red center
of the battlefield.

Demons dance there.
And your kingdom
is an unfailing harvest
of victorious wars.[7]

● **Kushan Gold Coin**
Kanishka I had coins made depicting a standing Buddha with his right hand raised in a gesture of renunciation. The reverse side shows the king performing a sacrifice, the legend reading "Kanishka the Kushan, king of kings." *(Courtesy of the Trustees of the British Museum)*

Code of Manu *The codification of Indian law from the second or third century C.E.; it lays down family, caste, and commercial law.*

Primary Source:
From **The Laws of Manu**

Chapter Summary

Key Terms

Harappan
Aryans
Rigveda
raja
Brahmans
caste system
varna
outcastes
samsara
karma
moksha
brahman
Four Noble Truths
Eightfold Path
nirvana
sutras
Mahayana
bodhisattvas
dharma
Code of Manu

• What does archaeology tell us about the earliest civilization in India?

From archaeology, we know that the Harappan civilization emerged in the Indus River valley in the third millennium B.C.E. The large cities that have been excavated were made of kiln-dried brick and were carefully planned, with straight streets and sewers. Although many intriguing artifacts have been excavated, many questions remain about this civilization, and its script has not been deciphered. Scholars can only speculate why Harappan cities were largely abandoned by 1800 B.C.E.

• What kind of society and culture did the Indo-European Aryans create?

From originally oral texts like the *Rigveda*, we know much about the values and social practices of the Aryans, speakers of an early form of Sanskrit (which is an Indo-European language). In the period 1500–500 B.C.E. Aryan warrior tribes fought using chariots and bronze swords and spears, gradually expanding into the Ganges River valley. The first stages of the Indian caste system date to this period, when warriors and priests were ranked above merchants, artisans, and farmers. Key religious ideas that date to this period are the notions of karma and rebirth and the importance of sacrifice.

• What ideas and practices were taught by the founders of Jainism, Buddhism, and Hinduism?

Beginning around 500 B.C.E. three of India's major religions emerged. Mahavira was the founder of the Jain religion. He taught his followers to live ascetic lives, avoid doing harm to any living thing, and renounce evil thoughts and actions. The founder of Buddhism, Siddhartha Gautama or the Buddha, similarly taught his followers a path to liberation that involved avoiding violence and freeing themselves from desires. The Buddha, however, did not think extreme asceticism was the best path and put more emphasis on mental detachment. In response to the popularity of Jainism and Buddhism, both of which rejected animal sacrifice and ignored the caste system, the traditional Brahmanic religion evolved in a devotional direction that has been called Hinduism. Hindu traditions validated sacrifice and caste but stressed the individual's relationship to the gods he or she worshiped.

• How did India respond to the expansion of the Persian and Greek empires?

In the sixth century B.C.E. the Persian empire expanded into the Indus River valley, and in the fourth century Alexander the Great's troops took the same region. From contact with the Persians and Greeks, new political techniques, ideas, and art styles entered the Indian repertoire.

• What were the consequences of the unification of much of India by Chandragupta and Ashoka?

Shortly after the arrival of the Greeks, much of north India was politically unified by the Mauryan Empire. Its greatest ruler was Ashoka, who converted to Buddhism and promoted its spread outside India. The inscriptions he had carved on stones and erected many places in his empire provide some of the best-dated sources on early Indian history.

• How was India shaped by political disunity and contacts with other cultures?

After the decline of the Mauryan empire, India was politically fragmented. Indian cultural identity remained strong, however, because of shared religious ideas and shared literature, including the great early epics. Trade and other contact with the outside world brought new elements into Indian civilization. And just as India came to absorb some Persian bureaucratic techniques and Greek artistic styles, other regions borrowed crops, textiles, inventions, and religious ideas from India.

Suggested Reading

Basham, A. L. *The Wonder That Was India,* 3d rev. ed. 1968. Classic, appreciative account of early Indian civilization by a scholar deeply immersed in Indian literature.

Embree, Ainslee, ed. *Sources of Indian Tradition,* 2d ed. 1988. An excellent introduction to Indian religion, philosophy, and intellectual history through translations of major sources.

Koller, John M. *The Indian Way,* 2d ed. 2004. An accessible introduction to the variety of Indian religions and philosophies.

Kulke, Hermann, and Dietmar Rothermund. *A History of India,* 3d ed. 1998. A good, balanced introduction to Indian history.

Lopez, Donald S., Jr. *The Story of the Buddha: A Concise Guide to Its History and Teachings.* 2001. Puts emphasis on Buddhist practice, drawing examples from many different countries and time periods.

Miller, Barbara, trans. *The Bhagavad-Gita: Krishna's Counsel in Time of War.* 1986. One of several excellent translations of India's classical literature.

Possehl, Gregory L. *The Indus Civilization.* 2002. Recent overview of Harappan civilization.

Renfew, Colin. *Archaeology and Language: The Puzzle of Indo-European Origins.* 1987. Analyzes the question of the origins of the Aryans in depth.

Scharff, Harmut. *The State in Indian Tradition.* 1989. A scholarly analysis of the period from the Aryans to the Muslims.

Thapar, Romilia. *Early India to 1300.* A freshly revised overview by a leading Indian historian.

Notes

1. Excerpt from Barbara Stoler Miller, trans., *The Bhagavad-gita: Krishna's Counsel in Time of War* (New York: Columbia University Press, 1986), pp. 31–32. Translation copyright © 1986 by Barbara Stoler Miller. Used by permission of Bantam Books, a division of Random House, Inc.

2. Arrian, *Anabasis* 5.8.2; Plutarch, *Alexander* 59.1. Translated by John Buckler.

3. *Strabo,* 15.1.55. Translated by John Buckler.

4. Quoted in H. Kulke and D. Rothermund, *A History of India,* 3d ed. (London: Routledge, 1998), p. 62.

5. Quoted in B. G. Gokhale, *Asoka Maurya* (New York: Twayne Publishers, 1966), p. 169.

6. Quoted ibid., pp. 168–169.

7. A. K. Ramanujan, ed. and trans., *Poems of Love and War: From the Eight Anthologies and the Ten Long Poems of Classical Tamil* (New York: Columbia University Press, 1985), p. 115. Copyright 1985 by Columbia University Press. Reproduced with permission of Columbia University Press in the format Textbook via Copyright Clearance Center.

Listening to the PAST

Rama and Sita

The Ramayana, *an epic poem of about fifty thousand verses, is attributed to the third-century* B.C.E. *poet Valmiki. Its main character, Rama, the oldest son of a king, is an incarnation of the great god Vishnu. As a young man, he wins the princess Sita as his wife when he alone among her suitors proves strong enough to bend a huge bow. Rama and Sita love each other deeply, but court intrigue disturbs their happy life. After the king announces that he will retire and consecrate Rama as his heir, the king's beautiful junior wife, wishing to advance her own son, reminds the king that he has promised her a favor of her choice. She then asks to have him appoint her son heir and to have Rama sent into the wilderness for fourteen years. The king is forced to consent, and Rama obeys his father.*

The passage below gives the conversations between Rama and Sita after Rama learns he must leave. In subsequent parts of the very long epic, the lovers undergo many other tribulations, including Sita's abduction by the lord of the demons, the ten-headed Ravana, and her eventual recovery by Rama with the aid of monkeys.

The Ramayana *eventually appeared in numerous versions in all the major languages of India. Hearing it recited was said to bring religious merit. Sita, passionate in her devotion to her husband, has remained the favorite Indian heroine. Rama, Sita, and the monkey Hanuman are cult figures in Hinduism, with temples devoted to their worship.*

"For fourteen years I must live in Dandaka, while my father will appoint Bharata prince regent. I have come to see you before I leave for the desolate forest. You are never to boast of me in the presence of Bharata. Men in power cannot bear to hear others praised, and so you must never boast of my virtues in front of Bharata. . . . When I have gone to the forest where sages make their home, my precious, blameless wife, you must earnestly undertake vows and fasts. You must rise early and worship the gods according to custom and then pay homage to my father Dasaratha, lord of men. And my aged mother Kausalya, who is tormented by misery, deserves your respect as well, for she has subordinated all to righteousness. The rest of my mothers, too, must always receive your homage. . . . My beloved, I am going to the great forest, and you must stay here. You must do as I tell you, my lovely, and not give offense to anyone."

So Rama spoke, and Sita, who always spoke kindly to her husband and deserved kindness from him, grew angry just because she loved him, and said, "My lord, a man's father, his mother, brother, son, or daughter-in-law all experience the effects of their own past deeds and suffer an individual fate. But a wife, and she alone, bull among men, must share her husband's fate. Therefore I, too, have been ordered to live in the forest. It is not her father or mother, not her son or friends or herself, but her husband, and he alone, who gives a woman permanent refuge in this world and after death. If you must leave this very day for the trackless forest, Rama, I will go in front of you, softening the thorns and sharp *kusa* grass. Cast out your anger and resentment, like so much water left after drinking one's fill. Do not be reluctant to take me, my mighty husband. There is no evil in me. The shadow of a husband's feet in any circumstances surpasses the finest mansions, an aerial chariot, or even flying through the sky. . . . O Rama, bestower of honor, you have the power to protect any other person in the forest. Why then not me? . . .

"If I were to be offered a place to live in heaven itself, Rama, tiger among men, I would refuse it if you were not there. I will go to the trackless forest teeming with deer, monkeys, and elephants, and live there as in my father's house, clinging to your feet alone, in strict self-discipline. I love no one else; my heart is so attached to you that were we to be parted I am resolved to die. Take me, oh please grant my request. I shall not be a burden to you." . . .

When Sita finished speaking, the righteous prince, who knew what was right and cherished it, attempted to dissuade her. . . .

"Sita, give up this notion of living in the forest. The name 'forest' is given only to wild regions where hardships abound. . . . There are lions that live in mountain caves; their roars are redoubled by mountain torrents and are a painful thing to hear—the forest is

Rama and Sita in the forest, from a set of miniature paintings done in about 1600. (*National Museum, New Delhi*)

a place of pain. At night worn with fatigue, one must sleep upon the ground on a bed of leaves, broken off of themselves—the forest is a place of utter pain. And one has to fast, Sita, to the limit of one's endurance, wear clothes of barkcloth and bear the burden of matted hair. . . . There are many creeping creatures, of every size and shape, my lovely, ranging aggressively over the ground. . . . Moths, scorpions, worms, gnats, and flies continually harass one, my frail Sita—the forest is wholly a place of pain. . . ."

Sita was overcome with sorrow when she heard what Rama said. With tears trickling down her face, she answered him in a faint voice. . . . "If from feelings of love I follow you, my pure-hearted husband, I shall have no sin to answer for, because my husband is my deity. My union with you is sacred and shall last even beyond death. . . . If you refuse to take me to the forest despite the sorrow that I feel, I shall have no recourse but to end my life by poison, fire, or water."

Though she pleaded with him in this and every other way to be allowed to go, great-armed Rama would not consent to taking her to the desolate forest. And when he told her as much, Sita fell to brooding, and drenched the ground, it seemed, with the hot tears that fell from her eyes. . . . She was nearly insensible with sorrow when Rama took her in his arms and comforted her. . . . "Without knowing your true feelings, my lovely, I could not consent to your living in the wilderness, though I am perfectly capable of protecting you. Since you are determined to live with me in the forest, Sita, I could no sooner abandon you than a self-respecting man his reputation. . . . My father keeps to the path of righteousness and truth, and I wish to act just as he instructs me. That is the eternal way of righteousness. Follow me, my timid one, be my companion in righteousness. Go now and bestow precious objects on the brahmans, give food to the mendicants and all who ask for it. Hurry, there is no time to waste."

Finding that her husband had acquiesced in her going, the lady was elated and set out at once to make the donations.

Questions for Analysis

1. What can you infer about early Indian family life and social relations from this story?

2. What do Sita's words and actions indicate about women's roles in Indian society of the time?

3. What do you think accounts for the continuing popularity of the story of Rama throughout Indian history?

Source: The Ramayana of Valmiki: An Epic of India, vol. 2: Ayodhyakanda, trans. Sheldon I. Pollock, ed. Robert P. Goldman (Princeton, N.J.: Princeton University Press, 1986), pp. 134–142, modified slightly. Copyright © 1986 by Princeton University Press. Reprinted by permission of Princeton University Press.

Bronze Vessel (twelfth century B.C.E.). About 10 inches tall, this bronze is covered with symmetrical animal imagery, including stylized *taotie* masks. *(The Metropolitan Museum of Art. Purchase, Arthur M. Sackler Gift, 1974 [1974.268.2ab]. Photograph © 1979 The Metropolitan Museum of Art)*

3 CHINA'S CLASSICAL AGE, TO 256 B.C.E.

Chapter Preview

The Emergence of Civilization in China
• *When, where, and how did writing, bronze technology, and other elements of civilization develop in China?*

The Early Zhou Dynasty (ca. 1050–500 B.C.E.)
• *How was China governed in the period looked back on as its golden age?*

The Warring States Period (500–221 B.C.E.)
• *What were the consequences of the breakup of Zhou unity and the rise of independent states?*

Confucius and His Followers
• *What ideas did Confucius teach, and how were they a response to his times?*

Daoism, Legalism, and Other Schools of Thought
• *What did those who opposed Confucianism argue?*

The early development of China's civilization occurred with little contact with the other early civilizations of Eurasia. The reason for China's relative isolation was geographic: communication with West and South Asia was very difficult, impeded by high mountains and vast deserts. Thus, in comparison to India and the ancient Middle East, there was less cross-fertilization through trade and other contact with other comparably advanced civilizations. Moreover, there were no cultural breaks comparable to the rise of the Aryans in India or the Assyrians in Mesopotamia; there were no new peoples bringing new languages.

The impact of early China's relative isolation is found in many distinctive or unique features of its culture. Perhaps the most important is its writing system. Unlike the other major societies of Eurasia, China retained a logographic writing system with a separate symbol for each word. This writing system shaped not only Chinese literature and thought but also key social and political processes, such as the nature of the ruling class and the way Chinese interacted with non-Chinese.

Chinese history is commonly discussed in terms of a succession of dynasties. The Shang Dynasty (ca. 1500–ca. 1050 B.C.E.) was the first to have writing, metalworking, cities, and chariots. The Shang kings played priestly roles, serving as intermediaries with both their royal ancestors and the high god Di. The Shang were overthrown by one of their vassal states, which founded the Zhou Dynasty (ca. 1050–256 B.C.E.). The Zhou rulers set up a decentralized feudal governmental structure. After several centuries, this structure evolved into a multistate system. As warfare between the states intensified from the sixth century B.C.E. on, social and cultural change also quickened. Aristocratic privileges declined, and China entered one of its most creative periods, when the philosophies of Confucianism, Daoism, and Legalism were developed.

THE EMERGENCE OF CIVILIZATION IN CHINA

When, where, and how did writing, bronze technology, and other elements of civilization develop in China?

The term *China,* like the term *India,* does not refer to the same geographical entity at all points in history. The historical China, also called China proper, was smaller than present-day China, not larger like the historical India. The contemporary People's Republic of China includes Tibet, Inner Mongolia, Turkestan, Manchuria, and other territories that in premodern times were not inhabited by Chinese or ruled directly by Chinese states (see Map 3.1).

China proper, about a thousand miles north to south and east to west, occupies much of the temperate zone of East Asia. The northern part, drained by the Huang (Yellow) River, is colder, flatter, and more arid than the south. Rainfall in many areas is less than twenty inches a year, making the land well suited to crops like wheat and millet. The dominant soil is **loess**—fine wind-driven earth that is fertile and easy to work even with primitive tools. Because so much of the loess ends up as silt in the Huang River, the riverbed rises and easily floods unless diked. Drought is another perennial problem for farmers in the north. The Yangzi River is the dominant feature of the warmer, wetter, and more lush south, a region well suited to rice cultivation and double cropping. The Yangzi and its many tributaries are navigable, so boats were traditionally the preferred means of transportation in the south.

Mountains, deserts, and grasslands separated China proper from other early civilizations. Between China and India lay Tibet, with its vast mountain ranges and high plateaus. North of Tibet are great expanses of desert where nothing grows except in rare oases, and north of the desert stretch grasslands from the Ukraine to eastern Siberia. Chinese civilization did not spread into any of these Inner Asian regions, above all because they were not suited to crop agriculture. Inner Asia, where raising animals is a more productive use of land than planting crops, became the heartland of China's traditional enemies, such as the Xiongnu and Mongols.

The Neolithic Age

From about 10,000 B.C.E. agriculture was practiced in China, apparently originating independently of somewhat earlier developments in Egypt and Mesopotamia, but perhaps influenced by developments in Southeast Asia, where rice was also cultivated very early. By 5000 B.C.E. there were Neolithic village settlements in several regions of China. The primary Neolithic crops were drought-resistant millet, grown in the loess soils of the north, and rice, grown in the wetlands of the lower reaches of the Yangzi River, where it was supplemented by fish. In both areas pigs, dogs, and cattle were domesticated, and by 3000 B.C.E. sheep had become important in the north and water buffalo in the south.

Over the course of the fifth to third millennia B.C.E., many distinct regional Neolithic cultures emerged. For instance, in the northwest during the fourth and third millennia B.C.E., people made fine red pottery vessels decorated in black pigment with bold designs, including spirals, sawtooth lines, and zoomorphic stick figures. At the same time in the east, pottery was rarely painted but was made into distinctive shapes, including three-legged, deep-bodied tripods. Jade ornaments, blades, and ritual objects, sometimes of extraordinary craftsmanship, have been found in several eastern sites but are rare in western ones.

loess *Soil deposited by wind. It is fertile and easy to work.*

● **Neolithic Jade Plaque** This small plaque (2.5 inches by 3.25 inches), dating from about 2000 B.C.E., is similar to others of the Liangzhu area near modern Shanghai. It is incised to depict a human figure who merges into a monster mask. The lower part could be interpreted as his arms and legs but at the same time resembles a monster mask with bulging eyes, prominent nostrils, and a large mouth. *(Zheijiang Provincial Institute of Archaeology/Cultural Relics Publishing House)*

Over time Neolithic cultures came to share more by way of material culture and social and cultural practices. Many practices related to treatment of the dead spread out of their original area, including use of coffins, ramped chambers, large numbers of grave goods, and divination based on interpreting cracks in cattle bones. Fortified walls, made of rammed earth, came to be built around settlements in many areas, suggesting not only increased contact but also increased conflict.

The Shang Dynasty (ca. 1500–ca. 1050 B.C.E.)

After 2000 B.C.E. a Bronze Age civilization appeared in north China with the traits found in Bronze Age civilizations elsewhere, such as writing, metalworking, domestication of the horse, class stratification, and cult centers. These findings can be linked to the Shang Dynasty, long known from early texts.

Shang civilization was not as densely urban as Mesopotamia, but Shang kings ruled from large settlements. The best excavated is **Anyang,** from which the Shang kings ruled for more than two centuries. At the center of Anyang were large palaces, temples, and altars. These buildings were constructed on rammed-earth foundations (a feature of Chinese building practice that would last for centuries). Outside the central core were industrial areas where bronzeworkers, potters, stone carvers, and other artisans lived and worked. Many homes were built partly below ground level, probably as a way to conserve heat. Beyond these urban settlements were farming areas and large forests. Deer, bears, tigers, wild boars, elephants, and rhinoceros were still plentiful in north China in this era.

The divinatory texts found in the royal tombs at Anyang show that Shang kings were military chieftains. The king regularly sent out armies of three thousand to five thousand men on campaigns, and when not at war they would go on hunts lasting for months. They fought rebellious vassals and foreign tribes, but the situation constantly changed as vassals became enemies and enemies accepted offers of alliance. War booty was an important source of the king's revenue, especially the war captives who could be made into slaves. Captives not needed as slaves might end up as sacrificial victims—or perhaps the demands of the gods and ancestors for sacrifices were a motive for going to war.

Bronze-tipped spears and halberds were widely used by Shang warriors. Bronze was also used for the fittings of the chariots that came into use around 1200 B.C.E., probably as a result of diffusion across Asia. The chariot provided commanders with a mobile station from which they could supervise their troops; it also gave archers and soldiers armed with long halberds increased mobility.

Shang power did not rest solely on military supremacy. The Shang king was also the high priest, the one best qualified to offer sacrifices to the royal ancestors and the high god Di. Royal ancestors were viewed as able to intervene with Di, send curses, produce dreams, assist the king in battle, and so on. The king divined his ancestors' wishes by interpreting the cracks made in heated cattle bones or tortoise shells prepared for him by professional diviners.

Chronology

ca. 1500–ca. 1050 B.C.E.	Shang Dynasty
ca. 1200 B.C.E.	Evidence of writing found in royal tombs
ca. 1050–256 B.C.E.	Zhou Dynasty
ca. 900	*Book of Songs, Book of Changes, Book of Documents*
771 B.C.E.	Zhou capital moved to Luoyang
551–479 B.C.E.	Confucius
ca. 500 B.C.E.	Iron technology in wide use
500–200 B.C.E.	Golden age of Chinese philosophy
453–403 B.C.E.	Sun Wu, *The Art of War*
ca. 450 B.C.E.	Mozi
ca. 370–ca. 300 B.C.E.	Mencius
369–286 B.C.E.	Zhuangzi
ca. 350 B.C.E.	Infantry armed with crossbows
ca. 310–ca. 215 B.C.E.	Xunzi
ca. 300–200 B.C.E.	*Laozi* written
ca. 280?–233 B.C.E.	Han Feizi of Legalist school

Anyang *One of the Shang Dynasty capitals.*

● **Royal Tomb at Anyang** Eleven large tombs and more than a thousand small graves have been excavated at the royal burial ground at Anyang. This grave, about 60 feet deep and 300 feet long, would have taken thousands of laborers many months to complete. But even more wealth was expended to fill it with bronze, stone, pottery, jade, and textile grave goods. Human victims were also placed in it. (*Academia Sinica, Institute of History and Philology, Taiwan*)

Shang palaces were undoubtedly splendid but were constructed of perishable material like wood, and nothing of them remains today, unlike the stone buildings and monuments so characteristic of the ancient West. What has survived are the lavish underground tombs built for Shang kings and their consorts. They were filled with bronze vessels and weapons, jade and ivory ornaments, and often people, some of whom were sacrificed and others who chose to follow their lord in death. Human sacrifice did not occur only at funerals. Inscribed bones report sacrifices of war captives in the dozens and hundreds.

Shang society was marked by sharp status distinctions. The Shang royal family and aristocracy lived in large houses built on huge platforms of rammed earth. The king and other noble families had family and clan names transmitted along patrilineal lines, from father to son. Kingship similarly passed along patrilines, from elder to younger brother and father to son, but never to or through sisters or daughters. The kings and the aristocracy owned slaves, many of whom had been captured in war. In the urban centers there were substantial numbers of craftsmen who worked in stone, bone, and bronze.

Shang farmers were essentially serfs of the aristocrats. Their life was not that different from that of their Neolithic ancestors, and they worked the fields with similar stone tools. They usually lived in small, compact villages surrounded by fields. Some new crops became common in Shang times, most notably wheat, which had spread from West Asia.

● **Jade Figure** Among the valuables placed in royal Shang tombs were many jade objects, such as this figure, 2¾ inches tall. Since Neolithic times, jade has had the place in China occupied by gold in many other cultures: it is valued for its beauty, rarity, and endurance. This figure was one of seven hundred jade pieces in the tomb of Lady Hao. (*Institute of Archaeology, Beijing/DNP Archives*)

Writing The survival of divination texts inscribed on bones from Shang tombs demonstrates that writing was already a major element in Chinese culture by 1200 B.C.E. Writing must have been developed earlier, but the early stages cannot be traced, probably because writing was done on wood, bamboo, silk, or other perishable materials.

Once writing was invented, it had profound effects on China's culture and government. A written language made possible a bureaucracy capable of keeping records and conducting correspondence with commanders and governors far from the palace. Hence literacy became the ally of royal rule, facilitating communication with and effective control over the realm. Literacy also preserved the learning, lore, and experience of early Chinese society and facilitated the development of abstract thought.

Like ancient Egyptian and Sumerian, the Chinese script was **logographic**: each word was represented by a single symbol. In the Chinese case, some of these symbols were pictures, but for the names of abstract concepts other methods were adopted. Sometimes the symbol for a different word was borrowed because the two words were pronounced alike. Sometimes two different symbols were combined; for instance, to represent different types of trees, the symbol for *tree* could be combined with another symbol borrowed for its pronunciation (see Figure 3.1).

In western Eurasia logographic scripts were eventually modified or replaced by phonetic scripts, but that never happened in China (although, because of changes in the spoken language, today many words are represented by two or three characters rather than a single one). Because China retained its logographic writing system, many years were required to gain full mastery of reading and writing, which added to the prestige of education.

Why did China retain a logographic writing system even after encounters with phonetic ones? Although phonetic systems have many real advantages, especially with

logographic *A language in which each word is represented by a single symbol, such as the Chinese script.*

MAP 3.1 **China Under the Shang and Zhou Dynasties** Chinese civilization developed in the temperate regions drained by the Huang (Yellow) and Yangzi Rivers. The early Zhou government controlled larger areas than the Shang did, but the independent states of the Warring States Period were more aggressive about pushing out their frontiers, greatly extending the geographical boundaries of Chinese civilization.

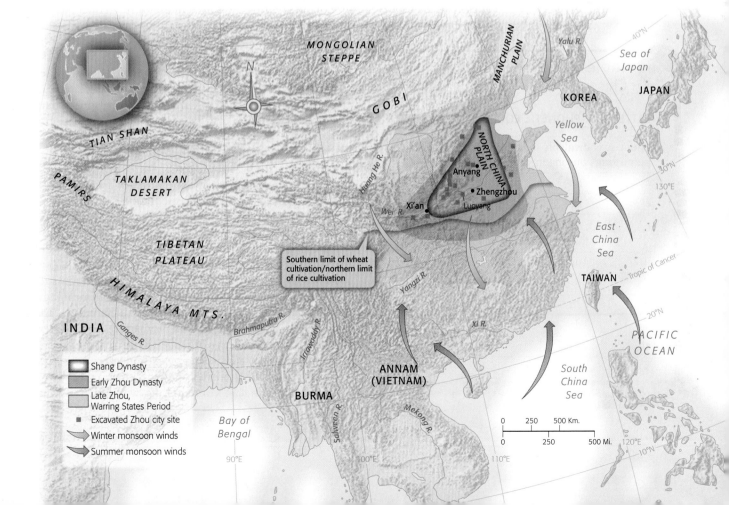

WORD	ox	goat, sheep	tree	moon	earth	water	to show, declare	then (men and bowl)	heaven	to pray
SHANG SYMBOL	Ψ	Ψ	朩	D	⌀	巛	丌	彡	⊼	禤
MODERN CHARACTER	牛	羊	木	月	土	水	示	就	天	祝

● FIGURE 3.1 **The Origins of Chinese Writing** The modern Chinese writing system (bottom row) evolved from the script employed by diviners in the Shang period (upper row). *(Source: Adapted from Patricia Buckley Ebrey,* The Cambridge Illustrated History of China *[Cambridge: Cambridge University Press, 1996], p. 26. Reprinted by permission of Cambridge University Press.)*

respect to ease of learning to read, there are some costs to dropping a logographic system. Those who learned to read Chinese could communicate with a wider range of people than those who read scripts based on speech. Since characters did not change when the pronunciation changed, educated Chinese could read texts written centuries earlier without the need for them to be translated. Moreover, as the Chinese language developed regional variants, readers of Chinese could read books and letters by contemporaries whose oral language they could not comprehend. Thus the Chinese script played a large role in holding China together and fostering a sense of connection with the past. In addition, many of China's neighbors (Japan, Korea, and Vietnam, in particular) adopted the Chinese script, allowing communication through writing between people whose languages were totally unrelated. In this regard, the Chinese language was like Arabic numerals, which have the same meaning however they are pronounced.

Bronzes As in Egypt, Mesopotamia, and India, the development of more complex forms of social organization in Shang China coincided with the mastery of metalworking, specifically bronze. Bronze, in Shang times, was used more for ritual than for war. Most surviving Shang bronze objects are vessels such as cups, goblets, steamers, and cauldrons that would have originally been used during sacrificial ceremonies. They were beautifully formed in a great variety of shapes and sizes. Complex designs were achieved through mold casting and prefabrication of parts. For instance, legs, handles, and other protruding members were cast first, before the body was cast onto them.

The decoration on Shang bronzes seems to say something interesting about Shang culture, but scholars do not agree about what it says. In the art of ancient Egypt, Assyria, and Babylonia, representations of agriculture (domesticated plants and animals) and of social hierarchy (kings, priests, scribes, and slaves) are very common, matching our understandings of the social, political, and economic development of those societies. In Shang China, by contrast, images of wild animals predominate. Some animal images readily suggest possible meanings. Jade cicadas were sometimes found in the mouths of the dead, and images of cicadas on bronzes are easy to interpret as images evocative of rebirth in the realm of ancestral spirits, as cicadas spend years underground before emerging. Birds, similarly, suggest to many the idea of messengers that can communicate with other realms,

Table 3.1 Pronouncing Chinese Words

LETTER	PHONETIC EQUIVALENT IN CHINESE
Phonetic equivalents for the vowels and especially perplexing consonants are given here.	
a	ah
e	uh
i	ee; except after *z, c,* and *ch,* when the sound is closer to *i* in *it*
u	oo; as in English *food*
c	ts (*ch,* however, is like English *ch*)
q	ch
z	dz
zh	j
x	sh

especially realms in the sky. More problematic is the most common image, the stylized animal face called the **taotie**. To some it is a monster—a fearsome image that would scare away evil forces. Others imagine a dragon—an animal whose vast powers had more positive associations. Some hypothesize that it reflects masks used in rituals. Others associate it with animal sacrifices, totemism, or shamanism. Still others see these images as hardly more than designs. Without new evidence, scholars can only speculate.

Bronze technology spread beyond Shang territories into areas the Shang would have considered enemy lands. In 1986, in the western province of Sichuan, discovery was made of a bronze-producing culture contemporaneous with the late Shang but very different from it. This culture did not practice human sacrifice, but two sacrificial pits contained the burned remains of elephant tusks and a wide range of gold, bronze, jade, and stone objects. Among them were a life-size statue and many life-size bronze heads, all with angular facial features and enormous eyes. No human sacrifices were found, leading some scholars to speculate that the masks were used to top wood or clay statues buried in place of humans in a sacrificial ceremony. Archaeologists are continuing to excavate in this region, and new discoveries may provide fuller understanding of the religion of the people who lived there.

● **Inscribed Pan** This bronze vessel, dating to before 900 B.C.E., was one of 103 vessels discovered in 1975 by farmers clearing a field. The inscription tells the story of the first six Zhou kings and of the family of scribes who served them. It was cast by Scribe Qiang. *(Zhou Yuan Administrative Office of Cultural Relics, Fufeng, Shaanxi Province)*

taotie *A common image in Chinese bronzes; it is a stylized animal face.*

THE EARLY ZHOU DYNASTY (CA. 1050–500 B.C.E.)

How was China governed in the period looked back on as its golden age?

The Shang campaigned constantly against enemies. To the west were the fierce Qiang, considered barbarian tribesmen by the Shang and perhaps speaking an early form of Tibetan. Between the Shang capital and the Qiang was a frontier state called Zhou, which seems to have both inherited cultural traditions from the Neolithic cultures of the northwest and absorbed most of the material culture of the Shang. In about 1050 B.C.E., the Zhou rose against the Shang and defeated them in battle.

Primary Source:
From Book of Documents

Zhou Politics

The early Zhou period is the first one for which transmitted texts exist in some abundance. The *Book of Documents* describes the Zhou conquest of the Shang as the victory of just and noble warriors over decadent courtiers who were led by a dissolute, sadistic king. At the same time, these documents show that the Zhou recognized the Shang as occupying the center of the world, were eager to succeed to that role themselves, and saw history as a major way to legitimate power. The three early Zhou rulers who are given the most praise are King Wen (the "cultured" or "literate" king), who expanded the Zhou domain; his son King Wu (the "martial" king), who conquered the Shang; and Wu's brother, the Duke of Zhou, who consolidated the conquest and served as loyal regent for Wu's heir.

Book of Documents One of the earliest of the "Confucian" classics, containing documents, speeches, and historical accounts.

Like the Shang kings, the Zhou kings sacrificed to their ancestors, but they also sacrificed to Heaven. The *Book of Documents* assumes a close relationship between Heaven and the king, who was called the Son of Heaven. Heaven gives the king a mandate to rule only as long as he rules in the interests of the people. Thus it was because the last king of the Shang had been decadent and cruel that Heaven took the mandate away from him and entrusted it to the virtuous Zhou kings. Because this theory of the **Mandate of Heaven** does not seem to have had any place in Shang cosmology, it may have been elaborated by the early Zhou rulers as a kind of propaganda to win over the conquered subjects of the Shang. Whatever its origins, it remained a central feature of Chinese political ideology from the early Zhou period on.

Rather than attempt to rule all their territories directly, the early Zhou rulers set up a decentralized feudal system. They sent out relatives and trusted subordinates with troops to establish walled garrisons in the conquered territories. Such a vassal was generally able to pass his position on to a son, so that in time the domains became hereditary fiefs. By 800 B.C.E. there were about two hundred lords with domains large and small. Each lord appointed officers to serve him in ritual, administrative, or military capacities. These posts and their associated titles tended to become hereditary as well.

The decentralized rule of the early Zhou period had from the beginning carried within it the danger that the regional lords would become so powerful that they would no longer obey the commands of the king. As generations passed and ties of loyalty and kinship grew more distant, this indeed happened. In 771 B.C.E. the Zhou king was killed by an alliance of Rong tribesmen and Zhou vassals. One of his sons was put on the throne, and then for safety's sake the capital was moved east out of the Wei River valley to modern Luoyang, just south of the Huang River in the heart of the central plains (see Map 3.1).

The revived Zhou Dynasty never fully regained control over its vassals, and China entered a prolonged period without a strong central authority. For a couple of centuries a code of chivalrous or sportsmanlike conduct still regulated warfare between the states: one state would not attack another while it was in mourning for its ruler; during battles one side would not attack before the other side had time to line up; ruling houses were not wiped out, so that successors could continue to sacrifice to their ancestors; and so on. Thereafter, however, such niceties were abandoned, and China entered a period of nearly constant conflict.

Zhou Society

During the Zhou Dynasty, Chinese society underwent radical changes. Early Zhou rule was highly aristocratic. Inherited ranks placed people in a hierarchy ranging downward from the king to the rulers of states with titles like duke and marquis, the hereditary great officials of the states, the lower ranks of the aristocracy (men who could serve in either military or civil capacities, known as **shi**), and finally to the ordinary people (farmers, craftsmen, and traders). Patrilineal family ties were very important in this society, and at the upper reaches, at least, sacrifices to ancestors were one of the key rituals used to forge social ties.

Glimpses of what life was like at various social levels in the early Zhou Dynasty can be found in the *Book of Songs*, which contains the earliest Chinese poetry. Some of the songs are hymns used in court religious ceremonies, such as offerings to ancestors. Others clearly had their origins in folk songs. Some of these folk songs depict farmers at work clearing fields, plowing and planting, gathering mulberry leaves for silkworms, and spinning and weaving. Farming life involved not merely the cultivation of crops like millet, hemp (for cloth), beans, and vegetables, but also hunting small animals and collecting grasses and rushes to make rope and baskets.

Many of the folk songs are love songs that depict a more informal pattern of courtship than prevailed in later China. One stanza reads:

Mandate of Heaven *The theory that Heaven gives the king a mandate to rule only as long as he rules in the interests of the people.*

shi *The lower ranks of Chinese aristocracy; these men could serve in either military or civil capacities.*

Book of Songs *The earliest collection of Chinese poetry; it provides glimpses of what life was like in the early Zhou Dynasty.*

Primary Source: *From* Book of Songs

Please, Zhongzi,
Do not leap over our wall,
Do not break our mulberry trees.
It's not that I begrudge the mulberries,
But I fear my brothers.
You I would embrace,
But my brothers' words—those I dread.[1]

There were also songs of complaint, such as this one in which the ancestors are rebuked for failing to aid their descendants:

The drought has become so severe
That it cannot be stopped.
Glowing and burning,
We have no place.
The great mandate is about at an end.
Nothing to look forward to or back upon.
The host of dukes and past rulers
Does not help us.
As for father and mother and the ancestors,
How can they bear to treat us so?[2]

Other songs in this collection are court odes that reveal attitudes of the aristocrats. One such ode expresses a deep distrust of women's involvement in politics:

Clever men build cities,
Clever women topple them.
Beautiful, these clever women may be
But they are owls and kites.
Women have long tongues
That lead to ruin.
Disorder does not come down from heaven;
It is produced by women.[3]

● **Bronze Relief of Hunters** Hunting provided an important source of food in the Zhou period, and hunters were often depicted on inlaid bronzes of the period. *(The Avery Brundage Collection/Laurie Platt Winfrey, Inc.)*

Part of the reason for distrust of women in politics was the practice of concubinage. Rulers regularly demonstrated their power and wealth by accumulating large numbers of concubines and thus would have children by several women. In theory, succession went to the eldest son of the wife, then to younger sons by her, and only in their absence to sons of concubines; but in actual practice, the ruler of a state or the head of a powerful ministerial family could select a son of a concubine to be his heir if he wished. This led to much scheming for favor among the various sons and their mothers and the common perception that women were incapable of taking a disinterested view of the larger good.

THE WARRING STATES PERIOD (500–221 B.C.E.)

What were the consequences of the breakup of Zhou unity and the rise of independent states?

Warring States Period *The period of Chinese history between 403 and 221 B.C.E. when states fought each other and one after another was destroyed until only one remained.*

crossbow *A powerful, mechanical bow developed during the Warring States Period.*

Social and economic change quickened after 500 B.C.E. Cities began appearing all over north China. Thick earthen walls were built around the palaces and ancestral temples of the ruler and other aristocrats, and often an outer wall was added to protect the artisans, merchants, and farmers who lived outside the inner wall. Accounts of sieges launched against these walled citadels, with scenes of the scaling of walls and the storming of gates, are central to descriptions of military confrontations in this period.

The old aristocratic social structure of the Zhou was being undermined by advances in military technology. Large, well-drilled infantry armies became a potent military force in the **Warring States Period,** able to withstand and defeat chariot-led forces. By 300 B.C.E. states were sending out armies of a couple hundred thousand drafted foot soldiers, usually accompanied by horsemen. Adding to the effectiveness of armies of drafted foot soldiers was the development of the **crossbow** around 350 B.C.E. The trigger of a crossbow was an intricate bronze mechanism that allowed a foot soldier to shoot farther than could a horseman carrying a light bow. One text of the period reports that a skilled soldier with a powerful crossbow and a sharp sword was the match of a hundred ordinary men. To defend against crossbows, soldiers began wearing armor and helmets. Most of the armor was made of leader strips tied with cords. Helmets were sometimes made of iron.

The introduction of cavalry in this period also reduced the need for a chariot-riding aristocracy. Shooting bows and arrows from horseback was first perfected by non-Chinese peoples to the north of China proper, who at that time were making the transition to a nomadic pastoral economy. The northern state of Jin, to defend itself from the attacks of these horsemen, developed its own cavalry armies. Once it started using cavalry against other Chinese states, they too had to master the new technology. From this time on, acquiring and pasturing horses was a key component of military preparedness.

● **Lacquer Cup** This 6-inch-long lacquer cup, decorated with images of two intertwined birds, was one of many lacquered eating vessels found in a third-century B.C.E. tomb. Lacquer is made from the sap of a tree native to China. It is remarkably light, strong, smooth, and waterproof. Lacquered dishes, cups, boxes, musical instruments, and sculptures became highly sought-after luxury items. *(Jingzhou Prefecture Museum/© Cultural Relics Publishing House)*

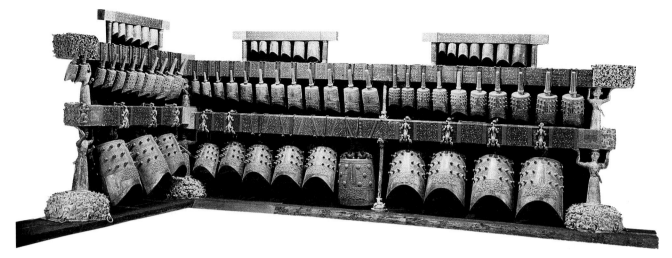

Because these developments made commoners and craftsmen central to military success, rulers tried to find ways to increase their populations. To increase agricultural output, they brought new land into cultivation, drained marshes, and dug irrigation channels. Rulers began surveying their land and taxing farmers. They wanted to undermine the power of lords over their subjects in order to get direct access to the peasants' labor power. Serfdom thus gradually declined. Registering populations led to the extension of family names to commoners at an earlier date than anywhere else in the world.

To encourage trade, rulers began casting coins. The development of iron technology in the early Zhou Dynasty also promoted economic expansion. By the fifth century B.C.E. iron was being widely used for both farm tools and weapons. By the third century B.C.E. the largest smelters employed two hundred or more workmen. A new powerful group also emerged in society—the rich who had acquired their wealth through trade or industry rather than inheritance or political favor. Late Zhou texts frequently mention cross-regional trade in objects such as furs, copper, dyes, hemp, salt, and horses.

Social mobility increased in this period. Rulers more often sent out their own officials rather than delegate authority to hereditary lesser lords. This trend toward centralized bureaucratic control created opportunities for social advancement for the shi on the lower end of the old aristocracy. Competition among such men guaranteed rulers a ready supply of able and willing subordinates, and competition among rulers for talent meant that ambitious men could be selective in deciding where to offer their services. (See the feature "Individuals in Society: Guan Zhong.")

The development of infantry armies also created the need for a new type of general, and rulers became less willing to let men lead troops merely because of aristocratic birth. Treatises on the art of war described the ideal general as a master of maneuver, illusion, and deception. In *The Art of War,* Master Sun argued that heroism is a useless virtue that leads to needless deaths. But discipline is essential, and he insisted that the entire army had to be trained to follow the orders of its commanders without questioning them.

States on the periphery that had been considered barbarian or semibarbarian during the early Zhou were gradually brought into the cultural sphere of the Central States, as the core region of China was called. For instance, the southern state of Chu expanded rapidly in the Yangzi Valley, defeating and absorbing fifty or more small states as it extended its reach north to the heartland of Zhou and east to absorb the old states of Wu and Yue. By the late Zhou period, Chu was on the forefront of cultural innovation and produced the greatest literary masterpiece of the era, the *Songs of Chu,* a collection of fantastical poems full of images of elusive deities and shamans who can fly through the spirit world.

● **Bells of the Marquis of Zeng** Music played a central role in court life in ancient China. The tomb of a minor ruler who died about 400 B.C.E. contained 124 musical instruments, including drums, flutes, mouth organs, pan pipes, zithers, a set of 32 chime stones, and this 64-piece bell set. The bells bear inscriptions that name the two tones each bell could make, depending on where it was struck. Five men, using poles and mallets and standing on either side of the set of bells, would have played the bells by hitting them from outside. (© Cultural Relics Publishing House)

> **Primary Source:**
> *Anecdotes from the Warring States Period*

By the third century B.C.E. there were only seven important states remaining. These states were much more centralized than their early Zhou predecessors. The kings of these states had eliminated indirect control through vassals and in its place dispatched royal officials to remote cities, controlling them from a distance through the transmission of documents and dismissing them at will.

CONFUCIUS AND HIS FOLLOWERS

What ideas did Confucius teach, and how were they a response to his times?

The Warring States Period was the era when the "Hundred Schools of Thought" contended. During the same period in which Indian sages and mystics were developing religious speculation about karma, souls, and eons of time, Chinese thinkers were arguing about the ideal forms of social and political organization and man's connections to nature.

Confucius (traditional dates: 551–479 B.C.E.) was one of the first men of ideas. As a young man, Confucius served in the court of his home state of Lu without gaining much influence. After leaving Lu, he set out with a small band of students and wandered through neighboring states in search of a ruler who would take his advice.

Confucius's ideas are known to us primarily through the sayings recorded by his disciples in the *Analects*. The thrust of his thought was ethical rather than theoretical or metaphysical. He talked repeatedly of an ideal age in the early Zhou Dynasty when everyone was devoted to fulfilling his or her role: superiors looked after those dependent on them; inferiors devoted themselves to the service of their superiors; parents and children, husbands and wives, all wholeheartedly embraced what was expected of them.

Confucius considered the family the basic unit of society. He extolled **filial piety,** which to him meant more than just reverent obedience of children to their parents:

The Master said, "You can be of service to your father and mother by remonstrating with them tactfully. If you perceive that they do not wish to follow your advice, then continue to be reverent toward them without offending or disobeying them; work hard and do not murmur against them."[4]

The relationship between father and son was one of the five cardinal relationships stressed by Confucius. The others were between ruler and subject, husband and wife, elder and younger brother, and friend and friend. Mutual obligations of a hierarchical sort underlay the first four of these relationships: the senior leads and protects; the junior supports and obeys. The exception was the relationship between friends, which was conceived in terms of mutual obligations between equals.

A man of moderation, Confucius was an earnest advocate of gentlemanly conduct. He redefined the term *gentleman* (*junzi*) to mean a man of moral cultivation rather than a man of noble birth. He repeatedly urged his followers to aspire to be gentlemen rather than petty men intent on personal gain. The gentleman, he said, "feels bad when his capabilities fall short of the task. He does not feel bad when people fail to recognize him."[5] Confucius did not advocate social equality, but his teachings minimized the importance of class distinctions and opened the way for intelligent and talented people to rise in the social scale. The Confucian gentleman found his calling in service to the ruler. Loyal advisers should encourage their rulers to govern through ritual, virtue, and concern for the welfare of their subjects, and much of the *Analects* concerns the way to govern well.

To Confucius the ultimate virtue was humanity (**ren**). A person of humanity cares about others and acts accordingly:

Zhonggong asked about humanity. The Master said, "When you go out, treat everyone as if you were welcoming a great guest. Employ people as though you were conducting a great

filial piety *Reverent attitude of children to their parents; it was extolled by Confucius.*

ren *The ultimate Confucian virtue; it is translated as perfect goodness, benevolence, humanity, human-heartedness, and nobility.*

Guan Zhong

By the time of Confucius, the success of states was often credited more to the lord's astute advisers than to the lord himself. To Confucius, the most praiseworthy political adviser was Guan Zhong (ca. 720–645 B.C.E.), the genius behind the rise of the state of Qi, in eastern China.

The earliest historical sources to recount Guan Zhong's accomplishments are the "commentaries" compiled in the Warring States Period to elaborate on the dry chronicle known as the *Spring and Autumn Annals.* The *Zuo Commentary,* for instance, tells us that in the year 660 B.C.E. Guan Zhong advised Duke Huan to aid the small state of Xing, then under attack by the non-Chinese Rong tribes: "The Rong and the Di are wolves who cannot be satiated. The Xia (Chinese) states are kin who should not be abandoned." In 652 B.C.E., it tells us, Guan Zhong urged the duke to maintain the respect of the other states by refusing the offer of the son of a recently defeated state's ruler to ally himself with Qi if Qi would help him depose his father. Because the duke regularly listened to Guan Zhong's sound advice, Qi brought the other states under its sway, and the duke came to be recognized as the first *hegemon,* or leader of the alliance of states.

Guan Zhong was also credited with strengthening the duke's internal administration. He encouraged the employment of officials on the basis of their moral character and ability rather than their birth. He introduced a system of drafting commoners for military service. In the history of China written by Sima Qian in about 100 B.C.E., Guan Zhong is also given credit for enriching Qi by promoting trade, issuing coins, and standardizing merchants' scales. He was credited with the statement "When the granaries are full, the people will understand ritual and moderation. When they have enough food and clothing, they will understand honor and disgrace."

Sima Qian's biography of Guan Zhong emphasizes his early poverty and the key role played by a friend, Bao Shuya, who recognized his worth. As young men, both Bao and Guan Zhong served brothers of the duke of Qi. When this duke was killed and a messy succession struggle followed, Bao's patron won out and became the next duke, while Guan Zhong's patron had to flee and in the end was killed. Bao, however, recommended Guan Zhong to the new duke, Duke Huan, and Guan Zhong took up a post under him.

The inlaid decoration on bronze vessels of the Warring States Period often shows people engaged in warfare, hunting, preparing food, performing rituals, and making music. *(From E. Consten,* Das alte China)

In the *Analects,* one of Confucius's disciples thought that Guan Zhong's lack of loyalty to his first lord made him a man unworthy of respect: "When Duke Huan killed his brother Jiu, Guan Zhong was unable to die with Jiu but rather became prime minister to Duke Huan." Confucius disagreed: "Guan Zhong became prime minister to Duke Huan and made him hegemon among the lords, uniting and reforming all under Heaven. The people, down to the present, continued to receive benefits from this. Were it not for Guan Zhong our hair would hang unbound and we would fold our robes on the left [that is, live as barbarians]."*

A book of the teachings associated with Guan Zhong, the *Guanzi,* was in circulation by the late Warring States Period. Although it is today not thought to reflect the teachings of the historical Guan Zhong, the fact that later statecraft thinkers would borrow his name is an indication of his fame as a great statesman.

Questions for Analysis

1. How did the form of government promoted by Guan Zhong differ from the early Zhou political system?

2. What can one infer about Chinese notions of loyalty from the story of Guan Zhong and his friend Bao Shuya?

3. Did Guan Zhong and Confucius share similar understandings of the differences between Chinese and barbarians?

*Analects, 14.18. Translated by Patricia Ebrey.

● **Serving Parents with Filial Piety** This illustration of a passage in the *Classic of Filial Piety* shows how commoners should serve their parents: by working hard at productive jobs such as farming and tending to their parents' daily needs. The married son and daughter-in-law bring food or drink to offer the older couple as their own children look on, thus learning how they should treat their own parents after they become aged themselves. *(National Palace Museum, Taipei, Taiwan)*

sacrifice. Do not do unto others what you would not have them do unto you. Then neither in your country nor in your family will there be complaints against you."[6]

Confucius encouraged the men who came to study with him to master the poetry, rituals, and historical traditions that we know today as Confucian classics. Many passages in the *Analects* reveal Confucius's confidence in the power of study:

The Master said, "I am not someone who was born wise. I am someone who loves the ancients and tries to learn from them."

The Master said, "I once spent a whole day without eating and a whole night without sleeping in order to think. It was of no use. It is better to study."[7]

The eventual success of Confucian ideas owes much to Confucius's followers in the three centuries following his death. The most important of them were Mencius (ca. 370–ca. 300 B.C.E.) and Xunzi (ca. 310–ca. 215 B.C.E.).

Mencius, like Confucius, traveled around offering advice to rulers of various states. (See the feature "Listening to the Past: The Book of Mencius" on pages 74–75.) Over and over he tried to convert them to the view that the ruler able to win over the people through benevolent government would succeed in unifying "all under Heaven." Mencius proposed concrete political and financial measures for easing tax burdens and otherwise improving the people's lot. Men willing to serve an unworthy ruler earned his contempt, especially when they worked hard to fill the ruler's coffers or expand his territory. With his disciples and fellow philosophers, Mencius also discussed other issues in moral philosophy, arguing strongly, for instance, that human nature is fundamentally good, as everyone is born with the capacity to recognize what is right and act on it.

Xunzi, a half century later, took the opposite view of human nature, arguing that people are born selfish and that it is only through education and ritual that they learn to put moral principle above their own interest. Much of what is desirable is not inborn but must be taught:

When a son yields to his father, or a younger brother yields to his elder brother, or when a son takes on the work for his father or a younger brother for his elder brother, their actions go against their natures and run counter to their feelings. And yet these are the way of the filial son and the principles of ritual and morality.[8]

Neither Confucius nor Mencius had had much actual political or administrative experience, but Xunzi had worked for many years in the court of his home state. Not surprisingly, he showed more consideration than either Confucius or Mencius for the difficulties a ruler might face in trying to rule through ritual and virtue. Xunzi was also a more rigorous thinker than his predecessors and developed the philosophical foundations of many ideas merely outlined by Confucius or Mencius. Confucius, for instance, had declined to discuss gods, portents, and anomalies and had spoken of sacrificing as if the spirits were present. Xunzi went farther and explicitly argued that Heaven does not intervene in human affairs. Praying to Heaven or to gods, he asserted, does not induce them to act. "Why does it rain after a prayer for rain? In my opinion, for no reason. It is the same as raining when you had not prayed."[9]

Even though he did not think praying could bring rain or other benefits from Heaven, Xunzi did not propose abandoning traditional rituals. In contrast to Daoists and Mohists (discussed below), who saw rituals as unnatural or extravagant, Xunzi saw them as an efficient way to attain order in society. Rulers and educated men should continue traditional ritual practices such as complex funeral protocols because the rites themselves have positive effects on performers and observers. Not only do they let people express feelings and satisfy desires in an orderly way, but because they specify graduated ways to perform the rites according to social rank, ritual traditions sustain the social hierarchy. Xunzi compared and contrasted ritual and music: music shapes people's emotions and creates feelings of solidarity, while ritual shapes people's sense of duty and creates social differentiation.

The Confucian vision of personal ethics and public service found a small but ardent following in the Warring States Period. In later centuries, rulers came to see men educated in Confucian virtues as ideal advisers and officials. Neither revolutionaries nor toadies, Confucian scholar-officials opposed bad government and upheld the best ideals of statecraft. Confucian political ideals shaped Chinese society into the twentieth century.

The Confucian vision also provided the moral basis for the Chinese family into modern times. Repaying parents and ancestors came to be seen as a sacred duty. Because people owe their very existence to their parents, they should reciprocate by respecting them, making efforts to please them, honoring their memories, and placing the interests of the family line above personal preferences. Since this family line is a patrilineal line from father to son to grandson, placing great importance on it has had the effect of devaluing women.

DAOISM, LEGALISM, AND OTHER SCHOOLS OF THOUGHT

What did those who opposed Confucianism argue?

During the Warring States Period, rulers took advantage of the destruction of states to recruit newly unemployed men to serve as their advisers and court assistants. Lively debate often resulted as these strategists proposed policies and defended their ideas against challengers. Followers took to recording their teachers' ideas, and the circulation of these "books" (rolls of silk, or strips of wood or bamboo tied together) served further to stimulate debate.

Many of these schools of thought directly opposed the ideas of Confucius and his followers. Mozi proposed that every idea should be tested on the basis of utility: does it benefit the people and the state? He objected to Confucian emphasis on ritual because it interrupts work and is wasteful. Mozi did not approve of Confucian emphasis on treating only one's family with special concern, saying that the principle should be concern for everyone equally. The Daoists and Legalists opposed other Confucian principles.

the Way *The Dao, the whole natural order.*

Daoism

Confucius and his followers believed in moral effort and statecraft. They thought men of virtue should devote themselves to making the government work to the benefit of the people. Those who came to be labeled Daoists disagreed. They thought striving to make things better generally makes them worse. Daoists defended private life and wanted the rulers to leave the people alone. They sought to go beyond everyday concerns and to let their minds wander freely. Rather than making human beings and human actions the center of concern, they focused on the larger scheme of things, the whole natural order identified as **the Way,** or Dao.

Early Daoist teachings are known from two surviving books, the *Laozi* and the *Zhuangzi,* both dating to the third century B.C.E. Laozi, the putative author of the *Laozi,* may not be a historical figure, but the text ascribed to him has been of enduring importance. A recurrent theme in this brief, aphoristic text is the mystical superiority of yielding over assertion and silence over words: "The Way that can be discussed is not the constant Way."[10] The highest good is like water: "Water benefits all creatures but does not compete. It occupies the places people disdain and thus comes near to the Way."[11]

Because purposeful action is counterproductive, the ruler should let people return to a natural state of ignorance and contentment:

Do not honor the worthy,
And the people will not compete.
Do not value rare treasures,
And the people will not steal.
Do not display what others want,
And the people will not have their hearts confused.
A sage governs this way:
He empties people's minds and fills their bellies.
He weakens their wills and strengthens their bones.
Keep the people always without knowledge and without desires,
For then the clever will not dare act.
Engage in no action and order will prevail.[12]

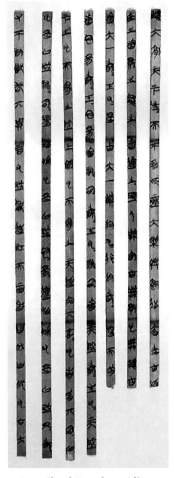

● **Inscribed Bamboo Slips** In 1993 Chinese archaeologists discovered a late-fourth-century B.C.E. tomb in Hubei province that contained 804 bamboo slips, bearing some 12,000 Chinese characters. Scholars have been able to reconstruct more than a dozen books from them, some of which match transmitted texts fairly closely, but others are books previously unknown. *(Courtesy, Jingmen City Museum, Hubei)*

In the philosophy of the *Laozi,* the people would be better off if they knew less, gave up tools, renounced writing, stopped envying their neighbors, and lost their desire to travel or engage in war.

Zhuangzi (369–286 B.C.E.), the author of the book of the same name, was a historical figure who shared many of the central ideas of the *Laozi.* He was proud of his disinterest in politics. In one of his many anecdotes, he reported that the king of Chu once sent an envoy to invite him to take over the government of his realm. In response Zhuangzi asked the envoy whether a tortoise that had been held as sacred for three thousand years would prefer to be dead with its bones venerated or alive with its tail dragging in the mud. When the envoy agreed that life was preferable, Zhuangzi told the envoy to leave. He preferred to drag his tail in the mud.

The *Zhuangzi* is filled with parables, flights of fancy, and fictional encounters between historical figures, including Confucius and his disciples. A more serious strain of Zhuangzi's thought concerned death. He questioned whether we can be sure life is better than death. People fear what they do not know, the same way a captive girl will be terrified when she learns she is to become the king's concubine. Perhaps people will discover that death has as many delights as life in the palace.

When a friend expressed shock that Zhuangzi was not weeping at his wife's death but rather singing, Zhuangzi explained:

When she first died, how could I have escaped feeling the loss? Then I looked back to the beginning before she had life. Not only before she had life, but before she had form. Not only before she had form, but before she had vital energy. In this confused amorphous realm, something changed and vital energy appeared; when the vital energy was changed, form appeared; with changes in form, life began. Now there is another change bringing death. This is like the progression of the four seasons of spring and fall, winter and summer. Here she was lying down to sleep in a huge room and I followed her, sobbing and wailing. When I realized my actions showed I hadn't understood destiny, I stopped.[13]

● **Embroidered Silk** From ancient times, silk was one of China's most famous products. Women traditionally did most of the work involved in making silk, from feeding mulberry leaves to the silkworms, to reeling and twisting the fibers, to weaving and embroidering. The embroidered silk depicted here is from a robe found in a fourth-century B.C.E. tomb in central China. The flowing, curvilinear design incorporates dragons, phoenixes, and tigers. *(Jingzhou Museum)*

Zhuangzi was similarly iconoclastic in his political ideas. In one parable a wheelwright insolently tells a duke that books are useless since all they contain are the dregs of men long dead. The duke, insulted, threatens to execute him if he cannot give an adequate explanation of his remark. The wheelwright replies:

I see things in terms of my own work. When I chisel at a wheel, if I go slow, the chisel slides and does not stay put; if I hurry, it jams and doesn't move properly. When it is neither too slow nor too fast, I can feel it in my hand and respond to it from my heart. My mouth cannot describe it in words, but there is something there. I cannot teach it to my son, and my son cannot learn it from me. So I have gone on for seventy years, growing old chiseling wheels. The men of old died in possession of what they could not transmit. So it follows that what you are reading are their dregs.[14]

To put this another way, truly skilled craftsmen respond to situations spontaneously; they do not analyze or reason or even keep in mind the rules they have

> **Primary Source:**
> **Laozi, *From* Dao De Jing: *Administering the Empire***

mastered. This strain of Daoist thought denies the validity of verbal reasoning and the sorts of knowledge conveyed through words.

Daoism can be seen as a response to Confucianism, a rejection of many of its basic premises. Nevertheless, over the course of Chinese history, many people felt the pull of both Confucian and Daoist ideas and studied the writings of both schools. Even Confucian scholars who had devoted much of their lives to public service might find that the teachings of the *Laozi* or *Zhuangzi* helped to put their frustrations in perspective. Whereas Confucianism often seems sternly masculine, Daoism is more accepting of feminine principles and even celebrates passivity and yielding. Those drawn to the arts were also often drawn to Daoism, with its validation of spontaneity and freedom. Rulers, too, were drawn to the Daoist notion of the ruler who can have great power simply by being himself without instituting anything.

Legalism

Legalists *Political theorists who emphasized the need for rigorous laws and laid the basis for China's later bureaucratic government.*

As one small state after another was conquered, the number of surviving states dwindled. Rulers fearful that their states might be next were ready to listen to political theorists who claimed expertise in the accumulation of power. These theorists, labeled **Legalists** because of their emphasis on the need for rigorous laws, argued that strong government depended not on the moral qualities of the ruler and his officials, as Confucians claimed, but on establishing effective laws and procedures. Legalism, though eventually discredited, laid the basis for China's later bureaucratic government.

In the fourth century B.C.E. the state of Qin, under the leadership of its chief minister, Lord Shang (d. 338 B.C.E.), adopted many Legalist policies. It abolished the aristocracy. Social distinctions were to be based on military ranks determined by the objective criterion of the number of enemy heads cut off in battle. In place of the old fiefs, Qin divided the country into counties and appointed officials to govern them according to the laws decreed at court. To increase the population, migrants were recruited from other states with offers of land and houses. To encourage farmers to work hard and improve their land, they were allowed to buy and sell it. Ordinary farmers were thus freed from serf-like obligations to the local nobility, but direct control by the state could be even more onerous. Taxes and labor service obligations were heavy. Travel required a permit, and vagrants could be forced into penal labor service. All families were grouped into mutual responsibility groups of five and ten families; whenever anyone in the group committed a crime, all the others were equally liable unless they reported it.

In the century after Lord Shang, Legalism found its greatest exponent in Han Feizi (ca. 280?–233 B.C.E.). Han Feizi had studied with the Confucian master Xunzi but had little interest in Confucian values of goodness or ritual. In his writings he warned rulers of the political pitfalls awaiting them. They had to be careful where they placed their trust, for "when the ruler trusts someone, he falls under that person's control."[15] This is true even of wives and concubines, who think of the interests of their sons. Given subordinates' propensities to pursue their own selfish interests, the ruler should keep them ignorant of his intentions and control them by manipulating competition among them. Warmth, affection, or candor should have no place in his relationships with others.

Han Feizi saw the Confucian notion that government could be based on virtue as naive:

Think of parents' relations to their children. They congratulate each other when a son is born, but complain to each other when a daughter is born. Why do parents have these divergent responses when both are equally their offspring? It is because they calculate their long-term advantage. Since even parents deal with their children in this calculating way, what can one expect where there is no parent-child bond? When present-day scholars counsel rulers, they all tell them to rid themselves of thoughts of profit and follow the path of mutual love. This is expecting rulers to go further than parents.[16]

If rulers would make the laws and prohibitions clear and the rewards and punishments automatic, then the officials and common people would be easy to govern. Uniform laws get people to do things they would not otherwise be inclined to do, such as work hard and fight wars, essential to the goal of establishing hegemony over all the other states.

The laws of the Legalists were designed as much to constrain officials as to regulate the common people. The third-century B.C.E. tomb of a Qin official has yielded statutes detailing the rules for keeping accounts, supervising subordinates, managing penal labor, conducting investigations, and many other responsibilities of officials. Infractions were generally punishable through the imposition of fines.

Legalism saw no value in intellectual debate or private opinion. Divergent views of right and wrong lead to weakness and disorder. The ruler should not allow others to undermine his laws by questioning them. In Legalism, there were no laws above or independent of the wishes of the rulers, no laws that might set limits on rulers' actions in the way that natural or divine laws did in Greek thought. Indeed, a ruler's right to exercise the law as he saw fit was demonstrated in the violent deaths of the two leading Legalist thinkers: Lord Shang was drawn and quartered by chariots in 338 B.C.E., and Han Feizi was imprisoned and forced to drink poison in 233 B.C.E.

Rulers of several states adopted some Legalist ideas, but only the state of Qin systematically followed them. The extraordinary but brief success Qin had with these policies is discussed in Chapter 6.

Yin and Yang

Cosmological speculation formed another important strain of early Chinese thought. The concepts of **yin and yang** are found in early form in the divination manual the *Book of Changes,* but late Zhou theorists developed much more elaborate theories based on them. Yin is the feminine, dark, receptive, yielding, negative, and weak; yang is the masculine, bright, assertive, creative, positive, and strong. Yin and yang are complementary poles rather than distinct entities or opposing forces. The movement of yin and yang accounts for the transition from day to night and from summer to winter. These models based on observation of nature were extended to explain not only phenomena we might classify as natural, such as illness, storms, and earthquakes, but also social phenomena, such as the rise and fall of states and conflict in families. In all these realms, unwanted things happen when the balance between yin and yang gets disturbed.

yin and yang *A concept of complementary poles, one of which represents the feminine, dark, and receptive, and the other the masculine, bright, and assertive.*

In recent decades archaeologists have further complicated our understanding of early Chinese thought by unearthing records of the popular religion of the time—astrological manuals, handbooks of lucky and unlucky days, medical prescriptions, exercises, and ghost stories. The tomb of an official who died in 316 B.C.E. has records of divinations showing that illness was seen as the result of unsatisfied spirits or malevolent demons, best dealt with through exorcisms or offering sacrifices to the astral god Taiyi (Grand One).

● **Dagger Depicting Taiyi** Recent archaeological excavations of manuscripts from the Warring States Period have given us a much clearer understanding of religious beliefs and practices in early China. The deity Taiyi ("Grand One"), depicted on this late-fourth-century B.C.E. drawing of a dagger, was the god of the pole star. Sacrifices were made to Taiyi to avert evil or gain his protection in battle. *(From Michael Loewe and Edward Shaughnessy, eds.,* Cambridge History of Ancient China *[New York: Cambridge University Press, 1999]. Reprinted with permission of Cambridge University Press)*

Chapter Summary

To assess your mastery of this chapter and read the primary sources listed in the margins, visit **bedfordstmartins.com/mckayworld** or see *Sources of World Societies*.

Key Terms

loess
Anyang
logographic
taotie
Book of Documents
Mandate of Heaven
shi
Book of Songs
Warring States Period
crossbow
filial piety
ren
the Way
Legalists
yin and yang

• When, where, and how did writing, bronze technology, and other elements of civilization develop in China?

After a long Neolithic period, China entered the Bronze Age with the Shang Dynasty. In Shang times, the kings served also as priests, and great wealth was invested in extraordinarily complex bronze ritual vessels. From Shang times on, the Chinese language has been written in a logographic script, which shaped the ways people have become educated and the value assigned to education.

• How was China governed in the period looked back on as its golden age?

The Zhou Dynasty, which overthrew the Shang in about 1050 B.C.E., parceled out its territory to lords, whose titles gradually became hereditary. The texts transmitted from this period present Heaven as the high god. Kings were called Sons of Heaven because they had to have Heaven's approval to gain the throne. If they did not rule in the interests of the people, Heaven could take the Mandate away from them and confer it on a worthier person.

• What were the consequences of the breakup of Zhou unity and the rise of independent states?

The ties between the Zhou king and his lords gradually weakened, and the domains over time came to act like independent states. After 500 B.C.E. China is best thought of as a multistate realm. Social and cultural change was particularly rapid under these conditions of intense competition. Changes in military technology included the introduction of cavalry, infantry armies, and the crossbow. Iron utensils came into use, as did metal coinage.

• What ideas did Confucius teach, and how were they a response to his times?

This Warring States Period was the golden age of Chinese philosophy. Confucius and his followers advocated a deeply moral view of the way to achieve order through the cultivation of virtues by everyone from the ruler on down. Key virtues were sincerity, loyalty, benevolence, and filial piety. Over the next two centuries Confucius's message was elaborated by important followers, including Mencius, who urged rulers to rule through goodness and argued that human nature is good, and Xunzi, who stressed the power of ritual and argued that human nature is selfish and must be curbed through education.

• What did those who opposed Confucianism argue?

In the contentious spirit of the age, many thinkers countered Confucian principles. Daoists like Laozi and Zhuangzi looked beyond the human realm to the entire cosmos and spoke of the relativity of concepts such as good and bad and life and death. The Legalists were hardheaded men who heaped ridicule on the idea that a ruler could get his people to be good by being good himself and proposed instead clear laws with strict rewards and punishments. Natural philosophers explored issues Confucius had neglected, such as the forces that bring about the changes in the seasons and health and illness.

Suggested Reading

Blunden, Caroline, and Mark Elvin. *Cultural Atlas of China.* 1983. Valuable both for its historical maps and its well-illustrated topical essays.

Chang, Kwang-chih. *Archeology of Ancient China,* 4th ed. 1986. An overview by a leading archaeologist.

de Bary, Wm. Theodore, and Irene Bloom. *Sources of Chinese Tradition.* 1999. Large collection of primary sources for Chinese intellectual history, with lengthy introductions.

Ebrey, Patricia Buckley. *Cambridge Illustrated History of China.* 1996. Well-illustrated brief overview of Chinese history.

Graham, A. C. *Disputers of the Tao: Philosophical Argument in Ancient China.* 1989. A philosophically rich overview of the intellectual flowering of the Warring States Period.

Ledderose, Lothar. *Ten Thousand Things: Module and Mass Production in Chinese Art.* 2000. A new interpretation of Chinese culture in terms of modules; offers fresh perspectives on the Chinese script and the production of bronzes.

Loewe, Michael, and Edward Shaughnessy, eds. *The Cambridge History of Ancient China: From the Origins of Civilization to 221 B.C.* 1999. An authoritative collection of chapters, half by historians, half by archaeologists.

Mote, F. W. *Intellectual Foundations of China.* 1989. Brief but stimulating introduction to early Chinese thought.

Thorp, Robert, and Richard Vinograd. *Chinese Art and Culture.* 2001. Broad coverage of all of China's visual arts.

Yang, Xin, ed. *The Golden Age of Chinese Archaeology.* 1999. The well-illustrated catalogue of a major show of Chinese archaeological finds.

Notes

1. *Chinese Civilization: A Sourcebook,* 2d ed., revised and expanded by Patricia Buckley Ebrey (New York: Free Press/Macmillan, 1993), p. 11. All quotations from this work reprinted and edited with the permission of The Free Press, a Division of Simon & Schuster Adult Publishing Group. Copyright © 1993 by Patricia Buckley Ebrey. All rights reserved.

2. Edward Shaughnessy, "Western Zhou History," in M. Loewe and E. Shaughnessy, eds., *The Cambridge History of Ancient China* (New York: Cambridge University Press, 1999), p. 336. Reprinted with the permission of Cambridge University Press and Edward L. Shaughnessy.

3. Patricia Buckley Ebrey, *The Cambridge Illustrated History of China* (Cambridge: Cambridge University Press, 1996), p. 34.

4. Ebrey, *Chinese Civilization,* p. 21.
5. Ibid., p. 19.
6. Ibid.
7. *Analects* 7.19, 15.30. Translated by Patricia Ebrey.
8. Ebrey, *Chinese Civilization,* p. 26.
9. Ibid., p. 24, modified.
10. Ibid., p. 27.
11. Ibid., p. 28, modified.
12. Ibid., p. 28.
13. Ibid., p. 31.
14. Ibid.
15. Ibid., p. 33.
16. Ibid., p. 35.

Listening to the PAST

The Book of Mencius

*T*he book that records the teachings of Mencius (ca. 370–ca. 300 B.C.E.) was modeled on the Analects of Confucius. It presents, in no particular order, conversations between Mencius and several rulers, philosophers, and disciples. Unlike the Analects, however, the Book of Mencius includes extended discussions of particular points, suggesting that Mencius had a hand in recording the conversations.

Mencius had an audience with King Hui of Liang. The king said, "Sir, you did not consider a thousand *li* too far to come. You must have some ideas about how to benefit my state."

Mencius replied, "Why must Your Majesty use the word 'benefit'? All I am concerned with are the benevolent and the right. If Your Majesty says, 'How can I benefit my state?' your officials will say, 'How can I benefit my family,' and officers and common people will say, 'How can I benefit myself?' Once superiors and inferiors are competing for benefit, the state will be in danger.

"When the head of a state of ten thousand chariots is murdered, the assassin is invariably a noble with a fief of a thousand chariots. When the head of a fief of a thousand chariots is murdered, the assassin is invariably head of a subfief of a hundred chariots. Those with a thousand out of ten thousand, or a hundred out of a thousand, had quite a bit. But when benefit is put before what is right, they are not satisfied without snatching it all. By contrast, there has never been a benevolent person who neglected his parents or a righteous person who put his lord last. Your Majesty perhaps will now also say, 'All I am concerned with are the benevolent and the right.' Why mention 'benefit'?"

After seeing King Xiang of Liang, Mencius said to someone, "When I saw him from a distance, he did not look like a ruler, and when I got closer, I saw nothing to command respect. But he asked, 'How can the realm be settled?'

"I answered, 'It can be settled through unity.'

"'Who can unify it?' he asked.

"I answered, 'Someone not fond of killing people.'

"'Who could give it to him?'

"I answered, 'Everyone in the world will give it to him. Your Majesty knows what rice plants are? If there is a drought in the seventh and eighth months, the plants wither, but if moisture collects in the sky and forms clouds and rain falls in torrents, the plants suddenly revive. This is the way it is; no one can stop the process. In the world today there are no rulers disinclined toward killing. If there were a ruler who did not like to kill people, everyone in the world would crane their necks to catch sight of him. This is really true. The people would flow toward him the way water flows down. No one would be able to repress them.'"

After an incident between Zou and Lu, Duke Mu asked, "Thirty-three of my officials died but no common people died. I could punish them, but I could not punish them all. I could refrain from punishing them, but they did angrily watch their superiors die without saving them. What would be the best course for me to follow?"

Mencius answered, "When the harvest failed, even though your granaries were full, nearly a thousand of your subjects were lost—the old and weak among them dying in the gutters, the able-bodied scattering in all directions. Your officials never reported the situation, a case of superiors callously inflicting suffering on their subordinates. Zengzi said, 'Watch out, watch out! What you do will be done to you.' This was the first chance the people had to pay them back. You should not resent them. If Your Highness practices benevolent government, the common people will love their superiors and die for those in charge of them."

King Xuan of Qi asked, "Is it true that Tang banished Jie and King Wu took up arms against Zhou?"

Mencius replied, "That is what the records say."

"Then is it permissible for a subject to assassinate his lord?"

Mencius said, "Someone who does violence to the good we call a villain; someone who does violence to the right we call a criminal. A person who is both a villain and a criminal we call a scoundrel. I have heard that the scoundrel Zhou was killed, but have not heard that a lord was killed."

King Xuan of Qi asked about ministers.

Mencius said, "What sort of ministers does Your Majesty mean?"

The king said, "Are there different kinds of ministers?"

"There are. There are noble ministers related to the ruler and ministers of other surnames."

The king said, "I'd like to hear about noble ministers."

Mencius replied, "When the ruler makes a major error, they point it out. If he does not listen to their repeated remonstrations, then they put someone else on the throne."

The king blanched. Mencius continued, "Your Majesty should not be surprised at this. Since you asked me, I had to tell you truthfully."

After the king regained his composure, he asked about unrelated ministers. Mencius said, "When the king makes an error, they point it out. If he does not heed their repeated remonstrations, they quit their posts."

Bo Gui said, "I'd like a tax of one part in twenty. What do you think?"

Mencius said, "Your way is that of the northern tribes. Is one potter enough for a state with ten thousand households?"

"No, there would not be enough wares."

"The northern tribes do not grow all the five grains, only millet. They have no cities or houses, no ritual sacrifices. They do not provide gifts or banquets for feudal lords, and do not have a full array of officials. Therefore, for them, one part in twenty is enough. But we live in the central states. How could we abolish social roles and do without gentlemen? If a state cannot do without potters, how much less can it do without gentlemen.

"Those who want to make government lighter than it was under Yao and Shun are to some degree barbarians. Those who wish to make government heavier than it was under Yao and Shun are to some degree [tyrants like] Jie."

Gaozi said, "Human nature is like whirling water. When an outlet is opened to the east, it flows east;

Opening page of a 1617 edition of the Book of Mencius. *(Rare Books Collections, Harvard-Yenching Library, Harvard University)*

when an outlet is opened to the west, it flows west. Human nature is no more inclined to good or bad than water is inclined to east or west."

Mencius responded, "Water, it is true, is not inclined to either east or west, but does it have no preference for high or low? Goodness is to human nature like flowing downward is to water. There are no people who are not good and no water that does not flow down. Still, water, if splashed, can go higher than your head; if forced, it can be brought up a hill. This isn't the nature of water; it is the specific circumstances. Although people can be made to be bad, their natures are not changed."

Questions for Analysis

1. Does Mencius give consistent advice to the kings he talks to?

2. Do you see a link between Mencius's views on human nature and his views on the true king?

3. What role does Mencius see for ministers?

Source: Reprinted and edited with the permission of The Free Press, a Division of Simon & Schuster Adult Publishing Group, from *Chinese Civilization: A Sourcebook,* Second Edition, revised and expanded by Patricia Buckley Ebrey. Copyright © 1993 by Patricia Buckley Ebrey. All rights reserved.

Tetrapylon of Aphrodisias. This monumental gate celebrates the beautiful and rich city of Aphrodisias in modern Turkey. *(John Buckler)*

4 THE GREEK EXPERIENCE (CA. 3500–146 B.C.E.)

The people of ancient Greece developed a culture that fundamentally shaped the civilization of the western part of Eurasia much as the Chinese did for the eastern part. The Greeks were the first in the Mediterranean and neighboring areas to explore most of the questions that still concern thinkers today. Going beyond mythmaking, the Greeks strove to understand the world in logical, rational terms. The result was the birth of philosophy and science, subjects as important to many of them as religion. From daily life they developed the concept of politics. Their contributions to the arts and literature still fertilize intellectual life today.

The history of the Greeks is divided into two broad periods: the Hellenic, roughly the time between the arrival of the Greeks and the triumph of Macedonia in 338 B.C.E.; and the Hellenistic, the years from Alexander the Great (336–323 B.C.E.) to the Roman conquest (200–146 B.C.E.).

HELLAS: THE LAND AND THE POLIS (CA. 3500–CA. 800 B.C.E.)

How did the geography of Greece divide the land so that small communities naturally developed?

Hellas, as the Greeks call their land, encompasses the Greek peninsula and the islands surrounding it, the area known as the Aegean basin. This basin in turn included the Greek settlements in Ionia in Asia Minor, the western coast of modern Turkey. Geography acts as an enormously divisive force in Greek life because the rugged terrain led to political fragmentation. Consequently, no strong central state became permanently dominant.

77

● Mycenaean Lion Hunt The Mycenaeans were a robust, warlike people who enjoyed the thrill and the danger of hunting. This scene on the blade of a dagger depicts hunters armed with spears and protected by shields defending themselves against charging lions. *(National Archaeological Museum/ Archaeological Receipts Fund)*

The Earliest Settlers

At the faint dawn of history, small farming communities worked much of the land. They prospered and expanded in a gradual process still little understood. Historians can, however, describe two well-documented early civilizations. The Minoan culture, the earlier of the two, arose about 3500 B.C.E. on the island of Crete. Its modern discoverers named it after the mythical king Minos. The second society, the Mycenaean, flourished between about 1575 and 1000 B.C.E. Its name, too, is modern, derived from the small Greek town where its remains were first discovered. Because both the Minoans and Mycenaeans used bronze instruments, modern scholars name this the Bronze Age.

At the head of Minoan society stood a king and his nobles governing a society of farmers and maritime merchants. Besides spreading throughout Crete, the Minoans traded with Egypt and the coastal cities of the ancient Near East. Their trading ventures also brought them into contact with the Mycenaeans on the Greek peninsula. The Mycenaeans founded numerous kingdoms from Thessaly in the north to the southern Peloponnesos. The kingdom was the basic Mycenaean political unit, headed by a king and his warrior aristocracy. Owners of most of the land, they relied on non-noble artisans, traders, and farmers to run the economy. Slaves, at the bottom of the social scale, were owned by the king and aristocrats. Mycenaean commerce quickly spread throughout the eastern Mediterranean, reaching Asia Minor, Cyprus, and Egypt. Prosperity, however, did not bring peace, and between 1300 and 1000 B.C.E. various kingdoms ravaged one another in a savage series of wars that destroyed both the Minoan and Mycenaean civilizations.

The fall of these first kingdoms ushered in a period of poverty and disruption usually called Greece's "Dark Age" (ca. 1100–800 B.C.E.). Despite daunting challenges, Greece actually became even more Greek during these years. Some Greeks entered the peninsula for the first time, the most important being the Dorians, who became the historical Spartans, Argives, and Messenians. Others migrated eastward to Asia Minor. By the end of the Dark Age Greeks and their culture had spread throughout the Aegean basin (see Map 4.1).

The Polis (ca. 800 B.C.E.)

polis *Generally translated as "city-state," it was the basic political and institutional unit of Greece.*

During the Dark Age, the Greeks developed the **polis,** which is generally translated as "city-state." More than a political institution, the polis was a community of citizens with their own customs and laws. Even though the physical, religious, and political form of the polis varied from place to place, it was the very badge of Greekness.

acropolis *An elevated point within a city on which stood temples, altars, public monuments, and various dedications to the gods of the polis.*

The polis included the town and its surrounding countryside. The people of the polis typically lived in a compact group of houses within a city, which by the fifth century B.C.E. was generally surrounded by a wall. The city contained a point, usually elevated, called the **acropolis,** and a public square or marketplace, the *agora.* On the acropolis stood the temples, altars, public monuments, and various dedications to the gods of the polis. The agora was originally the place where the warrior assembly met, and it became the political center of the polis. In the agora were porticoes, shops, public buildings, and courts.

The *chora*, which included the arable land, pastureland, and wasteland of the polis, was typically its source of wealth. Farmers left the city each morning to work their fields or tend their flocks of sheep and goats, and they returned at night. On the wasteland people often quarried stone or mined for precious metals. Thus the polis was the scene of both urban and agrarian life.

The size of the polis varied according to geographical circumstances. But regardless of its size or wealth, the polis was fundamental to Greek life. The very smallness of the polis enabled Greeks to see how the individual fit into the overall system—how the human parts made up the social whole. The Greeks were their own magistrates, administrators, and soldiers.

The polis could be governed in several ways. In a **monarchy,** a term derived from the Greek for "the rule of one man," a king represented the community, reigning according to law and respecting the rights of the citizens. The aristocracy could govern the state. A literal political translation of the term *aristocracy* means "power in the hands of the best." Or the running of the polis could be the prerogative of an **oligarchy,** which literally means "the rule of a few"—in this case a small group of wealthy citizens not necessarily of aristocratic birth. Still another form of government was **tyranny,** rule by a man who had seized power by extralegal means. Or the polis could be governed as a **democracy,** through the rule of the people, a concept that in Greece meant that all citizens, regardless of birth or wealth, administered the workings of government.

Because the bonds that held the polis together were so intimate, Greeks were extremely reluctant to allow foreigners to share fully in its life. Nor could women play political roles. Women participated in some religious ceremonies, and served as priestesses, but the polis had no room for them in state affairs. In Greek democracy, citizenship was extended to many but not all males whose families had long lived in the polis.

Although each polis was jealous of its independence, some Greeks banded together to create leagues of city-states. Here was the birth of Greek federalism, a political system in which several states formed a central government while remaining independent in their internal affairs. United in a league, a confederation of city-states was far stronger than any of the individual members and better able to withstand external attack.

The passionate individualism of the polis proved to be another serious weakness. The citizens of each polis were determined to remain free and autonomous. Since the Greeks were rarely willing to unite in larger political bodies, the political result was almost constant warfare. A polis could dominate, but unlike Rome it could not incorporate other cities.

Chronology

ca. 3500–338 B.C.E.   Hellenic period

ca. 3500–ca. 1000 B.C.E.   Minoan and Mycenaean civilizations

ca. 1100–800 B.C.E.   Evolution of the polis; Greece's "Dark Age"

ca. 800–500 B.C.E.   Rise of Sparta and Athens

776 B.C.E.   Foundation of the Olympic games

ca. 750–550 B.C.E.   Greek colonization of the Mediterranean

525–322 B.C.E.   Birth and development of tragedy, historical writing, and philosophy

499–404 B.C.E.   Persian and Peloponnesian Wars

ca. 470–322 B.C.E.   Philosophies of Socrates, Plato, and Aristotle

367–100 B.C.E.   Growth of mystery religions

340–262 B.C.E.   Rise of Epicurean and Stoic philosophies

336–100 B.C.E.   Hellenistic period

336–323 B.C.E.   Reign of Alexander the Great

326–146 B.C.E.   Spread of commerce from the Mediterranean Sea to India

310–212 B.C.E.   Period of scientific advancements

monarchy   *Derived from the Greek for "the rule of one man," it was a type of Greek government in which a king represented the community.*

oligarchy   *"The rule of a few," a type of Greek government in which a small group of wealthy citizens, not necessarily of aristocratic birth, ruled.*

MAP 4.1 **Ancient Greece** In antiquity the home of the Greeks included the islands of the Aegean and the western shore of Turkey as well as the Greek peninsula itself.

Map labels:
0 50 100 Km.
0 50 100 Mi.

THRACE
Byzantium
MACEDON
Pella
Amphipolis
Nestos R.
Strymon R.
Axius R.
Aliakmon R.
Sea of Marmara
CHALCIDICE
Thasos
Hebrus R.
Hellespont
40° N
Potidaea
Lemnos
Troy
Mt. Olympus
Aöus R.
PINDUS MTS.
Peneus R.
Mt. Ossa
ANATOLIA
Corcyra
Dodona
THESSALY
Saganus R.
EPIRUS
Mt. Pelion
Aegean Sea
Lesbos
LYDIA
Ionian Sea
ACARNANIA
Artemisium 480 B.C.E.
Hermus R.
Thermopylae 480 B.C.E.
AETOLIA
Mt. Parnassus
Chaeronea
Euboea
Chios
IONIA
Sardis
Achelous R.
Mt. Helicon
Delphi
BOEOTIA
Chalcis
Eretria
Smyrna
Ithaca
Gulf of Corinth
Leuctra
Thebes
Mt. Parnes
ACHAEA
Plataea 479 B.C.E.
Eleusis
Marathon 490 B.C.E.
Ephesus
Moeander R.
Elis
Sicyon
Megara
Athens
Samos
20° E
ELIS
Corinth
Nemea
Salamis ATTICA
Andros
Mycale 479 B.C.E.
Olympia
ARCADIA
Mycenae 480 B.C.E.
Aegina
Miletus
Mantinea
Argos
Saronic Gulf
Epidaurus
PELOPONNESUS
Tegea
CYCLADES
Paros
Delos
Halicarnassus
Mt. Ithome
Sparta
MESSENIA
LACONIA
Naxos
Cos
Pylos
TAYGETOS MTS.
Melos
Cythera
Rhodes
Mediterranean Sea
Sea of Crete
25° E
35° N
Crete
Knossos
Gortyn

Legend:
Ancient Greece
Plains
★ Major battle of the Persian Wars
▲ Mountain
🏛 Sanctuary

THE ARCHAIC AGE (CA. 800–500 B.C.E.)

What were the major accomplishments of the Archaic age, and why were they important?

The maturation of the polis coincided with an era that gave rise to two developments of lasting importance. The first was another geographical expansion of Greeks, who now ventured as far east as the Black Sea and as far west as the Atlantic Ocean. The next saw Sparta and Athens, the two poles of the Greek experience, rise to prominence.

Overseas Expansion

With stability and prosperity, the Greek world grew in wealth and numbers, which brought new problems. Given the infertility of Greece, the increase in population led to land hunger. The resulting social and political tensions drove many Greeks to seek new homes outside Greece (see Map 4.2).

From about 750 to 550 B.C.E. Greeks poured onto the coasts of the northern Aegean and the Black Sea, westward along the north Africa coast, Sicily, southern Italy, and beyond to Spain and the Atlantic. In all these places the Greeks established flourishing cities that turned the Mediterranean into a Greek lake. A later wave of colonization spread Greeks throughout the northern coast of the Black Sea as far east as southern Russia. Colonization on this scale meant that the future culture of this entire area would be Greek, and to this heritage Rome would later fall heir.

The Growth of Sparta

During the Archaic period the Spartans also faced problems of overpopulation and land hunger. They solved both by conquering the rich region of Messene in 715 B.C.E. They made the Messenians *helots,* state slaves, who soon rose in a revolt that took the Spartans thirty years to crush. Afterwards, non-nobles who had shared in the fighting demanded rights equal to those of the nobility. Under intense pressure the aristocrats agreed to remodel the state in a system called the Lycurgan regimen after Lycurgus, a legendary lawgiver. All Spartans were given equal political rights. Two kings ruled, assisted by a council of nobles. Executive power lay in the hands of five *ephors,* overseers, elected by the people. Economically, the helots did all the work, while Spartan citizens devoted their time to military training.

In the Lycurgan system every citizen owed primary allegiance to Sparta. Suppression of the individual together with emphasis on military prowess led to a barracks state. Family life itself was sacrificed to the polis. After long, hard military training that began at age seven, citizen men became lifelong soldiers, the best in Greece. Family life remained important to Spartan society, but it was second to the needs of military

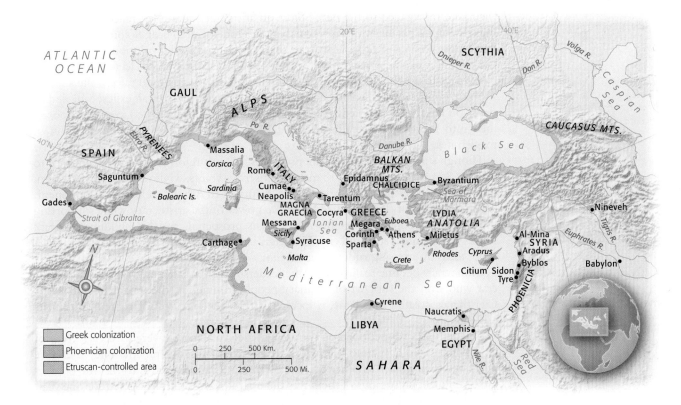

MAP 4.2 **Colonization of the Mediterranean**   Though the Greeks and Phoenicians colonized the Mediterranean basin at about the same time, the Greeks spread much farther.

hoplite *The heavily armed infantry man who was the backbone of the Greek army.*

Primary Source:
Homer, From Iliad: Hector Prepares to Meet His Destiny

defense. In battle Spartans were supposed to stand and die rather than retreat. **Hoplites,** heavily armed infantrymen, were urged to come back with their shields or be carried dead on them. In the Lycurgan regimen Spartans were expected to train vigorously, do with little, and like it.

In this martial atmosphere women were remarkably free. The Spartans viewed maternal health as crucial for the bearing of healthy children and thus encouraged women to participate in athletics and to eat well. With men in military service much of their lives, citizen women ran the estates and owned land in their own right. They were not physically restricted or secluded. Spartans expected them to be good wives and strict mothers of future soldiers. Not only in time of war but also in peace men often did not see their wives for long periods. Men's most meaningful relations were same-sex ones. The Spartan military leaders viewed such relationships as militarily advantageous because they felt that men would fight even more fiercely for lovers and comrades. Close links among men thus contributed to Spartan civic life, which was admired throughout the Greek world.

The Evolution of Athens

Like Sparta, Athens faced pressing social and economic problems during the Archaic period, but the Athenians eventually extended to all citizens the right and duty of governing the polis. The late seventh century B.C.E. was for Athens a time of turmoil because aristocrats had begun to seize the holdings of smaller landowners. In 621 B.C.E. the aristocrat Draco, under pressure from the peasants and with the consent of the nobles, published the first law code of the Athenian polis. Though harsh, his code nonetheless embodied the ideal that the law belonged to all citizens. Yet the aristocracy still governed Athens oppressively, and by the early sixth century B.C.E. the social and economic situation remained dire, as noble landholders forced small farmers into economic dependence. Many families were sold into slavery, while others were exiled and their land mortgaged to the rich. Solon, an aristocrat and a poet, railed against these injustices in his poems, which he recited in the agora for all to hear. Solon's sincerity and good sense convinced other aristocrats that he was no crazed revolutionary. Moreover, the common people trusted him. Around 594 B.C.E. the nobles elected him *archon,* chief magistrate of the polis, and gave him extraordinary power to reform the state.

Solon immediately freed all people enslaved for debt, recalled all exiles, canceled all debts on land, and made enslavement for debt illegal. He allowed even the poorest men into the old aristocratic assembly, where they could vote in the election of magistrates.

Though solving some immediate problems, Solon's reforms did not bring peace to Athens. Some aristocrats tried to make themselves tyrants, while others opposed them. In 546 B.C.E. Pisistratus, an exiled noble, returned to Athens, defeated his opponent, and became tyrant. Pisistratus reduced the power of the aristocracy while supporting the common people. Under his rule Athens prospered, and his building program made Athens into a splendid city. His reign as tyrant promoted the growth of democratic ideas by arousing rudimentary feelings of equality among many Athenians.

Democracy became reality under the leadership of Cleisthenes, a prominent aristocrat who won the support of ordinary people to emerge triumphant in 508 B.C.E. Cleisthenes created the **deme,** a local unit that kept the roll of citizens within its jurisdiction.

deme *A local unit that served as the basic element of Cleisthenes's political system.*

The democracy functioned on the ideal that all full citizens were sovereign. Yet not all citizens could take time from work to participate in government. They therefore delegated their power to other citizens by creating various offices to run the democracy. The most prestigious of them was the board of ten archons, elected for one year, who handled legal and military affairs. After leaving office, they entered the *Areopagos,* a select council of ex-archons who handled cases involving homicide, wounding, and arson.

Legislation was in the hands of two bodies, the *boule,* or council, composed of five hundred members, and the *ecclesia,* the assembly of all citizens. The boule, separate from the Areopagos, was perhaps the major institution of the democracy. By supervising the various committees of government and proposing bills to the assembly, it guided Athenian political life. It received foreign envoys and forwarded treaties to the assembly for ratification. The ecclesia by a simple majority vote, however, had the final word.

Athenian democracy demonstrated that a large group of people, not just a few, could efficiently run the affairs of state. Because citizens could speak their minds, they were not forced to rebellion or conspiracy to express their views. Like all democracies in ancient Greece, however, the Athenian was limited. Women, slaves, and outsiders could not be citizens. Their opinions were neither recorded nor legally binding.

THE CLASSICAL PERIOD (500–338 B.C.E.)

Although the classical period saw tremendous upheavals, what were its lasting achievements?

In the years between 500 and 338 B.C.E. Greek civilization reached its highest peak in politics, thought, and art. In this period the Greeks beat back the armies of the Persian Empire. Then, turning their spears against one another, they destroyed their own political system in a century of warfare. Some thoughtful Greeks recorded these momentous events. Herodotus (ca. 485–425 B.C.E.), "the father of history," described the Persian War of 490–479 B.C.E., followed by Thucydides (ca. 460–ca. 399 B.C.E.), whose account of the Peloponnesian War remains a literary classic. This era also saw the flowering of philosophy, as thinkers like Socrates (ca. 470–399 B.C.E.), Plato (427–347 B.C.E.), and Aristotle (384–322 B.C.E.) pondered the meaning of the universe and human nature. The Greeks invented drama, and Greek architects reached the zenith of their art. Because of these various intellectual and artistic achievements, this age is called the classical period.

Delian League *A grand naval alliance, created by the Athenians and aimed at liberating Ionia from Persian rule.*

The Deadly Conflicts (499–404 B.C.E.)

Warfare marked the entire classical period. In 499 B.C.E. the Ionian Greeks with feeble Athenian help unsuccessfully rebelled against the Persian Empire. In retaliation the Persians struck at Athens, only to be defeated at Marathon (see Map 4.1). In 480 B.C.E. the Persian king Xerxes invaded Greece on a massive scale. Under the leadership of Sparta by land and Athens by sea, many Greeks united to defeat the Persians in hard-fought battles at the pass of Thermopylae and in the waters off Artemisium in 480 B.C.E. In 479 B.C.E., after the loss of Athens, the Greeks defeated the Persians at the decisive battle of Salamis and finally again at Plataea later that year.

In 478 B.C.E. the victorious Athenians and their allies formed the **Delian League,** a grand naval alliance intended to liberate Ionia from Persian rule. While driving the Persians out of Asia Minor, the Athenians also turned the league into an Athenian empire. Under their great leader Pericles (ca. 494–429 B.C.E.) the Athenians grew so powerful and aggressive that they alarmed Sparta and its allies. In 431 B.C.E. Athenian imperialism finally drove Sparta into the conflict known as the Peloponnesian War. At its outbreak a Spartan ambassador warned the Athenians: "This day will be the beginning of great evils

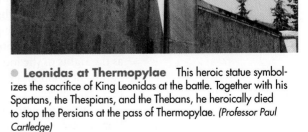

● **Leonidas at Thermopylae** This heroic statue symbolizes the sacrifice of King Leonidas at the battle. Together with his Spartans, the Thespians, and the Thebans, he heroically died to stop the Persians at the pass of Thermopylae. *(Professor Paul Cartledge)*

● **The Acropolis of Athens**
These buildings embody the noblest spirit of Greek architecture. From the entrance visitors walk through the Propylaea and its pillars. Ahead opens the grand view of the Parthenon, still noble in ruins. To the left stands the Erechtheum, the whole a monument to Athens itself. *(Courtesy, Sotiris Toumbis Editions)*

for the Greeks."[1] Few have ever spoken more prophetically. The Peloponnesian War lasted a generation (431–404 B.C.E.) and brought widespread destruction and huge loss of life. In 404 B.C.E. the Athenians finally surrendered, but not before Greek civilization had been struck a serious blow.

Athenian Arts in the Age of Pericles

In the last half of the fifth century B.C.E. Pericles turned Athens into the showplace of Greece by making the Acropolis a wonder for all time. He appropriated allied money to pay for a huge building program that erected temples and other buildings to honor Athena, the patron goddess of the city, and to show the Greek world the glory of Athens. The Propylaea is a magnificent gateway to a living cultural museum. The nearby temple of Athena Nike (Athena the Victorious) is a small gem. Above all, the Parthenon stands splendidly as a monumental gift to Athena. In many ways the Athenian Acropolis is the epitome of Greek art and its spirit. Although the buildings were dedicated to the gods and most of the sculptures portray gods, they all nonetheless express the Greek fascination with the human form. The Acropolis also exhibits the rational side of Greek art. Greek artists portrayed action in a balanced and restrained fashion, capturing the noblest aspects of human beings: their reason and dignity.

Other aspects of Athenian cultural life were also rooted in the life of the polis. The development of drama was tied to the religious festivals of the city. The polis sponsored the production of plays and required wealthy citizens to pay the expenses of their production. Although many plays were highly controversial, they were neither suppressed nor censored.

Aeschylus (525–456 B.C.E.) was the first dramatist to explore such basic questions as the rights of the individual, the conflict between society and the individual, and the nature of good and evil. In his trilogy of plays, *The Oresteia*, he treats the themes of betrayal, murder, and reconciliation, urging that reason and justice be applied to reconcile fundamental conflicts. The final play concludes with a prayer that civil dissension never be allowed to destroy the city.

Sophocles (496–406 B.C.E.) also deals with matters personal, political, and divine. In *Antigone* he emphasizes the precedence of divine law over political law and family custom. In *Oedipus the King* he tells the story of a good man doomed by the gods to kill his father and marry his mother. When Oedipus fails to avoid his fate, in despair he blinds himself and flees into exile. In *Oedipus at Colonus* Sophocles treats the last days of the broken man, whose patient suffering and uncomplaining piety ultimately win the blessings and honor of the gods. Sophocles urges people to obey the will of the gods even without fully understanding it, for the gods stand for justice and order.

Euripides (ca. 480–406 B.C.E.), the last of the three great tragic dramatists, likewise explored the theme of personal conflict within the polis and sounded the depths of the individual. With Euripides drama entered a new and more personal phase. To him the gods mattered far less than people. The essence of his tragedy is the flaws of people who bring disaster on themselves because their passions overwhelm reason.

Writers of Athenian comedy treated the affairs of the polis bawdily and often coarsely. Even so, their plays too were performed at religious festivals. They used humor as political commentary in an effort to suggest and support the proper policies of the polis. Best known of the comedians is Aristophanes (ca. 445–386 B.C.E.), a merciless critic of cranks, quacks, and fools. He used his art of sarcasm to dramatize his ideas on the right conduct of the citizen and his leaders for the good of the polis.

Despite the undeniable achievements of the Athenians, many modern historians have exaggerated their importance. This Athenocentrism fails to do justice to the other Greeks who also shaped society, culture, and history.

Aspects of Social Life in Athens

The Athenians, like other Greeks, lived comparatively simple lives with few material possessions. The Athenian house was rather simple. It consisted of a series of rooms opening onto a central courtyard that contained a well, an altar, and a washbasin. Larger houses often had a room at the front, where the men of the family ate and entertained guests, and women's quarters at the back. If the family lived in the country, stalls for animals faced the courtyard. Farmers kept oxen for plowing, various animals for food, and donkeys for transportation. Even in the city chickens and perhaps a goat or two roamed the courtyard with dogs and cats.

In the city a man might support himself as a craftsman, potter, bronzesmith, or tanner, or he could contract with the polis to work on public buildings. Certain crafts, including spinning and weaving, were generally done by women. Men and women without skills worked as paid laborers, but competed with slaves, who were usually foreigners or prisoners of war. Citizens and slaves were paid the same amount for their work.

The social conditions of Athenian women have been the subject of much debate and little agreement, in part because the sources are fragmentary. Women rarely played notable roles in public affairs, and we know the names of no female poets, artists, or philosophers from classical Athens. Women did manage the household and attend religious festivals. The status of a free woman was strictly protected by law. Only her children could be citizens. Only she was in charge of the household and the family's possessions, yet the law protected her primarily to protect her husband's interests. Women in Athens and elsewhere in Greece, like those in Mesopotamia, brought dowries to their husbands upon marriage, which legally remained their property.

> **Primary Source:**
> **Sappho, *A Lyric Poem Laments an Absent Lover***

● **Woman Grinding Grain**   Here a woman takes the grain raised on the family farm and grinds it by hand in a mill. She needed few tools to turn the grain into flour. *(National Archaeological Museum, Athens/Archaeological Receipts Fund)*

● **Sacrificial Scene** Much of Greek religion was simple and festive, as this scene demonstrates. The participants include women and boys dressed in their finest clothes and crowned with garlands. Musicians add to the festivities. Only the sheep will not enjoy the ceremony. *(National Archaeological Museum, Athens/ Archaeological Receipts Fund)*

A citizen woman's main functions were to bear and raise children. Respectable citizen women ideally lived secluded lives in which the only men they usually saw were relatives and tradesmen. How far this ideal was actually a reality is impossible to say, but prosperous women probably spent much of their time at home. There they oversaw domestic slaves and hired labor, and together with servants and friends worked wool into cloth. In a sense, poor and noncitizen women lived freer lives than did wealthier women. They performed manual labor in the fields or sold goods in the agora, going about their affairs much as men did. Prostitution was legal in Athens, and some prostitutes added intellectual accomplishments to physical beauty. These *hetairai* accompanied men in public settings where their wives would not have been welcome, serving men as social as well as sexual partners.

In classical Athens, part of a male adolescent citizen's training in adulthood was supposed to entail a hierarchical sexual and tutorial relationship with an older man, who most likely was married and may have had other female sexual partners as well. These relationships between adolescents and men were often celebrated in literature and art, in part because Athenians regarded perfection as possible only in the male. Women were generally seen as inferior to men, dominated by their bodies rather than their minds.

Same-sex relations did not mean that people did not marry, for Athenians saw the continuation of the family line as essential. Sexual desire and procreation were both important aspects of life, but they were not necessarily linked for ancient Greeks.

Greek Religion

It is extremely difficult to understand Greek religion, since, unlike modern peoples, the ancient Greeks had no uniform faith or creed. Although the Greeks usually worshiped the same deities—Zeus, Hera, Apollo, Athena, and others—the cults of these divinities varied from polis to polis. The Greeks had no sacred books such as the Bible, and Greek religion was often a matter more of ritual than belief. Nor did cults impose an ethical code of conduct. Unlike the Egyptians and Hebrews, the Greeks lacked a priesthood as the modern world understands the term. In Greece priests and priestesses existed to care for temples and sacred property and to conduct the proper rituals, but not to make religious rules or doctrines, much less to enforce them. In short, there existed in Greece no central ecclesiastical authority and no organized creed.

The most important members of the Greek pantheon were Zeus, the king of the gods, and his consort, Hera. Although they were the mightiest and most honored of the deities who lived on Mount Olympus, their divine children were closer to ordinary people. Apollo was especially popular. He represented the epitome of youth, beauty, benevolence, and athletic skill. He was also the god of music and culture, in many ways symbolizing the best of Greek culture. His sister Athena, who patronized women's crafts such as weaving, was also a warrior-goddess who had been born from the head of Zeus without a mother. Best known for her cult at Athens, to which she gave her name, she was highly revered throughout Greece. Besides these Olympian gods, each polis had its own minor deities, each with his or her own local cult. Much religion was local and domestic. Each village possessed its own cults and rituals, and individual families honored various deities in their homes.

Though Greek religion in general was individual or related to the polis, the Greeks also shared some Pan-Hellenic festivals, the chief of which were held at Olympia to honor Zeus and at Delphi to honor Apollo. The festivities at Olympia included the famous athletic contests that have inspired the modern Olympic games. Held every four years, they attracted visitors from all over the Greek world and lasted well into Christian times. The Pythian games at Delphi were also held every four years, but these contests included musical and literary competitions. Both the Olympic and Pythian games were unifying factors in Greek life.

The Flowering of Philosophy

The Greeks, like peoples before them, originally spun myths and epics to explain the origin of the universe. Yet going further, they created philosophy to understand the cosmos in purely physical terms. Some Greeks in Ionia began an intellectual revolution that still flourishes today. These thinkers are called the Pre-Socratics because their rational efforts preceded those of Socrates. Taking individual facts, they wove them into general theories. Despite appearances, they concluded, the universe is actually simple and subject to natural laws. Drawing on their observations, they speculated about the basic building blocks of the universe.

The first of these Pre-Socratic thinkers, Thales (ca. 600 B.C.E.) sought to determine the basic element of the universe from which all else sprang. He surmised that it was water. Although he was wrong, it was the beginning of the scientific method. Another Pre-Socratic, Anaximander (d. 547 B.C.E.) was the first to use general concepts, which are essential to abstract thought. Heraclitus (ca. 500 B.C.E.) declared the primal element to be fire, which is ever changing and eternal. Democritus (ca. 460 B.C.E.) created the atomic theory that the universe is made up of invisible, indestructible particles. The culmination of Pre-Socratic thought was the theory that four simple substances make up the universe: fire, air, earth, and water.

This stream of thought also branched into other directions. Hippocrates (ca. 470–400 B.C.E.), the father of medicine, sought natural explanations for diseases and natural means to treat them. He relied on empirical knowledge rather than religion or magic to further his work. The Sophists took the direction of making a distinction between science and philosophy. While differing on particulars, they all agreed that human beings were the proper subject of study. They also believed that excellence could be taught. They held that nothing is absolute; everything is relative.

Socrates (ca. 470–399 B.C.E.) shared the Sophists' belief that people are the essential subjects of philosophical inquiry. He started with a general topic and narrowed it

> **Primary Source:**
> **Plato, *From* Apologia**

to its essentials by posing questions, then sought answers. This is the Socratic method. He felt that through knowledge people could approach the supreme good and thus find happiness. Yet in 399 B.C.E. the Athenians executed him for corrupting the youth and for impiety.

Socrates' student Plato (427–347 B.C.E.) founded the Academy, a school dedicated to philosophy. Plato developed the theory that all tangible things are unreal and temporary, copies of "forms" or "ideas" that are constant and indestructible. The highest form is the idea of good, which he equated with god.

Aristotle (384–322 B.C.E.) went beyond his teacher Plato by using observation and analysis of natural phenomena to explain the cosmos. He argued that the universe was finite, spherical, and eternal. He postulated four principles: matter, form, movement, and goal. His theory of cosmology added ether as one of the building blocks of the universe. He wrongly concluded that the earth is the center of the universe and that the stars and planets revolve around it.

The philosophies of Plato and Aristotle both viewed women as inferior beings. Plato associated women with the body and emotions and men with superior faculties of mind and reason. Aristotle thought that women's primary purpose was to bear children. Even though Athenian philosophers pushed beyond the limited thinking of previous generations, they still reflected the accepted values and concepts of their times.

> **Primary Source:**
> **Aristotle, *From* Politics**

From Polis to Monarchy (404–323 B.C.E.)

MAP 4.3 **Alexander's Conquests** This map shows the course of Alexander's invasion of the Persian Empire and the speed of his progress. More important than the great success of his military campaigns was his founding of Hellenistic cities in the East.

Immediately after the Peloponnesian War, Sparta began striving for empire over the Greeks. Yet even with Persian help, Sparta could not maintain its hold on Greece. In 371 B.C.E. at Leuctra in Boeotia, a Theban army under Epaminondas destroyed the flower of the Spartans. But the Thebans were unable to bring peace to Greece. In 362 B.C.E. Epaminondas was killed in battle, and a period of stalemate followed. Philip II,

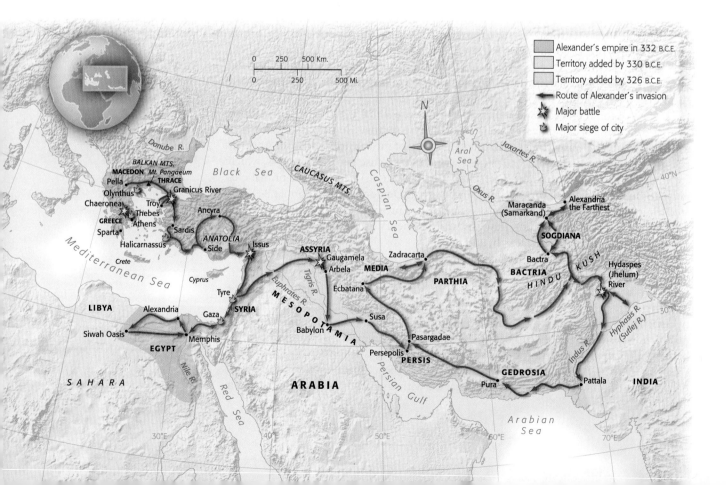

● **Alexander at the Battle of Issus**   At left, Alexander the Great, bareheaded and wearing a breastplate, charges King Darius, who is standing in a chariot. The moment marks the turning point of the battle, as Darius turns to flee from the attack. *(National Museum, Naples/Alinari/Art Resource, NY)*

king of Macedonia (r. 359–336 B.C.E.), turned the situation to his advantage. By clever use of his wealth and superb army, Philip won control of the northern Aegean, awakening fear in Athens. Finally, in 338 B.C.E. he defeated a combined Theban-Athenian army at Chaeronea. He had conquered Greece and become its arbiter. Because the Greeks could not put aside their quarrels, they fell to an invader.

Philip used his victory to unite the Greek states with his Macedonian kingdom to proclaim a crusade to liberate the Ionian Greeks from Persian rule. Before he could launch his crusade, Philip fell to an assassin's dagger in 336 B.C.E. His young son Alexander, soon to be known as "the Great," vowed to carry on Philip's mission. In 334 B.C.E. Alexander led an army of Macedonians and Greeks into western Asia. In the next three years he won three major battles—at the Granicus River, at Issus, and at Gaugamela—on his march to the east (see Map 4.3). Having overthrown the Persian Empire, in 326 B.C.E. he entered India. Finally, at the Hyphasis River his troops refused to go farther. Alexander reluctantly turned south to the Arabian Sea and then back west. In 324 B.C.E. Alexander returned to Susa, and died the next year Babylon.

The political consequence of Alexander's premature death was chaos. Since several of the chief Macedonian officers aspired to Alexander's position as emperor while others opposed them, civil war lasting forty-three years tore Alexander's empire apart. By the end of this conflict, the most successful generals had carved out their own smaller and generally stable monarchies.

Ptolemy immediately seized Egypt and transformed the native system into a Greco-Macedonian kingdom. Seleucus meanwhile won the bulk of Alexander's empire, his monarchy extending from western Asia to India. In the third century B.C.E., however, the eastern parts of Seleucus's monarchy gained their independence. The Parthians, a native people, came to power in Iran, and the Greeks created a monarchy of their own in Bactria. Antigonus maintained control of the Macedonian kingdom in Europe. Until the arrival of the Romans in the eastern Mediterranean in the second century B.C.E., the great monarchies waged frequent wars that brought no lasting results. The Hellenistic monarchy was no improvement on the Greek polis.

• • • • • • • • • • • • • • •

THE SPREAD OF HELLENISM (336–100 B.C.E.)

After Alexander the Great's conquest of the Persian Empire, how did Greek immigrants and the native peoples there create a new society?

When the Greeks and Macedonians entered Asia and Egypt, they encountered civilization older than their own. In some ways the Eastern cultures were more advanced than theirs, in others less so. Thus this third great tide of Greek migration differed from preceding waves that had spread over land inhabited by less-developed peoples. In this process both Greeks and native peoples confronted a new cultural reality. The Greeks saw themselves as "the West," while the peoples of the ancient Near East made up "the East." "East" as yet had no wider meaning for the Greeks, who had only just learned of India and knew nothing of China and lands beyond. Since the Eastern civilization was older and in some ways more sophisticated than the Greek, the newcomers had a great deal to learn from it. Yet the Greeks also proved surprisingly successful in spreading their own vibrant culture among the easterners. The result was the blending of Hellenism and Near Eastern cultures that is now called "Hellenistic." No comparable spread and sharing of cultures had occurred in this area since the days of the Mesopotamians.

Cities and Kingdoms

A major development in this new world was the supremacy of monarchy that for the Greeks replaced the polis as the chief political unit of society. Furthermore, these new kingdoms consisted of numerous different peoples who at first had little in common. Although the native populations found kingdoms traditional and familiar, to the Greeks monarchy was new and somewhat alien. To them civilized life without the polis was unthinkable. Hellenistic kings solved the problem by combining the concepts of monarchy and polis to embrace all their subjects. The kingdom became dominant in political affairs, and the polis, now only a city, served as the administrative and cultural unit. The Greek city thereby became the linchpin of the Hellenistic monarchy.

A problem, however, remained with this solution. The Greek polis had been **sovereign,** and in a monarchy only the king held sovereignty. Unwilling to create a real polis, Hellenistic kings gave their cities all the external trappings of a polis but none of the political power. Consequently, the Hellenistic city resembled a modern city. It was a cultural center with theaters, temples, and libraries—a seat of learning and a place for amusement. The Hellenistic city was also an economic center—a marketplace, a scene of trade and manufacturing. On these terms Hellenistic cities proved remarkably effective.

sovereign *An independent, autonomous state run by its citizens, free of any outside power or restraint.*

Building a Shared Society

Despite difficulties, Hellenistic monarchies successfully spread Greek culture. If the Hellenistic component was sometimes largely a veneer, it at least touched nearly every life. At the same time the Greeks became increasingly influenced by the societies they conquered. These two tendencies produced a mutually recognized common Hellenistic culture, remarkably widespread and healthy. Even so, Hellenistic kingdoms were never entirely unified in language, customs, and thought. Greek culture took firmest hold along the shores of the Mediterranean, where it thrived until the coming of the Arabs. It also prospered farther inland. In Bactria Greek and Iranian settlements led to an independent society that was soundly founded and well integrated. Bactria itself became an outpost of Hellenism, from which the Han Dynasty learned of civilized societies other than the Chinese (see page 137). Greco-Bactrians prospered until invaders from Central Asia overwhelmed their settlements in the first century B.C.E. Nonetheless, its cultural influence lasted another century.

The Seleucid kings most successfully built a shared society by their extensive colonization. Their military settlements spread from western Asia Minor along the banks of the Tigris and Euphrates and father east to India. Although the Seleucids had no elaborate plan for Hellenizing the native population, they nevertheless introduced a large and vigorous Greek population to these lands. Their presence alone had an impact. Seleucid military colonies were generally founded near native villages, thus exposing each to the other's culture. Farther east Greek kings won their independence from the Seleucids and extended their influence into India.

By contrast, the Ptolemies in Egypt at first made no effort to spread their culture, and unlike other Hellenistic kings they were not city builders. Indeed, they founded only the city of Ptolemais near Thebes. The native Egyptian population, the descendants of the pharaoh's people, originally kept their traditional language, religion, and way of life. They also continued to be the foundation of the state. They fed it by their labor in the fields and financed it with their taxes. In the second century B.C.E., however, Greeks and native Egyptians began to intermarry and mingle their cultures and languages. Some natives adopted Greek customs and language and began to play a role in the administration of the kingdom and even to serve in the army. Although more slowly than elsewhere, the overall result was the evolution of a widespread Greco-Egyptian culture.

For natives the prime advantage of Hellenistic culture was its very pervasiveness. The Greek language became the common speech of the entire eastern Mediterranean. A new Greek dialect called the **koine,** which means common, became the speech of the royal court, bureaucracy, and army. Everyone, Greek or easterner, who wanted to find an official position or compete in business had to learn it. As early as the third century B.C.E. some Greek cities granted citizenship to Hellenized natives.

koine *A common dialect of the Greek language that influenced the speech of all Greeks.*

Though Greeks and easterners adapted to each other's ways, there was never a true fusion of cultures. Nonetheless, each found many useful things in the civilization of the other, and they fertilized each other. This mingling of Greek and eastern elements made Hellenistic culture energetic and successful.

The Economic Scope of the Hellenistic World

Alexander's conquest not only changed the political face of the ancient world but also merged it into one broad economic sphere. Yet the period did not see a revolution in the way people lived and worked. The material demands of Hellenistic society remained as simple as before. Yet the spread of Greeks eastward created new markets and stimulated trade. The economic unity of the Hellenistic world, like its cultural bonds, later proved valuable to the Romans.

When Alexander conquered the Persian Empire, he found the royal treasury filled with vast sums of gold, silver, and other treasure. The victors used this wealth to finance the building of roads, the development of harbors, and most especially the founding of new cities. Whole new markets opened to all merchants, who eagerly took advantage of the unforeseen opportunities. In this fresh economic environment Greeks and local residents learned of each other's customs and traditions while forging new contacts. In the process they also spread immediate knowledge of their own cultures.

The Seleucid and Ptolemaic dynasties traded as far afield as India, Arabia, and sub-Saharan Africa. Overland trade with India and Arabia was conducted by caravan that was largely in the hands of easterners. The caravan trade never dealt in bulk goods or essential commodities. Once goods reached the Hellenistic monarchies, Greek merchants took a hand in the trade. Essential to this trade from the Mediterranean to Afghanistan and India was the southern route through Arabia. The desert of Arabia lies west of the Iranian plateau, from which trade routes stretched to the south and farther east to China. Commerce from the east arrived at Egypt and the harbors of Palestine, Phoenicia, and Syria. From these ports goods flowed to Greece, Italy, and Spain.

Over these routes traveled luxury goods that were light, rare, and expensive. In time these luxury items became necessities. This whole development was in part the result of an increased volume of trade. In the prosperity of the period, more people could afford to buy gold, silver, precious stones, and many other easily transportable goods. The most prominent goods in terms of volume were tea and silk. Indeed, the trade in silk gave the major route the name the **Great Silk Road.** In return the peoples of the eastern Mediterranean sent east manufactured items, especially metal weapons, cloth, wine, and olive oil. Although these caravan routes can trace their origins to earlier times, they became far more prominent in the Hellenistic period. Business customs developed and became standardized so that merchants of different nationalities, aided especially by koine, communicated in a way understandable to them all.

Great Silk Road *The name of the major route for the silk trade.*

More economically important than this exotic trade were commercial dealings in essential commodities like raw materials, grain, and industrial products. The Hellenistic monarchies usually raised enough grain for their own needs as well as a surplus for export. For the cities of the Aegean the trade in grain was essential, because many of them could not grow enough. Fortunately for them, abundant wheat supplies were available nearby in Egypt and in the Crimea in southern Russia.

The Greek cities paid for their grain by exporting olive oil and wine. Another significant commodity was fish, which for export was either salted, pickled, or dried. This trade was doubly important because fish provided poor people with an essential element of their diet. Important also was the trade in honey, dried fruit, nuts, and vegetables. Of raw materials wood was high in demand.

Throughout the Hellenistic world slaves almost always found a ready market. Only the Ptolemies discouraged both the trade and slavery itself, but they did so only for economic reasons. Their system had no room for slaves, who only would have competed with inexpensive free labor. Otherwise slave labor could be found in cities and temples, in factories and fields, and in the homes of wealthier people.

Most trade in bulk commodities was seaborne, and the Hellenistic merchant ship was the workhorse of the day. The merchant ship had a broad beam and relied on sails for propulsion. It was far more seaworthy than the Hellenistic warship, which was long, narrow, and built for speed. A small crew of experienced sailors easily handled the merchant vessel. Maritime trade also provided opportunities for workers in many other industries and trades, particularly shipbuilders, dockworkers, teamsters, and pirates. Piracy was a constant factor in the Hellenistic world and remained so until Rome cleared it from the seas.

While demand for goods increased during the period, few new techniques of production appeared. Manual labor far more than machinery continued to turn out agricultural produce, raw materials, and the few manufactured goods the Hellenistic world used. Typical was mining, where slaves, criminals, or forced laborers dug the ore under frightful conditions. The Ptolemies ran their gold mines along harsh lines. One historian gives a grim picture of the miners' lives:

The kings of Egypt condemn [to the mines] those found guilty of wrong-doing and those taken prisoner in war, those who are victims of false accusations and were put into jail because of royal anger. . . . The condemned—and they are very many—all of them are put in chains, and they work persistently and continually, both by day and throughout the night, getting no rest and carefully cut off from escape.[2]

The Ptolemies even condemned women and children to work in the mines. Besides gold and silver, used primarily for coins and jewelry, iron was the most important metal and saw the most varied use. Even so, the method of production never became very sophisticated. Despite these shortcomings, the volume of goods produced increased in this period. Small manufacturing establishments existed nearly everywhere.

All Hellenistic kings paid special attention to agriculture. Much of their revenue came from the produce of royal lands, rents paid by the tenants of royal lands, and taxation of them. The Ptolemies, who made the greatest strides in agriculture, sponsored experiments to improve seed grain. These efforts apart, most people supported themselves in the traditional ways that supplied their basic needs.

HELLENISTIC INTELLECTUAL ADVANCES

How did the intellectual meeting of two vibrant cultures lead to a very fertile intellectual development?

The peoples of the Hellenistic era advanced the ideas and ideals of the classical Greeks to new heights. Their achievements created the religious and intellectual atmosphere that deeply influenced Roman thinking and that of Judaism and early Christianity. Far from being stagnant, this was instead a period of vigorous growth, especially in the areas of philosophy, science, and medicine.

Religion in the Hellenistic World

In religion the most significant new ideas arose outside of Greece. The Hellenistic period saw at first the spread of Greek cults throughout the Near East. When Hellenistic kings founded cities, they also built temples with new cults and priesthoods for the old Olympian gods. Greek cults, as before, sponsored literary, musical, and athletic contests, which were staged in beautiful surroundings among splendid Greek buildings. On the whole, however, the civic cults were primarily concerned with ritual and neither appealed to religious emotions nor embraced matters such as sin and redemption. While lavish in pomp and display, the new cults could not satisfy deep religious feelings or spiritual yearnings.

Greek increasingly sought solace from other sources. Some relied on philosophy as a guide to life, while others turned to superstition, magic, or astrology. Still others shrugged and spoke of **Tyche,** which means "fate," "chance," or "doom"—a capricious and sometimes malevolent force.

Beginning in the second century B.C.E. some individuals were increasingly attracted to new **mystery religions,** so called because they featured a body of ritual and beliefs not divulged to anyone not initiated into the cult. These new mystery cults incorporated aspects of both Greek and Eastern religions and held broad appeal for people who yearned for personal immortality. Already familiar with old mystery cults such as the Eleusinian mysteries in Attica, the new cults did not strike the Greeks as alien. Familiar, too, was the concept of preparation for an initiation. Devotees of the Eleusinian mysteries and other such cults had to prepare themselves mentally, physically, and spiritually before entering the gods' presence. The mystery cults thus fit well with Greek practice.

The new religions enjoyed one tremendous advantage over the old Greek mystery cults. Whereas old Greek cults were tried to particular places, such as Eleusis, the new religions spread

Tyche *The Greek goddess of fate and luck, eventually identified with the Roman goddess Fortuna.*

mystery religions *Any of several religious systems in the Greco-Roman world characterized by secret doctrines and rituals of initiation.*

● **Hellenistic Magic** This magical text, written in Greek and Egyptian, displays a snake surrounding the magical incantation. The text is intentionally obscure. *(British Library)*

● **Hellenistic Mystery Cult** The scene depicts part of the ritual of initiation into the cult of Dionysus. The young woman here has just completed the ritual. She now dances in joy as the official with the sacred staff looks on. *(Scala/Art Resource, NY)*

throughout the Hellenistic world. People did not have to undertake long and expensive pilgrimages just to become members of the religion. In that sense the mystery religions came to the people, for temples of the new deities sprang up wherever Greeks lived.

The mystery religions all claimed to save their adherents from the worst that fate could do and promised life for the soul after death. They all had a single concept in common: the belief that by the rites of initiation devotees became united with a deity who had also died and risen from the dead. The sacrifice of the god and his victory over death saved the devotee from eternal death. Similarly, all mystery religions demanded a period of preparation in which the converts strove to become holy, that is, to live by the religion's precepts. Once aspirants had prepared themselves, they went through an initiation in which they learned the secrets of the religion. The initiation was usually a ritual of great emotional intensity, symbolizing the entry into a new life.

Among the mystery religions the Egyptian cults of Serapis and Isis took the Hellenistic world by storm. Serapis, who was invented by King Ptolemy, was believed to be the judge of souls who rewarded virtuous and righteous people with eternal life. The cult of Isis enjoyed even wider appeal than that of Serapis. Isis, wife of Osiris, was believed to have conquered Tyche and promised to save any mortal who came to her. She became the most important goddess of the Hellenistic world, especially among women. Her priests claimed that she had bestowed on humanity the gift of civilization and founded law and literature. She was the goddess of marriage, conception, and childbirth. Like Serapis, she promised to save the souls of her believers.

Mystery religions took care of the big things in life, but many people resorted to ordinary magic for daily matters. When a cat walked across their path, they threw three rocks across the road. People often purified their houses to protect them from Hecate, a sinister goddess associated with witchcraft. Many people had dreams that only seers and augurs could interpret. Some of these superstitions are familiar today because some old fears still live.

Epicureanism *A Greek system of philosophy founded on the teachings of Epicurus, which emphasized that a life of contentment, free from fear and suffering, was the greatest good.*

Philosophy and the People

During the Hellenistic period philosophy touched more people than ever before. Two significant philosophies caught the minds and hearts of many Greeks and easterners, as well as many later Romans. The first was **Epicureanism,** a practical philosophy of serenity in an often tumultuous world. Epicurus (340–270 B.C.E.) taught that the principal good of life is pleasure, which he defined as the absence of pain. He concluded that any violent emotion is undesirable. He advocated instead mild self-discipline and even considered poverty good so long as people had enough food, clothing, and shelter. Epicurus also taught that people can most easily attain peace and serenity by ignoring the outside world and looking instead into their personal feelings. His followers ignored politics, for it led to tumult, which would disturb the soul.

Opposed to the passivity of the Epicureans, Zeno (335–262 B.C.E.) came to Athens, where he formed his own school, **Stoicism,** named after the Stoa, the building where he taught. To the Stoics the important matter was not whether they achieved anything, but whether they lived virtuous lives. In that way they could triumph over Tyche, which could destroy their achievements but not the nobility of their lives. Stoicism became the most popular Hellenistic philosophy and the one that later captured the mind of Rome.

Zeno and his fellow Stoics considered nature an expression of divine will. In their view, people could be happy only when living in accordance with nature. They stressed "the brotherhood of man," the concept that all people were kindred who were obliged to help one another. The Stoics' most lasting practical achievement was the creation of the concept of natural law. The Stoics concluded that as all people were brothers, partook of divine reason, and were in harmony with the universe, one **natural law** governed them all.

Hellenistic Science

Hellenistic culture achieved its greatest triumphs in science. The most notable of the Hellenistic astronomers was Aristarchus of Samos (ca. 310–230 B.C.E.), who was educated at Aristotle's school. Aristarchus concluded that the sun is far larger than the earth and that the stars are enormously distant from the earth. He argued against Aristotle's view that the earth is the center of the universe. Aristarchus instead propounded the **heliocentric theory**—that the earth and planets revolve around the sun. His work is all the more impressive because he lacked even a rudimentary telescope. Aristarchus's theories, however, did not persuade the ancient world. His heliocentric theory lay dormant until resurrected in the sixteenth century by the brilliant astronomer Nicolaus Copernicus.

In geometry Euclid (ca. 300 B.C.E.), a mathematician living in Alexandria, compiled a valuable textbook of existing knowledge. His book *The Elements of Geometry* became the standard introduction to the subject. Generations of students from antiquity to the present have learned the essentials of geometry from it.

Stoicism   *The most popular of Hellenistic philosophies; it considers nature an expression of divine will and holds that people can be happy only when living in accordance with nature.*

natural law   *The belief that the laws governing ethical behavior are written into nature itself and therefore possess universal validity.*

heliocentric theory   *The belief that the earth revolves around the sun.*

● **Tyche**   The statue depicts Tyche as the bringer of bounty to people. Some Hellenistic Greeks worshiped Tyche in the hope that she would be kind to them. Philosophers tried to free people from her whimsies. Others tried to placate her. *(Fatih Cimok, Turkey)*

● **Catapult** This model shows a catapult as its crew would have seen it in action. The arrow was loaded on the long horizontal beam, its point fitting into the housing. There the torsion spring under great pressure released the arrow at the target, which could be some 400 yards away. *(Courtesy, Noel Kavan)*

The greatest thinker of the period was Archimedes (ca. 287–212 B.C.E.). A clever inventor, he devised new artillery for military purposes. In peacetime he created the Archimedian screw to draw water from a lower to a higher level. (See the feature "Individuals in Society: Archimedes and the Practical Application of Science.") He invented the compound pully to lift heavy weights. His chief interest, however, lay in pure mathematics. He founded the science of hydrostatics and discovered the principle that the weight of a solid floating in a liquid is equal to the weight of the liquid displaced by the solid.

Archimedes willingly shared his work with others, among them Eratosthenes (285–ca. 204 B.C.E.), who was the librarian of the vast royal library in Alexandria. Eratosthenes used mathematics to further the geographical studies for which he is most famous. He calculated the circumference of the earth geometrically, estimating it as about 24,675 miles. He was not wrong by much: the earth is actually 24,860 miles in circumference. Eratosthenes further concluded that the earth is a spherical globe and that the ocean surrounds the land mass.

Besides these tools for peace, Hellenistic science applied theories of mechanics to build machines that revolutionized warfare. The catapult shot large arrows and small stones against enemy targets. Engineers also built wooden siege towers as artillery platforms. Generals added battering rams to bring down large portions of walls. If these new engines made warfare more efficient, they also added to the misery of the people. War came to embrace the whole population.

Hellenistic Medicine

The study of medicine flourished during the Hellenistic period, and Hellenistic physicians carried the work of Hippocrates into new areas. Herophilus, who lived in the first half of the third century B.C.E., approached the study of medicine in a systematic, scientific fashion. He dissected corpses and measured what he observed. He discovered the nervous system and concluded that two types of nerves, motor and sensory, existed. Herophilus also studied the brain, which he considered the center of intelligence. In the process he discerned the cerebrum and cerebellum. His other work dealt with the liver, lungs, and uterus.

In about 280 B.C.E. Philinus and Serapion, pupils of Herophilus, concentrated on the observation and cure of illnesses rather than focusing on dissection. They also laid heavier stress on the use of drugs and medicines to treat illnesses. Heraclides of Tarentum (perhaps first century B.C.E.) carried on this tradition by discovering the benefits of opium and other drugs that relieved pain.

The Hellenistic world was also plagued by people who claimed to cure illnesses through incantations and magic. Quacks tried to heal and alleviate pain by administering weird potions and bogus concoctions. The medical abuses that arose during the period were so flagrant that many people developed an intense distrust of physicians. Nevertheless, the work of men like Herophilus and Serapion made valuable contributions to the knowledge of medicine, and the fruits of their work were handed on to posterity.

Archimedes and the Practical Application of Science

Archimedes' mill. A slave turns a large cylinder fitted with blades to form a screw that draws water from a well. *(Courtesy, Soprintendenza Archeologica di Pompei. Photograph by Penelope M. Allison)*

Throughout the ages generals have besieged cities to force them to surrender. Sieges were particularly hard and violent, bringing misery to soldiers and civilians alike. Between 213 and 211 B.C.E. the Roman general Marcellus laid close siege to the strongly walled city of Syracuse, the home of Archimedes. Not a soldier, Archimedes was the greatest scientist of his age. He towered above all others in abstract thought. The Roman siege challenged him to a practical response. Hiero, king of Syracuse and friend of Archimedes, turned to him for help.

The king persuaded Archimedes to prepare for him offensive and defensive engines to be used in every kind of warfare. These he had never used himself, because he spent the greater part of his life in freedom from war and amid the festal rites of peace. But at the present time his apparatus stood the Syracusans in good stead, and, with the apparatus, its fabricator. When, therefore, the Romans assaulted them by sea and land, the Syracusans were stricken dumb with terror. They thought that nothing could withstand so furious an onset by such forces.

Archimedes, however, began to ply his engines, and shot against the land forces of the attackers all sorts of missiles and immense masses of stones, which came down with incredible din and speed. Nothing whatever could ward off their weight, but they knocked down in heaps those who stood in their way, and threw their ranks into confusion. At the same time huge beams were suddenly projected over the ships from the walls, which sank some of them with great weights plunging down from on high. Others were seized at the prow by iron claws, or beaks like the beaks of cranes, drawn straight up into the air, and then plunged stern first into the depths, or were turned round and round by means of enginery within the city, and dashed upon the steep cliffs that jutted out beneath the wall of the city, with great destruction of the fighting men on board, who perished in the wrecks. Frequently, too, a ship would be lifted out of the water into mid-air, whirled here and there as it hung there, a dreadful spectacle, until its crew had been thrown out and hurled in all directions. Then it would fall empty upon the walls, or slip away from the clutch that had held it. As for the engine that Marcellus was bringing up on the bridge of ships, and which was called "sambuca" [large mechanically operated scaling ladders carried on ships].

While it was still some distance off in its approach to the wall, a stone of 500 pounds' weight was discharged at it, then a second and a third. Some of them, falling upon it with great noise and surge of wave, crushed the foundation of the engine, shattered its framework, and dislodged it from the platform, so that Marcellus, in perplexity, ordered his ships to sail back as fast as they could and his land forces to retire. . . .

Many of their ships, too, were dashed together, and they could not retaliate in any way upon their foes. For Archimedes had built most of his engines close behind the wall, and the Romans seemed to be fighting against the gods, now that countless mischiefs were poured out upon them from an invisible source.

At last the Romans became so fearful that whenever they saw a bit of rope or a stick of timber projecting a little over the wall. "There it is," they shouted, "Archimedes is training some engine upon us." They then turned their backs and fled. Seeing this, Marcellus desisted from all the fighting and assault, and thenceforth depended on a long siege.

For all his genius, Archimedes did not survive the siege. His deeds of war done, he returned to his thinking and his mathematical problems, even with the siege still in the background. When Syracuse was betrayed to the Romans, soldiers streamed in, spreading slaughter and destruction throughout the city. A Roman soldier came upon Archimedes in his study and killed him outright, thus ending the life of one of the world's greatest thinkers.

Questions for Analysis

1. How did Archimedes' engines repulse the Roman attacks?

2. What effect did his weapons have on the Roman attackers?

3. What is the irony of Archimedes' death?

Source: Reprinted by permission of the publishers and the Trustees of the Loeb Classical Library™ from *Plutarch: Volume V*, Loeb Classical Library™ Volume 87, trans. Bernadotte Perrin (Cambridge, Mass.: Harvard University Press), 1917. The Loeb Classical Library™ is a registered trademark of the President and Fellows of Harvard College.

Chapter Summary

Key Terms

polis
acropolis
monarchy
oligarchy
tyranny
democracy
hoplite
deme
Delian League
sovereign
koine
Great Silk Road
Tyche
mystery religions
Epicureanism
Stoicism
natural law
heliocentric theory

To assess your mastery of this chapter and read the primary sources listed in the margins, visit **bedfordstmartins.com/mckayworld** or see *Sources of World Societies*.

• How did the geography of Greece divide the land so that small communities naturally developed?

Terrain divided the land of Greece and the Aegean into small parcels that nurtured small communities. Some groups of people joined together in kingdoms, notably the Minoan kingdom in Crete and the Mycenaean on the mainland. The fall of these kingdoms led to a period known as the Greek Dark Age (ca. 1100–ca. 800 B.C.E.). Greek culture survived the collapse and developed the polis in which individuals governed themselves without elaborate political machinery. They created two prominent forms of governing—oligarchy, rule by a few citizens, and democracy, rule by all citizens. The success of the polis made it the ideal Greek government.

• What were the major accomplishments of the Archaic age, and why were they important?

In the Archaic period (ca. 800–500 B.C.E.), Greece prospered until it produced a burgeoning population that colonized the Mediterranean from the Atlantic Ocean to the Black Sea. Sparta created the most successful military polis, while the Athenian polis became democratic.

• Although the classical period saw tremendous upheavals, what were its lasting achievements?

The Greeks of the classical period (500–338 B.C.E.) successfully defended themselves from Persian invasions but nearly destroyed themselves in the Peloponnesian War. Yet they built comfortable cities decorated with architectural monuments and fine sculpture. They invented drama to explain individuals and their place in society. They refined their religious beliefs and evolved philosophy the better to understand life.

• After Alexander the Great's conquest of the Persian Empire, how did Greek immigrants and the native peoples there create a new society?

When Alexander the Great defeated the Persians, he opened western and central Asia to Greek expansion, resulting in the blending of these civilizations. In the Hellenistic period (336–146 B.C.E.) kingdoms and their cities sponsored a common culture linked by a common Greek dialect, the koine. Hellenistic society promoted commerce, and trade routes connected distant places as never before. Larger populations produced more goods, grew wealthier, and enjoyed broader outlooks. These developments led to greater advances in religion, which was marked by new mystery cults that promised eternal life.

• *How did the intellectual meeting of two vibrant cultures lead to a very fertile intellectual development?*

The new philosophies of Epicureanism and Stoicism helped people cope successfully with Tyche and the new demands of life. Hellenistic thinkers furthered knowledge of the earth and the entire universe. Advances in medicine made the Hellenistic world a healthier place. All these advances resulted in a large, generally satisfied, and worldly society.

Suggested Reading

Archibald, Z. H., et al. *Hellenistic Economics.* 2001. A very informative treatment of the subject.

Boardman, J. *The Greeks Overseas.* 2001. Very valuable coverage of Greek colonization.

Bosworth, A. B. *Conquest and Empire.* 1988. The most balanced discussion of Alexander the Great.

Buckler, J. *Aegean Greece in the Fourth Century BC.* 2003. The only modern study of this period.

Hansen, M. H. *Polis.* 2006. Already the classic treatment of the subject.

Hodkinson, S. *Property and Wealth in Classical Sparta.* 2000. Discusses many vital aspects of Spartan life.

Kingsley, P. *Ancient Philosophy.* 1996. A balanced survey of the entire field.

Patterson, C. B. *The Family in Greek History.* 2001. Treats public and private family relations.

Price, S. *Religions of the Ancient Greeks.* 1999. Covers all religions from ca. 800 B.C.E. to 500 C.E.

Thomas, C. G., and C. Conant. *Citadel to City-State.* 2003. An excellent treatment of early Greece and modern ideas about it.

Notes

1. Thucydides 2.12, translated by J. Buckler.
2. Diodoros 3.12.2–3, translated by J. Buckler.

Listening to the PAST

Alexander and the Brotherhood of Man

One historical problem challenged historians throughout the twentieth century and has yet to be solved to everyone's satisfaction. After returning to Opis, north of Babylon in modern Iraq, Alexander found himself confronted with a huge and unexpected mutiny by his Macedonian veterans. He held a banquet to pacify them, and he included in the festivities some Persians and other Asian followers, some nine thousand in all. During the festivities he offered a public prayer for harmony and partnership in rule between the Macedonians and Persians. Many modern scholars have interpreted this prayer as an expression of his desire to establish a "brotherhood of man." The following passage provides the evidence for this view. From it all readers can determine for themselves whether Alexander attempted to introduce a new philosophical ideal or whether he harbored his own political motives for political cooperation.

8. When [Alexander] arrived at Opis, he collected the Macedonians and announced that he intended to discharge from the army those who were useless for military service either from age or from being maimed in the limbs; and he said he would send them back to their own abodes. He also promised to give those who went back as much extra reward as would make them special objects of envy to those at home and arouse in the other Macedonians the wish to share similar dangers and labours. Alexander said this, no doubt, for the purpose of pleasing the Macedonians; but on the contrary they were, not without reason, offended by the speech which he delivered, thinking that now they were despised by him and deemed to be quite useless for military service. Indeed, throughout the whole of this expedition they had been offended at many other things; for his adoption of the Persian dress, thereby exhibiting his contempt for their opinion often caused them grief, as did also his accoutring the foreign soldiers called Epigoni in the Macedonian style, and the mixing of the alien horsemen among the ranks of the Companions. Therefore they could not remain silent and control themselves, but urged him to dismiss all of them from his army; and they advised him to prosecute the war in company with his father, deriding Ammon by

this remark. When Alexander heard this . . . , he ordered the most conspicuous of the men who had tried to stir up the multitude to sedition to be arrested. He himself pointed out with his hand to the shield-bearing guards those whom they were to arrest, to the number of thirteen; and he ordered these to be led away to execution. When the rest, stricken with terror, became silent, he mounted the platform again, and spoke as follows:

9. "The speech which I am about to deliver will not be for the purpose of checking your start homeward, for, so far as I am concerned, you may depart wherever you wish; but for the purpose of making you understand when you take yourselves off, what kind of men you have been to us who have conferred such benefits upon you. . . .

10. . . . Most of you have golden crowns, the eternal memorials of your valour and of the honour you receive from me. Whoever has been killed has met with a glorious end and has been honoured with a splendid burial. Brazen statues of most of the slain have been erected at home, and their parents are held in honour, being released from all public service and from taxation. But no one of you has ever been killed in flight under my leadership. And now I was intending to send back those of you who are unfit for service, objects of envy to those at home; but since you all wish to depart, depart all of you! Go back and report at home that your king Alexander, the conqueror of the Persians, Medes, Bactrians, and Sacians; the man who has subjugated the Uxians, Arachotians, and Drangians; who has also acquired the rule of the Parthians, Chorasmians, and Hyrcanians, as far as the Caspian Sea . . . —report that when you returned to Susa you deserted him and went away, handing him over to the protection of conquered foreigners. Perhaps this report of yours will be both glorious to you in the eyes of men and devout I ween in the eyes of the gods. Depart!"

11. Having thus spoken, he leaped down quickly from the platform, and entered the palace, where he paid no attention to the decoration of his person, nor was any of his Companions admitted to see him. Not

This gilded case for a bow and arrows indicates that Alexander's success came at the price of blood. These vigorous scenes portray more military conflict than philosophical compassion. *(Archaeological Museum Salonica/Dagli-Orti/ The Art Archive)*

even on the morrow was any one of them admitted to an audience; but on the third day he summoned the select Persians within, and among them he distributed the commands of the brigades, and made the rule that only those whom he proclaimed his kinsmen should have the honour of saluting him with a kiss. But the Macedonians who heard the speech were thoroughly astonished at the moment, and remained there in silence near the platform; nor when he retired did any of them accompany the king, except his personal Companions and the confidential body-guards. Though they remained most of them had nothing to do or say; and yet they were unwilling to retire. But when the news was reported to them . . . they were no longer able to restrain themselves; but running in a body to the palace, they cast their weapons there in front of the gates as signs of supplication to the king. Standing in front of the gates, they shouted, beseeching to be allowed to enter, and saying that they were willing to surrender the men who had been the instigators of the disturbance on that occasion, and those who had begun the clamour. They also declared they would not retire from the gates either day or night, unless Alexander would take some pity upon them. When he was informed of this, he came out without delay; and seeing them lying on the ground in humble guise, and hearing most of them lamenting with loud voice, tears began to flow also from his own eyes. He made an effort to say something to them, but they continued their importunate entreaties. At length one of them, Callines by name, a man conspicuous both for his age and because he was a captain of the Companion cavalry, spoke as follows, "O king, what grieves the Macedonians is that you have already made some of the Persians kinsmen to yourself, and that Persians are called Alexander's kinsmen, and have the honour of saluting you with a kiss; whereas none of the Macedonians have as yet enjoyed this honour." Then Alexander, interrupting him, said, "But all of you without exception I consider my kinsmen, and so from this time I shall call you." When he had said this, Callines advanced and saluted him with a kiss, and so did all those who wished to salute him. Then they took up their weapons and returned to the camp, shouting and singing a song of thanksgiving. After this Alexander offered sacrifice to the gods to whom it was his custom to sacrifice, and gave a public banquet, over which he himself presided, with the Macedonians sitting around him; and next to them the Persians; after whom came the men of the other nations, preferred in honour for their personal rank or for some meritorious action. The king and his guests drew wine from the same bowl and poured out the same libations, both the Grecian prophets and the Magians commencing the ceremony. He prayed for other blessings, and especially that harmony and community of rule might exist between the Macedonians and Persians.

Questions for Analysis

1. What was the purpose of the banquet at Opis?

2. Were all of the guests treated equally?

3. What did Alexander gain from bringing together the Macedonians and Persians?

Source: Arrian, *Anabasis of Alexander* 7.8.1–11.9 in F. R. B. Goldophin, ed., *The Greek Historians,* vol. 2. Copyright 1942 and renewed 1970 by Random House, Inc. Used by permission of Random House, Inc.

The Roman Forum. *(Josephine Powell, Photographer, Courtesy of Special Collections, Fine Arts Library, Harvard College Library)*

5 THE WORLD OF ROME (753 B.C.E.–479 C.E.)

Like the Persians under Cyrus and the Macedonians under Alexander, the Romans conquered vast territories in less than a century. Their singular achievement lay in their ability to incorporate conquered peoples into the Roman system. Unlike the Greeks, who refused to share citizenship, the Romans extended theirs first to the Italians and later to the peoples of the provinces. With that citizenship went Roman government and law. Rome created a state that embraced the entire Mediterranean area and extended northward. After a grim period of civil war, in 31 B.C.E. the emperor Augustus restored peace. He extended Roman power and law as far east as the Euphrates River and created the structure that the modern world calls the "Roman Empire."

Roman history is usually divided into two periods: the republic, the age in which Rome grew from a small city-state to ruler of an empire; and the empire, the period when the republican constitution gave way to a constitutional monarchy.

THE ROMANS IN ITALY (CA. 750–290 B.C.E.)

How did the Romans come to dominate Italy, and what political institutions did they create?

While the Greeks pursued their destiny in the eastern Mediterranean, two peoples—the Etruscans and Romans—entered the peninsula of Italy. The Etruscans developed the first cities and a rich cultural life, but the Romans eventually came to dominate the peninsula.

The Etruscans and Rome

The arrival of the Etruscans in the region of Etruria can reasonably be dated to about 750 B.C.E. The Etruscans established permanent settlements that evolved into the first Italian cities, which resembled the

Greek city-states in political organization. They spread their influence over the surrounding countryside, which they farmed and mined for its rich mineral resources. From an early period the Etruscans began to trade natural products, especially iron, with their Greek neighbors in the Mediterranean in exchange for luxury goods. They thereby built a rich cultural life that became the foundation of civilization throughout Italy. In the process they encountered a small collection of villages subsequently called Rome.

The Romans had settled in Italy by the eighth century B.C.E. According to one legend, Romulus and Remus founded the city in 753 B.C.E., Romulus making his home on the Palatine Hill, while Remus chose the Avertine. Under Etruscan influence the Romans prospered, occupying all of Rome's seven hills. Located at an easy crossing point on the Tibur River, Rome stood astride the main avenue of communications between northern and southern Italy. Its seven hills provided safety from attackers and from the floods of the Tibur (see Map 5.1).

From 753 to 509 B.C.E. a line of Etruscan kings ruled the city and introduced numerous customs. The Romans adopted the Etruscan alphabet, which the Etruscans themselves had adoped from the Greeks. The Romans later handed on this alphabet to medieval Europe and thence to the modern Western world. Even the **toga**, the white woolen robe won by citizens, came from the Etruscans. Under the Etruscans Rome enjoyed contacts with the larger Mediterranean world, while the city continued to grow. In the years 753 to 550 B.C.E. temples and public buildings began to grace the city. The **Forum** ceased to be a cemetery and began its history as a public meeting place similar to the Greek agora. Trade in metalwork became common, and wealthier Romans began to import fine Greek vases. The Etruscans had found Rome a collection of villages and made it a city.

The Roman Conquest of Italy (509–290 B.C.E.)

Legend held that the republic was established when the son of the Etruscan king raped Lucretia, a virtuous Roman wife, who committed suicide at the shame, causing the people to rise up in anger. The republic was actually founded in years after 509, when the Romans fought numerous wars with their Italian neighbors. Not until roughly a century after the founding of the republic did the Romans drive the Etruscans entirely out of Latium. The Romans very early learned the value of alliances with

> **Primary Source: Livy, *On the Founding of Rome and the Rape of the Sabine Women***

toga *The distinctive garment of Roman men, made of a long sash wrapped around the body. The wearing of the toga was forbidden to noncitizens.*

Forum *A public area in the center of Rome that served as focal point of the political, spiritual, and economic life of the city.*

● **Sarcophagus of Lartie Seianti** The woman portrayed on this lavish sarcophagus is the noble Etruscan Lartie Seianti. Although the sarcophagus is her place of burial, she is portrayed as in life, comfortable and at rest. The influence of Greek art on Etruscan is apparent in almost every feature of the sarcophagus. (*Archaeological Museum, Florence/Nimatallah/ Art Resource, NY*)

the Latin towns around them, which provided them all with security and the Romans with a large reservoir of manpower. These alliances involved the Romans in still other wars that took them farther afield in the Italian peninsula.

Around 390 B.C.E. the Romans suffered a major setback when a new people, the Celts—or Gauls, as the Romans called them—swept aside a Roman army and sacked Rome. More intent on loot than land, they agreed to abandon Rome in return for a thousand pounds of gold. In the century that followed the Romans rebuilt their city and recouped their losses. They brought Latium and their Latin allies fully under their control and conquered the Etruscans. In a series of bitter wars the Romans subdued southern Italy, all the while developing their superior military organization. That and the strength of Roman manpower led them to conquer all of Italy, where they stood unchallenged (see Map 5.1).

All the while, the Romans also spread their religious cults and culture throughout Italy. Although they did not force their beliefs on others, they welcomed their neighbors to religious places of assembly. The Romans and Italians grew closer by the mutual understanding of participation in religious rites.

In politics the Romans shared full Roman citizenship with many of their oldest allies, particularly the Latin cities. In other instances they granted citizenship without the **franchise,** that is, without the right to vote or hold Roman office. These allies were subject to Roman taxes and calls for military service but ran their own local affairs. The Latin allies could acquire full Roman citizenship by moving to Rome. Mundane but vital was Roman road-building. Roman roads, like the Persian Royal Road, facilitated the flow of communication, trade, and armies from the capital to outlying areas. They were the tangible sinews of unity.

The Roman Republic

The Romans summed up their political existence in a single phrase: *senatus populusque Romanus,* "the Roman senate and the people," which they abbreviated "SPQR." This sentiment reflects the republican ideal of shared government rather than power concentrated in a monarchy. It stands for the beliefs, customs, and laws of the republic—its unwritten constitution that evolved over two centuries to meet the demands of the governed.

In the early republic social divisions determined the shape of politics. Political power was in the hands of the aristocracy—the **patricians,** who were wealthy landowners. Patrician families formed clans, as did aristocrats in early Greece. Patricians dominated the affairs of state, provided military leadership in time of war, and monopolized knowledge of law and legal procedure. The common people of Rome, the **plebeians,** were free citizens with a voice in politics, but they could not hold high office or marry into patrician families. While some plebeian merchants rivaled the patricians in wealth, most plebeians were poor artisans, small farmers, and landless urban dwellers.

Chronology

735 B.C.E.   Traditional founding of Rome

ca. 750–509 B.C.E.   Etruscan rule of an evolving Rome

509–290 B.C.E.   Roman conquest of Italy

ca. 494–287 B.C.E.   Struggle of the Orders

264–45 B.C.E.   Punic Wars and conquest of the Mediterranean

88–31 B.C.E.   Civil war

44 B.C.E.   Assassination of Julius Caesar

31 B.C.E.   Triumph of Augustus

27 B.C.E.–68 C.E.   Julio-Claudian emperors, expansion in Europe, prosperity in the empire

ca. 3 B.C.E.–29 C.E.   Life of Jesus

30–312 C.E.   Spread of Christianity

96–180 C.E.   "Golden age" of peace and prosperity, reigns of the five good emperors

193–284 C.E.   Military monarchy, military conflict, and commercial contact with central and eastern Asia

284–337 C.E.   Diocletian and Constantine reconstruct the empire, dividing it into western and eastern halves, construction of Constantinople

380 C.E.   Christianity the official religion of the empire

franchise   *The rights, privileges, and protections of citizenship.*

patricians   *The aristocracy; wealthy landowners who held political power.*

plebeians   *The common people of Rome, who had few of the patricians' advantages.*

praetors *A new office created in 366 B.C.E.; these people acted in place of consuls when the consuls were away, although they primarily dealt with the administration of justice.*

MAP 5.1 **Roman Italy, ca. 265 B.C.E.** The geographical configuration of the Italian peninsula shows how Rome stood astride north-south communication routes and how the state that united Italy stood poised to move into Sicily and northern Africa.

The chief magistrates of the republic were the two consuls, elected for one-year terms. At first the consulship was open only to patrician men. The consuls commanded the army in battle, administered state business, and supervised financial affairs. When the consuls were away from Rome, **praetors** acted in their place. Otherwise, the praetors dealt primarily with the administration of justice. After the age of overseas conquest, the Romans divided the Mediterranean into provinces governed by ex-consuls and ex-praetors. Because of their experience in Roman politics, they were all suited to administer the affairs of the provincials and to fit Roman law and custom into new contexts.

Other officials included *quaestors,* who took charge of the public treasury and prosecuted criminals in the popular courts. *Censors* held many responsibilities including the supervision of public morals, the power to determine who could lawfully sit in the

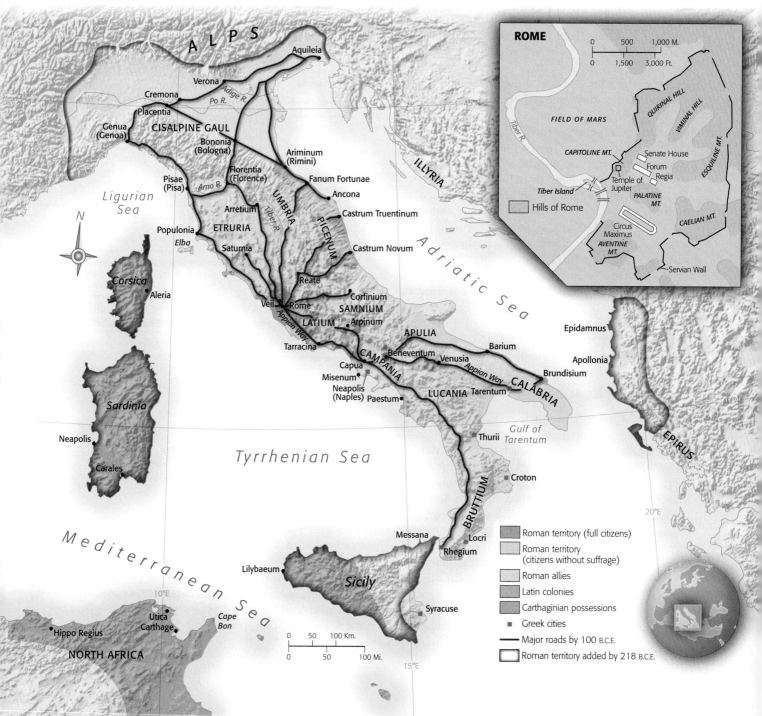

● **Guard Dog** The doorway of the house opened directly onto the street. This entrance is protected by a dog who is always on guard. The notice warns "CAVE CANEM" (beware of the dog). *(Robert Frerck/ Odyssey/Chicago)*

senate, the registration of citizens, and the leasing of public contracts. Lastly, the aediles supervised the streets and markets and presided over public festivals.

Perhaps the greatest institution of the republic was the senate, which had originated under the Etruscans as a council of noble elders who advised the king. During the republic the senate advised the consuls and other magistrates. Because the senate sat year after year, while magistrates changed annually, it provided stability. The senate could not technically pass legislation. It could only offer its advice. Yet increasingly, because of the senate's prestige, its advice came to have the force of law.

A lasting achievement of the Romans was their development of law. Roman civil law, the *ius civile,* consisted of statutes, customs, and forms of procedure that regulated the lives of citizens. As the Romans came into more frequent contact with foreigners, the praetors resorted to the law of equity, the *ius gentium,* the "law of the peoples," which they thought just to all parties. It led to a universal conception of law. By the late republic Roman jurists reached the concept of *ius naturale,* "natural law," based in part on Stoic beliefs, that applied to all societies.

Social Conflict in Rome

Inequality between plebeians and patricians led to a conflict known as the **Struggle of the Orders.** To solve their differences the plebeians nonviolently used the boycott to apply their power as a group. The patricians in turn generally responded peacefully by resorting to practical compromise.

The first showdown between the plebeians and patricians came, according to tradition, in 494 B.C.E. To force the patricians to grant concessions, the plebeians literally walked out of Rome and refused to serve in the army. The plebeians' general strike worked, and the patricians made important concessions. They allowed patricians and plebeians to marry one another. They recognized the right of plebeians to elect their own officials, the tribunes, who could bring plebeian grievances to the senate for resolution. Surrendering their legal monopoly, the patricians codified and published the Law of the

Struggle of the Orders
A great social conflict that developed between patricians and plebeians; the plebeians wanted real political representation and safeguards against patrician domination.

Primary Source:
The Twelve Tables

Twelve Tables, so called because they were inscribed on twelve bronze plaques. They also made public legal procedures so that plebeians could argue cases in court.

After a ten-year battle, the plebeians gained the Licinian-Sextian Rogations (or laws) that allowed wealthy plebeians access to all the magistracies of Rome. Once plebeians could hold the consulship, they could also sit in the senate and advise on policy. They also won the right to hold one of the two consulships. Though decisive, this victory did not automatically end the Struggle of the Orders. That happened only in 287 B.C.E. with the passage of the *lex Hortensia* that gave the resolutions of the *concilium plebis,* the Assembly of the People, the force of law for patricians and plebeians alike. This compromise established a new nobility of wealthy plebeians and patricians. Yet the Struggle of the Orders had made all citizens equal before the law, resulting in a Rome stronger and better united than before.

• • • • • • • • • • • • • • • • •

ROMAN EXPANSION AND ITS REPERCUSSIONS

How did Rome expand its power beyond Italy, and what were the effects of success on Rome?

With their internal affairs settled, the Romans turned their attention abroad. In a series of wars they conquered the Mediterranean, creating an overseas empire that brought them unheard of power and wealth. The new situation made many of them more cosmopolitan and comfortable. Yet it also caused social unrest at home and opened unprecedented opportunities for ambitious generals who wanted to rule Rome like an empire. Hard civil war ensued, which Julius Caesar quelled for a moment. Only his grandnephew Octavius, better known to history as Augustus, finally restored peace and order to Rome.

The Age of Overseas Conquest (264–45 B.C.E.)

In 282 B.C.E., when the Romans had reached southern Italy, they embarked upon a series of wars that left them the rulers of the Mediterranean world. Although they sometimes declared war reluctantly, they nonetheless felt the need to dominate, to eliminate any state that could endanger them. Yet they did not map out grandiose strategies to conquer the world. Rather they responded to situations as they arose.

Their presence in southern Italy brought the Romans to Sicily, next door. There they collided with the Carthaginians, Phoenician colonists living in North Africa (see Map 5.2). Conflicting ambitions in Sicily led to the First Punic War, which lasted from 264 to 241 B.C.E. Roman victory led to the island's becoming its first province. Still a formidable enemy, Carthage sent its brilliant general Hannibal (ca. 247–183 B.C.E.) against Rome. During the Second Punic War (218–201 B.C.E.) Hannibal won three major victories, including the devastating blow at Cannae in 216 B.C.E. Carrying the fighting to the very gates of Rome, he spread devastation farther across the Italian countryside. The Roman general Scipio Africanus (ca. 236–ca. 183 B.C.E.) led the counterattack to Carthage itself. In 202 B.C.E., near the town of Zama, Scipio defeated Hannibal in one of history's truly decisive battles. Scipio's victory meant that Rome's heritage would be passed on to posterity.

After defeating Carthage a last time in 146 B.C.E., the Romans turned east. After provocation from the king of Macedonia, Roman legions quickly conquered Macedonia and Greece and defeated the Seleucid monarchy. In 133 B.C.E. the king of Pergamum in Asia Minor willed his kingdom to Rome when he died. The Ptolemies of Egypt meekly obeyed Roman wishes. The Mediterranean had become *mare nostrum,* "our sea."

Primary Source:
Tacitus, *On the Roman Empire*

Old Values and Greek Culture

Rome had conquered the Mediterranean world, but some Romans considered that victory a misfortune. The historian Sallust (86–34 B.C.E.), writing from hindsight, complained that the acquisition of an empire was the beginning of Rome's troubles:

But when through labor and justice our Republic grew powerful . . . then fortune began to be harsh and to throw everything into confusion. The Romans had easily borne labor, danger, and hardship. To them leisure, riches—otherwise desirable—proved to be burdens and torments. So at first money, then desire for power, grew great. These things were a sort of cause of all evils.[1]

Instead, in the second century B.C.E. the Romans learned that they could not return to a simple life. Having become world rulers, they began to build a huge imperial system. They had to change their institutions, social patterns, and way of thinking to shape a new era. In the end Rome triumphed here just as on the battlefield, for out of turmoil came the *pax Romana*—"Roman peace" (see page 112).

Two attitudes represent the major ways in which the Romans met these challenges. One longed for the good old days and an idealized agrarian way of life. The other embraced the new urban culture.

In Roman society, whether traditional or new-fashioned, the head of the family was the **paterfamilias,** the oldest dominant male of the family. He held nearly absolute power over the lives of his wife and children as long as he lived. Until he died, his sons could not legally own property. To deal with important matters, he usually called a council of the adult males. In these councils the women of the family had no formal part, but they could inherit and own property. Romans viewed the family as important and thought that children should be raised by their mothers. Women who fulfilled these ideals were accorded respect. They handled the early education of the children. After the age of seven, sons and often daughters began their formal education.

An influx of slaves came from Rome's conquests. To the Romans slavery was a misfortune that befell some people, but it did not entail any racial theories. Not even later Christians questioned the institution of slavery. For loyal slaves the Romans always held out the possibility of freedom. **Manumission,** the freeing of individual slaves by their masters, became common.

For most Romans religion played an important role in life. Jupiter, the sky-god, and his wife, Juno, became equivalent to the Greek Zeus and Hera. Mars was the god of war but also guaranteed the welfare of the farm. In addition to the great gods, the Romans believed in spirits who haunted fields and even the home itself. Some of the deities were hostile, and only magic could ward them off. Some spirits were ghosts who haunted places where they had lived.

The new feeling of wealth and leisure is most readily seen in Rome, now a great city, where the spoils of war financed the building of baths, theaters, and other places of amusement. Romans developed new tastes and especially a liking for Greek culture. During this period the Greek custom of bathing became a Roman passion. Now large buildings containing pools and exercise rooms became essential parts of the Roman city. The baths were prominent places where men and women went to see and be seen. Despite the objections of the conservatives, these new social customs did not corrupt the Romans. They still continued efficiently to rule their empire.

The Late Republic (133–31 B.C.E.)

The wars of conquest created serious political problems for the Romans. When the legionaries returned home, they found their farms

paterfamilias *A term that means far more than merely "father"; it indicates the oldest dominant male of the family who holds nearly absolute power over the lives of family members as long as he lives.*

manumission *The freeing of individual slaves by their masters.*

● **African Acrobat** Conquest and prosperity brought exotic pleasure to Rome. Every feature of this sculpture is exotic. The young African woman and her daring gymnastic pose would catch anyone's attention. To add to the spice of her act, she performs using a live crocodile as her platform. Americans would have loved it. *(Courtesy of the Trustees of the British Museum)*

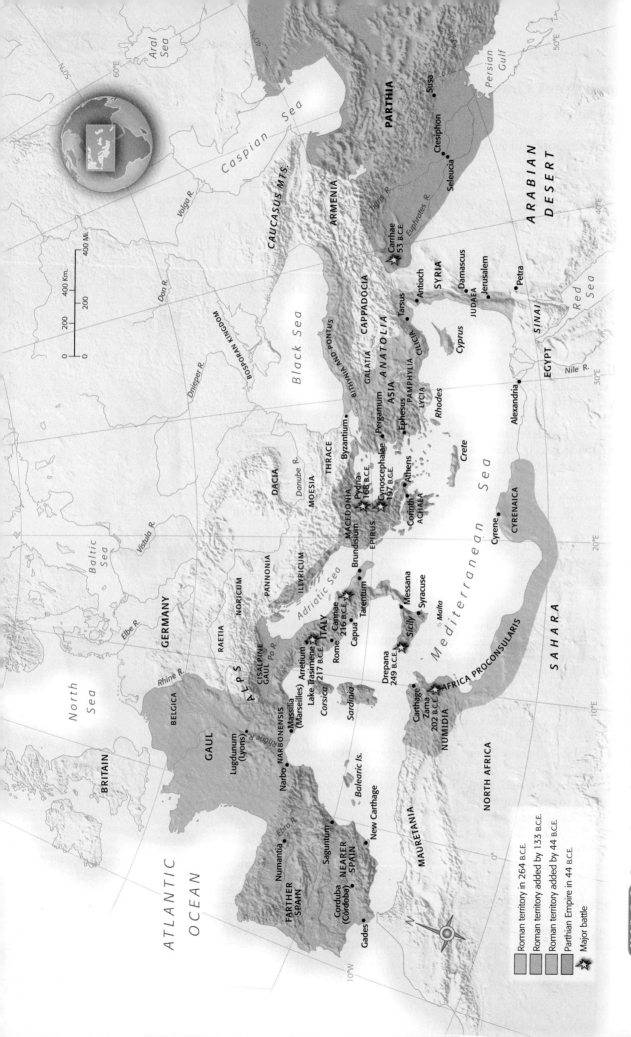

MAP 5.2 Roman Expansion During the Republic The main spurt of Roman expansion occurred between 264 and 133 B.C.E., when most of the Mediterranean fell to Rome, followed by the conquest of Gaul and the eastern Mediterranean by 44 B.C.E.

Roman territory in 264 B.C.E.

Roman territory added by 133 B.C.E.

Roman territory added by 44 B.C.E.

Parthian Empire in 44 B.C.E.

Major battle

ATLANTIC OCEAN

BRITAIN

North Sea

Baltic Sea

GERMANY

BELGICA

GAUL

Lugdunum (Lyons)

Narbo NARBONENSIS

Massilia (Marseilles)

ALPS

CISALPINE GAUL

Arretium

Lake Trasimene 217 B.C.E.

Rome

Corsica

Sardinia

Balearic Is.

New Carthage

Gades

Corduba (Córdoba) NEARER SPAIN

FARTHER SPAIN

Numantia

Saguntum

Ebro R.

Rhône R.

Rhine R.

Elbe R.

RAETIA

NORICUM

PANNONIA

ILLYRICUM

Po R.

ITALY

Capua

Cannae 216 B.C.E.

Tarentum

Brundisium

Adriatic Sea

Drepana 249 B.C.E.

Sicily

Messana

Syracuse

Malta

Carthage

Zama 202 B.C.E.

NUMIDIA

MAURETANIA

NORTH AFRICA

AFRICA PROCONSULARIS

SAHARA

Mediterranean Sea

DACIA

MOESIA

THRACE

Danube R.

MACEDONIA

Pydna 168 B.C.E.

Cynoscephalae 197 B.C.E.

EPIRUS

ACHAEA

Corinth

Athens

Byzantium

BITHYNIA AND PONTUS

GALATIA

CAPPADOCIA

ANATOLIA

ASIA

Pergamum

Ephesus

PAMPHYLIA

LYCIA

CILICIA

Tarsus

Crete

Rhodes

Cyprus

Cyrene

CYRENAICA

Black Sea

Caspian Sea

Aral Sea

CAUCASUS MTS.

ARMENIA

PARTHIA

Susa

Ctesiphon

Seleucia

Carrhae 53 B.C.E.

SYRIA

Antioch

Damascus

Jerusalem

JUDAEA

Petra

SINAI

EGYPT

Alexandria

Nile R.

Red Sea

ARABIAN DESERT

Persian Gulf

Euphrates R.

Tigris R.

Volga R.

Don R.

Dnieper R.

Vistula R.

BOSPORAN KINGDOM

400 Mi.

400 Km.

200

0

Roman Table Manners
This mosaic is a floor that can never be swept clean. It whimsically suggests what a dining room floor looked like after a lavish dinner and also tells something about the menu: a chicken head, a wishbone, and remains of various seafood, vegetables, and fruit are easily recognizable. *(Museo Gregoriano Profano, Vatican Museums/Scala/Art Resource, NY)*

looking like those of the people they had conquered. Many were forced to sell their land, and they found ready buyers in those who had grown rich from the wars. These wealthy men created huge estates called **latifundia**. Landless veterans moved to the cities, especially Rome, but could not find work. These developments threatened Rome's army because landless men were forbidden to serve.

The landless veterans were willing to follow any leader who promised help. Tiberius Gracchus (163–133 B.C.E.), an aristocrat who was appalled by the situation, was elected tribune in 133 B.C.E. Tiberius proposed dividing public land among the poor, but a group of wealthy senators murdered him, launching a long era of political violence that would destroy the republic. Still, Tiberius's brother Gaius Gracchus (153–121 B.C.E.) passed a law providing the urban poor with cheap grain and urged practical reforms. Once again senators tried to stem the tide of reform by murdering him.

The next reformer, Gaius Marius (ca. 157–86 B.C.E.) recruited landless men into the army to put down a rebel king in Africa. He promised them land for their service. But after his victory, the senate refused to honor his promise. From then on, Roman soldiers looked to their commanders, not to the senate or the state, to protect their interests. The turmoil continued until 88 B.C.E., when the Roman general Sulla made himself dictator. Although he voluntarily stepped down nine years later, it was too late to restore the republican constitution. The senate and other institutions of the Roman state had failed to meet the needs of empire. They had lost control of their generals and army. The soldiers put their faith in generals rather than the state, and that doomed the republic.

The history of the late republic is the story of power struggles among many famous Roman figures. Pompey used military success in Spain to force the senate to allow him to run for consul. In 59 B.C.E. he was joined in a political alliance called the **First Triumvirate** by Crassus and Julius Caesar (100–44 B.C.E.). Born of a noble family, Caesar, an able general, was also a brilliant politician with unbridled ambition. Recognizing that military success led to power, he led his troops to victory in Spain and Gaul, modern France. Having later defeated his Roman opponents, he made himself

latifundia *Huge Roman estates created by buying up several small farms.*

First Triumvirate *A political alliance between Caesar, Crassus, and Pompey in which they agreed to advance one another's interests.*

Primary Source:
**Plutarch, *On Julius Caesar,
A Man of Unlimited
Ambition***

dictator. Using his victory wisely, he enacted basic reforms. He extended citizenship to many provincials outside Italy who had supported him. To relieve the pressure of Rome's huge population, he sent eighty thousand poor people to plant colonies in Gaul, Spain, and North Africa. These new communities—formed of Roman citizens, not subjects—helped spread Roman culture.

In 44 B.C.E. a group of conspirators assassinated Caesar and set off another round of civil war. His grandnephew and heir, the eighteen-year-old Octavian, better known as Augustus, joined with two of Caesar's followers, Marc Antony and Lepidus, in the Second Triumvirate. After defeating Caesar's murderers, they had a falling-out. Octavian forced Lepidus out of office and waged war against Antony, who had become allied with Cleopatra, queen of Egypt. In 31 B.C.E., with the might of Rome at his back, Octavian defeated the combined forces of Antony and Cleopatra at the Battle of Actium in Greece. His victory ended the age of civil war. For his success the senate in 27 B.C.E. voted Octavian the name *Augustus*.

pax Romana *A period during the first and second centuries C.E. of security, order, harmony, flourishing culture, and expanding economy.*

The Pax Romana

When Augustus ended the civil wars, he faced the monumental problems of reconstruction. From 29–23 B.C.E. Augustus toiled to heal Rome's wounds. He first had to rebuild the constitution and the organs of government. He next had to demobilize much of the army and care for the welfare of the provinces. Then he had to meet the danger of barbarians on Rome's European frontiers. Augustus was highly successful in meeting these challenges. The world came to know this era as the **pax Romana**, the Roman peace. His gift of peace to a war-torn world sowed the seeds of the empire's golden age.

Augustus claimed that in restoring constitutional government he was also restoring the republic. Yet he had to modify republican forms and offices to meet the new circumstances. While expecting the senate to shoulder heavy administrative burdens, he failed to give it enough actual power to do the job. Many of the senate's prerogatives thus shifted by default to Augustus and his successors.

Augustus also had to fit his own position into the republican constitution. He became **princeps civitatis**, "First Citizen of the State," a prestigious title without power. His real power resided in the multiple magistracies he held and in the powers granted him by the senate. He held the consulship annually. The senate voted him the full power of the tribunes, giving him the right to call the senate into session, present legislation to the people, and defend their rights. He held control of the army, which he made a permanent, standing organization. He kept all this power in the background. Failing to restore the republic, he actually created a constitutional monarchy. Without saying so, he also created the office of emperor. Yet he failed to find a way to institutionalize his position with the army, which remained personal. Although the Augustan principate worked well at first, by the third century C.E. the army would make and break emperors at will.

● **Augustus as Imperator** Here Augustus, dressed in breastplate and uniform, emphasizes the imperial majesty of Rome and his role as imperator. The figures on his breastplate represent the restoration of peace, one of Augustus's greatest accomplishments and certainly one that he frequently stressed. *(Erich Lessing/Art Resource, NY)*

Augustus put provincial administration on an orderly basis and improved its functioning. He encouraged local self-government and urbanism. As a spiritual bond between the provinces and Rome, Augustus encouraged the cult of *Roma et Augustus,* "Rome and Augustus," as the guardians of the state. The cult spread rapidly and became a symbol of Roman unity.

One of the most momentous aspects of Augustus's reign was Roman expansion into northern and western Europe (see Map 5.3). Augustus completed the conquest of Spain. In Gaul he founded twelve new towns, and the Roman road system linked new settlements with one another and with Italy. After hard fighting, he made the Rhine River and the Roman frontier in Germany. Meanwhile, generals extended the Roman standards as far as the Danube. Roman legions penetrated the areas of modern Austria, southern Bavaria, and western Hungary. The regions of modern Serbia, Bulgaria, and Romania fell. Within this area the legionaries built fortified camps. Roads linked these camps with one another, and settlements grew up around the camps.

Amid the vast expanse of forests, Roman towns, trade, language, and law began to exert a civilizing influence on the barbarians. Many military camps became towns, and many modern European cities owe their origins to the forts of the Roman army. For the first time, the barbarian north came into direct and continuous contact with Mediterranean culture. The Romans maintained peaceful relations with the barbarians whenever possible, but Roman legions remained on the frontier to repel hostile barbarians.

THE COMING OF CHRISTIANITY

What was Christianity, and how did it affect life in the empire?

During the reign of the emperor Tiberius (14–37 C.E.), in the Roman province of Judaea, created out of the Jewish kingdom of Judah, Jesus of Nazareth preached, attracting a following, and was executed on the order of the Roman prefect Pontius Pilate. Much contemporary scholarship has attempted to understand who Jesus was and what he meant by his teachings. Views vary widely. Some see him as a visionary and a teacher, others as a magician and a prophet, and still others as a rebel and a revolutionary. A great many people believe that he was the son of God. The search for the historical Jesus is complicated by many factors. One is the difference between history and faith. History relies on evidence and proof for its conclusions; faith depends on belief. Thus, whether Jesus is divine is not an issue to be decided by historians. Their role is to understand his religious, cultural, social, and historical context.

Unrest in Judaea

The civil wars that destroyed the Roman republic left their mark on Judaea, where Jewish leaders had taken sides in the conflict. The turmoil created a climate of violence throughout the area. Among the Jews two movements spread. First was the rise of the Zealots, who fought to rid Judaea of the Romans. The second movement was the growth of militant apocalypticism, the belief that the coming of the Messiah was near. The Messiah would destroy the Roman legions and then inaugurate a period of happiness and plenty for Jews.

The pagan world played its part in the story of early Christianity. The term **pagan** refers to all those who believed in the Greco-Roman gods. Paganism at the time of Jesus' birth can be broadly divided into three spheres: the official state religion of Rome, the traditional Roman cults of hearth and countryside, and the new mystery religions that arose in the Hellenistic world (see pages 93–94). The mystery religions gave their adherents what neither the official religion nor traditional cults could, but they were exclusive. None of these religious sentiments met many people's spiritual needs.

princeps civitatis *A Latin term meaning "first citizen" used as an official title by the early Roman emperors, from Augustus through Diocletian, followed by a Latin term meaning a city under Roman imperial authority possessing some limited degree of autonomy.*

pagan *From a Latin term meaning "of the country," used to describe followers of a folk religion.*

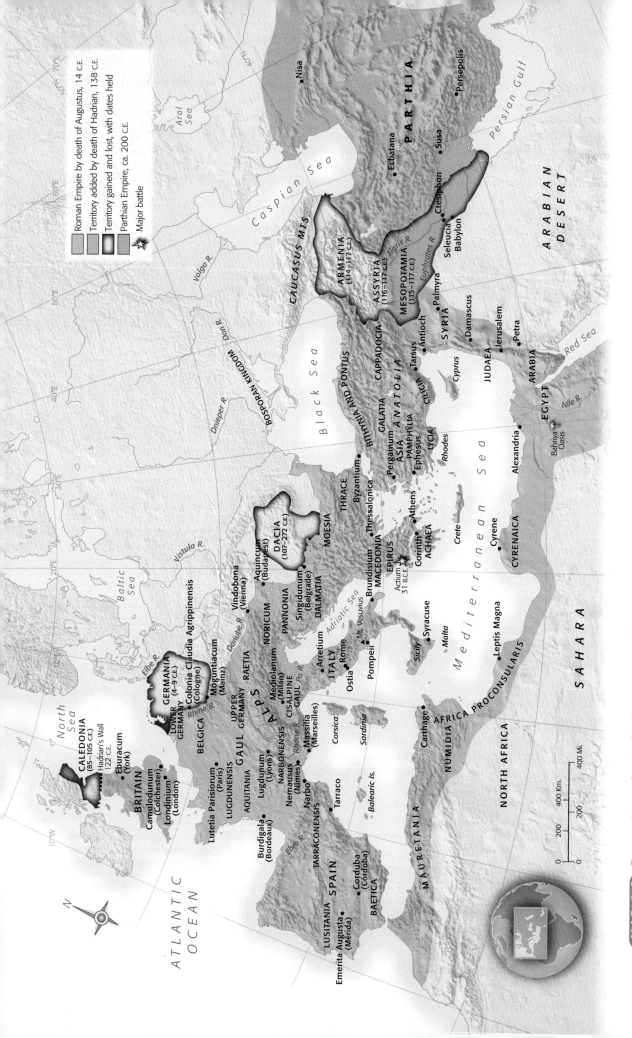

MAP 5.3 Roman Expansion Under the Empire Following Roman expansion during the republic, Augustus added vast tracts of Europe to the Roman Empire, which the emperor Hadrian later enlarged by assuming control over parts of central Europe, the Near East, and North Africa.

Roman Empire by death of Augustus, 14 C.E.

Territory added by death of Hadrian, 138 C.E.

Territory gained and lost, with dates held

Parthian Empire, ca. 200 C.E.

Major battle

ATLANTIC OCEAN

North Sea

Baltic Sea

CALEDONIA
(85–105 C.E.)
Hadrian's Wall
122 C.E.
Eburacum
(York)
BRITAIN
Camulodunum
(Colchester)
Londinium
(London)

GERMANIA
LOWER
GERMANY (4–9 C.E.)
Colonia Claudia Agrippinensis
(Cologne)
UPPER GERMANY
Moguntiacum
(Mainz)
BELGICA
GAUL
Lutetia Parisiorum
(Paris)
LUGDUNENSIS
AQUITANIA
Lugdunum
(Lyons)
NARBONENSIS
Nemausus
(Nîmes)
Narbo
Burdigala
(Bordeaux)
TARRACONENSIS
Tarraco
SPAIN
LUSITANIA
Emerita Augusta
(Mérida)
Corduba
(Córdoba)
BAETICA

Elbe R.
Rhine R.
Vistula R.
Danube R.
Don R.
Dnieper R.
Volga R.

Vindobona
(Vienna)
NORICUM
RAETIA
ALPS
Mediolanum
(Milan)
CISALPINE
GAUL
Po R.
Massilia
(Marseilles)
Rhône R.
Corsica
Sardinia
Balearic Is.
Ebro R.

Aquincum
(Budapest)
PANNONIA
Singidunum
(Belgrade)
DALMATIA
DACIA
(107–272 C.E.)
MOESIA
Adriatic Sea
Arretium
ITALY
Rome
Ostia
Pompeii
Mt. Vesuvius
Brundisium
MACEDONIA
Thessalonica
EPIRUS
Actium
31 B.C.E.
ACHAEA
Corinth
Athens
Sicily
Syracuse
Malta
Leptis Magna
Carthage
NUMIDIA
MAURETANIA
NORTH AFRICA
AFRICA PROCONSULARIS
SAHARA

Caspian Sea

BOSPORAN KINGDOM
Black Sea
THRACE
Byzantium
BITHYNIA AND PONTUS
CAPPADOCIA
GALATIA
ASIA ANATOLIA
Pergamum
Ephesus
PAMPHYLIA
LYCIA
CILICIA
Tarsus
Rhodes
Crete
Cyprus
Cyrene
CYRENAICA
Mediterranean Sea
Alexandria
EGYPT
Bahriya
Oasis
Nile R.
Red Sea

PARTHIA
Nisa
Ecbatana
Susa
Persepolis
Persian Gulf
CAUCASUS MTS.
ARMENIA
(114–117 C.E.)
ASSYRIA
(116–117 C.E.)
MESOPOTAMIA
(115–117 C.E.)
Tigris R.
Euphrates R.
Ctesiphon
Seleucia
Babylon
Palmyra
SYRIA
Antioch
Damascus
Jerusalem
JUDAEA
Petra
ARABIA
ARABIAN DESERT

Aral Sea

N

0   200   400 Km.
0   200   400 Mi.

The Life and Teachings of Jesus

Into this climate of Messianic hope and Roman religious yearning came Jesus of Nazareth (ca. 3 B.C.E.–29 C.E.). He was raised in Galilee, stronghold of the Zealots. The principal evidence for his life and deeds are the four Gospels of the New Testament. These Gospels—their name means "good news"—are records of his teachings and religious doctrines with certain details of his life. They are neither biographies of Jesus nor histories of his life. The earliest Gospels were written some seventy-five years after his death, and there are discrepancies among the four accounts. These differences indicate that early Christians had a diversity of beliefs about Jesus' nature and purpose. Only slowly, as the Christian church became an institution, were lines drawn more clearly between what was considered correct teaching and what was considered incorrect, or **heresy.**

Despite this diversity, there were certain things about Jesus' teachings that almost all the sources agree on: Jesus preached of a heavenly kingdom, one of eternal happiness in a life after death. His teachings were essentially Jewish. His orthodoxy enabled him to preach in the synagogue and the temple. His major deviation from orthodoxy was his insistence that he taught in his own name, not in the name of Yahweh. Was he then the Messiah? A small band of followers thought so, and Jesus claimed that he was. Yet Jesus had his own conception of the Messiah. He would establish a spiritual kingdom, not an earthly one.

● **Pontius Pilate and Jesus** This Byzantine mosaic from Ravenna illustrates a dramatic moment in Jesus' trial and crucifixion. Jesus stands accused before Pilate, but Pilate symbolically washes his hands of the whole affair. *(Scala/Art Resource, NY)*

heresy *A non-orthodox religious practice or belief.*

The prefect Pontius Pilate knew little about Jesus' teachings. He was concerned with maintaining peace and order. The crowds following Jesus at the time of Passover, a highly emotional time in the Jewish year, alarmed Pilate, who faced a volatile situation. Some Jews believed that Jesus was the long-awaited Messiah. Others hated and feared Jesus because they thought him religiously dangerous. To avert riot and bloodshed, Pilate condemned Jesus to death, and his soldiers carried out the sentence. On the third day after Jesus' crucifixion, some of his followers claimed that he had risen from the dead. For the earliest Christians and for generations to come, the resurrection of Jesus became a central element of faith: he had triumphed over death, and his resurrection promised all Christians immortality.

The Spread of Christianity

The memory of Jesus and his teachings survived and flourished. Believers in his divinity met in small assemblies or congregations, often in one another's homes, to discuss the meaning of Jesus' message. These earliest Christians defined their faith to fit the life of Jesus into an orthodox Jewish context. Only later did these congregations evolve into what can be called a church with a formal organization and set of beliefs.

The catalyst in the spread of Jesus' teachings and the formation of the Christian church was Paul of Tarsus, a Hellenized Jew who was comfortable in both the Roman and Jewish worlds. He had begun by persecuting the new sect, but on the road to Damascus he was converted to belief in Jesus. He was the single most important figure responsible for changing Christianity from a Jewish sect into a separate religion. He urged the Jews to include Gentiles, non-Jews, in the faith. His was the first universal message of Christianity.

Many early Christian converts were Gentile women, especially from the wealthier classes, and women were active in spreading Christianity. Paul greeted male and female converts by name in his letters and noted that women often provided financial support for his activities. Missionaries and others spreading the Christian message worked through families and friendship networks. The growing Christian communities differed in their ideas about the proper gender order; some favored giving women a larger role in church affairs, while others were more restrictive.

Christianity might have remained just another local sect had it not reached Rome, the capital of a far-flung empire. Rome proved to be a dramatic feature in the spread of Christianity for different reasons. First, Jesus had told his followers to spread his word throughout the world, thus making his teachings universal. The pagan Romans also considered their secular empire universal, and the early Christians combined the two concepts of **universalism**. Secular Rome provided another advantage to Christianity. If all roads led to Rome, they also led outward to the provinces. The very stability and extent of the Roman Empire enabled early Christians easily to spread their faith throughout the known world.

universalism *The belief that all human beings will ultimately be reconciled to God and achieve salvation.*

● **The Catacombs of Rome** The early Christians used underground crypts and rock chambers to bury their dead. The bodies were placed in these galleries and then sealed up. The catacombs became places of pilgrimage, and in this way the dead continued to be united with the living. *(Catacombe di Priscilla, Rome/Scala/Art Resource, NY)*

The Appeal of Christianity

Christianity offered its adherents the promise of salvation. Christians believed that Jesus had defeated evil and that he would reward his followers with eternal life after death. Christianity also offered the possibility of forgiveness. Human nature was weak, and even the best Christians would fall into sin. But Jesus loved sinners and forgave those who repented. Christianity was also attractive to many because it gave the Roman world a cause. Instead of passivity, Christians stressed the ideal of striving for a goal. By spreading the word of Christ, Christians played their part in God's plan for the triumph of Christianity on earth. They were not discouraged by temporary setbacks, believing Christianity to be invincible. Christianity likewise gave its devotees a sense of community. Believers met regularly to celebrate the **eucharist,** the Lord's Supper. Each individual community was in turn a member of a greater community. And that community, according to Christian Scripture, was indestructible, for Jesus had promised that "the gates of hell shall not prevail against it."[2]

eucharist *A Christian sacrament in which the death of Christ is communally remembered through a meal of bread and wine.*

THE "GOLDEN AGE"

How did efficient Roman rule lead to a "golden age" for the empire?

Augustus's success in creating solid political institutions was tested by the dynasty he created, but later in the first century Rome entered a period of political stability. This era later became known as the "golden age," a time of growing cities and economic well-being.

Politics in the Empire

For fifty years after Augustus's death the dynasty that he established—known as the Julio-Claudians because they were all members of the Julian and Claudian clans—provided the emperors of Rome. Some of the Julio-Claudians, such as Tiberius and Claudius, were sound rulers and able administrators. Others, including Caligula and Nero, were weak and frivolous men. Nonetheless, the Julio-Claudians for the most part gave the empire peace and prosperity.

In 68 C.E. Nero's inept rule led to military rebellion and widespread disruption. Yet only two years later Vespasian (9–79 C.E.), who established the Flavian dynasty, restored order. He also turned Augustus's principate into a monarchy. The Flavians (69–96 C.E.) repaired the damage of civil war to give the Roman world peace, and paved the way for the **five good emperors,** the golden age of the empire (96–180 C.E.). The era of the five good emperors was a period of almost unparalleled prosperity for the empire (see the feature "Individuals in Society: Plutarch of Chaeronea"). Wars generally ended victoriously and were confined to the frontiers. The five good emperors—Nerva, Trajan, Hadrian, Antoninus Pius, and Marcus Aurelius—were among the most dedicated and ablest men in Roman history.

five good emperors *Five consecutive Roman emperors (Nerva, Trajan, Hadrian, Antoninus Pius, and Marcus Aurelius) distinguished by their benevolence and moderation.*

In addition to the full-blown monarchy of the Flavians, other significant changes had occurred in Roman government since Augustus's day. Claudius had created an imperial bureaucracy, which Hadrian, who became emperor in 117 C.E., put on an organized, official basis. He established imperial administrative departments and separated civil from military service. His bureaucracy demanded professionalism from its members. These innovations made for more efficient running of the empire while increasing the authority of the emperor, who was now the ruling power of the bureaucracy.

In these years the Roman army changed from a mobile unit to a defensive force. The frontiers became firmly fixed and defended by a system of forts. Behind them

● **Canopus, Hadrian's Villa**   This view of Hadrian's villa embodies sublime and serene beauty. The columns and statues lend dignity, and the pond suggests rest. In the background a spacious house offers a retreat from the cares of imperial duties. *(Mark Edward Smith/ TIPS Images)*

roads were increased and improved both to supply the forts and to reinforce them in times of trouble. The army had evolved into a garrison force, with legions guarding specific areas for long periods.

Life in the Golden Age

This era of peace gave the empire unparalleled prosperity both in Rome and in the provinces. Rome was truly an extraordinary city. It was enormous, with a population somewhere between 500,000 and 750,000. Although it could boast of stately palaces, noble buildings, and beautiful residential areas, most people lived in jerrybuilt houses. Fire and crime were perennial problems even in Augustus's day. Sanitation was a serious problem. Under the five emperors, urban planning and new construction greatly improved the situation. By comparison with later European cities, Rome became a very attractive place to live.

Rome grew so large that it became ever more difficult to feed. The emperor solved the problem by providing citizens with free bread, oil, and wine. By doing so, he also kept their favor. He likewise entertained the people with gladiatorial contests and chariot races. Many gladiators were criminals, some the slaves of gladiatorial schools, others prisoners of war. A few free people, men and women, volunteered for the arena. The Romans actually preferred chariot racing to gladiatorial contests. Two-horse and four-horse chariots ran a course of seven laps, about five miles. Four permanent teams, each with its own color, competed against each other.

In the province and on the frontiers, the era of the five good emperors was one of extensive prosperity. Peace and security opened Britain, Gaul, Germany, and the lands of the Danube to immigration (see Map 5.4). Agriculture flourished in the hands of free tenant farmers. The holders of small parcels of land thrived as never before. Consequently, the small tenant farmer became the backbone of Roman agriculture.

In continental Europe the army was largely responsible for the new burst of expansion. The areas where legions were stationed became Romanized. Upon retirement, legionaries often settled where they had served. Having learned a trade in the army, they brought essential skills to areas that badly needed trained men. These veterans used their retirement pay to set themselves up in business.

Plutarch of Chaeronea

This Renaissance popularization of Plutarch depicts one of the favorite writers of that time period and today. *(Courtesy, Antiquity Project/Visual Connection Archive)*

During the era of the five good emperors (96–180 C.E.) people throughout the Roman Empire enjoyed nearly unparalleled peace and prosperity. The five good emperors encouraged Romans and non-Romans alike to embrace concepts and ideas beyond narrow, local boundaries. Plutarch (ca. 50–ca. 120 C.E.) provides an excellent example of this attitude and policy. Born in the small but lovely city of Chaeronea in Greece, he came from a prominent family, but one with only local prestige. He received a typical education in writing, literature, and mathematics. His exploration of the countryside in his spare hours inspired an interest in history. As a youth and later in his life he especially sought out small temples and abandoned battlefields.

When Plutarch reached young manhood, his family sent him to Athens, no longer a mighty military power but instead a center of philosophy and rhetoric. In Athens he polished his innate talents and took advantage of the opportunity to learn about and enjoy the cultural treasures of the city, all the while becoming acquainted with many wealthy and influential young men from elsewhere in the Roman Empire. In the era of the five good emperors, prominent Romans often sent their sons to Athens, not simply to learn but also to become culturally refined. These young men befriended Plutarch and widened his social horizon.

When Plutarch finished his studies, he began a tour of the Roman Empire beyond Athens. With enthusiasm he traveled abroad, forged new friendships, and became acquainted with new-to-him regions and their history. He also avidly read books previously unavailable to him.

Plutarch journeyed to the Peloponnesus, Asia Minor, Crete, and northern Egypt. All along the way he took notes describing what he saw and learned. Like tourists everywhere, he saw the sights; and from his articulate and well-educated friends he encountered information and lore not readily found elsewhere.

At Rome, the political and social center of the empire, Plutarch met leading figures and made many useful social connections. He learned enough Latin to read literary works but never became fluent enough to speak it easily. Consequently he gave public lectures in Greek, which his educated audiences had no difficulty understanding. His good nature opened many doors, and he took advantage of every opportunity to examine official records and other documents to gain information about the early years of the Roman republic and the first Roman emperors. His personal popularity afforded him an intimate glimpse of life among the Roman elite.

Plutarch returned to Chaeronea where he spent his days writing many influential and compelling biographies of eminent Greeks and Romans, including Themistocles, Pericles, Caesar, and Antony. Both a biographer and a literary artist, he used the careers of his subjects to explore their characters. He made these historical figures human beings. He had also mastered philosophy and wrote extensively on Plato and his teachings. His writings included treatises on moral philosophy as a guide to everyday life. Plutarch was the ideal type of the refined and learned man of his day, a genteel product of Greco-Roman culture. Very popular in his own day, his works hugely influenced the Renaissance and remain popular today.

In the tranquil surroundings of Chaeronea he spent his life. Even now, people visiting the museum at Delphi can see the inscription with which his fellow citizens honored him. Though remaining a lifelong citizen of Chaeronea, Plutarch also symbolizes the urbanity of the Roman Empire in the era of the five good emperors.

Questions for Analysis

1. What factors helped to propel Plutarch to prominence?

2. What does Plutarch's career indicate about social mobility in the Roman world?

3. Since Plutarch wrote biographies of both Greeks and Romans, does that indicate that he saw a basic unity in classical civilization?

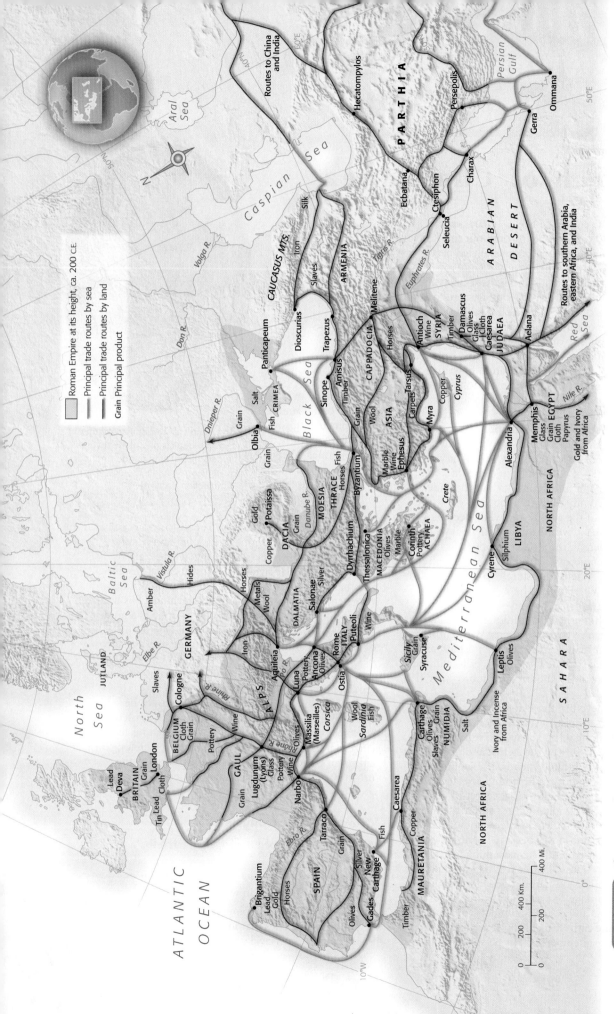

MAP 5.4 The Economic Aspect of the Pax Romana The Roman Empire was not merely a political and military organization but also an intricate economic network through which goods from Armenia and Syria were traded for Western products from as far away as Spain and Britain.

Roman Empire at its height, ca. 200 C.E.

Principal trade routes by sea

Principal trade routes by land

Grain Principal product

ATLANTIC OCEAN

North Sea

Baltic Sea

JUTLAND

Aral Sea

Caspian Sea

Black Sea

Mediterranean Sea

Persian Gulf

Red Sea

PARTHIA

ARMENIA

CAUCASUS MTS.

ARABIAN DESERT

SAHARA

NORTH AFRICA

LIBYA

EGYPT

SYRIA

JUDAEA

CAPPADOCIA

ASIA

THRACE

MOESIA

DACIA

MACEDONIA

ACHAEA

DALMATIA

ITALY

GERMANY

GAUL

BELGIUM

BRITAIN

SPAIN

MAURETANIA

NUMIDIA

CRIMEA

Crete

Cyprus

Corsica

Sardinia

Sicily

ALPS

Routes to China and India

Routes to southern Arabia, eastern Africa, and India

Hecatompylos

Persepolis

Ecbatana

Ctesiphon

Seleucia

Charax

Gerra

Ommana

Damascus

Antioch

Caesarea

Aelana

Alexandria

Memphis

Cyrene

Leptis

Carthage

Caesarea

New Carthage

Gades

Tarraco

Brigantium

Narbo

Massilia (Marseilles)

Lugdunum (Lyons)

Cologne

London

Deva

Rome

Ostia

Puteoli

Ancona

Luna

Aquileia

Salonae

Dyrrhachium

Thessalonica

Corinth

Byzantium

Ephesus

Myra

Tarsus

Melitene

Amisus

Sinope

Trapezus

Dioscurias

Panticapeum

Olbia

Potaissa

Syracuse

Silphium

Atlantic OCEAN

Rhine R.

Rhône R.

Po R.

Ebro R.

Danube R.

Elbe R.

Vistula R.

Don R.

Dnieper R.

Volga R.

Euphrates R.

Tigris R.

Nile R.

Tin Lead

Lead

Grain Cloth

Cloth Grain

Pottery

Wine

Glass Pottery

Grain

Olives

Silver

Horses

Gold

Lead

Olives

Timber

Copper

Fish

Grain

Silver

Olives

Slaves Grain

Olives Grain

Salt

Ivory and Incense from Africa

Gold and Ivory from Africa

Grain Glass Cloth Papyrus

Wine Olives Glass Cloth

Timber

Copper

Carpets

Wool

Grain

Fish

Horses

Marble Wine

Pottery Marble

Olives

Silver

Gold Copper

Grain

Fish

Salt

Iron

Slaves

Horses

Metals Wool

Hides

Amber

Slaves

Iron

Silk

Slaves

Wine

Horses

Wool Fish

Wine Pottery Olives

Wine

Grain

Grain Pottery

The Roman Provinces

The eastern part of the empire shared in the boom in part by trading with other areas and in part because of local industries. The cities of the east built extensively, beautifying themselves with new amphitheaters, temples, and other public buildings. Especially in the eastern empire this was the heyday of the city.

Trade among the provinces increased dramatically. Britain and Belgium became prime grain producers, much of their harvests going to the armies of the Rhine. Britain's wool industry probably got its start under the Romans. Italy and southern Gaul produced wine in huge quantities. Roman colonists introduced the olive to southern Spain and northern Africa, which soon produced most of the oil consumed in the western empire. In the east the oil production of Syrian farmers reached an all-time high. Egypt produced tons of wheat that fed the Roman populace. The Roman army in Mesopotamia consumed a high percentage of the raw materials and manufactured products of Syria and Asia Minor. During the time of the five good emperors the empire had become an economic as well as a political reality (see Map 5.4).

The growth of industry in the provinces was a striking feature of this period. Cities in Gaul and Germany eclipsed the old Mediterranean manufacturing centers. In the second century C.E. Gaul and Germany took over the pottery market. Lyons in Gaul and later Cologne in Germany became the new centers of the glassmaking industry. The cities of Gaul were nearly unrivaled in the manufacture of bronze and brass. Europe and western Asia had entered fully into a united economic, political, and cultural world.

● **Gladiatorial Games** Though hardly games, the contests were vastly popular among the Romans. Gladiators were usually slaves, but successful ones could gain their freedom. The fighting was hard but fair, and the gladiators shown here look equally matched. *(Interfoto Pressebildagentur/Alamy)*

Eastward Expansion

Their expansion took the Romans into Central Asia, which had two immediate effects. The first was a long military confrontation between the Romans and their Iranian neighbors. Second, Roman military movement eastward coincided with Chinese expansion to the west, resulting in a period when the major ancient civilizations of the world came into contact with each other (see page 144).

When their expansion took the Romans farther eastward, they encountered the Parthians, who had established a kingdom in Iran in the Hellenistic period (see page 89). The Romans tried unsuccessfully to drive the Parthians out of Armenia and Mesopotamia until the Parthians fell to the Sasanids, a people indigenous to southern Iran, in 226 C.E. When the Romans continued their attacks against this new enemy, the Sasanid king Shapur defeated the Roman legions of the emperor Valerius, whom he took prisoner. Not until the reign of Diocletian and Constantine was Roman rule again firmly established in western Asia.

Although warfare disrupted parts of Asia, it did not stop trade that had prospered from Hellenistic times (see pages 91–93). Rarely did a merchant travel the entire distance from China to Mesopotamia. Protecting their own profits, the Parthians acted as middlemen to prevent the Chinese and Romans from making direct contact. Chinese merchants sold their wares to the Parthians at the Stone Tower, located in modern Tashkughan in Afghanistan. The Parthians then carried the goods overland to Mesopotamia or Egypt, where they were shipped throughout the Roman Empire. Silk was still a major commodity from east to west, along with other luxury goods. In return the Romans traded glassware, precious gems, and slaves. The Parthians added exotic fruits, rare birds, and other products desired by the Chinese (see the feature "Global Trade: Pottery" on pages 124–125).

Contacts Between Rome and China

This was also an era of exciting maritime exploration. Roman ships sailed from Egyptian ports to the mouth of the Indus River, where they traded local merchandise and wares imported by the Parthians. Merchants who made the voyage contended with wind, shoal waters, and pirates. Despite such dangers and discomforts, hardy mariners pushed into the Indian Ocean and beyond, reaching Malaya, Sumatra, and Java, when they traded with equally hardy local sailors.

Maritime trade between Chinese and Roman ports began in the second century C.E., though no merchant traveled the entire distance. The period of this contact coincided with the era of Han greatness in China (see pages 135–144). The Han emperor Wu Ti encouraged trade by land as well as sea, and Chinese merchants traded in the Parthian Empire along what came to be known as the "Great Silk Road." Indeed, a later Han emperor sent an ambassador directly to the Roman Empire by sea. The ambassador, Kan Ying, sailed to the Roman province of Syria during the reign of the emperor Nerva (96–98 C.E.), the first Chinese official to see for himself the Greco-Roman world. Although he left a fascinating report of his travels to his emperor, the Romans paid no attention to the contact. For the Romans China remained more of a mythical than a real place, and they never bothered to learn more about it.

TURMOIL AND REFORM (284–337 C.E.)

How did barbarian invasions and political turmoil shape the Roman Empire in the third and fourth centuries?

The era of the five good emperors gave way to a period of chaos and stress. During the third century C.E. the Roman Empire was stunned by civil war and barbarian invasions. By the time peace was restored, the economy was shattered, cities had shrunk in size, and agriculture was becoming manorial. In the disruption of the third century and the reconstruction of the fourth, the transition from the classical to the medieval world began.

Reconstruction Under Diocletian and Constantine

At the close of the third century C.E. the emperor Diocletian (r. 284–305 C.E.) ended the period of chaos. Repairing the damage done in the third century was the major work of the emperor Constantine (r. 306–337 C.E.) in the fourth. But if the price was high, so was the prize.

Under Diocletian the princeps became *dominus,* "lord." The emperor claimed that he was "the elect of god," that he ruled because of divine favor. To underline the emperor's exalted position, Diocletian and Constantine adopted the court ceremonies and trappings of the Persian Empire.

Diocletian recognized that the empire had become too great for one man to handle and so divided it into a western and an eastern half (see Map 5.5). Diocletian assumed direct control of the eastern part, while giving the rule of the western part to a colleague along with the title *augustus,* which had become synonymous with emperor. Diocletian and his fellow augustus further delegated power by appointing two men to assist them. Each man was given the title of *caesar* to indicate his exalted rank. Although this system is known as the *Tetrarchy* because four men ruled the empire, Diocletian was clearly the senior partner and final source of authority.

MAP 5.5 **The Roman World Divided** Under Diocletian, the Roman Empire was first divided into a western and an eastern half, a development that foreshadowed the medieval division between the Latin West and the Byzantine East.

Diocletian's political reforms were a momentous step. The Tetrarchy soon failed, but Diocletian's division of the empire into two parts became permanent. Throughout the fourth century C.E. the eastern and western sections drifted apart. In later centuries the western part witnessed the decline of Roman government and the rise of barbarian kingdoms, while the eastern half evolved into the Byzantine Empire.

Economic Hardship and Consequences

Major economic, social, and religious problems also confronted Diocletian and Constantine. They needed additional revenues to support the army and the imperial court. Yet the wars and invasions had struck a serious blow to Roman agriculture. Christianity had become too strong either to ignore or to crush. The way Diocletian, Constantine, and their successors responded to these problems left a permanent impression on future developments.

The empire itself was less capable of recovery than in earlier times. Wars and invasions had disrupted normal commerce and the means of production. Mines were exhausted in the attempt to supply much-needed ores, especially gold and silver. In the

POTTERY

Today we often consider pottery in utilitarian and decorative terms, but it served a surprisingly large number of purposes in the ancient world. Families used earthen pottery for cooking and tableware, for storing grains and liquids, and for lamps. On a larger scale pottery was used for the transportation and protection of goods traded overseas.

The creation of pottery dates back to the Neolithic period. Pottery required few resources to make, as potters needed only abundant sources of good clay and wheels upon which to throw their vessels. Once made, the pots were baked in specially constructed kilns. Although the whole process was relatively simple, skilled potters formed groups that made utensils for entire communities. Later innovations occurred when the artisans learned to glaze their pots by applying a varnish before baking them in a kiln.

The earliest potters focused on coarse ware: plain plates, cups, and cooking pots that remained virtually unchanged throughout antiquity. Increasingly, however, potters began to decorate these pieces with simple designs. In this way pottery became both functional and decorative. One of the most popular pieces was the amphora, a large two-handled jar with a wide mouth, a round belly, and a base. It became the workhorse of maritime shipping because it protected contents from water and rodents, was easy and cheap to produce, and could be reused. Amphoras contained goods as different as wine and oil, spices and unguents, dried fish and

The Pottery Trade

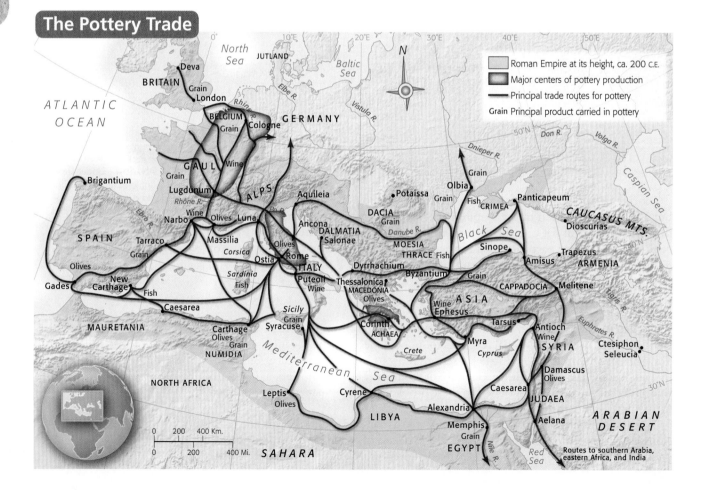

The Greeks captured Troy by concealing themselves in a wooden horse, which the Trojans pulled into the city. On this piece from a pot found in Mykonos, probably dating to the seventh century B.C.E., Greeks have just launched their attack from inside the horse. (Archaeological Receipts Fund, Athens)

pitch. The amphora's dependability and versatility kept it in use from the fourth century B.C.E. to the beginning of the Middle Ages.

In classical Greece individual potters sold their wares directly to local customers or traders; manufacturer and buyer alone determined the quantity of goods for sale and their price. In the Hellenistic and Roman periods amphoras became common throughout the Mediterranean and carried goods eastward to the Black Sea, Persian Gulf, and Red Sea. The Ptolemies of Egypt sent amphoras and their contents even farther, to Arabia, eastern Africa, and India. Thus merchants and mariners who had never seen the Mediterranean depended on these containers.

Other pots proved as useful as the amphora, and all became a medium of decorative art. By the eighth century B.C.E. Greek potters and artists began to decorate their wares by painting them with patterns and scenes from mythology, legend, and daily life. They portrayed episodes such as the chariot race at Patroclus's funeral or battles from the *Iliad*. Some portrayed the gods, such as Dionysos at sea. These images widely spread knowledge of Greek religion and culture. In the West, especially the Etruscans in Italy and the Carthaginians in North Africa eagerly welcomed the pots, their decora-

tion, and their ideas. The Hellenistic kings shipped these pots as far east as China. Pottery thus served as a cultural exchange among people scattered across huge portions of the globe.

The Romans took the manufacture of pottery to an advanced stage by introducing a wider range of vessels for new purposes. The Roman ceramic trade spread from Italy throughout the Mediterranean. The Roman army provides the best example of how this ordinary industry affected the broader culture. Especially on the European frontiers the army used its soldiers to produce the pottery it needed. These soldiers made their own Italian *terra sigallata,* which was noted for its smooth red glaze. Native potters immediately copied this style, thus giving rise to local industries. Indeed, terra sigallata remained the dominant pottery style in northern Europe until the seventh century C.E. When Roman soldiers retired, they often settled where they had served, especially if they could continue their trades. Such ordinary Romans added local ideas to their craft. This exchange resulted in a culture that was becoming European, rather than just Roman, and extended into Britain, France, the Low Countries, and southern Germany.

cities markets, trade, and industry were disrupted, and travel became dangerous. The devastation of the countryside increased the difficulty of feeding and supplying the cities. Merchant and artisan families rapidly left devastated regions. Economic hardship had been met by cutting the silver content of coins until money was virtually worthless. The immediate result was crippling inflation throughout the empire.

Diocletian's attempt to curb inflation illustrates the methods of absolute monarchy. In a move unprecedented in Roman history, Diocletian issued an edict that fixed maximum prices and wages throughout the empire. The emperors dealt with the tax system just as strictly and inflexibly. Taxes became payable in kind, that is, in goods and services instead of money. All those involved in the growing, preparation, and transportation of food and other essentials were locked into their professions. A baker or shipper could not go into any other business, and his son took up the trade at his death. In this period of severe depression, many localities could not pay their taxes. In such cases local tax collectors, who were themselves locked into service, had to make up the difference from their own funds. This system soon wiped out a whole class of moderately wealthy people.

Because of worsening conditions during the third century C.E., many free tenant farmers and their families were killed, fled the land to escape the barbarians or brigands, or abandoned farms ravaged in the fighting. Large tracts of land consequently lay deserted. Great landlords with ample resources began at once to reclaim as much of this land as they could. The huge estates that resulted, called villas, were self-sufficient. Since they produced more than they consumed, they successfully competed with the declining cities by selling their surplus in the countryside. They became islands of stability in an unsettled world.

The rural residents who remained on the land were exposed to the raids of barbarians and brigands and to the tyranny of imperial officials. In return for the protection and security landlords could offer, the small landholders gave over their lands and their freedom. They could no longer decide to move elsewhere. Henceforth, they and their families worked their patrons' land, not their own. Free people were becoming what would later be called serfs.

The Acceptance of Christianity

The Roman attitude toward Christianity evolved as well during this period of empire. At first many pagans genuinely misunderstood Christian practices and rites. They thought that such secret rites as the Lord's Supper, at which Christians said that they ate and drank the body and blood of Jesus, were acts of cannibalism. Pagans thought that Christianity was one of the worst of the mystery cults with immoral and indecent rituals. They also feared that the gods would withdraw their favor from the Roman Empire because of the Christian insistence that the pagan gods either did not exist or were evil spirits.

The Christians also exaggerated the degree of pagan hostility to them, and most of the gory stories about the martyrs are fictitious. There were indeed some cases of pagan persecution of the Christians, but with few exceptions they were local and sporadic in nature. Even Nero's notorious persecution was temporary and limited to Rome. No constant persecution of Christians occurred. As time went on, pagan hostility and suspicion decreased. Pagans realized that Christians were not working to overthrow the state and that Jesus was no rival of Caesar. The emperor Trajan forbade his governors to hunt down Christians. Though admitting that he considered Christianity an abomination, he preferred to leave Christians in peace.

The stress of the third century C.E., however, seemed to some emperors the punishment of the gods. Although the Christians depicted Diocletian as a fiend, he persecuted them in the hope that the gods would restore their blessing on Rome. Yet even his persecutions were never very widespread or long-lived. By the late third century C.E. pagans had become used to Christianity, and Constantine recognized Christianity as a legitimate religion. He himself died a Christian in 337 C.E. In time the Christian triumph would be complete. In 380 C.E. the emperor Theodosius made Christianity the official religion of the Roman Empire. At that point Christians began to persecute the pagans for their religion. History had come full circle.

The Construction of Constantinople

The triumph of Christianity was not the only event that made Constantine's reign a turning point in Roman history. Constantine took the bold step of building a new capital for the empire. Constantinople, the New Rome, was constructed on the site of Byzantium, the old Greek city on the Bosporus. Throughout the third century C.E. emperors had found Rome and western Europe hard to defend. The eastern part of the empire was more easily defensible and so escaped the worst of the barbarian devastation. It was wealthy and its urban life still vibrant. Moreover, Christianity was more widespread in the east than in the west, and the city of Constantinople was intended to be a Christian center.

● **Arch of Constantine** Though standing in stately surroundings, Constantine's arch in Rome is decorated with art plundered from the arches of Trajan and Marcus Aurelius. He robbed them rather than decorate his own with the inferior work of his own day. *(Michael Reed, photographer/www.mike-reed.com)*

From the Classical World to Late Antiquity

Although Constantine had restored order, he could not undo the past. Too much had changed forever. The two-faced Roman god Janus, who looked both ways, in this case looked both to the past and the future and well symbolizes this period. A great deal of the past remained through these years of change. People still lived under the authority of the emperors and the guidance of Roman law. They still communicated with one another as usual, in Latin throughout the west and Greek in the east. Grecoroman art, architecture, and literature surrounded them as part of daily life.

Yet changes were also underway. Government had evolved from the pagan republic of the past to the Christian monarchy of the new age. The empire itself was split into east and west. The east remained the world of urbanism and empire, while the west became the home of independent barbarian kingdoms built on classical foundations.

Paganism faded into the background as Christianity prevailed. Greek philosophy was replaced by Christian theology, as thinkers tried earnestly to understand Jesus' message. Through all these changes the lives of ordinary people did not change dramatically. They farmed, worked in cities, and nurtured their families. They took new ideas, blended them with the old, and created new cultural forms. The classical world gradually gave way to a new intellectual, spiritual, and political life that forever changed the face of western Eurasia.

Chapter Summary

To assess your mastery of this chapter and read the primary sources listed in the margins, visit bedfordstmartins.com/mckayworld or see *Sources of World Societies*.

Key Terms

toga
Forum
franchise
patricians
plebeians
praetors
Struggle of the Orders
paterfamilias
manumission
latifundia
First Triumvirate
pax Romana
princeps civitatis
pagan
heresy
universalism
eucharist
five good emperors

• *How did the Romans come to dominate Italy, and what political institutions did they create?*

The Etruscans and Romans both settled in Italy and the Etruscans developed the first cities and a rich cultural life. Ruling as kings, the Etruscans introduced Romans to urbanism, industry, trade, and the alphabet. The Romans fought numerous wars with the Etruscans, and in 509 B.C.E. the Romans won their independence and created the republic. The republic functioned through a shared government of the people directed by the senate, summarized by the expression SPQR—*senatus populusque Romanus,* the Roman senate and people. In resolving a social conflict known as the "Struggle of the Orders," Roman nobles and ordinary people created a state administered by magistrates elected from the entire population and a legal code common to all.

• *How did Rome expand its power beyond Italy, and what were the effects of success on Rome?*

Once united, the Romans launched a series of wars that took them from Spain in the west to Pergamum in Asia Minor. Their empire brought wealth, which led to a grand building program and a rich life for very many Romans. Increased power brought political problems, and during the late republic many poor people sought political and social reforms. Ambitious generals fought for power until Julius Caesar restored order. His adopted son Augustus transformed the republic into the empire by creating a constitutional monarchy in which he was the sole executive of the state. He directed the organs of government and the army, while encouraging local government.

• *What was Christianity, and how did it affect life in the empire?*

Christians developed as an offshoot of Judaism, when Jesus of Nazareth proclaimed himself the son of God. He taught that belief in his divinity led to eternal life. His followers spread their belief across the empire, transforming it from a Jewish sect into a new religion.

• *How did efficient Roman rule lead to a "golden age" for the empire?*

Augustus was followed by a series of efficient emperors who created an official bureaucracy to administer the empire. The five good emperors divided civil from military service, and made the army a garrison force to guard the frontiers. During this golden period Rome became the magnificent capital of the empire, increasingly adorned with beautiful buildings and improved urban housing, and harboring a well-fed populace. Rome also became a city of fun, marked by gladiatorial games and chariot racing. This was also a period of thriving agriculture and commercial expansion throughout the empire.

• *How did barbarian invasions and political turmoil shape the Roman Empire in the third and fourth centuries?*

When Rome expanded eastward from Europe, it met opposition, yet even during the fighting, commerce among the Romans, the Iranians, and the Chinese empire thrived through a series of trade routes, the most famous being the Great Silk Road. After the five good emperors, the empire fell prey to civil war and foreign invasion, both of which devastated the land and caused political chaos. Two gifted emperors, Diocletian and Constantine, restored order and then permanently divided the empire into western and eastern halves. Their rigid control of the economy was not successful. Rich landowners reclaimed land and created villas worked by tenants instead of free farmers. Meanwhile, the emperors legalized Christianity. The symbol of change became the new capital of the empire, Constantinople, the New Rome. The classical world gave way to the medieval.

Suggested Reading

Bruun, C., ed. *The Roman Middle Republic, ca. 400–133 B.C.* 2000. Treats the central issues of the period.

Burn, T. S. *Rome and the Barbarians, 100 B.C.–A.D. 400.* 2003. Analyzes the mutual impact of Romans and barbarians.

D'Ambra, E. *Roman Women.* 2007. A comprehensive and learned treatment of all aspects of women's life, private and public.

Esler, P. *The Early Christian World.* 2004. A collection of studies that cover all aspects of the topic.

Goldsworthy, A. *Roman Warfare.* 2000. A concise treatment of warfare from republican to imperial times.

Goodman, M. *The Roman World, 44 B.C.–A.D. 180.* 1997. A solid general treatment of the empire.

Kamm, A. *Julius Caesar.* 2006. An excellent brief biography that deals with all important aspects of his life.

MacMullen, R. *Roman Social Relations, 50 B.C.–A.D. 284.* 1981. Still an excellent discussion of the topic by a leading scholar.

Scullard, H. H. *A History of the Roman World,* 4th ed. 1993. Still the best single account of Roman history.

Turcam, R. *The Gods of Ancient Rome.* 2000. Provides a concise survey of the Roman pantheon.

Notes

1. Sallust, *War with Cataline* 10.1–3, translated by J. Buckler.
2. Matthew 16:18.

Listening to the PAST

Titus Flamininus and the Liberty of the Greeks

After his arrival in Greece in 197 B.C.E., Titus Flamininus defeated the Macedonians in Thessaly. He next sent his recommendations on the terms of the peace agreement to the Roman senate. The following year the senate sent him ten commissioners, who agreed with his ideas. The year 196 B.C.E. was also the occasion when the great Pan-Hellenic Isthmian games were regularly celebrated near Corinth. Many of the dignitaries and the most prominent people of the Hellenistic world were present. Among them was Flamininus, who came neither as a participant in the games nor solely as a spectator of them. Instead, he took the occasion to make a formal announcement about Roman policy. There in Isthmia he officially announced that Rome granted freedom to the Greeks. He assured his audience that Rome had not come as a conqueror. The eminent Greek biographer Plutarch has left a vivid account of the general response to this pronouncement.

Accordingly, at the Isthmian games, where a great throng of people were sitting in the stadium and watching the athletic contests (since, indeed, after many years Greece had at last ceased from wars waged in hopes of freedom, and was now holding festival in time of assured peace), the trumpet signalled a general silence, and the herald, coming forward into the midst of the spectators, made proclamation that the Roman senate and Titus Quinctius Flamininus proconsular general, having conquered King Philip and the Macedonians, restored to freedom, without garrisons and without imposts, and to the enjoyment of their ancient laws, the Corinthians, the Locrians, the Phocians, the Euboeans, the Achaeans of Phthiotis, the Magnesians, the Thessalians, and the Perrhaebians. At first, then, the proclamation was by no means generally or distinctly heard, but there was a confused and tumultuous movement in the stadium of people who wondered what had been said, and asked one another questions about it, and called out to have the proclamation made again; but when silence had been restored, and the herald in tones that were louder

than before and reached the ears of all, had recited the proclamation, a shout of joy arose, so incredibly loud that it reached the sea. The whole audience rose to their feet, and no heed was paid to the contending athletes, but all were eager to spring forward and greet and hail the saviour and champion of Greece.

And that which is often said of the volume and power of the human voice was then apparent to the eye. For ravens which chanced to be flying overhead fell down into the stadium. The cause of this was the rupture of the air; for when the voice is borne aloft loud and strong, the air is rent asunder by it and will not support flying creatures, but lets them fall, as if they were over a vacuum, unless, indeed, they are transfixed by a sort of blow, as of a weapon, and fall down dead. It is possible, too, that in such cases there is a whirling motion of the air, which becomes like a waterspout at sea with a refluent flow of the surges caused by their very volume.

Be that as it may, had not Titus, now that the spectacle was given up, at once foreseen the rush and press of the throng and taken himself away, it would seem that he could hardly have survived the concourse of so many people about him at once and from all sides. But when they were tired of shouting about his tent, and night was already come, then, with greetings and embraces for any friends and fellow citizens whom they saw, they betook themselves to banqueting and carousing with one another. And here, their pleasure naturally increasing, they moved to reason and discourse about Greece, saying that although she had waged many wars for the sake of her freedom, she had not yet obtained a more secure or more delightful exercise of it than now, when others had striven in her behalf, and she herself, almost without a drop of blood or a pang of grief, had borne away the fairest and most enviable of prizes. Verily, they would say, valour and wisdom are rare things among men, but the rarest of all blessings is the just man. For men like Agesilaüs, or Lysander, or Nicias, or Alcibiades could indeed conduct wars well, and understood how to be victorious commanders in battles by land and sea, but they would

This coin provides a contemporary profile of Titus Flamininus, which also illustrates Roman realism in portraiture. (Courtesy of the Trustees of the British Museum)

publicly proclaimed freedom to the Greeks. Then he visited the different cities, establishing among them law and order, abundant justice, concord, and mutual friendliness. He quieted their factions and restored their exiles, and plumed himself on his persuading and reconciling the Greeks more than on his conquest of the Macedonians, so that their freedom presently seemed to them the least of his benefactions. . . .

. . . In the case of Titus and the Romans, . . . gratitude for their benefactions to the Greeks brought them, not merely praises, but also confidence among all men and power, and justly too. For men not only received the officers appointed by them, but actually sent for them and invited them and put themselves in their hands. And this was true not only of peoples and cities, nay, even kings who had been wronged by other kings fled for refuge into the hands of Roman officials, so that in a short time—and perhaps there was also divine guidance in this—everything became subject to them. But Titus himself took most pride in his liberation of Greece.

not use their successes so as to win legitimate favour and promote the right. Indeed, if one excepts the action at Marathon, the sea-fight at Salamis, Plataea, Thermopylae, and the achievements of Cimon at the Eurymedon and about Cyprus, Greece has fought all her battles to bring servitude upon herself, and every one of her trophies stands as a memorial of her own calamity and disgrace, since she owed her overthrow chiefly to the baseness and contentiousness of her leaders. Whereas men of another race, who were thought to have only slight sparks and insignificant traces of a common remote ancestry, from whom it was astonishing that any helpful word or purpose should be vouchsafed to Greece—these men underwent the greatest perils and hardships in order to rescue Greece and set her free from cruel despots and tyrants.

So ran the thoughts of the Greeks; and the acts of Titus were consonant with his proclamations. For at once he sent Lentulus to Asia to set Bargylia free, and Stertinius to Thrace to deliver the cities and islands there from Philip's garrisons. Moreover, Publius Villius sailed to have a conference with Antiochus concerning the freedom of the Greeks who were under his sway. Titus himself also paid a visit to Chalcis, and then sailed from there to Magnesia, removing their garrisons and restoring to the peoples their constitutions. He was also appointed master of ceremonies for the Nemeian games at Argos, where he conducted the festival in the best possible manner, and once more

Questions for Analysis

1. Did Titus Flamininus really want peace for the Greeks, or was this a cynical propaganda gesture?

2. What caused Greek political difficulties in the first place?

3. Was the Greek response to Titus Flamininus's proclamation genuine and realistic?

Source: Reprinted by permission of the publishers and the Trustees of the Loeb Classical Library from *Plutarch: Volume X—Parallel Lives.* Loeb Classical Library Volume L 102, trans. B. Perrin (Cambridge, Mass.: Harvard University Press, 1921). The Loeb Classical Library® is a registered trademark of the President and Fellows of Harvard College.

The Chinese Buddhist Monk Ganjin (688–763 c.e.).
Ganjin was blind by the time he finally reached Japan on
the sixth attempt in 754 and began his missionary work.

(Suzanne Perrin/Japan Interlink)

6
EAST ASIA AND THE SPREAD OF BUDDHISM, 256 B.C.E.–800 C.E.

East Asia was transformed over the millennium from 200 B.C.E. to 800 C.E. In 200 B.C.E. only one of the societies in the region had writing, iron technology, large cities, and complex state organizations. Over the course of the next several centuries, this situation changed dramatically as war, trade, diplomacy, missionary activity, and pursuit of learning brought increased contact among the peoples of the region. Buddhism came to provide a common set of ideas and visual images for the entire area. Chinese was widely used as an international language outside its native area.

Increased communication stimulated state formation in Central Asia, Tibet, Korea, Manchuria, and Japan. The new states usually adopted political models from China. Nevertheless, by 800 each of these regions was well on its way to developing a distinct political and cultural identity. Ancient China is treated in Chapter 3; this is the first chapter to treat Korea and Japan.

THE AGE OF EMPIRE IN CHINA

What were the social, cultural, and political consequences of the unification of China under a strong centralized government?

In much the same period in which Rome created a huge empire, the Qin and Han rulers in China created an empire on a similar scale. Like the Roman Empire, the Chinese empire was put together through force of arms and held in place by sophisticated centralized administrative machinery.

The Qin Unification (221–206 B.C.E.)

In 221 B.C.E., after decades of constant warfare, the state of Qin, the state that had adopted Legalist policies (see pages 70–71), succeeded in defeating the last of its rivals. China was unified for the first time in many centuries. The king of Qin decided that the title

● **Army of the First Emperor** The thousands of life-size ceramic soldiers buried in pits about a half mile from the First Emperor's tomb help us imagine the Qin military machine. It was the Qin emperor's concern with the afterlife that led him to construct such a lifelike guard. The soldiers were originally painted in bright colors, and they held real bronze weapons. (*Robert Harding World Imagery*)

"king" was not grand enough and invented the title "emperor" (*huangdi*). He called himself the First Emperor (Shihuangdi) in anticipation of a long line of successors.

Once Qin ruled all of China, the First Emperor and his shrewd Legalist minister Li Si embarked on a sweeping program of centralization that touched the lives of nearly everyone in China. To cripple the nobility of the defunct states, the First Emperor ordered the nobles to leave their lands and move to the capital. To administer the territory that had been seized, he dispatched officials, then controlled them through a long list of regulations, reporting requirements, and penalties for inadequate performance. These officials owed their power and positions entirely to the favor of the emperor and had no hereditary rights to their offices.

To harness the enormous human resources of his people, the First Emperor ordered a census of the population. Census information helped the imperial bureaucracy to plan its activities—to estimate the costs of public works, the tax revenues needed to pay for them, and the labor force available for military service and building projects. To make it easier to administer all regions uniformly, the script was standardized, along with weights, measures, coinage, even the axle lengths of carts. Private possession of arms was outlawed to make it more difficult for subjects to rebel. To make it easier for Qin armies to move rapidly, thousands of miles of roads were built. Most of the labor on these projects came from farmers performing required corvée labor or convicts working their sentences.

Some twentieth-century Chinese historians glorified the First Emperor as a bold conqueror who let no obstacle stop him, but the traditional evaluation of him was almost entirely negative. For centuries Chinese historians castigated him as a cruel, arbitrary, impetuous, suspicious, and superstitious megalomaniac. Hundreds of thousands of subjects were drafted to build the **Great Wall,** a rammed-earth fortification along the northern border between the Qin realm and the land controlled by the

Great Wall *A rammed-earth fortification built along the northern border of China during the reign of the First Emperor.*

nomadic Xiongnu. After Li Si complained that scholars used records of the past to denigrate the emperor's achievements and undermine popular support, the emperor had all writings other than useful manuals on topics such as agriculture, medicine, and divination collected and burned. As a result of this massive book burning, many ancient texts were lost.

Three times assassins tried to kill the First Emperor, and perhaps as a consequence he became obsessed with discovering the secrets of immortality. He spent lavishly on a tomb designed to protect him in the afterlife. Although the central chambers have not yet been excavated, in nearby pits archaeologists have unearthed thousands of life-size terra-cotta figures of armed soldiers and horses lined up to protect him.

After the First Emperor died in 210 B.C.E., the Qin state unraveled. The Legalist institutions designed to concentrate power in the hands of the ruler made the stability of the government dependent on his strength and character. The First Emperor's heir was murdered by his younger brother, and uprisings soon followed.

The Han Dynasty (206 B.C.E.–220 C.E.)

The eventual victor in the struggle for power that ensued was Liu Bang, known in history as Emperor Gaozu (r. 202–195 B.C.E.). The First Emperor of Qin was from the Zhou aristocracy. Gaozu was, by contrast, from a modest family of commoners, so his elevation to emperor is evidence of how thoroughly the Qin Dynasty had destroyed the old order.

Gaozu did not disband the centralized government created by the Qin, but he did remove its most unpopular features. Harsh laws were canceled, taxes were sharply reduced, and a policy of laissez faire was adopted in an effort to promote economic recovery. With policies of this sort, relative peace, and the extension of China's frontiers, the Chinese population grew rapidly in the first two centuries of the Han Dynasty. The census of 2 C.E. recorded a population of 58 million, the earliest indication of the large size of China's population.

In contrast to the Qin promotion of Legalism, the Han came to promote Confucianism and recruit officials on the basis of their Confucian learning or Confucian moral qualities. Under the most activist of the Han emperors, Emperor Wu, the "Martial Emperor" (r. 141–87 B.C.E.), Confucian scholars were given a privileged position. The Han government's efforts to recruit men trained in the Confucian classics marked the beginning of the Confucian scholar-official system, one of the most distinctive features of imperial China. Chinese officials, imbued with Confucian values, did not comply automatically with the policies of the ruler, above all because they saw criticism of the government as one of their duties. Their willingness to stand up to the ruler also reflected the fact that most of the Confucian scholars selected to serve

Chronology

ca. 230–208 B.C.E.   Construction of Great Wall to protect against Xiongnu

221 B.C.E.   China unified under Qin Dynasty

206 B.C.E.–220 C.E.   Han Dynasty

145–ca. 85 B.C.E.   Sima Qian, Chinese historian

111 B.C.E.   Emperor Wu conquers Nam Viet

108 B.C.E.   Han government establishes colonies in Korea

105 C.E.   Chinese invention of paper

ca. 200 C.E.   Buddhism begins rapid growth in China

220–589 C.E.   Age of Division in China

313–668 C.E.   Three Kingdoms Period in Korea

372 C.E.   Buddhism introduced in Korea

538 C.E.   Buddhism introduced in Japan

581–618 C.E.   Sui Dynasty

604 C.E.   Prince Shōtoku's "Seventeen Principles" in Japan

618–907 C.E.   Tang Dynasty

668 C.E.   Silla unifies Korea

690 C.E.   Empress Wu declares herself emperor, becoming the only Chinese woman emperor

710 C.E.   Japan's capital moved to Nara

735–737 C.E.   Smallpox epidemic in Japan

845 C.E.   Tang emperor begins persecution of Buddhism

as officials came from landholding families, much like those who staffed the Roman government, which gave them some economic independence.

The Han government was supported largely by the taxes and labor service demanded of farmers, but this revenue regularly fell short of the government's needs. To pay for his military campaigns, Emperor Wu took over the minting of coins, confiscated the land of nobles, sold offices and titles, and increased taxes on private businesses. A widespread suspicion of commerce as an unproductive exploitation of the true producers made it easy to levy especially heavy assessments on merchants. The worst blow to businessmen, however, was the government's decision to enter into market competition with them by selling the commodities that had been collected as taxes. In 119 B.C.E. government monopolies were established in the production of iron, salt, and liquor. These enterprises had previously been sources of great profit for private entrepreneurs. Large-scale grain dealing also had been a profitable business, which the government now took over. Grain was to be bought where it was plentiful and its price low and to be either stored in granaries or transported to areas of scarcity. This procedure was supposed to eliminate speculation in grain, provide more constant prices, and bring profit to the government.

Inner Asia and the Silk Road

The difficulty of defending against the nomadic pastoral peoples to the north is a major reason China came to favor a centralized bureaucratic form of government. Resources from the entire subcontinent were needed to maintain control of the northern border.

Beginning long before the Han Dynasty, China's contacts with its northern neighbors had involved both trade and military conflict. China's neighbors sought Chinese products such as silk and lacquer ware. When they did not have goods to trade or when trading relations were disrupted, raiding was considered an acceptable alternative in the tribal cultures of the region. Chinese sources speak of defending against raids of "barbarians" from Shang times (ca. 1500–ca. 1050 B.C.E.) on, but not until the rise of nomadism in the mid-Zhou period (fifth–fourth centuries B.C.E.) did the horsemen of the north become China's main military threat.

The economy of these nomads was based on raising sheep, goats, camels, and horses. Families lived in tents that could be taken down and moved north in summer and south in winter as groups of families moved in search of pasture. Herds were tended on horseback, and everyone learned to ride from a young age. Especially awesome from the Chinese perspective was the ability of nomad horsemen to shoot arrows while riding horseback. The typical social structure of the steppe nomads was fluid, with family and clan units linked through loyalty to tribal chiefs selected for their military prowess. Charismatic tribal leaders could form large coalitions and mobilize the entire society for war.

Chinese farmers and Inner Asian herders had such different modes of life that it is not surprising that they had little respect for each other. For most of the imperial period, Chinese farmers looked on the northern non-Chinese horsemen as gangs of bullies who thought robbing was easier than working for a living. The nomads identified glory with military might and viewed farmers as contemptible weaklings.

● **Xiongnu Metalwork** The metal ornaments of the Xiongnu provide convincing evidence that they were in contact with nomadic pastoralists farther west in Asia, such as the Scythians, who also fashioned metal plaques and buckles in animal designs. This buckle or ornament is made of gold and is about 3 inches tall. (The Metropolitan Museum of Art, Gift of J. Pierpont Morgan, 1917 [17.190.1672]. Photograph © 1981 The Metropolitan Museum of Art)

In the late third century B.C.E. the Xiongnu (known in the West as the Huns) formed the first great confederation of nomadic tribes (see Map 6.1). The Qin's Great Wall was built to defend against them, and the Qin sent out huge armies against them. The early Han emperors tried to make peace with them, offering generous gifts of silk, rice, cash, and even imperial princesses as brides. But these policies were controversial, since critics thought they merely strengthened the enemy. Certainly Xiongnu power did not decline, and in 166 B.C.E. 140,000 Xiongnu raided to within a hundred miles of the Chinese capital.

Emperor Wu decided that China had to push the Xiongnu back. He sent several armies of one hundred thousand to three hundred thousand troops deep into Xiongnu territory. These costly campaigns were of limited value since the Xiongnu were a moving target: fighting nomads was not like attacking walled cities. If the Xiongnu did not want to fight the Chinese troops, they simply moved their camps. To try to find allies and horses, Emperor Wu turned his attention west, toward Central Asia. From the envoy he sent into Bactria, Parthia, and Ferghana in 139 B.C.E., the Chinese learned for the first time of other civilized states comparable to China (see Map 6.1). The envoy described Ferghana as an urban society ten thousand *li* (about three thousand miles) west of China, where grapes were grown for wine and the horses were particularly fine. In Parthia, he was impressed by the use of silver coins stamped with the image of the king's face. These regions, he reported, were familiar with Chinese products, especially silk, and did a brisk trade in them.

MAP 6.1 **The Han Empire** The Han Dynasty asserted sovereignty over vast regions from Korea in the east to Central Asia in the west and Vietnam in the south. Once garrisons were established, traders were quick to follow, leading to considerable spread of Chinese material culture in East Asia. Chinese goods, especially silk, were in demand far beyond East Asia, promoting long-distance trade across Eurasia.

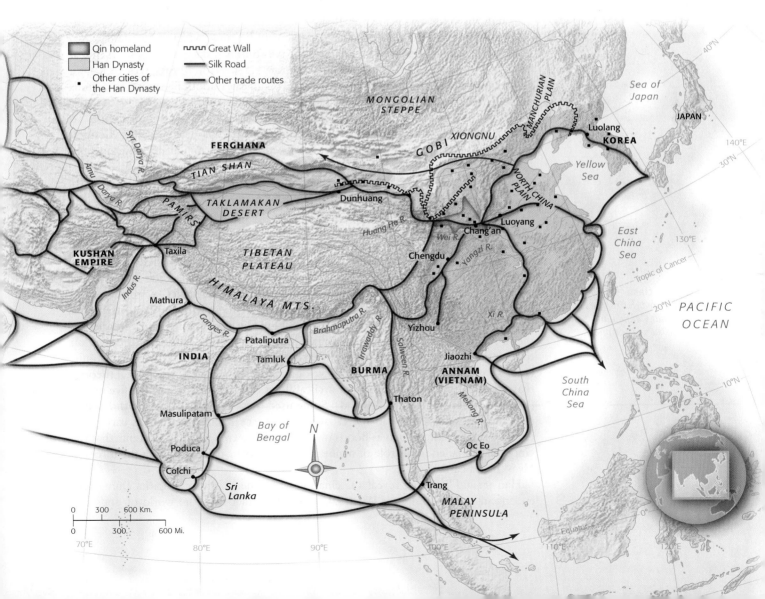

Silk Road *The trade routes across Central Asia through which Chinese silk and other items were traded.*

Emperor Wu sent an army into Ferghana and gained recognition of Chinese over-lordship in the area, thus obtaining control over the trade routes across Central Asia commonly called the **Silk Road.** The city-states along this route did not resist the Chinese presence. They could carry out the trade on which they depended more conveniently with Chinese garrisons to protect them than with rival tribes raiding them.

At the same time, Emperor Wu sent troops into northern Korea to establish military districts that would flank the Xiongnu on their eastern border. By 111 B.C.E. the Han government also had extended its rule south into what is now northern Vietnam. Thus during Emperor Wu's reign, the territorial reach of the Han state was vastly extended.

tributary system *A system used by China to regulate contact with foreign powers. States and tribes beyond its borders sent envoys bearing gifts and received gifts in return.*

During the Han Dynasty, China developed a **tributary system** to regulate contact with foreign powers. States and tribes beyond its borders sent envoys bearing gifts and received gifts in return. Over the course of the dynasty the Han government's outlay on these gifts was huge, perhaps as much as 10 percent of state revenue. In 25 B.C.E., for instance, the government gave tributary states twenty thousand rolls of silk cloth and about twenty thousand pounds of silk floss. Although the tribute system was a financial burden to the Chinese, it reduced the cost of defense and offered China confirmation that it was the center of the civilized world.

The silk given to the Xiongnu and other northern tributaries often entered the trading networks of Sogdian, Parthian, and Indian merchants, who carried it by caravans across Asia. There was a market both for skeins of silk thread and for silk cloth woven in Chinese or Syrian workshops. Caravans returning to China carried gold, horses, and occasionally handicrafts of West Asian origin, such as glass beads and cups. Through the trade along the Silk Road, the Chinese learned of new foodstuffs, including walnuts, pomegranates, sesame, and coriander, all of which came to be grown in China. This trade was largely carried by the two-humped Bactrian camel, which had been bred in Central Asia since the first century B.C.E. With a heavy coat of hair to withstand the bitter cold of winter, each camel could carry about five hundred pounds of cargo. (See the feature "Global Trade: Silk" on pages 140–141.)

Maintaining a military presence so far from the center of China was expensive. To cut costs, the government set up self-supporting military colonies, recruited Xiongnu tribes to serve as auxiliary forces, and established vast government horse farms. Still, military expenses threatened to bankrupt the Han government.

Han Intellectual and Cultural Life

Confucianism made a comeback during the Han Dynasty, but it was a changed Confucianism. Although Confucian texts had fed the First Emperor's bonfires, some dedicated scholars had hidden their books, and others had memorized whole works: one ninety-year-old man was able to recite two long books almost in their entirety. The ancient books recovered in this way (called the **Confucian classics**) were revered as repositories of the wisdom of the past. Scholars studied them with piety and attempted to make them more useful as sources of moral guidance by writing commentaries on them. Many Confucian scholars specialized in a single classic, and teachers passed on to their disciples their understanding of each sentence in the work. Other Han Confucians went to the opposite extreme, developing comprehensive cosmological theories that explained the world in terms of cyclical flows of yin and yang and the five phases (fire, water, earth, metal, and wood). Some used these theories to elevate the role of the emperor, who alone had the capacity to link the realms of Heaven, earth, and man. Natural disasters such as floods or earthquakes were viewed as portents that the emperor had failed in his role of maintaining the proper balance among the forces of Heaven and earth.

Confucian classics *The ancient texts recovered during the Han Dynasty that Confucian scholars treated as sacred scriptures.*

Han art and literature reveal a fascination with omens, portents, spirits, immortals, and occult forces. Emperor Wu tried to make contact with the world of gods and immortals through elaborate sacrifices, and he welcomed astrologers, alchemists, seers, and shamans to his court. He marveled at stories of the paradise of the Queen Mother of the West and the exploits of the Yellow Emperor, who had taken his entire court with him when he ascended to the realm of the immortals. Much of this interest in immortality and communicating with the spirit world was absorbed into the emerging religion of Daoism, which also drew on the philosophical ideas of Laozi and Zhuangzi.

A major intellectual accomplishment of the Han Dynasty was history writing. Sima Qian (145–ca. 85 B.C.E.) wrote a comprehensive history of China from the time of the mythical sage-kings of high antiquity to his own day, dividing his account into a chronology recounting political events, biographies of key individuals, and treatises on subjects such as geography, taxation, and court rituals. As an official of the emperor, he had access to important people and documents and to the imperial library. Like the Greeks Herodotus and Thucydides (see page 83), Sima Qian believed fervently in visiting the sites where history was made, examining artifacts, and questioning people about events. He was also interested in China's geography and local history. The result of his research, ten years in the making, was ***Records of the Grand Historian,*** a massive work of literary and historical genius. In the chapter devoted to "money-makers," he described how the Ping family made its fortune:

Lu people are customarily cautious and miserly, but the Ping family of Cao were particularly so. They started out by smelting iron and in time accumulated a fortune of a hundred million cash. All the members of the family from the father and elder brothers down to the sons and grandsons, however, made a promise that they would "Never look down without picking up something useful; never look up without grabbing something of value." They traveled about to all the provinces and kingdoms, selling goods on credit, lending money and trading. It was because of their influence that so many people in Zou and Lu abandoned scholarship and turned to the pursuit of profit.[1]

From examples like these Sima Qian concluded that wealth has no permanent master: "It finds its way to the man of ability like the spokes of a wheel converging upon the hub, and from the hands of the worthless it falls like shattered tiles."[2] For centuries to come, Sima Qian's work set the standard for Chinese historical writing, although most of the histories modeled after it covered only a single dynasty. The first of these was the work of three members of the Ban family in the first century C.E. (See the feature "Individuals in Society: The Ban Family.")

The circulation of books like Sima Qian's was made easier by the invention of paper, which the Chinese traditionally date to 105 C.E. Scribes had previously written on strips of bamboo and wood or rolls of silk. Cai Lun, to whom the Chinese attribute the invention of paper, worked the fibers of rags, hemp, bark, and other scraps into sheets of paper. Paper, thus, was somewhat similar to the papyrus made from pounded reeds in ancient Egypt. Though much less durable than wood, paper was far cheaper than silk and became a convenient means of conveying the written word. Compared to papyrus, it depended less on a specific source of plant fiber and so could be produced many places.

Records of the Grand Historian *A comprehensive history of China written by Sima Qian.*

Economy and Society in Han China

How were ordinary people's lives affected by the creation of a huge bureaucratic empire? The lucky ones who lived in Chang'an or Luoyang, the great cities of the empire, got to enjoy the material benefits of increased long-distance trade and a boom in the production of luxury goods.

The government did not promote trade per se. The Confucian elite, like ancient Hebrew wise men, considered trade necessary but lowly. Agriculture and crafts were more honorable because they produced something, but merchants merely took

SILK

Silk was one of the earliest commodities to stimulate international trade. By 2500 B.C.E. Chinese farmers had domesticated *Bombyx mori,* the Chinese silkworm, and by 1000 B.C.E. they were making fine fabrics with complex designs. Sericulture (silk making) is labor-intensive. In order for silkworms to spin their cocoons, they have to be fed leaves from mulberry trees. The leaves have to be picked and chopped, then fed to the worms every few hours, day and night, during the month between hatching and spinning. The cocoons consist of a single filament several thousand feet long but a minuscule 0.025 millimeter thick. More than two thousand cocoons are needed to make a pound of silk. After the cocoons are boiled to loosen the natural gum that binds the filament, several strands of filament are twisted together to make yarns.

What made silk the most valued of all textiles was its beauty and versatility. It could be made into sheer gauzes, shiny satins, multicolored brocades, and plush velvets. Fine Han silks have been found in Xiongnu tombs in northern Mongolia. Korea and Japan not only imported silk but also began silk production themselves, and silk came to be used in both places in much the way it was used in China—for the clothes of the elite,

The Silk Trade

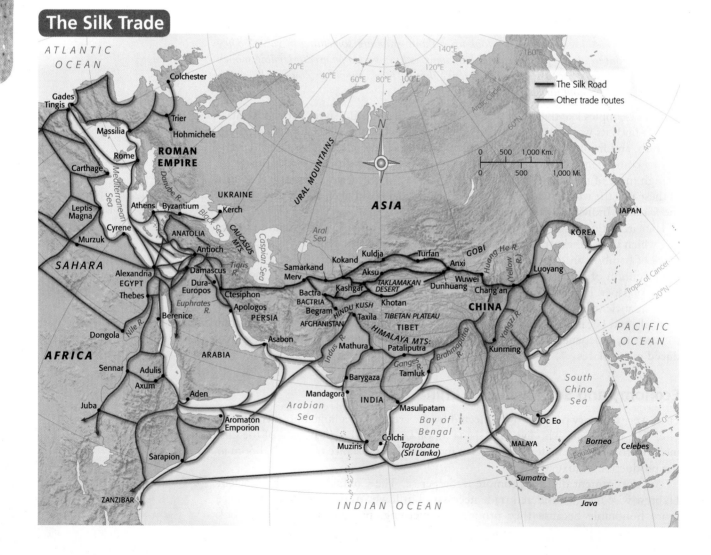

This fragment of a silk damask, about a foot square, was woven in China in the eleventh or twelfth century C.E., then transported by sea to Persia, where it was excavated along with southern Chinese porcelains of similar date. The design on the damask shows baby boys among pomegranates and flowers. Pomegranates have many seeds, making them symbols for ample progeny, a message conveyed even more concretely by the boys. (The Metropolitan Museum of Art. Purchase, Rogers Fund, 1952 [52.8]. Photograph © 1997 The Metropolitan Museum of Art)

for temple banners, and as a surface for writing and painting. Central Asia, Persia, India, and Southeast Asia also became producers of silk in distinctive local styles. Lacking suitable climates to produce silk, Mongolia and Tibet remained major importers of Chinese silks into modern times.

What makes the silk trade famous, however, is not the trade within Asia but the trade across Asia to Europe. In Roman times, silk carried by caravans across Asia or by ships across the Indian Ocean became a high-status luxury item, said to cost its weight in gold. To satisfy Roman taste, imported silk fabrics were unraveled and rewoven in Syrian workshops. Although the techniques of sericulture gradually spread through Asia, they remained a mystery in the West until the Byzantine emperor Justinian in the sixth century had two monks bring back silkworms from China along with knowledge of how to care for them and process their cocoons.

In medieval times, most of the silk imported into Europe came from Persia, the Byzantine Empire, or the Arab world. Venetian merchants handled much of the trade. Some of this fabric still survives in ancient churches, where it was used for vestments and altar clothes and to wrap relics. In the eleventh century, Roger I, king of Sicily, captured groups of silk-workers from Athens and Corinth and moved them to Sicily, initiating the production of silk in western Europe. Over the next couple of centuries, Italy became a major silk producer, joined by France in the fifteenth century.

When Marco Polo traveled across Asia in the late thirteenth century, he found local silk for sale in Baghdad, Georgia, Persia, and elsewhere, but China remained the largest producer. He claimed that more than a thousand cartloads of silk were brought into the capital of China every day.

With the development of the sea route between western Europe and China from the sixteenth century on, Europe began importing large quantities of Chinese silk, much of it as silk floss—raw silk—to supply Italian, French, and English silk weavers. In 1750 almost 70,000 kilograms (77.2 tons) of raw silk and nearly 20,000 lengths of silk cloth were carried from China to Europe. By this period the aristocracy of Europe regularly wore silk clothes, including silk stockings.

Mechanization of silk making began in Europe in the seventeenth century. The Italians developed machines to "throw" the silk—doubling and twisting raw silk into threads having the required strength and thickness. In the early nineteenth century, the introduction of Jacquard looms using punched cards made complex patterns easier to weave.

In the 1920s the silk industry was hit hard by the introduction of synthetic fibers, especially rayon and nylon. In the 1940s women in the United States and Europe switched from silk stockings to the much less expensive nylon stockings. European production of silk almost entirely collapsed.

In the 1980s silk made a comeback as China in the post-Mao era rapidly expanded its silk production. By 2003 there were more than two thousand silk enterprises in China, employing a million workers and supplying 80 percent of the total world trade in silk.

advantage of others' shortages to make profits as middlemen. This attitude justified the government's takeover of the grain, iron, and salt businesses. Still, the government indirectly promoted commerce by building cities and roads.

Markets were the liveliest places in the cities. Besides stalls selling goods of all kinds, markets offered fortunetellers and entertainers. People flocked to puppet shows and performances of jugglers and acrobats. The markets also were used for the execution of criminals, to serve as a warning to onlookers.

Government patronage helped maintain the quality of craftsmanship in the cities. By the beginning of the first century C.E., China had about fifty state-run ironworking factories. Chinese metalworking was the most advanced in the world at the time. In contrast to Roman blacksmiths, who hammered heated iron to make wrought iron tools, the Chinese knew how to liquefy iron and pour it into molds, producing tools with a higher carbon content that were harder and more durable. Han workmen turned out iron plowshares, agricultural tools with wooden handles, and weapons and armor.

Iron was replacing bronze in tools, but bronzeworkers still turned out a host of goods. Bronze was prized for jewelry, mirrors, and dishes. Bronze was also used for minting coins and for precision tools such as carpenters' rules and adjustable wrenches. Surviving bronze gear-and-cog wheels bear eloquent testimony to the sophistication of Han machinery. Han metal-smiths were mass-producing superb crossbows long before the crossbow was dreamed of in Europe.

The bulk of the population in Han times and even into the twentieth century consisted of peasants living in villages of a few hundred households. Since the Han empire, much like the contemporaneous Roman Empire, drew its strength from a large population of free peasants who contributed both taxes and labor services to the state, the government had to try to keep peasants independent and productive. The economic insecurity of small holders was described by one official in 178 B.C.E. in terms that could well have been repeated in most later dynasties:

They labor at plowing in the spring and hoeing in the summer, harvesting in the autumn and storing foodstuff in winter, cutting wood, performing labour service for the local government, all the while exposed to the dust of spring, the heat of summer, the storms of autumn, and the chill of winter. Through all four seasons they never get a day off. They need funds to cover such obligations as entertaining guests, burying the dead, visiting the sick, caring for orphans, and bringing up the young. No matter how hard they work they can be ruined by floods or droughts, or cruel and arbitrary officials who impose taxes at the wrong times or keep changing their orders. When taxes fall due, those with produce have to sell it at half price [to raise the needed cash], and those without [anything to sell] have to borrow [at such high rates] they will have to pay back twice what they borrowed. Some as a consequence sell their lands and houses, even their children and grandchildren.[3]

To fight peasant poverty, the government kept land taxes low (one-thirtieth of the harvest), provided relief in time of famine, and promoted up-to-date agricultural methods. Still, many hard-pressed peasants were left to choose between migration to areas where new lands could be opened and quasi-servile status as the dependents of a magnate. Throughout the Han period, Chinese farmers in search of land to till pushed into frontier areas, expanding Chinese domination at the expense of other ethnic groups, especially in central and south China.

The Chinese family in Han times was much like the Roman (see page 109) and the Indian (see pages 315–316) family. In all three societies, senior males had great authority, marriages were arranged by parents, and brides normally joined their husbands' families. Other practices were more distinctive to China, such as the universality of patrilineal family names, the practice of dividing land equally among the sons in a family, and the great emphasis placed on the virtue of filial piety. The brief *Classic of Filial Piety,* which claimed that filial piety was the root of all virtue, gained wide

The Ban Family

Ban Biao (3–54 C.E.), a successful official from a family with an envied library, had three highly accomplished children: his twin sons, the general Ban Chao (32–102) and the historian Ban Gu (32–92); and his daughter, Ban Zhao (ca. 45–120).

After distinguishing himself as a junior officer in campaigns against the Xiongnu, Ban Chao was sent in 73 C.E. to the Western Regions to see about the possibility of restoring Chinese overlordship there, lost since Wang Mang's time (early first century C.E.). Ban Chao spent most of the next three decades in Central Asia. Through patient diplomacy and a show of force, he reestablished Chinese control over the oasis cities of Central Asia, and in 92 he was appointed protector general of the area.

His twin brother Ban Gu was one of the most accomplished writers of his age, excelling in a distinctive literary form known as the rhapsody (*fu*). His "Rhapsody on the Two Capitals" is in the form of a dialogue between a guest from Chang'an and his host in Luoyang. It describes the palaces, spectacles, scenic spots, local products, and customs of the two great cities. Emperor Zhang (r. 76–88) was fond of literature and often had Ban Gu accompany him on hunts or travels. He also had him edit a record of the court debates he held on issues concerning the Confucian classics.

Ban Biao was working on a history of the Western Han Dynasty when he died in 54. Ban Gu took over this project, modeling it on Sima Qian's *Records of the Grand Historian.* He added treatises on law, geography, and bibliography, the last a classified list of books in the imperial library.

Because of his connection to a general out of favor, Ban Gu was sent to prison in 92, where he soon died. At that time the *History of the Former Han Dynasty* was still incomplete. The emperor called on Ban Gu's widowed sister, Ban Zhao, to finish it. She came to the palace, where she not only worked on the history but also became a teacher of the women of the palace. According to the *History of the Later Han,* she taught them the classics, history, astronomy, and mathematics. In 106 an infant succeeded to the throne, and the widow of an earlier emperor became regent. This empress frequently turned to Ban Zhao for advice on government policies.

Ban Zhao credited her own education to her learned father and cultured mother and became an advocate of the education of girls. In her *Admonitions for*

Ban Zhao continued to be considered the ideal woman teacher into the eighteenth century, when this imaginary portrait depicted her taking up her brush among women and children. *(National Palace Museum, Taipei, Taiwan)*

Women, Ban Zhao objected that many families taught their sons to read but not their daughters. She did not claim girls should have the same education as boys; after all, "just as yin and yang differ, men and women have different characteristics." Women, she wrote, will do well if they cultivate the womanly virtues such as humility. "Humility means yielding and acting respectful, putting others first and oneself last, never mentioning one's own good deeds or denying one's own faults, enduring insults and bearing with mistreatment, all with due trepidation."* In subsequent centuries, Ban Zhao's *Admonitions* became one of the most commonly used texts for the education of girls.

Questions for Analysis

1. What inferences would you draw from the fact that a leading general had a brother who was a literary man?

2. What does Ban Zhao's life tell us about women in her society? How do you reconcile her personal accomplishments with the advice she gave for women's education?

*Patricia Buckley Ebrey, ed., *Chinese Civilization: A Sourcebook,* rev. ed. (New York: Free Press, 1993), p. 75.

Primary Source:
Ban Zhao, *From* Lessons
for Women

circulation in Han times. The virtues of loyal wives and devoted mothers were extolled in the *Biographies of Exemplary Women,* which told the stories of women from China's past who were notable for giving their husbands good advice, knowing how to educate their sons, and sacrificing themselves when forced to choose between their fathers and husbands. The book also contained a few cautionary tales of scheming, jealous, manipulative women who brought destruction to all around them.

China and Rome

The empires of China and Rome have often been compared. Both were large, complex states governed by monarchs, bureaucracies, and standing armies. Both reached directly to the people through taxation and conscription policies. Both invested in infrastructure such as roads and waterworks. Both had to work hard to keep land from becoming too concentrated in the hands of hard-to-tax wealthy magnates. In both empires people in neighboring areas that came under political domination were attracted to the conquerors' material goods, productive techniques, and other cultural products, resulting in gradual cultural assimilation. Both China and Rome had similar frontier problems and tried similar solutions, such as using "barbarian" auxiliaries and settling soldier-colonists.

Nevertheless, the differences between Rome and Han China are worth as much notice as the similarities. The Roman Empire was linguistically and culturally more diverse than China. In China there was only one written language; but in the Roman Empire people still wrote in Greek and several other languages, and people from the East could claim more ancient civilizations. Politically, the dynastic principle was stronger in China than in Rome. Han emperors were never chosen by the army or by any institution comparable to the Roman senate, nor were there any republican ideals in China. In contrast to the graduated forms of citizenship in Rome, Han China drew no distinctions between original and added territories. The social and economic structures also differed in the two empires. Slavery was much more important in Rome than in China, and merchants were more favored. Over time these differences put Chinese and Roman social and political development on rather different trajectories.

The Fall of the Han and the Age of Division

In the second century C.E. the Han government suffered a series of blows. A succession of child emperors allowed their mothers' relatives to dominate the court. Emperors turned to **eunuchs** (castrated palace servants) for help in ousting the consort families (families of empresses), only to find that they were just as difficult to control. In 166 and 169 scholars who had denounced the eunuchs were arrested, killed, or banished from the capital and official life. Then in 184 a millenarian religious sect rose in massive revolt. The armies raised to suppress the rebels soon took to fighting among themselves. In 189 one general slaughtered two thousand eunuchs in the palace and took the Han emperor captive. After years of fighting, a stalemate was reached, with three warlords each controlling distinct territories in the north, the southeast, and the southwest. In 220 one of them forced the last of the Han emperors to abdicate, formally ending the Han Dynasty.

The period after the fall of the Han Dynasty is often referred to as the **Age of Division** (220–589). A brief reunification from 280 to 316 came to an end when non-Chinese who had been settling in north China since Han times seized the opportunity afforded by the political turmoil to take power. For the next two and a half centuries north China was ruled by one or more non-Chinese dynasty (the Northern Dynasties), and the south was ruled by a sequence of four short-lived Chinese dynasties (the Southern Dynasties) centered in the area of the present-day city of Nanjing.

In the south a hereditary aristocracy entrenched itself in the higher reaches of

eunuchs *Castrated males who played an important role as palace servants.*

Age of Division *The period after the fall of the Han Dynasty, during which time China was politically divided.*

officialdom. These families intermarried only with families of equivalent pedigree and compiled lists and genealogies of the most eminent families. They saw themselves as maintaining the high culture of the Han and looked on the emperors of the successive dynasties as upstarts—as military men rather than men of culture. In this aristocratic culture, the arts of poetry and calligraphy flourished, and people began collecting writings by famous calligraphers.

Establishing the capital at Nanjing, south of the Yangzi River, had a beneficial effect on the economic development of the south. To pay for an army and to support the imperial court and aristocracy in a style that matched their pretensions, the government had to expand the area of taxable agricultural land, whether through settling migrants or converting the local inhabitants into taxpayers. The south, with its temperate climate and ample supply of water, offered nearly unlimited possibilities for such development.

The Northern Dynasties are interesting as the first case of alien rule in China. Ethnic tensions flared from time to time. In the late fifth century the Northern Wei Dynasty (386–534) moved the capital from near the Great Wall to the ancient city of Luoyang, adopted Chinese-style clothing, and made Chinese the official language. The Xianbei tribesmen, who still formed the main military force, saw themselves as marginalized by these policies and rebelled in 524. For the next fifty years north China was torn apart by struggles for power. It had long been the custom of the northern pastoral tribes to enslave those they captured; sometimes the residents of entire cities were enslaved. In 554, when the city of Jiangling was taken, one hundred thousand civilians were enslaved and distributed to generals and officials.

THE SPREAD OF BUDDHISM OUT OF INDIA

How were both Buddhism and China changed by the spread of Buddhism across Asia?

In much the same period that Christianity was spreading out of its original home in ancient Israel, Buddhism was spreading beyond India. Like Christianity, Buddhism was shaped by its contact with cultures in the different areas into which it spread, leading to several distinct forms. The Mahayana form of Buddhism (see page 41) that spread via Central Asia to China, Korea, and Japan is distinct from the Theravada form that spread from India to Sri Lanka and Southeast Asia and the Tantric form that spread to Tibet.

Central Asia is a loose term used to refer to the vast area between the ancient civilizations of Persia, India, and China. Modern political borders are a product of competition among the British, Russians, and Chinese for empire in the mid-nineteenth century and have relatively little to do with the earlier history of the region. Through most of recorded history, the region was ethnically and culturally diverse; it was home to urban centers, especially at the oases along the Silk Road, and to pastoralists in the mountains and grasslands.

Under Ashoka (see pages 45–46) Buddhism began to spread to Central Asia. This continued under the Kushan empire (ca. 50–250 C.E.), especially under the greatest Kushan king, Kanishka I (ca. 100 C.E.). In this region, where the influence of Greek art was strong, artists began to depict the Buddha in human form. Over the next several centuries most of the city-states of Central Asia became centers of Buddhism, from Bamiyan, northwest of Kabul, to Kucha, Khotan, Loulan, Turfan, and Dunhuang (see Map 6.2). Because the remarkable Buddhist civilization of Central Asia was later supplanted by Islam, it was not until early in the twentieth century that European archaeologists discovered its traces. The main sites yielded not only numerous

Buddhist paintings but also thousands of texts in a variety of languages. In Khotan, for instance, an Indian language was used for administrative purposes long after the fall of the Kushan empire. Other texts were in various Persian languages, showing the cultural mix of the region.

The first translators of Buddhist texts into Chinese were not Indians but Parthians, Sogdians, and Kushans from Central Asia. One of the most important interpreters of Buddhism in China was the eminent Central Asian monk Kumarajiva (350–413) from Kucha, who settled in Chang'an and directed several thousand monks in the translation of Buddhist texts.

Why did Buddhism find so many adherents in China during the three centuries after the fall of the Han Dynasty in 220? There were no forced conversions, but still the religion spread rapidly. In the unstable political environment, many people were open to new ideas. To Chinese scholars the Buddhist concepts of the transmigration of souls, karma, and nirvana posed a stimulating intellectual challenge. To rulers the Buddhist religion offered a source of magical power and a political tool to unite

MAP 6.2 **The Spread of Buddhism** Buddhism spread throughout India in Ashoka's time and beyond India in later centuries. The different forms of Buddhism found in Asia today reflect this history. The Mahayana Buddhism of Japan came via Central Asia, China, and Korea, with a secondary later route through Tibet. The Theravada Buddhism of Southeast Asia came directly from India and indirectly through Sri Lanka.

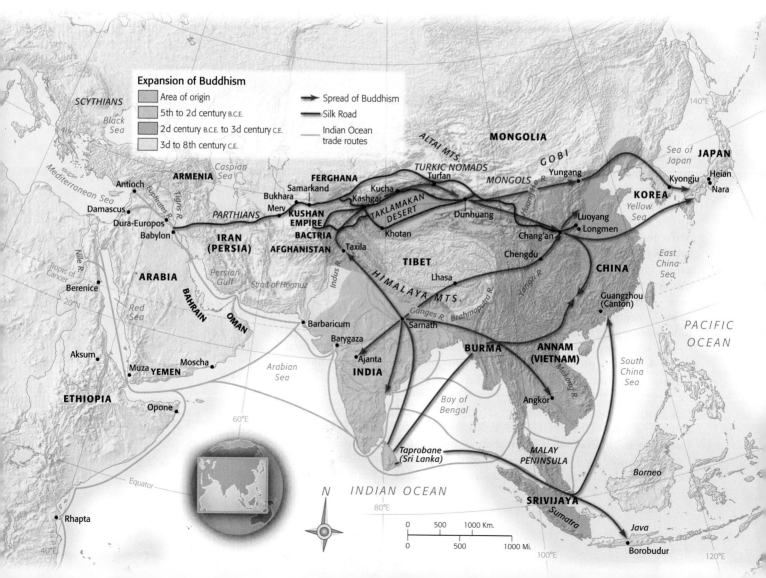

Chinese and non-Chinese. In a rough and tumultuous age Buddhism's emphasis on kindness, charity, and eternal bliss was deeply comforting. As in India, Buddhism posed no threat to the social order, and the elite who were drawn to Buddhism encouraged its spread to people of all classes. (See the feature "Listening to the Past: Copying Buddhist Sutras" on pages 160–161.)

The monastic establishment grew rapidly in China. Like their Christian counterparts in medieval Europe, Buddhist monasteries played an active role in social, economic, and political life. By 477 there were said to be 6,478 Buddhist temples and 77,258 monks and nuns in the north. Some decades later south China had 2,846 temples and 82,700 clerics. Given the importance of family lines in China, becoming a monk was a major decision, since a man had to give up his surname and take a vow of celibacy, thus cutting himself off from the ancestral cult. Those not ready to become monks or nuns could pursue Buddhist goals as pious laypeople by performing devotional acts and making contributions to monasteries. Among the most generous patrons were rulers in both the north and south.

In China women turned to Buddhism as readily as men. Although incarnation as a female was considered lower than incarnation as a male, it was also viewed as temporary, and women were encouraged to pursue salvation on terms nearly equal to men. Joining a nunnery became an alternative for a woman who did not want to marry or did not want to stay with her husband's family in widowhood.

● **Meditating Monk** This monk, wearing the traditional patchwork robe, sits in the crossed-legged meditation position. His small niche is to the left of the main image of the Buddha in cave 285 at Dunhuang, a cave completed in 539 under the patronage of a prince of the Northern Wei imperial house who was then the local governor. *(Photo: Lois Conner. Courtesy, Dunhuang Academy)*

Buddhism had an enormous impact on the visual arts in China, especially sculpture and painting. Before Buddhism, Chinese had not set up statues of gods in temples, but now they decorated temples with a profusion of images. Inspired by the cave-temples of India and Central Asia, in China, too, caves were carved into rock faces to make temples.

Buddhist temples were just as splendid in the cities. One author described the ceremony held each year on the seventh day of the fourth month at the largest monastery in the northern capital, Luoyang. All the Buddhist statues in the city, more than a thousand altogether, would be brought to the monastery, and the emperor would come in person to scatter flowers as part of the Great Blessing ceremony:

The gold and the flowers dazzled in the sun, and the jewelled canopies floated like clouds; there were forests of banners and a fog of incense, and the Buddhist music of India shook heaven and earth. All kinds of entertainers and trick riders performed shoulder to shoulder. Virtuous hosts of famous monks came, carrying their staves; there were crowds of the Buddhist faithful, holding flowers; horsemen and carriages were packed beside each other in an endless mass.[4]

● **Yungang Colossal Buddha** Beginning about 460 C.E. the Northern Wei rulers constructed a series of caves at Yungang, not far from their capital. The large Buddha shown here in a lotus meditation posture is 45 feet (13.7 meters) tall. Notice the long ears and the robe across the Buddha's shoulders, both features associated with the Buddha. *(Dean Conger/Corbis)*

Not everyone was won over by Buddhist teachings. Critics of Buddhism labeled it immoral, unsuited to China, and a threat to the state since monastery land was not taxed and monks did not perform labor service. Twice in the north orders were issued to close monasteries and force monks and nuns to return to lay life, but these suppressions did not last long, and no attempt was made to suppress belief in Buddhism.

THE CHINESE EMPIRE RE-CREATED: SUI (581–618) AND TANG (618–907)

In what ways was China's second empire different from its first?

In the 570s and 580s, the long period of division in China was brought to an end under the leadership of the Sui Dynasty. Yang Jian, who both founded the Sui Dynasty and oversaw the reunification of China, was from a Chinese family that had intermarried with the non-Chinese elite of the north. His conquest of the south involved naval as well as land battles, with thousands of ships on both sides contending for control of the Yangzi River. The Sui reasserted Chinese control over northern Vietnam and campaigned into Korea and against the new force on the steppe, the Turks. The Sui strengthened central control of the government by curtailing the power of local officials to appoint their own subordinates and by instituting competitive written examinations for the selection of officials.

The crowning achievement of the Sui Dynasty was the **Grand Canal**, which connected the Huang (Yellow) and Yangzi River regions. The canal facilitated the shipping of tax grain from the prosperous Yangzi Valley to the centers of political and military power in north China. Henceforth the rice-growing Yangzi Valley and south China played an ever more influential role in the country's economic and political life, strengthening China's internal cohesion.

Despite these accomplishments, the Sui Dynasty lasted for only two reigns. The ambitious projects of the two Sui emperors led to exhaustion and unrest, and in the ensuing warfare Li Yuan, a Chinese from the same northwest aristocratic circles as the founder of the Sui, seized the throne.

Grand Canal *A canal, built during the Sui Dynasty, that connected the Huang (Yellow) and Yangzi Rivers.*

The Tang Dynasty (618–907)

The dynasty founded by Li Yuan, the Tang, was one of the high points of traditional Chinese civilization. Especially during this dynasty's first century, its capital, Chang'an, was the cultural center of East Asia, drawing in merchants, pilgrims, missionaries, and students to a degree never matched before or after. This position of strength gave the Chinese the confidence to be open to what they could learn from the outside world, leading to a more cosmopolitan culture than in any other period before the twentieth century.

The first two Tang rulers, Gaozu (r. 618–626) and Taizong (r. 626–649), were able monarchs. Adding to their armies auxiliary troops composed of Turks, Tanguts, Khitans, and other non-Chinese led by their own chieftains, they campaigned into Korea, Vietnam, and Central Asia. In 630 the Chinese turned against their former allies, the Turks, gaining territory from them and winning for Taizong the title of Great Khan, so that he was for a short period simultaneously head of both the Chinese and the Turkish empires.

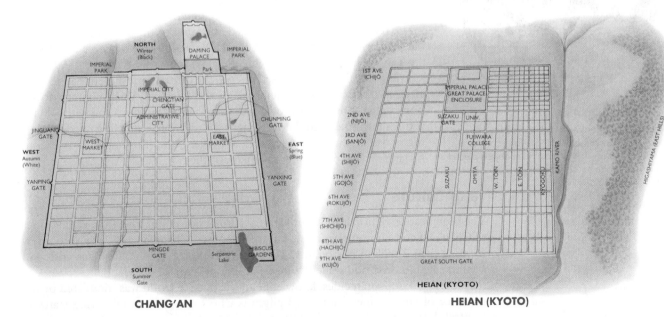

CHANG'AN

HEIAN (KYOTO)

● **Urban Planning** Chang'an in Tang times attracted merchants, pilgrims, and students from all over East Asia. The city was laid out on a square grid (*left*) and divided into walled wards, the gates to which were closed at night. Temples were found throughout the city, but trade was limited to two government-supervised markets. In the eighth and ninth centuries the Japanese copied the general plan of Chang'an in designing their capitals—first at Nara, then at Heian, shown on the right. *(From* Cradles of Civilization: China *[Weldon Owen Pty Limited, Australia])*

In the civil sphere Tang accomplishments far outstripped anything known in Europe until the growth of national states in the seventeenth century. Tang emperors subdivided the administration of the empire into departments, much like the numerous agencies of modern governments. They built on the Sui precedent of using written examinations to select officials. Although only about thirty men were recruited this way each year, the prestige of passing the examinations became so great that more and more men attempted them. Candidates had to master the Confucian classics and the rules of poetry, and they had to be able to analyze practical administrative and political matters. Government schools were founded to prepare the sons of officials and other young men for service as officials.

The mid-Tang Dynasty saw two women—Empress Wu and Consort Yang Guifei—rise to positions of great political power. Empress Wu was the consort of the weak and sickly Emperor Gaozong. After Gaozong suffered a stroke in 660, she took full charge. She continued to rule after Gaozong's death, summarily deposing her own two sons and dealing harshly with all opponents. In 690 she proclaimed herself emperor, the only woman who took that title in Chinese history. To gain support, she circulated a Buddhist sutra that predicted the imminent reincarnation of the Buddha Maitreya as a female monarch, during whose reign the world would be free of illness, worry, and disaster. Although despised by later historians as an evil usurper, Empress Wu was an effective leader. It was not until she was over eighty that members of the court were able to force her out in favor of her son.

Her grandson, the emperor Xuanzong (r. 713–756), in his early years presided over a brilliant court and patronized leading poets, painters, and calligraphers. In his later years, however, after he became enamored of his consort Yang Guifei, he let things slide. This was a period when ample and rounded proportions were much admired in women, and Yang was said to be such a full-figured beauty. The emperor allowed her to place friends and relatives in important positions in the government. One of her favorites was the general An Lushan, who, after getting into a quarrel with Yang's brother over control of the government, rebelled in 755. Xuanzong had to flee the capital, and the troops that accompanied him forced him to have Yang Guifei executed.

The rebellion of An Lushan was devastating to the Tang Dynasty. Peace was restored only by calling on the Uighurs, a Turkish people allied with the Tang, who looted the capital after taking it from the rebels. After the rebellion was finally suppressed in 763, the central government had to keep meeting the extortionate demands of the Uighurs. Many military governors came to treat their provinces as hereditary kingdoms and withheld tax returns from the central government. In addition, eunuchs gained increasing power at court and were able to prevent both the emperors and Confucian officials from doing much about them.

● **Five-Stringed Pipa/Biwa** This musical instrument, decorated with fine wood marquetry, was probably presented by the Tang court to a Japanese envoy. It was among the objects placed in a royal storage house (Shōsōin) in 756. *(Courtesy, Nara National Museum)*

Tang Culture

The reunification of north and south led to cultural flowering. The Tang capital cities of Chang'an and Luoyang became great metropolises; Chang'an and its suburbs grew to more than 2 million inhabitants. The cities were laid out in rectangular grids and contained a hundred-odd walled "blocks" inside their walls.

In these cosmopolitan cities, knowledge of the outside world was stimulated by the presence of envoys, merchants, and pilgrims who came from neighboring states in Central Asia, Japan, Korea, Tibet, and Southeast Asia. Because of the presence of foreign merchants, many religions were practiced, including Nestorian Christianity, Manichaeism, Zoroastrianism, Judaism, and Islam, although none of them spread into the Chinese population the way Buddhism had a few centuries earlier. Foreign fashions in hair and clothing were often copied, and foreign amusements such as polo found followings among the well-to-do. The introduction of new musical instruments

Primary Source:
Bishop Adam, *From* The Christian Monument

● **Woman Playing Polo**   Notions of what makes women attractive have changed over the course of Chinese history. The figurines found in Tang tombs reveal that active women, even women playing polo on horseback like the one shown here, were viewed as appealing. In earlier and later periods, female beauty was identified with slender waists and delicate faces, but in Tang times women were admired for their plump bodies and full faces. *(Chinese. Equestrienne [tomb figure], buff earthenware with traces of polychromy, first half 8th cent., 56.2 x 48.2 cm. Gift of Mrs. Pauline Palmer Wood, 1970.1073. Photograph © 1998, The Art Institute of Chicago)*

and tunes from India, Iran, and Central Asia brought about a major transformation in Chinese music.

The Tang Dynasty was the great age of Chinese poetry. Skill in composing poetry was tested in the civil service examinations, and educated men had to be able to compose poems at social gatherings. The pain of parting, the joys of nature, and the pleasures of wine and friendship were all common poetic topics. One of Li Bo's (701–762) most famous poems describes an evening of drinking with only the moon and his shadow for company:

A cup of wine, under the flowering trees;
I drink alone, for no friend is near.
Raising my cup I beckon the bright moon,
For he, with my shadow, will make three men.
The moon, alas, is no drinker of wine;
Listless, my shadow creeps about at my side.
. . .
Now we are drunk, each goes his way.
May we long share our odd, inanimate feast,
And we meet at last on the cloudy River of the sky.[5]

Primary Source:
**Han Yu, *Memorial on
Buddhism***

The poet Bo Juyi (772–846) often wrote of more serious subjects. At times he worried about whether he was doing his job justly and well:

From these high walls I look at the town below
Where the natives of Pa cluster like a swarm of flies.
How can I govern these people and lead them aright?
I cannot even understand what they say.
But at least I am glad, now that the taxes are in,
To learn that in my province there is no discontent.[6]

In Tang times Buddhism fully penetrated Chinese daily life. Stories of Buddhist origin became widely known, and Buddhist festivals, such as the festival for feeding hungry ghosts in the summer, became among the most popular holidays. Buddhist monasteries became an important part of everyday life. They ran schools for children. In remote areas they provided lodging for travelers. Merchants entrusted their money and wares to monasteries for safekeeping, in effect transforming the monasteries into banks and warehouses. The wealthy often donated money or land to support temples and monasteries, making monasteries among the largest landlords.

Pure Land *A school of Buddhism that taught that by paying homage to the Buddha Amitabha and his chief helper, one could achieve rebirth in Amitabha's paradise.*

At the intellectual and religious level, Buddhism was developing in distinctly Chinese directions. Two schools that thrived were Pure Land and Chan. **Pure Land** appealed to laypeople. The simple act of calling on the Buddha Amitabha and his chief helper, the compassionate bodhisattva Guanyin, could lead to rebirth in Amitabha's paradise, the Pure Land. Among the educated elite the **Chan** school (known in Japan as Zen) also gained popularity. Chan teachings rejected the authority of the scriptures and claimed the superiority of mind-to-mind transmission of Buddhist truths. The "northern" tradition emphasized meditation and monastic discipline. The "southern" tradition was even more iconoclastic, holding that enlightenment could be achieved suddenly through insight into one's own true nature, even without prolonged meditation.

Chan *A school of Buddhism (known in Japan as Zen) that rejected the authority of the sutras and claimed the superiority of mind-to-mind transmission of Buddhist truths.*

In the late Tang period, opposition to Buddhism reemerged. In addition to concerns about the fiscal impact of removing so much land from the tax rolls and so many men from the labor service force, there were concerns about Buddhism's foreign origins. As China's international position weakened, xenophobia emerged. During the persecution of 845, more than 4,600 monasteries and 40,000 temples and shrines were destroyed, and more than 260,000 Buddhist monks and nuns were forced to return to secular life. Although this ban was lifted after a few years, the monastic establishment never fully recovered. Among laypeople Buddhism retained a strong hold, and basic Buddhist ideas like karma and reincarnation had become fully incorporated into everyday Chinese thinking. But Buddhism was never again as central to Chinese life.

THE EAST ASIAN CULTURAL SPHERE

What elements of Chinese culture were adopted by Koreans, Vietnamese, and Japanese, and how did they adapt them to their own circumstances?

During the millennium from 200 B.C.E. to 800 C.E. China exerted a powerful influence on its immediate neighbors, who began forming states of their own. By Tang times China was surrounded by independent states in Korea, Manchuria, Tibet, the area that is now Yunnan province, Vietnam, and Japan. All of these states were much smaller than China in area and population, making China by far the dominant force politically and culturally until the nineteenth century. Nevertheless, each of these separate states developed a strong sense of uniqueness and independent identity.

The earliest information about each of these countries is found in Chinese sources. Han armies brought Chinese culture to Korea and Vietnam, but even in those cases much cultural borrowing was entirely voluntary as the elite, merchants, and craftsmen adopted the techniques, ideas, and practices they found appealing. In Japan much of the process of absorbing elements of Chinese culture was mediated via Korea. In Korea, Japan, and Vietnam the fine arts—painting, architecture, and ceramics in particular—were all strongly influenced by Chinese models. Tibet, though a thorn in the side of Tang China, was as much in the Indian sphere of influence as in the Chinese and thus followed a somewhat different trajectory. Most significant, it never adopted Chinese characters as its written language, nor was it as influenced by Chinese artistic styles as other areas. Moreover the form of Buddhism that became dominant in Tibet came directly from India, not through Central Asia and China.

In each area, literate Chinese-style culture was at first an upper-level overlay over an indigenous cultural base, but in time many products and ideas adopted from China became incorporated into everyday life, ranging from written language to chopsticks and soy sauce. By the eighth century the Chinese language was a written lingua franca among educated people throughout East Asia. Educated Vietnamese, Koreans, and Japanese could communicate in writing when they could not understand each other's spoken languages, and envoys to Chang'an could carry out "brush conversations" with each other. The books that educated people read included the Chinese classics, histories, and poetry, as well as Buddhist sutras translated into Chinese. The great appeal of Buddhism known primarily through Chinese translation was a powerful force promoting cultural borrowing.

Vietnam

Vietnam is today classed with the countries to its west as part of Southeast Asia, but its ties are at least as strong to China. The Vietnamese first appear in Chinese sources as a people of south China called the Yue, who gradually migrated farther south as the Chinese state expanded. The people of the Red River valley in northern Vietnam had achieved a relatively advanced level of Bronze Age civilization by the first century B.C.E. The bronze heads of their arrows often were dipped in poison to facilitate killing large animals such as elephants, whose tusks were traded to China for iron. Power was held by hereditary tribal chiefs who served as civil, religious, and military leaders, with the king as the most powerful chief.

The collapse of the Qin Dynasty in 206 B.C.E. had an impact on this area because a former Qin general, Zhao Tuo (Trieu Da in Vietnamese), finding himself in the far south, set up his own kingdom of Nam Viet (Nan Yue in Chinese). This kingdom covered much of south China and was ruled by Trieu Da from his capital near the present site of Guangzhou. Its population consisted chiefly of the Viet people. After killing all officials loyal to the Chinese emperor, Trieu Da adopted the customs of the Viet and made himself the ruler of a vast state that extended as far south as modern-day Da Nang.

After almost a hundred years of diplomatic and military duels between the Han Dynasty and Trieu Da and his successors, Nam Viet was conquered in 111 B.C.E. by Chinese armies. Chinese administrators were assigned to replace the local nobility. Chinese

● **Bronze Drum** By 300 B.C.E. large bronze drums were being cast in what is now northern Vietnam. They were regularly decorated with scenes of daily life, war, and rituals. This drum, called the Ngoc Lu Drum, has depictions of boats carrying warriors on its sides. The three concentric rings on top show birds, deer, houses, and pairs of people pounding rice. *(From A. J. Bernet Kempers, The Kettledrums of South Asia: A Bronze Age World and Its Aftermath [Leiden, The Netherlands: A. A. Balkema, 1988, Tozzer Library, Harvard College Library])*

political institutions were imposed, and Confucianism became the official ideology. The Chinese language was introduced as the medium of official and literary expression, and Chinese ideographs were adopted as the written form for the Vietnamese spoken language. The Chinese built roads, waterways, and harbors to facilitate communication within the region and to ensure that they maintained administrative and military control over it. Chinese art, architecture, and music had a powerful impact on their Vietnamese counterparts.

Chinese innovations that were beneficial to the Vietnamese were readily integrated into the indigenous culture, but the local elite were not reconciled to Chinese political domination. The most famous early revolt took place in 39 C.E., when two widows of local aristocrats, the Trung sisters, led an uprising against foreign rule. After overwhelming Chinese strongholds, they declared themselves queens of an independent Vietnamese kingdom. Three years later a powerful army sent by the Han emperor reestablished Chinese rule.

China retained at least nominal control over northern Vietnam through the Tang Dynasty, and there were no real borders between China proper and Vietnam during this time. The local elite became culturally dual, serving as brokers between the Chinese governors and the native people.

Korea

Korea is a mountainous peninsula some 600 miles long extending south from Manchuria and Siberia. At its tip it is about 120 miles from Japan (see Map 6.3). Archaeological, linguistic, and anthropological evidence indicates that the Korean people share a common ethnic origin with other peoples of North Asia, including those of Manchuria, Siberia, and Japan. Linguistically, Korean is not related to Chinese.

Bronze and iron technology spread from China and North Asia in the Zhou period. In about 194 B.C.E. Wiman, an unsuccessful rebel against the Han Dynasty, fled to Korea and set up a state called Chosŏn in what is now northwest Korea and southern Manchuria. In 108 B.C.E. this state was overthrown by the armies of the Han emperor Wu. Four commanderies were established there, and Chinese officials were dispatched to govern them.

The impact of the Chinese commanderies in Korea was similar to that of the contemporaneous Roman colonies in Britain in encouraging the spread of culture and political forms. The commanderies survived not only through the Han Dynasty, but also for nearly a century after the fall of the dynasty, to 313 C.E. The Chinese never controlled the entire Korean peninsula, however. The Han commanderies coexisted with the native Korean kingdom of Koguryŏ, founded in the first century B.C.E. Chinese sources describe this kingdom as a society of aristocratic tribal warriors who had under them a mass of serfs and slaves, mostly from conquered tribes. After the Chinese colonies were finally overthrown, the kingdoms of Paekche and Silla emerged farther south on the peninsula in the third and fourth centuries C.E., leading to what is called the Three Kingdoms Period (313–668 C.E.). In all three Korean kingdoms Chinese was used as the language of government and learning. Each of the three kingdoms had hereditary kings, but their power

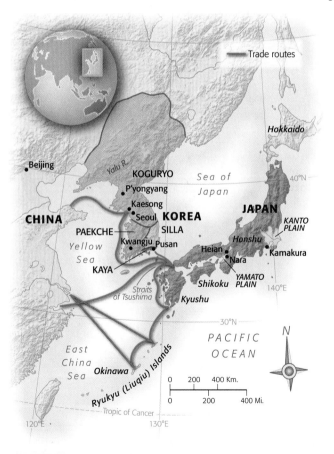

MAP 6.3 **Korea and Japan, ca. 600** Korea and Japan are of similar latitude, but Korea's climate is more continental, with harsher winters. Of Japan's four islands, Kyushu is closest to Korea and mainland Asia.

was curbed by the existence of very strong hereditary elites.

Buddhism was officially introduced in Koguryŏ from China in 372 and in the other states not long after. Buddhism placed Korea in a pan-Asian cultural context. Buddhist monks went back and forth between China and Korea. One even made the journey to India and back, and others traveled on to Japan to aid in the spread of Buddhism there.

When the Sui Dynasty finally reunified China in 589, it tried to establish control of at least a part of Korea. But the Korean kingdoms were much stronger than their predecessors in Han times, and they repeatedly repulsed Chinese attacks. The Tang government then tried allying itself with one state to fight another. Silla and Tang jointly destroyed Paekche in 660 and Koguryŏ in 668. The unification under Silla marks the first political unification of Korea.

Although Silla quickly forced the Tang to withdraw, for the next century Silla embarked on a policy of wholesale borrowing of Chinese culture and institutions. Annual embassies were sent to Chang'an, and large numbers of students studied in China. The Silla government was modeled on the Tang, although modifications were made to accommodate Korea's more aristocratic social structure.

Japan

Japan does not touch China as do Korea, Tibet, and Vietnam. The heart of Japan is four mountainous islands off the coast of Korea (see Map 6.3). Japan's early development was closely tied to that of the mainland, especially to Korea. Physical anthropologists have discerned several major waves of immigrants into Japan. People of the Jōmon culture, established by about 10,000 B.C.E. after an influx of people from Southeast Asia, practiced hunting and fishing and fashioned clay pots. New arrivals from northeast Asia brought agriculture and a distinct culture called Yayoi (ca. 300 B.C.E.–300 C.E.). Later Yayoi communities were marked by complex social organization with rulers, soldiers, artisans, and priests. Objects of Chinese and Korean manufacture found their way into Japan, an indication that people were traveling back and forth as well. In the third century C.E. Chinese histories begin to report on the land called Wa made up of mountainous islands. It had numerous communities, markets, granaries, tax collection, and class distinctions. The people ate with their fingers, used body paint, purified themselves by bathing after a funeral, and liked liquor. Of their rulers the Chinese historian wrote:

The country formerly had a man as ruler. For some seventy or eighty years after that there were disturbances and warfare. Thereupon the people agreed upon a woman for their ruler. Her name was Himiko. She occupied herself with magic and sorcery, bewitching the people. Though mature in age, she remained unmarried. She had a younger brother who assisted her in ruling the country. After she became the ruler, there were few who saw her. She had one thousand women as attendants, but only one man. He served her food and drink and acted as a medium of communication. . . .

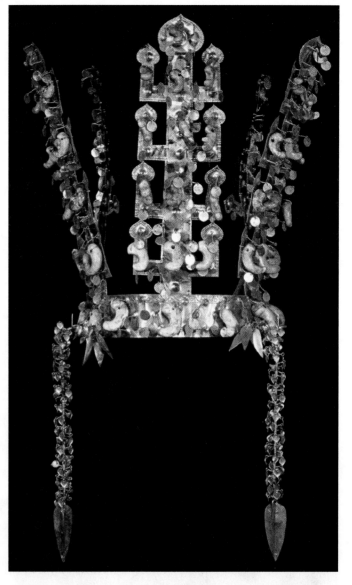

● **Gold Crown** Excavated from a fifth- to sixth-century royal Silla tomb, this magnificent crown reflects metalwork traditions found in scattered places across the Eurasian steppe. The crown is decorated with dangling gold disks and comma-shaped beads of jadeite. The upright bars at the top are thought to represent deer antlers. *(Kyongju National Museum, Kyongju)*

> When Himiko passed away, a great mound was raised, more than a hundred paces in diameter. Over a hundred male and female attendants followed her to the grave. Then a king was placed on the throne, but the people would not obey him. Assassination and murder followed; more than one thousand were thus slain.
>
> A relative of Himiko named Iyo, a girl of thirteen, was then made queen and order was restored.[7]

During the fourth through sixth centuries, new waves of migrants from Korea brought with them the language that evolved into Japanese. They also brought sericulture (silk making), bronze swords, crossbows, iron plows, and the Chinese written language. In this period, a social order similar to Korea's emerged, dominated by a warrior aristocracy organized into clans. Clad in helmet and armor, these warriors wielded swords, battle-axes, and often bows. Some of them rode into battle on horseback. Those vanquished in battle were made slaves. Each clan had its own chieftain, who marshaled clansmen for battle and served as chief priest. Over time the clans fought with each other, and their numbers were gradually reduced through conquest and alliance. By the fifth century the chief of the clan that claimed descent from

● **Hōryūji Temple** Japanese Buddhist temples, like those in China and Korea, consisted of several buildings within a walled compound. The buildings of the Hōryūji Temple (built 670–711; Prince Shōtoku's original temple burned down) include the oldest wooden structures in the world and house some of the best early Buddhist sculpture in Japan. The three main buildings depicted here are the pagoda, housing relics; the main hall, with the temple's principal images; and the lecture hall, for sermons. The five-story pagoda could be seen from far away, much like the steeples of cathedrals in medieval Europe. *(The Orion Press)*

the sun-goddess, located in the Yamato plain around modern Osaka, had come to occupy the position of Great King—or Queen, as female rulers were not uncommon in this period.

The Yamato rulers used their religion to subordinate the gods of their rivals, much as Hammurabi had used Marduk in Babylonia (see page 7). They established the chief shrine of the sun-goddess near the seacoast, where she could catch the first rays of the rising sun. Cults to other gods also were supported as long as they were viewed as subordinate to the sun-goddess. This native religion was later termed **Shinto,** the Way of the Gods.

In the sixth century Prince Shōtoku (574–622) undertook a sweeping reform of the state designed to strengthen Yamato rule by adopting Chinese-style bureaucratic practices. His "Seventeen Principles" of 604 drew from both Confucian and Buddhist teachings. In it he likened the ruler to Heaven and instructed officials to put their duty to the ruler above the interest of their families. He instituted a ladder of official ranks similar to China's, admonished the nobility to avoid strife and opposition, and urged adherence to Buddhist precepts. Near his seat of government, Prince Shōtoku built the magnificent Hōryūji Temple and staffed it with monks from Korea. He also opened direct relations with China, sending four missions during the brief Sui Dynasty.

State-building efforts continued through the seventh century and culminated in the establishment in 710 of Japan's first permanent capital at **Nara,** north of modern Osaka. Nara, which was modeled on the Tang capital of Chang'an, gave its name to an era that lasted until 794 and that was characterized by the avid importation of Chinese ideas and methods. Seven times missions with five hundred to six hundred men were sent on the difficult journey to Chang'an. Chinese and Korean craftsmen were often brought back to Japan, especially to help with the decoration of the many Buddhist temples then under construction. Musical instruments and tunes were imported as well, many originally from Central Asia. Chinese practices were instituted, such as the compilation of histories and law codes, the creation of provinces, and the appointment of governors to collect taxes from them. By 750 some seven thousand men staffed the central government.

Increased contact with the mainland had unwanted effects as well, such as the great smallpox epidemic of 735–737, which is thought to have reduced the population of about 5 million by 30 percent. (Smallpox did not become an endemic childhood disease in Japan until the tenth or eleventh century.)

The Buddhist monasteries that ringed Nara were both religious centers and wealthy landlords, and the monks were active in the political life of the capital. Copying the policy of the Tang Dynasty in China, the government ordered that every province establish a Buddhist temple with twenty monks and ten nuns to chant sutras and perform other ceremonies on behalf of the emperor and the state. When an emperor abdicated in 749 in favor of his daughter, he became a Buddhist priest, a practice many of his successors would later follow.

Many of the temples built during the Nara period still stand, the wood, clay, and bronze statues in them exceptionally well preserved. The largest of these temples was the Tōdaiji, with its huge bronze statue of the Buddha, which stood fifty-three feet tall and was made from more than a million pounds of metal. When the temple and statue were completed in 752, an Indian monk painted the eyes, and the ten thousand monks present for the celebration had a magnificent vegetarian feast. Objects from the dedication ceremony were placed in a special storehouse, the Shōsōin, and about ten thousand of them are still there, including books, weapons, mirrors, screens, and objects of gold, lacquer, and glass, most made in China but some coming from Central Asia and Persia via the Silk Road.

Shinto *The "Way of the Gods," it was the native religion espoused by the Yamato rulers.*

Nara *Japan's first true city; it was established in 710 north of modern Osaka.*

Primary Source:
From **Chronicles of Japan**

Chapter Summary

To assess your mastery of this chapter and read the primary sources listed in the margins, visit **bedfordstmartins.com/mckayworld** or see *Sources of World Societies*.

Key Terms

Great Wall
Silk Road
tributary system
Confucian classics
Records of the Grand Historian
eunuchs
Age of Division
Grand Canal
Pure Land
Chan
Shinto
Nara

• *What were the social, cultural, and political consequences of the unification of China under a strong centralized government?*

The unification of China in 221 B.C.E. by the Qin Dynasty had momentous consequences. During the four centuries of the subsequent Han Dynasty, unified government provided internal peace and promoted Confucian principles. It aided economic development by building roads and providing relief in cases of floods, droughts, and famines. It could draw on its vast resources to send huge armies against the nomadic Xiongnu, who regularly raided settlements in the north. These armies made possible a major expansion of Chinese territory both to the south and into Central Asia. Overlordship in Central Asia allowed trade along the Silk Road to flourish. The Han was so successful that its memory inspired many efforts to reunify China during the four centuries of division that followed.

• *How were both Buddhism and China changed by the spread of Buddhism across Asia?*

In the final years of the Han Dynasty, Buddhism reached China. Conquest had little to do with the spread of Buddhism in East Asia (in contrast with the spread of Christianity and Islam, which often followed a change of rulers). Rather it was merchants and missionaries who brought Buddhism across the Silk Road. By the time it reached China, Buddhism was a religion with a huge body of scriptures, celibate monks and nuns, traditions of depicting Buddhas and bodhisattvas in statues and paintings, and a strong proselytizing tradition, all of which distinguished it from China's indigenous religious traditions. Buddhism brought to China new philosophical concepts, new artistic styles, and the new social roles of celibate monks and nuns.

• *In what ways was China's second empire different from its first?*

After centuries of division, China was reunified in 589 by the Sui and Tang Dynasties. China regained overlordship along the Silk Road into Central Asia and once again had to deal with powerful northern neighbors, this time the Turks and Uighurs. But there was also much that was different between the Han and Tang empires. The south had become a much more major part of the economy, settled by many more Chinese. Perhaps in part because of the enormous popularity of Buddhism, Chinese culture in Tang times was highly receptive to influences from outside during this period, especially from Persia and India. Poetry played a much larger part in intellectual life, and the examination system was becoming steadily more important as well.

• What elements of Chinese culture were adopted by Koreans, Vietnamese, and Japanese, and how did they adapt them to their own circumstances?

In this era, China's neighbors, especially Korea, Japan, and Vietnam, began to adopt elements of China's material, political, and religious culture, including the Chinese writing system. Force of arms helped bring Chinese culture to both Korea and Vietnam. But military might was not the primary means by which culture spread in this period. Particularly in Korea and Japan, ambitious rulers sought out Chinese expertise and Chinese products, believing the adoption of the most advanced ideas and technologies to be to their advantage. They could pick and choose, adopting those elements of the more advanced cultures that suited them while retaining features of their earlier cultures, in the process developing distinctive national styles.

Suggested Reading

Barfield, Thomas. *Perilous Frontier: Nomadic Empires and China, 221 B.C.–A.D. 1757*. 1989. A bold interpretation of the relationship between the rise and fall of dynasties in China and the rise and fall of nomadic confederations that derived resources from them.

Elvin, Mark. *The Pattern of the Chinese Past*. 1973. Analyzes the military dimensions of China's unification.

Farris, Wayne. *Population, Disease, and Land in Early Japan, 645–900*. 1985. Shows the impact of the introduction of smallpox to Japan in the eighth century on the government and rural power structure.

Hardy, Grant. *Worlds of Bronze and Bamboo: Sima Qian's Conquest of History*. 1999. An excellent introduction to the methods of China's earliest historian. Although Sima Qian seems to present just the facts, Hardy shows how he brings out different perspectives and interpretations in different chapters.

Holcomb, Charles. *The Genesis of East Asia, 221 B.C.–A.D. 907*. 2001. A thought-provoking analysis of the connections between China and Korea, Japan, and Vietnam, which emphasizes the use of the Chinese script.

Schafer, Edward. *The Golden Peaches of Samarkand*. 1963. Draws on Tang literature to show the place of the western regions in Tang life and imagination.

Seth, Michael J. *A Concise History of Korea: From the Neolithic Period Through the Nineteenth Century*. 2006. An up-to-date and well-balanced introduction to Korean history.

Totman, Conrad. *A History of Japan*. 1999. A broad and up-to-date history of Japan.

Waley, Arthur. *The Life and Times of Po Chu-i, 772–846 A.D.* 1949. A lively biography of a Tang official, which draws heavily on his poetry.

Wright, Arthur. *Buddhism in Chinese History*. 1959. This short book remains a good introduction to China's encounter with Buddhism and the ways Buddhism was adapted to China.

Notes

1. Burton Watson, trans. *Records of the Grand Historian of China*, vol. 2 (New York: Columbia University Press, 1961), p. 496.
2. Ibid., p. 499.
3. Patricia Buckley Ebrey, *The Cambridge Illustrated History of China* (Cambridge: Cambridge University Press, 1996), p. 74.
4. W. F. Jenner, *Memories of Loyang: Yang Hsüan-chih and the Lost Capital (493–534)* (Oxford: Clarendon Press, 1981), p. 208.
5. Arthur Waley, trans., *More Translations from the Chinese* (New York: Knopf, 1919), p. 27. Reprinted by permission of the Arthur Waley Estate.
6. Ibid., p. 71.
7. *Sources of Japanese Tradition*, by de Bary, Keene, Tanabe, and Varley, eds. Copyright © 2001 by Columbia University Press. Reproduced with permission of COLUMBIA UNIVERSITY PRESS in the format Textbook via Copyright Clearance Center.

Listening to the

PAST

Copying Buddhist Sutras

Buddhism was not merely a set of ideas but also a set of practices. In Chinese, Japanese, and Korean monasteries, as in Western ones, monks and nuns, under the direction of an abbot or abbess, would read and copy scriptures as an act of devotion. Pious laypeople might pay to have sutras copied as a means of earning religious merit. Sometimes at the end of a sutra a copyist attached a statement explaining the circumstances that had surrounded the act of copying. Here are two such statements, one from a sutra found in Dunhuang, on the northwest fringe of China proper, dated 550, and the other from Korea, dated 755.

1.

Happiness is not fortuitous: pray for it and it will be found. Results are not born of thin air: pay heed to causes and results will follow. This explains how the Buddhist disciple and nun Daorong—because her conduct in her previous life was not correct—came to be born in her present form, a woman, vile and unclean.

Now if she does not honor the awesome decree of Buddha, how can future consequences be favorable for her? Therefore, having cut down her expenditures on food and clothing, she reverently has had the *Nirvana sutra* copied once. She prays that those who read it carefully will be exalted in mind to the highest realms and that those who communicate its meaning will cause others to be so enlightened.

She also prays that in her present existence she will have no further sickness or suffering, that her parents in seven other incarnations (who have already died or will die in the future) and her present family and close relatives may experience joy in the four elements [earth, water, fire, and air], and that whatever they seek may indeed come to pass. Finally, she prays that all those endowed with knowledge may be included within this prayer. Dated the 29th day of the fourth month of 550.

2.

The copying began on the first day of the eighth month of 754, and was completed on the fourteenth day of the second month of the following year.

One who made a vow to copy the scripture is Dharma master Yongi of Hwangnyong Monastery. His purposes were to repay the love of his parents and to pray for all living beings in the dharma realm to attain the path of the Buddha.

The scripture is made as follows: First scented water is sprinkled around the roots of a paper-bark mulberry tree to quicken its growth; the bark is then peeled and pounded to make paper with a clean surface. The copyists, the artisans who make the centerpiece of the scroll, and the painters who draw the images of buddhas and bodhisattvas all receive the bodhisattva ordination and observe abstinence. After relieving themselves, sleeping, eating, or drinking, they take a bath in scented water before returning to the work. Copyists are adorned with new pure garments, loose trousers, a coarse crown, and a deva crown. Two azure-clad boys sprinkle water on their heads and . . . azure-clad boys and musicians perform music. The processions to the copying site are headed by one who sprinkles scented water on their path, another who scatters flowers, a dharma master who carries a censer, and another dharma master who chants Buddhist verses. Each of the copyists carries incense and flowers and invokes the name of the Buddha as he progresses.

This gilt bronze image of Maitreya, not quite 3 feet tall, was made in Korea in about 600. It depicts the Buddha Maitreya, the Future Buddha who presides over Tushita Heaven. The rounded face, slender body, and gracefully draped robe help convey the idea that the Buddha is neither male nor female but beyond such distinctions. *(Courtesy, Yushin Yoo)*

Upon reaching the site, all take refuge in the three Jewels (the Buddha, the Dharma, and the Order), make three bows, and offer the *Flower Garland Scripture* and others to buddhas and bodhisattvas. Then they sit down and copy the scripture, make the centerpiece of the scroll, and paint the buddhas and bodhisattvas. Thus, azure-clad boys and musicians cleanse everything before a piece of relic is placed in the center.

Now I make a vow that the copied scripture will not break till the end of the future—even when a major chilicosm [millions of universes] is destroyed by the three calamities, this scripture shall be intact as the void. If all living things rely on this scripture, they shall witness the Buddha, listen to his dharma, worship the relic, aspire to enlightenment without backsliding, cultivate the vows of the Universally Worthy Bodhisattva, and achieve Buddhahood.

Questions for Analysis

1. How does the nun who wrote the first note explain her birth as a woman? Whom does she hope to benefit by the act of copying the sutra?

2. What do you make of the emphasis on rituals surrounding copying the sutra in the second statement?

Sources: Patricia Buckley Ebrey, ed., *Chinese Civilization: A Sourcebook* (New York: Free Press, 1993), pp. 102–103; Peter H. Lee, ed., *Sourcebook of Korean Civilization* (New York: Columbia University Press, 1993), pp. 201–202, modified.

Hagia Sophia ("Holy Wisdom"), built by the emperor Justinian in the sixth century, was the largest Christian cathedral in the world for a thousand years. After Constantinople was conquered by the Ottoman Turks in 1453, it became a mosque, and today it is a museum. *(Courtesy, Editore Sadea Sansoni, Florence)*

7 EUROPE AND WESTERN ASIA, CA. 350–850

From the third century onward, the Western Roman Empire slowly disintegrated. The last Roman emperor in the West, Romulus Augustus, was deposed by the Ostrogothic chieftain Odoacer in 476, but much of the empire had already come under the rule of various barbarian tribes well before this. Scholars have long seen this era as one of the great turning points in Western history, but during the last several decades, focus has shifted to continuities as well as changes. What is now usually termed "late antiquity" has been recognized as a period of creativity and adaptation in Europe and western Asia, not simply of decline and fall.

The two main agents of continuity were the Eastern Roman (or Byzantine) Empire and the Christian church. The Byzantine Empire lasted until 1453, a thousand years longer than the Western Roman Empire, and preserved and transmitted much of ancient law, philosophy, and institutions. Missionaries and church officials spread Christianity within and far beyond the borders of what had been the Roman Empire, transforming a small sect into the most important and wealthiest institution in Europe. The main agents of change in late antiquity were the barbarian groups migrating throughout much of Europe and western Asia. They brought different social, political, and economic structures with them, but as they encountered Roman and Byzantine culture and became Christian, their own ways of doing things were also transformed.

THE BYZANTINE EMPIRE

How was the Byzantine Empire able to survive for so long, and what were its most important achievements?

The Emperor Constantine (see page 122) had tried to maintain the unity of the Roman Empire, but during the fifth and sixth centuries the Western and Eastern halves drifted apart. From Constantinople, Eastern Roman emperors worked to hold the empire together and to reconquer at least some of the West from barbarian

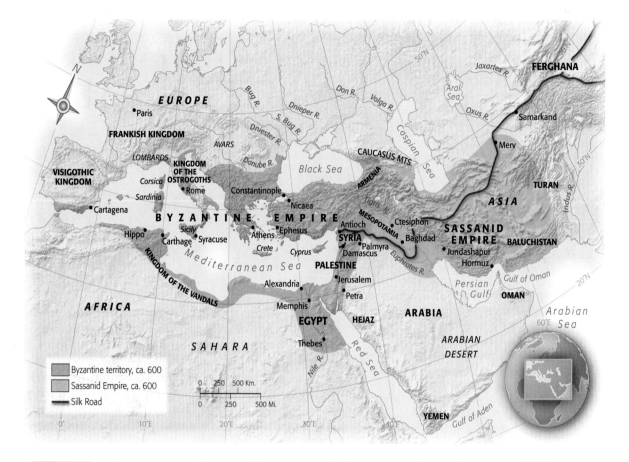

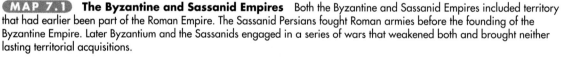

MAP 7.1 **The Byzantine and Sassanid Empires** Both the Byzantine and Sassanid Empires included territory that had earlier been part of the Roman Empire. The Sassanid Persians fought Roman armies before the founding of the Byzantine Empire. Later Byzantium and the Sassanids engaged in a series of wars that weakened both and brought neither lasting territorial acquisitions.

tribes. Justinian (r. 527–565) waged long wars against the Ostrogoths and temporarily regained Italy and North Africa, but the costs were high. Justinian's wars exhausted the resources of the state, destroyed Italy's economy, and killed a large part of Italy's population. Weakened, Italy fell easily to another Germanic tribe, the Lombards, shortly after Justinian's death. In the late sixth century, the territory of the Western Roman Empire came once again under Germanic sway.

However, the Roman Empire continued in the East. The Eastern Roman or Byzantine Empire (see Map 7.1) preserved the forms, institutions, and traditions of the old Roman Empire, and its people even called themselves Romans. Byzantium passed the intellectual heritage of Greco-Roman civilization on to later cultures and also developed its own distinctive characteristics.

Sources of Byzantine Strength

While the Western parts of the Roman Empire gradually succumbed to Germanic invaders, the Eastern Roman or Byzantine Empire survived. (The Byzantines themselves called their state the "Roman Empire," and only in the sixteenth century did people begin to use the term "Byzantine Empire.") Byzantine emperors traced their lines back past Constantine to Augustus (see page 112). While evolving into a Christian and Greek-speaking state with a multiethnic population centered in the eastern Mediterranean and the Balkans, the Byzantines retained the legal and administrative system of the empire centered at Rome. Thus, the senate that sat in Constantinople carried on the traditions and preserved the glory of the old Roman senate. The army that defended the empire was the direct descendant of the old Roman legions.

That army was kept very busy, for the Byzantine Empire survived waves of attacks. In 559 a force of Huns and Slavs reached the gates of Constantinople. In 583 the Avars, a mounted Mongol people who had swept across Russia and southeastern Europe, seized Byzantine forts along the Danube and also reached the walls of Constantinople. Between 572 and 630 the Greeks were repeatedly at war with the Sassanid Persians (see below). Beginning in 632 the Arabs pressured the Greek empire. Why didn't one or a combination of these enemies capture Constantinople, as the Germans had taken Rome? The answer lies, first, in the strong military leadership the Greeks possessed. General Priskos (d. 612) skillfully led Byzantine armies to a decisive victory over the Avars in 601. Then, after a long war, the well-organized emperor Heraclius I (r. 610–641) crushed the Persians at Nineveh in Iraq.

Second, the city's location and excellent fortifications proved crucial. The site of Constantinople was not absolutely impregnable, but it was almost so. Constantinople had the most powerful defenses in the ancient world. Massive triple walls protected the city from sea invasion. Within the walls huge cisterns provided water, and vast gardens and grazing areas supplied vegetables and meat. Such strong fortifications and provisions meant that if attacked by sea, a defending people could hold out far longer than a besieging army. The site chosen for the imperial capital in the fourth century enabled Constantinople to survive in the eighth century. Because the city survived, the empire, though reduced in territory, endured.

Chronology

226–651	Sassanid dynasty
312	Constantine legalizes Christianity in Roman Empire
340–419	Life of Saint Jerome; creation of the Vulgate
354–430	Life of Saint Augustine
380	Theodosius makes Christianity official religion of Roman Empire
385–461	Life of Saint Patrick
481–511	Reign of Clovis
527–565	Reign of Justinian
529	*The Rule of Saint Benedict*
541–543	"Justinian plague"
730–843	Iconoclastic controversy
768–814	Reign of Charlemagne; Carolingian Renaissance
1054	Schism between Roman Catholic and Greek Orthodox churches

The Sassanid Empire of Persia and Byzantium

For several centuries the Sassanid Empire of Persia was Byzantium's most regular foe. In 226, Ardashir I (r. 226–243) founded the Sassanid dynasty, which lasted until 651, when it was overthrown by the Muslims. Ardashir expanded his territory and absorbed the Roman province of Mesopotamia.

Centered in the fertile Tigris-Euphrates Valley, but with access to the Persian Gulf and extending south to Meshan (modern Kuwait), the Sassanid Empire's economic prosperity rested on agriculture; its location also proved well suited for commerce. A lucrative caravan trade from Ctesiphon north to Merv and then east to Samarkand linked the Sassanid Empire to the Silk Road and China (see page 138). Persian metalwork, textiles, and glass were exchanged for Chinese silks, and these goods brought about considerable cultural contact between the Sassanids and the Chinese.

Whereas the Parthians had tolerated many religions, the Sassanid Persians made Zoroastrianism the official state religion. Religion and the state were inextricably tied together. The king's power rested on the support of nobles and Zoroastrian priests, who monopolized positions in the court and in the imperial bureaucracy. A highly elaborate court ceremonial and ritual exalted the status of the king and emphasized his semidivine pre-eminence over his subjects. (The Byzantine monarchy, the Roman papacy, and the Muslim caliphate subsequently copied aspects of this Persian ceremonial.) Zoroastrianism promoted hostility toward Christians because of what was perceived as their connections to Rome and Constantinople, and the sizable Jewish population in Mesopotamia after the **diaspora** (dispersion of the Jews from Jerusalem between 132 and 135) suffered intermittent persecution.

An expansionist foreign policy brought Persia into frequent conflict with Byzantium, and neither side was able to achieve a clear-cut victory. The long wars financed by higher taxation, on top of the arrival of the bubonic plague (see page 168), compounded discontent in both Byzantine and Persian societies. Internal political instability weakened the Sassanid dynasty, and in the seventh century Persian territories were absorbed into the Islamic caliphate (see page 194).

The Law Code of Justinian

Byzantine emperors organized and preserved Roman law, making a lasting contribution to the medieval and modern worlds. Roman law had developed from many sources—decisions by judges, edicts of the emperors, legislation passed by the senate, and the opinions of jurists expert in the theory and practice of law. By the fourth century, Roman law had become a huge, bewildering mass. Its sheer bulk made it almost unusable.

● **Sassanid Silver and Gold Plate** This exquisitely wrought Sassanid plate shows a king hunting from horseback. Hunting was a favorite aristocratic pastime, and fine horses were exported from Persia to many parts of the world, as were Sassanid plates and drinking cups. *(Erich Lessing/Art Resource, NY)*

The emperor Justinian appointed a committee of eminent jurists to sort through and organize the laws. The result was the *Code,* which distilled the legal genius of the Romans into a coherent whole, eliminated outmoded laws and contradictions, and clarified the law itself.

diaspora *The dispersion of the Jews from Jerusalem between 132 and 135.*

Justinian next set about bringing order to the equally huge body of Roman *jurisprudence,* the science or philosophy of law. To harmonize the often differing opinions of Roman jurists, Justinian directed his jurists to clear up disputed points and to issue definitive rulings. Accordingly, in 533 his lawyers published the *Digest,* which codified Roman legal thought. Then Justinian's lawyers compiled a handbook of civil law, the *Institutes.* These three works—the *Code,* the *Digest,* and the *Institutes*—are the backbone of the **corpus juris civilis,** the "body of civil law," which is the foundation of law for nearly every modern European nation.

corpus juris civilis *The "body of civil law," it is composed of the* Code, *the* Digest, *and the* Institutes.

Byzantine Intellectual Life

The Byzantines prized education, and because of them many masterpieces of ancient Greek literature survived to influence the intellectual life of the modern world. The literature of the Byzantine Empire was predominately Greek, although Latin was long spoken by top politicians, scholars, and lawyers. Among members of the large reading public, history was a favorite subject.

The most remarkable Byzantine historian was Procopius (ca. 500–ca. 562), who left a rousing account of Justinian's reconquest of North Africa and Italy. Procopius's *Secret History,* however, is a vicious and uproarious attack on Justinian and his wife, the empress Theodora, which continued the wit and venom of earlier Greek and Roman writers. (See the feature "Individuals in Society: Theodora of Constantinople.")

Theodora of Constantinople

The empress Theodora shown with the halo symbolic of power in Eastern art. *(Scala/Art Resource, NY)*

The most powerful woman in Byzantine history was the daughter of a bear trainer for the circus. Theodora (ca. 497–548) grew up in what her contemporaries regarded as an undignified and morally suspect atmosphere, and she worked as a dancer and burlesque actress, both dishonorable occupations in the Roman world. Despite her background, she caught the eye of Justinian, who was then a military leader and whose uncle (and adoptive father) Justin had himself risen from obscurity to become the emperor of the Byzantine Empire. Under Justinian's influence, Justin changed the law to allow an actress who had left her disreputable life to marry whom she liked, and Justinian and Theodora married in 525. When Justinian was proclaimed co-emperor with his uncle Justin on April 1, 527, Theodora received the rare title of *augusta,* empress. Thereafter her name was linked with Justinian's in the exercise of imperial power.

Most of our knowledge of Theodora's early life comes from the *Secret History,* a tell-all description of the vices of Justinian and his court, written by Procopius (ca. 550), who was the official court historian and thus spent his days praising those same people. In the *Secret History,* he portrays Theodora and Justinian as demonic, greedy, and vicious, killing courtiers to steal their property. In scene after detailed scene, Procopius portrays Theodora as particularly evil, sexually insatiable, depraved, and cruel, a temptress who used sorcery to attract men, including the hapless Justinian.

In one of his official histories, *The History of the Wars of Justinian,* Procopius presents a very different Theodora. Riots between the supporters of two teams in chariot races—who formed associations somewhat like street gangs and somewhat like political parties—had turned deadly, and Justinian wavered in his handling of the perpetrators. Both sides turned against the emperor, besieging the palace while Justinian was inside it. Shouting N-I-K-A (Victory), the rioters swept through the city, burning and looting, and destroyed half of Constantinople. Justinian's counselors urged flight, but, according to Procopius, Theodora rose and declared:

For one who has reigned, it is intolerable to be an exile. . . . If you wish, O Emperor, to save yourself, there is no difficulty: we have ample funds and there are the ships. Yet reflect whether, when you have once escaped to a place of security, you will not prefer death to safety. I agree with an old saying that the purple [that is, the color worn only by emperors] is a fair winding sheet [to be buried in].

Justinian rallied, had the rioters driven into the hippodrome, and ordered between thirty and thirty-five thousand men and women executed. The revolt was crushed and Justinian's authority restored, an outcome approved by Procopius.

Other sources describe or suggest Theodora's influence on imperial policy. Justinian passed a number of laws that improved the legal status of women, such as allowing women to own property the same way that men could and to be guardians over their own children. He forbade the exposure of unwanted infants, which happened more often to girls than to boys, since boys were valued more highly. Theodora presided at imperial receptions for Arab sheiks, Persian ambassadors, Germanic princesses from the West, and barbarian chieftains from southern Russia. When Justinian fell ill from the bubonic plague in 542, Theodora took over his duties, banning those who discussed his possible successor. Justinian is reputed to have consulted her every day about all aspects of state policy, including religious policy regarding the doctrinal disputes that continued throughout his reign. Theodora's favored interpretation of Christian doctrine about the nature of Christ was not accepted by the main body of theologians in Constantinople—nor by Justinian—but she urged protection of her fellow believers and in one case hid an aged scholar in the women's quarters of the palace.

Theodora's influence over her husband and her power in the Byzantine state continued until she died, perhaps of cancer, twenty years before Justinian. Her influence may have even continued after death, for Justinian continued to pass reforms favoring women and, at the end of his life, accepted her interpretation of Christian doctrine. Institutions that she established, including hospitals, orphanages, houses for the rehabilitation of prostitutes, and churches, continued to be reminders of her charity and piety.

Theodora has been viewed as a symbol of the manipulation of beauty and cleverness to attain position and power, and also as a strong and capable co-ruler who held the empire together during riots, revolts, and deadly epidemics. Just as Procopius expressed both views, the debate has continued to today among writers of science fiction and fantasy as well as biographers and historians.

Questions for Analysis

1. How would you assess the complex legacy of Theodora?

2. Since the public and private views of Procopius are so different regarding the empress, should he be trusted at all as a historical source?

In mathematics and science, the Byzantines discovered little that was new, though they passed Greco-Roman learning on to the Arabs. The best-known Byzantine scientific discovery was an explosive compound known as "Greek fire" made of crude oil mixed with resin and sulfur, which was heated and propelled by a pump through a bronze tube. As the liquid jet left the tube, it was ignited, somewhat like a modern flamethrower. Greek fire saved Constantinople from Arab assault in 678.

The Byzantines devoted a great deal of attention to medicine, and the general level of medical competence was far higher in the Byzantine Empire than it was in western Europe. Yet their physicians could not cope with the terrible disease, often called "the Justinian plague," that swept through the Byzantine Empire and parts of western Europe between 541 and 543. Probably originating in northwestern India and carried to the Mediterranean region by ships, the disease was similar to modern forms of bubonic plague. Characterized by high fevers, chills, delirium, and enlarged lymph nodes, or by inflammation of the lungs that caused hemorrhages of black blood, the plague carried off tens of thousands of people. The epidemic had profound political as well as social consequences. It weakened Justinian's military resources, thus hampering his efforts to restore unity to the Mediterranean world. Losses from the plague also further weakened Byzantine and Persian forces that had badly damaged each other, contributing to their inability to offer more than token opposition to the Muslim armies (see pages 194–195).

● **Justinian and His Attendants** This mosaic detail is composed of thousands of tiny cubes of colored glass or stone called *tessarae*, which are set in plaster against a blazing golden background. Some attempt has been made at naturalistic portraiture. *(Scala/Art Resource, NY)*

Constantinople: The Second Rome

In the tenth century Constantinople was the greatest city in the Christian world: the seat of the imperial court and administration, a large population center, and the pivot of a large volume of international trade. As a natural geographical entrepôt between East and West, the city's markets offered goods from many parts of the world. Furs and timber flowed across the Black Sea from the Rus (Russia) to the capital, as did slaves across the Mediterranean from northern Europe and the Balkans via Venice. Spices, silks, jewelry, and luxury goods came to Constantinople from India and China by way of Arabia, the Red Sea, and the Indian Ocean. By the eleventh century, only Baghdad exceeded Constantinople in the quantity and value of goods exchanged there.

Jewish, Muslim, and Italian merchants controlled most foreign trade. Among the Greeks, aristocrats and monasteries usually invested their wealth in real estate, which involved little risk but brought little gain. As in western Europe and China, the landed aristocracy always held the dominant social position. Merchants and craftsmen, even when they acquired considerable wealth, never won social prominence.

Constantinople did not enjoy constant political stability. Between the accession of Heraclius in 610 and the fall of the city to Western Crusaders in 1204 (see page 364), four separate dynasties ruled at Constantinople. Imperial government involved such intricate court intrigue, assassinations, and military revolts that the word *byzantine* is sometimes used in English to mean extremely entangled and complicated politics.

What do we know about private life in Constantinople? Research has revealed a fair amount about the Byzantine *oikos,* or household. The Greek household included family members and servants, some of whom were slaves. Artisans lived and worked in their shops. Clerks, civil servants, minor officials, business people—those who today would be called middle class—commonly dwelt in multistory buildings perhaps comparable to the apartment complexes of modern American cities. Wealthy aristocrats resided in freestanding mansions that frequently included interior courts, galleries, large reception halls, small sleeping rooms, reading and writing rooms, baths, and chapels.

In the homes of the upper classes, the segregation of women seems to have been the first principle of interior design. As in ancient Athens, private houses contained a *gynaceum,* or women's apartment, where women were kept strictly separated from the outside world. The fundamental reason for this segregation was the family's honor: "An unchaste daughter is guilty of harming not only herself but also her parents and relatives. That is why you should keep your daughters under lock and key, as if proven guilty or imprudent, in order to avoid venomous bites," as an eleventh-century Byzantine writer put it.[1]

Marriage served as part of a family's strategy for social advancement. The family and the entire kinship group participated in the selection of brides and grooms, choosing spouses that might enhance the family's wealth or prestige.

● ● ● ● ● ● ● ● ● ● ● ● ● ●

THE GROWTH OF THE CHRISTIAN CHURCH

What factors enabled the Christian church to expand and thrive?

As the Western Roman Empire disintegrated in the fourth and fifth centuries, the Christian church survived and grew, becoming the most important institution in Europe. The able administrators and creative thinkers of the church gradually established an orthodox set of beliefs and adopted a system of organization based on that of the Roman state.

The Church and Its Leaders

dioceses *Geographic administrative districts of the Church, each under the authority of a bishop and centered around a cathedral.*

In early Christian communities believers elected their leaders, but as the centuries passed appointment by existing church leaders or secular rulers became the common pattern. During the reign of Diocletian (284–305), the empire had been divided for administrative purposes into geographical units called **dioceses,** and Christianity adopted this pattern. Each diocese was headed by a bishop who was responsible for organizing preaching, overseeing the community's goods, and maintaining orthodox (established or correct) doctrine. The center of a bishop's authority was his cathedral, a word deriving from the Latin *cathedra,* meaning "chair."

The early Christian church benefited from the brilliant administrative abilities of some bishops. Bishop Ambrose, for example, the son of the Roman prefect of Gaul, was a trained lawyer and the governor of a province. He is typical of the Roman aristocrats who held high public office, were converted to Christianity, and subsequently became bishops. The church received support from the emperors, and in return the emperors expected the support of the Christian church in maintaining order and unity.

Arianism *A theological belief, originating with Arius, a priest of Alexandria, that denied that Christ was divine and co-eternal with God the Father.*

In the fourth century, theological disputes frequently and sharply divided the Christian community. Some disagreements had to do with the nature of Christ. For example, **Arianism,** which originated with Arius (ca. 250–336), a priest of Alexandria, held that Jesus was created by the will of God the Father and thus was not co-eternal with him. Arius also reasoned that Jesus the Son must be inferior to God the Father, because the Father is incapable of suffering and did not die. Orthodox theologians branded Arius's position a *heresy*—denial of a basic doctrine of faith.

Arianism enjoyed such popularity and provoked such controversy that Constantine, to whom religious disagreement meant civil disorder, interceded. In 325 he summoned a council of church leaders to Nicaea in Asia Minor and presided over it personally. The council produced the Nicene Creed, which defined the orthodox position that Christ is "eternally begotten of the Father" and of the same substance as the Father. Arius and those who refused to accept the creed were banished, the first case of civil punishment for heresy. This participation of the emperor in a theological dispute within the church paved the way for later emperors to claim that they could do the same.

In 380 the emperor Theodosius went further than Constantine and made Christianity the official religion of the empire. Theodosius stripped Roman pagan temples of statues, made the practice of the old Roman state religion a treasonable offense, and persecuted Christians who dissented from orthodox doctrine. Most significant, he allowed the church to establish its own courts. Church courts began to develop their own body of law, called **canon law.** These courts, not the Roman government, had jurisdiction over the clergy and ecclesiastical disputes. The foundation for later growth in church power had been laid.

canon law *The body of internal law that governs the church.*

The Western Church and the Eastern Church

The position of the church differed considerably in the Byzantine East and the Germanic West. The fourth-century emperors Constantine and Theodosius had wanted the church to act as a unifying force within the empire, but the Germanic invasions made that impossible. The bishops of Rome repeatedly called on the emperors at Constantinople for military support against the invaders, but rarely could the emperors send it. The church in the West became less dependent on the emperors' power, and gradually took over political authority, charging taxes, sending troops, and enforcing laws.

Primary Source:
Tertullian, *From* Apologia

After the removal of the imperial capital and the emperor to Constantinople, the bishop of Rome exercised considerable influence in the West, in part because he had no real competitor there. In addition, successive bishops of Rome stressed their special role. According to tradition, Peter, the chief of Christ's first twelve followers, had lived and been executed in Rome. The popes claimed to be successors to Peter and heirs to his authority, based on Jesus' words: "You are Peter, and on this rock I will build my church. . . . Whatever you declare bound on earth shall be bound in heaven." Theologians call this statement the **Petrine Doctrine.** The bishops of Rome came to be known as popes—from the Latin *papa,* for "father"—and in the fifth century began to stress their supremacy over other Christian communities.

In the East, the bishops of Antioch, Alexandria, Jerusalem, and Constantinople had more power than other bishops, but the emperor's jurisdiction over the church was also fully acknowledged. The emperor in Constantinople nominated the *patriarch,* as the highest prelate of the Eastern church was called. The Eastern emperors looked on religion as a branch of the state. They considered it their duty to protect the faith not only against heathen enemies but also against heretics within the empire. Following the pattern set by Constantine, the emperors summoned councils of bishops and theologians to settle doctrinal disputes.

> **Petrine Doctrine** *The statement used by popes, bishops of Rome, based on Jesus' words, to substantiate their claim of being the successors of Saint Peter and heirs to his authority as chief of the apostles.*

The Iconoclastic Controversy

Several theological disputes split the Eastern Christian Church (also called the Orthodox Church) in the centuries after Constantine. The most serious was a controversy over *icons*—images or representations of God the Father, Jesus, the Virgin, or the saints in a painting, bas-relief, or mosaic. Since the third century the church had allowed people to venerate icons. Although all prayer had to be directed to God the Father, Christian teaching held that icons representing the saints fostered reverence and that Jesus and the saints could most effectively plead a cause to God the Father. *Iconoclasts,* those who favored the destruction of icons, argued that people were worshiping the image itself rather than what it signified. This, they claimed, constituted *idolatry,* a violation of the prohibition of images in the Ten Commandments.

The result of the controversy over icons was a terrible theological conflict that split the Byzantine world for a century. In 730 the emperor Leo III (r. 717–741) ordered the destruction of the images. The removal of icons from Byzantine churches provoked a violent reaction: entire provinces revolted, and the empire and Roman papacy severed relations. Since Eastern monasteries were the fiercest defenders of icons, Leo's son Constantine V (r. 741–775), nicknamed "Copronymous" ("Dung-name") by his enemies, took the war to the monasteries. He seized their property, executed some of the monks, and forced others into the army. Theological disputes and civil disorder over the icons continued intermittently until 843, when the icons were restored.

The implications of the **iconoclastic controversy** extended far beyond strictly theological issues. Iconoclasm raised the question of the right of the emperor to intervene in religious disputes—a central problem in the relations of church and state. Iconoclasm antagonized the pope and served to encourage him in his quest for an alliance with the Frankish monarchy (see page 182). This further divided the two parts of Christendom, and in 1054 a theological disagreement led the bishop of Rome and the patriarch of Constantinople to excommunicate each other. The outcome was a continuing **schism,** or split, between the Roman Catholic and the Greek Orthodox churches. Finally, the acceptance of icons profoundly influenced subsequent religious art within Christianity. That art rejected the Judaic and Islamic prohibition of figural representation and continued in the Greco-Roman tradition of human representation.

> **Primary Source:**
> **Liudprand of Cremona,**
> ***A Report on the Embassy to Constantinople***

> **iconoclastic controversy** *The conflict that resulted from the destruction of Christian images in Byzantine churches in 730.*

> **schism** *A division, or split, in church leadership; there were several major schisms in Christianity.*

Christian Monasticism

Like the great East Asian religions of Jainism and Buddhism (see pages 37–41), Christianity soon developed an ascetic component: monasticism. Christianity began and spread as a city religion. As early as the first century, however, some especially pious Christians felt that the only alternative to the decadence of urban life was complete separation from the world. This desire to withdraw from ordinary life led to the

eremitical *A form of monasticism that began in Egypt in the third century in which individuals and small groups withdrew from cities and organized society to seek God through prayer.*

coenobitic *Communal living in monasteries, encouraged by Saint Basil and the church because it provided an environment for training the aspirant in the virtues of charity, poverty, and freedom from self-deception.*

regular clergy *Clergy who live under the rule (Latin: regulus) of a monastic house; monks and nuns.*

secular clergy *Clergy who staffed the churches where people worshiped and were therefore not separated from the world (Latin: saeculum); priests and bishops.*

> **Primary Source:**
> **St. Benedict of Nursia,**
> ***The Rule of St. Benedict:***
> ***Work and Pray***

development of the monastic life, which took two forms: **eremitical** (isolated) and **coenobitic** (communal). The people who lived in caves and sought shelter in the desert and mountains were called *hermits,* from the Greek word *eremos.*

Monasticism began in Egypt in the third century. At first individuals and small groups withdrew from cities and organized society to seek God through prayer in caves and shelters in the desert or mountains. Gradually large colonies of monks emerged in the deserts of Upper Egypt. Many devout women also were attracted to this eremitical life. Although monks and nuns led isolated lives, ordinary people soon recognized them as holy people and sought them as spiritual guides.

Church leaders did not really approve of eremitical life. Hermits sometimes claimed to have mystical experiences—direct communications with God. If hermits could communicate directly with the Lord, what need had they for the priest and the institutional church? The church hierarchy encouraged coenobitic monasticism, communal living in monasteries, which provided an environment for training the aspirant in the virtues of charity, poverty, and freedom from self-deception. In the fourth, fifth, and sixth centuries, many different kinds of communal monasticism developed in Gaul, Italy, Spain, Anglo-Saxon England, and Ireland.

In 529 Benedict of Nursia (480–543), who had experimented with both the eremitical and the communal forms of monastic life, wrote a brief set of regulations for the monks who had gathered around him at Monte Cassino between Rome and Naples. Benedict's guide for monastic life, known as the *Rule,* slowly replaced all others. *The Rule of Saint Benedict* has influenced all forms of organized religious life in the Roman church.

Men and women who lived in monastic houses all followed sets of rules, first those of Benedict and later those written by other individuals, and because of this came to be called **regular clergy,** from the Latin word *regulus* (rule). Priests and bishops who staffed churches in which people worshiped and who were not cut off from the world were called **secular clergy.** (According to official church doctrine, women are not members of the clergy, but this distinction was not clear to most medieval people.)

The Rule of Saint Benedict offered a simple code for ordinary men. It outlined a monastic life of regularity, discipline, and moderation in an atmosphere of silence. Each monk had ample food and adequate sleep. The monk spent part of each day in formal prayer, chanting psalms and other prayers from the Bible. The rest of the day was passed in manual labor, study, and private prayer.

Why did the Benedictine form of monasticism eventually replace other forms of Western monasticism? The monastic life as conceived by Saint Benedict struck a balance between asceticism and activity. It thus provided opportunities for men of entirely different abilities and talents—from mechanics to gardeners to literary scholars. The Benedictine form of religious life also proved congenial to women. Five miles from Monte Cassino at Plombariola, Benedict's twin sister Scholastica (480–543) adapted the *Rule* for the use of her community of nuns.

Benedictine monasticism also succeeded partly because it was so materially successful. In the seventh and eighth centuries, monasteries pushed back forest and wasteland, drained swamps, and experimented with crop rotation. Such Benedictine houses made a significant contribution to the agricultural development of Europe, earning immense wealth in the process. The communal nature of their organization, whereby property was held in common and profits were pooled and reinvested, made this contribution possible.

Finally, monasteries conducted schools for local young people. Some learned about prescriptions and herbal remedies and went on to provide medical treatment for their localities. A few copied manuscripts and wrote books. Local and royal governments drew on the services of the literate men and able administrators the monasteries produced.

Monasticism in the Greek Orthodox world differed in fundamental ways from the monasticism that evolved in western Europe. First, while *The Rule of Saint Benedict* gradually became the universal guide for all western European monasteries, each individual house in the Byzantine world developed its own set of rules for organization and behavior. Second, education never became a central feature of the Greek houses. Monks and nuns had to be literate to perform the services of the choir, and children destined for the monastic life were taught to read and write, but no monastery assumed responsibility for the general training of the local young. Since bishops and patriarchs of the Greek church were recruited only from the monasteries, Greek houses did, however, exercise a cultural influence.

CHRISTIAN IDEAS AND PRACTICES

How did Christian thinkers and missionaries adapt Greco-Roman ideas to Christian theology and develop effective techniques to convert barbarian peoples to Christianity?

The evolution of Christianity was not simply a matter of institutions such as the papacy and monasteries, but also of ideas. Initially, Christians had believed that the end of the world was near and that they should dissociate themselves from the "filth" of Roman culture. Gradually, however, Christians developed a culture of ideas that drew on classical influences. At the same time, missionaries sponsored by bishops and monasteries spread Christian ideas and institutions far beyond the borders of the Roman Empire, often adapting them to existing notions as they assimilated pagan peoples to Christianity.

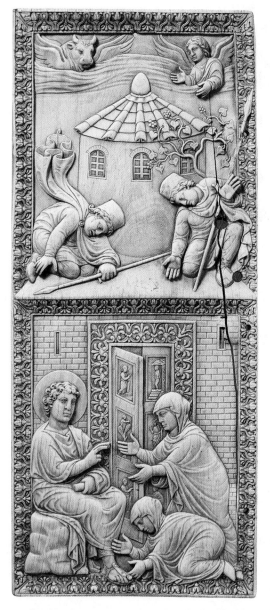

● **The Marys at Jesus' Tomb** This late-fourth-century ivory panel tells the story of Mary Magdalene and another Mary who went to Jesus' tomb to anoint the body (Matthew 28:1–7). At the top guards collapse when an angel descends from Heaven, and at the bottom the Marys listen to the angel telling them that Jesus had risen. Immediately after this, in Matthew's Gospel, Jesus appears to the women. Here the artist uses Roman artistic styles to convey Christian subject matter, an example of the assimilation of classical form and Christian teaching. *(Castello Sforzesco/Scala/Art Resource, NY)*

Adjustment to Classical Culture

Christians in the first and second centuries believed that Christ would soon fulfill his promise to return and that the end of the world was near. Thus they considered knowledge useless and learning a waste of time, and they preached the duty of Christians to prepare for the Second Coming of the Lord. The church father Tertullian (ca. 160–220) claimed: "We have no need for curiosity since Jesus Christ, nor for inquiry since the gospel."

On the other hand, Christianity encouraged adjustment to the ideas and institutions of the Roman world. Some biblical texts urged Christians to accept the existing social, economic, and political establishment. Christians really had little choice. Jewish and Roman cultures were the only cultures early Christians knew; they had to adapt their Roman education to their Christian beliefs. The result was compromise, as evidenced by the distinguished theologian Saint Jerome (340–419). He thought that Christians should study the best of ancient thought because it would direct their minds to God, and he translated the Old and New Testaments from Hebrew and Greek into vernacular Latin; his edition is known as the Vulgate.

Christian attitudes toward gender and sexuality provide a good example of the ways early Christians both adopted and adapted the views of their contemporary world. In his plan of salvation, Jesus considered women the equal of men. He attributed no disreputable qualities to women and did not refer to them as inferior creatures. On the contrary, women were among his earliest and most faithful converts.

Women took an active role in the spread of Christianity, preaching, acting as missionaries, being martyred alongside men, and perhaps even baptizing believers. Because early Christians believed that the Second Coming of Christ was imminent, they devoted their energies to their new spiritual family of co-believers. Early Christians often met in people's homes and called one another brother and sister, a metaphorical use of family terms that was new to the Roman Empire. Some women embraced the ideal of virginity and either singly or in monastic communities declared themselves "virgins in the service of Christ." All this made Christianity seem dangerous to many Romans, especially when becoming Christian actually led some young people to avoid marriage, which was viewed by Romans as the foundation of society and the proper patriarchal order.

Not all Christian teachings about gender were radical, however. In the first century C.E. male church leaders began to place restrictions on female believers. Paul and later writers forbade women to preach, and women were gradually excluded from holding official positions in Christianity other than in women's monasteries. In so limiting the activities of female believers Christianity was following classical Mediterranean culture, just as it patterned its official hierarchy after that of the Roman Empire.

Christian teachings about sexuality also built on classical culture. Many early church leaders, who are often called the church fathers, renounced marriage and sought to live chaste lives not only because they expected the Second Coming imminently, but also because they accepted the hostility toward the body that derived from certain strains of Hellenistic philosophy. Just as spirit was superior to matter, the mind was superior to the body. Though God had clearly sanctioned marriage, celibacy was the highest good. This emphasis on self-denial led to a strong streak of misogyny (hatred of women) in their writings, for they saw women and female sexuality as the chief obstacles to their preferred existence. They also saw intercourse as little more than animal lust, the triumph of the inferior body over the superior mind. Same-sex relations—which were generally acceptable in the Greco-Roman world, especially if they were between socially unequal individuals—were evil. The church fathers' misogyny and hostility toward sexuality had a greater influence on the formation of later attitudes than did the relatively egalitarian actions and words of Jesus.

Saint Augustine

The most influential church father in the West was Saint Augustine of Hippo (354–430). Saint Augustine was born into an urban family in what is now Algeria in North Africa. His father, a minor civil servant, was a pagan; his mother, Monica, a devout Christian. It was not until adulthood that he converted to his mother's religion. As bishop of the city of Hippo Regius, he was a renowned preacher, a vigorous defender of orthodox Christianity, and the author of more than ninety-three books and treatises.

Augustine's autobiography, *The Confessions,* is a literary masterpiece. Written in the rhetorical style and language of late Roman antiquity, it marks the synthesis of Greco-Roman forms and Christian thought. *The Confessions* describes Augustine's moral struggle, the conflict between his spiritual aspirations and his sensual self. Many Greek and Roman philosophers had taught that knowledge and virtue are the same: a person who knows what is right will do what is right. Augustine rejected this idea, arguing that people do not always act on the basis of rational knowledge. Instead the basic or dynamic force in any individual is the will. When Adam ate the fruit forbidden by God in the Garden of Eden (Genesis 3:6), he committed the "original sin" and corrupted the will, wrote Augustine. Adam's sin was not simply his own, but was passed on to all later humans through sexual intercourse; even infants were tainted. Augustine viewed sexual desire as the result of Adam and Eve's disobedience, linking sexuality even more clearly with sin than had earlier church fathers. Because Adam disobeyed God, all human beings have an innate tendency to sin: their will is weak. But according to Augustine, God restores the strength of the will through grace, which is transmitted in certain rituals that the church defined as **sacraments.** Augustine's ideas on sin, grace, and redemption became the foundation of all subsequent Western Christian theology, Protestant as well as Catholic.

> **Primary Source:**
> **Saint Augustine,**
> *From* **City of God:**
> *A Denunciation of Paganism*

sacraments *Certain rituals of the church believed to act as a conduit of God's grace. The Eucharist and baptism were among the sacraments.*

Missionary Activity

The word *catholic* derives from a Greek word meaning "general," "universal," or "worldwide." Christ had said that his teaching was for all peoples, and Christians sought to make their faith catholic—that is, worldwide or believed everywhere. The Mediterranean served as the highway over which Christianity spread to the cities of the empire (see Map 7.2). From there missionaries took Christian teachings to the countryside, and then to areas beyond the borders of the empire.

Religion was not a private or individual matter. It was a social affair, and the religion of the chieftain or king determined the religion of the people. Thus missionaries concentrated their initial efforts not on the people, but on kings or tribal chieftains. According to custom, kings negotiated with all foreign powers, including the gods. Because the Christian missionaries represented a "foreign" power (the Christian God), the king dealt with them. Barbarian kings accepted Christianity because they believed the Christian God was more powerful than pagan gods and the Christian God would deliver victory in battle; or because Christianity taught obedience to (kingly) authority; or because Christian priests possessed knowledge and a charisma that could be associated with kingly power. Kings who converted, such as Ethelbert of Kent and the Frankish chieftain Clovis, sometimes had wives who had converted first and influenced their husbands. Tradition identifies the conversion of Ireland with Saint Patrick (ca. 385–461). After a vision urged him to Christianize Ireland, Patrick studied in Gaul and in 432 was consecrated a bishop. He returned to Ireland, where he converted the Irish tribe by tribe, first baptizing the king.

The Christianization of the English really began in 597, when Pope Gregory I sent a delegation of monks to England. The conversion of the English had far-reaching consequences because Britain later served as a base for the Christianization of the European continent (see Map 7.2). Between the fifth and tenth centuries, the great

MAP 7.2 **The Spread of Christianity and Islam** Originating in the area near Jerusalem, Christianity spread throughout the cities of the Roman world along sea-lanes and roads, then into more rural areas. Islam spread from the Arabian peninsula into the Mediterranean, first by land and then by sea.

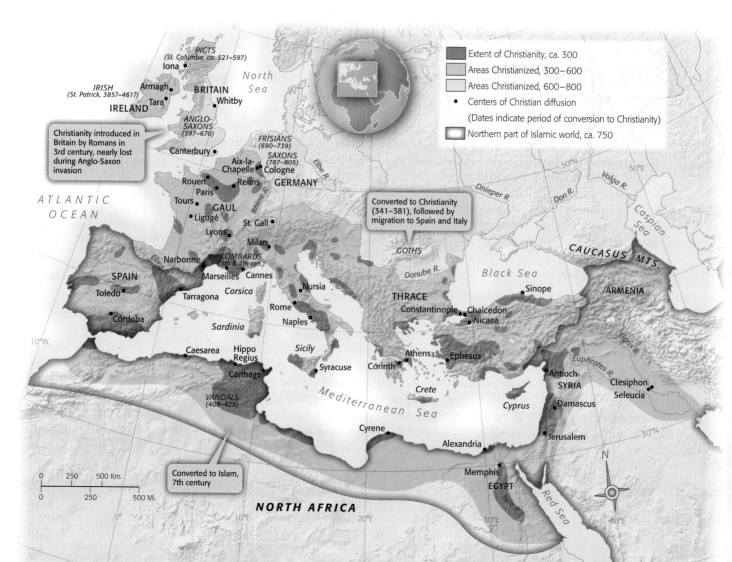

majority of peoples living on the European continent and the nearby islands accepted the Christian religion—that is, they received baptism, though baptism in itself did not automatically transform people into Christians.

In eastern Europe, missionaries traveled far beyond the boundaries of the Byzantine Empire. In 863 the emperor Michael III sent the brothers Cyril (826–869) and Methodius (815–885) to preach Christianity in Moravia (the region of modern central Czech Republic). Other missionaries succeeded in converting the Russians in the tenth century. Cyril invented a Slavic alphabet using Greek characters, and this script (called the "Cyrillic alphabet") is still in use today. Cyrillic script made possible the birth of Russian literature. Similarly, Byzantine art and architecture became the basis of and inspiration for Russian forms. The Byzantines were so successful that the Russians claimed to be the successors of the Byzantine Empire. For a time Moscow was even known as the "Third Rome" (the second Rome being Constantinople).

Conversion and Assimilation

Most of the peoples living in northern and eastern Europe idealized the military virtues of physical strength, ferocity in battle, and loyalty to the leader. Thus they had trouble accepting the Christian precepts of "love your enemies" and "turn the other cheek," and they found the Christian notions of sin and repentance virtually incomprehensible. How did missionaries and priests get masses of pagan and illiterate peoples to understand Christian ideals and teachings? They did it through preaching, through assimilation, and through the penitential system.

Preaching aimed at presenting the basic teachings of Christianity and strengthening the newly baptized in their faith through stories about the lives of Christ and the saints. Deeply ingrained pagan customs and practices, however, could not be stamped out by words alone or even by imperial edicts. Christian missionaries often pursued a policy of assimilation, easing the conversion of pagan men and women by stressing similarities between their customs and beliefs and those of Christianity. In the same way that classically trained scholars such as Jerome and Augustine blended Greco-Roman and Christian ideas, missionaries and converts mixed pagan ideas and practices with Christian ones. Bogs and lakes sacred to Germanic gods became associated with saints, as did various aspects of ordinary life, such as traveling, planting crops, and worrying about a sick child. Aspects of existing midwinter celebrations, which often centered on the return of the sun as the days became longer, were incorporated into celebrations of Christmas. Spring rituals involving eggs and rabbits (both symbols of fertility) were added to Easter.

Also instrumental in converting pagans was the rite of reconciliation in which the sinner was able to receive God's forgiveness. The penitent knelt individually before the priest, who asked about the sins the penitent might have committed. A penance such as fasting on bread and water for a period of time or saying specific prayers was imposed as medicine for the soul. The priest and penitent were guided by manuals known as **penitentials,** which included lists of sins and the appropriate penance. Penitentials gave pagans a sense of the behavior expected of Christians. The penitential system also encouraged the private examination of conscience and offered relief from the burden of sinful deeds.

Most religious observances continued to be community matters, however, as they had been in the ancient world. People joined with family members, friends, and neighbors to celebrate baptisms and funerals, presided over by a priest. They prayed to saints or to the Virgin Mary to intercede with God, or they simply asked the saints for protection and blessing. The entire village participated in processions marking saints' days or points in the agricultural year, often carrying images of saints or their **relics**—bones, articles of clothing, or other objects associated with the life of a saint—around the houses and fields.

penitentials *Manuals for the examination of conscience.*

relics *Bones, articles of clothing, or other material objects associated with the life of a saint, used as an expedient to worship or to invoke the blessing and protection of that particular saint.*

● **Procession to a New Church** In this sixth-century ivory carving, two men in a wagon, accompanied by a procession of people holding candles, carry a relic casket to a church under construction. Workers are putting tiles on the church roof. New churches often received holy items when they were dedicated, and processions were common ways in which people expressed community devotion. *(Cathedral Treasury, Trier/Photo: Ann Muenchow)*

MIGRATING PEOPLES

How did the barbarians shape social, economic, and political structures in Europe and western Asia?

The migration of peoples from one area to another has been a continuing feature of world history. The causes of early migrations varied and are not thoroughly understood by scholars. But there is no question that they profoundly affected both the regions to which peoples moved and the regions they left behind.

Celts, Huns, and Germans

In surveying the world around them, the ancient Greeks often conceptualized things in dichotomies, or sets of opposites: light and dark, hot and cold, wet and dry, mind and body, male and female, and so on. One of their key dichotomies was Greek and non-Greek, and the Greeks coined the word *barbaros* for those whose native language was not Greek, because they seemed to the Greeks to be speaking nonsense syllables—bar, bar, bar. ("Bar-bar" is the Greek equivalent to "blah-blah" or "yada-yada.") *Barbaros* originally meant simply someone who did not speak Greek, but gradually it also implied unruly, savage, and more primitive than the advanced civilization of Greece. The word brought this meaning with it when it came into Latin and other European languages, with the Romans referring to those who lived beyond the northeastern boundary of Roman territory as **"barbarians."**

barbarians *A name given by the Romans to all peoples living outside the frontiers of the Roman Empire (except the Persians).*

Migrating groups that the Romans labeled barbarians had pressed along the Rhine-Danube frontier of the Roman Empire since about 150 C.E. (see page 122). In the third and fourth centuries, increasing pressures on the frontiers from the east and north placed greater demands on Roman military manpower, which plague and a declining birthrate had reduced. Therefore, Roman generals recruited refugees and tribes allied with the Romans to serve in the Roman army, and some rose to the highest ranks.

Why did the barbarians migrate? In part, they were searching for more regular supplies of food, better farmland, and a warmer climate. Conflicts within and among barbarian groups also led to war and disruption, which motivated groups to move. Franks fought Alemanni in Gaul, while Visigoths fought Vandals in the Iberian peninsula and across North Africa. Pressure from Germanic-speaking groups caused Celtic-speaking peoples to move westward, settling in Brittany (modern northwestern France) and throughout the British Isles (England, Wales, Scotland, and Ireland). The Picts of Scotland as well as the Welsh, Britons, and Irish were peoples of Celtic descent (see Map 7.3).

A very significant factor in barbarian migration was pressure from nomadic steppe peoples from central Asia. This included the Alans, Avars, Bulghars, Khazars, and most prominently the Huns, who attacked the Black Sea area and the Eastern Roman Empire beginning in the fourth century. Under the leadership of their warrior-king Attila, the Huns swept into central Europe in 451, attacking Roman settlements in the Balkans and Germanic settlements along the Danube and Rhine Rivers. After Attila turned his army southward and crossed the Alps into Italy, a papal delegation,

● **Vandal Landowner** In this mosaic, a Vandal landowner rides out from his Roman-style house. His clothing—Roman short tunic, cloak, and sandals—reflects the way some Celtic and Germanic tribes accepted Roman lifestyles, though his beard is more typical of barbarian men's fashion. *(Courtesy of the Trustees of the British Museum)*

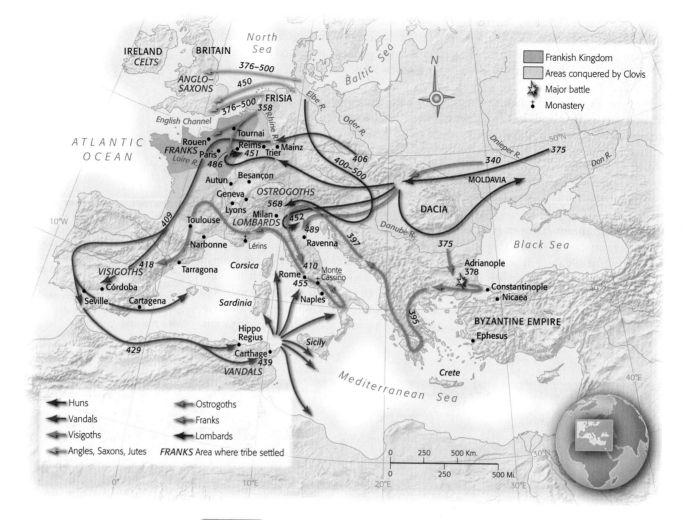

MAP 7.3 **The Barbarian Migrations** Various barbarian groups migrated throughout Europe and western Asia in late antiquity, pushed and pulled by a number of factors. Many of them formed loosely structured states, of which the Frankish Kingdom would become the most significant.

including Pope Leo I himself, asked him not to attack Rome. Though papal diplomacy was later credited with stopping the advance of the Huns, a plague that spread among Hunnic troops and their dwindling food supplies were probably much more important. The Huns retreated from Italy, and within a year Attila was dead. Later leaders were not as effective, and the Huns were never again an important factor in European history. Their conquests had slowed down the movements of various other groups, however, allowing barbarian peoples to absorb more of Roman culture as they picked the Western Roman Empire apart.

The largest group of barbarians were people who spoke Germanic languages. Many modern scholars have tried to explain who the Germans were. The present consensus, based on the study of linguistic and archaeological evidence, is that there were not one but rather many Germanic peoples with somewhat different cultural traditions.

Barbarian Society

Germanic and Celtic society had originated in the northern parts of central and western Europe and the southern regions of Scandinavia during the Iron Age (800–

500 B.C.E.). After the end of the Western Roman Empire, barbarian customs and traditions formed the basis of European society for centuries.

Barbarians generally had no notion of the state as we use the term today; they thought in social, not political, terms. The basic social unit was the tribe, a group whose members believed that they were all descended from a common ancestor. Blood united them; kinship protected them. Law was custom—unwritten, preserved in the minds of the elders of the tribe, and handed down by word of mouth from generation to generation.

Barbarian tribes were led by tribal chieftains, who are often called kings, though this implies broader power than they actually had. The chief was the member recognized as the strongest and bravest in battle and was elected from among the male members of the strongest family. He led the tribe in war, settled disputes among its members, conducted negotiations with outside powers, and offered sacrifices to the gods. The period of migrations and conquests of the Western Roman Empire witnessed the strengthening of kingship among tribes.

Early barbarian tribes had no written laws, but beginning in the late sixth century some tribal chieftains began to collect, write, and publish lists of their customs at the urging of Christian missionaries. The churchmen wanted to understand barbarian ways in order to assimilate the tribes to Christianity. Moreover, by the sixth century many barbarian kings needed regulations for the Romans under their jurisdiction as well as for their own people.

Today, if a person holds up a bank, American law maintains that the robber attacks both the bank and the state in which it exists—a sophisticated notion involving the abstract idea of the state. In early Germanic law, all crimes were regarded as crimes against a person.

According to the code of one Germanic tribe, the Salian Franks, every person had a particular monetary value to the tribe. This value was called the **wergeld**, which literally means "man-money" or "money to buy off the spear." Men of fighting age had the highest wergeld, then women of childbearing age, children, and finally the aged. Everyone's value reflected his or her potential military worthiness. If a person accused of a crime agreed to pay the wergeld and if the victim and his or her family accepted the payment, there was peace. If the accused refused to pay the wergeld or if the victim's family refused to accept it, a blood feud ensued.

wergeld   *"Man-money" or "money to buy off the spear"; according to the code of the Salian Franks, this is the particular monetary value of each member of the tribe.*

Social and Economic Structures

Barbarian groups usually resided in small villages, and climate and geography determined the basic patterns of agricultural and pastoral life. Many tribes lived in small settlements on the edges of clearings where they raised barley, wheat, oats, peas, and beans. Men and women tilled their fields with simple wooden scratch plows and harvested their grains with small iron sickles. The kernels of grain were eaten as porridge, ground up for flour, or fermented into strong, thick beer. The vast majority of people's caloric intake came from grain in some form.

Within the small villages, there were great differences in wealth and status. Free men and their families constituted the largest class. The number of cattle a man possessed indicated his wealth and determined his social status. Free men also shared in tribal warfare. Slaves (prisoners of war) worked as farm laborers, herdsmen, and household servants.

Barbarian tribes were understood as made up of kin groups, and those kin groups were made up of families, the basic social unit in barbarian society. Families were responsible for the debts and actions of their members and for keeping the peace in general. Germanic society was patriarchal: within each household the father had authority over his wife, children, and slaves. Some wealthy and powerful men had more than one wife, a pattern that continued even after they became Christian, but polygamy was not widespread among ordinary people. A woman was considered to be under the legal guardianship of a man, and she had fewer rights to own property than did Roman women in the late empire. However, once they were widowed (and there must have been many widows in such a violent, warring society), women sometimes assumed their husbands' rights over family property and held the guardianship of their children.

The Frankish Kingdom

Between 450 and 565, Germanic tribes established a number of kingdoms, but none other than the Frankish kingdom lasted very long. The Germanic kingdoms did not have definite geographical boundaries, and their locations are approximate. The Vandals, whose destructive ways are commemorated in the word *vandal,* settled in North Africa. In northern and western Europe in the sixth century, the Burgundians ruled over part of what is now France and the Ostrogoths much of what is now Italy.

The most enduring Germanic kingdom was established by the Frankish chieftain Clovis (r. 481–511). Originally only a petty chieftain in northwestern Gaul (modern Belgium), Clovis began to expand his territories in 486. His Catholic wife Clothild worked to convert her husband and supported the founding of churches and monasteries. Clothild typifies the role women played in the Christianization and Romanization of the Germanic kingdoms. Clovis's conversion to Orthodox Christianity in 496 won him the crucial support of the papacy and the bishops of Gaul. (See the feature "Listening to the Past: The Conversion of Clovis" on pages 188–189.) As the defender of Roman Catholicism against heretical Germanic tribes, Clovis went on to conquer the Visigoths, extending his domain to include much of what is now France and southwestern Germany. Because he was descended from the half-legendary chieftain Merovech, the dynasty that Clovis founded has been called **Merovingian.**

Merovingian *A dynasty founded in 481 by the Frankish chieftain Clovis in what is now France, so called because Clovis claimed descent from the semi-legendary leader Merovech.*

When Clovis died, following Frankish custom, his kingdom was divided among his four sons. For the next two centuries, the land was often wracked by civil war. So brutal were these wars that historians used to use the term *Dark Ages* to apply to the entire Merovingian period. Yet recent research has presented a more complex picture.

Merovingian kings based their administration on the *civitas,* the city and the surrounding territory over which a *count* presided. The count raised troops, collected royal revenues, and provided justice on the basis of local, not royal, law. At the king's court—that is, wherever the king was present—an official called the *mayor of the palace* supervised legal, financial, and household officials; the mayor of the palace also governed in the king's absence. In the seventh century, that position was held by members of an increasingly powerful family, the **Carolingians,** who further increased their power through advantageous marriages, a well-earned reputation for military strength, and the help of the church.

Carolingians *A Frankish family that increased its power through selective marriage, political acumen, and military victory to the point that it was able to replace the Merovingians as the rulers of the Frankish kingdom during the seventh century.*

The Carolingians replaced the Merovingians as rulers of the Frankish kingdom, cementing their authority when the Carolingian Charles Martel defeated Muslim invaders in 732 at the Battle of Poitiers in central France. Muslims and Christians have interpreted the battle differently. Muslims considered it a minor skirmish and attributed the Frankish victory to Muslim difficulties in maintaining supply lines over long distances and to ethnic conflicts and unrest in Islamic Spain. Charles Martel and later Carolingians used it to portray themselves as defenders of Christendom against the Muslims.

The battle of Poitiers helped the Carolingians acquire the support of the church, perhaps their most important asset. They further strengthened their ties to the church by supporting the work of missionaries who preached Christianity to pagan peoples, along with the Christian duty to obey secular authorities.

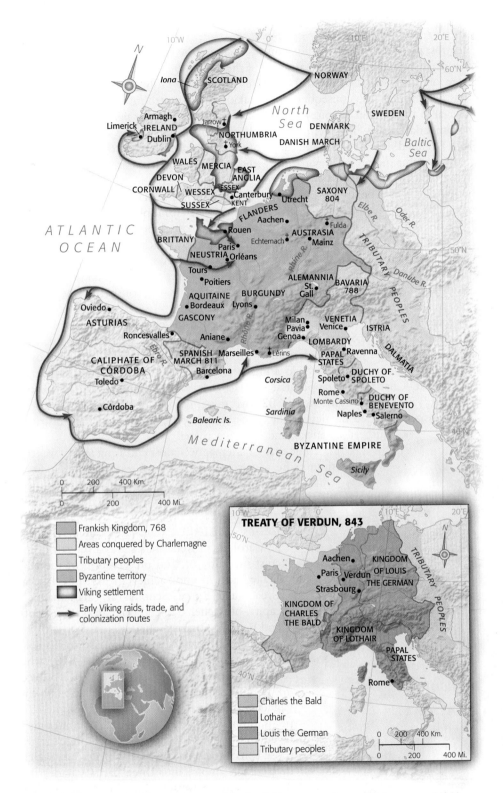

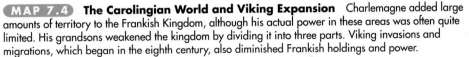

MAP 7.4 **The Carolingian World and Viking Expansion** Charlemagne added large amounts of territory to the Frankish Kingdom, although his actual power in these areas was often quite limited. His grandsons weakened the kingdom by dividing it into three parts. Viking invasions and migrations, which began in the eighth century, also diminished Frankish holdings and power.

Charlemagne

The most powerful of the Carolingians was Charles the Great (r. 768–814), generally known as Charlemagne. In the autumn of the year 800, Charlemagne visited Rome, where on Christmas Day Pope Leo III crowned him Holy Roman Emperor. The event had momentous consequences. In taking as his motto *Renovatio romani imperi* (Revival of the Roman Empire), Charlemagne was deliberately perpetuating old Roman imperial ideas while identifying with the new Rome of the Christian church. From Baghdad, Harun al Rashid, caliph of the Abbasid Empire (786–809), congratulated Charlemagne on his coronation with the gift of an elephant. But although the Muslim caliph recognized Charlemagne as a fellow sovereign, the Greeks regarded the papal acts as rebellious and Charlemagne as a usurper. The imperial coronation thus marks a decisive break between Rome and Constantinople.

> **Primary Source:**
> **Charlemagne, *From Capitulary on Saxony and A Letter to Pope Leo III***

Charlemagne built on the military and diplomatic foundations of his ancestors. His most striking characteristic was his phenomenal energy, which helps explain his great military achievements. Continuing the expansionist policies of his ancestors, Charlemagne fought more than fifty campaigns, and by around 805 the Frankish kingdom included all of continental Europe except Spain, Scandinavia, southern Italy, and the Slavic fringes of the East (see Map 7.4).

For administrative purposes, Charlemagne divided his entire kingdom into counties. Each of the approximately six hundred counties was governed by a count, who had full military and judicial power and held his office for life but could be removed by the emperor for misconduct. As a link between local authorities and the central government, Charlemagne appointed officials called *missi dominici,* "agents of the lord king." Each year beginning in 802, two missi, usually a count and a bishop or abbot, visited assigned districts. They checked up on the counts and their districts' judicial, financial, and clerical activities.

It is ironic that Charlemagne's most enduring legacy was the stimulus he gave to scholarship and learning. Barely literate, preoccupied with the control of vast territories, much more a warrior than a thinker, Charlemagne nevertheless set in motion a cultural revival that later historians called the "Carolingian Renaissance." The Carolingian Renaissance was a rebirth of interest in, study of, and preservation of the language, ideas, and achievements of classical Greece and Rome. Scholars at Charlemagne's capital of Aachen copied books and manuscripts and built up libraries.

Charlemagne left his vast empire to his sole surviving son, Louis the Pious (r. 814–840), who attempted to keep the empire intact. This proved to be impossible. Members of the nobility engaged in plots and open warfare against the emperor, often allying themselves with one of Louis's three sons. In 843, shortly after Louis's death, those sons agreed to the **Treaty of Verdun,** which divided the empire into three parts: Charles the Bald received the western part, Lothar the middle and the title of emperor, and Louis the eastern part, from which he acquired the title "the German." Though of course no one knew it at the time, this treaty set the pattern for political bound-

● **Germanic Bracteate (Gold Leaf) Pendant** This late-fifth-century piece, with the head of Rome above a wolf suckling Romulus and Remus, reflects Germanic assimilation of Roman legend and artistic design. *(Courtesy of the Trustees of the British Museum)*

aries in Europe that has been maintained until today. Other than brief periods under Napoleon and Hitler, Europe would never again see as large a unified state as it had under Charlemagne, which is one reason he has become a symbol of European unity in the twenty-first century.

The weakening of central power was hastened by invasions and migrations from the north, south, and east. Thus Charlemagne's empire ended in much the same way that the Roman Empire had earlier, a combination of internal weakness and external pressure.

Treaty of Verdun *A treaty, ratified in 843, that divided the territories of Charlemagne between his three surviving grandsons and formed the precursor states of modern Germany, France, and Italy.*

Chapter Summary

To assess your mastery of this chapter and read the primary sources listed in the margins, visit **bedfordstmartins.com/mckayworld** or see *Sources of World Societies*.

Key Terms

diaspora
corpus juris civilis
dioceses
Arianism
canon law
Petrine Doctrine
iconoclastic controversy
schism
eremitical
coenobitic
regular clergy
secular clergy
sacraments
penitentials
relics
barbarians
wergeld
Merovingian
Carolingians
Treaty of Verdun

• How was the Byzantine Empire able to survive for so long, and what were its most important achievements?

Late antiquity was a period of rupture and transformation in Europe and western Asia, but also of continuities and assimilation. In the east, the Byzantine Empire withstood attacks from Germanic tribes and steppe peoples and remained a state until 1453, a thousand years longer than the Western Roman Empire. Byzantium preserved the philosophical and scientific texts of the ancient world—which later formed the basis for study in science and medicine in both Europe and the Arabic world—and produced a great synthesis of Roman law, the Justinian *Code,* which shapes legal structures in much of Europe and former European colonies to this day.

• What factors enabled the Christian church to expand and thrive?

Christianity gained the support of the fourth-century emperors and gradually adopted the Roman system of hierarchical organization. The church possessed able administrators and leaders whose skills were tested in the chaotic environment of the end of the Roman Empire in the West. Bishops expanded their activities, and in the fifth century the bishops of Rome began to stress their supremacy over other Christian communities. Monasteries offered opportunities for individuals to develop deeper spiritual devotion and also provided a model of Christian living, a pattern of agricultural development, and a place for education and learning.

• How did Christian thinkers and missionaries adapt Greco-Roman ideas to Christian theology and develop effective techniques to convert barbarian peoples to Christianity?

Christian thinkers reinterpreted the classics in a Christian sense, incorporating elements of Greek and Roman philosophy and of various pagan religious groups into Christian teachings. Of these early thinkers, Augustine of Hippo was the most influential. His ideas about sin, free will, sexuality, and the role of government shaped western European thought from the fifth century on. Christianity had a dynamic missionary policy, and the church slowly succeeded in assimilating—that is, adapting—Germanic, Celtic, and Slavic peoples to Christian teaching. Christianity refashioned the Germanic and classical legacies, creating new rituals and practices that were meaningful to people.

• How did the barbarians shape social, economic, and political structures in Europe and western Asia?

The migration of barbarian groups into Europe from the east, caused by many factors, affected both the regions to which peoples moved and the ones they left behind. Barbarian customs and traditions formed the basis of European society for centuries. Most people lived in family groups in villages, where men, women, and children shared in the agricultural labor that sustained society. Barbarians are often divided into large linguistic groups, such as the Celtic and Germanic tribes, with ties to other tribes based on kinship and military alliances, not on loyalty to a particular government. Most barbarian states were weak and short-lived, though that of the Franks was relatively more unified and powerful. First rulers in the Merovingian dynasty, and then in the Carolingian, used military victories and strategic marriage alliances to enhance their authority. Carolingian government reached the peak of its development under Charlemagne, who built on the military and diplomatic foundations of his ancestors to build a state that controlled most of central and western continental Europe except for Muslim Spain.

Suggested Reading

Barbero, Allesandro. *Charlemagne: Father of a Continent.* 2004. A wonderful new biography of Charlemagne and a study of the times in which he lived that argues for the complexity of his legacy.

Brown, Peter. *Augustine of Hippo,* rev. ed. 2000. The best biography of Saint Augustine, which treats him as a symbol of change.

Brown, Peter. *The Body and Society: Men, Women, and Sexual Renunciation in Early Christianity.* 1988. Explores early Christian attitudes on sexuality and how they replaced Roman attitudes.

Brown, Peter. *The World of Late Antiquity,* A.D. 150–750, rev. ed. 1989. A lavishly illustrated survey that stresses social and cultural change and has clearly written introductions to the entire period.

Burns, Thomas S. *Rome and the Barbarians, 100 B.C.–400 A.D.* 2003. Argues that Germanic and Roman culture assimilated more than they conflicted.

Cameron, Averil. *The Mediterranean World in Late Antiquity,* A.D. 395–600. 1993. Focuses especially on political and economic changes.

Clark, Gilian. *Women in Late Antiquity: Pagan and Christian Lifestyles.* 1994. Explores law, marriage, and religious life.

Dunn, Marilyn. *The Emergence of Monasticism: From the Desert Fathers to the Early Middle Ages.* 2003. Focuses on the beginnings of monasticism.

Evans, James Allan. *The Empress Theodora: Partner of Justinian.* 2003. Provides a brief, yet balanced and thorough, treatment of the empress's life.

Fletcher, Richard. *The Barbarian Conversion: From Paganism to Christianity.* 1998. A superbly written analysis of conversion to Christianity.

Herrin, Judith. *The Formation of Christendom.* 1987. The best synthesis of the development of the Christian church from the third to the ninth centuries.

Macmullen, Ramsey. *Christianity and Paganism in the Fourth to Eighth Centuries.* 1998. Explores the influences of Christianity and paganism on each other.

Norwich, John Julius. *Byzantium: The Early Centuries.* 1989. An elegantly written brief survey.

Pelikan, Jaroslav. *The Excellent Empire: The Fall of Rome and the Triumph of the Church.* 1987. Describes how interpretations of the fall of Rome have influenced our understanding of Western culture.

Riche, Pierre. *Daily Life in the World of Charlemagne,* trans. JoAnn McNamara. 1978. A detailed study of many facets of Carolingian society.

Todd, Malcolm. *The Early Germans,* 2d ed. 2004. Uses archaeological and literary sources to analyze Germanic social structure, customs, and religion and to suggest implications for an understanding of migration and ethnicity.

Wells, Peter S. *The Barbarians Speak: How the Conquered Peoples Shaped Roman Europe.* 1999. Presents extensive evidence of Celtic and Germanic social and technical development.

Wood, Ian. *The Merovingian Kingdoms, 450–751.* 1994. The best general treatment of the Merovingians.

Notes

1. Quoted in E. Patlagean, "Byzantium in the Tenth and Eleventh Centuries," in *A History of Private Life.* Vol. 1: *From Pagan Rome to Byzantium,* ed. P. Ariès and G. Duby (Cambridge, Mass.: Harvard University Press, 1987), p. 573.

Listening to the PAST

The Conversion of Clovis

Modern Christian doctrine holds that conversion is a process, the gradual turning toward Jesus and the teachings of the Christian Gospels. But in the early medieval world, conversion was perceived more as a one-time event determined by the tribal chieftain. If he accepted baptism, the mass conversion of his people followed. The selection here about the Frankish king Clovis is from The History of the Franks *by Gregory, bishop of Tours (ca. 504–594), written about a century after the events it describes.*

The first child which Clotild bore for Clovis was a son. She wanted to have her baby baptized, and she kept urging her husband to agree to this. "The gods whom you worship are no good," she would say. "They haven't even been able to help themselves, let alone others. . . . Take your Saturn, for example, who ran away from his own son to avoid being exiled from his kingdom, or so they say; and Jupiter, that obscene perpetrator of all sorts of mucky deeds, who couldn't keep his hands off other men, who had his fun with all his female relatives and couldn't even refrain from intercourse with his own sister. . . .

"You ought instead to worship Him who created at a word and out of nothing heaven, and earth, the sea and all that therein is, who made the sun to shine, who lit the sky with stars, who peopled the water with fish, the earth with beasts, the sky with flying creatures, by whose hand the race of man was made, by whose gift all creation is constrained to serve in deference and devotion the man He made." However often the Queen said this, the King came no nearer to belief. . . .

The Queen, who was true to her faith, brought her son to be baptized. . . . The child was baptized; he was given the name Ingomer; but no sooner had he received baptism than he died in his white robes. Clovis was extremely angry. He began immediately to reproach his Queen. "If he had been dedicated in the name of my gods," he said, "he would have lived without question; but now that he has been baptized in the name of your God he has not been able to live a single day!"

"I give thanks to Almighty God," replied Clotild, "the Creator of all things who has not found me completely unworthy, for He has deigned to welcome into his Kingdom a child conceived in my womb. . . ."

Some time later Clotild bore a second son. He was baptized Chlodomer. He began to ail and Clovis said, "What else do you expect? It will happen to him as it happened to his brother: no sooner is he baptized in the name of your Christ than he will die!" Clotild prayed to the Lord and at His commands the baby recovered.

Queen Clotild continued to pray that her husband might recognize the true God and give up his idol-worship. Nothing could persuade him to accept Christianity. Finally war broke out against the Alamanni and in this conflict he was forced by necessity to accept what he had refused of his own free will. It so turned out that when the two armies met on the battlefield there was a great slaughter and the troops of Clovis were rapidly being annihilated. He raised his eyes to heaven when he saw this, felt compunction in his heart and was moved to tears. "Jesus Christ," he said, "you who Clotild maintains to be the Son of the living God, you who deign to give help to those in travail and victory to those who trust in you, in faith I beg the glory of your help. If you will give me victory over my enemies, and if I may have evidence to that miraculous power which the people dedicated to your name say that they have experienced, then I will believe in you and I will be baptized in your name. I have called upon my own gods, but, as I see only too clearly, they have no intention of helping me. I therefore cannot believe that they possess any power for they do not come to the assistance of those who trust them. I now call upon you. I want to believe in you, but I must first be saved from my enemies." Even as he said this the Alamanni turned their backs and began to run away. As soon as they saw that their King was killed, they submitted to Clovis. "We beg you," they said, "to put an end to this slaughter. We are prepared to obey you." Clovis stopped the war. He made a speech in which he called for peace. Then he went home. He

Ninth-century ivory carving showing Clovis being baptized by Saint Remi. *(Musée Condé, Chantilly/Laurie Platt Winfrey, Inc.)*

told the Queen how he had won a victory by calling on the name of Christ. This happened in the fifteenth year of his reign (496).

The Queen then ordered Saint Remigius, Bishop of the town of Rheims, to be summoned in secret. She begged him to impart the word of salvation to the King. The Bishop asked Clovis to meet him in private and began to urge him to believe in the true God, Maker of heaven and earth, and to forsake his idols, which were powerless to help him or anyone else. The King replied: "I have listened to you willingly, holy father. There remains one obstacle. The people under my command will not agree to forsake their gods. I will go and put to them what you have just said to me." He arranged a meeting with his people, but God in his power had preceded him, and before he could say a word all those present shouted in unison: "We will give up worshipping our mortal gods, pious King, and we are prepared to follow the immortal God about whom Remigius preaches." This news was reported to the Bishop. He was greatly pleased and he ordered the baptismal pool to be made ready. . . . The baptistry was prepared, sticks of incense gave off clouds of perfume, sweet-smelling candles gleamed bright and the holy place of baptism was filled with divine fragrance. God filled the hearts of all present with such grace that they imagined themselves to have been transported to some perfumed paradise. King Clovis asked that he might be baptized first by the Bishop.

Like some new Constantine he stepped forward to the baptismal pool, ready to wash away the sores of his old leprosy and to be cleansed in flowing water from the sordid stains which he had borne so long.

King Clovis confessed his belief in God Almighty, three in one. He was baptized in the name of the Father, the Son and the Holy Ghost, and marked in holy chrism [an anointing oil] with the sign of the Cross of Christ. More than three thousand of his army were baptized at the same time.

Questions for Analysis

1. Who took the initiative in urging Clovis's conversion? What can we deduce from that?

2. According to this account, why did Clovis ultimately accept Christianity?

3. For the Salian Franks, what was the best proof of divine power?

4. On the basis of this selection, do you consider *The History of the Franks* reliable history? Why?

Sources: L. Thorpe, trans., *The History of the Franks by Gregory of Tours* (Harmondsworth, England: Penguin, 1974), p. 159; P. J. Geary, ed., *Readings in Medieval History* (Peterborough, Ontario: Broadview Press, 1991), pp. 165–166.

The Patio of the Lions (fourteenth century), the Alhambra,
Granada, Spain. *(George Holton/Photo Researchers, Inc.)*

8 THE ISLAMIC WORLD, CA. 600–1400

Chapter Preview

The Origins of Islam
• Who was Muhammad, and what did he teach?

Islamic States and Their Expansion
• What forms of government did Islam establish, and how did they contribute to the rapid spread of Islam?

Fragmentation and Military Challenges (900–1400)
• How were the Muslim lands governed from 900 to 1400, and what new challenges did they face?

Muslim Society: The Life of the People
• What social distinctions were important in Muslim society?

Trade and Commerce
• Did Islamic teachings contribute to the thriving trade that passed through Muslim lands?

Cultural Developments
• What advances were made in the arts, sciences, and education?

Around 610 in the city of Mecca in what is now Saudi Arabia, a merchant called Muhammad began to have religious experiences. By the time he died in 632, most of Arabia had accepted his teachings. A century later his followers controlled Syria, Palestine, Egypt, what is now Iraq, Persia (present-day Iran), northern India, North Africa, Spain, and part of France. Within another century Muhammad's beliefs had been carried across Central Asia to the borders of China and India. In the ninth, tenth, and eleventh centuries, the Muslims created a brilliant civilization centered at Baghdad in Iraq, a culture that profoundly influenced the development of both Eastern and Western civilizations.

THE ORIGINS OF ISLAM
Who was Muhammad, and what did he teach?

The Arabian peninsula, about a third of the size of Europe or the United States, covers about a million square miles, much but not all of it desert. By the sixth century C.E., farming prevailed in the southwestern mountain valleys with their ample rainfall. In other areas scattered throughout the peninsula, oasis towns sustained sizable populations including artisans, merchants, and religious leaders. In Mecca the presence of the **Ka'ba,** a temple containing a black stone thought to be a god's dwelling place, attracted pilgrims and enabled Mecca to become the economic and cultural center of western Arabia.

Thinly spread over the entire peninsula were nomadic Bedouins who migrated from place to place, grazing their sheep, goats, and camels. Though always small in number, Bedouins were the most important political and military force in the region because of their toughness, solidarity, fighting traditions, possession of horses, and ability to control trade and lines of communication.

● **Qur'an with Kufic Script** Kufic takes its name from the town of Kufa, south of Baghdad in Iraq, at one time a major center of Muslim learning. Kufic scripts were angular and derived from inscriptions on stone monuments. *(Mashed Shrine Library, Iran/Robert Harding World Imagery)*

Ka'ba *The temple in Mecca containing a black stone thought to be God's dwelling place.*

Qur'an *The sacred book of Islam.*

caliph *The successor to Muhammad; the representative or deputy of God.*

For all Arabs, the basic social unit was the *tribe*—a group of blood relations connected through the male line. The tribe provided protection and support and in turn expected members' total loyalty. Like the Germanic peoples in the age of their migrations (see pages 178–180), Arab tribes were not static entities but continually evolving groups. A particular tribe might include both nomadic and sedentary members.

Strong economic links joined all Arab peoples. Nomads and seminomads depended on the agriculturally productive communities for food they could not produce, cloth, metal products, and weapons. Nomads paid for these goods with livestock, milk and milk products, hides, and hair, items in demand in oasis towns. Nomads acquired income by serving as desert guides and as guards for caravans. Plundering caravans and extorting protection money also yielded income.

In northern and central Arabia in the early seventh century, tribal confederations with their warrior elite were dominant. In the southern parts of the peninsula, religious aristocracies tended to hold political power. Many oasis or market towns contained members of one holy family who served the deity who resided in the town and acted as guardians of the deity's shrine. At the shrine, a *mansib,* or cultic leader, adjudicated disputes and tried to get agreements among warrior tribes. All Arabs respected the shrines because they served as neutral places for arbitration among warring tribes.

The power of the northern warrior class rested on its fighting skills. The southern religious aristocracy, by contrast, depended on its cultic and economic power. Located in agricultural areas that were also commercial centers, the religious aristocracy had a stronger economic base than the warrior-aristocrats. The political genius of Muhammad was to bind together these different tribal groups into a strong unified state.

Muhammad

Much like the earliest sources for Jesus, the earliest account of the life of Muhammad (ca. 570–632) comes from oral traditions passed down among followers and not recorded for several decades or generations. According to these traditions, Muhammad was orphaned at the age of six and brought up by his paternal uncle. As a young man, he became a merchant in the caravan trade. Later he entered the service of a wealthy widow, Khadija, and their subsequent marriage brought him financial security while she lived. Muhammad was extremely pious and devoted to contemplation. At about age forty, in a cave in the hills near Mecca where he was accustomed to pray, Muhammad had a vision of an angelic being who commanded him to preach the revelations that God would be sending him. Muhammad began to preach to the people of Mecca, urging them to give up their idols and submit to the one indivisible God. During his lifetime, Muhammad's followers jotted down his revelations haphazardly. After his death, scribes organized the revelations into chapters. In 651 they published the version of them that Muslims consider authoritative, the **Qur'an.** Muslims revere the Qur'an for its sacred message and for the beauty of its Arabic language.

After the death of Muhammad, two or three centuries passed before the emergence of a distinct Muslim identity, a period some writers call the Age of Arab Monotheism. Theological issues, such as the oneness of God, the role of angels, the prophets, the Scriptures, and Judgment Day, as well as political issues, such as the authority of Muhammad and that of the **caliph** (successor to Muhammad, representative or deputy of God), all had to be worked out. Likewise, legal issues relating to the **hadith,** collections of the sayings of or anecdotes about Muhammad, required investigation. Muhammad's example as revealed in the hadith became the legal basis for the conduct or behavior of every Muslim. The life of Muhammad, who is also known as the Prophet, provides the "normative example," or **Sunna,** for the Muslim believer. Once Islamic theology and law had evolved into a religious system, Muhammad was revealed as the perfect man, the embodiment of the will of God. The Muslim way of life rests on Muhammad's example.

The Islamic Faith

Islam, the strict monotheistic faith that is based on the teachings of Muhammad, rests on the principle of the absolute unity and omnipotence of God (Allah). The word *Islam* means "submission to God," and *Muslim* means "a person who submits." Muslims believe that Muhammad was the last of the prophets, completing the work begun by Abraham, Moses, and Jesus. According to the Qur'an, both Jewish and Christian authorities acknowledged the coming of a final prophet. The Qur'an asserts that the Prophet Muhammad descended from Adam, the first man, and that the Prophet Abraham built the Ka'ba. The Qur'an holds that the holy writings of both Jews and Christians represent divine revelation, but it claims that both Jews and Christians tampered with the books of God.

Muslims believe that they worship the same God as Jews and Christians. Monotheism had flourished in Middle Eastern Semitic and Persian cultures for centuries before Muhammad. Islam accepts much of the Old and New Testaments; it obeys the Mosaic law about circumcision, ritual bathing, and restrictions on eating pork and shellfish; and the Qur'an calls Christians "nearest in love" to Muslims. Muhammad insisted that he was not preaching a new message; rather, he was calling people back to the one true God, urging his contemporaries to reform their lives, to return to the faith of Abraham, the first monotheist.

Muhammad displayed genius as both a political strategist and a religious teacher. He gave Arabs the idea of a unique and unified **umma,** or community, which consisted of all those whose primary identity and bond was a common religious faith and commitment, not a tribal tie. The umma was to be a religious and political community led by Muhammad for the achievement of God's will on earth. In the early seventh century, the southern Arab tribal confederations lacked cohesiveness and unity and were constantly warring. The Islamic notion of an absolute higher authority transcended the boundaries of individual tribal units and fostered the political consolidation of the tribal confederations. All authority came from God through Muhammad. Within the umma, the law of God was discerned and applied through Muhammad.

The Qur'an prescribes a strict code of moral behavior. A Muslim must recite the profession of faith in God and in Muhammad as his prophet: "There is no God but

Chronology

622	Muhammad and followers emigrate from Mecca to Medina
632	Abu Bakr becomes first caliph
642	Muslim defeat of Persians marks end of Sassanid empire
650–1000	Evolution of core Muslim doctrines and beliefs
651	Publication of Qur'an
661	Ali assassinated; split between Shi'ites and Sunnis
711	Muslims defeat Visigothic kingdom in Spain
750–1258	Abbasid caliphate
762	Baghdad founded by Abbasids
869–883	Zanj (slave) revolts
900–1300	Height of Muslim learning and creativity
950–1100	Entry on a large scale of Turks into the Middle East
1000–1350	Foundation of many madrasas
1055	Baghdad falls to Seljuk Turks
1099–1187	Christian Crusaders hold Jerusalem
ca. 1100–1300	Progressive loss of most of Spain to the reconquista
1126–1198	Averroës writes on the works of Aristotle
1258	Mongols capture Baghdad and kill last Abbasid caliph

hadith *Collections of the sayings of and anecdotes about Muhammad.*

Sunna *An Arabic term meaning "trodden path." The term refers to the deeds and sayings of Muhammad, which constitute the obligatory example for Muslim life.*

umma *A community of those who share a religious faith and commitment rather than a tribal tie.*

God, and Muhammad is his Prophet." A believer must also pray five times a day, fast and pray during the sacred month of Ramadan, make a pilgrimage to the holy city of Mecca once during his or her lifetime, and give alms to the Muslim poor. These fundamental obligations are known as the **Five Pillars of Islam.**

Islam forbids alcoholic beverages and gambling. It condemns usury in business—that is, lending money and charging the borrower interest—and taking advantage of market demand for products by charging high prices. Most scholars hold that compared with earlier Arab standards, the Qur'an set forth an austere sexual code. Muslim jurisprudence condemned licentious behavior by both men and women and specified the same punishments for both. (By contrast, contemporary Frankish law punished prostitutes, but not their clients.)

Islam warns about Judgment Day and the importance of the life to come. Like the Christian Judgment Day, on that day God will separate the saved and the damned. The Qur'an describes in detail the frightful tortures with which God will punish the damned and the heavenly rewards of the saved and the blessed. The Muslim vision of Heaven features lush green gardens surrounded by refreshing streams. There the saved, clothed in rich silks, lounge on brocade couches, nibbling ripe fruits, sipping delicious beverages, and enjoying the companionship of physically attractive people.

Five Pillars of Islam *The basic tenets of the Islamic faith; they include reciting a profession of faith in God and in Muhammad as God's prophet, prayer five times daily, fasting and prayer during the month of Ramadan, a pilgrimage to Mecca once in one's lifetime, and contribution of alms to the poor.*

**Primary Source:
Muhammad, *Qur'an:
Muslim Devotion to God***

ISLAMIC STATES AND THEIR EXPANSION

What forms of government did Islam establish, and how did they contribute to the rapid spread of Islam?

According to Muslim tradition, Muhammad's preaching at first did not appeal to many people. Legend has it that for the first three years he attracted only fourteen believers. Muhammad preached a transformation of the social order and called for the destruction of the idols in the Ka'ba. The townspeople of Mecca turned against him, and he and his followers were forced to flee to Medina. This *hijra,* or emigration, occurred in 622, and Muslims later dated the beginning of their era from that event.

At Medina, Muhammad attracted increasing numbers of believers, and his teachings began to have an impact. By the time he died in 632, he had welded together all the Bedouin tribes. After the Prophet's death, Islam eventually emerged not only as a religious faith but also as a gradually expanding culture of worldwide significance (see Map 8.1).

In the sixth century, two powerful empires divided the Middle East: the Greek-Byzantine empire centered at Constantinople and the Persian-Sassanid empire concentrated at Ctesiphon (near Baghdad in present-day Iraq). The Byzantine Empire stood for Hellenistic culture and championed Christianity. The Sassanid empire espoused Persian cultural traditions and favored the religious faith known as Zoroastrianism. Although each empire maintained an official state religion, neither possessed religious unity. Both had sizable Jewish populations, and within Byzantium sects whom Orthodox Greeks considered heretical—Monophysites and Nestorians—served as a politically divisive force. Between the fourth and sixth centuries, these two empires had fought each other fiercely to expand their territories and to control and tax the rich trade coming from Arabia and the Indian Ocean region.

The second and third successors of Muhammad, Umar (r. 634–644) and Uthman (r. 644–656; see page 197), launched a two-pronged attack. One force moved north from Arabia against the Byzantine provinces of Syria and Palestine. The Greek armies there could not halt them (see page 165). From Syria, the Muslims conquered the rich province of Egypt, taking the commercial and intellectual hub of Alexandria in 642. Simultaneously, Arab armies swept into the Sassanid empire. The Muslim defeat of the Persians at Nihawand in 642 signaled the collapse of the Sassanid empire.[1]

● **Dome of the Rock, Jerusalem** Completed in 691 and revered by Muslims as the site where Muhammad ascended to Heaven, the Dome of the Rock is the oldest surviving Islamic sanctuary and, after Mecca and Medina, the holiest place in Islam. Although influenced by Byzantine and Persian architecture, the 700 feet of carefully selected Qur'anic inscriptions and vegetal motifs, however, represent distinctly Arabic features. *(Sonia Halliday Photographs)*

The Muslims continued their drive eastward. In the mid-seventh century, they occupied the province of Khurasan, where the city of Merv became the center of Muslim control over eastern Persia and the base for campaigns farther east. By 700 the Muslims had crossed the Oxus River and swept toward Kabul, today the capital of Afghanistan. They penetrated Kazakhstan and then seized Tashkent, one of the oldest cities in Central Asia. The clash of Muslim horsemen with a Chinese army at the Talas River in 751 marked the farthest Islamic penetration into Central Asia. From southern Persia, a Muslim force marched into the Indus Valley in northern India and in 713 founded an Islamic community there. Beginning in the eleventh century, Muslim dynasties from Ghazni in Afghanistan carried Islam deeper into the Indian subcontinent.

Likewise to the west, Arab forces moved across North Africa, crossed the Strait of Gibraltar, and in 711 at the Guadalete River easily defeated the Visigothic kingdom of Spain. A few Christian princes supported by Merovingian rulers held out in the Cantabrian Mountains, but the Muslims controlled most of Spain until the thirteenth century.

Reasons for the Spread of Islam

By the beginning of the eleventh century, the crescent of Islam flew from the Iberian heartlands to northern India. How can this rapid and remarkable expansion be explained? Muslim historians attribute Islamic victories to God's support for the Islamic faith. True, the Arabs possessed a religious fervor that their enemies could not equal. Perhaps they were convinced of the necessity of the **jihad,** or holy war. The Qur'an does not precisely explain the concept. Thus modern Islamicists, as well as early Muslims, have debated the meaning of jihad, sometimes called the sixth pillar of Islam. Some students hold that it signifies the individual struggle against sin and toward perfection on "the straight path" of Islam. Other scholars claim that jihad has a social and communal implication—a militancy as part of a holy war against unbelievers living in territories outside the control of the Muslim community. The Qur'an states, "Fight those in the way of God who fight you. . . . Fight those wheresoever you find them, and expel them from the place they had turned you out from. . . . Fight until

jihad *"Holy War," an Arabic term that some scholars interpret as the individual struggle against sin and others interpret as having a social and communal implication.*

MAP 8.1 **The Islamic World, ca. 900** The rapid expansion of Islam in a relatively short span of time testifies to the Arabs' superior fighting skills, religious zeal, and economic ambition as well as to their enemies' weakness. Plague, famine, and political troubles in Sassanid Persia contributed to Muslim victory there.

sedition comes to an end and the law of God [prevails]" (Qur'an 4:74–76).[2] Since the Qur'an suggests that God sent the Prophet to establish justice on earth, it would follow that justice will take effect only where Islam triumphs. Just as Christians have a missionary duty to spread their faith, so Muslims have the obligation, as individuals and as a community, to extend the power of Islam. For some Islam came to mean the struggle to expand Islam, and those involved in that struggle were assured happiness in the world to come.

The Muslim practice of establishing garrison cities or camps facilitated expansion. Rather than scattering as landlords of peasant farmers over conquered lands, Arab soldiers remained together in garrison cities, where their Arab ethnicity, tribal organization, religion, and military success set them apart.

diwān *Unit of government.*

All soldiers were registered in the **diwān**, an administrative organ adopted from the Persians or Byzantines. Soldiers received a monthly ration of food for themselves and their families and an annual cash stipend. In return, they had to be available for military service. Fixed salaries, regular pay, and the lure of battlefield booty attracted rugged tribesmen from Arabia. Except for the Berbers of North Africa, whom the Arabs could not pacify, Muslim armies initially did not seek to convert or recruit warriors from conquered peoples. Instead, conquered peoples became slaves. In later campaigns to the east, many recruits were recent converts to Islam from Christian, Persian, and Berber backgrounds. The assurance of army wages secured the loyalty of these very diverse men. Still, in the first two centuries of Muslim expansion, Arab military victories probably resulted as much from the weaknesses of their enemies (the Sassanid Persians and the Byzantines) as from Arab strength.

The Muslim conquest of Syria offers an example of the mixed motives that propelled early Muslim expansion. Syria had been under Byzantine Christian or Roman rule for centuries. Arab caravans knew the market towns of southern Syria and the rich commercial centers of the north, such as Edessa, Aleppo, and Damascus. Syria's economic prosperity probably attracted the Muslims, and perhaps Muhammad saw the land as a potential means of support for the poor who flooded Medina. Syria also contained sites important to the faith: Jerusalem, where Jesus and other prophets mentioned in the Qur'an had lived and preached, and Hebron, the traditional burial place of Abraham, the father of monotheism.

How did the conquered peoples make sense of their new subordinate situations? Defeated peoples almost never commented on the actions and motives of the Arabs. Jews and Christians both tried to minimize the damage done to their former status and played down the gains of their new masters. Christians regarded the conquering Arabs as God's punishment for their sins, while Jews saw the Arabs as instruments for their deliverance from Greek and Sassanid persecution.[3]

Primary Source:
Muhammad, *The Constitution of Medina: Muslims and Jews at the Dawn of Islam*

The Caliphate

When Muhammad died in 632, he left a large Muslim umma, but this community stood in danger of disintegrating into separate tribal groups. How was the vast empire that came into existence within one hundred years of his death to be governed? Neither the Qur'an nor the Sunna offered guidance for the succession.

In this crisis, according to tradition, a group of Muhammad's ablest followers elected Abu Bakr (573–634), a close supporter of the Prophet and his father-in-law, and hailed him as caliph, a term combining the ideas of leader, successor, and deputy (of the Prophet). This election marked the victory of the concept of a universal community of Muslim believers.

Because the law of the Qur'an was to guide the community, there had to be an authority to enforce the law. Muslim teaching held that the law was paramount. God is the sole source of the law, and the ruler is bound to obey the law. Government exists not to make law but to enforce it. Muslim teaching also maintained that there is no distinction between the temporal and spiritual domains: social law is a basic strand in the fabric of comprehensive religious law. Thus religious belief and political power are inextricably intertwined: the first sanctifies the second, and the second sustains the first. The creation of Islamic law in an institutional sense took three or four centuries and is one of the great achievements of medieval Islam.

In the two years of his rule (632–634), Abu Bakr governed on the basis of his personal prestige within the Muslim umma. He sent out military expeditions, collected taxes, dealt with tribes on behalf of the entire community, and led the community in prayer. Gradually, under Abu Bakr's first three successors, Umar (r. 634–644), Uthman (r. 644–656), and Ali (r. 656–661), the caliphate emerged as an institution. Umar succeeded in exerting his authority over the Bedouin tribes involved in ongoing conquests. Uthman asserted the right of the caliph to protect the economic interests of the entire umma. Uthman's publication of the definitive text of the Qur'an showed his concern for the unity of the umma. But Uthman's enemies accused him of nepotism—of using his position to put his family in powerful and lucrative jobs—and of unnecessary cruelty. Opposition coalesced around Ali, and when Uthman was assassinated in 656, Ali was chosen to succeed him.

The issue of responsibility for Uthman's murder raised the question of whether Ali's accession was legitimate. Uthman's cousin Mu'awiya, a member of the Umayyad family who had built a power base as governor of Syria, refused to recognize Ali as caliph. In the ensuing civil war, Ali was assassinated, and Mu'awiya (r. 661–680) assumed the caliphate. Mu'awiya founded the Umayyad Dynasty and shifted the capital of the Islamic state from Medina in Arabia to Damascus in Syria. When the Umayyad family assumed the leadership of Islam, there was no Muslim state, no formal impersonal institutions of government exercising jurisdiction over a very wide area. The first four caliphs were elected by their peers, and the theory of an elected caliphate remained the Islamic legal ideal. Three of the four "patriarchs," as they were called, were murdered, however, and civil war ended the elective caliphate. Beginning with Mu'awiya, the office of caliph was in fact, but never in theory, dynastic. Two successive dynasties, the Umayyad (661–750) and the Abbasid (750–1258), held the caliphate.

From its inception the caliphate rested on the theoretical principle that Muslim political and religious unity transcended tribalism. Mu'awiya sought to enhance the power of the caliphate by making the tribal leaders dependent on him for concessions and special benefits. At the same time, his control of a loyal and well-disciplined army enabled him to develop the caliphate in an authoritarian direction. Through intimidation he forced the tribal leaders to accept his son Yazid as his heir, thereby establishing the dynastic principle of succession. By distancing himself from a simple life within the umma and withdrawing into the palace that he built at Damascus, and by surrounding himself with symbols and ceremony, Mu'awiya laid the foundations for an elaborate caliphal court. Many of Mu'awiya's innovations were designed to protect him from assassination. A new official, the *hajib,* or chamberlain, restricted access to the caliph, who received visitors seated on a throne surrounded by bodyguards.

The assassination of Ali and the assumption of the caliphate by Mu'awiya had another profound consequence. It gave rise to a fundamental division in the umma and in Muslim theology. Ali had claimed the caliphate on the basis of family ties—he was Muhammad's cousin and son-in-law. When Ali was murdered, his followers argued—partly because of the blood tie, partly because Muhammad had designated Ali **imam,** or leader in community prayer—that Ali had been the Prophet's designated successor.

imam *The leader in community prayer.*

Shi'ites *Arabic term meaning "supporters of Ali"; they make up one of the two main divisions of Islam.*

Sunnis *Members of the larger of the two main sects of Islam; the division between Sunnis and Shi'ites began in a dispute about succession to Muhammad, but over time many differences in theology developed.*

ulama *A group of religious scholars whom Sunnis trust to interpret the Qur'an and the Sunna.*

These supporters of Ali were called **Shi'ites,** or *Shi'at Ali,* or simply *Shi'a*—Arabic terms all meaning "supporters" or "partisans" of Ali. In succeeding generations, opponents of the Umayyad Dynasty emphasized their blood descent from Ali and claimed to possess divine knowledge that Muhammad had given them as his heirs.

Other Muslims adhered to the practice and beliefs of the umma based on the precedents of the Prophet. They were called **Sunnis,** which derived from Sunna (examples from Muhammad's life). When a situation arose for which the Qur'an offered no solution, Sunni scholars searched for a precedent in the Sunna, which gained an authority comparable to the Qur'an itself.

Both Sunnis and Shi'ites maintain that authority within Islam lies first in the Qur'an and then in the Sunna. Who interprets these sources? Shi'ites claim that the imam does, for he is invested with divine grace and insight. Sunnis insist that interpretation comes from the consensus of the **ulama,** the group of religious scholars.

The Umayyad caliphs were Sunnis, and throughout the Umayyad period the Shi'ites constituted a major source of discontent. Shi'ite rebellions expressed religious opposition in political terms. The Shi'ites condemned the Umayyads as worldly and sensual rulers, in contrast to the pious true successors of Muhammad. The Abbasid clan, which based its claim to the caliphate on the descent of Abbas, Muhammad's uncle, exploited the situation. The Abbasids agitated the Shi'ites, encouraged dissension among tribal factions, and contrasted Abbasid piety with the pleasure-loving style of the Umayyads.

● **Qibla Compass** Religious precepts inspired Muslims to considerable scientific knowledge. For example, the Second Pillar of Islam requires them to pray five times a day facing the Ka'ba in Mecca. To determine the direction of Mecca, called the *qibla,* Muslims adapted the compass, first invented in China. Modern worshipers still use the qibla compass. *(Robert Selkowitz)*

The Abbasid Caliphate

In 747 Abu' al-Abbas led a rebellion against the Umayyads, and in 750 he won general recognition as caliph. Damascus had served as the headquarters of Umayyad rule. Abu' al-Abbas's successor, al-Mansur (r. 754–775), founded the city of Baghdad in 762 and made it his capital. Thus the geographical center of the caliphate shifted eastward to former Sassanid territories. The first three Abbasid caliphs crushed their opponents, eliminated their Shi'ite supporters, and created a new ruling elite drawn from newly converted Persian families that had traditionally served the ruler. The Abbasid revolution established a basis for rule and citizenship more cosmopolitan and Islamic than the narrow, elitist, and Arab basis that had characterized Umayyad government.

The Abbasids worked to identify their rule with Islam. They patronized the ulama, built mosques, and supported the development of Islamic scholarship. Moreover, under the Umayyads the Muslim state had been a federation of regional and tribal armies; during the Abbasid caliphate, provincial governors gradually won semi-independent power. Although at first Muslims represented only a small minority of the conquered peoples, Abbasid rule provided the religious-political milieu in which Islam gained, over time, the allegiance of the vast majority of the populations from Spain to Afghanistan.

The Abbasids also borrowed heavily from Persian culture. Following Persian tradition, the Abbasid caliphs claimed to rule by divine right, as reflected in the change of their title from "successor of the Prophet" to "deputy of God." A magnificent palace with hundreds of attendants and elaborate court ceremonial deliberately isolated the caliph from the people he ruled. Subjects had to bow before the caliph, kissing the ground, a symbol of his absolute power.

Under the third caliph, Harun al-Rashid (r. 786–809), Baghdad emerged as a flourishing commercial, artistic, and scientific center—the greatest city in Islam and one of the most cosmopolitan cities in the world. Its population of about 1 million people—an astoundingly large size in preindustrial times—represented a huge demand for goods and services. Baghdad served as an entrepôt for textiles, slaves, and foodstuffs coming from Oman, East Africa, and India. Harun al-Rashid established a library that translated Greek medical and philosophical texts. The scholar Hunayn ib Ishaq al-Ibadi (808–873) translated Galen's medical works into Arabic and made Baghdad a center for the study and practice of medicine. Likewise, impetus was given to the study of astronomy, and through a program of astronomical observations, Muslim astronomers sought to correct and complement Ptolemaic astronomy. Above all, studies in Qur'anic textual analysis, history, poetry, law, and philosophy—all in Arabic—reflected the development of a distinctly Islamic literary and scientific culture.

> **Primary Source:**
> **Benjamin ben Jonah of Tudela, *From* Book of Travels**

The early Abbasid caliphal court was magnificent. In the caliph's palace complexes, maintained by staffs numbering in the tens of thousands, an important visitor would be conducted through elaborate rituals and confronted with indications of the caliph's majesty and power: rank upon rank of lavishly appointed guards, pages, servants, slaves, and other retainers; lush parks full of exotic wild beasts; and fantastic arrays of gold and silver objects, ornamented furniture, precious carpets and tapestries, pools of mercury, and ingenious mechanical devices. The most famous of the mechanical devices was a gold and silver tree with leaves that rustled, branches that swayed, and mechanical birds that sang as the breezes blew.

An important innovation of the Abbasids was the use of slaves as soldiers. The caliph al-Mu'taşim (r. 833–842) acquired several thousand Turkish slaves who were converted to Islam and employed in military service. Scholars have offered varied explanations for this practice: that the use of slave soldiers was a response to a manpower shortage; that as heavy cavalry with expertise as horse archers, the Turks had military skills superior to those of the Arabs and other peoples; and that al-Mu'taşim felt he could trust the Turks more than the Arabs, Persians, Khurasans, and other recruits. In any case, slave soldiers—later including Slavs, Indians, and sub-Saharan blacks—became a standard feature of Muslim armies in the Middle East down to the twentieth century.

Administration of the Islamic Territories

emirs *Arab governors who were given overall responsibility for good order, maintenance of the armed forces, and tax collection.*

The Islamic conquests brought into being a new imperial system. The Muslims adopted the patterns of administration used by the Byzantines in Egypt and Syria and by the Sassanids in Persia. Arab **emirs,** or governors, were appointed and given overall responsibility for good order, maintenance of the armed forces, and tax collection. Below them, experienced native officials—Greeks, Syrians, Copts (Egyptian Christians)—remained in office. Thus there was continuity with previous administrations.

The Umayyad caliphate witnessed the further development of the imperial administration. At the head stood the caliph, who led the holy war against unbelievers. Theoretically, he had the ultimate responsibility for the interpretation of the sacred law. In practice, the ulama interpreted the law as revealed in the Qur'an and the Sunna. In the course of time, the ulama's interpretations constituted a rich body of law, the **shari'a,** which covered social, criminal, political, commercial, and ritual matters. The ulama enjoyed great prestige in the Muslim community and was consulted by the caliph on difficult legal and spiritual matters. The **qadis,** or judges, who were well versed in the sacred law, carried out the judicial functions of the state. Nevertheless, Muslim law prescribed that all people have access to the caliph, and he set aside special times for hearing petitions and for the direct redress of grievances.

shari'a *Muslim law, which covers social, criminal, political, commercial, and religious matters.*

qadis *Muslim judges who carried out the judicial functions of the state.*

The central administrative organ was the diwān, which collected the taxes that paid soldiers' salaries (see page 196) and financed charitable and public works that the caliph undertook, such as aid to the poor and the construction of mosques, irrigation works, and public baths. As Arab conquests extended into Spain, Central Asia, and Afghanistan, lines of communication had to be kept open. Emirs and other officials, remote from the capital at Damascus and later Baghdad, might revolt. Thus a relay network was established to convey letters and intelligence reports between the capital and the various outposts.

The early Abbasid period witnessed considerable economic expansion and population growth, so the work of government became more complicated. New and specialized departments emerged, each with a hierarchy of officials. The most important new official was the **vizier,** a position that the Abbasids adopted from the Persians. The vizier was the caliph's chief assistant, advising the caliph on matters of general policy, supervising the bureaucratic administration, and, under the caliph, overseeing the army, the provincial governors, and relations with foreign governments. As the caliphs withdrew from leading Friday prayers and other routine functions, the viziers gradually assumed power. But the authority and power of the vizier usually depended on the caliph's personality and direct involvement in state affairs. Many viziers used their offices for personal gain and wealth. Although some careers ended with the vizier's execution, there were always candidates seeking the job.

vizier *The caliph's chief assistant.*

FRAGMENTATION AND MILITARY CHALLENGES (900–1400)

How were the Muslim lands governed from 900 to 1400, and what new challenges did they face?

In theory, the caliph and his central administration governed the whole empire. In practice, the many parts of the empire enjoyed considerable local independence. As long as public order was maintained and taxes were forwarded, the central government rarely interfered. The enormous distance separating many provinces from the imperial capital, and the long time it took to travel between them by horse or camel,

● **Ivory Chest of Pamplona, Spain** The court of the Spanish Umayyads prized small, intricately carved ivory chests, often made in a royal workshop and used to store precious perfumes. This exquisite side panel depicts an eleventh-century caliph flanked by two attendants. An inscription on the front translates as "In the Name of God. Blessings from God, goodwill, and happiness." *(Museo Navarra, Pamplona/Institut Amatller d'Art Hispanic)*

made it difficult for the caliph to prevent provinces from breaking away. Particularism and ethnic or tribal loyalties, combined with strength and fierce ambition, led to the creation of local dynasties in much of the Islamic world, including Spain, Iran, Central Asia, northern India, and Egypt. None of these states repudiated Islam, but they did stop sending tax revenues to Baghdad. Moreover, most states became involved with costly wars against their neighbors in their attempts to expand. Sometimes these conflicts were worsened by Sunni-Shi'ite antagonisms.

One of the first to break away from the Baghdad-centered caliphate was Spain. In 755 an Umayyad prince who had escaped death at the hands of the triumphant Abbasids and fled to Spain set up an independent regime at Córdoba (see Map 8.1). Others soon followed. In 800 the emir in Tunisia in North Africa set himself up as an independent ruler and refused to place the caliph's name on the local coinage. In 820 Tahir, the son of a slave, was rewarded with the governorship of Khurasan because he had supported the caliphate. Once there, Tahir ruled independently of Baghdad, not even mentioning the caliph's name in the traditional Friday prayers in recognition of caliphal authority.

In 969 the Fatimids, a Shi'ite dynasty who claimed descent from Muhammad's daughter Fatima, conquered the Abbasid province of Egypt. The Fatimids founded the city of Cairo as their capital. They extended their rule over North Africa, with the result that for a century or so, Shi'ites were in ascendancy in much of the western parts of the Islamic world.

In 946 a Shi'ite Iranian clan overran Iraq and occupied Baghdad. The caliph was forced to recognize the leader as commander-in-chief and to allow the celebration of Shi'ite festivals—though the caliph and most of the people were Sunnis. A year later, the caliph was accused of plotting against his new masters, snatched from his throne, dragged through the streets, and blinded. Blinding was a practice adopted from the Byzantines as a way of rendering a ruler incapable of carrying out his duties. This incident marks the practical collapse of the Abbasid caliphate. Abbasid caliphs, however, remained as puppets of a series of military commanders and symbols of Muslim unity until the Mongols killed the last Abbasid caliph in 1258.

Egypt, too, saw successive overlords. The Ayyubids were able to take over Egypt from the Fatimids, and in 1250 the Mamluks replaced the Ayyubids and ruled Egypt until the Ottoman conquest in 1517. The Mamluks were originally slave soldiers, and they continued to staff their armies with slaves, mostly unconverted Turks or Christians, acquired from the northern fringes of Muslim lands.

The Ascendancy of the Turks

In the mid-tenth century, the Turks began to enter the Islamic world in large numbers. First appearing in Mongolia in the sixth century, groups of Turks gradually appeared across the grasslands of Eurasia (see Chapter 11). Skilled horsemen, they became prime targets for slave raids, as they made good slave soldiers. Once they understood that Muslims could not be captured for slaves, more and more of them

● **Great Mosque at Isfahan in Persia**   Begun in the late eighth century and added to over the centuries, the Great Mosque in Isfahan is one of the masterpieces of Islamic architecture. The huge dome and the vaulted niches around the courtyard are covered with blue, turquoise, white, and yellow tile. *(© Roger Wood/Corbis)*

converted to Islam (and often became *ghazi,* holy warriors, who raided unconverted Turks to capture slaves). The first to convert accepted Sunni Islam near Bukhara (then a great Persian commercial and intellectual center).

Seljuk Turks overran Persia in the 1020s and 1030s, then pushed into Iraq and Syria. Baghdad fell to them on December 18, 1055, and the caliph became a puppet of the Turkish *sultan*—literally, "he with authority." The Turks rapidly gave up pastoralism and took up the sedentary style of life of the people they governed.

The Turks brought to the Islamic world badly needed military strength. They played a major part in recovering Jerusalem after it was held by the European Crusaders for nearly a century between 1099 and 1187. They also were important in preventing the later Crusades from accomplishing much. Turks also became staunch Sunnis and led a campaign against Shi'ites.

The influx of Turks from 950 on also helped provide a new expansive dynamic. At the battle of Manzikert in 1071, Seljuk Turks broke through Byzantine border defenses, opening Anatolia to Turkish migration. Over the next couple of centuries, perhaps a million Turks entered the area—including bands of ghazis (holy warriors) and dervishes (Sufi brotherhoods). Seljuk Turks set up the Sultanate of Rum, which lasted until the Mongols invaded in 1243. With the Turks came many learned men from the Persian-speaking east. Over time, many of the Christians in Anatolia converted to Islam and became fluent in Turkish.

The Mongol Invasions

In the early thirteenth century the Mongols arrived in the Middle East. Originally from the grasslands of Mongolia (see pages 296–298), in 1206 they had elected Chinggis Khan (1162–1227) as their leader, and he welded Mongol, Tatar, and Turkish tribes into a strong confederation that rapidly subdued neighboring settled societies. After conquering much of north China, they swept westward, leaving a trail of blood and destruction. The Mongols used terror as a weapon, and out of fear many cities surrendered without a fight.

In 1219–1221, the years the Mongols first reached the Islamic lands, the areas from Iran through the central Asian cities of Herat and Samarkand were part of the kingdom of Khwarizm. The ruler—the son of a Turkish slave who had risen to governor of a province—was a conqueror himself, having conquered much of Persia. He had the audacity to execute Chinggis's envoy who demanded his surrender. Chinggis retaliated with a force of a hundred thousand soldiers that sacked city after city, often slaughtering the residents or enslaving them and sending them to Mongolia. Millions are said to have died. The irrigation systems that were needed for agriculture in this dry region were destroyed as well.

Not many Mongol forces were left in Persia after the campaign of 1219–1221, and another campaign was sent in 1237, which captured Isfahan. In 1251 the decision was taken to push farther west. Chinggis Khan's grandson Hülegü (1217–1265) led the attack on the Abbasids. His armies sacked and burned Baghdad and killed the last Abbasid caliph in 1258. Baghdad and the Abbasid caliphate fell in 1258, Damascus in 1260. Mamluk soldiers from Egypt, however, were able to withstand the Mongols and win a major victory at Ayn Jalut in Syria, which has been credited with saving Egypt and the Muslim lands in North Africa and perhaps Spain. It should be pointed out, however, that in 1260 the Great Khan died, and the top Mongol generals withdrew to Mongolia for the selection of the next Great Khan.

Hülegü and his descendants ruled the central Muslim lands (referred to as the Il-Khanate) for eighty years. In 1295 his descendant Ghazan embraced Islam and worked for the revival of Muslim culture. As the Turks had done earlier, the Mongols, once converted, injected new vigor into the faith and spirit of Islam. In the Il-Khanate, the Mongols governed through Persian viziers and native financial officials.

● **Jonah and the Whale**   When the Mongol ruler Ghazan asked his chief minister, the remarkable Persian polymath Rashid al-Din—a Jew by birth who converted to Islam and a physician by training—to write a history of the Mongols in Persia, he responded with the *Collection of Histories*, which treats China, India, the Jews, Muhammad and the caliphs, pre- and post-Islamic Persia, even the Franks (Europeans). To explain the section on the Jews, a Chinese artist inserted this illustration of the Old Testament prophet Jonah. The Chinese artist had never seen a whale, but he possessed imagination and mastery of movement. *(Courtesy of Edinburgh University Library, Or Ms 20, fol 23N)*

MUSLIM SOCIETY: THE LIFE OF THE PEOPLE

What social distinctions were important in Muslim society?

When the Prophet appeared, Arab society consisted of independent Bedouin tribal groups loosely held together by loyalty to a strong leader and by the belief that all members of a tribe were descended from a common ancestor. Heads of families elected the *sheik,* or tribal chief. He was usually chosen from among elite warrior families who believed their birth made them superior. According to the Qur'an, however, birth counted for nothing; zeal for Islam was the only criterion for honor: "O ye folk, verily we have created you male and female. . . . Verily the most honourable of you in the sight of God is the most pious of you."[4] The idea of social equality was a basic Muslim doctrine.

When Muhammad defined social equality, he was thinking about equality among Muslims alone. But even among Muslims, a sense of pride in ancestry could not be destroyed by a stroke of the pen. Claims of birth remained strong among the first Muslims, and after Islam spread outside of Arabia, full-blooded Arab tribesmen regarded themselves as superior to foreign converts.

The Classes of Society

In the Umayyad period, Muslim society consisted of several classes. At the top were the caliph's household and the ruling Arab Muslims. Descended from Bedouin tribespeople and composed of warriors, veterans, governing officials, and town settlers, this class constituted the ruling elite. Because birth continued to determine membership, it was more a caste than a class. It was also a relatively small group, greatly outnumbered by Muslim villagers and country people.

Converts constituted the second class in Islamic society. Converts to Islam had to attach themselves to one of the Arab tribes as clients. They greatly resented having to do this, since they believed they represented a culture superior to the culture of the Arab tribespeople. From the Muslim converts eventually came the members of the commercial and learned professions—merchants, traders, teachers, doctors, artists, and interpreters of the shari'a. Second-class citizenship led some Muslim converts to adopt Shi'ism (see page 198) and other unorthodox doctrines inimical to the caliphate. Over the centuries, Berber, Copt, Persian, Aramaean, and other converts to Islam intermarried with their Muslim conquerors. Gradually, assimilation united peoples of various ethnic and "national" backgrounds.

Dhimmis, or "protected peoples"—Jews, Christians, and Zoroastrians—formed the third class. They were allowed to practice their religions, maintain their houses of worship, and conduct their business affairs as long as they gave unequivocal recognition to Muslim political supremacy and paid a small tax. Because many Jews and Christians were found to be well educated, they were often appointed to high positions in provincial capitals as well as in Damascus and Baghdad. Restrictions placed on Christians and Jews were not severe, and both groups seem to have thrived under Muslim rule. Outbursts of violence against Christians and Jews were rare. The social position of the "protected peoples" deteriorated during the Crusades (see pages 362–365) and the Mongol invasions, when there was a general rise of religious loyalties. At those times, Muslims suspected the dhimmis, often rightly, of collaborating with the enemies of Islam.

> **dhimmis** *A term meaning "protected peoples"; they included Jews, Christians, and Zoroastrians.*

What was the fate of Jews living under Islam? How does their experience compare with that of Jews living in Christian Europe? Recent scholarship shows that in Europe, Jews were first marginalized in the Christian social order, then completely expelled from it. In Islam, though marginalized, Jews participated fully in commercial and professional activities, some attaining economic equality with their Muslim counterparts. The seventeenth Sura (chapter) of the Qur'an, titled Bani Isra'il, "The Children of Israel," accords to the Jews a special respect because they were "the people of the Book." Also, Islamic culture was an urban and commercial culture that gave the merchant considerable respect; medieval Christian culture was basically rural and agricultural and did not revere the business person.

Slavery

At the bottom of the social scale were slaves. Slavery had long existed in the ancient Middle East, and the Qur'an accepted slavery much the way the Old and New Testaments did. But the Qur'an prescribes just and humane treatment of slaves. A master should feed and clothe his slaves adequately; give them moderate, not excessive, work; and not punish them severely. The Qur'an also explicitly encourages the freeing of slaves and urges owners whose slaves ask for their freedom to give them the opportunity to buy it.

Muslim expansion ensured a steady flow of slaves captured in war. The great Muslim commander Musa ibn Nusayr, himself the son of a Christian enslaved in Iraq, is reputed to have taken three hundred thousand prisoners of war in his North African campaigns (708–818) and thirty thousand virgins from the Visigothic nobility of Spain. (These numbers are surely greatly inflated, as most medieval numbers are.) Every soldier, from general to private, had a share of slaves from captured prisoners.

Women slaves worked as cooks, cleaners, laundresses, and nursemaids. A few performed as singers, musicians, dancers, and reciters of poetry. Many women also served as concubines. Not only rulers but also high officials and rich merchants owned many

● **Slaves Dancing** A few women slaves performed as dancers, singers, and musicians, usually before an elite audience of rulers, officials, and wealthy merchants. This reconstructed wall-painting adorned a harem in a royal palace in Samarra. *(Bildarchiv Preussischer Kulturbesitz/Art Resource, NY)*

concubines. Down the economic ladder, artisans and tradesmen often had a few concubines who assumed domestic as well as sexual tasks.

According to tradition, the seclusion of women in the harem protected their virtue (see page 209), and when men had the means the harem was secured by eunuch guards. The use of eunuch guards seems to have been a practice Muslims adopted from the Byzantines and Persians. Early Muslim law forbade castration, so in the early Islamic period Muslims secured eunuchs from European, African, and Central Asian slave markets. In the tenth century the caliph of Baghdad had seven thousand black eunuchs and four thousand white ones in his palace. In contrast to China, where only the emperor could have eunuch servants, in the Muslim world, the well-to-do could purchase them to guard their harems. Because of the insatiable demand for eunuch guards, the cost of eunuchs was very high, perhaps seven times that of uncastrated male slaves.

Muslims also employed eunuchs as secretaries, tutors, and commercial agents, possibly because unlike men with ordinary desires, eunuchs were said to be more tractable and dependable. Besides administrative, business, or domestic services, male slaves, eunuchs or not, were also set to work as longshoremen on the docks, as oarsmen on ships, in construction crews, in factories, and in gold and silver mines.

Male slaves also fought as soldiers. Any free person could buy a slave, but only a ruler could own military slaves. In the ninth century, the rulers of Tunisia formed a special corps of black military slaves, and at the end of that century the Tulunid rulers of Egypt built an army of twenty-four thousand white and forty-five thousand black slaves. The Fatimid rulers of Egypt (969–1171) raised large black battalions, and a Persian visitor to Cairo between 1046 and 1049 estimated an army of a hundred thousand slaves, of whom thirty thousand were black soldiers.

Slavery in the Islamic world differed in at least two fundamental ways from the slavery later practiced in South and North America. First, Muslims did not identify slavery with blackness as Europeans did in the Americas. The general and widespread use of Caucasian slaves in Islamic societies made that connection impossible. Second, slavery in the Islamic world was not the virtual equivalent of commercial plantation agriculture as practiced in the southern United States, the Caribbean, and Brazil in the eighteenth and nineteenth centuries. True, in the tenth century, large numbers of black slaves worked on the date plantations in northeastern Arabia. But massive revolts of black slaves called Zanj from East Africa, provoked by mercilessly harsh labor conditions in the salt flats and on the sugar and cotton plantations of southwestern Persia, erupted in 869. Gathering momentum, the Zanj captured the rich cities of Ahwaz, Basra, and Wasit and threatened Baghdad. Only the strenuous efforts of the commander of the caliph's armies, which were composed of Turkish slaves and included naval as well as land forces, halted and gradually crushed the Zanj in 883. The long and destructive Zanj revolt ended the Muslim experiment with plantation agriculture.[5]

Women in Classical Islamic Society

Arab tribal law gave women virtually no legal status. At birth girls could be buried alive by their fathers. They were sold into marriage by their guardians. Their husbands could terminate the union at will. And women had virtually no property or succession rights. The Qur'an sought to improve the social position of women.

The hadith—records of what Muhammad said and did, and what believers in the first two centuries after his death believed he said and did (see page 193)—also provide information about his wives. Some hadith portray the Prophet's wives as subject to common human frailties, such as jealousy; other hadith report miraculous events in their lives. Most hadith describe the wives as "mothers of the believers"—models of piety and righteousness whose every act illustrates their commitment to promoting God's order on earth by personal example.

Although the hadith usually depict women in terms of moral virtue, domesticity, and saintly ideals, the hadith also show some prominent women in "public" and political roles. For example, Aisha, daughter of the first caliph and probably Muhammad's favorite wife, played a "leading role" in rallying support for the movement opposing Ali, who succeeded Uthman in 656 (see page 197). Likewise, Umm Salama, a member of a wealthy and prominent clan in Mecca, at first supported Ali, then switched sides and supported the Umayyads.[6] (See the feature "Listening to the Past: The Etiquette of Marriage" on pages 226–227.)

The Qur'an, like the religious writings of all traditions, represents moral precept rather than social practice, and the texts are open to different interpretations. Yet modern scholars tend to agree that the Islamic sacred book intended women to be the spiritual and sexual equals of men and gave them considerable economic rights. In the early Umayyad period, moreover, women played an active role in the religious, economic, and political life of the community. They owned property. They had freedom of movement and traveled widely. Women participated with men in the public religious rituals and observances. But this Islamic ideal of women and men of equal value to the community did not last.[7] As Islamic society changed, the precepts of the Qur'an were interpreted to meet different circumstances.

In the later Umayyad period, the status of women declined. The rapid conquest of vast territories led to the influx of large numbers of slave women. As wealth replaced birth as the criterion of social status, scholars speculate, men more and more viewed women as possessions, as a form of wealth. The increasingly inferior status of women is revealed in three ways: in the relationship of women to their husbands, in the practice of veiling women, and in the seclusion of women in harems (see page 209).

On the rights and duties of a husband to his wife, the Qur'an states that "men are in charge of women because Allah hath made the one to excel the other, and because they (men) spend of their property (for the support of women). So good women are obedient, guarding in secret that which Allah hath guarded."[8] A tenth-century interpreter, Abu Ja'far Muhammad ibn-Jarir al-Tabari, commented on that passage in this way:

Men are in charge of their women with respect to disciplining (or chastising) them, and to providing them with restrictive guidance concerning their duties toward God and themselves (i.e., the men), by virtue of that by which God has given excellence (or preference) to the men over their wives: i.e., the payment of their dowers to them, spending of their wealth on them, and providing for them in full.[9]

A thirteenth-century commentator on the same Qur'anic passage goes into more detail and argues that women are incapable of and unfit for any public duties, such as participating in religious rites, giving evidence in the law courts, or being involved in any public political decisions.[10] Muslim society fully accepted this view, and later interpreters further categorized the ways in which men were superior to women.

The Sunni aphorism "There shall be no monkery Islam" captures the importance of marriage in Muslim culture and the Muslim belief that a sexually frustrated person is dangerous to the community. Islam vehemently discourages sexual abstinence. Islam expects that every man and woman, unless physically incapable or financially unable, will marry: marriage is a safeguard of chastity, essential to the stability both of the family and of society.

As in medieval Europe and traditional India and China, marriage in Muslim society was considered too important an undertaking to be left to the romantic emotions of the young. Families or guardians, not the prospective bride and groom, identified suitable partners and finalized the contract. The official wedding ceremony consisted of an offer and its acceptance by representatives of the bride's and groom's parents at a meeting before witnesses. A wedding banquet at which men and women feasted separately followed; the quality of the celebration, of the gifts, and of the food depended on the relative wealth of the two families. Because it was absolutely essential that the bride be a virgin, marriages were arranged shortly after the onset of the girl's menarche at age twelve or thirteen. Husbands were perhaps ten to fifteen years older. Youthful marriages ensured a long period of fertility.

A wife's responsibilities depended on the financial status of her husband. A farmer's wife helped in the fields, ground the corn, carried water, prepared food, and did the myriad tasks necessary in rural life. Shopkeepers' wives in the cities sometimes helped in business. In an upper-class household, the lady supervised servants, looked after all domestic arrangements, and did whatever was needed for her husband's comfort.

In every case, children were the wife's special domain. A mother exercised authority over her children and enjoyed their respect. A Muslim tradition asserts that "Paradise is at the mother's feet." Thus, as in Chinese culture, the prestige of the young wife depended on the production of children—especially sons—as rapidly as possible. A wife's failure to have children was one of the main reasons for a man to take a second wife or to divorce his wife entirely.

Like the Jewish tradition, Muslim law permits divorce. The law prescribes that if a man intends to divorce his wife, he should avoid hasty action and not have intercourse with her for three months; hopefully, they will reconcile. If the woman becomes pregnant during that period, the father can be identified. Divorce was not, however, encouraged. The commentator Ibn Urnan reported the Prophet as saying, "The lawful thing which God hates most is divorce."

Interpretations of the Qur'an's statements on polygamy give an example of the declining status of women in Muslim society. The Qur'an permits a man to have four wives, provided "that all are treated justly. . . . Marry of the women who seem good to you, two or three or four; and if ye fear that you cannot do justice (to so many) then one (only) or the captives that your right hand possess."[11] Muslim jurists interpreted the statement as having legal force. The Prophet's emphasis on justice to the several wives, however, was understood as a mere recommendation.[12] Although the Qur'an allows polygamy, only very wealthy men could afford several wives. The vast majority of Muslim males were monogamous because women could not earn money and men had difficulty enough supporting one wife.

In contrast to the Christian view of sexual activity as something inherently shameful and even within marriage only a cure for concupiscence, Islam maintains a healthy acceptance of sexual pleasure for both males and females. Islam holds that sexual satisfaction for both partners in marriage is necessary to prevent extramarital activity. Men, however, are entitled to as many as four legal partners. Women have to be content with one.

In many present-day Muslim cultures, few issues are more sensitive than those of the veiling and the seclusion of women. These practices have their roots in pre-Islamic times, and they took firm hold in classical Islamic society. The head veil seems to have been the mark of freeborn urban women; wearing the veil distinguished free women from slave women. Country and desert women did not wear veils because they interfered with work. Probably of Byzantine or Persian origin, the veil indicated respectability and modesty. As the Arab conquerors subjugated various peoples, they adopted some of the vanquished peoples' customs, one of which was veiling. The Qur'an contains no specific rule about the veil, but its few vague references have been interpreted as sanctioning the practice. Gradually, all parts of a woman's body were considered *pudendal* (shameful because they are capable of arousing sexual desire) and were not allowed to be seen in public.

Even more restrictive of the freedom of women than veiling was the practice of *purdah*, literally, seclusion behind a screen or curtain—the **harem** system. The English word *harem* comes from the Arabic *haram*, meaning "forbidden" or "sacrosanct," which the women's quarters of a house or palace were considered to be. The practice of secluding women in a harem also derives from Arabic contacts with other Eastern cultures. Scholars do not know precisely when the harem system began, but by 800 women in more prosperous households stayed out of sight. The harem became another symbol of male prestige and prosperity, as well as a way to distinguish upper-class women from peasants.

harem *The separate quarters of a house or palace where women live and men are excluded.*

TRADE AND COMMERCE

Did Islamic teachings contribute to the thriving trade that passed through Muslim lands?

Islam had a highly positive disposition toward profit-making enterprises. In the period from 1000 to 1500, there was less ideological resistance to the striving for profit in trade and commerce in the Muslim world than there was in the Christian West or the Confucian East. Again in contrast to the social values of the medieval West and the Confucian East, Muslims tended to look with disdain on agricultural labor. Muhammad had earned his living in business as a representative of the city of Mecca, which carried on a brisk trade from southern Palestine to southwestern Arabia. According to the sayings of the Prophet:

The honest, truthful Muslim merchant will stand with the martyrs on the Day of Judgment. I commend the merchants to you, for they are the couriers of the horizons and God's trusted servants on earth.[13]

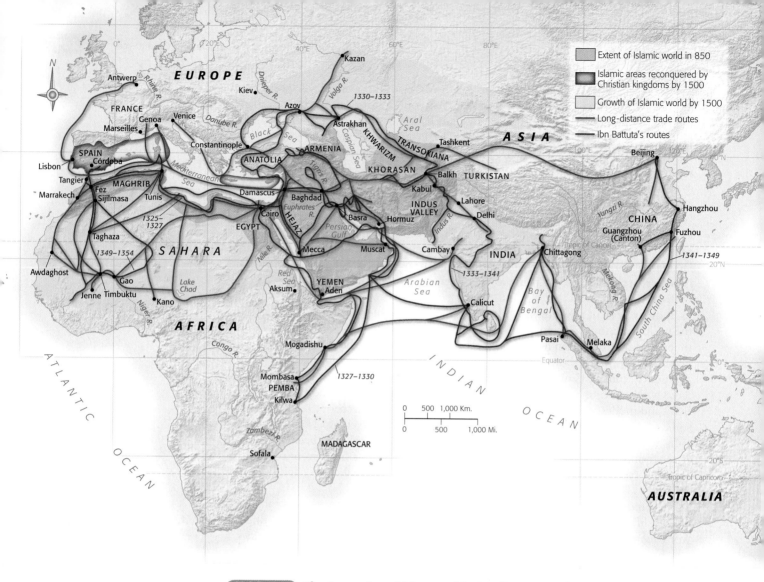

MAP 8.2 **The Expansion of Islam and Its Trading Networks in the Thirteenth and Fourteenth Centuries** By 1500 Islam had spread extensively in north and east Africa, into the Balkans, the Caucuses, Central Asia, India, and island Southeast Asia. Muslim merchants played a major role in bringing their religion as they extended their trade networks. They were active in the Indian Ocean long before the arrival of Europeans.

The Qur'an, moreover, has no prohibition against trade with Christians or other unbelievers.

Waterways served as the main commercial routes of the Islamic world (see Map 8.2). They ranged from the Mediterranean to the Black Sea; the Caspian Sea and the Volga River, which gave access deep into Russia; the Aral Sea, from which caravans departed for China; the Gulf of Aden; and the Arabian Sea and the Indian Ocean, which linked the Arabian gulf region with eastern Africa, the Indian subcontinent, and eventually Indonesia and the Philippines.

Cairo was a major Mediterranean entrepôt for intercontinental trade. An Egyptian official served as the legal representative of foreign merchants from Central Asia, Persia, Iraq, northern Europe (especially Venice), the Byzantine Empire, and Spain. They or their agents sailed up the Nile to the Aswan region, traveled east from Aswan by caravan to the Red Sea, and sailed down the Red Sea to Aden, whence they crossed the Indian Ocean to India. They exchanged textiles, glass, gold, silver, and copper for Asian spices, dyes, and drugs and for Chinese silks and porcelains. Muslim and Jewish merchants dominated the trade with India; both spoke and wrote Arabic. Their commercial practices included the *sakk,* an Arabic word that is the root of the English *check,* an order to a banker to pay money held on account to a third party; the practice can be traced to Roman Palestine. Muslims developed other business devices, such as the bill of exchange, a written order from one person to another to pay a specified sum of money to a designated person or party, and the idea of the joint stock company, an arrangement that lets a group of people invest in a venture and share its profits (and losses) in proportion to the amount each has invested.

Between 1250 and 1500, Islamic trade changed markedly. In maritime technology, the adoption from the Chinese of the magnetic compass, an instrument for determining directions at sea by means of a magnetic needle turning on a pivot, allowed greater reconnaissance of the Arabian Sea and the Indian Ocean. The construction of larger ships led to a shift in long-distance cargoes from luxury goods such as pepper, spices, and drugs to bulk goods such as sugar, rice, and timber. Venetian galleys sailing the Mediterranean came to carry up to 250 tons of cargo, but the *dhows* plying the Indian Ocean were built to carry even more, up to 400 tons. The teak forests of western India supplied the wood for Arab ships.

Commercial routes also shifted. The Mongol invasions, culminating in the capture of Baghdad and the fall of the Abbasid caliphate (see page 203), led to the decline of Iraq and the rise of Egypt as the center of Muslim trade. Beginning in the late twelfth century, Persian and Arab seamen sailed down the east coast of Africa and established trading towns between Somalia and Sofala (see page 249). These thirty to fifty urban centers—each merchant-controlled, fortified, and independent—linked Zimbabwe in southern Africa (see page 252) with the Indian Ocean trade and the Middle Eastern trade.

A private ninth-century list mentions a great variety of commodities transported into and through the Islamic world by land and by sea:

● **Arab Trade and Commerce** A mariner's compass determines direction at sea. Arab traders brought this Chinese south-pointing compass (*right*) to the West, probably in the twelfth century. In 1984, archaeologists unearthed these coins (*left*) on the island of Pemba, off the coast of modern Kenya. Deriving from Tunisian, Egyptian, and Syrian mints and bearing Arabic scripts, the coins testify to Muslim trade with the Swahili city-states. (*right: Ontario Science Center, Toronto; left: Ashmolean Museum, Oxford*)

Imported from India: tigers, leopards, elephants, leopard skins, red rubies, white sandal-wood, ebony, and coconuts

From China: aromatics, silk, porcelain, paper, ink, peacocks, fiery horses, saddles, felts, cinnamon

From the Byzantines: silver and gold vessels, embroidered cloths, fiery horses, slave girls, rare articles in red copper, strong locks, lyres, water engineers, specialists in plowing and cultivation, marble workers, and eunuchs

From Arabia: Arab horses, ostriches, thoroughbred she-camels, and tanned hides

From Barbary and Maghrib (the Arabic name for northwest Africa, an area that included Morocco, Algeria, and Tunisia): leopards, acacia, felts, and black falcons

From Egypt: ambling donkeys, fine cloths, papyrus, balsam oil, and, from its mines, high-quality topaz

From the Khazars (a people living on the northern shore of the Black Sea): slaves, slave women, armor, helmets, and hoods of mail

From Samarkand: paper

From Ahwaz (a city in southwestern Persia): sugar, silk brocades, castanet players and dancing girls, kinds of dates, grape molasses, and candy.[14]

Camels made long-distance land transportation possible. Stubborn and vicious, camels nevertheless proved more efficient for desert transportation than did horses or oxen. The use of the camel to carry heavy and bulky freight facilitated the development of overland commerce.

Did Muslim economic activity amount to a kind of capitalism? If by capitalism is meant private (not state) ownership of the means of production, the production of goods for market sale, profit as the main motive for economic activity, competition, a money economy, and the lending of money at interest, then, unquestionably, the medieval Muslim economy had capitalistic features. Students of Muslim economic life have not made a systematic and thorough investigation of Muslims' industries, businesses, and seaports, but the impressionistic evidence is overwhelming: "Not only did the Muslim world know a capitalist sector, but this sector was apparently the most extensive in history before the establishment of the world market created by the Western European bourgeoisie, and this did not outstrip it in importance until the sixteenth century."[15] Its only real competition was Song China (see pages 333–334).

One byproduct of the extensive trade through Muslim lands was the spread of useful plants. Cotton, sugar cane, and sugar spread from India to other places with suitable climates. A tenth-century geographer reported that cotton and rice were being planted in Iraq. Citrus fruits made their way to Muslim Spain from Southeast Asia and India.

CULTURAL DEVELOPMENTS

What advances were made in the arts, sciences, and education?

Long-distance trade provided the wealth that made possible a gracious and sophisticated culture in the cities of the Muslim world. (See the feature "Individuals in Society: Abu 'Abdallah Ibn Battuta.") Although cities and mercantile centers dotted the entire Islamic world, the cities of Baghdad and Córdoba at their peak in the tenth century stand out as the finest examples of cosmopolitan Muslim civilization. On Baghdad's streets thronged a kaleidoscope of races, creeds, costumes, and cultures, an almost infinite variety of peoples: returning travelers, administrative officials, slaves, visitors, and

Abu 'Abdallah Ibn Battuta

In 1354 the sultan of Morocco appointed a scribe to write an account of the travels of Ibn Battuta (1304–1368), who between 1325 and 1354 had traveled through most of the Islamic world. The two men collaborated. The result was a travel book written in Arabic and later hailed as the richest eyewitness account of fourteenth-century Islamic culture. It has often been compared to the slightly earlier *Travels* of the Venetian Marco Polo (see page 306).

Ibn Battuta was born in Tangiers to a family of legal scholars. As a youth, he studied Muslim law, gained fluency in Arabic, and acquired the qualities considered essential for a civilized Muslim gentleman: courtesy, manners, the social polish that eases relations among people.

At age twenty-one, he left Tangiers to make the *hajj* (pilgrimage) to Mecca. He crossed North Africa and visited Alexandria, Cairo, Damascus, and Medina. Reaching Mecca in October 1326, he immediately praised God for his safe journey, kissed the Holy Stone at the Ka'ba, and recited the ritual prayers. There he decided to see more of the world.

In the next four years, Ibn Battuta traveled to Iraq and to Basra and Baghdad in Persia, then returned to Mecca before sailing down the coast of Africa as far as modern Tanzania. On the return voyage, he visited Oman and the Persian Gulf region, then traveled by land across central Arabia to Mecca. Strengthened by his stay in the holy city, he decided to go to India by way of Egypt, Syria, and Anatolia; across the Black Sea to the plains of western Central Asia, detouring to see Constantinople; back to the Asian steppe; east to Khurasan and Afghanistan; and down to Delhi in northern India.

For eight years, Ibn Battuta served as a judge in the service of the sultan of Delhi. In 1341 the sultan chose him to lead a diplomatic mission to China. When the expedition was shipwrecked off the southeastern coast of India, Ibn Battuta used the disaster to travel through southern India, Sri Lanka, and the Maldive Islands. Thence he went on his own to China, stopping in Bengal and Sumatra before reaching the southern coast of China, then under Mongol rule. Returning to Mecca in 1346, he set off for home, getting to Morocco in 1349. After a brief trip across the Strait of Gibraltar to Granada, he undertook his last journey, by camel caravan across the Sahara to Mali in the

A traveler, perhaps Ibn Battuta, as depicted on a 1375 European map. *(Bibliothèque nationale de France)*

West African Sudan (see page 236), returning home in 1354. Scholars estimate that he had traveled about seventy-five thousand miles.

Ibn Battuta had a driving intellectual curiosity to see and understand the world. At every stop, he sought out the learned jurists and pious men at the mosques and madrasas. He marveled at the Lighthouse of Alexandria, eighteen hundred years old in his day; at the vast harbor at Kaffa (in southern Ukraine on the Black Sea) whose two hundred Genoese ships were loaded with silks and slaves for the markets at Venice, Cairo, and Damascus; and at the elephants in the sultan's procession in Delhi, which carried machines that tossed gold and silver coins to the crowds.

Ibn Battuta must have had an iron constitution. Besides walking long distances on his land trips, he endured fevers, dysentery, malaria, the scorching heat of the Sahara, and the freezing cold of the steppe. His thirst for adventure was stronger than his fear of nomadic warriors and bandits on land and the dangers of storms and pirates at sea.

Questions for Analysis

1. Trace the routes of Ibn Battuta's travels on a map.

2. How did a common Muslim culture facilitate his travels?

Source: R. E. Dunn, *The Adventures of Ibn Battuta: A Muslim Traveler of the Fourteenth Century* (Berkeley: University of California Press, 1986).

merchants from Asia, Africa, and Europe. Shops and marketplaces offered the rich and extravagant a dazzling and exotic array of goods from all over the world.

The caliph Harun al-Rashid (r. 786–809) presided over a glamorous court. He invited writers, dancers, musicians, poets, and artists to live in Baghdad, and he is reputed to have rewarded one singer with a hundred thousand silver pieces for a single song. This brilliant era provided the background for the tales that appear in *The Thousand and One Nights.*

The central plot of the fictional tales involves the efforts of Scheherazade to keep her husband, Schariar, legendary king of Samarkand, from killing her. She entertains him with one tale a night for 1,001 nights. The best-known tales are "Aladdin and His Lamp," "Sinbad the Sailor," and "Ali Baba and the Forty Thieves." Also known as *The Arabian Nights,* this book offers a sumptuous collection of caliphs, viziers, and genies, varieties of sexual experiences, and fabulous happenings. *The Arabian Nights,* though folklore, has provided many of the images that Europeans have used since the eighteenth century to describe the Islamic world.

Córdoba in southern Spain competed with Baghdad for the cultural leadership of the Islamic world. In the tenth century, no city in Asia or Europe could equal dazzling Córdoba. Its streets were well paved and lighted, and the city had an abundant supply of fresh water. With a population of about 1 million, Córdoba contained 1,600 mosques, 900 public baths, 213,177 houses for ordinary people, and 60,000 mansions for generals, officials, and the wealthy. In its 80,455 shops, 13,000 weavers produced silks, woolens, and brocades that were internationally famous. Córdoba utilized the Syrian process of manufacturing crystal. It was a great educational center with 27 free schools and a library containing 400,000 volumes. (By contrast, the great Benedictine abbey of Saint-Gall in Switzerland had about 600 books.) Through Iran and Córdoba, the Indian game of chess entered western Europe. Córdoba's scholars made contributions in chemistry, medicine and surgery, music, philosophy, and mathematics. Its fame was so great it is no wonder that the contemporary Saxon nun Hrosthwita of Gandersheim (d. 1000) described the city as the "ornament of the world."[16]

Education and Intellectual Life

Urban and sophisticated Muslim culture possessed a strong educational foundation. Muslim culture placed extraordinary emphasis on knowledge, especially religious knowledge. Knowledge provided the guidelines by which men and women should live.

Conquering Arabs took enormous pride in their Arabic language, and they feared their sons would adopt a corrupted Arabic by contact with subject peoples speaking other languages. Thus parents established elementary schools for the training of their sons. After the caliph Uthman (see page 197) ordered the preparation of an approved codex of the Qur'an, and after copies of it were made, the Qur'an became the basic text. From the eighth century onward, formal education for male children and youths involved reading, writing, and the study of the Qur'an, believed essential for its religious message and for its training in proper grammar and syntax.

Of great aid to learning was the Muslim transmission and improvement of papermaking techniques. The Chinese had been making paper for centuries from rags and woody fibers from such plants as hemp, jute, and bamboo. After their techniques spread westward, Muslim papermakers improved on Chinese techniques by adding starch to fill the pores in the surfaces of the sheets. Muslims carried this new method to Baghdad in Iraq, Damascus in Syria, Cairo in Egypt, and the Maghrib (North Africa), from which it entered Spain. Papermaking, even before the invention of printing, had a revolutionary impact on the collection and diffusion of knowledge and thus on the transformation of society.

madrasa *A school for the study of Muslim law and religious science.*

Islam is a religion of the law, and the institution for instruction in Muslim jurisprudence was the **madrasa,** the school for the study of Muslim law and religious science.

● **Teachers Disputing in a Madrasa** Although Islamic education relied heavily on memorization of the Qur'an, religious scholars frequently debated the correct interpretation of a particular text. Listening to this lively disputation, students in the audience are learning to think critically and creatively. *(Bibliothèque nationale de France, Ms. Arabe 6094, fol. 16)*

By 1193 thirty madrasas existed in Damascus; between 1200 and 1250, sixty more were established there. Aleppo, Jerusalem, Alexandria, and above all Cairo also witnessed the foundation of madrasas.

Schools were urban phenomena. Wealthy merchants endowed them, providing salaries for the teachers, stipends for students, and living accommodations for both. The teacher served as a guide to the correct path of living. All Islamic higher education rested on a close relationship between teacher and students, so in selecting a teacher, the student (or his father) considered the character and intellectual reputation of the teacher, not that of any institution. Students built their subsequent careers on the reputation of their teachers.

Learning depended heavily on memorization. In primary school, which was often attached to an institution of higher learning, a boy began his education by memorizing the entire Qur'an. Normally, he achieved this feat by the time he was seven or eight! In adolescence a student learned by heart an introductory work in one of the branches of knowledge, such as jurisprudence or grammar. Later he analyzed the texts in detail. Memorizing four hundred to five hundred lines a day was considered outstanding. Every class day, the teacher examined the student on the previous day's learning and determined whether the student fully understood what he had memorized. Students, of course, learned to write, for they had to write down the teacher's commentary on a particular text. But the overwhelming emphasis was on the oral transmission of knowledge.

Because Islamic education focused on particular books, when the student had mastered a text to his teacher's satisfaction, the teacher issued the student a certificate stating that he had studied the book or collection of traditions with his teacher. The certificate allowed the student to transmit a text to the next generation on the authority of his teacher.

Apart from the fundamental goal of preparing men to live wisely and in accordance with God's law, Muslim higher education aimed at preparing men to perform religious and legal functions as Qur'an—or hadith—readers; as preachers in the mosques; as professors, educators, copyists; and especially as judges. Judges issued *fatwas,* or legal opinions, in the public courts; their training was in the Qur'an, hadith, or some text forming part of the shari'a. Islam did not know the division between religious and secular knowledge characteristic of the modern Western world.

What educational opportunities were available to women? Although tradition holds that Muhammad said, "The seeking of knowledge is a duty of every Muslim," Islamic culture was ambivalent on the issue of female education. Because of the basic Islamic principle that "Men are the guardians of women, because God has set the one over the other," the law excluded women from participation in the legal, religious, or civic occupations for which the madrasa prepared young men. Moreover, educational theorists insisted that men should study in a sexually isolated environment because feminine allure would distract male students. Nevertheless, many young women received substantial educations from their parents or family members; the initiative invariably rested with their fathers or older brothers. The daughter of Ali ibn Muhammad al-Diruti al Mahalli, for example, memorized the Qur'an, learned to write, and received instruction in several sacred works. One biographical dictionary containing the lives of 1,075 women reveals that 411 had memorized the Qur'an, studied with a particular teacher, and received a certificate. After marriage, responsibility for a woman's education belonged to her husband.[17]

How does Islamic higher education compare with that available in Europe or China at the time (see pages 371–372, 334–336)? There are some striking similarities and some major differences. The church operated schools and universities in Europe. In China the government, local villages, and lineages all ran schools, and private tutoring was very common. In the Islamic world, as in China, the personal relationship of teacher and student was seen as key to education. In Europe the reward for satisfactory completion of a course of study was a degree granted by the university. In China, at the very highest levels, the imperial civil service examination tested candidates' knowledge and rewarded achievement with appoint-

● **Mechanical Hand Washer** Building on the work of the Greek engineer and inventor Archimedes (see page 97), the Arab scientist ibn al-Razzaz al-Raziri (ca. 1200) designed practical devices to serve general social needs and illustrated them in a mechanical engineering handbook. In this diagram, a device in the form of a servant pours water with his right hand and offers a towel with his left. The device resembles a modern faucet that releases water when hands are held under it. *(Courtesy of the Freer Gallery of Art, Smithsonian Institution, Washington, D.C. Purchase, F1930.75a)*

● **Pharmacist Preparing Drugs**   The translation of Greek scientific treatises into Arabic, combined with considerable botanical experimentation, gave Muslims virtually unrivaled medical knowledge. Treatment for many ailments was by prescription drugs. In this thirteenth-century illustration, a pharmacist prepares a drug in a cauldron over a brazier. It has been said that the pharmacy as an institution is an Islamic invention. *(The Metropolitan Museum of Art, Bequest of Cora Timken Burnett Collection of Persian Miniatures and Other Persian Art Objects, Bequest of Cora Timken Burnett, 1957 [57.51.21]. Photograph © 1991 The Metropolitan Museum of Art)*

ments in the state bureaucracy. In Muslim culture it was not the school or the state but the individual teacher whose evaluation mattered and who granted certificates.

In all three cultures education rested heavily on the study of basic religious, legal, or philosophical texts: the Old and New Testaments or the Justinian *Code* in Europe; the Confucian classics and commentaries in China; the Qur'an, hadith, and legal texts deriving from these in the Muslim world. Also in all three cultures memorization played a large role in the acquisition and transmission of information. In all three teachers lectured on particular passages, and sometimes leading teachers disagreed fiercely about the correct interpretations of a particular text, forcing students to question, to think critically, and to choose between divergent opinions. Finally, educated people in each culture shared the same broad literary and religious or ethical culture, giving that culture cohesion and stability. Just as a man who took a degree at Cambridge University in England shared the Latin language and general philosophical outlook of someone with a degree from Montpellier in France or Naples in Italy, so a Muslim gentleman from Cairo spoke and read the same Arabic and knew the same hadith as a man from Baghdad or Samarkand. In China those who had studied the Chinese classics from distant parts of China and even Korea, Japan, and Vietnam were less likely to be able to talk about them together, but they could have "brush conversations," the classical Chinese language serving as a lingua franca of the educated in East Asia the way Arabic did in the Muslim world and Latin did in Europe.

In the Muslim world the spread of the Arabic language, not only among the educated classes but also among all people, was the decisive element in the creation of a common means of communication and a universal culture. Recent scholarship demonstrates that after the establishment of the Islamic empire, the major influence in the cultural transformation of the Byzantine–Sassanid–North African and the Central Asian worlds was language. The Arabic language proved more important than religion in this regard. Whereas conversion to Islam was gradual, linguistic conversion went much faster. Arabic became the official language of the state and its bureaucracies in former Byzantine and Sassanid territories. Muslim conquerors forbade Persian-speaking people to use their native language. Islamic rulers required tribute from monotheistic peoples—the Persians and Greeks—but they did not force them to change their religions. Conquered peoples were, however, compelled to submit to a linguistic conversion—to adopt the Arabic language.[18] In time Arabic produced a cohesive and "international" culture over a large part of the Eurasian world.

As a result of Muslim creativity and vitality, modern scholars consider about 900 to 1300 one of the most brilliant periods in the world's history. The Persian scholar al-Khwarizmi (d. ca. 850) harmonized Greek and Indian findings to produce astronomical tables that formed the basis for later Eastern and Western research. Al-Khwarizmi also studied mathematics, and his textbook on algebra (from the Arabic *al-Jabr*) was the first work in which the word *algebra* is used to mean the "transposing of negative terms in an equation to the opposite side."

Muslim medical knowledge far surpassed that of the West. The Baghdad physician al-Razi (865–925) produced an encyclopedic treatise on medicine that was translated into Latin and circulated widely in the West. Al-Razi was the first physician to make the clinical distinction between measles and smallpox. The great surgeon of Córdoba, al-Zahrawi (d. 1013), produced an important work in which he discussed the cauterization of wounds (searing with a branding iron) and the crushing of stones in the bladder. In Ibn Sina of Bukhara (980–1037), known in the West as Avicenna, Muslim science reached its peak. His *al-Qanun* codified all Greco-Arabic medical thought, described the contagious nature of tuberculosis and the spreading of diseases, and listed 760 pharmaceutical drugs. Muslim scholars also wrote works on geography and jurisprudence. Al-Kindi (d. ca. 870) was the first Muslim thinker to try to harmonize Greek philosophy and the religious precepts of the Qur'an. He sought to integrate Islamic concepts of human beings and their relations to God and the universe with the principles of ethical and social conduct discussed by Plato and Aristotle.

Inspired by Plato's *Republic* and Aristotle's *Politics,* the distinguished philosopher al-Farabi (d. 950) wrote a political treatise describing an ideal city whose ruler is morally and intellectually perfect and who has as his goal the citizens' complete happiness. Avicenna maintained that the truths found by human reason cannot conflict with the truths of revelation as given in the Qur'an. Ibn Rushid, or Averroës (1126–1198), of Córdoba, a judge in Seville and later royal court physician, paraphrased and commented on the works of Aristotle. He insisted on the right to subject all knowledge, except the dogmas of faith, to the test of reason and on the essential harmony between religion and philosophy.

Sufism

Like the world's other major religions—Buddhism, Hinduism, Judaism, and Christianity—Islam also developed a mystical tradition. It arose in the ninth and tenth

● **Sufi Collective Ritual** Collective or group rituals, in which Sufis tried through ecstatic experiences to come closer to God, have always fascinated outsiders, including non-Sufi Muslims. Here the sixteenth-century Persian painter Sultan Muhammad illustrates the writing of the fourteenth-century lyric poet Hafiz. Just as Hafiz's poetry moved back and forth between profane and mystical themes, so it is difficult to determine whether the ecstasy achieved here is alcoholic or spiritual. Notice the various musical instruments and the delicate floral patterns so characteristic of Persian art. *(Courtesy of the Arthur M. Sackler Museum, Harvard University Art Museums. Promised gift of Mr. and Mrs. Stuart Cary Welch, Jr. Partially owned by the Metropolitan Museum of Art and the Arthur M. Sackler Museum, Harvard University, 1988. In honor of the students of Harvard University and Radcliffe College, 1988.460.3. Photo: Imaging Department, © President and Fellows of Harvard College)*

centuries as a popular reaction to the materialism of the Umayyad regime. *Sufis* were ascetics. They wanted a personal union with God—divine love and knowledge through intuition rather than through rational deduction and study of the shari'a. They followed an ascetic routine (denial of physical desires to gain a spiritual goal), dedicating themselves to fasting, prayer, meditation on the Qur'an, and the avoidance of sin.

The woman mystic Rabi'a (717–801) epitomized this combination of renunciation and devotion. An attractive woman who refused marriage so that nothing would distract her from a total commitment to God, Rabi'a attracted followers, whom she served as a spiritual guide. Her poem captures her deep devotion: "O my lord, if I worship thee from fear of hell, and if I worship thee in hope of paradise, exclude me thence, but if I worship thee for thine own sake, then withhold not from me thine eternal beauty."[19]

In the twelfth century groups of Sufis gathered around teachers. A member of a Sufi order was called a *dervish*. The ritual of Sufi brotherhoods directed the dervish to a hypnotic or ecstatic trance, either through the constant repetition of certain prayers or through physical exertions such as whirling or dancing (hence the English phrase "whirling dervish" for one who dances with abandonment). Some Sufis acquired reputations as charismatic holy men to whom ordinary Muslims came seeking spiritual consolation, healing, charity, or political mediation between tribal and factional rivals.

Probably the most famous medieval Sufi was the Spanish mystic-philosopher Ibn al-'Arabi (1165–1240). He traveled widely in Spain, North Africa, and Arabia seeking masters of Sufism. He visited Mecca, where he received a "divine commandment" to begin his major work, *The Meccan Revelation,* which evolved into a personal encyclopedia of 560 chapters. At Mecca the wisdom of a beautiful young girl inspired him to write a collection of love poems, *The Interpreter of Desires,* for which he composed a mystical commentary. In 1223, after visits to Egypt, Anatolia, Baghdad, and Aleppo, Ibn al-'Arabi concluded his pilgrimage through the Islamic world at Damascus, where he produced *The Bezels [Edges] of Wisdom,* considered one of the greatest works of Sufism.

Muslim-Christian Encounters

During the early centuries of the development of Islam, it came into contact with the other major religions of Eurasia—Hinduism in India, Buddhism in Central Asia, Zoroastrianism in Persia, and Judaism and Christianity both at home in Western Asia and to the west in Europe. As Islam developed, the relationship that did the most to define Muslim identity was its relationship with Christianity. To put this another way, the most significant "other" to Muslims in the heartland of Islam was Christendom. The close physical proximity and the long history of military encounters undoubtedly contributed to making the Christian-Muslim encounter so important to both sides.

In the classical period of Islam, Muslims learned about Christianity from the Christians they met in conquered territories; from biblical texts, the Old and New Testaments; from Jews; and from Jews and Christians who converted to Islam. Before 1500 a wide spectrum of Muslim opinion about Jesus and Christians existed. At the time of the Crusades (see pages 362–365) and of the Christian reconquest of Muslim Spain (see page 362), polemical anti-Christian writings understandably appeared. In other periods, Muslim views were more positive.

In the medieval period Christians and Muslims met frequently in business and trade. Commercial contacts, especially when European merchants resided for a long time in the Muslim East, gave Europeans, notably the Venetians, familiarity with Muslim art and architecture. Likewise, when in the fifteenth century Muslim artists in the Ottoman Empire and in Persia became acquainted with Western artists, such as Gentile Bellini, they admired and imitated them. We have already seen the striking parallels

Primary Source: Zakariya al-Qazwini, *From Monuments of the Lands: An Islamic View of the West*

---

between aspects of Western and Muslim higher education; Christians had very probably borrowed from Islam.

Christian Europeans and Middle Eastern Muslims were geographical neighbors. They shared a common cultural heritage from the Judeo-Christian past. In the Christian West, Islam had the greatest cultural impact in Andalusia in southern Spain. Between roughly the eighth and twelfth centuries, Muslims, Christians, and Jews lived in close proximity in Andalusia, and some scholars believe the period represents a remarkable era of interfaith harmony. Many Christians adopted Arabic patterns of speech and dress, gave up the practice of eating pork, and developed a special appreciation for Arabic music and poetry. Some Christian women of elite status chose the Muslim practice of going out in public with their faces veiled. Records describe Muslim and Christian youths joining in celebrations and merrymaking. These assimilated Christians, called **Mozarabs,** did not attach much importance to the doctrinal differences between the two religions.

Mozarabs soon faced the strong criticism of both Muslim scholars and Christian clerics. Muslim teachers feared that close contact between the two peoples would lead to Muslim contamination and become a threat to the Islamic faith. Christian bishops worried that a knowledge of Islam would lead to ignorance of essential Christian doctrines. Both Muslim scholars and Christian theologians argued that assimilation led to sensuality and that sensuality was ruining their particular cultures.

Thus, beginning in the late tenth century, Muslim regulations closely defined what Christians and Muslims could do. A Christian, however much assimilated, remained an **infidel.** An infidel was an unbeliever, and the word carried a pejorative or disparaging connotation. Mozarabs had to live in special sections of cities; could not learn the Qur'an, employ Muslim workers or servants, or build new churches; and had to be buried in their own cemeteries. A Muslim who converted to Christianity immediately incurred a sentence of death. By about 1250 the Christian reconquest of Muslim Spain had brought most of the Iberian Peninsula under Christian control. Christian kings set up schools that taught both Arabic and Latin, but these schools were intended to produce missionaries.

Beyond Andalusian Spain, mutual animosity restricted contact between the two peoples. The Muslim assault on Christian Europe in the eighth and ninth centuries—with villages burned, monasteries sacked, and Christians sold into slavery—left a legacy of bitter hostility. Christians felt threatened by a faith that acknowledged God as creator of the universe but denied the doctrine of the Trinity; that accepted Jesus as a prophet but denied his divinity; that believed in the Last Judgment but seemed to make sensuality Heaven's greatest reward. Europeans' perception of Islam as a menace helped inspire the Crusades of the eleventh through thirteenth centuries.

Muslim scholars often wrote sympathetically about Jesus. For example, the great historian al Tabari (d. 923), relying on Arabic sources, wrote positively of Jesus' life, focusing on his birth and crucifixion; at the same time, al Tabari used Old Testament

● **Lusterware Bowl from Egypt** An outstanding example of brightly glazed pottery with sharply etched figures, this bowl by a Muslim potter named Sa'ad shows a Christian priest swinging a censer with burning incense to purify a religious space. After the Islamic conquest, most of Egypt's Coptic Christians held on to their faith, but the Crusades bred Muslim suspicions and led to the forced conversion of many Egyptian Copts. *(Courtesy of the Trustees of the Victoria & Albert Museum)*

Mozarabs *Christians who adopted some Arabic customs but did not convert.*

infidel *An unbeliever; the Muslim term for a Christian, no matter how assimilated.*

books to prove Muhammad's prophethood and stressed the truth of Islam over Christianity. Ikhwan al-Safa, an eleventh-century Islamic brotherhood, held that in his preaching Jesus deliberately rejected the harsh punishments reflected in the Jewish Torah and tried to be the healing physician teaching by parables and trying to touch people's hearts by peace and love. The prominent theologian and qadi (judge) of Teheran, Abd al-Jabbar (d. 1024), though not critical of Jesus, argued that Christians had rejected Jesus' teachings: they failed to observe ritual purity of prayer, substituting poems by Christian scholars for scriptural prayers; they gave up circumcision, the sign of their covenant with God and Abraham; they replaced the Sabbath with Sunday; they allowed the eating of pork and shellfish; and they adopted a Greek idea, the Trinity, defending it by quoting Aristotle. Thus, al-Jabbar maintained—and he was followed later by many other Muslim theologians and scholars—that Christians failed to observe the laws of Moses and Jesus and distorted Jesus' message.

By the thirteenth century Western literature sometimes displayed a sympathetic view of Islam. The Bavarian knight Wolfram von Eschenbach's *Parzival* and the Englishman William Langland's *Piers the Plowman*—two poems that survive in scores of manuscripts, suggesting that they circulated widely—reveal broad-mindedness and tolerance toward Muslims. Some travelers in the Middle East were impressed by the kindness and generosity of Muslims and with the strictness and devotion with which Muslims observed their faith.[20] Frequently, however, Christian literature portrayed Muslims as the most dreadful of Europe's enemies, guilty of every kind of crime. In his *Inferno,* the great Florentine poet Dante (1265–1321) placed the Muslim philosophers Avicenna and Averroës with other virtuous "heathens," among them Socrates and Aristotle, in the first circle of Hell, where they endured only moderate punishment. Muhammad, however, Dante consigned to the ninth circle, near Satan himself, where he was condemned as a spreader of discord and scandal. His punishment was to be continually torn apart from his chin to his anus.

The Christian and Muslim worlds had an impact on each other even when they rejected each other most forcefully. Art styles, technology, and even institutional practices were frequently adopted or adapted. During the Crusades, Muslims adopted Frankish weapons and methods of fortification. Christians in contact with Muslim scholars recovered ancient Greek philosophical texts that survived only in Arabic translation.

Chapter Summary

To assess your mastery of this chapter and read the primary sources listed in the margins, visit **bedfordstmartins.com/mckayworld** or see *Sources of World Societies*.

Key Terms

Ka'ba
Qur'an
caliph
hadith
Sunna
umma
Five Pillars of Islam
jihad
diwān
imam
Shi'ites
Sunnis
ulama
emirs
shari'a
qadis
vizier
dhimmis
harem
madrasa
Mozarabs
infidel

• Who was Muhammad, and what did he teach?

Muhammad was born in the Arabian peninsula among the traders, farmers, and nomadic pastoralists of the region. He taught strict monotheism—there is one and only one God, and believers must submit to God's will. This God is the same God of the Christians and Jews, and Muhammad was familiar with the Old and New Testaments. A few decades after his death, his followers recorded both his revealed teachings—the Qur'an—and traditions about his words and actions.

• What forms of government did Islam establish, and how did they contribute to the rapid spread of Islam?

The spread of Islam was one of the most momentous developments in world history. Driven by the religious zeal of the jihad, Muslims carried their faith from the Arabian peninsula through the Middle East to North Africa, Spain, and southern France in the west and to the borders of China and northern India in the east—all within the short span of a century. Successors to Muhammad established the caliphate, which coordinated rule of all Muslim lands until about 900 under two successive dynasties—the Umayyad, centered at Damascus in Syria, and the Abbasid, with its capital at Baghdad in Iraq.

• How were the Muslim lands governed from 900 to 1400, and what new challenges did they face?

As provincial governors acquired independent power, which the caliphs could not check, centralized authority within the Islamic state disintegrated, and after 900 the Islamic lands are more accurately viewed as composed of many local dynasties, often in competition with each other. Turks played more and more important roles in the armies and came to be the effective rulers in many places. In the mid-thirteenth century the central Muslim lands from Damascus to Afghanistan and Central Asia fell to the Mongols, who ruled the region for about eighty years.

• What social distinctions were important in Muslim society?

Even in periods of political division, the Muslim lands shared much of their culture. Muhammad had insisted that birth was unimportant; what mattered was religious piety. Still, as in virtually every other society, social distinctions made a large difference in how people lived. At the top were the Arabs, descended from the original followers of the Prophet. Next were converts, such as the Copts, Berbers, and Persians who adopted Islam in subsequent centuries. Below them were Jews, Christians, and Zoroastrians, recognized as "protected people" because they recognized only one God; they were allowed to continue their religions. Below them were a substantial number of slaves, many of whom had been enslaved as war captives. Slaves normally were converted to Islam and might come to hold important positions, especially in the army. Distinctions between men and women in Islamic society were strict. In the Qur'an men were said to be in charge of women because they excel them, and women were enjoined to be obedient. In time, seclusion and veiling of women became common practices, especially among the well-to-do.

• Did Islamic teachings contribute to the thriving trade that passed through Muslim lands?

Islam developed and flourished in a mercantile milieu. By land and sea Muslim merchants transported a rich variety of goods across Asia, the Middle East, Africa, and western Europe. Muslim business procedures and terminology greatly influenced the West.

• What advances were made in the arts, sciences, and education?

On the basis of the wealth that trade generated, a gracious, sophisticated, and cosmopolitan culture developed with centers at Baghdad and Córdoba. In the tenth and eleventh centuries the Islamic world witnessed enormous intellectual vitality and creativity. Muslim scholars produced important work in many disciplines, especially mathematics, medicine, and philosophy. Muslim civilization in the Middle Ages was far in advance of that of Christian Europe, and Muslims, with some justification, looked on Europeans as ignorant barbarians. By 1400 Islamic learning as revealed in astronomy, mathematics, medicine, architecture, and philosophical investigation was highly advanced, perhaps the most creative in the world. In the development and transmission of ancient Egyptian, Persian, and Greek wisdom, Muslims played a vital role, as they did in the transmission of innovations from China and India.

Suggested Reading

Berkey, Jonathan *The Transmission of Knowledge in Medieval Cairo.* 1992. A study of religious education and its social context.

Cohen, Mark R. *Under Crescent and Cross: The Jews in the Medieval Ages.* 1994. Argues that Jews were less marginalized and persecuted under Islamic states than under Christian states.

Constable, Olivia Remie. *Trade and Traders in Muslim Spain: The Commercial Realignment of the Iberian Peninsula, 900–1500.* 1994. An excellent study of Muslim trade and commerce, drawing on a wide range of both Western and Arabic sources.

Ettinghausen, Richard, Oleg Grabar, and Marilyn Jenkins-Madina. *The Art and Architecture of Islam, 650–1250.* 2001. A stunningly illustrated overview of Islamic art.

Fletcher, Richard. *The Cross and the Crescent.* 2003. A balanced, fascinating, and lucidly written short account of the earliest contacts between Christians and Muslims.

Hourani, Albert, and Malise Ruthven. *A History of the Arab Peoples,* 2d ed. 2003. An important synthesis.

Lewis, Bernard. *Race and Slavery in the Middle East.* 1990. Explores the culture of slavery beginning from before Islam, with particular attention to slaves from Africa.

Long, Pamela O. *Technology and Society in the Medieval Centuries: Byzantium, Islam, and the West, 500–1300.* 2003. A useful survey of Arab scientific and military developments.

Peters, F. E. *The Hajj: The Muslim Pilgrimage to Mecca and the Holy Places.* 1994. Covers the social, commercial, and political significance of the obligatory Muslim pilgrimage to Mecca.

Stowasser, Barbara Freyer. *Women in the Qur'an: Traditions and Interpretation.* 1994. A fine analysis of the Qur'an's statement on women.

Notes

1. See F. M. Donner, "Muhammad and the Caliphate," in *The Oxford History of Islam*, ed. J. L. Esposito (New York: Oxford University Press, 1999), pp. 3–13.

2. F. E. Peters, *A Reader on Classical Islam* (Princeton: Princeton University Press, 1994), pp. 154–155.

3. R. G. Hoyland, ed., *Seeing Islam as Others Saw It: A Survey and Evaluation of Christian, Jewish and Zoroastrian Writings on Early Islam* (Princeton, N.J.: Darwin Press, 1997), pp. 524–525.

4. Quoted in R. Levy, *The Social Structure of Islam,* 2d ed. (Cambridge: Cambridge University Press, 1957), p. 56.

5. R. Segal, *Islam's Black Slaves* (New York: Farrar, Straus, and Giroux, 2001), p. 44.

6. See B. F. Stowasser, *Women in the Qur'an, Tradition, and Interpretation* (New York: Oxford University Press, 1994), pp. 94–118.

7. N. Coulson and D. Hinchcliffe, "Women and Law Reform in Contemporary Islam," in *Women in the Muslim World,* ed. L. Beck and N. Keddie (Cambridge, Mass.: Harvard University Press, 1982), p. 37.

8. Quoted in B. F. Stowasser, "The Status of Women in Early Islam," in *Muslim Women,* ed. F. Hussain (New York: St. Martin's Press, 1984), p. 25.

9. Quoted ibid., pp. 25–26.

10. Ibid., p. 26.

11. Ibid., p. 16.

12. G. Nashat, "Women in Pre-Revolutionary Iran: A Historical Overview," in *Women and Revolution in Iran,* ed. G. Nashat (Boulder, Colo.: Westview Press, 1983), pp. 47–48.

13. Quoted in B. Lewis, ed. and trans., *Islam: From the Prophet Muhammad to the Capture of Constantinople,* vol. 2: *Religion and Society* (New York: Harper & Row, 1975), p. 126.

14. Adapted from ibid, pp. 154–157.

15. M. Rodinson, *Islam and Capitalism,* trans. Brian Pearce (Austin: University of Texas Press, 1981), p. 56.

16. R. Hillenbrand, "Cordoba," in *Dictionary of the Middle Ages,* vol. 3, ed. J. R. Strayer (New York: Scribner's, 1983), pp. 597–601.

17. I have leaned here on the important study of J. Berkey, *The Transmission of Knowledge in Medieval Cairo: A Social History of Islamic Education* (Princeton, N.J.: Princeton University Press, 1992), pp. 22–43, 161–181; the quotations are on p. 161.

18. A. Dallal, "Science, Medicine, and Technology: The Making of a Scientific Culture," in *The Oxford History of Islam,* ed. J. L. Esposito (New York: Oxford University Press, 1999), pp. 158–159.

19. Margaret Smith, *Readings from the Mystics of Islam* (London; Luzac and Co., 1950), p. 11.

20. JoAnn Hoeppner Moran Cruz, "Western Views of Islam in Medieval Europe," in *Perceptions of Islam,* ed. D. Blanks and M. Frassetto (New York: St. Martin's Press, 1999), pp. 55–81.

Listening to the PAST

The Etiquette of Marriage

Abu Hamid Al-Ghazali (1058–1111) was a Persian philosopher, theologian, jurist, Sufi, and prolific author of more than seventy books. His magnum opus, The Revival of the Religious Sciences, *is divided into four parts:* Acts of Worship, Norms of Daily Life, The Ways to Perdition, *and* The Ways of Salvation. *His lengthy discussion of marriage falls under the* Norms of Daily Life. *The passages selected here are only a small part of this lengthy treatise, full of quotations from the Qur'an and the traditions about the words and actions of Muhammad.*

There are five advantages to marriage: procreation, satisfying sexual desire, ordering the household, providing companionship, and disciplining the self in striving to sustain them. The first advantage—that is, procreation—is the prime cause, and on its account marriage was instituted. The aim is to sustain lineage so that the world would not want for humankind. . . .

It was for the purpose of freeing the heart that marriage with the bondmaid was permitted when there was fear of hardship, even though it results in enslaving the son, which is a kind of attrition; such marriage is forbidden to anyone who can obtain a free woman. However, the enslaving of a son is preferable to destroying the faith, for enslavement affects temporarily the life of the child, while committing an abomination results in losing the hereafter; in comparison to one of its days the longest life is insignificant. . . .

It is preferable for a person with temperament so overcome by desire that one woman cannot curb it to have more than one woman, up to four. For God will grant him love and mercy, and will appease his heart by them; if not, replacing them is recommended. Seven nights after the death of Fatimah, Ali got married. It is said that al-Hasan, the son of Ali, was a great lover having married more than two hundred women. Perhaps he would marry four at a time, and perhaps he would divorce four at a time replacing them with others. . . .

The fourth advantage [of marriage]: being free from the concerns of household duties, as well as of preoccupation with cooking, sweeping, making beds, cleaning utensils, and means for obtaining support. . . .

Ali used to say, "The worst characteristics of men constitute the best characteristics of women; namely, stinginess, pride, and cowardice. For if the woman is stingy, she will preserve her own and her husband's possessions; if she is proud, she will refrain from addressing loose and improper words to everyone; and if she is cowardly, she will dread everything and will therefore not go out of her house and will avoid compromising situations for fear of her husband. . . ."

Some God-fearing men as a precaution against delusion would not marry off their daughters until they are seen. Al-Amash said, "Every marriage occurring without looking ends in worry and sadness." It is obvious that looking does not reveal character, religion, or wealth; rather, it distinguishes beauty from ugliness. . . .

The Messenger of God declared that "The best women are those whose faces are the most beautiful and whose dowries are the smallest." He enjoined against excessiveness in dowries. The Messenger of God married one of his wives for a dowry of ten dirhams and household furnishings that consisted of a hand mill, a jug, a pillow made of skin stuffed with palm fibers, and a stone; in the case of another, he feasted with two measures of barley; and for another, with two measures of dates and two of mush. . . .

It is incumbent upon the guardian also to examine the qualities of the husband and to look after his daughter so as not to give her in marriage to one who is ugly, ill-mannered, weak in faith, negligent in upholding her rights, or unequal to her in descent. The Prophet has said, "Marriage is enslavement; let one, therefore, be careful in whose hands he places his daughter." . . .

The Prophet asked his daughter Fatimah, "What is best for a woman?" She replied, "That she should see no man, and that no man should see her." So he hugged her and said they were "descendants one of another" [Qur'an 3:33]. Thus he was pleased with her answer. . . .

The Prophet permitted women to go to the mosques; the appropriate thing now, however, is to prevent them [from doing so], except for the old [ones]. Indeed such [prevention] was deemed proper during the days of the companions; A'ishah declared, "If the Prophet only knew of the misdeeds that women would bring about after his time, he would have prevented them from going out." . . .

If [a man] has several wives, then he should deal equitably with them and not favor one over the other; should he go on a journey and desire to have one [of his wives] accompany him, he should cast lots among them, for such was the practice of the Messenger. If he cheats a woman of her night, he should make up for it, for making up for it is a duty upon him. . . .

Let [a man] proceed with gentle words and kisses. The Prophet said, "Let none of you come upon his wife like an animal, and let there be an emissary between them." He was asked, "What is this emissary, O Messenger of God?" He said, "The kiss and [sweet] words."

One should not be overjoyed with the birth of a male child, nor should he be excessively dejected over the birth of a female child, for he does not know in which of the two his blessings lie. Many a man who has a son wishes he did not have him, or wishes that he were a girl. The girls give more tranquility and [divine] remuneration, which are greater.

Concerning divorce, let it be known that it is permissible; but of all permissible things, it is the most detestable to Almighty God. . . .

Questions for Analysis

1. In what ways are the views toward marriage and gender expressed by Al-Ghazali similar to those seen in other traditions?

2. Did the author think it was always appropriate to do what Muhammad and his early followers did?

Source: Madelain Farah, *Marriage and Sexuality in Islam: A Translation of Al-Ghazāli's Book on the Etiquette of Marriage from the Ihyā'* (Salt Lake City: University of Utah Press, 1984), pp. 53, 63, 64, 66, 85–86, 88–89, 91, 95–96, 100, 103, 106, 113, 116, slightly modified.

Last page of the manuscript of the *Munquidh min al Dalah*, contained in no. 1712 of the Sehid Ali Pasa of Istanbul. *(From Richard Joseph McCarthy, S.J., Deliverance from Error [Louisville, Ky.: Fons Vitae])*

Oni of Ife. Bronze striated head (marked with stripes, grooves, or ridges in parallel lines) showing an Oni of Ife, thirteenth to fourteenth century. *(© Jerry Thompson)*

9 AFRICAN SOCIETIES AND KINGDOMS, CA. 400–1450

Until fairly recently, ethnocentrism and racism limited what the outside world knew about Africa. But as recent scholarship has allowed us to learn more about early African civilizations, we can now appreciate the richness, diversity, and dynamism of those cultures. We know now that between about 400 and 1500, some highly centralized, bureaucratized, and socially stratified civilizations developed in Africa alongside communities that had a looser form of social organization and functioned as lineage or descent groups.

THE LAND AND PEOPLES OF AFRICA

What patterns of social and political organization prevailed among the peoples of Africa, and what types of agriculture and commerce did Africans engage in?

Africa is immense. The world's second largest continent (after Asia), it covers 20 percent of the earth's land surface. Five climatic zones roughly divide the continent (see Map 9.1). Fertile land with unpredictable rainfall borders parts of the Mediterranean coast in the north and the southwestern coast of the Cape of Good Hope in the south. Inland from these areas lies dry steppe country with little plant life. The steppe gradually gives way to Africa's great deserts: the Sahara in the north and the Namib and Kalahari in the south. The vast Sahara—3.5 million square miles—takes its name from the Arabic word for "tan," the color of the desert. (Folk etymology ascribes the word *Sahara* to an ancient Arabic word that sounds like a parched man's gasp for water.) The Sahara's southern fringe is called the Sahel. The Savanna—flat grassland—extends in a swath across the widest part of the continent, across parts of south-central Africa and along the eastern coast. It is one of the richest habitats in the world, accounting for perhaps 55 percent of the African continent. Dense, humid tropical rain forests stretch along coastal West Africa and on both sides of the equator in central Africa. Africa's climate is mostly tropical, with subtropical climates limited to the northern and southern coasts and to regions of high elevation. Rainfall is seasonal on most of the continent and is very sparse in desert and semidesert areas.

Geography and climate have significantly shaped African economic development. In the eastern African plains, the earliest humans hunted wild animals. The drier steppe regions favored herding. Wetter Savanna regions, like the Nile Valley, encouraged grain-based agriculture. Tropical forests favored hunting and gathering and, later, root-based agriculture. Rivers and lakes supported economies based on fishing.

Africa's peoples are as diverse as the continent's topography. In North Africa, contacts with Asian and European civilizations date back to the ancient Phoenicians, Greeks, and Romans. The native Berbers, living along the Mediterranean, have intermingled with many different peoples—with Muslim Arabs, who first conquered North Africa in the seventh and eighth centuries C.E.; with Spanish Muslims and Jews, many of whom settled in North Africa after their expulsion from Spain in 1492 (see page 402); and with sub-Saharan blacks.[1] The peoples living along the east, or Swahili, coast developed a maritime civilization and had rich commercial contacts with southern Arabia, the Persian Gulf, India, China, and the Malay Archipelago.

Black Africans inhabited the region south of the Sahara, an area of savanna and rain forest. The ancient Greeks called them *Ethiopians,* which means "people with burnt faces." The Berbers coined the term *Akal-n-Iquinawen,* which survives today as *Guinea.* The Arabs introduced another term, *Bilad al-Sudan,* which survives as *Sudan.* The Berber and Arab terms both mean "land of the blacks." Short-statured peoples, sometimes inaccurately referred to as Pygmies, inhabited the equatorial rain forests. South of those forests, in the continent's southern third, lived the Khoisan, a small people of yellow-brown skin color who primarily were hunters but also had domesticated livestock.

Egypt, Africa, and Race

Popular usage of the term *race* has often been imprecise and inaccurate. Unfortunately, the application of general characteristics and patterns of behavior to peoples based on perceptions of physical differences is one of the legacies of imperialism and colonialism. Anthropologists insist that when applied to geographical, national, religious, linguistic, or cultural groups, the concept of race is inappropriate and has been refuted by the scientific data. But the issue of race continues to engender fierce debate, as the example of Egypt shows.

Geographically, Egypt is obviously a part of the African continent. But from the days of the ancient Greek historian Herodotus of Halicarnassus, who visited Egypt (see page 8), down to the present, scholars have vigorously, even violently, debated whether racially and culturally Egypt is part of the Mediterranean world or part of the African world. Were Egyptians of the first century B.C.E.—who made enormous contributions to the Western world in architecture (the pyramids), mathematics, philosophy (the ideas of Socrates), science, and religion (the idea of divine kingship)—black people? The late Senegalese scholar Cheikh Anta Diop argued that much Western historical writing since the eighteenth century has been a "European racist plot" to destroy evidence showing that the people of the pharaohs were black. Diop and his followers in Africa and the United States have amassed architectural and linguistic evidence, as well as a small mountain of quotations from Greek and Roman writers and from the Bible, to insist that the ancient Egyptians belonged to the black race. Diop claimed to have examined the skin of ancient Egyptian mummies and said that on the basis of "infallible scientific techniques . . . the epidermis of those mummies was pigmented in the same way as that of all other (sub-Saharan) African negroes."[2]

Against this view, another group of scholars holds that the ancient Egyptians were Caucasians. They believe that Phoenician, Berber, Libyan, Hebrew, and Greek peoples populated Egypt and created its civilization. These scholars claim that Diop badly misunderstood the evidence. For example, whereas Diop relied on the book of Genesis to support his thesis, his detractors argue that the Hebrew Scriptures are not an anthropological treatise but a collection of Hebrew, Mesopotamian, and Egyptian legends concerned with the origins of all human peoples—by which the Hebrew writers meant ethnic groups, not racial groups in the twentieth-century sense. They point out that the pharaohs of the first century B.C.E. descended from the Macedonian generals whom Alexander the Great had placed over Egypt. They were white. A few scholars presenting a "white thesis" assert that Egypt exercised a "civilizing mission" in sub-Saharan Africa. Genetic theories, perhaps inevitably, have been challenged on many fronts, notably an archaeological one that proves no direct Egyptian influence in tropical Africa. Rather, the evidence suggests that indigenous cultures south of the Sahara developed independently, without any Egyptian influence. Both the "black thesis" and the "white thesis" are extremist.

A third proposition, perhaps the most plausible, holds that ancient Egypt, at the crossroads of three continents, was a melting pot of different cultures and peoples. To attribute Egyptian civilization to any one group is blatant racism. Many diverse peoples contributed to the great achievements of Egyptian culture. Moderate scholars believe that black Africans resided in ancient Egypt, primarily in Upper Egypt (south of what is now Cairo), but that other racial groups constituted the majority of the population.[3] On this complex issue, the jury is still out.

In the seventh and early eighth centuries, the Arabs conquered all of North Africa, taking control of Egypt between 639 and 642 (see page 194); ever since, Egypt has been an integral part of the Muslim world. Egypt's strategic location and commercial importance made it a logical target for Crusaders in the Middle Ages. In 1250 the Mamluks, a military warrior caste that originated in Anatolia, took over Egypt. With their slave soldiers, the Mamluks ruled until they were overthrown by the Ottoman Turks in 1517.

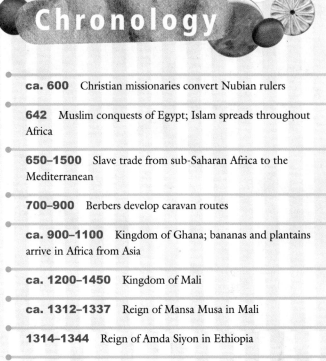

Chronology

ca. 600   Christian missionaries convert Nubian rulers

642   Muslim conquests of Egypt; Islam spreads throughout Africa

650–1500   Slave trade from sub-Saharan Africa to the Mediterranean

700–900   Berbers develop caravan routes

ca. 900–1100   Kingdom of Ghana; bananas and plantains arrive in Africa from Asia

ca. 1200–1450   Kingdom of Mali

ca. 1312–1337   Reign of Mansa Musa in Mali

1314–1344   Reign of Amda Siyon in Ethiopia

1324–1325   Mansa Musa's pilgrimage to Mecca

Early African Societies

Agriculture began very early in Africa. Archaeologists suggest that knowledge of plant cultivation moved west from ancient Judaea (southern Palestine), arriving in the Nile Delta in Egypt about the fifth millennium B.C.E. Settled agriculture then traveled down the Nile Valley and moved west across the Sahel to the central and western Sudan. By the first century B.C.E., settled agriculture existed in West Africa. From there it spread to the equatorial forests. African farmers learned to domesticate plants, including millet, sorghum, and yams. Cereal-growing people probably taught forest people to plant regular fields. Gradually African farmers also learned to clear land by burning. They evolved a sedentary way of life: living in villages, clearing fields, relying on root crops, and fishing.

● **Tassili Rock Painting**
This scene of cattle grazing near the group of huts (represented on the left by stylized white ovals) reflects the domestication of animals and the development of settled pastoral agriculture. Women and children seem to perform most of the domestic chores. Tassili is a mountainous region in the Sahara. *(Henri Lhote, Montrichard, France)*

Between 1500 and 1000 B.C.E., settled agriculture also spread southward from Ethiopia along the Rift Valley of present-day Kenya and Tanzania. Archaeological evidence reveals that the peoples of this region grew cereals, raised cattle, and used wooden and stone tools. Cattle raising spread more quickly than did planting. Early African peoples prized cattle highly. Many trading agreements, marriage alliances, political compacts, and treaties were negotiated in terms of cattle.

Cereals such as millet and sorghum are indigenous to Africa. Scholars speculate that traders brought bananas, taros (a type of yam), sugar cane, and coconut palms to Africa from Southeast Asia. Because tropical forest conditions were ideal for banana trees, their cultivation spread rapidly; they were easier to raise than cereal grains. Africans also domesticated donkeys, pigs, chickens, geese, and ducks.

The evolution to a settled life had profound effects. In contrast to nomadic conditions, settled societies made shared or common needs more apparent, and those needs strengthened ties among extended families. Population also increased:

The change from a hunter-gatherer economy to a settled farming economy affected population numbers. . . . What remains uncertain is whether in the agricultural economy there were more people, better fed, or more people, less well fed. . . . In precolonial Africa agricultural and pastoral populations may not have increased steadily over time, but fluctuated cyclically, growing and declining, though overall slowly growing.[4]

Scholars dispute the route by which ironworking spread to sub-Saharan Africa. Some believe the Phoenicians brought the iron-smelting technique to northwestern Africa, from where it spread southward. Others insist it spread from the Meroë region on the Nile westward. Most of West Africa had acquired knowledge of ironworking by 250 B.C.E., however, and archaeologists believe Meroë achieved pre-eminence as an iron-smelting center only in the first century B.C.E. Thus a stronger case can probably be made for the Phoenicians. The great trans-Saharan trade routes may have carried ironworking south from the Mediterranean coast. In any case, ancient iron tools found at the village of Nok on the Jos Plateau in present-day Nigeria seem to prove a

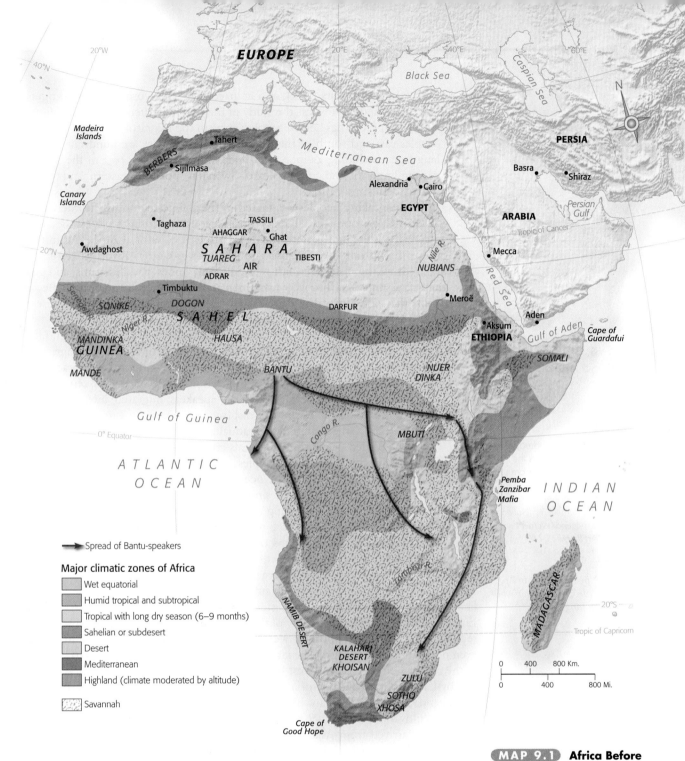

Spread of Bantu-speakers

Major climatic zones of Africa

- Wet equatorial
- Humid tropical and subtropical
- Tropical with long dry season (6–9 months)
- Sahelian or subdesert
- Desert
- Mediterranean
- Highland (climate moderated by altitude)
- Savannah

knowledge of ironworking in West Africa. The Nok culture, which enjoys enduring fame for its fine terra-cotta (baked clay) sculptures, flourished from about 800 B.C.E. to 200 C.E.

Bantu Migrations

The spread of ironworking is linked to the migrations of Bantu-speaking peoples. Today the overwhelming majority of the 70 million people living south of the Congo River speak a **Bantu** language. Because very few Muslims or Europeans penetrated into the interior, very few written sources for the early history of central and southern Africa survive. Lacking written sources, modern scholars have tried to reconstruct the history of the Bantu-speakers on the basis of linguistics, oral traditions (rarely reliable

● **Nok Woman** Hundreds of terra-cotta sculptures such as the head of this woman survive from the Nok culture, which originated in the central plateau of northern Nigeria in the first millennium B.C.E. *(National Museum, Lagos, Nigeria/Werner Forman Archive/Art Resource, NY)*

Bantu *The people living in Africa south of the Congo River who speak a Bantu language.*

beyond three hundred years back), and archaeology. The word *Bantu* is a linguistic classification, and linguistics (the study of the nature, structure, and modification of human speech) has helped scholars explain the migratory patterns of African peoples east and south of the equatorial forest. There are hundreds of Bantu languages, including Zulu, Sotho, and Xhosa, which are part of the southern African linguistic and cultural nexus. Swahili is spoken in eastern, and to a limited extent central, Africa.

Bantu-speaking peoples originated in the Benue region, the borderlands of modern Cameroon and Nigeria. In the second millennium B.C.E., they began to spread south and east into the forest zone of equatorial Africa. From there, groups moved onto the Savanna along the lower Congo River. Since they had words for fishing, fishhooks, fish traps, dugout canoes, paddles, yams, and goats, linguists assume that they were fishermen and that they cultivated roots. Because initially they lacked words for grains and cattle herding, they probably were not involved in those activities.

During the next fifteen hundred years, Bantu-speakers migrated throughout the Savanna, adopted mixed agriculture, and learned ironworking. Mixed agriculture (cultivating cereals and raising livestock) and ironworking were practiced in western East Africa (the region of modern Burundi) in the first century B.C.E. In the first millennium C.E., Bantu-speakers migrated into eastern and southern Africa. They did not displace earlier peoples but assimilated with them. The earlier inhabitants gradually adopted a Bantu language.

The settled cultivation of cereals and the keeping of livestock, together with intermarriage with indigenous peoples, apparently led over a long time to considerable population increases and the need to migrate further. The so-called Bantu migrations should not be seen as a single movement of cultivating, ironworking, Bantu-speaking black people sweeping across Africa from west to east and displacing all peoples in their path. Rather, those migrations were "a series of interrelated diffusions and syntheses, as small groups of Bantu-speakers interacted with preexisting peoples and new technical developments to produce a range of distinct cultural syntheses across the southern half of Africa."[5]

The Bantu-speakers' expansion and subsequent land settlement that dominated the first millennium and a half C.E. of eastern and southern African history was uneven. Enormous differences in the quality of the environment conditioned settlement. Some regions were well watered; others were very arid. This situation resulted in very uneven population distribution. The largest concentration of people seems to have been in the region bounded on the west by the Congo River and on the north, south, and east by Lakes Edward and Victoria and Mount Kilimanjaro, comprising parts of modern Uganda, Rwanda, and Tanzania. There the agricultural system rested on sorghum and yam cultivation. Between 900 and 1100, bananas and plantains (a starchy form of the banana) arrived from Asia. Because little effort was needed for their cultivation and the yield was much higher than for yams, bananas soon became the staple crop. The rapidly growing Bantu-speaking population led to further migration southward and eastward.[6] By the eighth century Bantu-speaking people had reached the region of present-day Zimbabwe, and by the fifteenth century Africa's southeastern coast.

Kingdoms of the Western Sudan (ca. 1000 B.C.E.–1500 C.E.)

Sudan *The African region surrounded by the Sahara, the Gulf of Guinea, the Atlantic Ocean, and the mountains of Ethiopia.*

The **Sudan** is that region bounded by the Sahara to the north, the Gulf of Guinea to the south, the Atlantic Ocean to the west, and the mountains of Ethiopia to the east. In the Savanna of the western Sudan—where the Bantu migrations originated—a series of dynamic kingdoms emerged in the millennium before European intrusion.

Between 1000 B.C.E. and 200 C.E., the peoples of the western Sudan made the momentous shift from nomadic hunting to settled agriculture. The rich Savanna proved ideally suited to the production of cereals, especially rice, millet, and sorghum. People situated near the Senegal River and Lake Chad supplemented their diet with fish. Food supply affects population, and the peoples of the region—known as the Mande-speakers and the Chadic-speakers, or Sao—increased dramatically in number. By 400 C.E. the entire Savanna, particularly the areas around Lake Chad, the Niger River bend, and present-day central Nigeria (see Map 9.1), had a large population.

Families and clans affiliated by blood kinship lived together in villages or small city-states. The basic social unit was the extended family. A chief, in consultation with a council of elders, governed a village. Some villages seem to have formed kingdoms. Village chiefs were responsible to regional heads, who answered to provincial governors, who in turn were responsible to a king. The chiefs and their families formed an aristocracy.

Kingship in the Sudan may have emerged from the priesthood, whose members were believed to make rain and to have contact with spirit powers. African kings always had religious sanction or support for their authority and were often considered divine. In this respect, early African kingship bears a strong resemblance to Germanic kingship of the same period: the king's authority rested in part on the ruler's ability to negotiate with outside powers, such as the gods.

African religions were animistic and polytheistic. Most people believed that a supreme being had created the universe and was the source of all life. The supreme being breathed spirit into all living things, and the *anima,* or spirit, residing in such things as trees, water, and earth had to be appeased. During the annual agricultural cycle, for example, all the spirits had to be propitiated from the time of clearing the land through sowing the seed to the final harvest. Because special ceremonies were necessary to satisfy the spirits, special priests with the knowledge and power to communicate with them through sacred rituals were needed. Thus the heads of families and villages were likely to be priests. Each family head was responsible for maintaining the family ritual cults—ceremonies honoring the dead and living members of the family.[7]

In sum, the most prominent feature of early African society was a strong sense of community based on blood relationship and on religion. Extended families made up the villages that collectively formed small kingdoms. What spurred the expansion of these small kingdoms into formidable powers controlling sizable territory was the development of long-distance trade. And what made long-distance or trans-Saharan trade possible was the camel.

The Trans-Saharan Trade

The expression "trans-Saharan trade" refers to the north-south trade across the Sahara (see Map 9.2). The camel had an impact on this trade comparable to the very important impact of the horse on European agriculture. Although scholars dispute exactly when the camel was introduced from Central Asia—first into North Africa, then into the Sahara and the Sudan—they agree that it was before 200 C.E. Camels can carry about five hundred pounds as far as twenty-five miles a day and can go for days without drinking, living on the water stored in their stomachs. Sometimes stupid and vicious, camels had to be loaded on a daily, sometimes twice-daily, basis. And much of the cargo for a long trip was provisions for the journey itself. Nevertheless, camels proved more efficient for desert transportation than horses or oxen, and the use of this beast to carry heavy and bulky freight not only brought economic and social change to Africa but also affected the development of world commerce.

Sometime in the fifth century, the North African **Berbers** fashioned a saddle for use on the camel. This saddle had no direct effect on commercial operations, for a merchant usually walked and guided the camel on foot. But the saddle gave the Berbers and later the region's Arabian inhabitants maneuverability on the animal and thus a powerful political and military advantage: they came to dominate the desert and to create lucrative routes across it. The Berbers determined who could enter the desert,

Berbers *North African peoples who were the first to develop saddles for use on the camel.*

and they extracted large sums of protection money from merchant caravans in exchange for a safe trip.

Between 700 and 900 C.E., the Berbers developed a network of caravan routes between the Mediterranean coast and the Sudan (see Map 9.1). The Morocco-Niger route ran from Fez to Sijilmassa on the desert's edge and then south by way of Taghaza and Walata and back to Fez. Another route originated at Sijilmassa and extended due south to Timbuktu with a stop at Taghaza. A third route ran south from Tripoli to Lake Chad. A fourth ran from Egypt to Gao by way of the Saharan oases of Ghat and Agades and then on to Takedda.

The long expedition across the Sahara testifies to the spirit of the traders and to their passion for wealth. Because of the blistering sun and daytime temperatures reaching 110 degrees, caravan drivers preferred night travel, when temperatures might drop to the low 20s. Ibn Battuta, an Arab traveler in the fourteenth century when the trade was at its height, left us one of the best descriptions of the trans-Saharan traffic (see page 213).

Nomadic raiders, the Tuareg Berbers, posed a serious threat. The Tuaregs lived in the desert uplands and preyed on the caravans as a way of life. Thus merchants made safe-conduct agreements with them and selected guides from among them. Caravans of twelve thousand camels were reported in the fourteenth century. Large numbers of merchants crossed the desert together to discourage attack. Blinding sandstorms often isolated part of a line of camels and on at least one occasion buried alive some camels and drivers. Water was the biggest problem. The Tuaregs sometimes poisoned wells to wipe out caravans and steal their goods. To satisfy normal thirst and to compensate for constant sweating, each person required a gallon of water per day. Desperate thirst sometimes forced the traders to kill camels and drink the foul, brackish water in their stomachs. It took Ibn Battuta twenty-five days to travel from Sijilmassa to the oasis of Taghaza and another sixty-five days to travel from Taghaza to the important market town of Walata.

The Arab-Berber merchants from North Africa who controlled the caravan trade carried manufactured goods—silk and cotton cloth, beads, mirrors—as well as dates and salt (essential in tropical climates to replace the loss from perspiration) from the Saharan oases and mines to the Sudan. These products were exchanged for the much-coveted commodities of the West African savanna—gold, ivory, gum, kola nuts (eaten as a stimulant), and captive slaves.

The steady growth of trans-Saharan trade had three important effects on West African society. The trade stimulated gold mining and the search for slaves. Parts of modern-day Senegal, Nigeria, and Ghana contained rich veins of gold. Both sexes shared in mining it. Men sank the shafts, hacked out gold-bearing rocks, and crushed them, separating the gold from the soil. Women washed the gold in gourds. Alluvial gold (mixed with soil, sand, or gravel) was separated from the soil by panning. Scholars estimate that by the eleventh century nine tons were exported to Europe annually—a prodigious amount for the time, since even with modern machinery and sophisticated techniques, the total gold exports from the same region in 1937 amounted to only twenty-one tons. A large percentage of this metal went to Egypt. From there it was transported down the Red Sea and eventually to India (see Map 8.2 on page 210) to pay for the spices and silks demanded by Mediterranean commerce. West African gold proved "absolutely vital for the monetization of the medieval Mediterranean economy and for the maintenance of its balance of payments with South Asia."[8] African gold linked the entire world, exclusive of the Western Hemisphere.

Slaves were West Africa's second most valuable export (after gold). African slaves, like their early European and Asian counterparts, seem to have been peoples captured in war. In the Muslim cities of North Africa, southern Europe, and southwestern Asia, there was a high demand for household slaves among the elite. Slaves also worked the gold and salt mines. Recent research suggests, moreover, that large numbers of black slaves were recruited through the trans-Saharan trade for Muslim military service.

Primary Source: Ibn Battuta, *From* Travels in Asia and Africa

Table 9.1 Estimated Magnitude of Trans-Saharan Slave Trade, 650–1500

YEARS	ANNUAL AVERAGE OF SLAVES TRADED	TOTAL
650–800	1,000	150,000
800–900	3,000	300,000
900–1100	8,700	1,740,000
1100–1400	5,500	1,650,000
1400–1500	4,300	430,000

Source: From R. A. Austen, "The Trans-Saharan Slave Trade: A Tentative Census," in *The Uncommon Market: Essays in the Economic History of the Atlantic Slave Trade,* ed. H. A. Gemery and J. S. Hogendorn (New York: Academic Press, 1979). Used with permission.

High death rates from disease, manumission, and the assimilation of some blacks into Muslim society meant that the demand for slaves remained high for centuries. Table 9.1 shows one scholar's tentative conclusions, based on many kinds of evidence, about the scope of the trans-Saharan slave trade. The total number of blacks enslaved over an 850-year period may be tentatively estimated at more than 4 million.[9]

Slavery in Muslim societies, as in European and Asian countries before the fifteenth century, was not based on skin color. Muslims also enslaved Caucasians who had been purchased, seized in war, or kidnapped from Europe. Wealthy Muslim households in Córdoba, Alexandria, and Tunis often included slaves of a number of races, all of whom had been completely cut off from their cultural roots. Likewise, West African kings who sold blacks to northern traders also bought a few white slaves—Slavic, British, and Turkish—for their domestic needs. Race had little to do with the phenomenon of slavery.[10]

The trans-Saharan trade also stimulated the development of vigorous urban centers in West Africa. Scholars date the growth of African cities from around the early ninth century. Families that had profited from trade tended to congregate in the border zones between the Savanna and the Sahara. They acted as middlemen between the miners to the south and Muslim merchants from the north. By the early thirteenth century, these families had become powerful black merchant dynasties. Muslim traders from the Mediterranean settled permanently in the trading depots, from which they organized the trans-Saharan caravans. The concentration of people stimulated agriculture and the craft industries. Gradually cities of sizable population emerged. Jenne, Gao, and Timbuktu, which enjoyed commanding positions on the Niger River bend, became centers of the export-import trade. Sijilmassa grew into a thriving market center. Kumbi, with between fifteen thousand and twenty thousand inhabitants, was probably the largest city in the western Sudan in the twelfth century. (By European standards, Kumbi was a metropolis; London and Paris achieved its size only in the late thirteenth century.) Between 1100 and 1400, these cities played a dynamic role in the commercial life of West Africa and Europe and became centers of intellectual creativity.

Perhaps the most influential consequence of the trans-Saharan trade was the introduction of Islam to West African society. In the eighth century, Arab invaders overran all of coastal North Africa. The Berbers living there gradually became Muslims. As traders, these Berbers carried Islam to sub-Saharan West Africa, the region known in Arabic as Bilad al-Sudan, "Land of the Blacks." From the eleventh century onward,

Primary Source:
**Abu Ubaydallah al-Bakri,
From The Book of Routes
and Realms**

militant Almoravids, a coalition of fundamentalist western Saharan Berbers, preached Islam to the rulers of Ghana, Mali, Songhai, and Kanem-Bornu, who, admiring Muslim administrative techniques and wanting to protect their kingdoms from Muslim attacks, accepted Islamic conversion. Some merchants also sought to preserve their elite mercantile status by adopting Islam. By the tenth century, Muslim Berbers controlled the north-south trade routes to the Savanna. By the eleventh century, African rulers of Gao and Timbuktu had accepted Islam. The king of Ghana was also influenced by Islam. Muslims quickly became integral to West African government and society. Hence in the period from roughly 1000 to 1400, Islam in West Africa was a class-based religion with conversion inspired by political or economic motives. Rural people retained their traditional animism.

Conversion to Islam introduced West Africans to a rich and sophisticated culture. By the late eleventh century, Muslims were guiding the ruler of Ghana in the operation of his administrative machinery. The king of Ghana adopted the Muslim diwān, the agency for keeping financial records (see page 196). Because efficient government depends on the preservation of records, the arrival of Islam in West Africa marked the advent of written documents there. Arab Muslims also taught the rulers of Ghana how to manufacture bricks, and royal palaces and mosques began to be built of brick. African rulers corresponded with Muslim architects, theologians, and other intellectuals, who advised them on statecraft and religion. Islam accelerated the development of the West African empires of the ninth through fifteenth centuries.

After the Muslim conquest of Egypt in 642 (see page 194), Islam spread southward from Egypt up the Nile Valley and west to Darfur and Wadai. This Muslim penetration came not by military force but, as in the trans-Saharan trade routes in West Africa, by gradual commercial passage.

Mogadishu *A Muslim port city founded between the eighth and tenth centuries; today it is the capital of Somalia.*

Muslim expansion from the Arabian peninsula across the Red Sea to the Horn of Africa, then southward along the coast of East Africa, represents a third direction of Islam's growth in Africa. From ports on the Red Sea and the Gulf of Aden, maritime trade carried the Prophet's teachings to East Africa and the Indian Ocean. Muslims founded the port city of **Mogadishu,** today Somalia's capital. In the twelfth century, Mogadishu developed into a Muslim sultanate, a monarchy that employed a slave military corps against foreign and domestic enemies. Archaeological evidence, confirmed by Arabic sources, reveals a rapid Islamic expansion along Africa's east coast in the thirteenth century. Many settlers came from Yemen in the southern Arabian peninsula, and one family set up the Abul-Mawahib dynasty in Kilwa.[11] Ibn Battuta discovered a center for Islamic law when he visited Kilwa in 1331.

• • • • • • • • • • • • • • • • • • • •

AFRICAN KINGDOMS AND EMPIRES (CA. 800–1450)

What values do Africans' art, architecture, and religions express?

All African societies shared one basic feature: a close relationship between political and social organization. Ethnic or blood ties bound clan members together. What scholars call **stateless societies** were culturally homogeneous ethnic societies. The smallest ones numbered fewer than a hundred people and were nomadic hunting groups. Larger stateless societies of perhaps several thousand people lived a settled and often agricultural or herding life.

stateless societies *African societies bound together by ethnic or blood ties rather than being political states.*

The period from about 800 to 1450 witnessed the flowering of several powerful African states. In the western Sudan, the large empires of Ghana and Mali developed, complete with large royal bureaucracies. On the east coast emerged powerful city-states based on sophisticated mercantile activities and, like Sudan, very much influenced by Islam. In Ethiopia, in central East Africa, kings relied on the Christian faith of their people to strengthen political authority. In South Africa, the empire of Great Zimbabwe, built on the gold trade with the east coast, flourished.

The Kingdom of Ghana (ca. 900–1100)

So remarkable was the kingdom of **Ghana** during the age of Africa's great empires that writers throughout the medieval world, such as the fourteenth-century Muslim historian Ibn Khaldun, praised it as a model for other rulers. Medieval Ghana also holds a central place in the historical consciousness of the modern state of Ghana. Since this former British colony attained independence in 1957, its political leaders have hailed the medieval period as a glorious heritage. The name of the modern republic of Ghana—which in fact lies far from the site of the old kingdom—was selected to signify the rebirth of an age of gold in black Africa.

> **Ghana** *The name of a great African kingdom inhabited by the Soninke people.*

The nucleus of the territory that became the kingdom of Ghana was inhabited by Soninke people who called their ruler **ghana,** or war chief. By the late eighth century, Muslim traders and other foreigners applied the word to the region where the Soninke lived, the black kingdom south of the Sahara. The Soninke themselves called their land "Aoukar" or "Awkar," by which they meant the region north of the Senegal and Niger Rivers. Only the southern part of Aoukar received enough rainfall to be agriculturally productive, and it was in this area that the civilization of Ghana developed. Skillful farming and an efficient system of irrigation led to the production of abundant crops, which eventually supported a population of as many as two hundred thousand.

> **ghana** *The name used by the Soninke people for their ruler.*

The Soninke name for their king—war chief—aptly describes the king's major preoccupation in the tenth century. In 992 Ghana captured the Berber town of Awdaghost, strategically situated on the trans-Saharan trade route (see Map 9.1). Thereafter Ghana controlled the southern portion of a major caravan route. Before the year 1000, the rulers of Ghana had extended their influence almost to the Atlantic coast and had captured a number of small kingdoms in the south and east. By the early eleventh century, the king exercised sway over a territory approximately the size of Texas. No other power in the West African region could successfully challenge him.

Throughout this vast West African area, all authority sprang from the king. Religious ceremonies and court rituals emphasized the king's sacredness and were intended to strengthen his authority. The king's position was hereditary in the matrilineal line—that is, the ruling king's heir was one of the king's sister's sons (presumably the eldest or fittest for battle). According to the eleventh-century Spanish Muslim geographer al-Bakri (1040?–1094), "This is their custom . . . the kingdom is inherited only by the son of the king's sister. He the king has no doubt that his successor is a son of his sister, while he is not certain that his son is in fact his own."[12]

A council of ministers assisted the king in the work of government, and from the ninth century on most of these ministers were Muslims. Detailed evidence about the early Ghanaian bureaucracy has not survived, but scholars suspect that separate agencies were responsible for taxation, royal property, foreigners, forests, and the army. The royal administration was well served by Muslim ideas, skills, and especially literacy. The king and his people, however, clung to their ancestral religion and basic cultural institutions.

The king of Ghana held his court in **Kumbi.** Al-Bakri provides a valuable picture of the city in the eleventh century:

> **Kumbi** *The city where the king of Ghana held his court.*

The city of Ghana consists of two towns lying on a plain, one of which is inhabited by Muslims and is large, possessing twelve mosques—one of which is a congregational mosque for Friday prayer; each has its imam, its muezzin and paid reciters of the Quran. The town possesses a large number of jurisconsults and learned men.[13]

Either for their own protection or to preserve their special identity, the Muslims lived separate from the African artisans and tradespeople. The Muslim community in Ghana must have been large and prosperous to have supported twelve mosques. The *imam* was the religious leader who conducted the ritual worship, especially the main prayer service on Fridays (see page 198). The *muezzin* led the prayer responses after the imam; he needed a strong voice so that those at a distance and the women in the harems, or enclosures, could hear (see page 209). Muslim religious leaders exercised civil authority over their coreligionists. Their presence and that of other learned Muslims also suggests vigorous intellectual activity.

Al-Bakri describes the town where the king lived and the royal court:

The town inhabited by the king is six miles from the Muslim one and is called Al Ghana. . . . The residence of the king consists of a palace and a number of dome-shaped dwellings, all of them surrounded by a strong enclosure, like a city wall. In the town . . . is a mosque, where Muslims who come on diplomatic missions to the king pray. The town where the king lives is surrounded by domed huts, woods, and copses where priest-magicians live; in these woods also are the religious idols and tombs of the kings. Special guards protect this area and prevent anyone from entering it so that no foreigners know what is inside. Here also are the king's prisons, and if anyone is imprisoned there, nothing more is heard of him.[14]

The king adorns himself, as do the women here, with necklaces and bracelets; on their heads they wear caps decorated with gold, sewn on material of fine cotton stuffing. When he holds court in order to hear the people's complaints and to do justice, he sits in a pavilion around which stand ten horses wearing golden trappings; behind him ten pages stand, holding shields and swords decorated with gold; at his right are the sons of the chiefs of the country, splendidly dressed and with their hair sprinkled with gold. The governor of the city sits on the ground in front of the king with other officials likewise sitting around him. Excellently pedigreed dogs guard the door of the pavilion. . . . The noise of a sort-of drum, called a daba, and made from a long hollow log, announces the start of the royal audience. When the king's coreligionists appear before him, they fall on their knees and toss dust on their heads—this is their way of greeting their sovereign. Muslims show respect by clapping their hands.[15]

What sort of juridical system did Ghana have? How was the guilt or innocence of an accused person determined? Justice derived from the king, who heard cases at court or on his travels throughout his kingdom. As al-Bakri recounts:

When a man is accused of denying a debt or of having shed blood or some other crime, a headman (village chief) takes a thin piece of wood, which is sour and bitter to taste, and pours upon it some water which he then gives to the defendant to drink. If the man vomits, his innocence is recognized and he is congratulated. If he does not vomit and the drink remains in his stomach, the accusation is accepted as justified.[16]

This appeal to the supernatural for judgment was very similar to the justice by ordeal that prevailed among the Germanic peoples of western Europe at the same time. Complicated cases in Ghana seem to have been appealed to the king, who often relied on the advice of Muslim legal experts.

The king's elaborate court, the administrative machinery he built, and the extensive territories he governed were all expensive. Ghana's king needed a lot of money, and he apparently had four main sources of support. The royal estates—some hereditary, others conquered in war—produced annual revenue, mostly in the form of foodstuffs for the royal household. The king also received tribute annually from subordinate chieftains (lack of evidence prevents an estimate of the value of this tax). Customs duties on goods entering and leaving the country generated revenues. Salt was the largest import. Berber merchants paid a tax to the king on the cloth, metalwork, weapons, and other goods that they brought into the country from North Africa; in return these traders received royal protection from bandits. African traders bringing gold into Ghana from the south also paid the customs duty.

Finally, the royal treasury held a monopoly on the export of gold. The gold industry was undoubtedly the king's largest source of income. It was on gold that the fame of medieval Ghana rested. The ninth-century geographer al-Ya-qubi wrote, "Its king

is mighty, and in his lands are gold mines. Under his authority are various other kingdoms—and in all this region there is gold."[17]

The governing aristocracy—the king, his court, and Muslim administrators—occupied the highest rung on the Ghanaian social ladder. On the next rung stood the merchant class. Considerably below the merchants stood the farmers, cattle breeders, gold mine supervisors, and skilled craftsmen and weavers—what today might be called the middle class. Some merchants and miners must have enjoyed great wealth, but, as in all aristocratic societies, money alone did not suffice. High status was based on blood and royal service. On the social ladder's lowest rung were slaves, who worked in households, on farms, and in the mines. As in Asian and European societies of the time, slaves accounted for only a small percentage of the population.

Apart from these social classes stood the army. According to al-Bakri, "the king of Ghana can put 200,000 warriors in the field, more than 40,000 being armed with bow and arrow." Like most medieval estimates, this is probably a gross exaggeration. Even a modern industrialized state with sophisticated means of transportation, communication, and supply lines would have enormous difficulty mobilizing so many men for battle. The king of Ghana, however, was not called "war chief" for nothing. He maintained at his palace a crack standing force of a thousand men, comparable to the Roman Praetorian Guard. These thoroughly disciplined, well-armed, totally loyal troops protected the king and the royal court. They lived in special compounds, enjoyed the king's favor, and sometimes acted as his personal ambassadors to subordinate rulers. In wartime, this regular army was augmented by levies of soldiers from conquered peoples and by the use of slaves and free reserves. The force that the king could field was sizable, if not as huge as al-Bakri estimated.

The Kingdom of Mali (ca. 1200–1450)

During the century after the collapse of Kumbi, a cloud of obscurity hung over the western Sudan. The kingdom of Ghana split into several small kingdoms that feuded among themselves. One people, the Mandinke, lived in the kingdom of Kangaba on the upper Niger River. The Mandinke had long been part of the Ghanaian empire, and the Mandinke and Soninke belonged to the same language group. Kangaba formed the core of the new empire of Mali. Building on Ghanaian foundations, Mali developed into a better-organized and more powerful state than Ghana.

● **The Great Friday Mosque, Jenne** The mosque at Jenne was built in the form of a parallelogram. Inside, nine long rows of adobe columns run along a north-south axis and support a flat roof of palm logs. A pointed arch links each column to the next in its row, forming nine east-west archways facing the *mihrab*, the niche indicating the direction of Mecca and from which the *imam* (prayer leader) speaks. This mosque (rebuilt in 1907 on a thirteenth-century model) testifies to the considerable wealth, geometrical knowledge, and manpower of the region. *(Copyright Carollee Pelos. From Spectacular Vernacular: The Adobe Tradition, Chapter 11, "Histories of the Great Mosques of Djenné" [New York: Aperture, 1996])*

● **Dogon Couple** This seated couple, made of wood and metal, tells us a great deal about the culture of the people living in the Dogon region at the Niger River bend in West Africa, in what is now Mali. The man's right arm circles the woman's shoulder and rests on her breast; his left hand points toward his genitals. He carries a quiver on his back; she bears an infant on hers. The mutually dependent figures indicate that the man is progenitor, protector, and provider; the woman is child-bearer and nurturer. Dogon society was strongly patrilineal and famous for its artwork. This piece was done between the sixteenth and twentieth centuries. (The Metropolitan Museum of Art, Gift of Lester Wunderman, 1977 [1977.394.15]. Photograph © 1993 The Metropolitan Museum of Art)

The kingdom of Mali (see Map 9.2) owed its greatness to two fundamental assets. First, its strong agricultural and commercial base provided for a large population and enormous wealth. Second, Mali had two rulers, Sundiata and Mansa Musa, who combined military success with exceptionally creative personalities.

The earliest surviving evidence about the Mandinke, dating from the early eleventh century, indicates that they were extremely successful at agriculture. Consistently large harvests throughout the twelfth and thirteenth centuries meant a plentiful supply of food, which encouraged steady population growth. The geographical location of Kangaba also placed the Mandinke in an ideal position in West African trade. Earlier, during the period of Ghanaian hegemony, the Mandinke had acted as middlemen in the gold and salt traffic flowing north and south. In the thirteenth century Mandinke traders formed companies, traveled widely, and gradually became a major force in the entire West African trade.

Sundiata (r. ca. 1230–1255) set up his capital at Niani, transforming the city into an important financial and trading center. He then embarked on a policy of imperial expansion. Through a series of military victories, Sundiata and his successors absorbed into Mali other territories of the former kingdom of Ghana and established hegemony over the trading cities of Gao, Jenne, and Walata.

These expansionist policies were continued in the fourteenth century by Sundiata's descendant Mansa Musa (r. ca. 1312–1337), early Africa's most famous ruler. In the language of the Mandinke, *mansa* means "emperor." Mansa Musa fought many campaigns and checked every attempt at rebellion. Ultimately his influence extended northward to several Berber cities in the Sahara, eastward to Timbuktu and Gao, and westward as far as the Atlantic Ocean. Throughout his territories, he maintained strict royal control over the rich trans-Saharan trade. Thus this empire, roughly twice the size of the Ghanaian kingdom and containing perhaps 8 million people, brought Mansa Musa fabulous wealth.

Mansa Musa built on the foundations of his predecessors. The stratified aristocratic structure of Malian society perpetuated the pattern set in Ghana, as did the system of provincial administration and annual tribute. The emperor took responsibility for the territories that formed the heart of the empire and appointed governors to rule the outlying provinces or dependent kingdoms. But Mansa Musa made a significant innovation: in a practice strikingly similar to a system used in both China and France at that time, he appointed members of the royal family as provincial governors. He could count on their loyalty, and they received valuable experience in the work of government.

In another aspect of administration, Mansa Musa also differed from his predecessors. He became a devout Muslim. Although most of the Mandinke clung to their ancestral animism, Islamic practices and influences in Mali multiplied.

The most celebrated event of Mansa Musa's reign was his pilgrimage to Mecca in 1324–1325, during which he paid a state visit to the sultan of Egypt. Mansa Musa's entrance into Cairo was magnificent. Preceded by five hundred slaves, each carrying a six-pound staff of gold, he followed with a huge host of retainers, including one hundred elephants each bearing one hundred pounds of gold. The emperor lavished his wealth on the citizens of the Egyptian capital. Writing twelve years later, al-Omari, one of the sultan's officials, recounts:

This man Mansa Musa spread upon Cairo the flood of his generosity: there was no person, officer of the court, or holder of any office of the Sultanate who did not receive a sum of gold from him. The people of Cairo earned incalculable sums from him, whether by buying and selling or by gifts. So much gold was current in Cairo that it ruined the value of money.[18]

Mansa Musa's gold brought about terrible inflation throughout Egypt. For the first time, the Mediterranean world gained concrete knowledge of Mali's wealth and power, and the black kingdom began to be known as one of the world's great empires. Mali retained this international reputation into the fifteenth century.

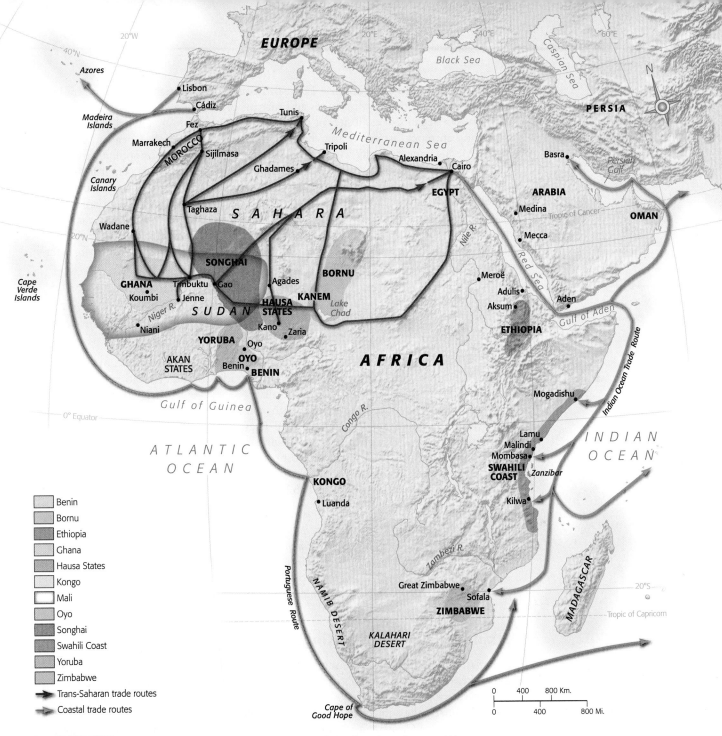

MAP 9.2 **Sub-Saharan African Kingdoms and Trade** Throughout world history powerful kingdoms have generally been closely connected to far-flung trade networks. Here we can see how the large empires in western, central, and southern Africa were linked either to the great trans-Saharan trade network, the Indian Ocean trade network, or, in the case of the Congo, to the massive interior trade network of central Africa and the Congo River basin. Although not a kingdom, the large and wealthy Swahili city-states along the East African coast owed their existence to the trade reaching across the Indian Ocean to India, Southeast Asia, and China.

Musa's pilgrimage also had significant consequences within Mali. He gained some understanding of the Mediterranean countries and opened diplomatic relations with the Muslim rulers of Morocco and Egypt. His zeal for the Muslim faith and Islamic culture increased. Musa brought back from Arabia the distinguished architect al-Saheli, whom he commissioned to build new mosques at Timbuktu and other cities. These mosques served as centers for the conversion of Africans. Musa employed

Muslim engineers to build in brick. He also encouraged Malian merchants and traders to wear the distinctive flowing robes and turbans of Muslim males.

Timbuktu began as a campsite for desert nomads. Under Mansa Musa, it grew into a thriving entrepôt, attracting merchants and traders from North Africa and all parts of the Mediterranean world. These people brought with them cosmopolitan attitudes and ideas. In the fifteenth century, Timbuktu developed into a great center for scholarship and learning. Architects, astronomers, poets, lawyers, mathematicians, and theologians flocked there. One hundred fifty schools were devoted to Qur'anic studies. The school of Islamic law enjoyed a distinction in Africa comparable to the prestige of the school at Cairo (see page 215). A vigorous trade in books flourished in Timbuktu. Leo Africanus, a sixteenth-century Muslim traveler and writer who later converted to Christianity, recounts that around 1500 Timbuktu had a

great store of doctors, judges, priests, and other learned men that are bountifully maintained at the king's cost and charges. And hitherto are brought diverse manuscripts or written books out of Barbarie the north African states, from Egypt to the Atlantic Ocean which are sold for more money than any other merchandise.

It is easy to understand why the university at Timbuktu was called by a contemporary writer "the Queen of the Sudan." Timbuktu's tradition and reputation for African scholarship lasted until the eighteenth century.

Moreover, in the fourteenth and fifteenth centuries, many Muslim intellectuals and Arab traders married native African women. These unions brought into being a group of racially mixed people. The necessity of living together harmoniously, the traditional awareness of diverse cultures, and the cosmopolitan atmosphere of Timbuktu all contributed to a rare degree of racial toleration and understanding. After visiting the court of Mansa Musa's successor in 1352–1353, Ibn Battuta observed that

the Negroes possess some admirable qualities. They are seldom unjust, and have a greater abhorrence of injustice than any other people. Their sultan shows no mercy to anyone who is guilty of the least act of it. There is complete security in their country. Neither traveler nor inhabitant in it has anything to fear from robbers. . . . They do not confiscate the property of any white man who dies in their country, even if it be uncounted wealth. On the contrary, they give it into the charge of some trustworthy person among the whites.[19]

Ethiopia: The Christian Kingdom of Aksum

Egyptian culture exerted a profound influence on the sub-Saharan kingdom of Nubia in northeastern Africa. Nubia's capital was at Meroë (see Map 9.2); thus the country is often referred to as the Nubian kingdom of Meroë. As part of the Roman Empire, Egypt was naturally subject to Hellenistic and Roman cultural forces, and it became an early center of Christianity. Nubia, however, was never part of the Roman Empire; its people clung to ancient Egyptian religious ideas. Christian missionaries went to the Upper Nile region and succeeded in converting the Nubian rulers around 600 C.E. By that time, there were three separate Nubian states, of which the kingdom of Nobatia, centered at Dongola, was the strongest. The Christian rulers of Nobatia had close ties with **Ethiopia**.

Two-thirds of the country consists of the Ethiopian highlands, the rugged plateau region of East Africa. The Great Rift Valley divides this territory into two massifs (mountain masses), of which the Ethiopian Plateau is the larger. Sloping away from each side of the Great Rift Valley are a series of mountains and valleys. Together with this mountainous environment, the three Middle Eastern religions—Judaism, Christianity, and Islam—have conditioned Ethiopian society, bringing symbols of its cultural identity.

In the first century C.E., the author of the *Periplus of the Erythraean Sea* (see page 248) described the kingdom of **Aksum** in northwestern Ethiopia as a sizable trading

Timbuktu *Originally a campsite for desert nomads, it grew into a thriving city under Mansa Musa.*

Ethiopia *The first black African society that can be studied from written records; it was the site of the kingdom of Aksum.*

Aksum *A kingdom in northwestern Ethiopia that was a sizable trading state and the center of Christian culture.*

state. Merchants at Adulis, its main port on the Red Sea, sold ivory, gold, emeralds, rhinoceros horns, shells, and slaves to the Sudan, Arabia, Yemen, and various cities across the Indian Ocean in exchange for glass, ceramics, fabrics, sugar, oil, spices, and precious gems. Adulis contained temples, stone-built houses, and irrigated agriculture. Between the first and eighth centuries, Aksum served as the capital of an empire extending over much of what is now northern Ethiopia. The empire's prosperity rested on trade. Aksum even minted specie (coins) modeled on the Roman *solidus;* at that time, only the Roman Empire, Persia, and some Indian states issued coins that circulated in Middle Eastern trade.

The expansion of Islam into northern Ethiopia in the eighth century (see page 237) weakened Aksum's commercial prosperity. The Arabs first imposed a religious test on Byzantine merchants who traded on the Dahklak Islands (in the southern Red Sea), thereby ousting the Greeks. Then, Muslims attacked and destroyed Adulis. Some Aksumites converted to Islam; many others found refuge in the rugged mountains north of Lasta and Tigray, where they were isolated from outside contacts. Thus began the insularity that characterized later Ethiopian society.

Tradition ascribes to Frumentius (ca. 300–380 C.E.), a Syrian Christian trader, the introduction of Christianity into Ethiopia. Kidnapped en route from India to Tyre (now a town in southern Lebanon), Frumentius was taken to Aksum and appointed tutor to the future king, Ezana. Later, Frumentius went to Alexandria in Egypt, where he was consecrated the first bishop of Aksum. Thus Christianity came to Ethiopia from Egypt in the Monophysite form. Shortly after members of the royal court accepted Christianity, it became the Ethiopian state religion. Ethiopia's future was to be inextricably tied up with Christianity, a unique situation in black Africa.

Ethiopia's acceptance of Christianity led to the production of ecclesiastical documents and royal chronicles, making Ethiopia the first black African society that can be studied from written records. The Scriptures were translated into Ge'ez, the language of Aksum; pagan temples were dedicated to Christian saints; and, as in early medieval Ireland and in the Orthodox Church of the Byzantine world, the monasteries were the main cultural institutions of the Christian faith in Ethiopia. From the monasteries, monks went out to preach and convert the people, who resorted to the monasteries in times of need. As the Ethiopian state expanded, vibrant monasteries provided inspiration for the establishment of convents for nuns, as in medieval Europe (see page 172).

Monastic records provide fascinating information about early Ethiopian society. Settlements were made on the warm and moist plateau lands, not in the arid lowlands or the river valleys. Farmers used a scratch plow (unique in sub-Saharan Africa) to cultivate wheat and barley and to rotate those cereals. Plentiful rainfall seems to have helped produce abundant crops, which in turn led to population growth. In contrast to most of sub-Saharan Africa, both sexes probably married

Primary Source:
Ezana, King of Aksum,
Stele of Ezana

● **Christianity and Islam in Ethiopia** The prolonged contest between the two religions in Ethiopia was periodically taken to the battlefield. This drawing by an Ethiopian artist shows his countrymen advancing victoriously (*from left to right*) and celebrates national military success. (© British Library Board. All rights reserved. OR 533 f50v)

● **The Queen of Sheba and King Solomon** The queen often figured prominently in European, as well as Ethiopian, art. Here, sitting enthroned in Jerusalem, Solomon receives gifts from Sheba's servants. Both are dressed in late medieval European garb, and in his left hand he holds a scepter (staff), symbol of his royal and Christian authority. Aside from the anachronistic costumes and scepter (what Jewish king would carry a Christian cross?), the inscription surrounding the scene—"Solomon joins himself to the Queen of Sheba and introduces her to his faith"—combines a number of myths. *(Erich Lessing/Art Resource, NY)*

young. Because of ecclesiastical opposition to polygyny, monogamy was the norm, except for kings and the very rich. The abundance of land meant that young couples could establish independent households. Widely scattered farms, with the parish church as the central social unit, seem to have been the usual pattern of existence.

Above the broad class of peasant farmers stood warrior-nobles. Their wealth and status derived from their fighting skills, which kings rewarded with grants of estates and with the right to collect tribute from the peasants. To acquire lands and to hold warriors' loyalty, Ethiopian kings had to pursue a policy of constant territorial expansion. (See the feature "Individuals in Society: Amda Siyon.") Nobles maintained order in their regions, supplied kings with fighting men, and displayed their superior status by the size of their households and their generosity to the poor.

Sometime in the fourteenth century, six scribes in the Tigrayan highlands, combining oral tradition, apocryphal texts, Jewish and Islamic commentaries, and Christian patristic writings, produced the *Kebre Negast* (*The Glory of Kings*). This history served the authors' goals: it became an Ethiopian national epic, glorifying a line of rulers descended from the Hebrew king Solomon (see page 17), arousing patriotic feelings, and linking Ethiopia's identity to the Judeo-Christian tradition. The book mostly deals with the origins of Emperor Menilek I in the tenth century B.C.E.

The *Kebre Negast* asserts that Queen Makeda of Ethiopia (called Sheba in the Jewish tradition) had little governmental experience when she came to the throne. So she sought the advice and wise counsel of King Solomon (r. 961–922 B.C.E.) in Jerusalem. Makeda learned Jewish statecraft, converted to Judaism, and expressed her gratitude to Solomon with rich gifts of spices, gems, and gold. Desiring something more precious, Solomon prepared a lavish banquet for his attractive pupil. Satiated with spicy food and rich wines, Makeda fell asleep. Solomon placed jugs of water near her couch. When she woke up, she gulped down some water, and Solomon satisfied his lust. Their son, Menilek, was born some months later. When Menilek reached maturity, he visited Solomon in Jerusalem. There Solomon anointed him crown prince of Ethiopia and sent a retinue of young Jewish nobles to accompany him home as courtiers. They, however, unable to face life without the Hebrews' Ark of the Covenant, stole the cherished wooden chest, which the Hebrews believed contained the Ten Commandments. God apparently approved the theft, for he lifted the youths, pursued by Solomon's army, across the Red Sea and into Ethiopia. Thus, according to the *Kebre Negast*, Menilek avenged his mother's shame, and God gave his legal covenant to Ethiopia, Israel's successor.[20] Although much of this narrative is myth and legend, it effectively served the purpose of building nationalistic fervor.

Consuming a spiked drink may not be the most dignified or auspicious way to found an imperial dynasty, but from the tenth to the sixteenth century, and even in the Ethiopian constitution of 1955, rulers of Ethiopia claimed that they belonged to the Solomonic line of succession. Church and state in Ethiopia were inextricably linked.

Ethiopia's high mountains encouraged an inward concentration of attention and hindered access from the outside. Twelfth-century Crusaders returning from the

Amda Siyon

Scholars consider Amda Siyon (r. 1314–1344) the greatest ruler of Ethiopia's Solomonic dynasty. Yet we have no image or representation of him. We know nothing of his personal life, though if he followed the practice of most Ethiopian kings, he had many wives and children. Nor do we know anything of his youth and education. The evidence of what he did, however, suggests a tough military man who personified the heroic endurance and physical pain expected of warriors. Once, surrounded by enemies, his face set hard as stone, he

clove the ranks of the rebels and struck so hard that he transfixed two men as one with the blow of his spear, through the strength of God. Thereupon the rebels scattered and took to flight, being unable to hold their ground in his presence.

Amda Siyon reinforced control over his kingdom's Christian areas. He then expanded into neighboring regions of Shewa, Gojam, and Damot. Victorious there, he gradually absorbed the Muslim states of Ifat and Hedya to the east and southeast. These successes gave him effective control over the central highlands and also over the Indian Ocean trade routes to the Red Sea (see Map 9.2). He governed in a quasi-feudal fashion (see page 352). Theoretically the owner of all land, he assigned *gults,* or fiefs, to his ablest warriors. In return for nearly complete authority in their regions, these warrior-nobles conscripted soldiers for the king's army, required agricultural services from the farmers working on their land, and collected taxes in kind.

Ethiopian rulers received imperial coronation at Aksum, but their kingdom had no permanent capital. Rather, the ruler and court were peripatetic. They constantly traveled around the country to check up on the warrior-nobles' management of the gults, to crush revolts, and to impress ordinary people with royal dignity.

Territorial expansion had important economic and religious consequences. Amda Siyon concluded trade agreements with Muslims by which Muslims were allowed to trade with his country in return for Muslim recognition of his authority, and their promise to accept his administration and to pay taxes. Economic growth followed. As a result of these agreements, the flow of Ethiopian gold, ivory, and slaves to Red Sea ports for export to the Islamic heartlands and to South Asia accelerated. Profits from commercial exchange improved people's lives, or at least the lives of the upper classes. Monk-missionaries from traditional Christian areas flooded newly conquered regions,

A monk entering the Holy of Holies in the Urai Kidane Miharet church, one of the many monasteries established by Amda Siyon. *(Kazuyoshi Nomachi/Pacific Press Service)*

stressing that Ethiopia was a new Zion, a second Israel, a Judeo-Christian nation defined by religion. Ethiopian Christianity focused on the divinity of the Old Testament Jehovah, rather than on the humanity of the New Testament Jesus. Jewish dietary restrictions, such as the avoidance of pork and shellfish, shaped behavior, and the holy Ark of the Covenant had a prominent place in the liturgy. But the monks also taught New Testament values, especially the importance of charity and spiritual reform. Following the Byzantine pattern, the Ethiopian priest-king claimed the right to summon church councils and to issue doctrinal degrees. Christianity's stress on monogamous marriage, however, proved hard to enforce. As in other parts of Africa (and in Islamic lands, China, and South Asia), polygyny remained common, at least among the upper classes.

Questions for Analysis

1. What features mark Ethiopian culture as unique and distinctive among early African societies?
2. Referring to Solomonic Ethiopia, assess the role of legend in history.
3. The German ruler Charles (r. 768–814) was also called "the Great"—or "Charlemagne" (see pages 184–185). Compare and contrast him with Amda Siyon of Ethiopia with respect to territorial expansion, relations with the church, and methods of governing.

Sources: H. G. Marcus, *A History of Ethiopia,* updated ed. (Berkeley: University of California Press, 2002); J. Iliffe, *Africans: The History of a Continent,* 2d ed. (New York: Cambridge University Press, 2007).

ተንበላቶ፡እንባርቲ፡   እዚ፡ይኩኖ፡አምላክ፡

● **Emperor Yekuno Amlak**
The Ethiopian emperor's claim of
possessing Solomon's blood won
him considerable popular support
in his war against the decaying
Zagwe dynasty, which he overthrew
in 1270. Here he receives Muslim
ambassadors while slaves attend
him.

Middle East told of a powerful Christian ruler, Prester John, whose lands lay behind Muslim lines and who was eager to help restore the Holy Land to Christian control. Europeans identified that kingdom with Ethiopia. In the later thirteenth century, the dynasty of the Solomonic kings witnessed a literary and artistic renaissance particularly notable for works of hagiography (biographies of saints), biblical exegesis, and manuscript illumination. The most striking feature of Ethiopian society in the period from 500 to 1500 was the close relationship between the church and the state. Christianity inspired fierce devotion and tended to equate doctrinal heresy with political rebellion, thus reinforcing central monarchical power.

The East African City-States

In the first century C.E., a merchant seaman from Alexandria in Egypt sailed down the Red Sea and out into the Indian Ocean. Along the coasts of East Africa and India, he found seaports. He took careful notes on all he observed, and the result, *Periplus of the Erythraean Sea* (as the Greeks called the Indian Ocean), is the earliest surviving literary evidence of the city-states of the East African coast. Although primarily preoccupied with geography and navigation, the *Periplus* includes accounts of the local peoples and their commercial activities. Even in the days of the Roman emperors, the *Periplus* testifies, the East African coast had strong commercial links with India and the Mediterranean.

Greco-Roman ships traveled from Adulis on the Red Sea around the tip of the Gulf of Aden and down the African coast that the Greeks called "Azania" in modern-day Kenya and Tanzania (see Map 9.2). These ships carried manufactured goods—cotton cloth, copper and brass, iron tools, and gold and silver plate. At the African coastal emporiums, Mediterranean merchants exchanged these goods for cinnamon, myrrh and frankincense, captive slaves, and animal byproducts such as ivory, rhinoceros horns, and tortoise shells. Somewhere around Cape Guardafui on the Horn of Africa, the ships caught the monsoon winds eastward to India (see page 425), where ivory was in great demand.

An omission in the *Periplus* has created a debate over the racial characteristics of the native peoples in East Africa and the dates of Bantu migrations into the area. The author, writing in the first century, did not describe the natives; apparently he did not find their skin color striking enough to comment on. Yet in the fifth century, there are references to these peoples as "Ethiopians." Could this mean that migrating black Bantu-speakers reached the east coast between the first and fifth centuries? Possibly. The distinguished archaeologist Neville Chittick, however, thinks not: "The writer of the *Periplus* made few comments on the physical nature of the inhabitants of the countries which he described . . . therefore nothing can be based on the mere omission of any mention of skin color."[21]

In the early centuries of the Christian era, many merchants and seamen from the Mediterranean settled in East African coastal towns. Succeeding centuries saw the arrival of more traders. The great emigration from Arabia after the death of Muhammad accelerated Muslim penetration of the area, which the Arabs called the *Zanj*, "land of the blacks." Along the coast, Arabic Muslims established small trading colonies whose local peoples were ruled by kings and practiced various animistic religions. Eventually—whether through Muslim political hegemony or gradual assimilation—the coastal peoples slowly converted to Islam. Indigenous African religions, however, remained strong in the continent's interior. (See the feature "Listening to the Past: A Tenth-Century Muslim Traveler Describes Parts of the East African Coast" on pages 254–255.)

Beginning in the late twelfth century, fresh waves of Arabs and of Persians from Shiraz poured down the coast, first settling at Mogadishu, then pressing southward to Kilwa (see Map 9.2). Everywhere they landed, they introduced Islamic culture to the indigenous population. Similarly, from the earliest Christian centuries through the Middle Ages, Indonesians crossed the Indian Ocean and settled on the African coast and on the large island of Madagascar, or Malagasy, an Indonesian name. All these immigrants intermarried with Africans, and the resulting society combined Asian, African, and especially Islamic traits. The East African coastal culture was called **Swahili,** after a Bantu language whose vocabulary and poetic forms exhibit a strong Arabic influence. The thirteenth-century Muslim mosque at Mogadishu and the fiercely Muslim populations of Mombasa and Kilwa in the fourteenth century attest to strong Muslim influence.

By the late thirteenth century, **Kilwa** had become the most powerful city on the coast, exercising political hegemony as far north as Pemba and as far south as Sofala

Swahili *The East African coastal culture, named after a Bantu language whose vocabulary and poetic forms exhibit strong Arabic influences.*

Kilwa *The most powerful city on the coast of Africa by the late thirteenth century.*

● **Great Mosque at Kilwa** Built between the thirteenth and fifteenth centuries to serve the Muslim commercial aristocracy of Kilwa on the Indian Ocean, the mosque attests to the wealth and power of the East African city-states. *(Karen Samson Photography)*

(see Map 9.2). In the fourteenth and fifteenth centuries, the coastal cities were great commercial empires comparable to Venice (see page 370). Like Venice, Kilwa, Mombasa, and Mafia were situated on offshore islands. The tidal currents that isolated them from the mainland also protected them from landside attack.

Much current knowledge about life in the East African trading societies rests on the account of Ibn Battuta. When he arrived at Kilwa, he found, in the words of a modern historian,

the city large and elegant, its buildings, as was typical along the coast, constructed of stone and coral rag [roofing slate]. Houses were generally single storied, consisting of a number of small rooms separated by thick walls supporting heavy stone roofing slabs laid across mangrove poles. Some of the more formidable structures contained second and third stories, and many were embellished with cut stone decorative borders framing the entranceways. Tapestries and ornamental niches covered the walls and the floors were carpeted. Of course, such appointments were only for the wealthy; the poorer classes occupied the timeless mud and straw huts of Africa, their robes a simple loincloth, their dinner a millet porridge.[22]

On the mainland were fields and orchards of rice, millet, oranges, mangoes, and bananas and pastures and yards for cattle, sheep, and poultry. Yields were apparently high; Ibn Battuta noted that the rich enjoyed three enormous meals a day and were very fat.

From among the rich mercantile families that controlled the coastal cities arose a ruler who by the fourteenth century had taken the Arabic title *sheik*. The sheik governed both the island city and the nearby mainland. Farther inland, tribal chiefs ruled with the advice of councils of elders.

The Portuguese, approaching the East African coastal cities in the late fifteenth century, were astounded at their enormous wealth and prosperity. This wealth rested on monopolistic control of all trade in the area. Some coastal cities manufactured goods for export: Mogadishu produced cloth for the Egyptian market; Mombasa and Malindi processed iron tools; and Sofala made cottons for the interior trade. The bulk of the cities' exports, however, consisted of animal products—leopard skins, tortoise shell, ambergris, ivory—and gold. The gold originated in the Mutapa region south of the Zambezi River, where the Bantu mined it. As in tenth-century Ghana, gold was a royal monopoly in the fourteenth-century coastal city-states. The Mutapa kings received it as annual tribute, prohibited outsiders from entering the mines or participating in the trade, and controlled shipments down the Zambezi to the coastal markets. Kilwa's prosperity rested on its traffic in gold.

African goods satisfied the widespread aristocratic demand for luxury goods. In Arabia leopard skins were made into saddles, shells were made into combs, and ambergris was used in the manufacture of perfumes. Because African elephants' tusks were larger and more durable than the tusks of Indian elephants, African ivory was in great demand in India for sword and dagger handles, carved decorative objects, and the ceremonial bangles used in Hindu marriage rituals. Wealthy Chinese valued African ivory for use in the construction of sedan chairs.

In exchange for these natural products, the Swahili cities bought pottery, glassware and beads, and many varieties of cloth. Swahili kings imposed enormous duties on imports, perhaps more than 80 percent of the value of the goods themselves. Even so, traders who came to Africa made fabulous profits.

Slaves were another export from the East African coast. Reports of slave trading began with the *Periplus*. The trade accelerated with the establishment of Muslim settlements in the eighth century and continued down to the arrival of the Portuguese in the late fifteenth century. In fact, the East African coastal slave trade persisted at least to the beginning of the twentieth century.

● **Copper Coin from Mogadishu, Twelfth Century** Islamic proscriptions against representation of the human form, combined with a deep veneration for writing, prevented the use of rulers' portraits on coinage, unlike the practice of the Romans, Byzantines, and Sassanids. Instead, Islamic coins since the Umayyad period were decorated exclusively with writing. Sultan Haran ibn Sulayman of Kilwa on the East African coast minted this coin, a symbol of the region's Muslim culture and of its rich maritime trade. *(Courtesy of the Trustees of the British Museum)*

As in West Africa, traders obtained slaves primarily through raids and kidnapping. As early as the tenth century, Arabs from Oman enticed hungry children with dates. When the children accepted the sweet fruits, they were abducted and enslaved. Profit was the traders' motive.

The Arabs called the northern Somalia coast *Ras Assir* (Cape of Slaves). From there, Arab traders transported slaves northward up the Red Sea to the markets of Arabia and Persia. Muslim dealers also shipped blacks from the region of Zanzibar across the Indian Ocean to markets in India. Rulers of the Deccan Plateau in central India used large numbers of black slave soldiers in their military campaigns. Slaves also worked on the docks and *dhows* (typical Arab lateen-rigged ships) in the Muslim-controlled Indian Ocean and as domestic servants and concubines throughout South and East Asia.

As early as the tenth century, sources mention persons with "lacquer-black bodies" in the possession of wealthy families in Song China.[23] In 1178 a Chinese official noted in a memorial to the emperor that Arab traders were shipping thousands of blacks from East Africa to the Chinese port of Guangzhou (Canton) by way of the Malay Archipelago. The Chinese employed these slaves as household servants, as musicians, and, because East Africans were often expert swimmers, as divers to caulk the leaky seams of ships below the water line.

By the thirteenth century, Africans living in many parts of South and East Asia had made significant economic and cultural contributions to their societies. Neither Asian nor Western scholars have adequately explored this subject. It appears, however, that in Indian, Chinese, and East African markets, slaves were never as valuable a commodity as ivory. Thus the volume of the Eastern slave trade did not approach that of the trans-Saharan slave trade.[24]

Southern Africa

Southern Africa, bordered on the northwest by the Kalahari Desert and on the northeast by the Zambezi River (see Map 9.2), enjoys a mild and temperate climate. Desert conditions prevail along the Atlantic coast, which gets less than five inches of annual rainfall. Eastward, rainfall increases, though some areas receive less than twenty inches a year. Although the Limpopo Valley in the east is very dry, temperate grasslands characterize the highlands in the interior. Considerable variations in climate occur throughout much of southern Africa from year to year.

Located at the southern extremity of the Afro-Eurasian landmass, southern Africa has a history that is very different from the histories of West Africa, the Nile Valley, and the east coast. Over the centuries, North and West Africa felt the influences of Phoenician, Greek, Roman, and Muslim cultures; the Nile Valley experienced the impact of major Egyptian, Assyrian, Persian, and Muslim civilizations; and the coast of East Africa had important contacts across the Indian Ocean with southern and eastern Asia and across the Red Sea with Arabia and Persia. Southern Africa, however,

● **Ruins of Great Zimbabwe** Considered the most impressive monument in the African interior south of the Ethiopian highlands, these ruins of Great Zimbabwe consist of two complexes of dry-stone buildings, some surrounded by a massive serpentine wall 32 feet high and 17 feet thick at its maximum. Great Zimbabwe was the center of a state whose wealth rested on gold. Towers were probably used for defensive purposes. *(Werner Forman Archive/Art Resource, NY)*

● **Bird at Top of Monolith, Great Zimbabwe, ca. 1200–1400 C.E.** The walls and buildings at Great Zimbabwe seem intended to reflect the ruler's wealth and power. Among the archaeological finds there are monoliths crowned by soapstone birds. This monolith (14½ inches high) also appears to have an alligator-like creature on its side. Scholars debate the significance of these birds: Were they symbols of royal power? eagles? messengers from the spiritual world to the terrestrial? And what does the alligator mean? *(Courtesy of the National Archives of Zimbabwe)*

Great Zimbabwe *A ruined African city discovered by a German explorer in 1871; it is considered the most powerful monument south of the Nile Valley and Ethiopian highlands.*

remained far removed from the outside world until the Portuguese arrived in the late fifteenth century—with one important exception. Bantu-speaking people reached southern Africa in the eighth century. They brought with them skills in ironworking and mixed farming (settled crop production plus cattle and sheep raising) and immunity to the kinds of diseases that later decimated the Amerindians of South America (see page 445).

Southern Africa has enormous mineral resources: gold, copper, diamonds, platinum, and uranium. Preindustrial peoples mined some of these deposits in open excavations down several feet, but fuller exploitation required modern technology. Today, gold mining operations can penetrate two miles below the surface.

The earliest residents of southern Africa were hunters and gatherers. In the first millennium C.E., new farming techniques from the north arrived. Lack of water and of timber (both needed to produce the charcoal used in iron smelting) slowed the spread of iron technology and tools and thus of crop production in southwestern Africa. These advances, however, reached the western coastal region by 1500. By that date, Khoisan-speakers were farming in the arid western regions. The area teemed with wild game—elephants, buffalo, lions, hippopotami, leopards, zebras, and many varieties of antelope. To the east, descendants of Bantu-speaking immigrants grew sorghum, raised cattle and sheep, and fought with iron-headed spears. Disease-bearing insects, such as the tsetse fly, which causes sleeping sickness, however, attacked these animals and retarded their domestication.

The nuclear family was the basic social unit among early southern African peoples, who practiced polygyny and traced descent in the male line. Several families numbering between twenty and eighty people formed bands. Such bands were not closed entities; people in neighboring territories identified with bands speaking the same language. As in most preindustrial societies, a division of labor existed whereby men hunted and women cared for children and raised edible plants. People lived in caves or in camps made of portable material, and they moved from one watering or hunting region to another as seasonal or environmental needs required.

In 1871 a German explorer came upon the ruined city of **Great Zimbabwe** southeast of what is now Nyanda in Zimbabwe. Archaeologists consider Great Zimbabwe the most impressive monument in Africa south of the Nile Valley and the Ethiopian highlands. The ruins consist of two vast complexes of dry-stone buildings, a fortress, and an elliptically shaped enclosure commonly called the Temple. Stone carvings, gold and copper ornaments, and Asian ceramics once decorated the buildings. The ruins extend over sixty acres and are encircled by a massive wall. The entire city was built from local granite between the eleventh and fifteenth centuries without any outside influence.

These ruins tell a remarkable story. Great Zimbabwe was the political and religious capital of a vast empire. During the first millennium C.E., settled crop cultivation, cattle raising, and work in metal led to a steady buildup in population in the Zambezi-Limpopo region. The area also contained a rich gold-bearing belt. Gold ore lay near the surface; alluvial gold lay in the Zambezi River tributaries. In the tenth century, the inhabitants collected the alluvial gold by panning and washing; after the year 1000, the gold was worked in open mines with iron picks. Traders shipped the gold eastward to Sofala (see Map 9.2). Great Zimbabwe's wealth and power rested on this gold trade.[25]

Great Zimbabwe declined in the fifteenth century, perhaps because the area had become agriculturally exhausted and could no longer support the large population. Some people migrated northward and settled in the Mazoe River valley, a tributary of the Zambezi. This region also contained gold, and there the settlers built a new empire in the tradition of Great Zimbabwe. This empire's rulers were called "Mwene Mutapa," and their power too was based on the gold trade down the Zambezi River to Indian Ocean ports. It was this gold that the Portuguese sought when they arrived on the East African coast in the late fifteenth century.

Chapter Summary

To assess your mastery of this chapter and read the primary sources listed in the margins, visit **bedfordstmartins.com/mckayworld** or see *Sources of World Societies*.

Key Terms

Bantu
Sudan
Berbers
Mogadishu
stateless societies
Ghana
ghana
Kumbi
Timbuktu
Ethiopia
Aksum
Swahili
Kilwa
Great Zimbabwe

• What patterns of social and political organization prevailed among the peoples of Africa, and what types of agriculture and commerce did Africans engage in?

In the fifteenth century, the African continent contained a number of very different societies and civilizations and many diverse ethnic groups. All of North Africa, from Morocco in the west to Egypt in the east, was part of the Muslim world. In West Africa, Mali continued the brisk trade in salt, gold, and slaves that had originated many centuries earlier. Islam, which had spread to sub-Saharan Africa through the caravan trade, had a tremendous influence on the peoples of the western Sudan, their governmental bureaucracies, and their vibrant urban centers. Between the first and eighth centuries, Christianity had penetrated the mountainous kingdom of Aksum (Ethiopia), beginning an enduring identification of the Ethiopian kingdom with the Judeo-Christian tradition. By virtue of their claim to Solomonic blood and by force of arms, kings of Ethiopia ruled a uniquely Christian state. Flourishing trade with Egypt, Arabia, and the East African city-states gave Aksum cultural access to much of southwestern Asia. The impact of the Islamic faith was also felt in East Africa, whose bustling port cities were in touch with the cultures of the Indian Ocean and the Mediterranean Sea. While the city-states along the eastern coast— Kilwa, Mombasa, and Mogadishu—conducted complicated mercantile activities with foreign societies, the mountain-protected kingdom of Ethiopia increasingly led an isolated, inward-looking existence. In southern Africa, the vast empire of Great Zimbabwe was yielding to yet another kingdom whose power was based on precious gold.

• What values do Africans' art, architecture, and religions express?

The student beginning the study of African history should bear in mind the enormous diversity of African peoples and cultures, a diversity both within and across regions. It is, therefore, difficult and often dangerous to make broad generalizations about African life. Statements such as "African culture is . . ." or "African peoples are . . ." are virtually meaningless. African peoples are not now and never have been homogeneous. This rich diversity helps explain why the study of African history is so exciting and challenging.

Suggested Reading

Allen, J. de Vere. *Swahili Origins.* 1993. A study of the problem of Swahili identity.

Austen, Ralph. *African Economic History.* 1987. Classic study of Africa's economic history.

Beck, Roger B. *The History of South Africa.* 2000. Introduction to this large and important country.

Bouvill, E.W., and Robin Hallett. *The Golden Trade of the Moors: West African Kingdoms in the Fourteenth Century.* 1995. Classic description of the trans-Saharan trade.

Bulliet, R. W. *The Camel and the Wheel.* 1995. The importance of the camel to African trade.

(continued on page 256)

Listening to the PAST

A Tenth-Century Muslim Traveler Describes Parts of the East African Coast

Except for Ethiopia, early African societies left no written accounts of their institutions and cultures. So modern scholars rely for information on the chronicles of travelers and merchants. Outsiders, however, come with their own preconceptions, attitudes, and biases. They tend to measure what they visit and see by the conditions and experiences with which they are familiar.

Sometime in the early tenth century, the Muslim merchant-traveler Al Mas'udi (d. 945 C.E.), in search of African ivory, visited Oman, the southeast coast of Africa, and Zanzibar. He referred to all the peoples he encountered as Zanj, a term that earlier had meant all the black slaves seized in the East Africa coastal region and that later was applied to the maritime Swahili culture of the area's towns. What does Al Mas'udi's report, excerpted here, tell us about these peoples?

The pilots of Oman pass by the channel [of Berbera] to reach the island of Kanbalu, which is in the Zanj sea. It has a mixed population of Muslims and Zanj idolaters. . . . The aforesaid Kanbalu is the furthest point of their voyages on the Zanj sea, and the land of Sofala and the Waqwaq, on the edge of the Zanj mainland and at the end of this branch of the sea. . . . I have sailed much on the seas, those of China, Rum, the Khazar, Qulzum and Yemen, but I do not know of one more dangerous than that of the Zanj, of which I have just spoken. There the whale is found. . . . There are also many other kinds of fish, with all sorts of shapes. . . . Amber* is found in great quantities on the Zanj coast and also near Shihr in Arabia. . . . The best amber is that found in the islands and on the shores of the Zanj sea: it is round and pale blue, sometimes as big as an ostrich egg, sometimes slightly less. The fish called the whale, which I have already mentioned, swallows it: when the sea is very rough it vomits up pieces of amber as large as rocks, and this fish swallows them. It is asphyxiated by them and then swims up to the surface. Then the Zanj, or men from other

*A fossil resin used in the manufacture of ornamental objects such as beads and women's combs.

lands, who have been biding their time in their boats, seize the fish with harpoons and tackle, cut its stomach open, and take the amber out. The pieces found near the bowels have a nauseating smell, and are called *nedd* by the Iraqi and Persian chemists: but the pieces found near the back are purer than those which have been a long time in the inner part of the body. . . .

The land of Zanj produces wild leopard skins. The people wear them as clothes, or export them to Muslim countries. They are the largest leopard skins and the most beautiful for making saddles. The sea of Zanj and that of Abyssinia lie on the right of the sea of India, and join up. They also export tortoise-shell for making combs, for which ivory is likewise used. The most common animal in these countries is the giraffe. . . . They [the Zanj] settled in that area, which stretches as far as Sofala, which is the furthest limit of the land and the end of the voyages made from Oman and Siraf on the sea of Zanj. In the same way that the sea of China ends with the land of Japan, the sea of Zanj ends with the land of Sofala and the Waqwaq, which produces gold and many other wonderful things. It has a warm climate and is fertile. The Zanj capital is there and they have a king called the *Mfalme*. This is the ancient name of their kings, and all the other Zanj kings are subject to him: he has 300,000 horsemen. The Zanj use the ox as a beast of burden, for they have no horses, mules or camels in their land, and do not know of their existence. . . . The land of Zanj begins with the branch which leaves the upper Nile and continues to the land of Sofala and the Waqwaq. The villages stretch for 700 parasangs and the same distance inland: the country is cut up into valleys, mountains and stony deserts. There are many wild elephants but no tame ones. The Zanj do not use them for war or anything else, but only hunt and kill them. When they want to catch them, they throw down the leaves, bark and branches of a certain tree which grows in their country: then they wait in ambush until the elephants come to drink. The water burns them and makes them drunk. They fall down and cannot get up: their limbs will not articulate. The Zanj rush upon them armed with very long spears,

An ancient mosque near Ras Mkumbuu in Pemba, which Al Mas'udi called Kanbalu. *(Visual Connection Archives)*

and kill them for their ivory. It is from this country that come tusks weighing fifty pounds and more. They usually go to Oman, and from there are sent to China and India. This is the chief trade route, and if it were not so, ivory would be common in Muslim lands.

In China the kings and military and civil officers use ivory palanquins†: no officer or notable dares to come into the royal presence in an iron palanquin, and ivory alone can be used. Thus they seek after straight tusks in preference to the curved, to make the things we have spoken of. They also burn ivory before their idols and cense their altars with it, just as Christians use the Mary incense and other perfumes. The Chinese make no other use of the elephant, and consider it unlucky to use it for domestic purposes or war. This fear has its origin in a tradition about one of their most ancient military expeditions. In India ivory is much sought after. It is used for the handles of daggers called *harari* or *harri* in the singular: and also for the curved sword-scabbards called *kartal,* in the plural *karatil.* But the chief use of ivory is making chessmen and backgammon pieces. . . .

The Zanj, although always busied hunting the elephant and collecting its ivory, make no use of it for domestic purposes. They use iron instead of gold and silver, just as they use oxen, as we said before, both for beasts of burden and for war. These oxen are harnessed like a horse. . . .

To go back to the Zanj and their kings, these are known as *Wafalme,* which means son of the Great Lord, since he is chosen to govern them justly. If he is tyrannical or strays from the truth, they kill him and exclude his seed from the throne; for they consider that in acting wrongfully he forfeits his position as the son of the Lord, the King of Heaven and Earth. They call God *Maliknajlu,* which means Great Lord.

The Zanj have an elegant language and men who preach in it. One of their holy men will often gather a crowd and exhort his hearers to please God in their lives and to be obedient to him. He explains the punishments that follow upon disobedience, and reminds them of their ancestors and kings of old. These people have no religious law: their kings rule by custom and by political expediency.

The Zanj eat bananas, which are as common among them as they are in India; but their staple food is millet and a plant called *kalari* which is pulled out of the earth like truffles. It is plentiful in Aden and the neighbouring part of Yemen near to the town. It is like the cucumber of Egypt and Syria. They also eat honey and meat. Every man worships what he pleases, be it a plant, an animal or a mineral.‡ They have many islands where the coconut grows: its nuts are used as fruit by all the Zanj peoples. One of these islands, which is one or two days' sail from the coast, has a Muslim population and a royal family. This is the island of Kanbalu of which we have already spoken.

Questions for Analysis

1. Identify on a map the places that Al Mas'udi mentions.

2. What commodities were most sought after by Muslim traders? Why? Where were they sold?

3. How would you describe Al Mas'udi's attitude toward the Zanj peoples and their customs?

Source: "10th Century Muslim Traveler Describes Part of the East African Coast," from Al Mas'udi, as appeared in G. S. P. Freeman-Grenville, *The East African Coast,* 1962, 14–17.

†An enclosed litter attached to poles that servants supported on their shoulders.

‡These are forms of animism.

Ehret, Christopher. *An African Classical Age: Eastern and Southern Africa in World History, 1000 B.C. to 400 A.D.* 2001. Solid introduction by a renowned African scholar.

Ehret, Christopher. *The Civilizations of Africa: A History to 1800.* 2002. The best study of pre-1800 African history.

Gilbert, Erik, and Jonathan Reynolds. *Africa in World History.* 2007. Best study of Africa's place in world history.

Iliffe, John. *Africans: The History of a Continent.* 2d ed. 2007. Thoughtful introduction to African history.

Levtzion, Nehemia, and Randall L. Pouwels. *History of Islam in Africa.* 2000. Comprehensive survey of Islam's presence in Africa.

Marcus, H. G. *A History of Ethiopia.* 2002. Standard introduction to Ethiopian history.

Mitchell, Peter. *African Connections: Archaeological Perspectives on Africa and the Wider World.* 2005. Places ancient Africa and its history in a global context.

Newman, J. L. *The Peopling of Africa: A Geographic Interpretation.* 1995. Explores population distribution and technological change down to the late nineteenth century.

Reader, J. *Africa: A Biography of a Continent.* 1997. Well-researched, popular account.

Schmidt, Peter R. *Historical Archaeology in Africa: Representation, Social Memory, and Oral Traditions.* 2006. An excellent introduction to archaeology and the reconstruction of Africa's history.

Notes

1. J. Hiernaux, *The People of Africa* (New York: Scribner's, 1975), pp. 46–48.
2. C. A. Diop, "The African Origins of Western Civilization," and R. Mauny, "A Review of Diop," in *Problems in African History: The Precolonial Centuries,* ed. R. O. Collins et al. (New York: Markus Weiner Publishing, 1994), pp. 32–40, 41–49; the quotations are on p. 42.
3. Mauny, "A Review of Diop." For contrasting views of Afrocentrism in American higher education, see T. Martin, *The Jewish Onslaught: Dispatches from the Wellesley Battlefront* (Dover, Mass.: The Majority Press, 1993), and M. Lefkowitz, *Not Out of Africa: How Afrocentrism Became an Excuse to Teach Myth as History* (New York: Basic Books, 1996).
4. "African Historical Demography," in *Proceedings of a Seminar Held in the Centre of African Studies,* University of Edinburgh, April 29–30, 1977, p. 3.
5. T. Spear, "Bantu Migrations," in *Problems in African History: The Precolonial Centuries,* p. 98.
6. J. Iliffe, *Africans: The History of a Continent,* 2d ed. (Cambridge: Cambridge University Press, 2007), pp. 100–110; J. L. Newman, *The Peopling of Africa: A Geographic Interpretation* (New Haven, Conn.: Yale University Press, 1995), pp. 140–147.
7. J. S. Trimingham, *Islam in West Africa* (Oxford: Oxford University Press, 1959), pp. 6–9.
8. R. A. Austen, *African Economic History* (London: James Currey/Heinemann, 1987), p. 36.
9. R. A. Austen, "The Trans-Saharan Slave Trade: A Tentative Census," in *The Uncommon Market: Essays in the Economic History of the Atlantic Slave Trade,* ed. H. A. Gemery and J. S. Hogendorn (New York: Academic Press, 1979), pp. 1–71, esp. p. 66.
10. R. N. July, *Precolonial African Economic and Social History* (New York: Scribner's, 1975), pp. 124–129.
11. See N. Levtzion, "Islam in Africa to 1800: Merchants, Chiefs, and Saints," in *The Oxford History of Islam,* ed. J. L. Esposito (New York: Oxford University Press, 1999), pp. 502–504.
12. Quoted in J. O. Hunwick, "Islam in West Africa, A.D. 1000–1800," in *A Thousand Years of West African History,* ed. J. F. Ade Ajayi and I. Espie (New York: Humanities Press, 1972), pp. 244–245.
13. Quoted in A. A. Boahen, "Kingdoms of West Africa, c. A.D. 500–1600," in *The Horizon History of Africa* (New York: American Heritage, 1971), p. 183.
14. Al-Bakri, *Kitab al-mughrib fdhikr bilad Ifriqiya wa'l-Maghrib (Description de l'Afrique Septentrionale),* trans. De Shane (Paris: Adrien-Maisonneuve, 1965), pp. 328–329.
15. Quoted in R. Oliver and C. Oliver, eds., *Africa in the Days of Exploration* (Englewood Cliffs, N.J.: Prentice-Hall, 1965), p. 10.
16. Quoted in Boahen, "Kingdoms of West Africa, c. A.D. 500–1600," p. 184.
17. This quotation and the next appear in E. J. Murphy, *History of African Civilization* (New York: Delta, 1972), pp. 109, 111.
18. Quoted ibid., p. 120.
19. Quoted in Oliver and Oliver, *Africa in the Days of Exploration,* p. 18.
20. See H. G. Marcus, *A History of Ethiopia,* updated ed. (Berkeley: University of California Press, 2002), pp. 17–20.
21. H. N. Chittick, "The Peopling of the East African Coast," in *East Africa and the Orient: Cultural Syntheses in Pre-Colonial Times,* ed. H. N. Chittick and R. I. Rotberg (New York: Africana Publishing, 1975), p. 19.
22. July, *Precolonial Africa,* p. 209.
23. Austen, "The Trans-Saharan Slave Trade," p. 65; J. H. Harris, *The African Presence in Asia* (Evanston, Ill.: Northwestern University Press, 1971), pp. 3–6, 27–30; and P. Wheatley, "Analecta Sino-Africana Recensa," in Chittick and Rotberg, *East Africa and the Orient,* p. 109.
24. I. Hrbek, ed., *General History of Africa,* vol. 3, *Africa from the Seventh to the Eleventh Century* (Berkeley: University of California Press; New York: UNESCO, 1991), pp. 294–295, 346–347.
25. P. Curtin et al., *African History,* rev. ed. (New York: Longman, 1984), pp. 284–287.

Engraved Mississippian Copper Plate. This ornamental copper plate was excavated in Etowah Mound, Georgia, a Mississippian site first settled in about 1000 C.E. The copper may have been mined along the shore of Lake Superior in what is now northern Michigan, the largest source of copper in North America. *(National Museum of American History, Smithsonian Institution, Washington, D.C.)*

10 CIVILIZATIONS OF THE AMERICAS, 2500 B.C.E.—1500 C.E.

From the beginning of recorded history—that is, from the earliest invention of writing systems—the Eastern and Western Hemispheres developed in isolation from one another. In both areas people initially gathered and hunted their food, and then some groups began to plant crops, adapting plants that were native to the areas they settled. Techniques of plant domestication spread, allowing for greater density of population because harvested crops provided a more regular food supply than did gathered food. In certain parts of both hemispheres, efficient production and transportation of food supplies allowed for the development of cities, with monumental buildings constructed to honor divine and human power, specialized production of a wide array of products, and marketplaces where those products were exchanged. New products included improved military equipment, which leaders used to enhance their power and build up the large political entities we call "kingdoms" and "empires." The power of those leaders also often rested on religious ideas, in which providing service to a king was viewed as a way to honor divine power. These large political units did not develop everywhere in either hemisphere, however, nor was settled agriculture the only economic system. In many places, particularly where the climate or environment made growing crops difficult or impossible, gathering and hunting, sometimes combined with raising animals for food, continued to provide for human sustenance.

The separate but parallel paths of the two hemispheres were radically changed by Columbus's voyage and the events that followed. The greater availability of metals, especially iron, in the Eastern Hemisphere meant that the military technology of the Europeans who came to the Western Hemisphere was more deadly than anything indigenous peoples had developed. Even more deadly, however, were the germs Europeans brought with them: measles, mumps, bubonic plague, influenza, and smallpox. Because the two hemispheres had been out of contact for so long, indigenous people had no resistance, and they died in astounding numbers. Population estimates of the Western Hemisphere in the 1400s vary,

ATLANTIC OCEAN

PACIFIC OCEAN

PIRO People

MAP 10.1 **The Peoples of Mesoamerica and South America** The major indigenous peoples of Mesoamerica and South America represented a great variety of languages and cultures adapted to a wide range of environments. *(Source: Adapted from* The Times Atlas of World History, *3d ed., p. 149. Reprinted by permission of HarperCollins Publishers Ltd.)*

but many demographers place the total population at about 70 million people. They also estimate that in many parts of the Western Hemisphere, 90 percent of the population died within the first decades of European contact.

Disease often spread ahead of actual groups of conquerors or settlers, when a few or even one native person came into contact with a European landing party and then returned to the village. Germs spread to other people as they did normal things like preparing food, carrying children, or talking about what they had seen. People became sick and died quickly, so that when Europeans got to an area several weeks or months later, they found people who were already weak and fewer in number.

The history of the Western Hemisphere *after* Columbus shapes all the words we use to describe it. About a decade after Columbus's first voyage, another Italian explorer and adventurer, Amerigo Vespucci, wrote a letter to his old employers, the Medici rulers in Italy, trumpeting the wonders of the "new world" he had seen. He claimed to have been the first to see what is now Venezuela on a voyage in 1497, a year before Columbus got there. This letter was published many times in many different languages, and the phrase "New World" began to show up on world maps around 1505. Shortly after that the word *America,* meaning "the land of Amerigo," also appeared, because mapmakers read and believed Vespucci's letter. By just a few years later, mapmakers and others knew that Columbus had been the first to this new world. They wanted to omit the label "America" from future maps, but the name had already stuck.

Our use of the word *Indian* for the indigenous peoples of the Americas stems from another mistake. Columbus was trying to reach Asia by sailing west and thought he was somewhere in the East Indies when he landed, which is why he called the people he met "Indians." They apparently called themselves "Tainos," and people who lived on nearby islands called themselves other things. In many cases people died so fast that we have no idea now what they actually called themselves, so the words we use for various indigenous groups come from other indigenous groups or from European languages and were sometimes originally insulting or derogatory nicknames. Many indigenous groups today are returning to designations from their own languages, and scholars are attempting to use terminology that is historically accurate, so certain groups are known by multiple names. The use of the word *Indian* is itself highly controversial, and various other terms are often used, including Native Americans, Amerindians, and (in Canada) First Peoples. Each of these substitutes has supporters and opponents, including people who are themselves of indigenous background. There is no term for all the inhabitants of the Western Hemisphere that is universally accepted, though in the United States "American Indians" is now preferred. The many peoples of the Americas did not think of themselves as belonging to a single group, any more than the peoples living in sixteenth-century Europe thought of themselves as Europeans (see Map 10.1).

All these issues were in the future in 1492, of course. Columbus's voyage resulted in a devastating chain of events for the inhabitants of the Western Hemisphere and determined the language we use to talk about them. In fact, even Western Hemisphere is a post-Columbus concept, as it requires setting an arbitrary line that divides the two halves of the world. Many different points were proposed over the centuries, and only in the nineteenth century was the current prime meridian at Greenwich—a suburb of London—agreed on.

This huge area had a highly complex history for millennia before Columbus, however, and a great diversity of peoples, cultures, and linguistic groups. New information about these cultures is emerging every year, provoking vigorous debates among scholars. In no other chapter of this book are the basic outlines of what most people agree happened changing as fast as they are for this chapter.

Chronology

40,000–15,000 B.C.E.   Initial human migration to the Americas (date disputed)

ca. 8000 B.C.E.   Beginnings of agriculture

ca. 2500 B.C.E.   First cities in Norte Chico; earliest mound building in North America

ca. 1500–300 B.C.E.   Olmec civilization

ca. 1200 B.C.E.   Emergence of Chavin culture

ca. 200 B.C.E.– 600 C.E.   Hopewell culture

ca. 100 B.C.E.–750 C.E.   Height of Teotihuacán civilization

ca. 600–900 C.E.   Peak of Maya civilization

ca. 1050–1250   Construction of mounds at Cahokia

1325   Construction of Aztec city of Tenochtitlán begins

mid-1400s   Height of Aztec culture

ca. 1500   Inca Empire reaches its largest extent

THE EARLY PEOPLES OF THE AMERICAS

How did early peoples in the Americas adapt to their environment as they created economic and political systems?

Mesoamerica *The term used by scholars to designate the area of present-day Mexico and Central America.*

As in the development of early human cultures in Afroeurasia (Chapter 1), the environment shaped the formation of human settlements in the Americas. North America includes arctic tundra, dry plains, coastal wetlands, woodlands, deserts, and temperate rain forests. **Mesoamerica,** a term scholars use to designate the area of present-day Mexico and Central America, is dominated by high plateaus with a temperate climate and good agricultural land bounded by coastal plains. The Caribbean coast of Central America—modern Belize, Guatemala, Honduras, Nicaragua, El Salvador, Costa Rica, and Panama—is characterized by thick jungle lowlands, heavy rainfall, and torrid heat. South America is a continent of extremely varied terrain. The entire western coast is edged by the Andes, the highest mountain range in the Western Hemisphere. Three-fourths of South America—almost the entire interior of the continent—is lowland plains. The Amazon River, at four thousand miles the second-longest river in the world, is bordered by tropical lowland rain forests with dense growth and annual rainfall in excess of eighty inches. All these environments have supported extensive human settlement at various times, though it is easier to learn about those in dryer areas because artifacts survive longer there.

Settling the Americas

The traditions of many American Indian peoples teach that the group originated independently, often through the actions of a divine figure. Many creation accounts, including that of the book of Genesis in the Bible, begin with people who are created out of earth and receive assistance from supernatural beings—who set out certain ways people are supposed to behave. Both Native American and biblical creation accounts continue to have deep spiritual importance for many people.

Archaeological and DNA evidence indicates that the earliest humans came to the Americas from Siberia and East Asia, but exactly when and how this happened is currently being hotly debated. The traditional account is that people crossed the Bering Strait from what is now Russian Siberia to what is now Alaska about fifteen thousand years ago, mostly by walking. This was the end of the last Ice Age, so that more of the world's water was frozen and ocean levels were much lower than they are today. (This situation is the opposite of what is occurring today; global warming is melting polar ice, which will raise water levels around the world.) The people migrated southward through North America between two large ice sheets that were slowly melting and retreating, and relatively quickly they spread through the entire hemisphere. They lived by gathering and hunting, using spears with stone tips that archaeologists term *Clovis points* after the town in New Mexico where they were first discovered.

Clovis points have been found widely throughout the Americas, and many archaeologists see the Clovis people as the ancestors of most indigenous people in the Western Hemisphere. There is some difference of opinion about exactly when the Clovis culture flourished, for various methods of carbon-14 dating produce slightly different results, with some scholars accepting 11,000 B.C.E. as the height of Clovis technology and others 9000 B.C.E. (Carbon-14 dating uses the rate at which the radioactive isotope of carbon—present in all living things—breaks down into a nonradioactive form to determine how old things are.)

Disagreements regarding the age of the Clovis culture are significant because they are part of a much broader debate about the traditional account of migration to the Americas. Archaeologists working at Monte Verde along the coast of Chile have excavated a site that they date to about 9000 B.C.E., and perhaps much earlier. This site is ten thousand miles from the Bering Land bridge, which would have meant a very fast walk. Monte Verde and a few other sites are leading increasing numbers of archaeologists to conclude that migrants over the land bridge were preceded by people who traveled along the coast in skin boats, perhaps as early as forty thousand years ago. They lived by fishing and gathering rather than hunting big game, and they slowly worked their way southward. The coasts that they traveled along are today far under water, so archaeological evidence is difficult to obtain, but DNA and other genetic evidence has lent support to this idea. (DNA evidence has generally not supported various other theories of early migrations from Europe or Australia.)

However and whenever people got to the Western Hemisphere—and a consensus about this may emerge in the next decade—they lived by gathering, fishing, and hunting, as did everyone throughout the world at that point. Some groups were nomadic and followed migrating game, while others did not have to travel to be assured of a regular food supply. Coastal settlements from the Pacific Northwest to the southern end of South America relied on fish and shellfish, and some also hunted seals and other large marine mammals.

The Development of Agriculture

About 8000 B.C.E., people in some parts of the Americas began raising crops as well as gathering wild produce. As in the development of agriculture in Afroeurasia, people initially planted the seeds of native plants. Pumpkins and other members of the gourd family were one of the earliest crops, as were chilies, beans, and avocados. At some point, people living in what is now southern Mexico also began raising what would become the most important crop in the Americas—maize, which we generally call "corn." Exactly how this happened is not clear. In contrast to other grain crops such as wheat and rice, the kernels of maize—which are the seeds as well as the part that is eaten for food—are wrapped in a husk, so that the plant cannot propagate itself easily. In addition, no wild ancestor of maize has been found. What many biologists now think happened is that a related grass called *teosinte* developed mutant forms with large kernels enclosed in husks, and people living in the area quickly realized its benefits. They began to intentionally plant these kernels and crossbred the results to get a better crop each year.

People bred various types of maize for different purposes and for different climates, making it the staple food throughout the highlands of Mesoamerica. They often planted maize along with squash, beans, and other crops in a field called a **milpa;** the beans use the maize stalks for support as they both grow and also fix nitrogen in the soil, acting as a natural fertilizer. Crops can be grown in milpas year after year, in contrast to single-crop planting in which rotation is needed so as not to exhaust the soil. Maize came to have a symbolic and religious meaning; it was viewed as the source of human life and was a prominent feature in sculptures of kings and gods.

In central Mexico, along with milpas, people also built *chinampas,* floating gardens. They dredged soil from the bottom of a lake or pond, placed the soil on mats of woven twigs, and then planted crops in the soil. Chinampas were enormously productive, yielding up to three harvests a year.

Knowledge of maize cultivation, and maize seeds themselves, spread out from Mesoamerica into both North and South America. By 3000 B.C.E. farmers in what is now Peru and Uruguay were planting maize, and by 2000 B.C.E. farmers in southwest North America were as well. The crop then spread into the Mississippi Valley and to northeastern North America, where farmers bred slightly different variants for the different growing conditions. After 1500 C.E. maize cultivation spread to Europe, Africa, and Asia as well, becoming an essential food crop there. (In the twentieth century maize became even more successful; about one-quarter of the nearly fifty thousand items in the average American supermarket now contain corn.)

milpa *A system of effective agriculture used throughout Mesoamerica that relies on crop rotation and the planting of multiple crops in a single field. The term is derived from a Nahuatl word meaning "field."*

The expansion of maize was the result of contacts between different groups that can be traced through trade goods as well. Copper from the Great Lakes was a particularly valuable item and was traded throughout North America, reaching Mexico by 3000 B.C.E. Obsidian from the Rocky Mountains, used for blades, was traded widely, as were shells and later pottery.

Different cultivars of maize could be developed for many different climates, but maize was difficult to grow in high altitudes. Thus in the high Andes, people relied on potatoes, terracing the slopes with stone retaining walls to keep the hillsides from sliding. High-altitude valleys were connected to mountain life and vegetation to form a single interdependent agricultural system called "vertical archipelagoes" capable of supporting large communities. Such vertical archipelagoes often extended more than thirty-seven miles from top to bottom. The terraces were shored up with earthen walls to retain moisture, enabling the production of bumper crops of many different types of potatoes. Potatoes ordinarily cannot be stored for long periods, but Andean

● **Inca Terraces** In order to create more land for farming and limit soil erosion, Andean peoples built terraces up steep slopes. Later the Incas built systems of aqueducts and canals to bring water to terraced fields. *(Wolfgang Kaehler/Corbis)*

peoples developed a product called *chuñu,* freeze-dried potatoes made by subjecting potatoes alternately to nightly frosts and daily sun. Chuñu will keep unspoiled for several years. Coca (the dried leaves of a plant native to the Andes from which cocaine is derived), chewed in moderation as a dietary supplement, enhanced people's stamina and their ability to withstand the cold.

Maize will also not grow in hot, wet climates very well. In Amazonia, manioc, a tuber that can be cooked in many ways, became the staple food. It was planted along with other crops, including fruits, nuts, and various types of palm trees. People domesticated peach palms, for example, which produce fruit, pulp that is made into flour, heart of palm that is eaten raw, and juice that can be fermented into beer. Just how many people Amazonian agriculture supported before the introduction of European diseases is an issue hotly debated by anthropologists, but increasing numbers see the original tropical rain forest not as a pristine wilderness, but as an ecosystem managed effectively by humans for thousands of years. The oldest known pottery in the Americas has been found along the Amazon River, as well as in the Andes.

Farming in the Americas was not limited to foodstuffs. Beginning about 2500 B.C.E., people living along the coast of Peru used irrigation to raise cotton, and textiles became an important part of Peruvian culture. Agriculture in the Americas was extensive, though it was limited by the lack of an animal that could be harnessed to pull a plow. People throughout the Americas domesticated dogs, and in the Andes they domesticated llamas and alpacas to carry loads through the mountains. But no native species allowed itself to be harnessed as horses, oxen, and water buffalo did in Asia and Europe, which meant that all agricultural labor was human-powered.

Colombian Lime Container The use of coca in rituals and to withstand bodily discomfort is an ancient tradition in South America. Pieces of coca leaves were placed in the mouth with small amounts of powdered lime made from seashells. The lime helped release the hallucinogens in the coca. This 9-inch gold bottle for holding lime shows a seated figure with rings in the ears and beads across the forehead and at the neck, wrists, knees, and ankles. A tiny spatula would be used to secure the lime through the bottle's narrow neck. *(The Metropolitan Museum of Art, Jan Mitchell and Sons Collection, Gift of Jan Mitchell, 1991 [1991.419.22]. Photograph © 1992 The Metropolitan Museum of Art)*

EARLY CIVILIZATIONS

What physical, social, and intellectual features characterized early civilizations in the Americas?

Agricultural advancement had definitive social and political consequences. Careful cultivation of the land brought a reliable and steady food supply, which contributed to a relatively high fertility rate and in turn to a population boom. Population in the Americas grew steadily and may have been about 15 million people by the first century B.C.E. This growth in population allowed for greater concentrations of people and the creation of the first urban societies.

Mounds, Towns, and Trade in North and South America

In North America by 2500 B.C.E., some groups began to build massive earthworks, mounds of earth and stone. The mounds differed in shape, size, and purpose: some were conical, others elongated or wall-like, others pyramidical, and still others, called effigy mounds, in serpentine, bird, or animal form. The Ohio and Mississippi Valleys

● **Inca Khipu, ca. 1400 c.e.**   This khipu, a collection of colored, knotted strings, recorded numeric information and allowed Inca administrators to keep track of the flow of money, goods, and people in their large empire. Every aspect of the khipu—the form and position of the knots, the colors and spin of the string—may have provided information. Administrators read them visually and by running their hands through them, as Braille text is read today. *(Museo Arqueologico Rafael Larco Herrera, Lima, Peru)*

Norte Chico *A region along the coast of Peru that possessed a highly developed urban culture characterized by massive stepped pyramids and extensive use of cotton as early as 2500 B.C.E.*

khipu *A intricate system of knotted and colored strings used by early Peruvian cultures to store information such as census and tax records.*

contain the richest concentration of mounds, but they have been found from the Great Lakes down to the Gulf of Mexico (see Map 10.3 on page 273). One early large mound at Poverty Point, Louisiana, on the banks of the Mississippi, dates from about 1300 B.C.E. and consists of six octagonal ramparts, one within the other, that measure 6 feet high and more than 400 yards across. The area was home to perhaps five thousand people and was inhabited for hundreds of years, with trade goods brought in by canoe and carved stone beads exported.

Large structures for political and religious purposes began to be built earlier in South America than in North America. By about 2500 B.C.E. cities grew along river valleys on the coast of Peru in the region called **Norte Chico.** Stepped pyramids, some more than ten stories high, dominated these settlements, which were built at about the same time the pyramids were being constructed in Egypt. Cities in Norte Chico often used irrigation to produce crops of squash, beans, cotton, and other crops. Those along the coast relied extensively on fish and shellfish, which they traded with inland cities for the cotton needed to make nets. The largest city, Caral, had many plazas, houses, and temples, built with quarried stone using woven cotton and grass bags filled with smaller stones for support. Cotton was used in Norte Chico for many things, including the earliest example yet discovered of a **khipu** (also spelled *quipu*), a collection of knotted strings that was used to record information. Later Peruvian cultures, including the Incas, developed ever more complex khipu, using the colors of the string and the style and position of the knots to represent tax obligations, census records, and other numeric data.

Along with khipu, Norte Chico culture also developed religious ideas that may have been adopted by later Andean cultures. The oldest religious image yet found in the Americas, a piece of gourd with a drawing of a fanged god holding a staff, comes from Norte Chico, dating about 2250 B.C.E. This Staff God became a major deity in many Andean cultures, one of a complex pantheon of deities. Religious ceremonies, as well as other festivities, in Norte Chico involved music, as a large number of bone flutes have been discovered.

The earliest cities in the Andes were built by the **Chavin** people beginning about 1200 B.C.E. They built pyramids and other types of monumental architecture, quarrying and trimming huge blocks of stone and assembling them without mortar. They worked gold and silver into human and animal figurines, trading these and other goods to coastal peoples.

Chavin *A culture that developed in the Andes Mountains of Peru around 1200 B.C.E. and was responsible for the earliest cities in the region.*

The Olmecs

The **Olmecs** created the first society with cities in Mesoamerica. The word *Olmec* comes from an Aztec term for the peoples living in southern Veracruz and western Tabasco, Mexico, between about 1500 and 300 B.C.E. They did not call themselves Olmecs or consider themselves a unified group, but their culture penetrated and influenced all parts of Mesoamerica. Until 1993 knowledge of the Olmecs rested on archaeological evidence—pyramids, jade objects, axes, figurines, and stone monuments—but that year two linguists deciphered Olmec writing. Since then, understanding of Olmec and other contemporary Mesoamerican cultures such as the Zapotecs also comes from the written records they left.

Olmecs *The oldest of the early advanced Amerindian civilizations.*

The Olmecs cultivated maize, squash, beans, and other plants and supplemented that diet with wild game and fish. Originally they lived in egalitarian societies that had no distinctions based on status or wealth. After 1500 B.C.E. more complex, hierarchical societies evolved. Most peoples continued to live in small villages along the rivers of the region, while the leaders of the societies resided in the large cities today known as San Lorenzo, La Venta, Tres Zapotes, and Laguna de los Cerros. These cities contained palaces (large private houses) for the elite, large plazas, temples (ritual centers), ball courts, water reservoirs, and carved stone drains for the disposal of wastes. Like the Chavin (with whom they had no contact), the Olmecs created large pyramid-shaped buildings. They also carved huge stone heads of rulers or gods, beginning a tradition of monumental stone sculptures adopted by later Mesoamerican civilizations. In order to trace celestial phenomena—which they believed influenced human life—they developed a complex calendar involving three different ways of counting time. The need to record time led to the development of a writing system. Whereas the earliest written records from Mesopotamia are tax records for payments to the temple (see page 4), the earliest written records from Mesoamerica, dating from about 700 B.C.E., are dates. Many early records also record the deeds of kings, so that the political history of Mesoamerica is becoming more detailed as scholars learn to read various writing systems.

The Olmecs had sacred ceremonial sites where they sometimes practiced human sacrifice, another tradition adopted by later Mesoamerican cultures. They erected special courts on which men played a game with a hard rubber ball that was both religious ritual and sport. Finally, the Olmecs engaged in long-distance trade, exchanging rubber, cacao (from which chocolate is made), pottery, figurines, jaguar pelts, and the services of painters and sculptors for obsidian (a hard, black volcanic glass from which paddle-shaped weapons were made), basalt, iron ore, shells, and various perishable goods. Commercial networks extended as far away as central and western Mexico and the Pacific coast.

Around 900 B.C.E. San Lorenzo, the center of early Olmec culture, was destroyed, probably by migrating peoples from the north, and power passed to La Venta in Tabasco. Archaeological excavation at La Venta has uncovered a huge volcano-shaped pyramid. Standing 110 feet high at an inaccessible site on an island in the Tonala River, the so-called Great Pyramid was the center of the Olmec religion. The upward thrust of this monument, like ziggurats in Mesopotamia or cathedrals of medieval Europe, may have represented the human effort to get closer to the gods. Built of huge stone slabs, the Great Pyramid required, scholars estimated, some eight hundred thousand man-hours of labor. It testifies to the region's bumper harvests, which were able to support a labor force large enough to build such a monument.

CLASSICAL ERA MESOAMERICA AND NORTH AMERICA

How did Mesoamerican and North American peoples develop prosperous and stable societies in the classical era?

The urban culture of the Olmecs and other Mesoamerican peoples influenced subsequent Mesoamerican societies. Especially in what became known as the classical era (300–900 C.E.), various groups developed large states centered on cities, with high levels of technological and intellectual achievement. Of these, the **Maya** were the most long-lasting, but other city-states were significant as well. Peoples living in North America built communities that were smaller than those in Mesoamerica, but many also used irrigation techniques to enhance agricultural production and built earthwork mounds for religious purposes.

Maya *A highly developed Mesoamerican culture centered in the Yucatán peninsula of Mexico. The Maya created the most intricate writing system in the Western Hemisphere.*

Maya Technology and Trade

The word *Maya* seems to derive from *Zamna,* the name of a Maya god. Linguistic evidence leads scholars to believe that the first Maya were a small North American Indian group that emigrated from the area that is now southern Oregon and northern California to the western highlands of Guatemala. Between the third and second millennia B.C.E., various groups, including the Cholans and Tzeltalans, broke away from the parent group and moved north and east into the Yucatán peninsula. The Cholan-speaking Maya, who occupied the area during the time of great cultural achievement, apparently created the culture.

Maya culture rested on agriculture. The staple crop in Mesoamerica was maize, often raised in multiple-crop milpas with other foodstuffs, including beans, squash, chili peppers, some root crops, and fruit trees. The Maya also practiced intensive agriculture in raised, narrow, rectangular plots that they built above the low-lying, seasonally flooded land bordering rivers.

The raised-field and milpa systems of intensive agriculture yielded food sufficient to support large population centers. The entire Maya region could have had as many as 14 million inhabitants. At Uxmal, Uaxactún, Copán, Piedras Negras, Tikal, Palenque, and Chichén Itzá (see Map 10.2), archaeologists have uncovered the palaces of nobles, elaborate pyramids where nobles were buried, engraved *steles* (stone-slab monuments), masonry temples, altars, sophisticated polychrome pottery, and courts for games played with a rubber ball. The largest site, Tikal, may have had forty thousand people and served as a religious and ceremonial center.

Public fairs for trading merchandise accompanied important religious festivals. Jade, obsidian, beads of red spiny oyster shell, lengths of cloth, and cacao beans—all in high demand in the

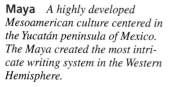

● **Palace Doorway Lintel at Yaxchilan, Mexico** Lady Xoc, principal wife of King Shield-Jaguar, who holds a torch over her, pulls a thorn-lined rope through her tongue to sanctify with her blood the birth of a younger wife's child—reflecting the importance of blood sacrifice in Maya culture. The elaborate headdresses and clothes of the couple show their royal status. (© Justin Kerr 1985)

Mesoamerican world—served as media of exchange. The extensive trade among Maya communities, plus a common language, promoted the union of the peoples of the region and gave them a common sense of identity. Merchants trading beyond Maya regions, such as with the Zapotecs of the Valley of Oaxaca and the Teotihuacános of the central valley of Mexico, were considered state ambassadors bearing "gifts" to royal neighbors, who reciprocated with their own "gifts." Since this long-distance trade played an important part in international relations, the merchants conducting it were high nobles or even members of the royal family.

The extensive networks of rivers and swamps in the area ruled by the Maya were the main arteries of transportation; over them large canoes carved out of hardwood trees carried cargoes of cloth and maize. Wide roads also linked Maya centers; on the roads merchants and lords were borne in litters, goods and produce on human backs. Trade produced considerable wealth that seems to have been concentrated in a noble class, for the Maya had no distinctly mercantile class. They did have a sharply defined hierarchical society. A hereditary elite owned private land, defended society, carried on commercial activities, exercised political power, and directed religious rituals. Artisans and scribes made up the next social level. The rest of the people were workers, farmers, and slaves, the latter including prisoners of war.

Wars were fought in Maya society for a variety of reasons. Long periods without rain caused crop failure, which led to famine and then war with other centers for food. Certain cities, such as Tikal, extended their authority over larger areas through warfare with neighboring cities. Within the same communities, domestic strife between factions over the succession to the kingship or property led to violence.

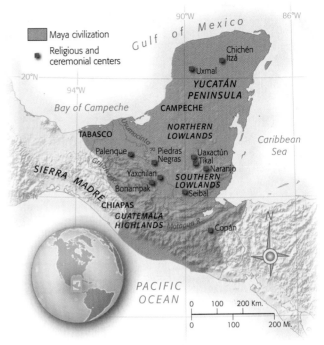

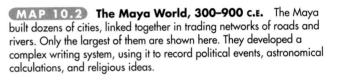

MAP 10.2 **The Maya World, 300–900 C.E.** The Maya built dozens of cities, linked together in trading networks of roads and rivers. Only the largest of them are shown here. They developed a complex writing system, using it to record political events, astronomical calculations, and religious ideas.

Maya Science and Religion

The Maya developed the most complex writing system in the Americas, a script with nearly a thousand characters that represent concepts and sounds. They used it to record chronology, religion, and astronomy in books made of bark paper and deerskin, on stone pillars archaeologists term "steles," on pottery, and on the walls of temples and other buildings. The deciphering of this writing over the last fifty years has demonstrated that inscriptions on steles are historical documents recording the births, accessions, marriages, wars, and deaths of Maya kings. The writing and pictorial imagery often represent the same events and have allowed for a fuller understanding of Maya dynastic history.

Learning about Maya religion through written records is more difficult. In the sixteenth century Spanish religious authorities ordered all books of Maya writing to be destroyed, viewing them as demonic. Only three (and part of a fourth) survived, because they were already in Europe. These texts do provide information about religious rituals and practices, as well as astronomical calculations. Further information comes from the **Popul Vuh,** or Book of Council, a book of mythological narratives and dynastic history written in the Maya language but in Roman script in the middle of the sixteenth century. Like the Bible in Judeo-Christian tradition, the *Popul Vuh* gives

Popul Vuh *The Book of Council, a collection of mythological narratives and dynastic histories that constitutes the primary record of the Maya civilization.*

● **Maya Ballplayers** Two teams of two players each face off in this lively scene on a painted ceramic vessel. Note that the ballplayers are wearing deer and vulture headdresses, Maya symbols of hunting and war. War was sometimes called the "hunting of men." *(Chrysler Museum of Art, Norfolk, Va., © Justin Kerr)*

Primary Source:
Antonio de Herrera y Tordesillas, *On the Mayan Ball Game Tlachtli*

the Maya view of the creation of the world, concepts of good and evil, and the entire nature and purpose of the living experience. Because almost all religious texts from Mesoamerica—not just Maya texts, but those from other cultures as well—were destroyed by Spanish Christian authorities, its significance is enormous.

Maya religious practice emphasized performing rituals at specific times, which served as an impetus for further refinements of the calendar. From careful observation of the earth's movements around the sun, the Maya devised a calendar of eighteen 20-day months and one 5-day month, for a total of 365 days. Their religious calendar, like that of the Olmecs, was a cycle of 260 days based perhaps on the movement of the planet Venus. When these two calendars coincided, which happened once every fifty-two years, the Maya celebrated a period of feasting, ballgame competitions, and religious observance. These observances—and those at other times as well—included human sacrifice to honor the gods and demonstrate the power of earthly kings.

Using a system of bars (— = 5) and dots (∘ = 1), the Maya devised a form of mathematics based on the vigesimal (20) rather than the decimal (10) system. More unusual was their use of the number zero, which allows for more complex calculations than are possible in number systems without it. The zero may have actually been "discovered" by the Olmecs, who used it in figuring their calendar, but the Maya used it mathematically as well. (At about the same time, mathematicians in India also began using zero.) They proved themselves masters of abstract knowledge—notably in astronomy, mathematics, calendric development, and the recording of history.

Maya civilization lasted about a thousand years, reaching its peak between approximately 600 and 900 C.E., the period when the Tang Dynasty was flourishing in China, Islam was spreading in the Middle East, and Carolingian rulers were extending their sway in Europe. Between the eighth and tenth centuries, the Maya abandoned their cultural and ceremonial centers, and Maya civilization collapsed. Archaeologists and historians attribute the decline to a combination of agricultural failures due to land exhaustion and drought; overpopulation; disease; and constant wars fought as an extension of economic and political goals. These wars brought widespread destruction, which aggravated agrarian problems. Maya royal ideology also played a role in their decline: just as in good times kings attributed moral authority and prosperity to themselves, so in bad times, when military, economic, and social conditions deteriorated, they became the objects of blame.

Teotihuacán and the Toltecs

The Maya were not alone in creating a complex culture in Mesoamerica during the classic period. In the isolated valley of Oaxaca at modern-day Monte Albán in southern Mexico, Zapotecan-speaking peoples established a great religious center whose temples and elaborately decorated tombs testify to the wealth of the nobility. To the north of Monte Albán, **Teotihuacán** in central Mexico witnessed the flowering of a remarkable civilization built by a new people from regions east and south of the Valley of Mexico. The city of Teotihuacán had a population of over two hundred thousand—larger than any European city at the time. The inhabitants were stratified into distinct social classes. The rich and powerful resided in houses of palatial splendor in a special precinct. Ordinary working people, tradespeople, artisans, and obsidian craftsmen lived in apartment compounds, or *barrios,* on the edge of the city. Agricultural laborers lived outside the city. Teotihuacán was a great commercial center, the entrepôt for trade and culture for all of Mesoamerica. It was also the ceremonial center, a capital filled with artworks, a mecca that attracted thousands of pilgrims a year.

Teotihuacán   *A city in central Mexico that became a great commercial center during the classic period.*

In the center of the city stood the Pyramids of the Sun and the Moon. The Pyramid of the Sun is built of sun-dried bricks and faced with stone. Each of its sides is seven hundred feet long and two hundred feet high. The smaller Pyramid of the Moon is similar in construction. In lesser temples, natives and outlanders worshiped the rain-god and the feathered serpent later called Quetzalcoatl. These gods were associated with the production of corn, the staple of the people's diet.

Toltecs   *An heir to Teotihuacán, this confederation extended its hegemony over most of central Mexico under the reign of Topiltzin.*

Around 750 C.E. less-developed peoples from the southwest burned Teotihuacán, and the city-state fell apart. This collapse, plus that of the Maya, marks the end of the classical period in Mesoamerica for most scholars, just as the end of the Roman Empire in the west marks the end of the classical era in Europe. As in Europe, a period characterized by disorder, militarism, and domination by smaller states followed.

Whereas nature gods and their priests seem to have governed the great cities of the earlier period, militant gods and warriors dominated the petty states that now arose. Among these states, the most powerful heir to Teotihuacán was the Toltec confederation, a weak union of strong states. The **Toltecs** admired the culture of their predecessors and sought to absorb and preserve it. Through intermarriage, they assimilated with the Teotihuacán people. In fact, every new Mesoamerican confederation became the cultural successor of earlier confederations.

Under Topiltzin (r. ca. 980–1000), the Toltecs extended their hegemony over most of central Mexico. Topiltzin established his capital at Tula. Its splendor and power became legendary during his reign. After the reign of Topiltzin, troubles beset the Toltec state. Drought led to crop failure. Northern peoples, the Chichimecas, attacked the borders in waves. Weak, incompetent rulers could not quell domestic uprisings. When the last Toltec king committed suicide in 1174, the Toltec state collapsed.

● **Maya Burial Urn**   After tightly wrapping the bodies of royal and noble persons in cloth, the K'iché Maya people of Guatemala placed them in urns and buried them in pyramids or sacred caves. The lid represents a divine being through whose mouth gifts may have been offered to the deceased. The figure with corncobs on top of the lid is the maize-god, a sacred figure to all Mesoamerican peoples. *(Museum of Fine Arts, Boston, Gift of Landon T. Clay [1988.1290]. © 2008 Museum of Fine Arts, Boston)*

● **Zapotec Deity** This Zapotec image of a god was found at Monte Albán, the primary Zapotec religious center. Made to be worn as a breast ornament, it was created through lost-wax casting, in which a mold is made from a wax model, and molten gold poured in to replace the wax. (Giraudon/The Bridgeman Art Library)

Hohokam *A Native American culture that emerged around 300 B.C.E. and was centered around the Gila River in Arizona. The Hohokam practiced a system of agriculture that relied on irrigation trenches, dams, and terraces to cultivate their arid land.*

Anasazi *A Native American culture that dominated the Four Corners region of the southwestern United States; remarkable for their construction of numerous cliff-dwellings in the region.*

Hopewell *An important mound-building Native American culture that thrived between 200 B.C.E. and 600 C.E. The culture was centered near the town of Hopewell, Ohio, and was noted for extensive canals and a trade network that extended from the Caribbean to Illinois.*

Hohokam, Hopewell, and Mississippian

Mesoamerican trading networks extended into southwestern North America, where by 300 B.C.E. the **Hohokam** people and other groups were using irrigation canals, dams, and terraces to enhance their farming of the arid land (see Map 10.3). The Hohokam built platforms for ceremonial purposes and played ballgames with rubber balls similar to those of the Olmecs and other Mesoamerican people. The rubber balls themselves were imported, for rubber trees do not grow in the desert, with turquoise and other precious stones exported in return. Religious ideas came along with trade goods, as the feathered serpent god became important to desert peoples. Other groups, including the **Anasazi**, Yuma, and later Pueblo, also built settlements in this area, using large sandstone blocks and masonry to construct thick-walled houses that offered protection from the heat. Mesa Verde, the largest Anasazi town, had a population of about twenty-five hundred living in houses built into and on cliff walls. Roads connected Mesa Verde to other Anasazi towns, allowing timber and other construction materials to be brought in more easily. Drought, deforestation, and soil erosion led to decline in both the Hohokam and Anasazi cultures, increasing warfare between towns.

To the east, the mound building that had first been developed at settlements along the Mississippi around 2000 B.C.E. spread more widely along many river basins. The most important mound-building culture in the first several centuries B.C.E. was the **Hopewell** culture, named for a town in Ohio near where the most extensive mounds were built. Some mounds were burial chambers for priests, leaders, and other high-status individuals, or for thousands of more average people. Others were platforms for the larger houses of important people. Still others were simply huge mounds of earth shaped like animals or geometric figures. Mound building thus had many purposes: it was a way to honor the gods, to remember the dead, and to make distinctions between leaders and common folk

Hopewell earthwork construction also included canals that enabled trading networks to expand, bringing products from the Caribbean far into the interior. Those

MAP 10.3 **Major North American Agricultural Societies, 600–1500 C.E.** Many North American groups used agriculture to increase the available food supply and allow for greater population density and the development of urban centers. Shown here are three of these cultures: the Mississippian, Anasazi, and Hohokam. Most mound-building cultures raised crops, and many were connected in an extensive trading network.

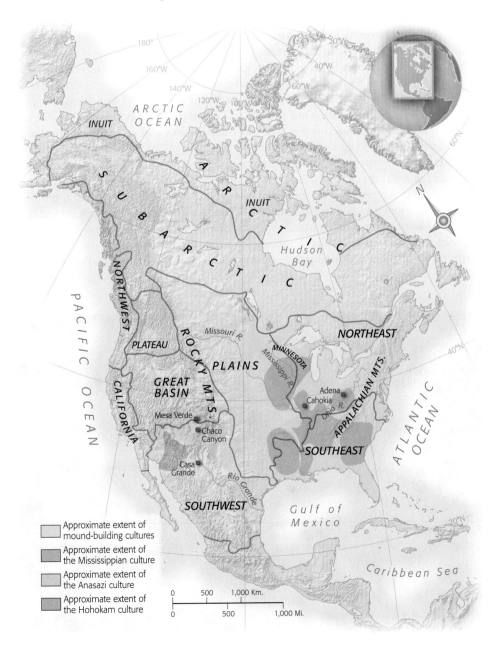

trading networks also carried maize, allowing more intensive agriculture to spread throughout the eastern woodlands of North America.

At Cahokia, near the confluence of the Mississippi and Missouri Rivers in Illinois, archaeologists have uncovered the largest mound of all. Begun about 1050 C.E. and completed about 1250 C.E., the complex at Cahokia covered five and a half square miles and was the ceremonial center for perhaps thirty-eight thousand people. A fence of wooden posts surrounded the core. More than five hundred rectangular mounds or houses, inside and outside the fence, served as tombs and as the bases for temples and palaces. Within the fence, the largest mound rose in four stages to a height of one hundred feet and was more than one thousand feet long, larger than the largest Egyptian pyramid. At its top, a small conical platform supported a wooden fence and a rectangular temple. The mounds at Cahokia represent the culture of the **Mississippian** mound builders.

Mississippian *An important mound-building culture that thrived between 800 and 1500 C.E. in a territory that extended from the Mississippi River to the Appalachian Mountains. The largest mound produced by this culture is found at Cahokia, Illinois.*

What do the mounds tell us about Mississippian societies? The largest mounds served as burial chambers for leaders and, in many cases, the women and retainers who were sacrificed in order to assist the leader in the afterlife. Mounds also contain valuable artifacts, such as jewelry made from copper from Michigan, mica (a mineral used in building) from the Appalachians, obsidian from the Rocky Mountains, conch shells from the Caribbean, and pipestone from Minnesota.

From these burial items, archaeologists have deduced that mound culture was hierarchical. The leader had religious responsibilities and also managed long-distance trade and gift-giving. The exchange of goods was not perceived as a form of commerce, but as a means of showing respect and of establishing bonds among diverse groups. Large towns housed several thousand inhabitants and served as political and ceremonial centers. They controlled surrounding villages of a few hundred people, but did not grow into politically unified city-states the way Tikal or Teotihuacán did.

Pottery in the form of bowls, jars, bottles, and effigy pipes in various shapes best reveals Mississippian peoples' art and religious ideas. Designs showing eagles, plumed serpents, warriors decapitating victims, and ceremonially ornamented priests suggest a strong Mesoamerican influence. At its peak, about 1150, Cahokia and its environs probably housed between thirty thousand and fifty thousand people, the largest city north of Mesoamerica. Building the interior wooden fence had denuded much of the

● **Great Serpent Mound, Adams County, Ohio** Made by people in the Hopewell culture, this 1,254-foot-long mound in the form of a writhing snake has its "head" at the highest point, suggesting an open mouth ready to swallow a huge egg formed by a heap of stones. *(Georg Gerster/ Photo Researchers, Inc.)*

MAP 10.4 **The Aztec (Mexica) Empire** The Mexica migrated into the central valley of what is now Mexico from the north, conquering other groups and establishing an empire, later called the Aztec Empire. The capital of the Aztec Empire was Tenochtitlán, built on islands in Lake Texcoco.

surrounding countryside of trees, however, which made spring floods worse and destroyed much of the city. An earthquake at the beginning of the thirteenth century knocked down more, and the city never recovered. Thus ecological crises appear to have played a part in bringing an end to various North American cultures, though their technologies and religious ideas were often maintained by those that developed later in the same areas.

Mississippian mound builders relied on agriculture to support their complex cultures, and by the time Cahokia was built, maize agriculture had spread to the Atlantic coast. Particularly along riverbanks and the coastline, fields of maize, beans, and squash surrounded large, permanent villages. Hunting provided meat protein, but the bulk of people's foodstuffs came from farming. The earliest European reports from Virginia and New England describe these villages and sometimes show illustrations of rows of houses within walls. By several decades after contact, disease had destroyed village life.

> **Primary Source:**
> **Father le Petite, *On the Customs of the Natchez***

THE AZTECS

How did the Aztecs both build on the achievements of earlier Mesoamerican cultures and develop new traditions to create their large empire?

The **Aztecs** provide a spectacular example of a culture that adopted many things from earlier peoples and also adapted them to create an even more powerful state. Around 1300, a group of **Nahuatl**-speaking people are believed to have migrated southward from what is now northern Mexico, settling on the shores and islands in Lake Texcoco in the central valley of Mexico (see Map 10.4). Here they built the twin cities of Tenochtitlán and Tlatelolco, which by 1500 were probably larger than any city in Europe except Istanbul. As they migrated, these people conquered many neighboring city-states and established an empire. This empire was later termed the "Aztec" Empire and the people called the "Aztecs." This was not a word used at the time,

Aztec *A term coined by nineteenth-century historians to describe the Mexica people.*

Nahuatl *The language of both the Toltecs and the Aztecs.*

Mexica *Another term for Aztec; it is a pre-Columbian term designating the dominant ethnic people of the island capital of Tenochtitlán-Tlatelolco.*

however, and now most scholars prefer the term **Mexica** to refer to the empire and its people; we use both terms here.

Religion and War in Aztec Society

In Mexica society, religion was the dynamic factor that transformed other aspects of the culture: economic security, social mobility, education, and especially war. War was an article of religious faith. The state religion of the Aztecs initially gave them powerful advantages over other groups in central Mexico; it inspired them to conquer vast territories in a remarkably short time. War came to be seen as a religious duty to the Mexicas, through which nobles, and occasionally commoners, honored the gods, gained prestige, and often acquired wealth.

The Mexicas worshiped a number of gods and goddesses as well as some deities that had dual natures as both male and female. The basic conflict in the world was understood as one between order and disorder, though the proper life balances these two, as disorder could never be completely avoided. Disorder was linked to dirt and uncleanness, so temples, shrines, and altars were kept very clean; rituals of purification often involved sweeping or bathing. Like many polytheists, Mexicas took the deities of people they encountered into their own pantheon, or mixed their attributes with those of existing gods. Quetzalcoatl, for example, the feathered serpent god found among many Mesoamerican groups, was generally revered by the Mexicas as a creator deity and source of knowledge.

Huitzilopochtli *The chief among the Aztecs' many gods, who symbolized the sun blazing at high noon.*

Among the deities venerated by Mexica and other Mesoamerican groups was **Huitzilopochtli**, a young warrior god whose name translates fully as "Blue Hummingbird of the South" (or "on the Left") and who symbolized the sun blazing at high noon. The sun, the source of all life, had to be kept moving in its orbit if darkness was not to overtake the world. To keep it moving, Aztecs believed, the sun had to be frequently fed precious fluids—that is, human blood. Human sacrifice was a sacred duty, essential for the preservation and prosperity of humankind. (See the feature "Individuals in Society: Tlacaélel.")

Most victims were war captives, for the Aztecs controlled their growing empire by sacrificing prisoners seized in battle, by taking hostages from among defeated peoples as ransom against future revolt, and by demanding from subject states an annual tribute of people to be sacrificed to Huitzilopochtli. Unsuccessful generals, corrupt judges, and careless public officials, even people who accidentally entered forbidden precincts of the royal palaces, were routinely sacrificed. In some years it was difficult to provide enough war captives, so other types of people, including criminals, slaves, and people supplied as tribute, were sacrificed as well. Such victims did not have the same status as captives, however, and Mexicas engaged in special wars simply to provide victims for sacrifices, termed "flower (or flowery) wars." Flowers were frequently associated metaphorically with warfare in Mexica culture, with blood described as a flower of warfare, swords and banners as blooming like flowers, and a warrior's life as fleeting like a flower's blooming. The objective of flower wars was capturing warriors from the other side, not killing them.

The Mexica state religion required constant warfare for two basic reasons. One was to meet the gods' needs for human sacrifice; the other was to acquire warriors for the next phase of imperial expansion. The sacred campaigns of Huitzilopochtli were synchronized with the political and economic needs of the Mexica nation as a whole. Moreover, defeated peoples had to pay tribute in foodstuffs to support rulers, nobles, warriors, and the imperial bureaucracy. The vanquished supplied laborers for agriculture, the economic basis of Mexica society. Likewise, conquered peoples had to produce workers for the construction and maintenance of the entire Aztec infrastructure—roads, dike systems, aqueducts, causeways, and the royal palaces. Finally, merchants also benefited, for war opened new markets for traders' goods in subject territories.

Tlacaélel

The hummingbird god Huitzilopochtli was originally a somewhat ordinary god of war and of young men, but in the fifteenth century he was elevated in status among the Mexica. He became increasingly associated with the sun and gradually became the Mexicas' most important deity. This change was primarily the work of Tlacaélel, the very long-lived chief adviser to the emperors Itzcóatl (r. 1427–1440), Montezuma I (r. 1440–1469), and Axayacatl (r. 1469–1481). Tlacaélel first gained influence during wars in the 1420s in which the Mexicas defeated the rival Tepanecs, after which he established new systems of dividing military spoils and enemy lands. At the same time, he advised the emperor that new histories were needed in which the destiny of the Mexica people was made clearer. Older historical texts were destroyed, and in these new chronicles the fate of the Mexicas was directly connected to Huitzilopochtli. Mexica writing was primarily pictographic, drawn and then read by specially trained scribes, who used written records as an aid to oral presentation, especially for legal issues, historical chronicles, religious and devotional poetry, and astronomical calculations.

According to these new texts, the Mexicas had been guided to Lake Texcoco by Huitzilopochtli; there they saw an eagle perched on a cactus, which a prophecy had told would mark the site of their new city. Huitzilopochtli kept the world alive by bringing the sun's warmth, but to do this he required the Mexicas, who increasingly saw themselves as the "people of the sun," to provide a steady offering of human blood.

The worship of Huitzilopochtli became linked to cosmic forces as well as daily survival. In Nahua tradition, the universe was understood to exist in a series of five suns, or five cosmic ages. Four ages had already passed, and their suns had been destroyed; the fifth sun, the age in which the Mexicas were now living, would also be destroyed unless the Mexicas fortified the sun with the energy found in blood. Warfare thus not only brought new territory under Mexica control, but also provided sacrificial victims for their collaboration with divine forces. With these ideas, Tlacaélel created what Miguel León-Portilla, a leading contemporary scholar of Nahuatl religion and philosophy, has termed a "mystico-militaristic" conception of Aztec destiny.

Human sacrifice was practiced in many cultures of Mesoamerica, including the Olmec and the Maya as well as the Mexica, before the changes introduced by Tlacaélel, but the number of victims is believed to have

Tlacaélel emphasized human sacrifice as one of the Aztecs' religious duties. *(Scala/Art Resource, NY)*

increased dramatically during the last period of Mexica rule. A huge pyramid-shaped temple in the center of Tenochtitlán, dedicated to Huitzilopochtli and the water god Tlaloc, was renovated and expanded many times, the last in 1487. Each expansion was dedicated by priests sacrificing war captives. Similar ceremonies were held regularly throughout the year on days dedicated to Huitzilopochtli and were attended by many observers, including representatives from neighboring states as well as masses of Mexicas. According to many accounts, victims were placed on a stone slab and their hearts cut out with an obsidian knife; the officiating priest then held the heart up as an offering to the sun. Sacrifices were also made to other gods at temples elsewhere in Tenochtitlán, and perhaps in other cities controlled by the Mexicas.

Estimates about the number of people sacrificed to Huitzilopochtli and other Mexica gods vary enormously and are impossible to verify. Both Mexica and later Spanish accounts clearly exaggerated the numbers, but most historians today assume that between several hundred and several thousand people were killed each year.

Questions for Analysis

1. How did the worship of Huitzilopochtli contribute to Aztec expansion? To hostility toward the Aztecs?

2. Why might Tlacaélel have seen it as important to destroy older texts as he created this new Aztec mythology?

Sources: León-Portilla, Miguel. *Pre-Columbian Literatures of Mexico* (Norman: University of Oklahoma Press, 1969); Clendinnen, Inga. *Mexicas: An Interpretation* (Cambridge: Cambridge University Press, 1991).

● **The Goddess Tlazolteotl** The Aztecs believed that cleanliness was a way to honor the gods, and that Tlazolteotl (sometimes called "Mother of the Gods") consumed the sins of humankind by eating refuse. She was also the goddess of childbirth. Notice the squatting position for childbirth, then common all over the world. (Dumbarton Oaks, Pre-Columbian Collection, Washington, D.C.)

tecuhtli *Provincial governors who exercised full political, judicial, and military authority on the Aztec emperor's behalf.*

The Life of the People

A wealth of information has survived about fifteenth- and sixteenth-century Mexico. The Aztecs wrote many books recounting their history, geography, and religious practices. They loved making speeches, which scribes wrote down. The Aztecs also preserved records of their legal disputes, which alone amounted to vast files. The Spanish conquerors subsequently destroyed much of this material. But enough documents remain to construct a picture of the Mexica people at the time of the Spanish intrusion.

No sharp social distinctions existed among the Aztecs during their early migrations. All were equally poor. The head of a family was both provider and warrior, and a sort of tribal democracy prevailed in which all adult males participated in important decision making. By the early sixteenth century, however, Aztec society had changed. A stratified social structure had come into being, and the warrior aristocracy exercised great authority.

Scholars do not yet understand precisely how this change occurred. According to Aztec legend, the Mexica admired the Toltecs and chose their first king, Acamapichti, from among them. The many children he fathered with Mexica women formed the nucleus of the noble class. At the time of the Spanish intrusion into Mexico, men who had distinguished themselves in war occupied the highest military and social positions in the state. Generals, judges, and governors of provinces were appointed by the emperor from among his servants who had earned reputations as war heroes. These great lords, or **tecuhtli**, dressed luxuriously and lived in palaces. The provincial governors exercised full political, judicial, and military authority on the emperor's behalf. In their territories they maintained order, settled disputes, and judged legal cases; oversaw the cultivation of land; and made sure that tribute—in food or gold—was paid. The governors also led troops in wartime. These functions resembled those of feudal lords in western Europe during the Middle Ages (see pages 367–368). Just as only nobles in France and England could wear fur and carry swords, just as gold jewelry and elaborate hairstyles for women distinguished royal and noble classes in African kingdoms, so in Mexica societies only the tecuhtli could wear jewelry and embroidered cloaks. The growth of a strong mercantile class as the empire expanded led to an influx of tropical wares and luxury goods: cotton, feathers, cocoa, skins, turquoise jewelry, and gold. The upper classes enjoyed an elegant and extravagant lifestyle.

Beneath the great nobility of soldiers and imperial officials was the class of warriors. Theoretically every free man could be a warrior, and parents dedicated their male children to war, burying a male child's umbilical cord with some arrows and a shield on the day of his birth. In actuality the sons of nobles enjoyed advantages deriving from their fathers' position and influence in the state. At the age of six, boys entered a school that trained them for war. Future warriors were taught to fight with a *macana,* a paddle-shaped wooden club edged with bits of obsidian. Youths were also trained in the use of spears, bows and arrows, and lances fitted with obsidian points. They learned to live on little food and sleep and to accept pain without complaint. At about age eighteen, a warrior fought his first campaign. If he captured a prisoner for ritual sacrifice, he acquired the title *iyac,* or warrior. If in later campaigns he succeeded in killing or capturing four of the enemy, he became a *tequiua*—one who shared in the booty and thus was a member of the nobility. If a young man failed in several campaigns to capture the required four prisoners, he joined the **maceualtin,** the plebeian or working class.

The maceualtin were the ordinary citizens—the backbone of Aztec society and the vast majority of the population. The word *maceualti* means "worker" and implies boorish speech and vulgar behavior. Members of this class performed all sorts of agricultural, military, and domestic services and carried heavy public burdens not required of noble warriors. Government officials assigned the maceualtin work on the temples, roads, and bridges. Army officers called them up for military duty, but Mexica considered this an honor and a religious rite, not a burden. Unlike nobles, priests, orphans, and slaves, maceualtin paid taxes. Maceualtin in the capital, however, possessed certain rights: they held their plots of land for life, and they received a small share of the tribute paid by the provinces to the emperor.

Beneath the maceualtin were the *tlalmaitl,* the landless workers or serfs. Some social historians speculate that this class originated during the period of migrations and upheavals following the end of the classical period (see page 271), when weak and defenseless people placed themselves under the protection of strong warriors, just as European peasants had become serfs after the end of the Roman Empire (see page 126). The tlalmaitl provided agricultural labor, paid rents in kind, and were bound to the soil—they could not move off the land. The tlalmaitl resembled in many ways the serfs of western Europe, but unlike serfs they performed military service when called on to do so. They enjoyed some rights as citizens and generally were accorded more respect than slaves.

Slaves were the lowest social class. Like Asian, European, and African slaves, most were prisoners captured in war or kidnapped from enemy tribes. But Aztecs who stole from a temple or private house or plotted against the emperor could also be enslaved, and people in serious debt sometimes voluntarily sold themselves into slavery. Female

maceualtin *The vast majority of the Aztec population; the ordinary citizens or members of the working class.*

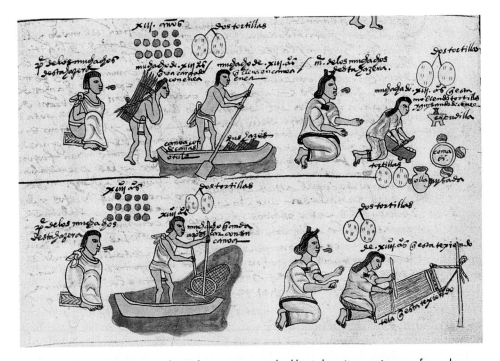

● **Aztec Youth** As shown in this codex, Aztec society had basic learning requirements for each age (indicated by dots) of childhood and youth. In the upper panel, boys of age thirteen gather firewood and collect reeds and herbs in a boat, while girls learn to make tortillas on a terra-cotta grill. At fourteen (lower panel), boys learn to fish from a boat, and girls are taught to weave. *(The Bodleian Library, University of Oxford, MS Arch. Selden. A.1, fol. 60r)*

slaves often became their masters' concubines. Mexica slaves, however, differed fundamentally from European ones, for they could possess goods, save money, buy land and houses and even slaves for their own service, and purchase their freedom. If a male slave married a free woman, their offspring were free, and a slave who escaped and managed to enter the emperor's palace was automatically free. Most slaves eventually gained their freedom. Mexica slavery, therefore, had some humane qualities and resembled slavery in Islamic societies (see pages 205–207).

Women of all social classes played important roles in Mexica society, but those roles were restricted entirely to the domestic sphere. As the little hands of the newborn male child were closed around a tiny bow and arrow indicating his warrior destiny, so the infant female's hands were wrapped around miniature weaving instruments and a small broom: weaving was a sacred and exclusively female art; the broom signaled a female's responsibility for the household shrines and for keeping the household swept and free of contamination. Almost all of the Mexica people married, a man at about twenty when he had secured one or two captives, a woman a couple of years earlier. As in premodern Asian and European societies, parents selected their children's spouses, using neighborhood women as go-betweens. Save for the few women vowed to the service of the temple, marriage and the household were a woman's fate; marriage represented social maturity for both sexes. Pregnancy became the occasion for family and neighborhood feasts, and a successful birth launched celebrations lasting from ten to twenty days.

Women were expected to pray for their husbands' success in battle while they were gone. As one prayer to Huitzilopochtli went:

O great Lord of All Things, remember your servant
Who has gone to exalt your honor and the greatness of your name.
He will offer blood in that sacrifice that is war.
Behold, Lord, that he did not go out to work for me
Or for his children . . . He went for your sake,
In your name, to obtain glory for you . . .
Give him victory in this war so that he may return
To rest in his home and so that my children and I may see
His countenance again and feel his presence."[1]

Alongside the secular social classes stood the temple priests. Huitzilopochtli and each of the numerous lesser gods had many priests to oversee the upkeep of the temple, assist at religious ceremonies, and perform ritual sacrifices. The priests also did a brisk business in foretelling the future from signs and omens. Aztecs consulted priests on the selection of wives and husbands, on the future careers of newborn babies, and before leaving on journeys or for war. Temples possessed enormous wealth in gold and silver ceremonial vessels, statues, buildings, and land. From the temple revenues and resources, the priests supported schools, aided the poor, and maintained hospitals. The chief priests had the ear of the emperor and often exercised great power and influence.

At the peak of the social pyramid stood the emperor. The various Aztec historians contradict one another about the origin of the imperial dynasty, but modern scholars tend to accept the verdict of one sixteenth-century authority that the "custom has always been preserved among the Mexicans (that) the sons of kings have not ruled by right of inheritance, but by election."[2] A small oligarchy of the chief priests, warriors, and state officials made the selection. If none of the sons proved satisfactory, a brother or nephew of the emperor was chosen, but election was always restricted to the royal family.

The Aztec emperor was expected to be a great warrior who had led Mexica and allied armies into battle. All his other duties pertained to the welfare of his people. It was up to the emperor to see that justice was done—he was the final court of appeal. He also held ultimate responsibility for ensuring an adequate food supply. The emperor Montezuma I (r. 1440–1467) distributed twenty thousand loads of stock-piled grain when a flood hit Tenochtitlán. The records show that the Aztec emperors took their public duties seriously.

The Cities of the Aztecs

When the Spanish entered **Tenochtitlán** (which they called Mexico City) in November 1519, they could not believe their eyes. According to Bernal Díaz, one of Cortés's companions:

> when we saw all those cities and villages built in the water, and other great towns on dry land, and that straight and level causeway leading to Mexico, we were astounded. These great towns and cues (temples) and buildings rising from the water, all made of stone, seemed like an enchanted vision. . . . Indeed, some of our soldiers asked whether it was not all a dream.[3]

Tenochtitlán had about sixty thousand households. The upper class practiced polygamy and had many children, and many households included servants and slaves. The total population probably numbered around 250,000. At the time, no European city and few Asian ones could boast a population even half that size. The total Aztec Empire has been estimated at around 5 million inhabitants, with the total population of Mesoamerica estimated at between 20 and 30 million.

Originally built on salt marshes, Tenochtitlán was approached by four great highways that connected it with the mainland. Bridges stood at intervals (comparable to modern Paris). Stone and adobe walls surrounded the city itself, making it (somewhat like medieval Constantinople; see page 169) highly defensible and capable of resisting

Tenochtitlán   *A large and prosperous Aztec city that was admired by the Spanish when they entered in 1519.*

● **Tenochtitlán**   The great Mexican archaeologist Ignacio Marquina designed this reconstruction of the central plaza of the Mexica city as it looked in 1519. The temple precinct, an area about 500 square yards, contained more than eighty structures, pyramids, pools, and homes of gods and of the men and women who served them. Accustomed to the clutter and filth of Spanish cities, the Spaniards were amazed by the elegance and cleanliness of Tenochtitlán. *(Enrique Franco-Torrijos)*

a prolonged siege. Wide, straight streets and canals crisscrossed the city. Boats and canoes plied the canals. Lining the roads and canals stood thousands of rectangular one-story houses of mortar faced with stucco. Although space was limited, many small gardens and parks were alive with the colors and scents of flowers.

A large aqueduct whose sophisticated engineering astounded Cortés carried pure water from distant springs and supplied fountains in the parks. Streets and canals opened onto public squares and marketplaces. Tradespeople offered every kind of merchandise. Butchers hawked turkeys, ducks, chickens, rabbits, and deer; grocers sold kidney beans, squash, avocados, corn, and all kinds of peppers. Artisans sold intricately designed gold, silver, and feathered jewelry. Seamstresses offered sandals, loincloths and cloaks for men, and blouses and long skirts for women—the clothing customarily worn by ordinary people—and embroidered robes and cloaks for the rich. Slaves for domestic service, wood for building, herbs for seasoning and medicine, honey and sweets, knives, jars, smoking tobacco, even human excrement used to cure animal skins—all these wares made a dazzling spectacle.

At one side of the central square of Tenochtitlán stood the great temple of Huitzilopochtli. Built as a pyramid and approached by three flights of 120 steps each, the temple was about one hundred feet high and dominated the city's skyline. According to Cortés, it was "so large that within the precincts, which are surrounded by a very high wall, a town of some five hundred inhabitants could easily be built. All round inside this wall there are very elegant quarters with very large rooms and corridors where their priests live."[4]

Travelers, perhaps inevitably, compare what they see abroad with what is familiar to them at home. Tenochtitlán thoroughly astounded Cortés, and in his letter to the emperor Charles V, he describes the city in comparison to his homeland: "the market square," where sixty thousand people a day came to buy and sell, "was twice as big as Salamanca"; the beautifully constructed "towers," as the Spaniards called the pyramids, rose higher "than the cathedral at Seville"; Montezuma's palace was "so marvelous that it seems to me to be impossible to describe its excellence and grandeur[;] . . . in Spain there is nothing to compare with it." Accustomed to the squalor and filth of Spanish cities, the cleanliness of Tenochtitlán dumbfounded the Spaniards, as did all the evidence of its ordered and elegant planning.[5]

> **Primary Source:**
> **Diego Durán, *From* Book of the Gods and Rites**

● ● ● ● ● ●

THE INCAS

What were the sources of strength and prosperity, and of problems, for the Incas as they created their enormous empire?

In the center of Peru rise the cold highlands of the Andes. Six valleys of fertile and wooded land at altitudes ranging from eight thousand to eleven thousand feet punctuate highland Peru. The largest of these valleys are the Huaylas, Cuzco, and Titicaca. It was there that Inca civilization developed and flourished. Like the Aztecs, the **Incas** were a small militaristic group that came to power, conquered surrounding groups, and established one of the most extraordinary empires in the world. Gradually, Inca culture spread throughout Peru.

> **Incas** *The Peruvian empire that was at its peak from 1438 until 1532.*

Earlier Peruvian Cultures

Inca achievements built on those of cultures that preceded them in the Andes and the Peruvian coast. These included the Chavin and the **Moche** civilization, which flourished along a 250-mile stretch of Peru's northern coast between 100 and 800 C.E. Rivers that flowed out of the Andes into the valleys allowed the Moche people to develop complex irrigation systems for agricultural development. Each Moche valley contained a large ceremonial center with palaces and pyramids surrounded by settlements of up to ten thousand people. The dazzling gold and silver artifacts, elaborate

> **Moche** *A Native American culture that thrived along Peru's northern coast between 100 and 800 C.E. The culture existed as a series of city-states rather than a single empire and is distinguished by an extraordinarily rich and diverse pottery industry.*

headdresses, and ceramic vessels display a remarkable skill in metalwork and pottery.

Politically, Moche culture was a series of small city-states rather than one unified state, which increased warfare. As in Aztec culture, war provided victims for human sacrifice, frequently portrayed on Moche pottery. Beginning about 500, the Moche suffered several severe *El Niños,* the change in ocean current patterns in the Pacific that brings both searing drought and flooding. Their leaders were not able to respond effectively, and the cities lost population.

In the Andes, various states developed after Chavin that were each able to carve out a slightly larger empire. They built cities around large public plazas, with temples, palaces, and elaborate stonework. Using terraces and other means to increase the amount of arable soil, they grew potatoes and other crops, even at very high altitudes. Enough food was harvested to feed not only the farmers themselves but also massive armies and administrative bureaucracies and thousands of industrial workers. These cultures were skilled at using fibers for a variety of purposes, including building boats to use on Lake Titicaca and bridges for humans and pack llamas to cross steep valleys.

Inca Imperialism

Who were the Incas? *Inca* was originally the name of the governing family of an Amerindian group that settled in the basin of Cuzco (see Map 10.5). From that family, the name was gradually extended to all peoples living in the Andes valleys. The Incas themselves used the word to identify their ruler or emperor. Here the term is used for both the ruler and the people. As with the Aztecs, so with the Incas: religious ideology was the force that transformed the culture. Religious concepts created pressure for imperialist expansion.

The Incas believed their ruler descended from the sun-god and that the health and prosperity of the state depended on him. Dead rulers were thought to link the people to the sun-god. When the ruler died, his corpse was preserved as a mummy in elaborate clothing and housed in a sacred and magnificent chamber. His royal descendants as a group managed his lands and sources of income for him and used the revenues to care for his mummy, maintain his cult, and support themselves. New rulers did not inherit these riches, so they had to win their own possessions by means of war and imperial expansion.

Around 1000 C.E. the Incas were one of many small groups fighting among themselves for land and water. The cult of royal mummies provided the impetus for expansion. The desire for conquest provided incentives for courageous (or ambitious) nobles: those who were victorious in battle and gained new territories for the state could expect lands, additional wives, servants, herds of llamas, gold, silver, fine clothes, and other symbols of high status. Even common soldiers who distinguished themselves in battle could be rewarded with booty and raised to noble status. The imperial interests of the emperor paralleled those of other social groups. Under Pachacuti Inca (1438–1471) and his successors, Inca domination was gradually extended by warfare to the frontier of present-day Ecuador and Colombia in the north and to the Maule River in present-day Chile in the south (see Map 10.5), an area of about 350,000 square miles. Eighty provinces, scores of ethnic groups, and 16 million people came under Inca control. A remarkable system of roads held the empire together.

MAP 10.5 **The Inca Empire, 1532** Beginning in the fifteenth century, the Incas expanded their holdings through warfare. They built an extensive network of roads to hold their ethnically diverse empire together.

● **Portrait Vessel of a Ruler** Artisans of the Moche culture on the northern coast of Peru produced objects representing many aspects of their world, including this flat-bottomed stirrup-spout jar with a ruler's face. The commanding expression conveys a strong sense of power, as does the elaborate headdress with the geometric designs of Moche textiles worn only by elite persons. *(South America, Peru, North Coast, Moche Culture, Portrait Vessel of a Ruler, earthenware with pigmented clay slip, 300–700, 35.6 x 24.1, Kate S. Buckingham Endowment, 1955.2338, 3/4 view. Photograph by Robert Hashimoto. Photograph © 1999, The Art Institute of Chicago)*

Quechua *First deemed the official language of the Incas under Pachacuti, it is still spoken by most Peruvians today.*

Primary Source:
Pedro de Cieza de León,
From **Chronicles:** *On the Inca*

Before Inca civilization, each group that entered the Andes valleys had its own distinct language. These languages were not written and have become extinct. Scholars will probably never understand the linguistic condition of Peru before the fifteenth century when Pachacuti made the Inca language, which the Spanish called **Quechua** (pronounced "keshwa"), the official language of his people and administration. Conquered peoples were forced to adopt the language, and Quechua spread the Inca way of life throughout the Andes. Though not written until the Spanish in Peru adopted it as a second official language, Quechua had replaced local languages by the seventeenth and eighteenth centuries and is still spoken by most Peruvians today.

Both the Aztecs and the Incas ruled very ethnically diverse peoples. Whereas the Aztecs tended to control their subject peoples through terror, the Incas governed by means of imperial unification. They imposed not only their language but also their entire panoply of gods. Magnificent temples scattered throughout the expanding empire housed images of these gods. Priests led prayers and elaborate rituals, and on such occasions as a terrible natural disaster or a great military victory, they sacrificed human beings to the gods. Subject peoples were required to worship the state gods.

Imperial unification was also achieved through the forced participation of local chieftains in the central bureaucracy and through a policy of colonization. To prevent rebellion in newly conquered territories, Pachacuti Inca and subsequent rulers transferred all their inhabitants to other parts of the empire, replacing them with workers who had lived longer under Inca rule. They drafted local men for distant wars, breaking up kin groups that had existed in Andean society for centuries.

An excellent system of roads—averaging three feet in width, some paved and others not—facilitated the transportation of armies and the rapid communication of royal orders by runners. The roads followed straight lines wherever possible but also crossed pontoon bridges and tunneled through hills. This great feat of Inca engineering bears striking comparison with Roman roads, which also linked an empire.

Ruling an empire requires a bureaucracy as well as an army, and Inca officials, tax collectors, and accountants traveled throughout the empire. They made increasingly elaborate khipus (see page 266) to record financial and labor obligations, the output of fields, population levels, land transfers, and other numerical records. Scholars have deciphered the way numbers were recorded on khipus, finding a base-ten system. Khipus may also have been used to record narrative history, but this is more speculative, as knowledge of how to read them died out after the Spanish conquest. Just as the Spanish destroyed books in Mesoamerica, they destroyed khipus in the Andes because they thought they might contain religious messages and encourage people to resist Spanish authority. About 750 Inca khipus survive today, more than half in museums in Europe.

Rapid Inca expansion, however, produced stresses. Although the pressure for growth remained unabated, open lands began to be scarce. Attempts to penetrate the tropical Amazon forest east of the Andes led to repeated military disasters. The Incas waged wars with highly trained armies drawn up in massed formation and fought pitched battles on level ground, often engaging in hand-to-hand combat. But in dense jungles, the troops could not maneuver or maintain order against enemies using guerrilla tactics and sniping at them with deadly blowguns. Another source of stress was revolts among subject peoples in conquered territories. Even the system of roads and trained runners eventually caused administrative problems. The average runner could cover about 50 leagues, or 175 miles, per day—a remarkable feat of physical endurance, especially at high altitude—but the larger the empire became, the greater the distances to be covered. The roundtrip from the capital at Cuzco to Quito in Ecuador, for example, took from ten to twelve days, so that an emperor might have to base urgent decisions on incomplete or out-of-date information. The empire was overextended.

When the Inca Huayna Capac died in 1525, his throne was bitterly contested by two of his sons, Huascar and Atauhualpa. Huascar's threat to do away with the cult of royal mummies led the nobles—who often benefited from managing land and wealth for a deceased ruler—to throw their support behind Atauhualpa. In the civil war that began in 1532, Atauhualpa's veteran warriors easily defeated Huascar's green recruits, but the conflict weakened the Incas. On his way to his coronation at Cuzco, Atauhualpa encountered Pizarro and 168 Spaniards who had recently entered the kingdom. The Spaniards quickly became the real victors in the Inca kingdom (see pages 442–443).

● **Machu Picchu**   The Inca city of Machu Picchu, surrounded by mountains in the clouds, clings to a spectacular crag in upland Peru. It was built around 1450, at the point that the Inca Empire was at its height, and abandoned about a century later. *(Will McIntyre/Photo Researchers, Inc.)*

● **An Inca Cape** Inca artisans could produce gorgeous textiles, and on ceremonial occasions nobles proudly paraded in brightly colored feathers or in garments made of luxurious alpaca wool. This exquisite cape is fashioned from the feathers of a blue and yellow macaw; the pattern, befitting aristocratic tastes, features lordly pelicans carried on litters by less exalted birds. *(The Textile Museum, Washington, D.C., 91.395. Acquired by George Hewitt Myers in 1941)*

Inca Society

ayllu *A clan; it served as the fundamental social unit of Inca society.*

curacas *The headman of the Inca clan; he was responsible for conducting relations with outsiders.*

The **ayllu,** or clan, served as the fundamental social unit of Inca society. All members of the ayllu owed allegiance to the **curacas,** or headman, who conducted relations with outsiders. The ayllu held specific lands, granted it by village or provincial authorities on a long-term basis, and individual families tended to work the same plots for generations. Cooperation in the cultivation of the land and intermarriage among members of the ayllu wove people there into a tight web of connections.

In return for the land, all men had to perform public duties and pay tribute to the authorities. Their duties included building and maintaining palaces, temples, roads, and irrigation systems. Tribute consisted of potatoes, corn, and other vegetables paid to the village head, who in turn paid them to the provincial governor. A draft rotary system called **mita** (turn) determined when men of a particular village performed public works. As the Inca Empire expanded, this pattern of social and labor organization was imposed on other, newly conquered indigenous peoples. After the conquest, the Spaniards adopted and utilized the Incas' ways of organizing their economy and administration, just as the Incas (and, in Mesoamerica, the Aztecs) had built on earlier cultures.

mita *A draft rotary system that determined when men of a particular hamlet performed public works.*

The Incas had well-established mechanisms for public labor drafts and tribute collection. The emperors sometimes gave newly acquired lands to victorious generals, distinguished civil servants, and favorite nobles. These lords subsequently exercised authority previously held by the native curacas. Whether long-time residents or new colonists, common people had the status of peasant farmers, which entailed heavy agricultural or other obligations. Just as in medieval Europe peasants worked several days each week on their lord's lands, so the Inca people had to work on state lands (that is, the emperor's lands) or on lands assigned to the temple. Peasants also labored on roads and bridges; terraced and irrigated new arable land; served on construction crews for royal palaces, temples, and public buildings such as fortresses; acted as runners on the post roads; and excavated in the imperial gold, silver, and copper mines. The imperial government annually determined the number of laborers needed for these various undertakings, and each district had to supply an assigned quota. The government also made an ayllu responsible for the state-owned granaries and for the production of cloth for army uniforms.

The state required everyone to marry and even decided when and sometimes whom a person should marry. Men married around the age of twenty, women a little younger. The Incas did not especially prize virginity; premarital sex was common. The marriage ceremony consisted of the joining of hands and the exchange of a pair of sandals. This ritual was followed by a large wedding feast at which the state presented the bride and groom with two sets of clothing, one for everyday wear and one for festive occasions. If a man or woman did not find a satisfactory mate, the provincial governor selected one for him or her. Travel was forbidden, so couples necessarily came from the same region. Like most warring societies with high male death rates, the Incas practiced polygamy, though the cost of supporting many wives restricted it largely to the upper classes.

The Incas relied heavily on local authorities and cultural norms for day-to-day matters. In some ways, however, the common people were denied choice and initiative and led regimented lives. The Incas did, however, take care of the poor and aged, distribute grain in times of shortage and famine, and supply assistance in natural disasters. Scholars have debated whether Inca society was socialistic, totalitarian, or a forerunner of the welfare state; it may be merely a matter of definition. Although the Inca economy was strictly regulated, there certainly was not an equal distribution of wealth. Everything above and beyond the masses' basic needs went to the emperor and the nobility.

The backbreaking labor of ordinary people in the fields and mines made possible the luxurious lifestyle of the great Inca nobility. The nobles—called *oregones,* or "big ears," by the Spanish because they pierced their ears and distended the lobes with heavy jewelry—were the ruling Inca's kinsmen. Lesser nobles included the curacas, royal household servants, public officials, and entertainers.

In the fifteenth century Inca rulers superimposed imperial institutions on those of kinship. They ordered allegiance to be paid to the ruler at Cuzco rather than to the curacas and relocated the entire populations of certain regions. Entirely new ayllus were formed, based on residence rather than kinship. As the empire expanded, there arose a noble class of warriors, governors, and local officials whose support the ruling Inca secured with gifts of land, precious metals, and llamas and alpacas (llamas were used as beasts of burden; alpacas were raised for their long fine wool). The nobility was exempt from agricultural work and from other kinds of public service.

Chapter Summary

Key Terms

Mesoamerica
milpa
Norte Chico
khipu
Chavin
Olmecs
Maya
Popul Vuh
Teotihuacán
Toltecs
Hohokam
Anasazi
Hopewell
Mississippian
Aztec
Nahuatl
Mexica
Huitzilopochtli
tecuhtli
maceualtin
Tenochtitlán
Incas
Moche
Quechua
ayllu
curacas
mita

> To assess your mastery of this chapter and read the primary sources listed in the margins, visit **bedfordstmartins.com/mckayworld** or see *Sources of World Societies.*

• How did early peoples in the Americas adapt to their environment as they created economic and political systems?

The environment shaped the formation of human settlements in the Americas, which began when people crossed into the Western Hemisphere from Asia. All the highly varied environments, from polar tundra to tropical rain forests, came to support human settlement. About 8000 B.C.E., people in some parts of the Americas began raising crops as well as gathering wild produce. Maize became the most important crop, with knowledge about its cultivation spreading out from Mesoamerica into North and South America.

• What physical, social, and intellectual features characterized early civilizations in the Americas?

Agricultural advancement led to an increase in population, which allowed for greater concentrations of people and the creation of the first urban societies. In certain parts of North and South America, towns dependent on agriculture flourished, especially in coastal areas and river valleys. Some in North America began to build large earthwork mounds, while those in South America practiced irrigation. The Olmecs created the first society with cities in Mesoamerica, with large ceremonial buildings, an elaborate and accurate calendar, and a system of writing.

• How did Mesoamerican and North American peoples develop prosperous and stable societies in the classical era?

The urban culture of the Olmecs and other Mesoamerican peoples influenced subsequent societies. Especially in what became known as the classical era (300–900 C.E.), various groups developed large states centered on cities, with high levels of technological and intellectual achievement. Of these, the Maya were the most long-lasting, creating a complex written language and elegant art. Peoples living in North America built communities that were smaller than those in Mesoamerica, but many also used irrigation techniques to enhance agricultural production and continued to build earthwork mounds for religious purposes.

• How did the Aztecs both build on the achievements of earlier Mesoamerican cultures and develop new traditions to create their large empire?

The Aztecs, also known as the Mexica, built a unified culture based heavily on the heritage of earlier Mesoamerican societies and distinguished by achievements in engineering, sculpture, and architecture. In Mexica society, religion was the dynamic factor that transformed other aspects of the culture: economic security, social mobility, education, and especially war. War was an article of religious faith, providing riches and land, and also sacrificial victims for ceremonies honoring the Aztec gods. Aztec society was hierarchical, with nobles and priests having special privileges. The Aztec empire centered on Tenochtitlán, the most spectacular and one of the largest cities in the world in 1500.

• What were the sources of strength and prosperity, and of problems, for the Incas as they created their enormous empire?

The Peruvian coast and Andean highlands were home to a series of cultures that cultivated cotton as well as food crops. Of these, the largest empire was created by the Incas, who began as a small militaristic group and conquered surrounding groups. The Incas established a far-flung empire that stretched along the Andes, keeping this together through a system of roads, along which moved armies and administrators. Andean society was dominated by clan groups, and Inca measures to disrupt these and move people great distances created resentment.

Suggested Reading

Clendinnen, I. *Aztecs: An Interpretation.* 1992. Pays particular attention to the role that rituals and human sacrifice played in Aztec culture.

Coe, M. *The Mayas.* 2005. A new edition of a classic survey that incorporates the most recent scholarship.

Conrad, G. W., and A. A. Demarest. *Religion and Empire: The Dynamics of Aztec and Inca Expansionism.* 1993. Compares the two largest American empires.

D'Altroy, T. *The Incas.* 2003. Examines the ways in which the Incas drew on earlier traditions to create their empire; by a leading scholar.

Freidel, D. *A Forest of Kings: The Untold Story of the Ancient Maya.* 1990. A splendidly illustrated work providing expert treatment of the Maya world.

Kehoe, Alice Beck. *America Before the European Invasion.* 2002. An excellent survey of North America before the coming of the Europeans, by an eminent anthropologist.

Knight, A. *Mexico: From the Beginnings to the Spanish Conquest.* 2002. Provides information on many Mesoamerican societies.

León-Portilla, M. *The Aztec Image of Self and Society: An Introduction to Nahua Culture.* 1992. The best appreciation of Aztec religious ritual and symbolism.

Mann, Charles C. *1491: New Revelations of the Americas Before Columbus.* 2005. A thoroughly researched overview of all the newest scholarship, written for a general audience.

Milner, G. *The Moundbuilders: Ancient Peoples of Eastern North America.* 2005. Beautifully illustrated book that discusses the mounds and the societies that built them; could also be used as a tourist guide.

Wright, R. *Time Among the Mayas.* 1989. A highly readable account of Maya agricultural and religious calendars.

Notes

1. Fray Diego Durán, *Mexicas: The History of the Indies of New Spain,* translated, with notes, by Doris Heyden and Fernand Horcasitas (New York: Orion Press, 1964), p. 203.

2. Quoted in J. Soustelle, *Daily Life of the Aztecs on the Eve of the Spanish Conquest,* trans. P. O'Brian (Stanford, Calif.: Stanford University Press, 1970), p. 89.

3. B. Díaz, *The Conquest of New Spain,* trans. J. M. Cohen (New York: Penguin Books, 1978), p. 214.

4. Quoted in J. H. Perry, *The Discovery of South America* (New York: Taplinger, 1979), pp. 161–163.

5. Quoted in I. Clendinnen, *Aztecs: An Interpretation* (New York: Cambridge University Press, 1992), pp. 16–17.

Listening to the PAST

The Death of Inca Yupanque (Pachacuti Inca) in 1471

In 1551 the Spaniard Juan de Betanzos began to write Narrative of the Incas. *Although Betanzos had only the Spanish equivalent of a grade school education when he arrived in Peru, and although he lacked dictionaries and grammar books, he had two powerful assets. First, he learned Quechua and earned a reputation for being the best interpreter and translator in postconquest Peru. Second, Betanzos had married Angelina Yupanque, an Inca noblewoman (her Inca name was Cuxirimay Ocllo) who was the widow of Atahualpa. Through her, Betanzos gained immediate and firsthand access to the Inca oral tradition. When he finished his book six years later, modern scholars believe he had produced "the most authentic chronicle that we have."*

Narrative of the Incas *provides a gold mine of information about Inca customs and social history. There is so much description of marriage, childbirth, and raising children—activities that were seen as the realm of women in both Inca and Spanish society—that scholars suspect Angelina Yupanque provided her husband with much of his information. Here is his account of the death of Inca Yupanque (Pachacuti Inca) in 1471.*

Since there were instructions for the idolatries and activities that you have heard about, Inca Yupanque ordered that immediately after he died these activities and sacrifices should be done. In addition, as soon as this was done, word should be sent to all the land, and from all the provinces and towns they should bring again all that was necessary for the service of the new lord, including gold, silver, livestock, clothing, and the rest of the things needed to replenish all the storehouses that, because of his death, had been emptied for the sacrifices and things he ordered to be done, and it should be so abundant because he realized that the state of the one who was thus Inca was growing greater.

While Inca Yupanque was talking and ordering what was to be done after he died, he raised his voice in a song that is still sung today in his memory by those of his generation. This song went as follows: "Since I bloomed like the flower of the garden, up to now I have given order and justice in this life and world as long as my strength lasted. Now I have turned into earth." Saying these words of his song, Inca Yupanque Pachacuti expired, leaving in all the land justice and order, as already stated. And his people were well supplied with idols, idolatries, and activities. After he was dead, he was taken to a town named Patallacta, where he had ordered some houses built in which his body was to be entombed. He was buried by putting his body in the earth in a large new clay urn, with him very well dressed. Inca Yupanque ordered that a golden image made to resemble him be placed on top of his tomb. And it was to be worshiped in place of him by the people who went there. Soon it was placed there. He ordered that a statue be made of his fingernails and hair that had been cut in his lifetime. It was made in that town where his body was kept. They very ceremoniously brought this statue on a litter to the city of Cuzco for the fiestas in the city. This statue was placed in the houses of Topa Inca Yupanque. When there were fiestas in the city, they brought it out for them with the rest of the statues. What is more laughable about this lord Inca Yupanque is that, when he wanted to make some idol, he entered the house of the Sun [the temple to the sun in Cuzco] and acted as though the Sun spoke to him, and he himself answered the Sun to make his people believe that the Sun ordered him to make those idols and *guacas** and so that they would worship them as such.

When the statue was in the city, Topa Inca Yupanque ordered those of his own lineage to bring this statue out for the feasts that were held in Cuzco. When they brought it out like this, they sang about the things that the Inca did in his life, both in the wars and in his city. Thus they served and revered him, changing its garments as he used to do, and serving it as he was served when he was alive. All of which was done thus.

This statue, along with the gold image that was on top of his tomb, was taken by Manco Inca from

---

*Any object, place, or person worshiped as a deity.

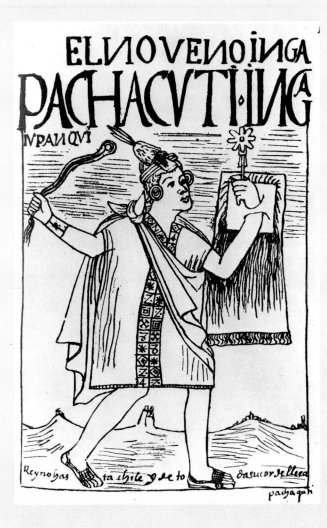

EL NOVENO INGA
PACHACVTI INGA
IVPANQVI

Reyno has · ta chile · y · se · to · · · · dasucor se lleca

pachaguh

Revered as a great conqueror and lawgiver, Pachacuti Inca here wears the sacred fringed headband symbolizing his royal authority and the large earrings of the *oregones*, the nobility. *(Pachacuti Inca, from* Nueva Coronica & Buen Gobierno, *by Guaman Poma de Ayala. Courtesy, Musée du Quai Branly/ Scala Picture Library)*

the city when he revolted. On the advice that Doña Angelina Yupanque gave to the Marquis Don Francisco Pizarro, he got it and the rest of the wealth with it. Only the body is in Patallacta at this time, and judging by it, in his lifetime he seems to have been a tall man. They say that he died at the age of one hundred twenty years. After his father's death, Topa Inca Yupanque ordered that none of the descendants of his father, Inca Yupanque, were to settle the area beyond the rivers of Cuzco. From that time until today the descendants of Inca Yupanque were called *Capacaillo Ynga Yupanque haguaynin,* which means "lineage of kings," "descendants and grandchildren of Inca Yupanque." These are the most highly regarded of all the lineages of Cuzco. These are the ones who were ordered to wear two feathers on their heads.

As time passed, this generation of *orejones* [*or-egones*]† multiplied. There were and are today many who became heads of families and renowned as firstborn. Because they married women who were not of their lineage, they took a variety of family names. Seeing this, those of Inca Yupanque ordered that those who had mixed with other people's blood should take

new family names and extra names so that [only] those of his lineage could clearly be called *Capacaillo* and descendants of Inca Yupanque.

Questions for Analysis

1. Juan de Betanzos clearly shows his disapproval of the cult of the royal mummies through his choice of words, but he also includes details that help explain its power. Judging by his description, why did people honor deceased rulers? Why did rulers (or at least Inca Yupanque) think they deserved such honors?

2. In the last paragraph, Inca Yupanque's descendants seek to limit their special title of *Capacaillo.* Why might they have done this? What effect might this have on marriage patterns among the descendants of an Inca king?

Source: Narrative of the Incas by Juan de Betanzos, trans. and ed. Roland Hamilton and Dana Buchanan from the Palma de Mallorca manuscript (Austin: University of Texas Press, 1996), pp. 138–139. Copyright © 1996. Used by permission of the University of Texas Press.

†Nobles.

Mongol Army Attacking a Walled City, from a Persian manuscript. Note the use of catapults on both sides. *(Bildarchiv Preussischer Kulturbesitz/Art Resource, NY)*

11 CENTRAL AND SOUTHERN ASIA, TO 1400

The large chunks of Asia treated in this chapter underwent profound changes during the centuries examined here. The Central Asian grasslands gave birth to nomadic confederations capable of dominating major states—first the Turks, then later, even more spectacularly, the Mongols. In the Indian subcontinent regional cultures flourished and the area had its first encounter with Islam. Southeast Asia developed several distinct cultures, most of them adopting Buddhism and other ideas and techniques from India.

Ancient India is covered in Chapter 2. This is the first chapter to treat Southeast Asia and to look at Central Asia on its own terms rather than as a problem for nearby agricultural societies.

CENTRAL ASIAN NOMADS

What gave the nomadic pastoralists of Central Asia military advantages over nearby settled civilizations?

One experience Rome, Persia, India, and China all shared was conflict with **nomads** who came from the very broad region referred to as Central Asia. This broad region was dominated by the arid **grasslands** (also called the **steppe**) that stretched from Hungary, through southern Russia and across Central Asia (today's Tajikistan, Turkmenistan, Kazakhstan, Kyrgyzstan, and Uzbekistan) and adjacent parts of China, to Mongolia and parts of north China. Easily crossed by horses but too dry for crop agriculture, the grasslands could support only a thin population of nomadic herders who lived off their flocks of sheep, goats, camels, horses, or other animals. At least twice a year they would break camp and move their animals to new pastures, in the spring moving north, in the fall south.

In their search for water and good pastures, nomadic groups often came into conflict with other nomadic groups pursuing the same resources,

nomads *Groups of people who move from place to place in search of food, water, and pasture for their animals, usually following the seasons.*

grasslands *Also called the steppe, these lands are too dry for crops but support pasturing animals.*

steppe *Another name for the grasslands that are common across much of the center of Eurasia.*

which the two would then fight over, as there was normally no higher political authority able to settle disputes. Groups on the losing end, especially if they were small, faced the threat of extermination or slavery, which prompted them to make alliances with other groups or move far away. Thus, over the centuries, the ethnic groups living in particular sections of the grasslands would change. Groups on the winning end of intertribal conflicts could exact tribute from those they defeated, sometimes so much that they could devote themselves entirely to war, leaving to their slaves and vassals the work of tending herds.

To get the products of nearby agricultural societies, especially grain, woven textiles, iron, tea, and wood, nomadic herders would trade their own products, such as horses and furs. When trade was difficult, they would turn to raiding to seize what they needed. Much of the time nomadic herders raided other nomads, but nearby agricultural settlements were common targets as well. The nomads' skill as horsemen and archers made it difficult for farmers and townsmen to defend against them. It was largely to defend against the raids of the Xiongnu nomads, for example, that the Chinese built the Great Wall (see page 134).

Political organization among nomadic herders was generally very simple. Clans had chiefs, as did tribes (which were coalitions of clans, often related to each other). Leadership within a group was based on military prowess and was often settled by fighting. Occasionally a charismatic leader would emerge who was able to extend alliances to form confederations of tribes. From the point of view of the settled societies, which have left most of the records about these nomadic groups, large confederations were much more of a threat, since they could plan coordinated attacks on cities and towns. Large confederations rarely lasted more than a century or so, however, and when they broke up, tribes again spent much of their time fighting with each other, relieving some of the pressure on their settled neighbors.

The three most wide-ranging and successful confederations were those of the Xiongnu/Huns, who emerged in the third century B.C.E. in the area near China; the Turks, who had their origins in the same area in the fourth and fifth centuries C.E.; and the Mongols, who did not become important until the late twelfth century. In all three cases, the entire steppe region was eventually swept up in the movement of peoples and armies.

The Turks

The Turks are the first of the Inner Asian peoples to have left a written record in their own language; the earliest Turkish documents date from the eighth century. Turkic languages may have already been spoken in dispersed areas of the Eurasian steppe when the Turks first appeared; today these languages are spoken by the Uighurs in western China, the Uzbeks, Kazakhs, Kyrghiz, and Turkmens of Central Asia, and the Turks of modern Turkey. The original religion of the Turks was shamanistic and involved worship of Heaven, making it similar to the religions of many other groups in the steppe region.

In 552 a group called Turks who specialized in metalworking rebelled against their overlords, the Rouruan, whose empire then dominated the region from the eastern Silk Road cities of Central Asia through Mongolia. The Turks quickly supplanted the Rouruan as overlords. When the first Turkish khagan (ruler) died a few years later, the Turkish Empire was divided between his younger brother, who took the western part (modern Central Asia), and his son, who took the eastern part (modern Mongolia). Sogdians working for the Western Turks convinced them to send embassies to both the Persian and the Byzantine courts. Repeat embassies in both directions did not prevent hostilities, however, and in 576 the Western Turks captured the Byzantine city of Bosporus in the Crimea.

The Eastern Turks frequently raided into China and just as often fought among themselves. The Chinese history of the Sui Dynasty records that "The Turks prefer to destroy each other rather than to live side-by-side. They have a thousand, nay ten thousand clans who are hostile to and kill one another. They mourn their dead with much grief and swear vengeance."[1] In the early seventh century the empire of the Eastern Turks ran up against the growing military might of the Tang Dynasty in China and soon broke apart. In the eighth century a Turkic people called the Uighurs formed a new empire based in Mongolia that survived about a century. It had close ties to Tang China, providing military aid but also extracting large payments in silk. During this period many Uighurs adopted religions then current along the Silk Road, notably Buddhism, Nestorian Christianity, and Manichaeism. In the ninth century this Uighur empire was destroyed by another Turkic people from north of Mongolia called the Kyrgyz. Some fled to what is now western China (Kansu and Xinjiang provinces). Setting up their capital city in Kucha, these Uighurs created a remarkably stable and prosperous kingdom that lasted four centuries (ca. 850–1250). Because of the dry climate of the region, many buildings, wall paintings, and manuscripts written in a variety of languages have been preserved from this era. They reveal a complex, urban civilization in which Buddhism, Manichaeism, and Christianity existed side by side, practiced by Turks as well as by Tokharians, Sogdians, and other Iranian peoples.

Farther west in Central Asia other groups of Turks, such as the Karakhanids, Ghaznavids, and Seljuks, rose to prominence. Often local Muslim forces would try to capture them, convert them, and employ them as slave soldiers (see pages 206–207). By the mid- to late tenth century many were serving in the Abbasid armies. It was also in the tenth century that Central Asian Turks began converting to Islam (which protected them from being abducted as slaves). Then they took to raiding unconverted Turks.

In the mid-eleventh century the Turks had gained the upper hand in the caliphate, and the caliphs became little more than figureheads. From there Turkish power was extended into Syria, Palestine, and other parts of the realm. (Asia Minor is now called Turkey because Turks migrated there by the thousands over several centuries.) In 1071 Seljuk Turks inflicted a devastating defeat on the Byzantine army in eastern Anatolia and even took the Byzantine emperor captive. Other Turkish confederations established themselves in Afghanistan and extended their control into north India (see page 312).

In India, Persia, and Anatolia, the formidable military skills of nomadic Turkish warriors made it possible for them to become overlords of settled societies. By the end of the thirteenth century nomad power prevailed through much of Eurasia. Just as the Uighurs developed a hybrid urban culture along the eastern end of the Silk Road, adopting many elements from the mercantile Sogdians, the Turks of Central and Western Asia created an Islamic culture that drew from both Turkish and Iranian sources. Often Persian was used as the administrative language of the states they formed. Nevertheless, despite the presence of Turkish overlords all along the southern fringe of the steppe, no one group of Turks was able to unite them all into a single

Chronology

ca. 320–480	Gupta Empire in India
ca. 380–450	Life of India's greatest poet, Kalidasa
ca. 450	White Huns invade India
ca. 500–1400	India's medieval age; caste system reaches its mature form
552	Turks rebel against Rouruan and rise to power
ca. 780	Borobudur temple complex begun in Srivijaya (modern Java)
802–1432	Khmer Empire of Cambodia
ca. 850–1250	Kingdom of the Uighurs
870–1030	Turks raid north India
939	Vietnamese gain independence from China
12th century	Buddhism declines in India
1206	Chinggis proclaimed Great Khan; Mongol language recorded
ca. 1240	*The Secret History of the Mongols*
1276	Mongol conquest of China
ca. 1300	Plague spreads throughout Mongol Empire
1405	Death of Tamerlane

political unit. That feat had to wait for the next major power on the grasslands, the Mongols.

The Mongols

In Mongolia in the twelfth century ambitious Mongols did not aspire to match the Turks or other groups that had migrated west, but rather the groups that had stayed in the east and mastered ways to extract resources from China, the largest and richest country in the region. In the tenth and eleventh centuries the Khitans had accomplished this; in the twelfth century the Jurchens had overthrown the Khitans and extended their reach even deeper into China. The Khitans and Jurchens formed hybrid nomadic-urban states, with northern sections where tribesmen continued to live in the traditional way and southern sections politically controlled by the non-Chinese rulers but settled largely by tax-paying Chinese. The Khitans and Jurchens had scripts created to record their languages and adopted many Chinese governing practices. They built cities in pastoral areas as centers of consumption and trade. In both cases, their elite became culturally dual, adept in Chinese ways as well as in their own traditions.

The Mongols lived north of these hybrid nomadic-settled societies and maintained their traditional ways. Chinese, Persian, and European observers have all left descriptions of the daily life of the Mongols, which they found strikingly different from their own. The daily life of the peasants of China, India, Vietnam, and Japan had much more in common with each other than with the Mongol pastoralists. Before considering the military conquests of the Mongols, it is useful to look more closely at their way of life.

Daily Life

Before their great conquests the Mongols did not have cities, towns, or villages. Rather, they moved with their animals between winter and summer pastures. They had to keep their belongings to a minimum because they had to be able to pack up and move everything they owned when it was time to move.

yurts *Tents in which the pastoral nomads lived; they could be quickly dismantled and loaded onto animals or carts.*

To make their settlements portable, the Mongols lived in tents called **yurts** rather than in houses. The yurts, about twelve to fifteen feet in diameter, were constructed of light wooden frames covered by layers of wool felt, greased to make them waterproof. The yurts were always round, since this shape held up better against the strong winds that blew across the treeless grasslands. They could be dismantled and loaded onto pack animals or carts in a short time. The floor of the yurt would be covered with dried grass or straw, then felt, skins, or rugs. In the center would be the hearth, directly under the smoke hole. Usually the yurt was set up with the entrance facing south. The master's bed would be on the north. Goat horns would be attached to the frame of the yurt and used as hooks to hang joints of meat, cooking utensils, bows, quivers of arrows, and the like. A group of families traveling together would set up their yurts in a circle open to the south and draw up their wagons in a circle around the yurts for protection.

For food the Mongols ate mostly animal products. Without granaries to store food for years of famine, the Mongols' survival was endangered whenever weather or diseases of their animals threatened their food supply. The most common meat was mutton, supplemented with wild game. When grain or vegetables could be obtained through trade, they were added to the diet. Wood was scarce, so the common fuel for the cook fires was dried animal dung or grasses.

The Mongols milked sheep, goats, cows, and horses and made cheese and fermented alcoholic drinks from the milk. A European visitor to Mongolia in the 1250s described how they milked mares, a practice unfamiliar to Europeans:

They fasten a long line to two posts standing firmly in the ground, and to the line they tie the young colts of the mares which they mean to milk. Then come the mothers who stand by their foals, and allow themselves to be milked. And if any of them be too unruly, then one takes her colt and puts it under her, letting it suck a while, and presently taking it away again, and the milker takes its place.[2]

He also described how they made the alcoholic drink kumiss from the milk, a drink that "goes down very pleasantly, intoxicating weak brains."[3]

Because of the intense cold of the grasslands in the winter, the Mongols made much use of furs and skins for clothing. Both men and women usually wore silk trousers and tunics (the silk obtained from China). Over these they wore robes of fur, for the very coldest times in two layers—an inner layer with the hair on the inside and an outer layer with the hair on the outside. Hats were of felt or fur, boots of felt or leather. Men wore leather belts to which their bows and quivers could be attached. Women of high rank wore elaborate headdresses decorated with feathers.

Mongol women had to work very hard and had to be able to care for the animals when the men were away hunting or fighting. They normally drove the carts and set up and dismantled the yurts. They were also the ones who milked the sheep, goats, and cows and made the butter and cheese. In addition, they made the felt, prepared the skins, and sewed the clothes. Because water was scarce, clothes were not washed with water, nor were dishes. Women, like men, had to be expert riders, and many also learned to shoot. Women participated actively in family decisions, especially as wives and mothers. In *The Secret History of the Mongols,* a work written in Mongolian in the mid-thirteenth century, Chinggis Khan's mother and wife frequently make impassioned speeches on the importance of family loyalty. (See the feature "Listening to the Past: The Abduction of Women in *The Secret History of the Mongols*" on pages 324–325.)

Mongol men kept as busy as the women. They made carts and wagons and the frames for the yurts. They also made harnesses for the horses and oxen, leather saddles, and the equipment needed for hunting and war, such as bows and arrows. Men

● **Mongol Yurt** A Chinese artist captured the essential features of a Mongol yurt to illustrate the story of a Chinese woman who married a nomad. *(The Metropolitan Museum of Art, Ex coll.: C. C. Wang Family, Gift of The Dillon Fund, 1973 [1973.120.3]. Photograph © 1994 The Metropolitan Museum of Art)*

also had charge of the horses, and they milked the mares. Young horses were allowed to run wild until it was time to break them in. Catching them took great skill in the use of a long springy pole with a noose at the end. One specialist among the nomads was the blacksmith, who made stirrups, knives, and other metal tools.

Kinship underlay most social relationships among the Mongols. Normally each family occupied a yurt, and groups of families camping together were usually related along the male line (brothers, uncles, nephews, and so on). More distant patrilineal relatives were recognized as members of the same clan and could call on each other for aid. People from the same clan could not marry each other, so men had to get wives from other clans. When a woman's husband died, she would be inherited by another male in the family, such as her husband's brother or his son by another woman. Tribes were groups of clans, often distantly related. Both clans and tribes had recognized chiefs who would make decisions on where to graze and when to retaliate against another tribe that had stolen animals or people. Women were sometimes abducted for brides. When tribes stole men from each other, they normally made them into slaves, and slaves were forced to do much of the heavy work. They would not necessarily remain slaves their entire lives, however, as their original tribes might be able to recapture them or make exchanges for them, or their masters might free them.

Even though population was sparse in the regions where the Mongols lived, conflict over resources was endemic, and each camp had to be on the alert for attacks. Defending against attacks and retaliating against raids was as much a part of the Mongols' daily life as caring for their herds and trading with nearby settlements.

Mongol children learned to ride at a young age, first riding on goats. The horses they later rode were short and stocky, almost like ponies, but nimble and able to endure long journeys and bitter cold. Even in the winter they survived by grazing, foraging beneath the snow. The prime weapon boys had to learn to use was the compound bow, which had a pull of about 160 pounds and a range of more than 200 yards. Other commonly used weapons were small battle-axes and lances fitted with hooks to pull enemies off their saddles.

From their teenage years Mongol men participated in battles, and among the Mongols courage in battle was essential to male self-esteem. Hunting was a common form of military training. Each year there would be one big hunt when mounted hunters would form a vast ring perhaps ten or more miles in circumference, then gradually shrink it down, trapping all the animals before killing them. On military campaigns a Mongol soldier had to be able to ride for days without stopping to cook food; he had to carry a supply of dried milk curd and cured meat, which could be supplemented by blood let from the neck of his horse. When time permitted, the soldiers would pause to hunt, adding to their food dogs, wolves, foxes, mice, and rats.

A common specialist among the Mongols was the shaman, a religious expert able to communicate with the gods. The high god of the Mongols was Heaven, but they recognized many other gods as well. Some groups of Mongols, especially those closer to settled communities, converted to Buddhism, Nestorian Christianity, or Manichaeism.

CHINGGIS KHAN AND THE MONGOL EMPIRE

How was the world changed by the Mongol conquests of much of Eurasia?

In the mid-twelfth century the Mongols were just one of many peoples in the eastern grasslands, neither particularly numerous nor especially advanced. Why did the Mongols suddenly emerge on the historical stage? One explanation is ecological. A drop in the mean annual temperature created a subsistence crisis. As pastures shrank, the Mongols and other nomads had to get more of their food from the agricultural world.

But the Mongols ended up getting much more than enough to eat. A second reason for their sudden rise is the appearance of a single individual, the brilliant but utterly ruthless Temujin (ca. 1162–1227), later called Chinggis.

Chinggis's early career was recorded in *The Secret History of the Mongols,* written within a few decades of his death. In Chinggis's youth his father had built up a modest following. When Chinggis's father was poisoned by a rival, his followers, not ready to follow a boy of twelve, drifted away, leaving Chinggis and his mother and brothers in a vulnerable position. In 1182 Chinggis was captured and carried in a cage to a rival's camp. After a daring midnight escape, he led his followers to join a stronger chieftain whom his father had once aided. With the chieftain's help, Chinggis began avenging the insults he had received.

As Chinggis subdued the Tartars, Kereyids, Naimans, Merkids, and other Mongol and Turkish tribes, he built up an army of loyal followers. He mastered the art of winning allies through displays of personal courage in battle and generosity to his followers. He also was willing to turn against former allies who proved troublesome. To those who opposed him, he could be merciless. He once asserted that nothing gave more pleasure than massacring one's enemies, seizing their horses and cattle, and ravishing their women. Sometimes Chinggis would kill all the men in a defeated tribe to prevent any later vendettas. At other times he would take them on as soldiers in his own armies. Courage impressed him. One of his leading generals, Jebe, first attracted his attention when he held his ground against overwhelming opposition and shot Chinggis's horse out from under him. Another prominent general, Mukhali, became Chinggis's personal slave at age twenty-seven after his tribe was defeated by Chinggis in 1197. Within a few years he was leading a corps of a thousand men from his own former tribe.

In 1206, at a great gathering of tribal leaders, Chinggis was proclaimed the **Great Khan.** He decreed that Mongol, until then an unwritten language, be written down in the script used by the Uighur Turks. With this script a record was made of the Mongol laws and customs, ranging from the rules for the annual hunt to punishments of death for robbery and adultery. Another measure adopted at this assembly was a postal relay system to send messages rapidly by mounted courier.

Great Khan *The title given to the Mongol ruler Chinggis in 1206 and later to his successors.*

With the tribes of Mongolia united, the energies previously devoted to infighting and vendettas were redirected to exacting tribute from the settled populations nearby, starting with the Jurchen (Jin) state that extended into north China (see Map 12.2 on page 334). In this Chinggis was following the precedent of the Jurchens, who had defeated the Khitans to get access to China's wealth a century earlier.

After Chinggis subjugated a city, he would send envoys to cities farther out to demand submission and threaten destruction. Those who opened their city gates and submitted without fighting could become allies and retain local power, but those who resisted faced the prospect of mass slaughter. He despised city dwellers and would sometimes use them as living shields in the next battle. After the Mongol armies swept across north China in 1212–1213, ninety-odd cities lay in rubble. Beijing, captured in 1215, burned for more than a month. Not surprisingly many governors of cities and rulers of small states hastened to offer submission.

Chinggis preferred conquest to administration and did not stay in north China to set up an administrative structure. He left that to subordinates and turned his attention westward, to Central Asia and Persia, then dominated by different groups of Turks. In 1218 Chinggis proposed to the Khwarizm shah of Persia that he accept Mongol overlordship and establish trade relations. The shah, to show his determination to resist, ordered the envoy and the merchants who had accompanied him killed. The next year Chinggis led an army of one hundred thousand soldiers west to retaliate. Mongol forces destroyed the shah's army and sacked one Persian city after another, demolishing buildings and massacring hundreds of thousands of people.

After returning from Central Asia, Chinggis died in 1227 during the siege of a city in northwest China. Before he died, he instructed his sons not to fall out among themselves but instead to divide the spoils.

Chinggis's Successors

khanates *The states ruled by a khan; the four units into which Chinggis divided the Mongol Empire.*

Although Mongol tribal leaders traditionally had had to win their positions, after Chinggis died the empire was divided into four **khanates,** with one of the lines of his descendants taking charge of each one. Chinggis's third son, Ögödei, became Great Khan, and he directed the next round of invasions.

In 1237 representatives of all four lines led 150,000 Mongol, Turkish, and Persian troops into Europe. During the next five years they gained control of Moscow and Kievan Russia and looted cities in Poland and Hungary. They were poised to attack deeper into Europe when they learned of the death of Ögödei in 1241. To participate in the election of a new khan, the army returned to the Mongols' new capital city, Karakorum.

Once Ögödei's son was certified as his successor, the Mongols turned their attention to Persia and the Middle East. In 1256 a Mongol army took northwest Iran, then pushed on to the Abbasid capital of Baghdad. When it fell in 1258, the last Abbasid caliph was murdered, and the population was put to the sword. The Mongol onslaught was successfully resisted, however, by both the Delhi sultanate (see page 312) and the Mamluk rulers in Egypt (see page 203).

Under Chinggis's grandson Khubilai (r. 1260–1294) the Mongols completed their conquest of China. South China had never been captured by non-Chinese, in large part because horses were of no strategic advantage in a land of rivers and canals. Perhaps because they were entering a very different type of terrain, the Mongols proceeded deliberately. First they surrounded the Song empire by taking its westernmost province in 1252, destroying the Nanzhao kingdom in modern Yunnan in 1254, and then continuing south and taking Annam (northern Vietnam) in 1257. A surrendered Song commander advised them to build a navy to attack the great Song cities located on rivers. During the five-year siege of a central Chinese river port, both sides used thousands of boats and tens of thousands of troops. The Mongols employed experts in naval and siege warfare from all over their empire—Chinese, Korean, Jurchen, Uighur, and Persian. Catapults designed by Muslim engineers launched a barrage of rocks weighing up to a hundred pounds each. During their advance toward the Chinese capital of Hangzhou, the Mongols ordered the total slaughter of the people of the major city of Changzhou, and in 1276 the Chinese empress dowager surrendered in hopes of sparing the people of the capital a similar fate.

Having overrun China and Korea, Khubilai turned his eyes toward Japan. In 1274 a force of 30,000 soldiers and support personnel sailed from Korea to Japan. In 1281 a combined Mongol and Chinese fleet of about 150,000 made a second attempt to conquer Japan. On both occasions the Mongols managed to land but were beaten back by Japanese samurai armies. Each time fierce storms destroyed the Mongol fleets. The Japanese claimed that they had been saved by the *kamikaze,* the "divine wind" (which later lent its name to the thousands of Japanese aviators who crashed their airplanes into American warships during World War II). A decade later, in 1293, Khubilai tried sending a fleet to the islands of Southeast Asia, including Java, but it met with no more success than the fleets sent to Japan.

Why were the Mongols so successful against so many different types of enemies? Even though their population was tiny compared to the populations of the large agricultural societies they conquered, their tactics, their weapons, and their organization all gave them advantages. Like other nomads before them, they were superb horsemen and excellent archers. Their horses were extremely nimble, able to change direction quickly, thus allowing the Mongols to maneuver easily and ride through infantry forces armed with swords, lances, and javelins. Usually the only armies that could stand up well against the Mongols were other nomadic ones like the Turks.

Marco Polo left a vivid description of the Mongol soldiers' endurance and military skill:

Mongol Conquests

1206	Chinggis made Great Khan
1215	Fall of Beijing (Jurchens)
1219–1220	Fall of Bukhara and Samarkand in Central Asia
1227	Death of Chinggis
1237–1241	Raids into eastern Europe
1257	Conquest of Annam (northern Vietnam)
1258	Conquest of Abbasid capital of Baghdad Conquest of Korea
1260	Accession of Khubilai
1274	First attempt at invading Japan
1276	Surrender of Song Dynasty (China)
1281	Second attempt at invading Japan
1293	Expedition to Java
mid-14th century	Decline of Mongol power; ouster or absorption

They are brave in battle, almost to desperation, setting little value upon their lives, and exposing themselves without hesitation to all manner of danger. Their disposition is cruel. They are capable of supporting every kind of privation, and when there is a necessity for it, can live for a month on the milk of their mares, and upon such wild animals as they may chance to catch. The men are habituated to remain on horseback during two days and two nights, without dismounting, sleeping in that situation whilst their horses graze. No people on earth can surpass them in fortitude under difficulties, nor show greater patience under wants of every kind.[4]

Primary Source: Marco Polo, *From* Travels: *Description of the World*

The Mongols were also open to new military technologies and did not insist on fighting in their traditional ways. To attack walled cities, they learned how to use catapults and other engines of war. At first they employed Chinese catapults, but when they later learned that those used by the Turks in Afghanistan were half again as powerful, they quickly adopted the better model. The Mongols also used exploding arrows and gunpowder projectiles developed by the Chinese.

Because of his early experiences with intertribal feuding, Chinggis mistrusted traditional Mongol tribal loyalties, and as he fashioned a new army, he gave it a new, nontribal structure. Chinggis also created an elite bodyguard of ten thousand sons and brothers of commanders, which served directly under him. Chinggis allowed commanders to pass their posts to their sons, but he could remove them at will. Marco Polo explained the decimal hierarchy of his armies this way:

When one of the great Tartar chiefs proceeds on an expedition, he puts himself at the head of an army of a hundred thousand horses, and organizes them in the following manner. He appoints an officer to the command of every ten men, and others to command a hundred, a thousand, and ten thousand men, respectively. Thus ten of the officers commanding ten men take their orders from him who commands a hundred; of these, each ten, from him who commands a thousand; and each ten of these latter, from him who commands ten thousand. By this arrangement each officer has only to attend to the management of ten men or ten bodies of men.[5]

The Mongols also made good use of intelligence and tried to exploit internal divisions in the countries they attacked. Thus, in north China they appealed to the Khitans, who had been defeated by the Jurchens a century earlier, to join them in attacking the Jurchens. In Syria they exploited the resentment of Christians against their Muslim rulers.

The Mongols as Rulers

The success of the Mongols in ruling vast territories was due in large part to their willingness to incorporate other ethnic groups into their armies and governments. Whatever their original country or religion, those who served the Mongols loyally were rewarded and given important posts. Uighurs, Tibetans, Persians, Chinese, and Russians came to hold powerful positions in the Mongol government. Chinese helped breach the walls of Baghdad in the 1250s, and Muslims operated the catapults that helped reduce Chinese cities in the 1270s. Mongol armies incorporated the armies they vanquished and in time had large numbers of Turkish troops.

Since, in Mongol eyes, the purpose of fighting was to gain riches, they regularly would loot the settlements they conquered, taking whatever they wanted, including the residents. Land would be granted to military commanders, nobles, and army units, to be governed and exploited as the recipients wished. Those who had worked on the land would be given to them as serfs. The Mongols built a capital city called Karakorum in modern Mongolia, and to bring it up to the level of the cities they

● **Gold-Decorated Saddle** The Mongols, like earlier nomads, prized fine metalwork. The gold panels that decorate this saddle were found in the tomb of a Mongol girl of about eighteen. The central motif of the front arch is a reclining deer; surrounding it are peonies. *(Collection of Inner Mongolia Autonomous Region Museum, Hohhot City, China)*

conquered, they transported skilled workers from those cities. For instance, after Bukhara and Samarkand were captured in 1219–1220, some thirty thousand artisans were seized and transported to Mongolia (see Map 11.1). Sometimes these slaves gradually improved their status. A French goldsmith working in Budapest named Guillaume Boucher was captured by the Mongols in 1242 and taken to Karakorum, where he lived for at least the next fifteen years. He gradually won favor and was put in charge of fifty workers to make gold and silver vessels for the Mongol court.

The traditional nomad disdain for farmers led some commanders to suggest turning north China into a gigantic pasture after it was conquered. In time, though, the Mongols came to realize that simply appropriating the wealth and human resources of the settled lands was not as good as extracting regular revenue from them. A Sinified Khitan who had been working for the Jurchens in China explained to the Mongols that collecting taxes from farmers would be highly profitable: they could extract a revenue of 500,000 ounces of silver, 80,000 bolts of silk, and more than 20,000 tons of grain from the region by taxing it. The Mongols gave this a try, but soon political rivals convinced the khan that he would gain even more by letting Central Asian Muslim merchants bid against each other for licenses to collect taxes any way they could, a system called **tax-farming**. Ordinary Chinese found this method of tax collecting much more oppressive than traditional Chinese methods, since there was little to keep the tax collectors from seizing everything they could.

tax-farming *Assigning the collection of taxes to whoever bids the most for the privilege.*

By the second half of the thirteenth century there was no longer a genuine pan-Asian Mongol Empire. Much of Asia was in the hands of Mongol successor states, but these were generally hostile to each other. Khubilai was often at war with the khanate of Central Asia, then held by his cousin Khaidu, and he had little contact with the khanate of the Golden Horde in south Russia. The Mongols adapted their methods of government to the existing traditions of each place they ruled, and the regions now went their separate ways.

In China the Mongols resisted assimilation and purposely avoided many Chinese social and political practices. The rulers conducted their business in the Mongol language and spent their summers in Mongolia. Khubilai discouraged Mongols from marrying Chinese and took only Mongol women into the palace. Some Mongol princes preferred to live in yurts erected on the palace grounds rather than in the grand palaces constructed at Beijing. Chinese were treated as legally inferior not only to the Mongols but also to all other non-Chinese.

In Central Asia, Persia, and Russia the Mongols tended to merge with the Turkish groups already there and like them converted to Islam. Russia in the thirteenth century was not a strongly centralized state, and the Mongols were satisfied to see Russian princes and lords continue to rule their territories as long as they turned over adequate tribute (which, of course, added to the burden on peasants). The city of Moscow became the center of Mongol tribute collection and grew in importance at the expense of Kiev. In the Middle East the Mongol Il-khans were more active as rulers, again continuing the traditions of the caliphate. In Mongolia itself, however, Mongol traditions were maintained.

Mongol control in each of the khanates lasted about a century. In the mid-fourteenth century the Mongol dynasty in China deteriorated into civil war, and in the 1360s the Mongols withdrew back to Mongolia. There was a similar loss of Mongol power in Persia and Central Asia. Only on the south Russian steppe was the Golden Horde able to maintain its hold for another century. As Mongol rule in Central Asia declined, a new conqueror emerged, known as Tamerlane (Timur the Lame). Not a nomad but a highly civilized Turkish noble, Tamerlane in the 1360s struck out from his base in Samarkand into Persia, north India, southern Russia, and beyond. His armies used the terror tactics that the Mongols had perfected, massacring the citizens of cities that resisted. With his death in 1405, however, Tamerlane's empire fell apart.

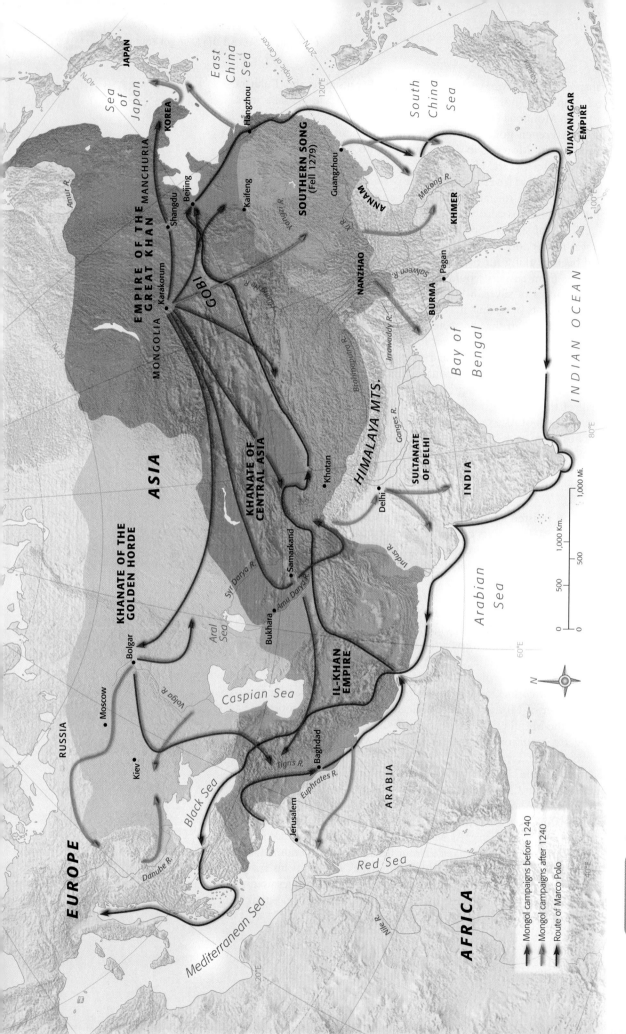

MAP 11.1 The Mongol Empire The creation of the vast Mongol Empire facilitated communication across Eurasia and led to both the spread of deadly plagues and the transfer of technical and scientific knowledge. After the death of Chinggis in 1227, the empire was divided into four khanates, ruled by different lines of his successors. In the 1270s the Mongols conquered southern China, but most of their subsequent campaigns did not lead to further territorial gains.

Mongol campaigns before 1240
Mongol campaigns after 1240
Route of Marco Polo

EAST-WEST COMMUNICATION DURING THE MONGOL ERA

How did the Mongol conquests facilitate the spread of ideas, religions, inventions, and diseases?

The Mongol governments did more than any earlier political entities to encourage the movement of people and goods across Eurasia. The Mongols had never looked down on merchants the way the elites of many traditional states did, and they welcomed the arrival of merchants from distant lands. Even when different groups of Mongols were fighting among themselves, they usually allowed caravans to pass unharassed.

The Mongol practice of transporting skilled people from the lands they conquered also brought people into contact with each other in new ways. Besides those forced to move, the Mongols recruited administrators from all over. Chinese, Persians, and Arabs served the Mongols, and the Mongols often sent them far from home. Especially prominent were the Uighur Turks of Chinese Central Asia, whose familiarity with Chinese civilization and fluency in Turkish were extremely valuable in facilitating communication. Literate Uighurs were many of the clerks and administrators running the Mongol administration.

One of the most interesting of those who served the Mongols was Rashid al-Din (ca. 1247–1318). A Jew from Persia and the son of an apothecary, Rashid al-Din converted to Islam at the age of thirty and entered the service of the Mongol Il-khan of Persia as a physician. He rose in government service, traveled widely, and eventually became prime minister. Rashid al-Din became friends with the ambassador from China, and together they arranged for translations of Chinese works on medicine, agronomy, and statecraft. He had ideas on economic management that he communicated to Mongol officials in Central Asia and China. Aware of the great differences between cultures, he believed that the Mongols should try to rule in accord with the moral principles of the majority in each land. On that basis he convinced the Mongol khan of Persia to convert to Islam. Rashid al-Din undertook to explain the great variety of cultures by writing a history of the world that was much more comprehensive than any previously written.

The Mongols were remarkably open to religious experts from all the lands they encountered. More Europeans made their way as far as Mongolia and China in the Mongol period than ever before. Popes and kings sent envoys to the Mongol court in the hope of enlisting the Mongols on their side in their long-standing conflict with Muslim forces over the Holy Land. These and other European visitors were especially interested in finding Christians who had been cut off from the West by the

● **Depictions of Europeans**   The Mongol Empire, by facilitating travel across Asia, increased knowledge of faraway lands. Rashid al-Din's *History of the World* included a history of the Franks, illustrated here with images of Western popes (*left*) conferring with Byzantine emperors (*right*). (*Topkapi Saray Museum, Ms. H.1654, fol. 303a*)

spread of Islam, and in fact there were considerable numbers of Nestorian Christians in Central Asia. In 1245 Pope Innocent IV wrote two letters to the "King and people of the Tartars" that were delivered to a Mongol general in Armenia. The next year another envoy, Giovanni di Pian de Carpine, reached the Volga River and the camp of Batu, the khan of the Golden Horde. Batu sent him on to the new Great Khan in Karakorum with two Mongol guides, riding so fast that they had to change horses five to seven times a day. Their full journey of more than three thousand miles took five and a half months. Carpine spent four months at the Great Khan's court but never succeeded in convincing the Great Khan to embrace Christianity or drop his demand that the pope appear in person to tender his submission. When Carpine returned, he wrote a report that urged preparation for a renewed Mongol attack on Europe. The Mongols had to be resisted "because of the harsh, indeed intolerable, and hitherto unheard-of slavery seen with our own eyes, to which they reduce all peoples who have submitted to them."[6]

A few years later, in 1253, Flemish friar William of Rubruck set out with the permission of King Louis IX of France as a missionary to convert the Mongols. He too made his way to Karakorum, where he found many Europeans. At Easter, Hungarians, Russians, Georgians, Armenians, and Alans all took communion in a Nestorian church. Rubruck also gathered some information about China while in Mongolia, such as the Chinese use of paper money and practice of writing with a brush.

The most famous European visitor to the Mongol lands was the Venetian Marco Polo. In his famous *Travels,* Marco Polo described all the places he visited or learned about during his seventeen years away from home. He reported being warmly received by Khubilai, who impressed him enormously. He was also awed by the wealth and splendor of Chinese cities and spread the notion of Asia as a land of riches. Even in Marco Polo's lifetime, some skeptics did not believe his tale, and today some scholars speculate that he may have learned about China from Persian merchants he met in the Middle East without actually going to China. But Marco Polo also has staunch

● **Horse and Groom** Zhao Mengfu (1254–1322), the artist of this painting and a member of the Song imperial family, took up service under the Mongol emperor Khubilai. The Mongol rulers, great horsemen themselves, would likely have appreciated this depiction of a horse buffeted by the wind. *(National Palace Museum, Taipei, Taiwan)*

defenders, even though they admit that he stretched the truth in more than one place to make himself look good. One leading Mongol scholar titled his review of the controversy "Marco Polo Went to China."[7] Regardless of the final verdict on Marco Polo's veracity, there is no doubt that the great popularity of his book contributed to European interest in finding new routes to Asia.

The more rapid transfer of people and goods across Central Asia spread more than ideas and inventions. It also spread diseases, the most deadly of which was the plague known in Europe as the Black Death. Scholars once thought that this plague was the bubonic plague, transmitted through rats and fleas, but some scholars now question that supposition. What is known is that it spread from Central Asia into West Asia, the Mediterranean, and western Europe. When the Mongols were assaulting the city of Kaffa in the Crimea in 1346, they themselves were infected by the plague and had to withdraw. They purposely spread the disease to their enemy by catapulting the bodies of victims into the city. Soon the disease was carried from port to port throughout the Mediterranean by ship. The confusion of the mid-fourteenth century that led to the loss of Mongol power in China, Iran, and Central Asia undoubtedly owes something to the effect of the spread of the plague and other diseases.

Traditionally, the historians of each of the countries conquered by the Mongols portrayed them as a scourge. Russian historians, for instance, saw this as a period of bondage that set Russia back and cut it off from western Europe. Today it is more common to celebrate the genius of the Mongol military machine and treat the spread of ideas and inventions as an obvious good, probably because we see global communication as a good in our own world. There is no reason to assume, however, that every person or every society benefited equally from the improved communications and the new political institutions of the Mongol era. Merchants involved in long-distance trade prospered, but those enslaved and transported hundreds or thousands of miles from home would have seen themselves not as the beneficiaries of opportunities to encounter cultures different from their own, but rather as the most pitiable of victims.

The places that were ruled by Mongol governments for a century or more—China, Central Asia, Persia, and Russia—do not seem to have advanced at a more rapid rate during that century than they did in earlier centuries, either economically or culturally. By Chinese standards Mongol imposition of hereditary status distinctions was a step backward from a much more mobile and open society, and placing Persians, Arabs, or Tibetans over Chinese did not arouse interest in foreign cultures. Much more foreign music and foreign styles in clothing, art, and furnishings were integrated into Chinese civilization in Tang times than in Mongol times.

In terms of the spread of technological and scientific ideas, Europe seems to have been by far the main beneficiary of increased communication, largely because in 1200 it lagged farther behind than the other areas. Chinese inventions such as printing, gunpowder, and the compass spread westward. Persian and Indian expertise in astronomy and mathematics also spread. In terms of the spread of religions, Islam

● **Kalyan Minaret** The Silk Road city of Bukhara (in today's Uzbekistan) is still graced by a 48-meter-tall minaret completed in 1127. Made of baked bricks laid in ornamental patterns, it is topped by a rotunda with sixteen arched windows, from which local Muslims were called to prayer five times a day. In times of war, the minaret could also serve as a watchtower. *(C. Rennie/Robert Harding World Imagery)*

probably gained the most. It spread into Chinese Central Asia, which had previously been Buddhist.

Perhaps because it was not invaded itself, Europe also seems to have been energized by the Mongol-imposed peace in ways that the other major civilizations were not. The goods from China and elsewhere in the East brought by merchants like Marco Polo to Europe whetted the appetites of Europeans for increased contacts with the East, and the demand for Asian goods eventually culminated in the great age of European exploration and expansion (see Chapter 15). By comparison, in areas the Mongols had directly attacked, protecting their own civilization became a higher priority than drawing from the outside to enrich or enlarge it.

INDIA (300–1400)

How did India respond to its encounters with Turks, Mongols, and Islam?

South Asia, far from the heartland of the steppe, still felt the impact of developments there. Over the course of many centuries, the Shakas, Huns, Turks, and Mongols all sent armies south to raid or invade north India.

Chapter 2 traces the early development of Indian civilization, including the emergence of the principal religious traditions of Hinduism, Buddhism, and Jainism; the impact of the Persian and Greek invasions; and the Mauryan Empire, with its great pro-Buddhist king, Ashoka. As discussed at the end of that chapter, after the Mauryan Empire broke apart in 184 B.C.E., India was politically divided into small kingdoms for several centuries.

The Gupta Empire (ca. 320–480)

In the early fourth century a state emerged in the Ganges plain that was able to bring large parts of north India under its control. The rulers of this Indian empire, the Guptas, consciously modeled their rule after that of the Mauryan Empire, and the founder took the name of the founder of that dynasty, Chandragupta. Although the Guptas never controlled as much territory as the Mauryans had, they united north India and received tribute from states in Nepal and the Indus Valley, thus giving large parts of India a period of peace and political unity.

The Guptas' administrative system was not as centralized as that of the Mauryans. In the central regions they drew their revenue from a tax on agriculture of one-quarter of the harvest and maintained monopolies on key products such as metals and salt (reminiscent of Chinese practice). They also exacted labor service for the construction and upkeep of roads, wells, and irrigation systems. More distant areas were assigned to governors who were allowed considerable leeway, and governorships often became hereditary. Areas still farther away were encouraged to become vassal states, able to participate in the splendor of the capital and royal court in subordinate roles and to engage in profitable trade, but not required to turn over much in the way of revenue.

The Gupta kings were patrons of the arts. Poets composed epics for the courts of the Gupta kings, and other writers experimented with prose romances and popular tales. India's greatest poet, Kalidasa (ca. 380–450), like Shakespeare, wrote poems as well as plays in verse. His most highly esteemed play, *Shakuntala,* concerns a daughter of a hermit who enthralls a king out hunting. The king sets up house with her, then returns to his court and owing to a curse forgets her. Only much later does he acknowledge their child as his true heir. Equally loved is Kalidasa's one-hundred-verse poem "The Cloud Messenger," about a demigod who asks a passing cloud to carry a message to his wife, from whom he has long been separated. At one point he instructs the cloud to tell her:

● **Wall Painting at Ajanta**   Many of the best surviving examples of Gupta period painting are found at the twenty-nine Buddhist cave temples at Ajanta in central India. The walls of these caves were decorated in the fifth and sixth centuries with scenes from the former lives of the Buddha. These two scenes, showing a royal couple on the right and a princess and her attendants on the left, offer us glimpses of what the royal courts of the period must have looked like. *(Benoy K. Behl)*

I see your body in the sinuous creeper, your gaze in the startled eyes of deer,
your cheek in the moon, your hair in the plumage of peacocks,
and in the tiny ripples of the river I see your sidelong glances,
but alas, my dearest, nowhere do I see your whole likeness.[8]

In mathematics, too, the Gupta period could boast of impressive intellectual achievements. The so-called Arabic numerals were actually of Indian origin. Indian mathematicians developed the place-value notation system, with separate columns for ones, tens, and hundreds, as well as a zero sign to indicate the absence of units in a given column. This system greatly facilitated calculation and spread as far as Europe by the seventh century.

The Gupta rulers were Hindus but tolerated all faiths. Buddhist pilgrims from other areas of Asia reported that Buddhist monasteries with hundreds or even thousands of monks and nuns flourished in the cities.

The great crisis of the Gupta Empire was the invasion of the Huns. The migration of these nomads from Central Asia shook much of Eurasia. Around 450 a group of them known as the White Huns thundered into India. Mustering his full might, the ruler Skandagupta (r. ca. 455–467) threw back the invaders. Although the Huns failed to uproot the Gupta Empire, they dealt the dynasty a fatal blow.

> **Primary Source:**
> **Fa-hsien, *From* A Record of Buddhistic Kingdoms**

India's Medieval Age (ca. 500–1400) and the First Encounter with Islam

After the decline of the Gupta Empire, India once again broke into separate kingdoms that were frequently at war with each other. Most of the dynasties were short-lived, but a balance of power was maintained between the four major regions of India, with none gaining enough of an advantage to conquer the others. Particularly notable are

MAP 11.2 **South and Southeast Asia in the Thirteenth Century** The extensive coastlines of South and Southeast Asia and the predictable monsoon winds aided seafaring in this region. Note the Strait of Malacca, through which most east-west sea trade passed.

the Cholas, who dominated the southern tip of the peninsula, Sri Lanka, and much of the eastern Indian Ocean to the twelfth century (see Map 11.2).

Political division fostered the development of regional cultures. Literature came to be written in regional languages, among them Marathi, Bengali, and Assamese. Commerce continued as before, and the coasts of India remained important in the sea trade of the Indian Ocean.

The first encounters with Islam occurred in this period. In 711, after pirates had plundered a richly laden Arab ship near the mouth of the Indus, the Umayyad governor of Iraq sent a force with six thousand horses and six thousand camels to seize the Sind area. The western part of India remained a part of the caliphate for centuries, but Islam did not spread much beyond this foothold. During the ninth and tenth centuries Turks from Central Asia moved into the region of today's northeastern Iran and western Afghanistan, then known as Khurasan. Converts to Islam, they first served as military forces for the caliphate in Baghdad, but as its authority weakened (see pages 200–203), they made themselves rulers of an effectively independent Khurasan and frequently sent raiding parties into north India. Beginning in 997, Mahmud of Ghazni (r. 997–1030) led seventeen annual forays into India from his base in modern Afghanistan. His goal was plunder to finance his wars against other Turkish rulers in

Central Asia. Toward this end, he systematically looted Indian palaces and temples, viewing religious statues as infidels' idols. Eventually even the Arab conquerors of the Sind fell to the Turks. By 1030 the Indus Valley, the Punjab, and the rest of northwest India were in the grip of the Turks.

The new rulers encouraged the spread of Islam, but the Indian caste system made it difficult to convert higher-caste Indians. Al-Biruni (d. 1048), a Persian scholar who spent much of his later life at the court of Mahmud and learned Sanskrit, gave some thought to the obstacles to Hindu-Muslim communication. The most basic barrier, he wrote, was language, but the religious gulf was also fundamental:

They totally differ from us in religion, as we believe in nothing in which they believe, and vice versa. On the whole, there is very little disputing about theological topics among them; at the utmost they fight with words, but they will never stake their soul or body or property on religious controversy. . . . They call foreigners impure and forbid having any connection with them, be it by intermarriage or any kind of relationship, or by sitting, eating, and drinking with them, because thereby, they think, they would be polluted.[9]

protected people *The Muslim classification used for Hindus, Christians, and Jews; they were allowed to follow their religions but had to pay a special tax.*

After the initial period of raids and destruction of temples, the Muslim Turks came to an accommodation with the Hindus, who were classed as a **protected people,** like the Christians and Jews, and allowed to follow their religion. They had to pay a special tax but did not have to perform military service. Local chiefs and rajas were often allowed to remain in control of their domains as long as they paid tribute. Most Indians looked on the Muslim conquerors as a new ruling caste, capable of governing and taxing them but otherwise peripheral to their lives. The myriad castes largely governed themselves, isolating the newcomers. Nevertheless, over the course of several centuries Islam gained a strong hold on north India, especially in the Indus Valley (modern Pakistan) and in Bengal at the mouth of the Ganges River (modern Bangladesh). Moreover, the sultanate seems to have had a positive effect on the economy. Much of the wealth confiscated from temples was put to more productive use, and India's first truly large cities emerged. The Turks also were eager to employ skilled workers, giving new opportunities to low-caste manual and artisan labor.

The Muslim rulers were much more hostile to Buddhism than to Hinduism, seeing Buddhism as a competitive proselytizing religion. In 1193 a Turkish raiding party destroyed the great Buddhist university at Nalanda in Bihar. Buddhist monks were killed or forced to flee to Buddhist centers in Southeast Asia, Nepal, and Tibet. Buddhism, which had thrived for so long in peaceful and friendly competition with Hinduism, was forced out of its native land.

Hinduism, however, remained as strong as ever. South India was largely unaffected by these invasions, and traditional Hindu culture flourished

● **Hindu Temple** Medieval Hindu temples were frequently decorated with scenes of sexual passion. Here Vishnu caresses Lakshami at the Parshvinath Temple. *(Richard Ashworth/Robert Harding World Imagery)*

there under native kings ruling small kingdoms (see the feature "Individuals in Society: Bhaskara the Teacher"). Temple-centered Hinduism flourished, as did devotional cults and mystical movements. This was a great age of religious art and architecture in India. Extraordinary temples covered with elaborate bas-relief were built in many areas. Sexual passion and the union of men and women were frequently depicted, symbolically representing passion for and union with the temple god.

In the twelfth century a new line of Turkish rulers arose in Afghanistan, led by Muhammad of Ghur (d. 1206). Muhammad captured Delhi and extended his control nearly throughout north India. When Muhammad of Ghur fell to an assassin in 1206, one of his generals, the former slave Qutb-ud-din, seized the reins of power and established a government at Delhi, separate from the government in Afghanistan. This sultanate of Delhi lasted for three centuries, even though dynasties changed several times.

The North African Muslim world traveler Ibn Battuta (1304–1368) (see page 213), who journeyed through Africa and Asia from 1325 to 1354, served for several years as a judge at the court of one of the Delhi sultans. He praised the sultan for his insistence on the observance of ritual prayers and many acts of generosity to those in need, but he also considered the sultan overly violent. Here is just one of many examples he offered of how quick the sultan was to execute:

During the years of the famine, the Sultan had given orders to dig wells outside the capital, and have grain crops sown in those parts. He provided the cultivators with the seed, as well as with all that was necessary for cultivation in the way of money and supplies, and required them to cultivate these crops for the [royal] grain-store. When the jurist 'Afif al-Din heard of this, he said, "This crop will not produce what is hoped for." Some informer told the Sultan what he had said, so the Sultan jailed him, and said to him, "What reason have you to meddle with the government's business?" Some time later he released him, and as 'Afif al-Din went to his house he was met on the way by two friends of his, also jurists, who said to him, "Praise be to God for your release," to which our jurist replied, "Praise be to God who has delivered us from the evildoers." They then separated, but they had not reached their houses before this was reported to the Sultan, and he commanded all three to be fetched and brought before him. "Take out this fellow," he said, referring to 'Afif al-Din, "and cut off his head baldrickwise," that is, the head is cut off along with an arm and part of the chest, "and behead the other two." They said to him, "He deserves punishment, to be sure, for what he said, but in our case for what crime are you killing us?" He replied, "You heard what he said and did not disavow it, so you as good as agreed with it." So they were all put to death, God Most High have mercy on them.[10]

A major accomplishment of the Delhi sultanate was holding off the Mongols. Chinggis Khan and his troops entered the Indus Valley in 1221 in pursuit of the shah of Khurasan. The sultan wisely kept out of the way, and when Chinggis left some troops in the area, the sultan made no attempt to challenge them. Two generations later, in 1299, a Mongol khan launched a campaign into India with two hundred thousand men, but the sultan of the time was able to defeat them. Two years later the Mongols returned and camped at Delhi for two months, but they eventually left without taking the sultan's fort. Another Mongol raid in 1306–1307 also was successfully repulsed.

Although the Turks by this time were highly cosmopolitan, they had retained their martial skills and understanding of steppe warfare. They were expert horsemen, and horses thrived in northwest India. The south and east of India, like the south of China, were less hospitable to raising horses and generally had to import them. In India's case, though, the climate of the south and east was well suited to elephants, which had been used as weapons of war in India since early times. Rulers in the northwest imported elephants from more tropical regions. The Delhi sultanate is said to have had as many as one thousand war elephants at its height.

During the fourteenth century, however, the Delhi sultanate was in decline and proved unable to ward off the armies of Tamerlane (see page 303), who took Delhi in

Individuals IN SOCIETY

Bhaskara the Teacher

In India, as in many other societies, astronomy and mathematics were closely linked, and many of the most important mathematicians served their rulers as astronomers. Bhaskara (1114–ca. 1185) was such an astronomer-mathematician. For generations his Brahman family had been astronomers at the Ujjain astronomical observatory in north-central India, and his father had written a popular book on astrology.

Bhaskara was a highly erudite man. A disciple wrote that he had thoroughly mastered eight books on grammar, six on medicine, six on philosophy, five on mathematics, and the four Vedas. Bhaskara eventually wrote six books on mathematics and mathematical astronomy. They deal with solutions to simple and quadratic equations and show his knowledge of trigonometry, including the sine table and relationships between different trigonometric functions, and even some of the basic elements of calculus. Earlier Indian mathematicians had explored the use of zero and negative numbers. Bhaskara developed these ideas further, in particular improving on the understanding of division by zero.

A court poet who centuries later translated Bhaskara's book titled *The Beautiful* explained its title by saying Bhaskara wrote it for his daughter named Beautiful (Lilavati) as consolation when his divination of the best time for her to marry went awry. Whether or not Bhaskara wrote this book for his daughter, many of the problems he provides in it have a certain charm:

On an expedition to seize his enemy's elephants, a king marched two yojanas the first day. Say, intelligent calculator, with what increasing rate of daily march did he proceed, since he reached his foe's city, a distance of eighty yojanas, in a week? *

Out of a heap of pure lotus flower, a third part, a fifth, and a sixth were offered respectively to the gods Siva, Vishnu, and the Sun; and a quarter was presented to Bhavani. The remaining six lotuses were given to the venerable preceptor. Tell quickly the whole number of lotus. †

If eight best variegated silk scarfs, measuring three cubits in breadth and eight in length, cost a hundred nishkas, say quickly, merchant, if thou understand trade, what a like scarf, three and a half cubits long and half a cubit wide will cost. ‡

In the conclusion to *The Beautiful*, Bhaskara wrote:

Joy and happiness is indeed ever increasing in this world for those who have The Beautiful *clasped to their*

throats, decorated as the members are with neat reduction of fractions, multiplication, and involution, pure and perfect as are the solutions, and tasteful as is the speech which is exemplified.

The observatory where Bhaskara worked in Ujjain today stands in ruins. *(Dinodia Picture Agency)*

Bhaskara had a long career. His first book on mathematical astronomy, written in 1150 when he was thirty-six, dealt with such topics as the calculation of solar and lunar eclipses or planetary conjunctions. Thirty-three years later he was still writing on the subject, this time providing simpler ways to solve problems encountered before. Bhaskara wrote his books in Sanskrit, already a literary language rather than a vernacular language, but even in his own day some of them were translated into other Indian languages.

Within a couple of decades of his death, a local ruler endowed an educational institution to study Bhaskara's works, beginning with his work on mathematical astronomy. In the text he had inscribed at the site, the ruler gave the names of Bhaskara's ancestors for six generations, as well as of his son and grandson, who had continued in his profession.

Questions for Analysis

1. What are the advantages of making occupations like astronomer hereditary?

2. Do you think there are connections between Bhaskara's broad erudition and his accomplishments as a mathematician?

*Quotations from Haran Chandra Banerji, *Colebrooke's Translation of the Lilanvanti*, 2d ed. (Calcutta: The Book Co., 1927), pp. 80–81, 30, 51, 200. The answer is that each day he must travel 22/7 yojanas farther than the day before.

†The answer is 120.

‡The answer, from the formula $x = (1 \times 7 \times 1 \times 100) / (8 \times 3 \times 8 \times 2 \times 2)$, is given in currencies smaller than the nishka: 14 drammas, 9 panas, 1 kakini, and 6⅔ cowry shells. (20 cowry shells = 1 kakini, 4 kakini = 1 pana, 16 panas = 1 dramma, and 16 drammas = 1 nishka.)

● **The God Ganesha** Known as the Destroyer of Obstacles, the elephant-headed Ganesha is one of the best-loved gods in the Hindu pantheon, invoked by those in need of a solution to a difficult situation. This stone sculpture was carved in southern India in the thirteenth century and is 37 inches tall. *(Gift of the de Young Museum Society Auxiliary, B68S4. © Asian Art Museum of San Fransisco. Used by permisson)*

1398. Tamerlane's chronicler reported that when the troops drew up for battle outside Delhi, the sultanate had 10,000 horsemen, 20,000 foot soldiers, and 120 war elephants with archers riding on them. Though alarmed at the sight of the elephants, Tamerlane's men dug trenches to trap them and also shot at their drivers. The sultan fled, leaving the city to surrender. Tamerlane took as booty all the elephants, loading them with treasures seized from the city. Ruy Gonzalez de Clavijo, an ambassador from the king of Castile who arrived in Samarkand in 1403, was greatly impressed by these well-trained elephants. "When all the elephants together charged abreast, it seemed as though the solid earth itself shook at their onrush," he observed, noting that he thought each elephant was worth a thousand foot soldiers in battle.[11]

Daily Life in Medieval India

To the overwhelming majority of people in medieval India, the size of the territory controlled by their king did not matter much. Local institutions played a much larger role in their lives than did the state. Guilds oversaw conditions of work and trade; local councils handled law and order at the town or village level; local castes gave members a sense of belonging and identity.

Like peasant societies elsewhere, including in China, Japan, and Southeast Asia, agricultural life in India ordinarily meant village life. The average farmer worked a small plot of land outside the village. All the family members pooled their resources—human, animal, and material—under the direction of the head of the family. Joint struggles strengthened family solidarity.

The agricultural year began with spring plowing. The ancient plow, drawn by two oxen wearing yokes and collars, had an iron-tipped share and a handle with which the farmer guided it. Rice, the most important and popular grain, was sown at the beginning of the long rainy season. Beans, lentils, and peas were the farmer's friends, for they grew during the cold season and were harvested in the spring when fresh food was scarce. Cereal crops such as wheat, barley, and millet provided carbohydrates and other nutrients. Sugar cane was another important crop. Some families cultivated vegetables, spices, fruit trees, and flowers in their gardens.

Cattle were raised for plowing and milk, hides, and horns, but Hindus did not slaughter them for meat. Like the Islamic and Jewish prohibition on the consumption of pork, the eating of beef was forbidden among Hindus.

Local craftsmen and tradesmen lived and worked in specific parts of a town or village. They were frequently organized into guilds, with guild heads and guild rules. The textile industries were particularly well developed. Silk (which had entered India from China), linen, wool, and cotton fabrics were produced in large quantities and traded throughout India and beyond. The cutting and polishing of precious stones was another industry associated closely with foreign trade.

In the cities shops were open to the street; families lived on the floors above. The busiest tradesmen dealt in milk and cheese, oil, spices, and perfumes. Equally prominent but disreputable were tavern keepers. Indian taverns were haunts of criminals and con artists, and in the worst of them fighting was as common as drinking. In addition to these tradesmen and merchants, a host of peddlers shuffled through towns and villages selling everything from needles to freshly cut flowers.

The Chinese Buddhist pilgrim Faxian, during his six years in Gupta India, described India as a peaceful land where people could move about freely without needing passports and where the upper castes were vegetarians. He was the first to make explicit reference to "untouchables," remarking that they hovered around the margins of Indian society, carrying gongs to warn upper-caste people of their polluting presence.

Villages were often walled, as in north China and the Middle East. The streets were unpaved, and the rainy season turned them into a muddy soup. Cattle and sheep roamed as freely as people. Some families kept pets, such as cats or parrots. Half-wild mongooses served as effective protection against snakes. The pond outside the village was its main source of water and also a spawning ground for fish, birds, and mosquitoes. Women drawing water frequently encountered water buffalo wallowing in the shallows. After the farmers returned from the fields in the evening, the village gates were closed until morning.

> **Primary Source:**
> *To Commemorate Building a Well*

In this period the caste system reached its mature form. Within the broad division into the four *varna* (strata) of Brahman, Kshatriya, Vaishya, and Shudra, the population was subdivided into numerous castes, or **jati**. Each caste had a proper occupation. In addition, its members married only within the caste and ate only with other members. Members of high-status castes feared pollution from contact with lower-caste individuals and had to undertake rituals of purification to remove the taint. Eventually Indian society comprised perhaps as many as three thousand castes. Each caste had its own governing body, which enforced the rules of the caste. Those incapable of living up to the rules were expelled, becoming outcastes. These unfortunates lived hard lives, performing tasks that others considered unclean or lowly.

jati *Indian castes.*

The life of the well-to-do is described in the *Kamasutra* (Book on the Art of Love). Comfortable surroundings provided a place for men to enjoy poetry, painting, and music in the company of like-minded friends. Well-trained courtesans added to the pleasures of the wealthy. A man who had more than one wife was advised not to let one speak ill of the other and to try to keep each of them happy by taking them to gardens, giving them presents, telling them secrets, and loving them well.

For all members of Indian society, regardless of caste, marriage and the family were the focus of life. As in China, the joint family was under the authority of the eldest male, who might take several wives. The family affirmed its solidarity by the religious ritual of honoring its dead ancestors—a ritual that linked the living and the dead, much like ancestor worship in China. People commonly lived in extended families: grandparents, uncles and aunts, cousins, and nieces and nephews all lived together in the same house or compound.

Children were viewed as a great source of happiness. The poet Kalidasa depicts children as the greatest joy of their father's life:

With their teeth half-shown in causeless laughter,
and their efforts at talking so sweetly uncertain,
when children ask to sit on his lap
a man is blessed, even by the dirt on their bodies.[12]

Children in poor households worked as soon as they were able. Children in wealthier households faced the age-old irritations of reading, writing, and arithmetic. Less attention was paid to daughters, though in more prosperous families they were often literate. Because girls who had lost their virginity could seldom hope to find good husbands and thus would become financial burdens and social disgraces to their families, daughters were customarily married as children, with consummation delayed until they reached puberty.

Wives' bonds with their husbands were so strong that it was felt a wife should have no life apart from her husband. A widow was expected to lead the hard life of the ascetic, sleeping on the ground; eating only one simple meal a day, without meat, wine, salt, or honey; wearing plain undyed clothes without jewelry; and shaving her head. She was viewed as inauspicious to everyone but her children, and she did not attend family festivals. Among high-caste Hindus, a widow would be praised for throwing herself on her husband's funeral pyre. Buddhist sects objected to this practice, called **sati,** but some writers declared that by self-immolation a widow could expunge both her own and her husband's sins, so that both would enjoy eternal bliss in Heaven.

sati *A practice whereby a high-caste Hindu woman would throw herself on her husband's funeral pyre.*

Within the home the position of a wife often depended chiefly on her own intelligence and strength of character. Wives were traditionally supposed to be humble, cheerful, and diligent even toward worthless husbands. As in other patriarchal societies, however, occasionally a woman ruled the roost. For women who did not want to accept the strictures of married life, the main way out was to join a Buddhist or Jain religious community.

SOUTHEAST ASIA, TO 1400

How did states develop along the maritime trade routes of Southeast Asia?

Much as Roman culture spread to northern Europe and Chinese culture spread to Korea, Japan, and Vietnam, in the first millennium C.E. Indian learning, technology, and material culture spread to Southeast Asia, both mainland and insular.

Southeast Asia is a tropical region that is more like India than China, with temperatures hovering around 80°F and rain falling dependably throughout the year. The topography of mainland Southeast Asia is marked by north-south mountain ranges separated by river valleys. It was easy for people to migrate south along these rivers but harder for them to cross the heavily forested mountains that divided the region into areas that had limited contact with each other. The indigenous population was originally mostly Malay, but migrations over the centuries brought many other peoples, including speakers of Austro-Asiatic, Austronesian, and Sino-Tibetan-Burmese languages, some of whom moved on to the islands offshore.

● **Bayan Relief, Angkor Wat**   Among the many relief sculptures at the amazing complex of Angkor Wat are depictions of royal processions, armies at war, trade, cooking, cockfighting, and other scenes of everyday life. In the relief shown here, the boats and fish convey something of the significance of the sea to life in Southeast Asia. *(Robert Wilson, photographer)*

The northern part of modern Vietnam was under Chinese political control off and on from the second century B.C.E. to the tenth century C.E. (see pages 153–154), but for the rest of Southeast Asia, Indian influence was of much greater significance. The first state to appear in Southeast Asia, called Funan by Chinese visitors, had its capital in southern Vietnam. In the first to sixth centuries C.E. Funan extended its control over much of Indochina and the Malay Peninsula. Merchants from northwest India would offload their goods and carry them across the narrowest part of the Malay Peninsula. The ports of Funan offered food and lodging to the merchants as they waited for the winds to shift to continue their voyages. Brahman priests and Buddhist monks from India settled along with the traders, serving the Indian population and attracting local converts. Rulers often invited Indian priests and monks to serve under them, using them as foreign experts knowledgeable about law, government, architecture, and other fields.

Sixth-century Chinese sources report that the Funan king lived in a multistory palace and the common people lived in houses built on piles with roofs of bamboo leaves. The king rode about on an elephant, but narrow boats measuring up to ninety feet long were a more important means of transportation. The people enjoyed both cockfighting and pig fighting. Instead of drawing water from wells, as the Chinese did, they made pools, from which dozens of nearby families would draw water.

After the decline of Funan, maritime trade continued to grow, and petty kingdoms appeared in many places. Indian traders frequently established small settlements, generally located on the coast. Contact with the local populations led to intermarriage and the creation of hybrid cultures. Local rulers often adopted Indian customs and values, embraced Hinduism and Buddhism, and learned **Sanskrit,** India's classical

Sanskrit *India's classical literary language.*

GLOBAL TRADE

SPICES

From ancient times on, for both Europeans and Chinese, a major reason to trade with South and Southeast Asia was to acquire spices, especially pepper, nutmeg, cloves, and cinnamon. These and other spices were in high demand not only because they could be used to flavor food but also because they were thought to have positive pharmacological properties. Unlike other highly desired products of India and farther east—such as sugar, cotton, rice, and silk—no way was found to produce the spices close to where they were in demand. Because of the location where

these spices were produced, this trade was from earliest times largely a maritime trade conducted through a series of middlemen. The spices were transported from where they were grown to nearby ports, and from there to major entrepôts, where merchants would take them in many different directions.

Two types of pepper grew in India and Southeast Asia. Black pepper is identical to our familiar pepper corns. "Long pepper," from a related plant, was hotter. The Mediterranean world imported its pepper from India; China imported it from Southeast Asia. After the discovery of the New World the importation of long pepper declined, as the chili pepper found in

The Spice Trade

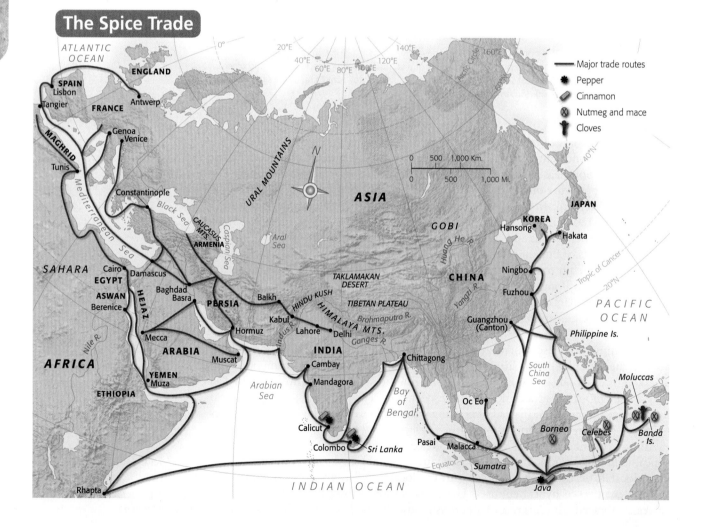

Major trade routes — Pepper — Cinnamon — Nutmeg and mace — Cloves

Mexico was at least as spicy and grew well in Europe and China.

Already in Greek and Roman times trade in pepper was substantial. According to the Greek geographer Strabo (64 B.C.E.–24 C.E.), 120 ships a year made the trip to India to acquire pepper, the round trip taking a year because they had to wait for the monsoon winds to be blowing in the right direction. Pliny in about 77 C.E. complained that the Roman Empire wasted fifty million sesterces per year on long pepper and white and black pepper combined.

Cloves and nutmeg entered the repertoire of spices somewhat later than pepper. They are interesting because they could be grown in only a handful of small islands in the eastern part of the Indonesian archipelago. Merchants in China, India, Arab lands, and Europe got them through intermediaries and did not know where they were grown. An Arab source from about 1000 C.E. reported that cloves came from an island near India that had a Valley of Cloves, and that they were acquired by a silent barter. The sailors would lay out on the beach the items they were willing to trade, and the next morning they would find cloves in their place.

The demand for these spices in time encouraged Chinese, Indian, and Arab seamen to make the trip to the Straits of Malacca or east Java. Malay seamen in small craft such as outrigger canoes would bring the spices the thousand or more miles to the major ports where foreign merchants would purchase them. This trade was important to the prosperity of the Srivijaya kingdom. The trade was so profitable, however, that it also attracted pirates.

In the Mongol era travelers like Marco Polo, Ibn Battuta, and Odoric of Pordenone reported on the cultivation and marketing of spices in the various places they visited. Ibn Battuta described pepper plants as vines planted to grow up coconut palms. He also reported seeing the trunks of cinnamon trees floated down rivers in India. Odoric reported that pepper was picked like grapes from groves so huge it would take eighteen days to walk around them. Marco Polo referred to the 7,459 islands in the China Sea that local mariners could navigate and that produced a great variety of spices as well as aromatic wood. He also reported that spices could be acquired at the great island of Java, including pepper, nutmeg, and cloves, perhaps not understanding that these had often been shipped from the innumerable small islands to Java.

Gaining direct access to the spices of the East was one of the motivations behind Christopher Columbus's voyages. Not long after, Portuguese sailors did reach India by sailing around Africa, and soon the Dutch were competing with them for control of the spice trade and setting up rival trading posts. Pepper was soon successively planted in other tropical places, including Brazil. India, however, has remained the largest exporter of spices to this day.

literary language. Sanskrit gave different peoples a common mode of written expression, much as Chinese did in East Asia and Latin did in Europe.

When the Indians entered mainland Southeast Asia, they encountered both long-settled peoples and migrants moving southward from the frontiers of China. As in other such extensive migrations, the newcomers fought one another as often as they fought the native populations. In 939 the Vietnamese finally became independent of China and extended their power southward along the coast of present-day Vietnam. The Thais had long lived in what is today southwest China and north Burma. In the eighth century the Thai tribes united in a confederacy and even expanded northward against Tang China. Like China, however, the Thai confederacy fell to the Mongols in 1253. Still farther west another tribal people, the Burmese, migrated to the area of modern Burma in the eighth century. They also established a state, which they ruled from their capital, Pagan, and came into contact with India and Sri Lanka.

The most important mainland state was the Khmer Empire of Cambodia (802–1432), which controlled the heart of the region. The Khmers were indigenous to the area. Their empire, founded in 802, eventually extended south to the sea and the northeast Malay Peninsula. Indian influence was pervasive; the impressive temple complex at Angkor Wat was dedicated to the Hindu god Vishnu. Social organization, however, was modeled not on the Indian caste system but on indigenous traditions. A large part of the population was of servile status, many descended from non-Khmer mountain tribes defeated by the Khmers. Generally successful in a long series of wars with the Vietnamese, the Khmers reached the peak of their power in 1219 and then gradually declined.

Srivijaya *A maritime empire that held the Strait of Malacca and the waters around Sumatra, Borneo, and Java.*

Far different from these land-based states was the maritime empire of **Srivijaya,** based on the island of Sumatra. From the sixth century on, it held the important Strait of Malacca, through which most of the sea traffic between China and India passed. (See the feature "Global Trade: Spices" on pages 318–319.) This state, held together as much by alliances as by direct rule, was in many ways like the Gupta state in India, securing its prominence and binding its vassals and allies through its splendor and the promise of riches through trade.

Much as the Korean and Japanese rulers adapted Chinese models (see page 157), the Srivijayan rulers drew on Indian traditions to justify their rule and organize their state. The Sanskrit writing system was used for government documents, and Indians were often employed as priests, scribes, and administrators. Using Sanskrit overcame the barriers raised by the many different native languages of the region. Indian mythology took hold, as did Indian architecture and sculpture. Kings and their courts, the first to embrace Indian culture, consciously spread it to their subjects. The Chinese Buddhist monk Yixing (d. 727) stopped at Srivijaya for six months in 671 on his way to India and for four years on his return journey. He found a thousand monks there, some of whom helped him translate Sanskrit texts.

Borobudur, the magnificent Buddhist temple complex, was begun around 780. This stone monument depicts the ten tiers of Buddhist cosmology. When pilgrims made the three-mile-long winding ascent, they passed numerous sculpted reliefs depicting the journey from ignorance to enlightenment.

After several centuries of prosperity, Srivijaya suffered a stunning blow in 1025. The Chola state in south India launched a large naval raid and captured the Srivijayan king and capital. Unable to hold their gains, the Indians retreated, but the Srivijaya Empire never regained its vigor.

Buddhism became progressively more dominant in Southeast Asia after 800. Mahayana Buddhism became important in Srivijaya and Vietnam, but Theravada Buddhism, closer to the original Buddhism of early India, became the dominant form in the rest of mainland Southeast Asia. Buddhist missionaries from India and Sri Lanka played a prominent role in these developments. Local converts continued the process by making pilgrimages to India and Sri Lanka to worship and to observe Indian life for themselves.

The Spread of Indian Culture in Comparative Perspective

The social, cultural, and political systems developed in India, China, and Rome all had enormous impact on neighboring peoples whose cultures were originally not as advanced. Some of the mechanisms for cultural spread were similar in all three cases, but differences were important as well.

In the case of Rome and both Han and Tang China, strong states directly ruled outlying regions, bringing their civilizations with them. India's states, even its largest empires, such as the Mauryan and Gupta, did not have comparable bureaucratic reach. Outlying areas tended to be in the hands of local lords who had consented to recognize the overlordship of the stronger state. Moreover, most of the time India was politically divided.

The expansion of Indian culture into Southeast Asia thus came not from conquest and extending direct political control, but from the extension of trading networks, with missionaries following along. This made it closer to the way Japan adopted features of Chinese culture, often through the intermediary of Korea. In both cases, the cultural exchange was largely voluntary, as the Japanese or Southeast Asians sought to adopt more up-to-date technologies (such as writing) or were persuaded of the truth of religious ideas they learned from foreigners.

Chapter Summary

To assess your mastery of this chapter and read the primary sources listed in the margins, visit **bedfordstmartins.com/mckayworld** or see *Sources of World Societies*.

Key Terms

nomads
grasslands
steppe
yurts
Great Khan
khanates
tax-farming
protected people
jati
sati
Sanskrit
Srivijaya

• *What gave the nomadic pastoralists of Central Asia military advantages over nearby settled civilizations?*

The nomadic pastoral societies that stretched across Eurasia had the great military advantage of being able to raise horses in large numbers and support themselves from their flocks. Their mastery of the horse and mounted archery allowed them repeatedly to overawe or conquer their neighbors. Nomadic pastoralists generally were organized on the basis of clans and tribes that selected chiefs for their military talent. Much of the time these tribes fought with each other, but several times in history leaders rose who formed larger confederations capable of coordinated attacks on cities and towns. From the fifth to the twelfth centuries, the most successful nomadic groups on the Eurasian grasslands were Turks of one sort or another.

• *How was the world changed by the Mongol conquests of much of Eurasia?*

The greatest of the nomadic military leaders was the Mongol Chinggis Khan. In the early thirteenth century, through his charismatic leadership and military genius, he was able to lead victorious armies from one side of Eurasia to another. The initial conquests were quite destructive, with the inhabitants of many cities enslaved or killed. After the empire was divided into four khanates ruled by different lines of Chinggis's descendants, more stable forms of government were developed. The Mongols rewarded loyalty and gave important positions to those willing to serve them faithfully. The Mongols did not try to change the cultures or religions of the countries they conquered. In Mongolia and China the Mongol rulers welcomed those learned in all religions. In Central Asia and Persia the Mongol khans converted to Islam and gave it the support earlier rulers there had done.

• How did the Mongol conquests facilitate the spread of ideas, religions, inventions, and diseases?

For a century Mongol hegemony fostered unprecedented East-West trade and contact. The Mongols encouraged trade and often moved craftsmen and other specialists from one place to another. More Europeans made their way east than ever before, and Chinese inventions such as printing and the compass made their way west. Because Europe was further behind in 1200, it benefited most from the spread of technical and scientific ideas. Diseases also spread, including, it seems, the plague referred to as the Black Death in Europe.

• How did India respond to its encounters with Turks, Mongols, and Islam?

India was invaded by the Mongols, but not conquered. After the fall of the Gupta Empire in about 480, India was for the next millennium ruled by small kingdoms, which allowed regional cultures to flourish. The north and northwest were frequently raided by Turks from Afghanistan or Central Asia, and for several centuries Muslim Turks ruled a state in north India called the Delhi Sultanate. Over time Islam gained adherents throughout South Asia. Hinduism continued to flourish, but Buddhism went into decline.

• How did states develop along the maritime trade routes of Southeast Asia?

Throughout the medieval period India continued to be the center of a very active seaborne trade, and this trade helped carry Indian ideas and practices to Southeast Asia. Local rulers used experts from India to establish strong states, such as the Khmer kingdom in Cambodia and the Srivijaya kingdom in Malaysia and Indonesia. Buddhism became the dominant religion throughout the region, though Hinduism also played an important role.

Suggested Reading

Abu-Lughod, Janet L. *Before European Hegemony: The World System A.D. 1250–1350.* 1989. Examines the period of Mongol domination from a global perspective.

Ali, Daud. *Courtly Culture and Political Life in Early Medieval India.* 2004. Explores the growth of royal households and the development of a courtly worldview in India from 350 to 1200.

Chaudhuri, K. N. *Asia Before Europe.* 1990. Discusses the economy and civilization of cultures within the basin of the Indian Ocean.

Findley, Carter Vaughn. *The Turks in World History.* 2005. Covers both the early Turks and the connections between the Turks and the Mongols.

Franke, Herbert, and Denis Twitchett, eds. *The Cambridge History of China,* vol. 6, *Alien Regimes and Border States.* 1994. Clear and thoughtful accounts of the Mongols and their predecessors in East Asia.

Jackson, Peter. *The Delhi Sultanate.* 2003. Provides a close examination of north India in the thirteenth and fourteenth centuries.

Jackson, Peter. *The Mongols and the West, 1221–1410.* 2005. A close examination of many different types of connections between the Mongols and both Europe and the Islamic lands.

Ratchnevsky, Paul. *Genghis Khan: His Life and Legacy.* 1992. A reliable account by a major Mongolist.

Rossabi, Morris. *Khubilai Khan: His Life and Times.* 1988. Provides a lively account of the life of one of the most important Mongol rulers.

Shaffer, Lynda. *Maritime Southeast Asia to 1500.* 1996. A short account of early Southeast Asia from a world history perspective.

Notes

1. Trans. in Denis Sinor, "The Establishment and Dissolution of the Türk Empire," in *The Cambridge History of Early Inner Asia,* ed. Denis Sinor (Cambridge: Cambridge University Press, 1990), p. 307.

2. Manuel Komroff, ed., *Contemporaries of Marco Polo* (New York: Dorset Press, 1989), p. 65.

3. Ibid.

4. *The Travels of Marco Polo, the Venetian,* ed. Manuel Komroff (New York: Boni and Liveright, 1926), p. 93.

5. Ibid., pp. 93–94.

6. Cited in John Larner, *Marco Polo and the Discovery of the World* (New Haven, Conn.: Yale University Press, 1999), p. 22.

7. Igor de Rachewiltz, "Marco Polo Went to China," *Zentralasiatische Studien* 27(1997): 34–92. See also Larner, *Marco Polo and the Discovery of the World.*

8. Quoted in A. L. Basham, *The Wonder That Was India,* 2d ed. (New York: Grove Press, 1959), p. 420. All quotations from this work are reprinted by permission of Pan Macmillan, London.

9. Edward C. Sachau, *Alberuni's India,* vol. 1 (London: Kegan Paul, 1910), pp. 19–20, slightly modified.

10. H. A. R. Gibb, *The Travels of Ibn Battuta* (Cambridge: Cambridge University Press for the Hukluyt Society, 1971), pp. 700–701.

11. Guy le Strang, trans., *Clavijo, Embassy to Tamerlane, 1403–1406* (London: Routledge, 1928), pp. 265–266.

12. Quoted in Basham, *The Wonder That Was India,* p. 161.

Listening to the
PAST

The Abduction of Women in *The Secret History of the Mongols*

Within a few decades of Chinggis Khan's death, oral traditions concerning his rise were written down in the Mongolian language. They begin with the cycles of revenge among the tribes in Mongolia, many of which began when women were abducted for wives. These passages relate how Temujin's (Chinggis's) father Yesugei seized Hogelun, Temujin's future mother, from a passing Merkid; how twenty years later three Merkids in return seized women from Temujin; and Temujin's revenge.

That year Yesugei the Brave was out hunting with his falcon on the Onan. Yeke Chiledu, a nobleman of the Merkid tribe, had gone to the Olkhunugud people to find himself a wife, and he was returning to the Merkid with the girl he'd found when he passed Yesugei hunting by the river. When he saw them riding along Yesugei leaned forward on his horse. He saw it was a beautiful girl. Quickly he rode back to his tent and just as quick returned with his two brothers, Nekun Taisi and Daritai Odchigin. When Chiledu saw the three Mongols coming he whipped his dun-colored horse and rode off around a nearby hill with the three men behind him. He cut back around the far side of the hill and rode to Lady Hogelun, the girl he'd just married, who stood waiting for him at the front of their cart. "Did you see the look on the faces of those three men?" she asked him. "From their faces it looks like they mean to kill you. As long as you've got your life there'll always be girls for you to choose from. There'll always be women to ride in your cart. As long as you've got your life you'll be able to find some girl to marry. When you find her, just name her Hogelun for me, but go now and save your own life!" Then she pulled off her shirt and held it out to him, saying: "And take this to remember me, to remember my scent." Chiledu reached out from his saddle and took the shirt in his hands. With the three Mongols close behind him he struck his dun-colored horse with his whip and took off down the Onan River at full speed.

The three Mongols chased him across seven hills before turning around and returning to Hogelun's cart. Then Yesugei the Brave grasped the reins of the cart, his elder brother Nekun Taisi rode in front to guide them, and the younger brother Daritai Odchigin rode along by the wheels. As they rode her back toward their camp, Hogelun began to cry, . . . and she cried till she stirred up the waters of the Onan River, till she shook the trees in the forest and the grass in the valleys. But as the party approached their camp Daritai, riding beside her, warned her to stop: "This fellow who held you in his arms, he's already ridden over the mountains. This man who's lost you, he's crossed many rivers by now. You can call out his name, but he can't see you now even if he looks back. If you tried to find him now you won't even find his tracks. So be still now," he told her. Then Yesugei took Lady Hogelun to his tent as his wife. . . .

[Some twenty years later] one morning just before dawn Old Woman Khogaghchin, Mother Hogelun's servant, woke with a start, crying: "Mother! Mother! Get up! The ground is shaking, I hear it rumble. The Tayichigud must be riding back to attack us. Get up!"

Mother Hogelun jumped from her bed, saying: "Quick, wake my sons!" They woke Temujin and the others and all ran for the horses. Temujin, Mother Hogelun, and Khasar each took a horse. Khachigun, Temuge Odchigin, and Belgutei each took a horse. Bogorchu took one horse and Jelme another. Mother Hogelun lifted the baby Temulun onto her saddle. They saddled the last horse as a lead and there was no horse left for [Temujin's wife] Lady Borte. . . .

Old Woman Khogaghchin, who'd been left in the camp, said: "I'll hide Lady Borte." She made her get into a black covered cart. Then she harnessed the cart to a speckled ox. Whipping the ox, she drove the cart away from the camp down the Tungelig. As the first light of day hit them, soldiers rode up and told them to stop. "Who are you?" they asked her, and Old Woman Khogaghchin answered: "I'm a servant of Temujin's. I've just come from shearing his sheep. I'm on my way back to my own tent to make felt

This portrait of Chinggis's wife, Borte, is found in a shrine to her in Mongolia. *(Courtesy of Genghis Khan Shrine, Yijinhuoluo Banner)*

from the wool." Then they asked her: "Is Temujin at his tent? How far is it from here?" Old Woman Khogaghchin said: "As for the tent, it's not far. As for Temujin, I couldn't see whether he was there or not. I was just shearing his sheep out back." The soldiers rode off toward the camp, and Old Woman Khogaghchin whipped the ox. But as the cart moved faster its axletree snapped. "Now we'll have to run for the woods on foot," she thought, but before she could start the soldiers returned. They'd made [Temujin's half brother] Belgutei's mother their captive, and had her slung over one of their horses with her feet swinging down. They rode up to the old woman shouting: "What have you got in that cart!" "I'm just carrying wool," Khogaghchin replied, but an old soldier turned to the younger ones and said, "Get off your horses and see what's in there." When they opened the door of the cart they found Borte inside. Pulling her out, they forced Borte and Khogaghchin to ride on their horses, then they all set out after Temujin. . . .

The men who pursued Temujin were the chiefs of the three Merkid clans, Toghtoga, Dayin Usun, and Khagatai Darmala. These three had come to get their revenge, saying: "Long ago Mother Hogelun was stolen from our brother, Chiledu." When they couldn't catch Temujin they said to each other: "We've got our revenge. We've taken their wives from them," and they rode down from Mount Burkhan Khaldun back to their homes. . . .

Having finished his prayer Temujin rose and rode off with Khasar and Belgutei. They rode to [his father's sworn brother] Toghoril Ong Khan of the Kereyid camped in the Black Forest on the Tula River. Temujin spoke to Ong Khan, saying: "I was attacked by surprise by the three Merkid chiefs. They've stolen my wife from me. We've come to you now to say, 'Let my father the Khan save my wife and return her.'" . . .

[Temujin and his allies] moved their forces from Botoghan Bogorjin to the Kilgho River where they built rafts to cross over to the Bugura Steppe, into [the Merkid] Chief Toghtoga's land. They came down on him as if through the smoke-hole of his tent, beating down the frame of his tent and leaving it flat, capturing and killing his wives and his sons. They struck at his door-frame where his guardian spirit lived and broke it to pieces. They completely destroyed all his people until in their place there was nothing but emptiness. . . .

As the Merkid people tried to flee from our army running down the Selenge with what they could gather in the darkness, as our soldiers rode out of the night capturing and killing the Merkid, Temujin rode through the retreating camp shouting out: "Borte! Borte!"

Lady Borte was among the Merkid who ran in the darkness and when she heard his voice, when she recognized Temujin's voice, Borte leaped from her cart. Lady Borte and Old Woman Khogaghchin saw Temujin charge through the crowd and they ran to him, finally seizing the reins of his horse. All about them was moonlight. As Temujin looked down to see who had stopped him he recognized Lady Borte. In a moment he was down from his horse and they were in each other's arms, embracing. . . .

Questions for Analysis

1. What do you learn from these stories about the Mongol way of life?

2. "Marriage by capture" has been practiced in many parts of the world. Can you infer from these stories why such a system would persist? What was the impact of such practices on kinship relations?

3. Can you recognize traces of the oral origins of these stories?

Source: Paul Kahn, trans., *The Secret History of the Mongols: The Origin of Chinghis Khan,* © Paul Kahn (Boston: Cheng & Tsui Company, 1998) Permission granted by Cheng & Tsui Company.

City Life. A well-developed system of river and canal transport kept the Song capital well supplied with goods from across China. *(The Palace Museum, Beijing)*

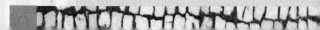

12 EAST ASIA, CA. 800–1400

Chapter Preview

The Medieval Chinese Economic Revolution (800–1100)
• *What allowed China to become a world leader economically and intellectually in this period?*

China During the Song Dynasty (960–1279)
• *How did the civil service examinations and the scholar-official class shape Chinese society and culture?*

Japan's Heian Period (794–1185)
• *How did the Heian form of government contribute to the cultural flowering of the period?*

The Samurai and the Kamakura Shogunate (1185–1333)
• *What were the causes and consequences of military rule in Japan?*

During the six centuries between 800 and 1400, East Asia was the most advanced region of the world. For several centuries the Chinese economy had grown spectacularly, and in fields as diverse as rice cultivation, the production of iron and steel, and the printing of books, China's methods of production were highly advanced. Its system of government was also advanced for its time. In the Song period the principle that the government should be in the hands of highly educated scholar-officials, selected through competitive written civil service examinations, became well established.

During the previous millennium basic elements of Chinese culture had spread beyond China's borders, creating a large cultural sphere centered on the use of Chinese as the language of civilization. Beginning around 800, however, the pendulum shifted toward cultural differentiation in East Asia, as Japan, Korea, and Vietnam developed in distinctive ways. This is particularly evident in the case of Japan, which in the samurai developed a military elite that was radically different from the Chinese scholar-official class.

THE MEDIEVAL CHINESE ECONOMIC REVOLUTION (800–1100)

What allowed China to become a world leader economically and intellectually in this period?

Chinese historians traditionally viewed dynasties as following a standard pattern. Founders were vigorous men able to recruit able followers to serve as officials and generals. Externally they would extend China's borders; internally they would bring peace. They would collect low but fairly assessed taxes. Over time, however, emperors born in the palace would get used to luxury and lack the founders' strength and wisdom. Entrenched interests would find ways to avoid taxes, forcing the government to impose heavier taxes on the poor. Impoverished peasants would flee; the morale of those in the

dynastic cycle *The theory that Chinese dynasties go through a predictable cycle, from early vigor and growth to subsequent decline as administrators become lax and the well-off find ways to avoid paying taxes, cutting state revenues.*

> **Primary Source:**
> **Chen Pu, *On the Craft of Farming***

paper money *Legal currency issued on paper; it developed in China as a convenient alternative to metal coins.*

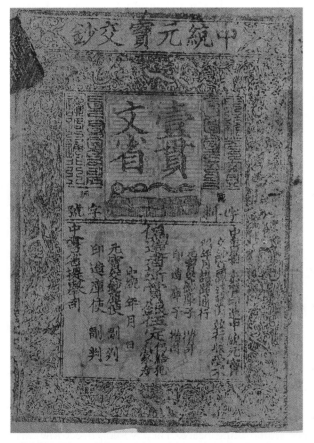

● **Chinese Paper Money** Chinese paper currency indicated the unit of currency and the date and place of issue. The Mongols continued the use of paper money; this note dates from the Mongol period. *(DNP Archives)*

government and armies would decline; and the dynasty would find itself able neither to maintain internal peace nor to defend its borders.

Viewed in terms of this theory of the **dynastic cycle**, by 800 the Tang Dynasty was in decline. It had ruled China for nearly two centuries, and its high point was in the past. A massive rebellion had wracked it in the mid-eighth century, and the Uighur Turks and Tibetans were menacing its borders. Many of the centralizing features of the government had been abandoned, with power falling more and more to regional military governors.

Chinese political theorists always made the assumption that a strong, centralized government was better than a weak one or political division, but if anything the late Tang period seems to have been both intellectually and economically more vibrant than the early Tang. Less control from the central government seems to have stimulated trade and economic growth.

In 742 China's population was still approximately 50 million, very close to what it had been in 2 C.E. Over the next three centuries, with the expansion of rice cultivation in central and south China, the country's food supply steadily increased, and so did its population, which reached 100 million by 1100. China was certainly the largest country in the world at the time; its population probably exceeded that of all of Europe (as it has ever since).

Agricultural prosperity and denser settlement patterns aided commercialization of the economy. Peasants in Song China did not aim at self-sufficiency. They had found that producing for the market made possible a better life. Peasants sold their surpluses and bought charcoal, tea, oil, and wine. In many places, farmers specialized in commercial crops, such as sugar, oranges, cotton, silk, and tea. (See the feature "Global Trade: Tea" on pages 330–331.) The need to transport the products of interregional trade stimulated the inland and coastal shipping industries, providing employment for shipbuilders and sailors and business opportunities for enterprising families with enough capital to purchase a boat. Marco Polo, the Venetian merchant who wrote of his visit to China in the late thirteenth century, was astounded at the boat traffic on the Yangzi River. He claimed to have seen no fewer than fifteen thousand vessels at one city on the river, "and yet there are other towns where the number is still greater."[1]

As marketing increased, demand for money grew enormously, leading eventually to the creation of the world's first **paper money**. The late Tang government's decision to abandon the use of bolts of silk as supplementary currency had increased the demand for copper coins. By 1085 the output of coins had increased tenfold to more than 6 billion coins a year. To avoid the weight and bulk of coins for large transactions, local merchants in late Tang times started trading receipts from deposit shops where they had left money or goods. The early Song authorities awarded a small set of shops a monopoly on the issuing of these certificates of deposit, and in the 1120s the government took over the system, producing the world's first government-issued paper money. Marco Polo was amazed:

The coinage of this paper money is authenticated with as much form and ceremony as if it were actually of pure gold or silver; for to each note a number of officers, specially appointed, not only subscribe their names, but affix their signets also; and when this has been regularly done by the whole of them, the principal officer . . . having dipped into vermilion the royal seal committed to his custody, stamps with it the piece of paper, so that the form of the seal tinged with the vermilion remains impressed upon it.[2]

With the intensification of trade, merchants became progressively more specialized and organized. They set up partnerships and joint stock companies, with a separation of owners (shareholders) and managers. In the large cities merchants were organized into guilds according to the type of product sold, and they arranged sales from wholesalers to shop owners and periodically set prices. When government officials wanted to requisition supplies or assess taxes, they dealt with the guild heads.

Foreign trade also flourished in the Song period. In 1225 the superintendent of customs at the coastal city of Quanzhou wrote an account of the foreign places Chinese merchants visited. It includes sketches of major trading cities from Srivijaya to Malabar, Cairo, and Baghdad. Pearls were said to come from the Persian Gulf, ivory from Aden, pepper from Java and Sumatra, and cotton from the various kingdoms of India. In this period Chinese ships began to displace Indian and Arab merchants in the South Seas. Ship design was improved in several ways. Watertight bulkheads improved buoyancy and protected cargo. Stern-mounted rudders improved steering. Some of the ships were powered by both oars and sails and were large enough to hold several hundred men.

Also important to oceangoing travel was the perfection of the **compass**. The way a magnetic needle would point north had been known for some time, but in Song times the needle was reduced in size and attached to a fixed stem (rather than floated in water). In some cases it was put in a small protective case with a glass top, making it suitable for sea travel. The first reports of a compass used in this way date to 1119.

The Song also witnessed many advances in industrial techniques. Heavy industry, especially iron, grew astoundingly. With advances in metallurgy, iron production reached around 125,000 tons per year in 1078, a sixfold increase over the output in 800. At first charcoal was used in the production process, leading to deforestation of parts of north China. By the end of the eleventh century, however, bituminous coke had largely taken the place of charcoal. Much of this iron was put to military purposes. Mass-production methods were used to make iron armor in small, medium, and large sizes. High-quality steel for swords was made through high-temperature metallurgy. Huge bellows, often driven by water wheels, were used to superheat the molten ore. The needs of the army also brought Chinese engineers to experiment with the use of gunpowder. In the wars against the Jurchens, those defending a besieged city used gunpowder to propel projectiles at the enemy.

The quickening of the economy fueled the growth of cities. Dozens of cities had fifty thousand or more residents, and quite a few had more than a hundred thousand. Both the capitals, Kaifeng and Hangzhou, are estimated to have had in the vicinity of

Chronology

794–1185	Heian period in Japan
804	Two Japanese Buddhist monks, Saichō and Kūkai, travel to China
960–1279	Song Dynasty in China; emergence of scholar-official class; invention of movable type
995–1027	Fujiwara Michinaga is dominant at Heian court
ca. 1010	*The Tale of Gengi,* world's first novel
1069	Wang Anshi introduces sweeping political and economic reforms
1100–1400	Zen Buddhism flourishes in Japan
1119	First reported use of compass
1120s	First government-issued paper money introduced by Song
1126	Loss of north China to the Jurchens; capital relocated to Hangzhou
1130–1200	Zhu Xi, Neo-Confucian philosopher
1185–1333	Kamakura Shogunate in Japan
ca. 1275–1292	Marco Polo travels in China

compass *A tool developed in Song times to aid in navigation at sea; it consisted of a magnetic needle that would point north in a small protective case.*

TEA

Tea is made from the young leaves and leaf buds of *Camellia sinensis,* a plant native to the hills of southwest China. As an item of trade, tea has a very long history. Already by Han times (206 B.C.E.–220 C.E.), tea was being grown and drunk in southwest China, and for several centuries thereafter it was looked on as a local product of the region with useful pharmacologic properties, such as countering the effects of wine. By Tang times (608–907) it was being widely cultivated in the Yangzi River valley and was a major item of interregional trade. Tea was common enough in Tang life that poets often mentioned it in their poems. In the eighth century Lu Yu wrote an entire treatise on the wonders of tea.

During the Tang Dynasty tea was a major commercial crop, especially in the southeast. The most intensive time for tea production was the harvest season, since young leaves were of much more value than mature ones. Mobilized for about a month each year, women would come out to help pick the tea. Not only were tea merchants among the wealthiest merchants, but from the late eighth century on, taxes on tea became a major source of government revenue.

Tea circulated in several forms, loose and compressed (brick), powder and leaf. The cost of tea varied both by form and by region of origin. In Song times (960–1279), the cheapest tea could cost as little as 18 cash per catty, the most expensive 275. In Kaifeng in the 1070s the most popular type was loose tea

The Tea Trade

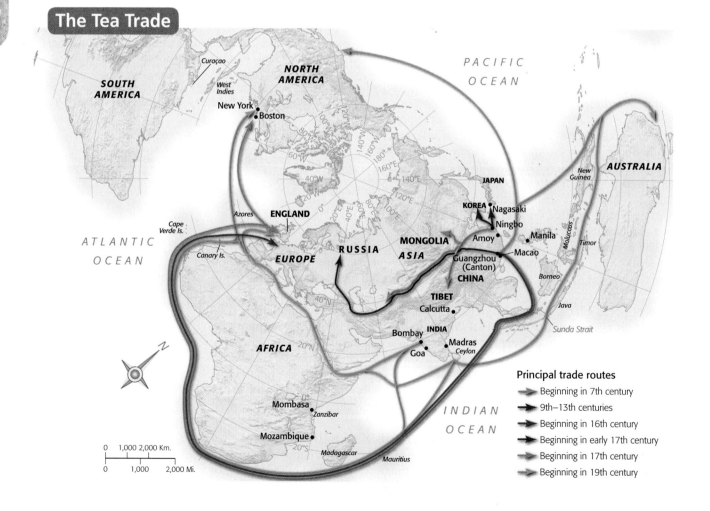

Principal trade routes

- Beginning in 7th century
- 9th–13th centuries
- Beginning in 16th century
- Beginning in early 17th century
- Beginning in 17th century
- Beginning in 19th century

powdered at water mills. The tea exported from Sichuan to Tibet, however, was formed into solid bricks.

The Song Dynasty established a government monopoly on tea. Only those who purchased government licenses could legally trade in tea. The dynasty also used its control of tea to ensure a supply of horses, needed for military purposes. The government could do this because the countries on its borders that produced the best horses—Tibet, Central Asia, Mongolia, and so on—were not suitable for growing tea. Thus the Song government insisted on horses for tea.

Tea reached Korea and Japan as a part of Buddhist culture. Buddhist monks drank it to help them stay awake during long hours of recitation or meditation. The priest Saichō, patriarch of Tendai Buddhism, visited China in 804–805 and reportedly brought back tea seeds. Tea drinking did not become widespread in Japan, however, until the twelfth century, when Zen monasteries popularized its use. By the fourteenth century tea imported from China was still prized, but the Japanese had already begun to appreciate the distinctive flavors of teas from different regions of Japan. With the development of the tea ceremony, tea drinking became an art in Japan, with much attention to the selection and handling of tea utensils. In both Japan and Korea, offerings of tea became a regular part of offerings to ancestors.

Tea did not become important in Europe until the seventeenth century. Tea first reached Russia in 1618, when a Chinese embassy presented some to the tsar. Under agreements between the Chinese and Russian governments, camel trains would arrive in China laden with furs and would return carrying tea, taking about a year for the round trip.

By 1700 Russia was receiving more than 600 camel loads of tea annually. By 1800 it was receiving more than 6,000 loads, amounting to more than 3.5 million pounds. Tea reached western Europe in the sixteenth century, both via Arabs and via Jesuit priests traveling on Portuguese ships.

In Britain, where tea drinking would become a national institution, tea was first drunk in coffeehouses. In his famous diary Samuel Pepys recorded having his first cup of tea in 1660. By the end of the seventeenth century tea made up more than 90 percent of China's exports to England. In the eighteenth century tea drinking spread to homes and tea gardens. Queen Anne (r. 1702–1714) was credited with starting the custom of drinking tea instead of ale for breakfast. In the nineteenth century afternoon tea became a central feature of British social life.

Already by the end of the eighteenth century Britain imported so much tea from China that it worried about the outflow of silver to pay for it. Efforts to balance trade with China involved promoting the sale of Indian opium to China and efforts to grow tea in British colonies. Using tea seeds collected in China and a tea plant indigenous to India's Assam province, both India and Sri Lanka eventually grew tea successfully. By the end of the nineteenth century huge tea plantations had been established in India, and India surpassed China as an exporter of tea.

The spread of the popularity of drinking tea also stimulated the desire for fine cups to drink it from. Importation of Chinese ceramics, therefore, often accompanied adoption of China's tea customs.

Primary Source:
**Zhau Rugua, *A
Description of Foreign
Peoples***

a million residents. Marco Polo described Hangzhou as the finest and most splendid city in the world. He reported that it had ten marketplaces, each half a mile long, where forty thousand to fifty thousand people would go to shop on any given day. There were also bathhouses; permanent shops selling things such as spices, drugs, and pearls; and innumerable courtesans—"adorned in much finery, highly perfumed, occupying well-furnished houses, and attended by many female domestics."[3]

The medieval economic revolution shifted the economic center of China south to the Yangzi River drainage area. This area had many advantages over the north China plain. Rice, which grew in the south, provides more calories per unit of land and therefore allows denser settlement. The milder temperatures often allowed two crops to be grown on the same plot of land, a summer and then a winter crop. The abundance of rivers and streams facilitated shipping, which reduced the cost of transportation and thus made regional specialization economically more feasible. In the first half of the Song Dynasty, the capital was still in the north, but on the Grand Canal, which linked it to the rich south.

The economic revolution of Song times cannot be attributed to intellectual change, as Confucian scholars did not reinterpret the classics to defend the morality of commerce. But neither did scholar-officials take a unified stand against economic development. As officials they had to work to produce revenue to cover government expenses such as defense, and this was much easier to do when commerce was thriving.

Ordinary people benefited from the Song economic revolution in many ways. There were more opportunities for the sons of farmers to leave agriculture and find work in cities. Those who stayed in agriculture had a better chance to improve their situations by taking up sideline production of wine, charcoal, paper, or textiles. Energetic farmers who grew cash crops such as sugar, tea, mulberry leaves (for silk), and cotton (recently introduced from India) could grow rich. Greater interregional trade led to the availability of more goods at the rural markets held every five or ten days.

Of course, not everyone grew rich. Poor farmers who fell into debt had to sell their

● **City Life**   In Song times many cities in China grew to fifty thousand or more people, and the capital, Kaifeng, reached over a million. The bustle of a commercial city is shown here in a detail from a 17-foot-long handscroll painted in the twelfth century. *(The Palace Museum, Beijing)*

● **Transplanting Rice** To get the maximum yield per plot and to make it possible to grow two crops in the same field, Chinese farmers grew rice seedlings in a seed bed and then, when a field was free, transplanted the seedlings into the flooded field. Because the Song government wanted to promote up-to-date agricultural technology, in the twelfth century it commissioned a set of twelve illustrations of the steps to be followed. This painting comes from a later version of those illustrations. *(Courtesy of the Freer Gallery of Art, Smithsonian Institution, Washington, D.C. [54.21])*

land, and if they still owed money, they could be forced to sell their daughters as maids, concubines, or prostitutes. The prosperity of the cities created a huge demand for women to serve the rich in these ways, and Song sources mention that criminals would kidnap girls and women to sell in distant cities at huge profits.

CHINA DURING THE SONG DYNASTY (960–1279)

How did the civil service examinations and the scholar-official class shape Chinese society and culture?

In the tenth century Tang China broke up into separate contending states, some of which had non-Chinese rulers. The two states that proved to be long lasting were the Song, which came to control almost all of China proper south of the Great Wall, and the Liao, whose ruling house was Khitan and who held the territory of modern Beijing and areas north (see Map 12.1). Although the Song Dynasty had a much larger population, the Liao was militarily the stronger of the two.

The founder of the Song Dynasty, Taizu (r. 960–976), was a general whose troops elevated him to emperor (somewhat reminiscent of Roman practice). Taizu worked to make sure that such an act could not happen in the future by placing the armies under central government control. He retired or rotated his own generals and assigned civil officials to supervise them. In time civil bureaucrats came to dominate every aspect of Song government and society. The civil service examination system was greatly expanded to provide the dynasty with a constant flow of men trained in the Confucian classics.

Curbing the generals ended warlordism but did not solve the military problem of defending against the Khitans to the north. After several attempts to push them back beyond the Great Wall, the Song concluded a peace treaty with them. The Song agreed to make huge annual payments of gold and silk to the Khitans, in a sense paying them

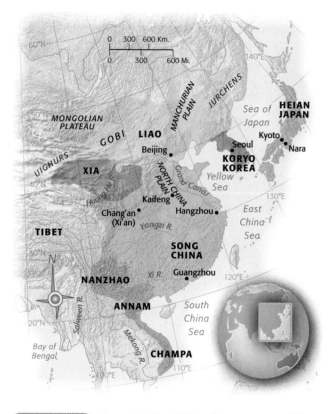

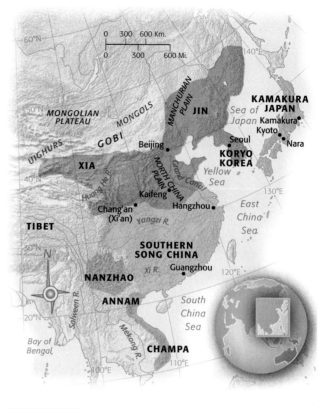

MAP 12.1 **East Asia in 1000** The Song Empire did not extend as far as its predecessor, the Tang, and faced powerful rivals to the north—the Liao Dynasty of the Khitans and the Xia Dynasty of the Tanguts. Korea under the Koryo Dynasty maintained regular contact with Song China, but Japan, by the late Heian period, was no longer deeply involved with the mainland.

MAP 12.2 **East Asia in 1200** By 1200 military families dominated both Korea and Japan, but their borders were little changed. On the mainland, the Liao Dynasty had been overthrown by the Jurchens' Jin Dynasty, which also seized the northern third of the Song Empire. Because the Song relocated its capital to Hangzhou in the south, this period is called the Southern Song period.

not to invade. Even so, the Song rulers had to maintain a standing army of more than a million men. By the middle of the eleventh century military expenses consumed half the government's revenues. Song had the industrial base to produce swords, armor, and arrowheads in huge quantities, but had difficulty maintaining enough horses and well-trained horsemen. Even though China was the economic powerhouse of the region with by far the largest population, in this period, when the horse was a major weapon of war, it was not easy to convert wealth to military advantage.

In the early twelfth century the military situation rapidly worsened when the Khitan state was destroyed by another tribal confederation led by the Jurchens. Although the Song allied with the Jurchens, the Jurchens quickly realized how easy it would be to defeat the Song. When they marched into the Song capital in 1126, they captured the emperor and took him and his entire court hostage. Song forces rallied around a prince who reestablished a Song court in the south at Hangzhou (see Map 12.2). This Southern Song Dynasty controlled only about two-thirds of the former Song territories, but the social, cultural, and intellectual life there remained vibrant until the Song fell to the Mongols in 1279.

The Scholar-Officials and Neo-Confucianism

The Song period saw the full flowering of one of the most distinctive features of Chinese civilization, the scholar-official class certified through highly competitive civil service examinations. This elite was both broader and better educated than the elites of earlier periods in Chinese history. Once the **examination system** was fully developed, aristocratic habits and prejudices largely disappeared.

The invention of printing should be given some credit for this development. Tang craftsmen developed the art of carving words and pictures into wooden blocks, inking the blocks, and then pressing paper onto them. Each block held an entire page of text and illustrations. Such whole-page blocks were used for printing as early as the middle of the ninth century, and in the eleventh century **movable type** (one piece of type for each character) was invented. Movable type was never widely used in China because whole-block printing was cheaper. In China as in Europe, the introduction of printing dramatically lowered the price of books, thus aiding the spread of literacy.

Among the upper class the availability of cheaper books enabled scholars to amass their own libraries. Song publishers printed the classics of Chinese literature in huge editions to satisfy scholarly appetites. Works on philosophy, science, and medicine also were avidly consumed, as were Buddhist texts. Han and Tang poetry and historical works became the models for Song writers. One popular literary innovation was the encyclopedia, which first appeared in the Song period, at least five centuries before publication of a European encyclopedia.

The examination system came to carry such prestige that the number of scholars entering each competition escalated rapidly, from fewer than 30,000 early in the eleventh century, to nearly 80,000 by the end of that century, to about 400,000 by the dynasty's end. To prepare for the examinations, men had to memorize the classics in order to be able to recognize even the most obscure passages. They also had to master specific forms of composition, including poetry, and be ready to discuss policy issues, citing appropriate historical examples. Those who became officials this way had usually tried the exams several times and were on average a little over thirty years of age when they succeeded. The great majority of those who devoted years to preparing for the exams, however, never became officials.

The life of the educated man involved more than study for the civil service examinations. Many took to refined pursuits such as collecting antiques or old books and

examination system *A system of selecting officials based on competitive written examinations.*

movable type *A system of printing in which one piece of type was used for each unique character.*

● **On a Mountain Path in Spring** With spare, sketchy strokes, the court painter Ma Yuan (ca. 1190–1225) depicts a scholar on an outing accompanied by his boy servant carrying a lute. The scholar gazes into the mist, his eyes attracted by a bird in flight. The poetic couplet was inscribed by Emperor Ningzong (r. 1194–1124), at whose court Ma Yuan served. *(National Palace Museum, Taipei, Taiwan)*

practicing the arts—especially poetry writing, calligraphy, and painting. For many individuals these cultural interests overshadowed any philosophical, political, or economic concerns; others found in them occasional outlets for creative activity and aesthetic pleasure. In the Song period the engagement of the elite with the arts led to extraordinary achievement in calligraphy and painting, especially landscape painting. A large share of the informal social life of upper-class men was centered on these refined pastimes, as they gathered to compose or criticize poetry, to view each other's treasures, and to patronize young talents.

The new scholar-official elite produced some extraordinary men, able to hold high court offices while pursuing diverse intellectual interests. (See the feature "Individuals in Society: Shen Gua.") Ouyang Xiu spared time in his busy official career to write love songs, histories, and the first analytical catalogue of rubbings of ancient stone and bronze inscriptions. Sima Guang, besides serving as prime minister, wrote a narrative history of China from the Warring States Period (403–221 B.C.E.) to the founding of the Song Dynasty. Su Shi wrote more than twenty-seven hundred poems and eight hundred letters while active in opposition politics. He was also an esteemed painter, calligrapher, and theorist of the arts. Su Song, another high official, constructed an eighty-foot-tall mechanical clock. He adapted the water-powered clock invented in the Tang period by adding a chain-driven mechanism. The clock told not only the time of day but also the day of the month, the phase of the moon, and the position of certain stars and planets in the sky. At the top was a mechanically rotated armillary sphere.

These highly educated men accepted the Confucian responsibility to aid the ruler in the governing of the country. In this period, however, this commitment tended to embroil them in unpleasant factional politics. In 1069 the chancellor Wang Anshi proposed a series of sweeping reforms designed to raise revenues and help small farmers. Many well-respected scholars and officials thought that Wang's policies would do more harm than good and resisted enforcing them. Animosities grew as critics were assigned far from the capital. Those sent away later got the chance to retaliate, escalating the conflict.

Besides politics, scholars also debated issues in ethics and metaphysics. For several centuries Buddhism had been more vital than Confucianism. Beginning in the late Tang period Confucian teachers began claiming that the teachings of the Confucian sages contained all the wisdom one needed and a true Confucian would reject Buddhist teachings. During the eleventh century many Confucian teachers gathered around them students whom they urged to set their sights not on exam success but on the higher goals of attaining the wisdom of the sages. Metaphysical theories about the workings of the cosmos in terms of *li* (principle) and *qi* (vital energy) were developed in response to the challenge of the sophisticated metaphysics of Buddhism.

Neo-Confucianism *The revival of Confucian thinking that began in the eleventh century.*

Neo-Confucianism, as this movement is generally termed, was more fully developed in the twelfth century by the immensely learned Zhu Xi (1130–1200). Besides serving in office, he wrote, compiled, or edited almost a hundred books; corresponded with dozens of other scholars; and still regularly taught groups of disciples, many of whom stayed with him for years at a time. Although he was treated as a political threat during his lifetime, within decades of his death his writings came to be considered orthodox, and in subsequent centuries candidates for the examinations had to be familiar with his commentaries on the classics.

Women's Lives

With the spread of printing, more books and more types of books survive from the Song period than from earlier periods, letting us catch more glimpses of women's lives. Song stories, documents, and legal cases show us widows who ran inns, maids sent out by their mistresses to do errands, midwives who delivered babies, pious women who spent their days chanting Buddhist sutras, nuns who called on such

Shen Gua

In the eleventh century it was not rare for Chinese men of letters to have broad interests, but few could compare to Shen Gua (1031–1095), a man who tried his hand at everything from mathematics, geography, economics, engineering, medicine, divination, and archaeology to military strategy and diplomacy.

In his youth Shen Gua traveled widely with his father, who served as a provincial official. His own career as an official, which started when he was only twenty, also took him to many places, adding to his knowledge of geography. He received a post in the capital in 1066, just before Wang Anshi's rise to power, and he generally sided with Wang in the political disputes of the day. He eventually held high astronomical, ritual, and financial posts and became involved in waterworks and the construction of defense walls. He was sent as an envoy to the Khitans in 1075 to try to settle a boundary dispute. When a military campaign that he advised failed in 1082, he was demoted and later retired to write.

It is from his book of notes that we know the breadth of his interests. In one note Shen describes how, on assignment to inspect the frontier, he made a relief map of wood and glue-soaked sawdust to show the mountains, roads, rivers, and passes. The emperor was so impressed when he saw it that he ordered all the border prefectures to make relief maps. Elsewhere Shen describes the use of petroleum and explains how to make movable type from clay. Shen Gua often applied a mathematical approach to issues that his contemporaries did not think of in those terms. He once computed the total number of possible situations on a go board, and another time he calculated the longest possible military campaign given the limits of human carriers, who had to carry their own food as well as food for the soldiers.

Shen Gua is especially known for what might be called scientific explanations. In one place, he explains the deflection of the compass from due south. In another, he identifies petrified bamboo and from its existence argues that the region where it was found must have been much warmer and more humid in ancient times. He argued against the theory that tides are caused by the rising and setting of the sun, demonstrating that they correlate rather with the cycles of the moon. He proposed switching from a lunar calendar to a solar one of 365 days, saying that even though his contemporaries would reject his idea, "surely in the fu-

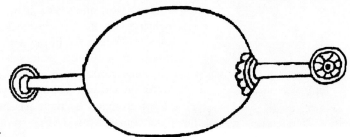

Among the advances of the Song period was the development of gunpowder. An eleventh-century manual on military technology illustrated this "thunderbolt ball," filled with gunpowder and iron scraps and hurled at the enemy with a catapult. (*Zeng Gongliang and Ding Du*, Wujing zongyao [*Zhong-guo bingshu jicheng, 1988 ed.*], 12:59, p. 640)

ture some will adopt my idea." To convince his readers that the sun and the moon were spherical, not flat, he suggested that they cover a ball with fine powder on one side and then look at it obliquely. The powder was the part of the moon illuminated by the sun, and as the viewer looked at it obliquely, the white part would be crescent shaped, like a waxing moon. Shen Gua, however, did not realize that the sun and moon had entirely different orbits, and he explained why they did not collide by positing that both were composed of *qi* (vital energy) and had form but not substance.

Shen Gua also wrote on medicine and criticized his contemporaries for paying more attention to old treatises than to clinical experience. Yet he, too, was sometimes stronger on theory than on observation. In one note he argues that longevity pills could be made from cinnabar. He reasoned that if cinnabar could be transformed in one direction, it ought to be susceptible to transformation in the opposite direction as well. Therefore, since melted cinnabar causes death, solid cinnabar should prevent death.

Questions for Analysis

1. Do you think Shen Gua's wide travels added to his curiosity about the material world?

2. In what ways could Shen Gua have used his scientific interests in his work as an official?

3. How does Shen Gua's understanding of the natural world compare to that of the early Greeks?

women to explain Buddhist doctrine, girls who learned to read with their brothers, farmers' daughters who made money by weaving mats, childless widows who accused their nephews of stealing their property, wives who were jealous of the concubines their husbands brought home, and women who used part of their own large dowries to help their husbands' sisters marry well.

Families who could afford it usually tried to keep their wives and daughters at home, where there was plenty for them to do. Not only was there the work of tending children and preparing meals, but spinning, weaving, and sewing also were considered women's work and took a great deal of time. Families that raised silkworms also needed women to do much of the work of coddling the worms and getting them to spin their cocoons. Within the home women generally had considerable say and took an active interest in issues such as the selection of marriage partners for their children.

Women tended to marry between the ages of sixteen and twenty. The husbands were, on average, a couple of years older than they were. The marriage would have been arranged by their parents, who would have either called on a professional matchmaker (most often an older woman) or turned to a friend or relative for suggestions. Before the wedding took place, written agreements would be exchanged, which would list the prospective bride's and groom's birth dates, parents, and grandparents; the gifts that would be exchanged; and the dowry the bride would bring. The goal was to match families of approximately equal status, but a young man who had just passed the civil service exams would be considered a good prospect even if his family had little wealth.

A few days before the wedding the bride's family would send to the groom's family her dowry, which at a minimum would contain boxes full of clothes and bedding. In better-off families, the dowry also would include items of substantial value, such as gold jewelry or deeds to land. On the day of the wedding the groom and some of his friends and relatives would go to the bride's home to get her. She would be elaborately dressed and would tearfully bid farewell to everyone in her family. She would be carried to her new home in a fancy sedan chair to the sound of music, alerting everyone on the street that a wedding was taking place. Meanwhile the groom's family's friends and relatives would have gathered at his home, and when the bridal party arrived, they would be there to greet them. The bride would have to kneel and bow to her new parents-in-law and later also to the tablets representing her husband's ancestors. A classical ritual still practiced was for the new couple to drink wine from the same cup. A ritual that had become popular in Song times was to attach a string to both of them, literally tying them together. Later they would be shown to their new bedroom, where the bride's dowry had already been placed, and people would toss beans or rice on the bed, symbolizing the desired fertility. After teasing them, the guests would leave them alone and go out to the courtyard for a wedding feast.

The young bride's first priority was to try to win over her mother-in-law, since everyone knew that mothers-in-law were hard to please. One way to do this was to quickly bear a son for the family. Within the patrilineal system, a woman fully secured her position in the family by becoming the mother of one of the men. Every community had older women skilled in midwifery who could be called to help when a woman went into labor. If the family was well-to-do, arrangements might be made for a wet nurse to help her take care of the newborn.

Women frequently had four, five, or six children, but likely one or more would die in infancy. If a son reached adulthood and married before the woman herself was widowed, she would be considered fortunate, for she would have always had an adult man who could take care of business for her—first her husband, then her grown son. But in the days when infectious diseases took many

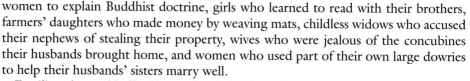

● **Woman Attendant** The Song emperors were patrons of a still-extant temple in northern China that enshrined a statue of the "holy mother," the mother of the founder of the ancient Zhou Dynasty. The forty-two maids who attend her, one of whom is shown here, seem to have been modeled on the palace ladies who attended Song emperors. (© Cultural Relics Press)

people in their twenties and thirties, it was not uncommon for a woman to be widowed while in her twenties, when her children were still very young.

A woman with a healthy and prosperous husband faced another challenge in middle age: her husband could bring home a **concubine** (more than one if he could afford it). Moralists insisted that it was wrong for a wife to be jealous of her husband's concubines, but everyone agreed that jealousy was very common. Wives outranked concubines and could give them orders in the house, but a concubine had her own ways of getting back through her hold on the husband. The children born to a concubine were considered just as much children of the family as the wife's children, and if the wife had had only daughters and the concubine had a son, the wife would find herself dependent on the concubine's son in her old age.

As a woman's children grew up, she would start thinking of suitable marriage partners. Many women liked the idea of bringing a woman from her natal family—perhaps her brother's daughter—to be her daughter-in-law. No matter who was selected, her life became easier once she had a daughter-in-law to do the cooking and cleaning. Many found more time for religious devotions at this stage of their lives. Their sons, still living with them, could be expected to look after them and do their best to make their late years comfortable.

Neo-Confucianism is sometimes blamed for a decline in the status of women in Song times, largely because one of the best known of the Neo-Confucian teachers, Cheng Yi, once told a follower that it would be better for a widow to die of starvation than to lose her virtue by remarrying. In later centuries this saying was often quoted to justify pressuring widows, even very young ones, to stay with their husbands' families and not remarry. In Song times, however, widows frequently remarried.

It is true that **foot binding** began during the Song Dynasty, but it was not recommended by Neo-Confucian teachers; rather it was associated with the pleasure quarters and with women's efforts to beautify themselves. Mothers bound the feet of girls aged five to eight with long strips of cloth to keep them from growing and to bend the four smaller toes under to make the foot narrow and arched. The hope was that the girl would be judged more beautiful. Foot binding spread gradually during Song times but was probably still largely an elite practice. In later centuries it became extremely common in north and central China, eventually spreading to all classes. Women with bound feet were less mobile than women with natural feet, but only those who could afford servants bound their feet so tightly that walking was difficult.

> **concubine** *A woman contracted to a man as a secondary spouse; although subordinate to the wife, her sons were considered legitimate heirs.*

> **foot binding** *The practice of binding the feet of girls with long strips of cloth to keep them from growing large.*

> **Primary Source:**
> **Widows Loyal Unto Death**

JAPAN'S HEIAN PERIOD (794–1185)

How did the Heian form of government contribute to the cultural flowering of the period?

As discussed in Chapter 6, during the seventh and eighth centuries the Japanese ruling house pursued a vigorous policy of adopting useful ideas, techniques, and policies from the more advanced civilization of China. The rulers built a splendid capital along Chinese lines in Nara and fostered the growth of Buddhism. Monasteries grew so powerful in Nara, however, that in less than a century the court decided to move away from them and encourage other sects of Buddhism.

The new capital was built not far away at Heian (modern Kyoto). Heian was, like Nara, modeled on the Tang capital of Chang'an (although neither of the Japanese capitals had walls, a major feature of Chinese cities), and for the first century at Heian the government continued to follow Chinese models. With the decline of the Tang Dynasty in the late ninth century, the Japanese turned away from dependence on Chinese models. The last official embassy to China made the trip in 894.

Fujiwara Rule

Only the first two Heian emperors were activists. Thereafter political management was taken over by a series of regents from the Fujiwara family, who supplied most of the empresses in this period. The emperors continued to be honored, even venerated, because of their presumed divine descent, but it was the Fujiwaras who ruled. Fujiwara dominance represented the privatization of political power and a reversion to clan politics. Political history thus took a very different course in Japan than in China, where political contenders sought the throne and successful contenders deposed the old emperor and founded new dynasties. In Japan for the next thousand years, political contenders sought to manipulate the emperors rather than supplant them.

The Fujiwaras reached the apogee of their glory under Fujiwara Michinaga (966–1027). Like many aristocrats of the period, he was learned in Buddhism, music, poetry, and Chinese literature and history. He dominated the court for more than thirty years as the father of four empresses, the uncle of two emperors, and the grandfather of three emperors. He acquired great landholdings and built fine palaces for himself and his family. After ensuring that his sons could continue to rule, he retired to a Buddhist monastery, all the while continuing to maintain control himself.

By the end of the eleventh century several emperors who did not have Fujiwara mothers found a device to counter Fujiwara control: they abdicated but continued to exercise power by controlling their young sons on the throne. This system of rule has been called **cloistered government** because the retired emperors took Buddhist orders. Thus for a time the imperial house was a contender for political power along with other aristocratic groups.

cloistered government
A system in which an emperor retired to a Buddhist monastery, but continued to exercise power by controlling his young son on the throne.

Aristocratic Culture

A brilliant aristocratic culture developed in the Heian period. It was strongly focused on the capital, where nobles, palace ladies, and imperial family members lived a highly refined and leisured life. Their society was one in which niceties of birth, rank, and breeding counted for everything. From their diaries we know of the pains aristocratic women took in selecting the color combinations of the kimonos they wore, layer upon layer. Even among men, knowing how to dress tastefully was more important than skill with a horse or sword. The elegance of one's calligraphy and the allusions in one's poems were matters of intense concern to both men and women at court. Courtiers did not like to leave the capital, and some like the court lady Sei Shonagon shuddered at the sight of ordinary working people. In her *Pillow Book,* she wrote of encountering a group of commoners on a pilgrimage: "They looked like so many basket-worms as they crowded together in their hideous clothes, leaving hardly an inch of space between themselves and me. I really felt like pushing them all over sideways."[4] (See the feature "Listening to the Past: *The Pillow Book* of Sei Shonagon" on pages 348–349.)

In this period a new script was developed for writing Japanese phonetically. Each symbol, based on a simplified Chinese character, represented one of the syllables used in Japanese (such as *ka, ki, ku, ke, ko*). Although "serious" essays, histories, and government documents continued to be written in Chinese, less formal works such as poetry and memoirs were written in Japanese. Mastering the new writing system took much less time than mastering writing in Chinese and aided the spread of literacy, especially among women in court society.

In Heian, women played important roles at all levels of society. Women educated in the arts and letters could advance at court as attendants to the rulers' consorts. Women could inherit property from their parents, and they would compete with their brothers for shares of the family property. In political life, marrying a daughter to an emperor or shogun was one of the best ways to gain power, and women often became major players in power struggles.

The literary masterpiece of this period is **The Tale of Genji**, written in Japanese by Lady Murasaki over several years (ca. 1000–1010). This long narrative depicts a cast of characters enmeshed in court life, with close attention to dialogue and personality. Murasaki also wrote a diary that is similarly revealing of aristocratic culture. In one passage she tells of an occasion when word got out that she had read the Chinese classics:

Worried what people would think if they heard such rumors, I pretended to be unable to read even the inscriptions on the screens. Then Her Majesty asked me to read to her here and there from the collected works of [the Tang Chinese poet] Bo Juyi, and, because she evinced a desire to know much more about such things, we carefully chose a time when other women would not be present and, amateur that I was, I read with her the two books of Bo Juyi's New Ballads in secret; we started the summer before last.[5]

Despite the reluctance of Murasaki and the lady she served to let others know of their learning, there were, in fact, quite a few women writers in this period. The wife of a high-ranking court official wrote a poetic memoir of her unhappy twenty-year marriage to him and his rare visits. One woman wrote both an autobiography that related her father's efforts to find favor at court and a love story of a hero who travels to China. Another woman even wrote a history that concludes with a triumphal biography of Fujiwara Michinaga.

Buddhism remained very strong throughout the Heian period. A mission sent to China in 804 included two monks in search of new texts. Saichō spent time at Mount Tiantai and brought back Tendai teachings. Tendai's basic message is that all living beings share the Buddha nature and can be brought to salvation. Tendai practices include strict monastic discipline, prayer, textual study, and meditation. Once back in Japan, Saichō established a monastery on Mount Hiei, outside Kyoto, which grew to be one of the most important monasteries in Japan. By the twelfth century this monastery and its many branch temples had vast lands and a powerful army of monk-soldiers to protect its interests. Whenever the monastery felt that its interests were at risk, it sent the monk-soldiers into the capital to parade its sacred symbols in an attempt to intimidate the civil authorities.

Kūkai, the other monk on the 804 mission to China, came back with texts from another school of Buddhism—Shingon, "True Word," a form of **Esoteric Buddhism.** Esoteric Buddhism is based on the idea that teachings containing the secrets of enlightenment had been secretly transmitted from the Buddha. An adept can gain access to these mysteries through initiation into the mandalas (cosmic diagrams), mudras (gestures), and mantras (verbal formulas). On his return to Japan, Kūkai attracted many followers and was allowed to establish a monastery at Mount Kōya, south of Osaka. The popularity of Esoteric Buddhism proved a great stimulus to art.

The Tale of Genji *A Japanese literary masterpiece written by Lady Murasaki about court life.*

Primary Source: Murasaki Shikibu, *From* **The Tale of Genji**

Primary Source: *From* **Okagami**

Esoteric Buddhism *A sect of Buddhism that maintains that the secrets of enlightenment have been secretly transmitted from the Buddha and can be accessed through initiation into the mandalas, mudras, and mantras.*

THE SAMURAI AND THE KAMAKURA SHOGUNATE (1185–1333)

What were the causes and consequences of military rule in Japan?

The rise of a warrior elite finally brought an end to the domination of the Fujiwaras and other Heian aristocratic families. In 1156 civil war broke out between the Taira and Minamoto clans, warrior clans with bases in western and eastern Japan, respectively. Both clans relied on skilled warriors, later called samurai, who were rapidly becoming a new social class. A samurai and his lord had a double bond: in return for the samurai's loyalty and service, the lord granted him land or income. From 1159 to 1181 a Taira named Kiyomori dominated the court, taking the position of prime minister and marrying his daughter to the emperor. His relatives became governors of more than thirty provinces, managed some five hundred tax-exempt estates, and amassed a fortune in the trade with Song China and Koryŏ Korea. Still, the Minamoto clan managed to defeat them, and the Minamoto leader, Yoritomo, became shogun, or general-in-chief. With him began the Kamakura Shogunate (1185–1333). This period is often referred to as Japan's feudal period because it was dominated by a military class whose members were tied to their superiors by bonds of loyalty and supported by landed estates rather than salaries.

Military Rule

The similarities between military rule in Japan and feudalism in medieval Europe have fascinated scholars, as have the very significant differences. In Europe feudalism emerged out of the fusion of Germanic and Roman social institutions and flowered under the impact of Muslim and Viking invasions. In Japan military rule evolved from a combination of the native warrior tradition and Confucian ethical principles of duty to superiors.

The emergence of the samurai was made possible by the development of private landholding. The government land allotment system, copied from Tang China, began breaking down in the eighth century (much as it did in China). By the ninth century local lords began escaping imperial taxes and control by formally giving (commending) their land to tax-exempt entities such as monasteries, the imperial family, and certain high-ranking officials. The local lord then received his land back as a tenant and paid his protector a small rent. The monastery or privileged individual received a steady income from the land, and the local lord escaped imperial taxes and control. By the end of the thirteenth century most land seems to have been taken off the tax rolls this way. Each plot of land could thus have several people with rights to shares of its produce, ranging from the cultivator, to a local lord, to an estate manager working for him, to a regional strongman, to a noble or temple in the capital. Unlike peasants in medieval Europe, where similar practices of commendation occurred, the cultivators in Japan never became serfs. Moreover, Japanese lords rarely lived on the lands they had rights in, unlike English or French lords who lived on their manors.

Samurai resembled European knights in several ways. Both were armed with expensive weapons, and both fought on horseback. Just as the knight was supposed to live according to the chivalric code, so Japanese samurai were expected to live according to **Bushido,** or "Way of the Warrior," a code that stressed military honor, courage, stoic acceptance of hardship, and, above all, loyalty. Physical hardship was accepted as routine, and soft living was despised as weak and unworthy. Disloyalty brought social disgrace, which the samurai could avoid only through *seppuku,* ritual suicide by slashing his belly.

The Kamakura Shogunate derives its name from Kamakura, a city near modern Tokyo that was the seat of the Minamoto clan. The founder, Yoritomo, ruled the country much the way he ran his own estates, appointing his retainers to newly created offices. To cope with the emergence of hard-to-tax estates, he put **military land stewards** in charge of seeing to the estates' proper operation. To bring order to the lawless countryside, he appointed **military governors** to oversee the military and enforce the law in the provinces. They supervised the conduct of the land stewards in peacetime and commanded the provincial samurai in war.

Bushido *Literally, the "Way of the Warrior," this was the code of conduct by which samurai were expected to live.*

military land stewards *Officials placed in charge of overseeing estates.*

military governors *Officials appointed to enforce the law in the provinces and oversee the samurai there.*

● **Samurai Armor** A member of the Taira clan once wore this twelfth-century set of armor. Armor had to serve the practical purpose of defense, but as in medieval Europe and medieval Islam, it was often embellished, turning armor into works of art. (*Suzanne Perrin/Japan Interlink*)

Yoritomo's wife Masako protected the interests of her own family, the Hōjōs, especially after Yoritomo died. She went so far as to force her first son to abdicate when he showed signs of preferring the family of his wife to the family of his mother. She later helped her brother take power away from her father. Thus the process of reducing power holders to figureheads went one step further in 1219 when the Hōjō family reduced the shogun to a figurehead. The Hōjō family held the reins of power until 1333.

The Mongols' two massive seaborne invasions in 1274 and 1281 (see page 300) were a huge shock to the shogunate. The Kamakura government was hard-pressed to gather adequate resources for its defense. Temples were squeezed, farmers taken away from their fields to build walls, and warriors promised generous rewards. Although the Hōjō regents, with the help of a "divine wind" (*kamikaze*), repelled the Mongols, they were unable to reward their vassals in the traditional way because little booty was found among the wreckage of the Mongol fleets. Discontent grew among the samurai, and by the fourteenth century the entire political system was breaking down. Both the imperial and the shogunate families were fighting among themselves. As land grants were divided, samurai became impoverished and took to plunder and piracy, or shifted their loyalty to local officials who could offer them a better living.

The factional disputes among Japan's leading families remained explosive until 1331, when the emperor Go-Daigo tried to recapture real power. His attempt sparked an uprising by the great families, local lords, samurai, and even Buddhist monasteries, which had thousands of samurai retainers. Go-Daigo destroyed the Kamakura Shogunate in 1333 but soon lost the loyalty of his followers. By 1338 one of his most important military supporters, Ashikaga Takauji, had turned on him and established the Ashikaga Shogunate, which lasted until 1573. Takauji's victory was also a victory for the samurai, who took over civil authority throughout Japan.

Zen *A school of Buddhism that emphasized meditation and truths that could not be conveyed in words.*

Cultural Trends

The cultural distance between the elites and the commoners narrowed a little during the Kamakura period. In this period Buddhism was vigorously spread to ordinary Japanese by energetic preachers. Hōnen propagated the Pure Land teaching (see page 152), preaching that paradise could be reached through simple faith in the Buddha and repeating the name of the Buddha Amitabha. Neither philosophical understanding of Buddhist scriptures nor devotion to rituals was essential. His follower Shinran taught that monks should not shut themselves off in monasteries but should marry and have children. Nichiren, a fiery and intolerant preacher, proclaimed that to be saved people had only to invoke sincerely the Lotus Sutra. These lay versions of Buddhism found a receptive audience among ordinary people in the countryside.

It was also during the Kamakura period that **Zen** (Chan) came to flourish in Japan. As mentioned in Chapter 6, Zen teachings originated in Tang China. Rejecting the authority of the sutras, Zen teachers claimed the superiority of mind-to-mind transmission of Buddhist truth. When Japanese monks went to

● **The Shogun Minamoto Yoritomo in Court Dress** This wooden sculpture, 27.8 inches tall (70.6 cm), was made about a half century after Yoritomo's death for use in a shrine dedicated to his memory. The bold shapes convey Yoritomo's dignity and power. *(Tokyo National Museum/image: TNM Image Archives; http://TnmArchives.jp/)*

● **The Itinerant Preacher Ippen** The monk Ippen traveled through Japan urging people to call on the Amida Buddha through song and dance. This detail from a set of twelve paintings done in 1299, a decade after his death, shows him with his belongings on his back as he approaches a village. *(Tokyo National Museum/ image: TNM Image Archives; http://TnmArchives.jp/)*

China in the twelfth century looking for ways to revitalize Japanese Buddhism, they were impressed by the rigorous monastic life of the Chan/Zen monasteries. One school of Zen held that enlightenment could be achieved suddenly through insight into one's own true nature. This school taught rigorous meditation and the use of kōan riddles to unseat logic and free the mind for enlightenment. This teaching found eager patrons among the samurai, who were attracted to its discipline and strong master-disciple bonds.

Buddhism remained central to the visual arts. Many temples in Japan still house fine sculptures done in this period. In painting, narrative handscrolls brought to life the miracles that faith could bring and the torments of Hell awaiting unbelievers. All forms of literature could be depicted in these scrolls, including *The Tale of Genji*, war stories, and humorous anecdotes.

During the Kamakura period the tradition of long narrative prose works was continued with the war tale. *The Tale of the Heike*, written by a courtier in the early thirteenth century, tells the story of the fall of the Taira family and the rise of the Minamoto clan. The tale reached a large audience because blind minstrels would chant sections of the tale to the accompaniment of the lute. The story is suffused with the Buddhist idea of the transience of life and the illusory nature of glory. Yet it also celebrates strength, courage, loyalty, and pride. The Minamoto warriors from the east are portrayed as the toughest. In one scene one of them dismisses his own prowess with the bow, claiming that other warriors from his region could pierce three sets of armor with their arrows. He then brags about the martial spirit of warriors from the east: "They are bold horsemen who never fall, nor do they let their horses stumble on the roughest road. When they fight they do not care if even their parents or children are killed; they ride over their bodies and continue the battle."[6] In this they stood in contrast to the warriors of the west who in good Confucian fashion would retire from battle to mourn their parents.

After stagnating in the Heian period, agricultural productivity began to improve in the Kamakura period, and the population grew, reaching perhaps 8.2 million by 1333. Much like farmers in contemporary Song China, Japanese farmers in this period adopted new strains of rice, often double-cropped in warmer regions, made increased use of fertilizers, and improved irrigation for paddy rice. Besides farming, ordinary people could make their livings as artisans, traders, fishermen, and entertainers. Although trade in human beings was banned, those who fell into debt might sell themselves or their children, and professional slave traders kidnapped women and children. A vague category of outcastes occupied the fringes of society. Buddhist strictures against killing and Shinto ideas of pollution probably account for the exclusion of butchers, leatherworkers, morticians, and lepers, but other groups, such as bamboo whisk makers, were also traditionally excluded for no obvious reason.

● **Zen Rock Garden** Rock gardens, such as this one at Ryoanji in Kyoto, capture the austere aesthetic of Zen Buddhism. *(Ryoanji Temple/DNP Archives)*

Chapter Summary

To assess your mastery of this chapter and read the primary sources listed in the margins, visit **bedfordstmartins.com/mckayworld** or see *Sources of World Societies*.

• What allowed China to become a world leader economically and intellectually in this period?

In the period from 800 to 1100, China's population doubled to 100 million, and its economy became increasingly commercialized. There was a huge increase in the use of money and even the introduction of paper money. Cities grew, and the economic center of China shifted from the north China plain to the south, the region drained by the Yangzi River.

• How did the civil service examinations and the scholar-official class shape Chinese society and culture?

China's great wealth could not be easily converted to military supremacy, and Song had to pay tribute to its northern neighbors. The booming economy and

Key Terms

dynastic cycle
paper money
compass
examination system
movable type
Neo-Confucianism
concubine
foot binding
cloistered government
The Tale of Genji
Esoteric Buddhism
Bushido
military land stewards
military governors
Zen

the invention of printing did allow a great expansion in the size of the educated class in the Song period, which came to dominate the government. The life of the educated class in Song times was strongly shaped by the civil service examinations, which most educated men spent a decade or more studying for, often unsuccessfully. Their high levels of education fostered interests in literature, antiquities, philosophy, and art, but may well have been a disadvantage when the times called for military leadership. Because there were more educated men, more books were written, and because of the spread of printing, a much greater share of them have survived to the present, making it possible to see dimensions of life poorly documented for earlier periods, such as the lives of women.

• *How did the Heian form of government contribute to the cultural flowering of the period?*

In marked contrast to Song China, in Heian Japan a tiny aristocracy dominated government and society. More important than the emperors were a series of regents, most of them from the Fujiwara family and fathers-in-law of the emperors. The aristocratic court society put great emphasis on taste and refinement. Women were influential at the court and wrote much of the best literature of the period. The Heian aristocrats had little interest in life in the provinces, which gradually came under the control of military clans.

• *What were the causes and consequences of military rule in Japan?*

After a civil war between the two leading military clans, a military government, called the shogunate, was established in the east. Emperors were still placed on the throne, but they had little power. During this period of military rule, culture was no longer so capital-centered, and Buddhism was vigorously spread to ordinary people. Arts that appealed to the samurai, such as war stories and Zen Buddhism, all flourished.

Suggested Reading

Bol, Peter K. *"This Culture of Ours": Intellectual Transitions in T'ang and Sung China.* 1992. A challenging inquiry into how intellectuals evaluated learning and culture.

Chaffee, John W. *The Thorny Gates of Learning in Sung China: A Social History of Examinations.* 1985. Documents the wide-ranging impact of the examination system and the ways men could improve their chances.

Ebrey, Patricia Buckley. *The Inner Quarters: Marriage and the Lives of Chinese Women in the Sung Period.* 1993. Overview of the many facets of women's lives, from engagements to dowries, childrearing, and widowhood.

Egan, Ronald. *Word, Image, and Deed in the Life of Su Shi.* 1994. A sympathetic portrait of one of the most talented men of the age.

Farris, Wayne W. *Heavenly Warriors.* 1992. Argues against Western analogies in explaining the dominance of the samurai.

Friday, Karl F. *Hired Swords.* 1992. Treats the evolution of state military development in connection with the emergence of the samurai.

Gernet, Jacques. *Daily Life in China on the Eve of the Mongol Invasion, 1250–76.* 1962. An accessible, lively introduction to the Song period.

Hansen, Valerie. *Changing the Gods in Medieval China, 1127–1276.* 1990. A portrait of the religious beliefs and practices of ordinary people in Song times.

Morris, Ivan. *The World of the Shining Prince: Court Life in Ancient Japan.* 1964. An engaging portrait of Heian culture based on both fiction and nonfiction sources.

Souyri, Pierre François. *The World Turned Upside Down: Medieval Japanese Society.* 2001. A thought-provoking analysis of both the social system and the mentalities of Japan's Middle Ages.

Notes

1. *The Travels of Marco Polo, the Venetian,* ed. Manuel Komroff (New York: Boni and Liveright, 1926), p. 227.
2. Ibid., p. 159.
3. Ibid., p. 235.
4. Ivan Morris, trans., *The Pillow Book of Sei Shonagon* (New York: Penguin Books, 1970), p. 258.
5. Quoted in M. Collcott, M. Jansen, and I. Kumakura, *Cultural Atlas of Japan* (New York: Facts on File, 1988), p. 82, slightly modified.
6. Ibid., p. 101.

Listening to the
PAST

The Pillow Book of Sei Shonagon

Beginning in the late tenth century, Japan produced a series of great women writers. At the time women were much freer than men to write in vernacular Japanese, giving them a large advantage. Lady Murasaki, author of the novel The Tale of Genji, *is the most famous of the women writers of the period, but her contemporary Sei Shonagon is equally noteworthy. Sei Shonagon served as a lady in waiting to Empress Sadako during the last decade of the tenth century (990–1000). Her only known work is* The Pillow Book, *a collection of notes, character sketches, anecdotes, descriptions of nature, and eccentric lists such as boring things, awkward things, hateful things, and things that have lost their power.*

The Pillow Book portrays the lovemaking/marriage system among the aristocracy more or less as it is depicted in The Tale of Genji. *Marriages were arranged for family interests, and men could have more than one wife. Wives and their children commonly stayed in their own homes, where their husbands and fathers would visit them. But once a man had an heir by his wife, there was nothing to prevent him from establishing relations with other women. Some relationships were long-term, but many were brief, and men often had several lovers at the same time. Some women became known for their amorous conquests, others as abandoned women whose husbands ignored them. The following passage from* The Pillow Book *looks on this lovemaking system with amused detachment.*

It is so stiflingly hot in the Seventh Month that even at night one keeps all the doors and lattices open. At such times it is delightful to wake up when the moon is shining and to look outside. I enjoy it even when there is no moon. But to wake up at dawn and see a pale sliver of a moon in the sky—well, I need hardly say how perfect that is.

I like to see a bright new straw mat that has just been spread out on a well-polished floor. The best place for one's three-foot curtain of state is in the front of the room near the veranda. It is pointless to put it in the rear of the room, as it is most unlikely that anyone will peer in from that direction.

It is dawn and a woman is lying in bed after her lover has taken his leave. She is covered up to her head with a light mauve robe that has a lining of dark violet; the colour of both the outside and the lining is fresh and glossy. The woman, who appears to be asleep, wears an unlined orange robe and a dark crimson skirt of stiff silk whose cords hang loosely by her side, as if they have been left untied. Her thick tresses tumble over each other in cascades, and one can imagine how long her hair must be when it falls freely down her back.

Nearby another woman's lover is making his way home in the misty dawn. He is wearing loose violet trousers, an orange hunting costume, so lightly coloured that one can hardly tell whether it has been dyed or not, a white robe of still silk, and a scarlet robe of glossy, beaten silk. His clothes, which are damp from the mist, hang loosely about him. From the dishevelment of his side locks one can tell how negligently he must have tucked his hair into the black lacquered headdress when he got up. He wants to return and write his next-morning letter before the dew on the morning glories has had time to vanish; but the path seems endless, and to divert himself he hums "the sprouts in the flax fields."

As he walks along, he passes a house with an open lattice. He is on his way to report for official duty, but cannot help stopping to lift up the blind and peep into the room. It amuses him to think that a man has probably been spending the night here and has only recently got up to leave, just as happened to himself. Perhaps that man too had felt the charm of the dew.

Looking around the room, he notices near the woman's pillow an open fan with a magnolia frame and purple paper; and at the foot of her curtain of state he sees some narrow strips of Michinoku paper and also some other paper of a faded colour, either orange-red or maple.

The woman senses that someone is watching her and, looking up from under her bedclothes, sees a gentleman leaning against the wall by the threshold, a smile on his face. She can tell at once that he is the

During the Heian period, noblewomen were fashion-conscious. Wearing numerous layers of clothing gave women the opportunity to choose different designs and colors for their robes. The layers also kept them warm in drafty homes. *(The Museum Yamato Bunkakan)*

sort of man with whom she need feel no reserve. All the same, she does not want to enter into any familiar relations with him, and she is annoyed that he should have seen her asleep.

"Well, well, Madam," says the man, leaning forward so that the upper part of his body comes behind her curtains, "what a long nap you're having after your morning adieu! You really are a lie-abed!"

"You call me that, Sir," she replied, "only because you're annoyed at having had to get up before the dew had time to settle."

Their conversation may be commonplace, yet I find there is something delightful about the scene.

Now the gentleman leans further forward and, using his own fan, tries to get hold of the fan by the woman's pillow. Fearing his closeness, she moves further back into her curtain enclosure, her heart pounding. The gentleman picks up the magnolia fan and, while examining it, says in a slightly bitter tone, "How standoffish you are!"

But now it is growing light; there is a sound of people's voices, and it looks as if the sun will soon be up. Only a short while ago this same man was hurrying home to write his next-morning letter before the mists had time to clear. Alas, how easily his intentions have been forgotten!

While all this is afoot, the woman's original lover has been busy with his own next-morning letter, and now, quite unexpectedly, the messenger arrives at her house. The letter is attached to a spray of bush-clover, still damp with dew, and the paper gives off a delicious aroma of incense. Because of the new visitor, however, the woman's servants cannot deliver it to her.

Finally it becomes unseemly for the gentleman to stay any longer. As he goes, he is amused to think that a similar scene may be taking place in the house he left earlier that morning.

Questions for Analysis

1. What sorts of images does Sei Shonagon evoke to convey an impression of a scene?

2. What can you learn from this passage about the material culture of Japan in this period?

3. Why do you think Sei Shonagon was highly esteemed as a writer?

Source: Ivan Morris, trans., *The Pillow Book of Sei Shonagon* (New York: Penguin Books, 1970), pp. 60–62. Copyright © 1970. Reprinted by permission of Oxford University Press.

Scenes of Agricultural Work, ca. 1190, from a German
manuscript, *Speculum Virginum.* The artist shows many tasks
and portrays the way these were shared by men, women, and
children. *(Landschaftsverband Rheinland/Rheinisches Landesmuseum, Bonn)*

EUROPE IN THE MIDDLE AGES, 850–1400

Chapter Preview

Political Developments
• How did medieval rulers overcome internal divisions and external threats, and work to create larger and more stable territories?

Revival and Reform in the Christian Church
• How did the Christian church enhance its power and create new institutions and religious practices?

The Crusades
• What were the motives, course, and consequences of the Crusades?

The Changing Life of the People
• What was life like for the common people of medieval Europe, and how were the lives of nobles and townspeople different?

The Culture of the Middle Ages
• What were the primary new cultural institutions and forms developed in medieval Europe?

Crises of the Later Middle Ages
• Why has the late Middle Ages been seen as a time of calamity and crisis?

The Italian Renaissance humanist Francesco Petrarch (1304–1374) coined the term *Middle Ages* to describe the period in European history from the end of the Roman Empire until his own time. Petrarch believed that his own age was a golden age marked by intellectual and cultural brilliance that recaptured the cultural splendor of ancient Roman civilization. Between the Roman world and the Renaissance, Petrarch believed, were the "Middle Ages," a time of Gothic barbarism and intellectual stagnation. Petrarch's terminology and time divisions have been widely adapted, but he had it wrong about barbarism and stagnation. Europeans developed new political and economic structures in the medieval period and displayed enormous intellectual energy and creative vitality.

One of the concepts that became more widely used was, in fact, the notion of "Europe." Classical geographers used the term *Europe* to distinguish this landmass from Africa and Asia, but in the medieval period the idea that there was a distinctive European culture began to take shape. While the peoples living there did not define themselves as European for centuries, a European identity began to be forged in the medieval period. That identity was shaped by interactions with other parts of the world and by Europeans' own expansion in this era.

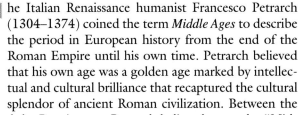

POLITICAL DEVELOPMENTS

How did medieval rulers overcome internal divisions and external threats, and work to create larger and more stable territories?

Petrarch dated the beginning of the Middle Ages to the fifth century, the time of the fall of the Roman Empire in the West. The growth of Germanic kingdoms such as those of the Merovingians and Carolingians (see page 182) are thus generally viewed as the beginning of "medieval" politics in Europe. After a period of disruption in the ninth and tenth centuries, rulers built on Carolingian models to restore order and create new systems of law and justice.

Feudalism and Manorialism

vassal *A knight who has sworn loyalty to a particular lord. Vassal is derived from a Celtic word meaning "servant."*

fief *A portion of land, the use of which was given by a lord to a vassal in exchange for the latter's oath of loyalty.*

feudalism *A medieval European political system that defines the military obligations and relations between a lord and his vassals and involves the granting of fiefs.*

manorialism *The economic system that governed rural life in medieval Europe, in which the landed estates of a lord were worked by the peasants under his jurisdiction in exchange for his protection.*

serf *A peasant who lost his freedom and became permanently bound to the landed estate of a lord.*

The large-scale division of Charlemagne's empire was accompanied by a decentralization of power at the local level. Civil wars weakened the power and prestige of kings who could do little about domestic violence. Likewise, the great invasions of the ninth century, especially the Viking invasions (see page 353), weakened royal authority. The Frankish kings could do little to halt the invaders, and the local aristocracy had to assume responsibility for defense. Common people turned for protection to the strongest power, the local counts, whom they considered their rightful rulers. Thus, in the ninth and tenth centuries great aristocratic families increased their authority.

The most powerful nobles were those able to gain the allegiance of warriors, often symbolized in an oath-swearing ceremony of homage and fealty that grew out of earlier Germanic oaths of loyalty. In this ceremony, a warrior (knight) swore his loyalty as a **vassal**—from a Celtic term meaning "servant"—to the more powerful individual, who became his lord. In return for the vassal's loyalty, aid, and military assistance, the lord promised him protection and material support. This support might be a place in the lord's household but was more likely land of the vassal's own, called a **fief** (*feudum* in Latin). The fief might contain forests, churches, and towns. The fief theoretically still belonged to the lord, and the vassal only had the use of it. Peasants living on a fief produced the food and other goods necessary to maintain the knight.

Though historians debate this, fiefs appear to have been granted extensively first by Charles Martel and then by his successors, including Charlemagne and his grandsons. These fiefs went to their most powerful nobles, who often took the title of count. As the Carolingians' control of their territories weakened, the practice of granting fiefs moved to the local level, with lay lords, bishops, and abbots as well as kings granting fiefs. This system, later named **feudalism,** was based on personal ties of loyalty cemented by grants of land rather than on allegiance to an abstract state or governmental system.

Feudalism concerned the rights, powers, and lifestyles of the military elite. **Manorialism** involved the services of the peasant class. The two were linked. The economic power of the warrior class rested on landed estates, which were worked by peasants. Peasants needed protection, and lords demanded something in return for that protection. Free farmers surrendered themselves and their land to the lord's jurisdiction. The land was given back to them to farm, but they were tied to the land by various payments and services. Those obligations varied from place to place, but certain practices became common everywhere. The peasant had to give the lord a percentage of the annual harvest, pay a fine to marry someone from outside the lord's estate, and pay a fine—usually the best sheep or cow owned—to inherit property. Most significant, the peasant lost his freedom and became a **serf,** part of the lord's permanent labor force, bound to the land and unable to leave it without the lord's permission. With large tracts of land and a small pool of labor, the most profitable form of capital was not land but laborers.

● **Homage and Fealty** Although the rite of entering a feudal relationship varied widely across Europe and sometimes was entirely verbal, we have a few illustrations of it. Here the vassal kneels before the lord, places his clasped hands between those of the lord, and declares, "I become your man." Sometimes the lord handed over a clump of earth, representing the fief, and the ceremony concluded with a kiss, symbolizing peace between them. *(Osterreichische Nationalbibliothek)*

The transition from freedom to serfdom was slow, depending on the degree of political order in a given region. By the year 800, though, perhaps 60 percent of the population of western Europe had been reduced to serfdom. While there were many economic levels within this serf class, from the highly prosperous to the desperately poor, all had lost their freedom.

Invasions and Migrations

From the moors of Scotland to the mountains of Sicily, there arose in the ninth century the prayer, "Save us, O God, from the violence of the Northmen." The Northmen, also known as Normans or Vikings, were pagan Germanic peoples from Norway, Sweden, and Denmark who had remained beyond the sway of the Christianizing and civilizing influences of the Carolingian Empire. Some scholars believe that the name *Viking* derives from the Old Norse word *vik,* meaning "creek." A Viking, then, was a pirate who waited in a creek or bay to attack passing vessels.

Viking assaults began around 800, and by the mid-tenth century the Vikings had brought large sections of continental Europe and Britain under their sway. In the east, they pierced the rivers of Russia as far as the Black Sea. In the west, they established permanent settlements on Iceland and short-lived ones in Greenland and Newfoundland in Canada (see Map 13.1).

The Vikings were superb seamen with advanced methods of boatbuilding. Propelled either by oars or by sails, deckless, and about sixty-five-feet long, a Viking ship could carry between forty and sixty men—quite enough to harass an isolated monastery or village. Against these ships navigated by thoroughly experienced and utterly fearless sailors, the Carolingian Empire, with no navy, was helpless. At first the Vikings attacked and sailed off laden with booty. Later, on returning, they settled down and colonized the areas they had conquered.

Along with the Vikings, groups of central European steppe peoples known as Magyars also raided villages in the late ninth century, taking plunder and captives and forcing leaders to pay tribute in an effort to prevent further looting and destruction. Moving westward, small bands of Magyars on horseback reached as far as Spain and the Atlantic coast. They subdued northern Italy, compelled Bavaria and Saxony to pay tribute, and penetrated even into the Rhineland and Burgundy. People thought of them as returning Huns, so the Magyars came to be known as Hungarians. They settled in the area that is now Hungary, became Christian, and in the eleventh century allied with the papacy.

From the south, the Muslims also began new encroachments, concentrating on the two southern peninsulas, Italy and Spain. In Italy the Muslims held Sicily, then drove northward and sacked Rome in 846. Most of Spain had remained under their domination since the eighth century. Expert seamen, they sailed around the Iberian Peninsula and braved the dangerous shoals and winds of the Atlantic coast. They also attacked Mediterranean settlements along the coast of Provence.

Chronology

ca. 800–950 Viking, Magyar, and Muslim attacks on Europe

1066–1087 Reign of William the Conqueror

1075–1122 Investiture controversy

1085–1248 Reconquista, the Christian reconquest of Spain from Muslims

1086 *Domesday Book*

1095–1270 Crusades

1180–1270 Height of construction of cathedrals in France

1215 Magna Carta

1225–1274 Life of Saint Thomas Aquinas, author of *Summa Theologica*

1309–1376 Papacy in Avignon

1315–1322 Famine in northern Europe

ca. 1337–1453 Hundred Years' War

1347 Black Death arrives in Europe

1358 Jacquerie peasant uprising in France

1378–1417 Great Schism

1431 Joan of Arc declared a heretic and burned at the stake

Viking, Magyar, and Muslim attacks accelerated the development of feudalism. Lords capable of rallying fighting men, supporting them, and putting up resistance to the invaders did so. They also assumed political power in their territories. Weak and defenseless people sought the protection of local strongmen. From the perspective of a person in what had been Charlemagne's empire, this was a period of chaos.

People in other parts of Europe might have had a different opinion, however. In Muslim Spain scholars worked in thriving cities, and new crops such as cotton and sugar enhanced ordinary people's lives. In eastern Europe states such as Moravia and Hungary became strong kingdoms. A Viking point of view might be the most positive, for by 1100 descendants of the Vikings not only ruled their homelands in Denmark, Norway, and Sweden, but also ruled northern France (a province known as Normandy), England, Sicily, Iceland, and Kievan Rus, with an outpost in Greenland and occasional voyages to North America.

MAP 13.1 **Invasions and Migrations of the Ninth Century** Vikings, Magyars, and Muslims all moved into central and western Europe in the ninth century, and Viking ships also sailed the rivers of Russia and the northern Atlantic ocean

● **The Bayeux Tapestry**   William's conquest of England was recorded in thread on a narrative embroidery panel measuring 231 feet by 19 inches. In this scene, two nobles and a bishop acclaim Harold Godwinson, William's rival, as king of England. The nobles hold a sword, symbol of military power, and the bishop holds a stole, symbol of clerical power. Harold himself holds a scepter and an orb, both symbols of royal power. The embroidery provides an important historical source for the clothing, armor, and lifestyles of the Norman and Anglo-Saxon warrior class. It eventually ended up in Bayeux in northern France, where it is displayed in a museum today, and is incorrectly called a "tapestry," which is a different kind of needlework. *(Tapisserie de Bayeux et avec autorisation spéciale de la Ville de Bayeux)*

The Restoration of Order

The eleventh century witnessed the beginnings of political stability in western Europe. Foreign invasions gradually declined, and in some parts of Europe rulers began to strengthen and extend their authority, creating more unified states out of the feudal system. Medieval rulers had common goals. To increase public order, they wanted to establish an effective means of communication with all peoples. They also wanted more revenue and efficient bureaucracies. The solutions they found to these problems laid the foundations for modern national states.

Political developments in England, France, and Germany provide good examples of the beginnings of the national state in the central Middle Ages. Under the pressure of Viking invasions in the ninth and tenth centuries, the seven kingdoms of Anglo-Saxon England united under one king. At the same time, England was divided into local shires, or counties, each under the jurisdiction of a sheriff appointed by the king. The kingdom of England, therefore, had a political head start on the rest of Europe.

When Edward the Confessor (r. 1042–1066) died, his cousin, Duke William of Normandy, claimed the English throne and won it by defeating his Anglo-Saxon rival at the Battle of Hastings. As William the Conqueror (r. 1066–1087) subdued the rest of the country, he distributed land to his Norman followers and required all feudal lords to swear an oath of allegiance to him as king. He retained the Anglo-Saxon institution of sheriff. The sheriff had the responsibility of catching criminals, collecting taxes, and raising soldiers for the king when ordered.

In 1085 William decided to conduct a systematic survey of the entire country to determine how much wealth there was and who had it. Groups of royal officials or judges were sent to every part of England. A priest and six local people swore an oath to answer truthfully. Because they swore (Latin, *juror*), they were called **jurors,** and from this small body of local people, the jury system in English-speaking countries gradually evolved. The records collected from the entire country, called *Domesday*

jurors   *In William the Conqueror's reign, a priest and six local people who swore an oath to answer truthfully all questions about their wealth.*

Book, provided William and his descendants with vital information for governing the country.

In 1128 William's granddaughter Matilda married Geoffrey of Anjou. Their son, who became Henry II of England, inherited the French provinces of Normandy, Anjou, and Touraine in northwestern France. When Henry married the great heiress Eleanor of Aquitaine in 1152, he claimed lordship over Aquitaine, Poitou, and Gascony in southwestern France as well. The histories of England and France were thus closely intertwined in the central Middle Ages.

In the early twelfth century France consisted of a number of nearly independent provinces, each governed by its local ruler. The work of unifying France began under Philip II (r. 1180–1223), called "Augustus" because he vastly enlarged the territory of the kingdom. By the end of his reign, Philip was effectively master of northern France. His descendants acquired important holdings in southern France, and by 1300 most of the provinces of modern France had been added to the royal domain through diplomacy, marriage, war, and inheritance.

In central Europe, the German king Otto I (r. 936–973) defeated many other lords to build up his power. The basis of Otto's power was an alliance with and control of the church. Otto asserted the right to control church appointments. Bishops and abbots had to perform feudal homage for the lands that accompanied the church office. This practice, later called **lay investiture,** led to a grave crisis in the eleventh century (see page 360). German rulers were not able to build up centralized power. Under Otto I and his successors, a sort of confederacy (a weak union of strong principalities), later called the Holy Roman Empire, developed in which the emperor shared power with princes, dukes, counts, archbishops, and bishops.

Frederick Barbarossa (r. 1152–1190) of the house of Hohenstaufen tried valiantly to make the Holy Roman Empire a united state. He made alliances with the great lay princes and even compelled the great churchmen to become his vassals. Unfortunately, Frederick did not concentrate his efforts and resources in one area. He became embroiled in the affairs of Italy, hoping to cash in on the wealth Italian cities had gained through trade. He led six expeditions into Italy, but his brutal methods provoked revolts, and the cities, allied with the papacy, defeated him in 1176. Frederick was forced to recognize the autonomy of the cities. Meanwhile, back in Germany, Frederick's absence allowed the princes and other rulers of independent provinces to consolidate their power.

lay investiture *The selection and appointment of church officials by secular authorities.*

Law and Justice

Throughout Europe in the twelfth and thirteenth centuries, the law was a hodge-podge of customs, feudal rights, and provincial practices. Kings wanted to blend these elements into a uniform system of rules acceptable and applicable to all their peoples. In France and England, kings successfully contributed to the development of national states through the administration of their laws.

The French king Louis IX (r. 1226–1270) was famous in his time for his concern for justice. Each French province, even after being made part of the kingdom of France, retained its unique laws and procedures, but Louis IX created a royal judicial system. He established the Parlement of Paris, a kind of supreme court that welcomed appeals from local administrators and from the courts of feudal lords throughout France.

Under Henry II (r. 1154–1189), England developed and extended a **common law**—a law common to and accepted by the entire country. No other country in medieval Europe did so. Each year Henry sent out *circuit judges* (royal officials who traveled in a given circuit or district) to hear civil and criminal cases. Wherever the king's judges sat, there sat the king's court. Slowly, the king's court gained jurisdiction over all property disputes and criminal actions.

common law *A law that originated in, and was applied by, the king's court.*

Proving guilt or innocence in criminal cases could pose a problem. Where there was no specific accuser, the court sought witnesses, then looked for written evidence. If the judges found neither and the suspect had a bad reputation in the community, the person went to trial by ordeal. He or she was bound hand and foot and dropped into a lake or river. Because water was supposed to be a pure substance, it would reject anything foul or unclean. Thus the innocent person would sink and the guilty person float. Because God determined guilt or innocence, a priest had to be present to bless the water. Henry disliked the system because the clergy controlled the procedure and because many suspicious people seemed to beat the system and escape punishment, but he had no alternative. Then in 1215 the church's Fourth Lateran Council forbade priests' participation in such trials, effectively ending them. Royal justice was desacralized. In the course of the thirteenth century, the king's judges adopted the practice of calling on twelve people to decide the accused's guilt or innocence. Trial by jury was only gradually accepted; medieval Europeans had more confidence in the judgment of God than in that of ordinary people.

Henry's son John (r. 1199–1216) met with serious disappointment. He lost the French province of Normandy to Philip Augustus in 1204 and spent the rest of his reign trying to win it back. Saddled with heavy debt from his father and brother Richard (r. 1189–1199), John tried to squeeze more money from nobles and town-dwellers, which created an atmosphere of resentment.

When John's military campaign failed in 1214, it was clear that the French lands that had once belonged to the English king were lost for good. His ineptitude as a soldier in a culture that idealized military glory turned the people against him. The barons revolted and in 1215 forced him to attach his seal to Magna Carta—the "Great Charter," which became the cornerstone of English justice and law.

Magna Carta signifies the principle that the king and the government shall be under the law and that everyone, including the king, must obey the law. If a government is to be legitimate, the theory emerged, then government must operate according to the *rule of law*. Some clauses of Magna Carta contain the germ of the ideas of *due process of law* and the right to a fair and speedy trial. A person may not be arbitrarily arrested and held indefinitely in prison without being accused of crime and brought to trial. Every English king in the Middle Ages reissued Magna Carta as evidence of his promise to observe the law. Centuries later, ideas of the rule of law and due process had global consequences.

> **Primary Source:**
> **King John of England,** *From* **Magna Carta:** *The Great Charter of Liberties*

REVIVAL AND REFORM IN THE CHRISTIAN CHURCH

How did the Christian church enhance its power and create new institutions and religious practices?

The eleventh century witnessed the beginnings of a remarkable religious revival. Monasteries remodeled themselves, and new religious orders were founded. After a century of corruption and decadence, the papacy reformed itself. The popes worked to clarify church doctrine and codify church law. Religion structured people's daily lives and the yearly calendar. Christianity expanded into Europe's northern and eastern regions, and Christian rulers expanded their holdings in Muslim Spain.

Monastic Reforms

The Viking, Magyar, and Muslim invaders attacked and ransacked many monasteries across Europe. Some religious communities fled and dispersed. In the period of political disorder that followed the disintegration of the Carolingian Empire, many religious houses fell under the control and domination of local feudal lords. Powerful laymen appointed themselves as abbots but kept their wives or mistresses. They took for themselves the lands and goods of monasteries, spending monastic revenues and selling monastic offices. The level of spiritual observance and intellectual activity declined.

An opportunity for reform came in 909, when William the Pious, duke of Aquitaine, established the abbey of Cluny in Burgundy. Duke William declared that the monastery was to be free from any feudal responsibilities to him or any other lord, its members subordinate only to the pope. The first two abbots of Cluny set very high standards of religious behavior and stressed strict observance of *The Rule of Saint Benedict.* Cluny gradually came to stand for clerical celibacy and the suppression of *simony* (the sale of church offices). In a disorderly world, Cluny represented religious and political stability. Laypersons placed lands under Cluny's custody and monastic houses under its jurisdiction for reform.

Deeply impressed laypeople showered gifts on monasteries with good reputations, but with this wealth came lay influence. And as the monasteries became richer, the lifestyle of the monks grew increasingly luxurious. Monastic observance and spiritual fervor declined. Soon fresh demands for reform were heard. The result was the founding of new religious orders in the late eleventh and early twelfth centuries.

The best representative of the new reforming spirit was the Cistercian order. The Cistercians combined a very simple liturgical life, a radical rejection of the traditional feudal sources of income (such as the possession of mills and serfs), and many innovative economic practices. The Cistercians' dynamic growth and rapid expansion had a profound impact on European society.

Throughout the Middle Ages, social class defined the kinds of religious life open to women and men in Europe. Kings and nobles often established convents for their daughters, sisters, aunts, or aging mothers. Entrance was restricted to women of the founder's class. (See the feature "Individuals in Society: Hildegard of Bingen.") Monks and nuns came into the convent or monastery as children.

The pattern of life within individual monasteries varied widely from house to house and from region to region. One central activity, however, was performed everywhere. Daily life centered on the *liturgy* or *Divine Office,* psalms, and other prayers, which monks and nuns prayed seven times a day and once during the night. Prayers were offered for peace, rain, good harvests, the civil authorities, the monks' and nuns' families, and their benefactors. Monastic patrons in turn lavished gifts on the monasteries, which often became very wealthy, controlling large tracts of land and the peasants who farmed them.

In the thirteenth century the growth of cities provided a new challenge for the church. Many urban people thought that the church did not fulfil their spiritual needs. They turned instead to heresies, many of which, somewhat ironically, denied the value of material wealth. Combating heresy became a principal task of new types of religious orders, most prominently the Dominicans and Franciscans, who preached, ministered to city dwellers, and also staffed the papal Inquisition, a special court designed to root out heresy. Dominicans and Franciscans also acted as missionaries in border areas of Europe, and beginning in the sixteenth century would be important agents of the spread of Christianity into European colonies around the world.

Papal Reforms

Serious efforts at papal reform began under Pope Leo IX (r. 1049–1054). He traveled widely, holding councils that issued decrees against violence, simony, and clerical marriage. Although celibacy had technically been an obligation for ordination since the fourth century, in the tenth and eleventh centuries probably a majority of European priests were married or living with a woman.

A church council produced another reform—removing the influence of Roman aristocratic factions in papal elections. Since the eighth century the priests of the

Hildegard of Bingen

The tenth child of a lesser noble family, Hildegard (1098–1179) was given when eight years old as an oblate to an abbey in the Rhineland, where she learned Latin and received a good education. She spent most of her life in various women's religious communities, two of which she founded herself. When she was a child, she began having mystical visions, often of light in the sky, but told few people about them. In middle age, however, her visions became more dramatic: "And it came to pass . . . when I was 42 years and 7 months old, that the heavens were opened and a blinding light of exceptional brilliance flowed through my entire brain. And so it kindled my whole heart and breast like a flame, not burning but warming . . . and suddenly I understood of the meaning of expositions of the books."* She wanted the church to approve of her visions and wrote first to St. Bernard of Clairvaux, who answered her briefly and dismissively, and then to Pope Eugenius, who encouraged her to write them down. Her first work was *Scivias* (Know the Ways of the Lord), a record of her mystical visions that incorporates vast theological learning (see the illustration).

Obviously possessed of leadership and administrative talents, Hildegard left her abbey in 1147 to found the convent of Rupertsberg near Bingen. There she produced *Physica* (On the Physical Elements) and *Causa et Curae* (Causes and Cures), scientific works on the curative properties of natural elements; poems; a mystery play; and several more works of mysticism. She carried on a huge correspondence with scholars, prelates, and ordinary people. When she was over fifty, she left her community to preach to audiences of clergy and laity, and she was the only woman of her time whose opinions on religious matters were considered authoritative by the church.

Hildegard's visions have been explored by theologians and also by neurologists, who judge that they may have originated in migraine headaches, as she reports many of the same phenomena that migraine sufferers do: auras of light around objects, areas of blindness, feelings of intense doubt and intense euphoria. The interpretations that she develops come from her theological insight and learning, however, not her illness. That same insight also emerges in her music, which is what she is best known for today. Eighty of her compositions survive—a huge number for a medieval composer—most of them written to be sung by the nuns in her convent, so they have strong lines for female voices. Many of her songs and chants

In one of her visions, Hildegard saw the Synagogue (the building where Jews worship) metaphorically as a very tall woman who holds in her arms Moses with the stone tablets of the Ten Commandments. *(Rheinisches Bildarchiv, Koln)*

have been recorded recently by various artists and are available on compact disk, as downloads, and on several websites.

Questions for Analysis

1. Why do you think Hildegard might have kept her visions secret? Why do you think she sought church approval for them?

2. In what ways might Hildegard's vision of Synagogue have been shaped by her own experiences? How does this vision compare with other ideas about the Jews that you have read about in this chapter?

*From *Scivias*, trans. Mother Columba Hart and Jane Bishop, *The Classics of Western Spirituallity* (New York/Mahwah: Paulist Press, 1990).

major churches around Rome had constituted a special group, called a "college," that advised the pope. They were called "cardinals," from the Latin *cardo,* or "hinge." They were the hinges on which the church turned. The Lateran Synod of 1059 decreed that these cardinals had the sole authority and power to elect the pope and that they would govern the church when the office was vacant.

By 1073 the reform movement was well advanced. That year, Cardinal Hildebrand was elected as Pope Gregory VII, and reform took on a political character. Gregory believed that the pope, as the successor of Saint Peter, was the vicar of God on earth and that papal orders were the orders of God. He insisted that the church should be completely free of lay control, and in 1075 he ordered clerics who accepted investiture from laymen to be deposed, and laymen who invested clerics to be *excommunicated*—cut off from the sacraments and the Christian community. The rulers of Europe immediately protested this restriction of their power.

The strongest reaction came from Henry IV of the Holy Roman Empire. Gregory excommunicated church officials who supported Henry, and suspended him from the emperorship. In January 1077 Henry arrived at the pope's residence in Canossa in northern Italy and, according to legend, stood outside in the snow for three days seeking forgiveness. As a priest, Gregory was obliged to grant absolution and readmit the emperor into the Christian community. Although the emperor, the most powerful ruler in Europe, bowed before the pope, Henry actually won a victory—albeit a temporary one. He regained the emperorship and authority over his subjects, but the controversy encouraged German nobles to resist any expansion in the emperor's power. The nobles gained power, subordinating knights and reducing free men and serfs to servile status. When the investiture issue was finally settled in 1122 by a compromise, the nobility held the balance of power in Germany.

Popular Religion

Religion was not simply a matter of institutions and officials in medieval Europe, but of everyday practice. Apart from the land, the weather, and local legal and social conditions, religion had the greatest impact on the daily lives of ordinary people. Religious practices varied widely from country to country and even from province to province. But nowhere was religion a one-hour-a-week affair. Most people in medieval Europe were Christian, but there were small Jewish communities scattered in many parts of Europe, as well as Muslims in the Iberian peninsula, Sicily, other Mediterranean islands, and southeastern Europe.

For Christians, the village church was the center of community life—social, political, and economic as well as religious—with the parish priest in charge of a host of activities. Every Sunday and on holy days, the villagers stood at Mass or squatted on the floor (there were no chairs), breaking the painful routine of work. The feasts that accompanied baptisms, weddings, funerals, and other celebrations were commonly held in the churchyard. Popular religion consisted largely of rituals heavy with symbolism. Before slicing a loaf of bread, the pious woman tapped the sign of the cross on it with her knife. Before planting, the village priest customarily went out and sprinkled the fields with water, symbolizing refreshment and life. Everyone participated in village processions. The entire calendar was designed with reference to Christmas, Easter, and Pentecost, events in the life of Jesus and his disciples.

Along with days marking events in the life of Jesus, the Christian calendar was filled with saints' days. **Saints** were individuals who had lived particularly holy lives and were honored locally or more widely for their connection with the divine. The cult of the saints, which developed in a rural and uneducated environment, represents a central feature of popular culture in the Middle Ages. People believed that the saints possessed supernatural powers that enabled them to perform miracles, and the saint became the special property of the locality in which his or her relics rested. Relics such as bones, articles of clothing, the saint's tears, saliva, and even the dust from the

saints *Individuals who had lived particularly holy lives and were consequently accorded great honor by medieval Christians. Saints were believed to possess the power to work miracles and were frequently invoked for healing and protection.*

saint's tomb were enclosed in the church altar. In return for the saint's healing and support, peasants would offer the saint prayers, loyalty, and gifts.

People had a strong sense of the presence of God. They believed that God rewarded the virtuous with peace, health, and material prosperity and punished sinners with disease, poor harvests, and war. Sin was caused by the Devil, who lurked everywhere and constantly incited people to evil deeds.

Increasing suspicion and hostility marked relations between religious groups throughout the Middle Ages, but there were also important similarities in the ways Christians, Jews, and Muslims in Europe understood and experienced their religions. In all three traditions, every major life transition was marked by a ceremony that included religious elements. Weddings often involved religious officials, and religious ceremonies welcomed children into the community. Death was marked by religious rituals, and the living had obligations to the dead, including prayers and special mourning periods, in all three religions.

The Expansion of Latin Christendom

The eleventh and twelfth centuries not only saw reforms in monasticism and the papacy, but also an expansion of Christianity into Scandinavia, the Baltic lands, eastern Europe, and Spain that had profound cultural consequences. Wars of expansion, the establishment of new Christian bishoprics, and the vast migration of colonists, together with the papal emphasis on a unified Christian world, brought about the gradual Europeanization of the frontier.

Latin Christian influences entered Scandinavia and the Baltic lands primarily through the creation of dioceses. This took place in Denmark in the tenth and eleventh centuries, and the institutional church spread rather quickly due to the support offered by the strong throne. Dioceses were established in Norway and Sweden in the eleventh century, and in 1164 Uppsala, long the center of the pagan cults of Odin and Thor, became a Catholic archdiocese.

Otto I (see page 356) planted a string of dioceses along his northern and eastern frontiers, hoping to pacify the newly conquered Slavs in eastern Europe. Frequent Slavic revolts illustrate the people's resentment of German lords and clerics and indicate that the church did not easily penetrate the region.

The church also moved into central Europe, first in Bohemia in the tenth century and from there into Poland and Hungary in the eleventh century. In the twelfth and thirteenth centuries thousands of settlers poured into eastern Europe. They settled in Silesia, Mecklenburg, Bohemia, Poland, Hungary, and Transylvania. New immigrants were German in descent, name, language, and law. Hundreds of small market towns populated by these newcomers supplied the needs of the rural countryside. Larger towns such as Cracow and Riga engaged in long-distance trade and gradually grew into large urban centers.

● **Almohad Banner** This finely worked embroidered banner is typical of Muslim style; it incorporates Arabic lettering on the edges and includes no representation of the human form. The Almohads were a strict Muslim dynasty from North Africa that had ruled about half of Spain in the twelfth century. In 1212 King Alfonso VIII of Castile won a decisive victory over Almohad forces at Las Navas de Tolosa, and Christian holdings in Spain increased. *(Institut Amatller d'Art Hispanic)*

The Iberian peninsula was another area of Christian expansion. About 950 Caliph Abd al-Rahman III (912–961) of the Umayyad Dynasty of Córdoba ruled most of the Iberian Peninsula. Christian Spain consisted of the small kingdoms of Castile, León, Catalonia, Aragon, Navarre, and Portugal. When civil wars erupted among Rahman's descendants, though, Muslim lands were split among several small kingdoms, and the Christian reconquest was made easier.

Fourteenth-century clerics used the term **reconquista** (reconquest) to describe what they called a sacred and patriotic crusade to wrest Spain from "alien" Muslim hands. This religious myth became part of Spanish national psychology. The reconquest took several centuries, but by 1248 Christians held all of the peninsula save for the small state of Granada.

As the Christians advanced, they changed the face of Spanish cities, transforming mosques into cathedrals and, in the process, destroying Muslim art—just as the Muslims, in the eighth century, had destroyed the pagan temples they found. The reconquista also meant the establishment of the Roman institutional church throughout Spain. Behind the advancing Christian armies came immigrants who settled in the cities that were depopulated with the expulsion of Muslims.

reconquista *A fourteenth-century term used to describe the Christian crusade to wrest Spain back from the Muslims; clerics believed it was a sacred and patriotic mission.*

Toward a Christian Society

By about 1300 frontier areas of northern and eastern Europe and Spain shared a broad cultural uniformity with the core regions of western Christendom: France, Germany, England, and Italy. The papal reform movement of the eleventh century had increased the prestige of the papacy and loyalty to it. Loyalty meant, on the local level, following the Roman liturgy, which led to a broad uniformity of religious practice across Europe.

During the reign of Pope Innocent III (1198–1216), papal directives and legates flowed to all parts of Europe. The papacy was recognized as the nerve center of a homogeneous Christian society. Europeans identified themselves as Christians and even described themselves as belonging to "the Christian race." As in the Islamic world, religion had replaced tribal and political structures as the essence of culture.

Migration and colonization, however, had a dark side. At first, legal and cultural pluralism existed: native peoples remained subject to their traditional laws, and newcomers lived under the laws of the countries from which they had come. Then, in the fourteenth century, economic tensions following the great famine and the Black Death (see pages 374–375) caused ethnic and "national" tensions to surface and multiply. In frontier regions immigrants settled in the towns, and native-born people lived in the countryside. Success in competition for openings in the guilds and for ecclesiastical offices came to be based on blood descent. Intermarriage was forbidden. Guild regulations were explicitly racist, with protectionist laws for some, exclusionist rules for others. Rulers of the Christian kingdoms of Spain passed legislation discriminating against Muslims and Jews living under Christian rule. Perhaps the harshest racial laws were in Ireland, imposed by the ruling English on the native Irish, who were denied access to the courts and basic rights and liberties.

• • • • • • • • • •

THE CRUSADES

What were the motives, course, and consequences of the Crusades?

Crusades *Holy wars sponsored by the papacy for the recovery of the Holy Land from the Muslims in the late eleventh and early twelfth centuries.*

The expansion of Christianity in the Middle Ages was not limited to Europe, but extended to the eastern Mediterranean in what were later termed **Crusades**. Crusades in the late eleventh and early twelfth centuries were wars sponsored by the papacy for the recovery of the Holy Land from the Muslims. The word *crusade* was not actually used at the time and did not appear in English until the late sixteenth century. It means

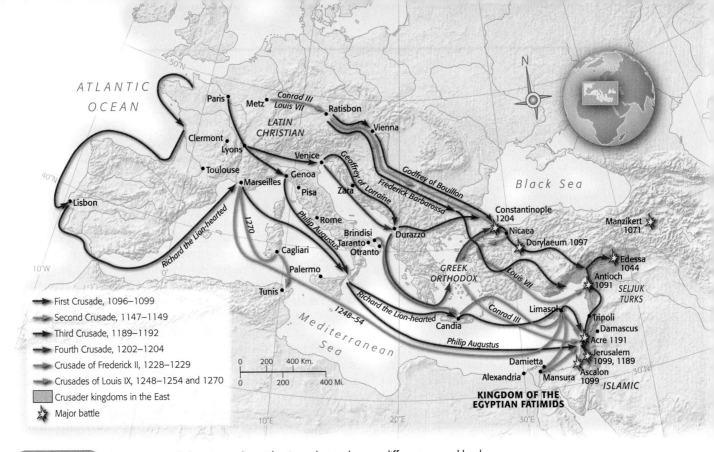

MAP 13.2 **The Routes of the Crusades** The Crusaders took many different sea and land routes on their way to Jerusalem, often crossing the lands of the Byzantine Empire, which led to conflict with eastern Christians. The Crusader kingdoms in the East lasted only briefly.

literally "taking the cross," from the cross that soldiers sewed on their garments as a Christian symbol. At the time people going off to fight simply said they were taking "the way of the cross" or "the road to Jerusalem." Although people of all ages and classes participated in the Crusades, so many knights did so that crusading became a distinctive feature of the upper-class lifestyle. In an aristocratic, military society, men coveted reputations as Crusaders; the Christian knight who had been to the Holy Land enjoyed great prestige.

Background of the Crusades

In the eleventh century the papacy had strong reasons for wanting to launch an expedition against Muslims in the East. It had been involved in the bitter struggle over church reform and lay investiture. If the pope could muster a large army against the enemies of Christianity, his claim to be leader of Christian society in the West would be strengthened. Moreover, in 1054 a serious theological disagreement had split the Greek church of Byzantium and the Roman church of the West. The pope believed that a crusade would lead to strong Roman influence in Greek territories and eventually the reunion of the two churches.

In 1071 at Manzikert in eastern Anatolia, Turkish soldiers defeated a Greek army and occupied much of Asia Minor. The emperor at Constantinople appealed to the West for support. Shortly afterward, the holy city of Jerusalem fell to the Turks. Pilgrimages to holy places in the Middle East became very dangerous, and the papacy claimed to be outraged that the holy city was in the hands of unbelievers. Since the Muslims had held Palestine since the eighth century, the papacy actually feared that the Seljuk Turks would be less accommodating to Christian pilgrims than the previous Muslim rulers had been.

In 1095 Pope Urban II called for a great Christian holy war against the infidels. He urged Christian knights who had been fighting one another to direct their energies against the true enemies of God, the Muslims. At the same time Crusaders could acquire spiritual merit and earn themselves a place in paradise. Ideas about pilgrimage, holy warfare, and the threat to Christendom were not new; Urban tied them all together.

The Course of the Crusades

Thousands of people of all classes joined the crusade. Although most of the Crusaders were French, pilgrims from many regions streamed southward from the Rhineland, through Germany and the Balkans. Of all of the developments of the High Middle Ages, none better reveals Europeans' religious and emotional fervor and the influence of the reformed papacy than the extraordinary outpouring of support for the First Crusade.

The First Crusade was successful, mostly because of the dynamic enthusiasm of the participants. The Crusaders had little more than religious zeal. They knew little of the geography or climate of the Middle East. Although there were several counts with military experience, the Crusaders could never agree on a leader. Lines of supply were never set up. Starvation and disease wracked the army, and the Turks slaughtered hundreds of noncombatants. Nevertheless, convinced that "God wills it," the war cry of the Crusaders, the army pressed on and in 1099 captured Jerusalem. Although the Crusaders fought bravely, Arab disunity was a chief reason for their victory. At Jerusalem, Edessa, Tripoli, and Antioch, Crusader kingdoms were founded on the Western feudal model (see Map 13.2).

Primary Source:
**Nicetas Choniates,
From Annals**

Between 1096 and 1270, the crusading ideal was expressed in eight papally approved expeditions to the East. Despite the success of the First Crusade, none of the later ones accomplished very much. During the Fourth Crusade (1202–1204), careless preparation and inadequate financing had disastrous consequences for Latin-Byzantine relations. In April 1204 the Crusaders and Venetians stormed Constantinople; sacked the city, destroying its magnificent library; and grabbed thousands of relics, which were later sold in Europe. The Byzantine Empire, as a political unit, never recovered from this destruction. The empire splintered into three parts and soon consisted of little more than the city of Constantinople. Moreover, the assault of one Christian people on another—when one of the goals of the crusade was reunion of the Greek and Latin churches—made the split between the churches permanent and discredited the entire crusading movement.

Much of medieval warfare consisted of the besieging of towns and castles. Help could not enter nor could anyone leave; the larger the number of besiegers, the greater was the chance the fortification would fall. Women swelled the numbers of besiegers. Women assisted in filling with earth the moats surrounding fortified places so that ladders and war engines could be brought close. In war zones some women concealed their sex by donning chain mail and helmets and fought with the knights.

In the late thirteenth century Turkish armies gradually conquered all other Muslim rulers and then turned against the Crusader states. In 1291 their last stronghold, the port of Acre, fell in a battle that was just as bloody as the first battle for Jerusalem two centuries earlier. Knights then needed a new battlefield for military actions, which some found in Spain, where the rulers of Aragon and Castile continued fighting Muslims until 1492.

Consequences of the Crusades

The Crusades provided an outlet for nobles' dreams of glory. Wars of foreign conquest had occurred before the Crusades, as the Norman Conquest of England in 1066 illustrates (see page 377), but for many knights migration began with the taking of the cross. The Crusades introduced some Europeans to Eastern luxury goods, but their immediate cultural impact on the West remains debatable. By the late eleventh century strong economic and intellectual ties with the East had already been made. The Crusades were a boon to Italian merchants, however, who profited from outfitting military expeditions as well as from the opening of new trade routes and the establishment of trading communities in the Crusader states.

The Crusades proved to be a disaster for Jewish-Christian relations. In the eleventh century Jews played a major role in the international trade between the Muslim Middle East and the West. Jews also lent money to peasants, townspeople, and nobles. When the First Crusade was launched, many poor knights had to borrow from Jews to equip themselves for the expedition. Debt bred resentment. Hostility to Jews was further enhanced by Christian beliefs that they engaged in the ritual murder of Christians to use their blood in religious rituals. Such accusations led to the killing of Jewish families and sometimes entire Jewish communities, sometimes by burning people alive in the synagogue or Jewish section of town.

Legal restrictions on Jews gradually increased. Jews were forbidden to have Christian servants or employees, to hold public office, to appear in public on Christian holy days, or to enter Christian parts of town without a badge marking them as Jews.

The Crusades also left an inheritance of deep bitterness in Christian-Muslim relations. Each side dehumanized the other, viewing those who followed the other religion as unbelievers. (See the feature "Listening to the Past: An Arab View of the Crusades" on pages 384–385.) Whereas Europeans perceived the Crusades as sacred religious movements, Muslims saw them as expansionist and imperialistic. The ideal of a sacred mission to conquer or convert Muslim peoples entered Europeans' consciousness and became a continuing goal. When in 1492 Christopher Columbus sailed west, hoping to reach India, he used the language of the Crusades in his diaries, which show that he was preoccupied with the conquest of Jerusalem (see Chapter 15). Columbus wanted to establish a Christian base in India from which a new crusade against Islam could be launched.

● ● ● ● ● ● ● ● ● ● ● ● ● ● ● ●

THE CHANGING LIFE OF THE PEOPLE

What was life like for the common people of medieval Europe, and how were the lives of nobles and townspeople different?

In the late ninth century medieval intellectuals described Christian society as composed of those who pray (the monks), those who fight (the nobles), and those who work (the peasants). This image of society became popular in the Middle Ages, especially among people who were worried about the changes they saw around them. They asserted that the three orders had been established by God and that every person had been assigned a fixed place in the social order.

The tripartite model does not fully describe medieval society, however. There were degrees of wealth and status within each group. The model does not take townspeople and the emerging commercial classes into consideration. It completely excludes those who were not Christian, such as Jews, Muslims, and pagans. Those who used the model, generally bishops and other church officials, ignored the fact that each of these groups was made up of both women and men; they spoke only of warriors, monks, and farmers. Despite—or perhaps because of—these limitations, the model of the three orders was a powerful mental construct. We can use it to organize our investigation of life in the Middle Ages, though we can broaden our categories to include groups and issues that medieval authors did not. (See page 358 for discussion of the life of monks—"those who pray.")

Those Who Work

The men and women who worked the land in the twelfth and thirteenth centuries made up the overwhelming majority of the population, probably more than 90 percent. The evolution of localized feudal systems into more centralized states had relatively little impact on the daily lives of peasants except when it involved warfare. While only nobles fought, their battles often destroyed the houses, barns, and fields of ordinary people, who might also be killed either directly or as a result of the famine and disease that often accompanied war. People might seek protection in the local castle during times of warfare, but typically they worked and lived without paying much attention to the political developments underway there.

This lack of attention went in the other direction as well. Since villagers did not perform what were considered "noble" deeds, the aristocratic monks and clerics who wrote the records that serve as historical sources did not spend time or precious writing materials on them. So it is more difficult to find information on the vast majority of Europeans who were peasants than on the small group at the top of society.

Medieval theologians lumped everyone who worked the land into the category of "those who work," but in fact there were many levels of peasants, ranging from complete slaves to free and very rich farmers. Slaves were found in western Europe in the central Middle Ages, but in steadily declining numbers. That the word *slave* derives from *Slav* attests to the widespread trade in men and women from the Slavic areas. Legal language differed considerably from place to place, and the distinction between slave and serf was not always clear. Both lacked freedom—the power to do as they wished—and both were subject to the arbitrary will of one person, the lord. A serf, however, could not be bought and sold like an animal or an inanimate object, as a slave could.

The serf was required to perform labor services on the lord's land. The number of workdays varied, but it was usually three days a week except in the planting or harvest seasons, when it increased. Serfs frequently had to pay arbitrary levies, as for marriage or inheritance. The precise amounts of tax paid to the lord depended on local custom and tradition. A free person had to do none of these things. For his or her landholding, rent had to be paid to the lord, and that was often the sole obligation. A free person could move and live as he or she wished.

Serfdom was a hereditary condition. A person born a serf was likely to die a serf, though many serfs did secure their freedom. More than anything else, the economic revival that began in the eleventh century (see pages 368–371) advanced the cause of freedom for serfs. The revival saw the rise of towns, increased land productivity, the growth of long-distance trade, and the development of a money economy. With the advent of a money economy, serfs could save money and, through a third-person intermediary, use it to buy their freedom. Many energetic and hard-working serfs acquired their freedom through this method of manumission in the High Middle Ages.

The thirteenth century witnessed enormous immigration to many parts of Europe that previously had been sparsely settled. Immigration and colonization provided the opportunity for freedom and social mobility.

Another opportunity for increased personal freedom, or at least for a reduction in traditional manorial obligations and dues, was provided by the reclamation of wasteland and forestland in the eleventh and twelfth centuries. Marshes and fens were drained and slowly made arable. This type of agricultural advancement frequently improved the peasants' social and legal condition.

In the Middle Ages most European peasants, free and unfree, lived on a manor, the estate of a lord (see page 352). The manor was the basic unit of medieval rural organization and the center of rural life. The arable land of the manor was divided into two sections. The *demesne,* or home farm, was cultivated by the peasants for the lord. The other, usually larger, section was held by the peasantry. All the arable land, both the lord's and the peasants', was divided into strips, and the strips belonging to any

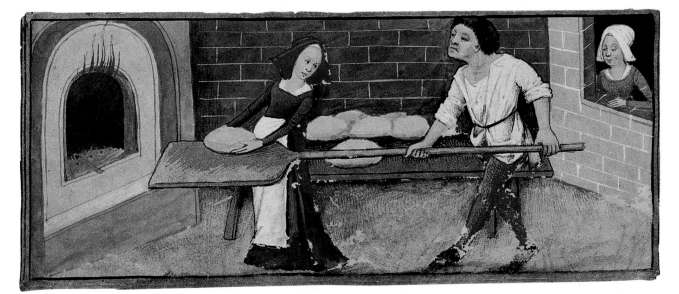

● **Baking Bread** Bread and beer or ale were the main manorial products for local consumption. While women dominated the making of ale and beer, men and women cooperated in the making and baking of bread—the staple of the diet. Most people did not have ovens in their own homes because of the danger of fire, but used the communal manorial oven, which, like a modern pizza oven, could bake several loaves at once. *(Bibliothèque nationale de France)*

given individual were scattered throughout the manor. All peasants cooperated in the cultivation of the land, working it as a group. All shared in any disaster as well as in any large harvest.

The peasants' work was typically divided according to gender. Men were responsible for clearing new land, plowing, and caring for large animals, and women were responsible for the care of small animals, spinning, and food preparation. Both sexes harvested and planted, though often there were gender-specific tasks within each of these major undertakings. Women and men worked in the vineyards and in the harvest and preparation of crops needed by the textile industry—flax and plants used for dyeing cloth.

Scholars have recently spent much energy investigating the structure of medieval peasant households. It appears that in western and central Europe a peasant household consisted of a simple nuclear family: a married couple alone or with a couple of children, or a widow or widower with children. The typical household numbered about five people, and blended households with half-siblings and step-parents were common, as death frequently took a first spouse and the survivor remarried.

The mainstay of the diet for peasants everywhere—and for all other classes—was bread. The diet of those living in an area with access to a river, lake, or stream was supplemented with fish, which could be preserved by salting. In many places, severe laws against hunting and trapping in the forests restricted deer and other game to the king and nobility. Except for the rare chicken or illegally caught wild game, meat appeared on the table only on the great feast days of the Christian year: Christmas, Easter, and Pentecost. Some scholars believe that by the mid-thirteenth century, there was a great increase in the consumption of meat generally. If so, this improvement in diet is evidence of an improved standard of living.

Those Who Fight

The nobility, though a small fraction of the total population, strongly influenced all aspects of medieval culture—political, economic, religious, educational, and artistic.

● **Saint Maurice** Certain individuals were held up to young men as models of ideal chivalry. One of these was Saint Maurice (d. 287), a soldier apparently executed by the Romans for refusing to renounce his Christian faith. He first emerges in the Carolingian period, and later he was held up as a model knight and declared a patron of the Holy Roman Empire and protector of the imperial (German) army in wars against the pagan Slavs. Until 1240 he was portrayed as a white man, but after that he was usually represented as a black man, as in this sandstone statue from Magdeburg Cathedral (ca. 1250). We have no idea why this change happened. Who commissioned this statue? Who carved it? Did an actual person serve as the model, and if so what was he doing in Magdeburg? *(Image of the Black Project, Harvard University/ Hickey-Robertson, Houston)*

chivalry *A code of conduct that governed the conduct of a knight, characterized by the virtues of bravery, generosity, honor, graciousness, mercy, and gallantry toward women.*

Despite political, scientific, and industrial revolutions, the nobility continued to hold real political and social power in Europe down to the nineteenth century.

Members of the nobility enjoyed a special legal status. A nobleman was free personally and in his possessions. He was limited only by his military obligation to king, duke, or prince. As the result of his liberty, he had certain rights and responsibilities. He raised troops and commanded them in the field. He held courts that dispensed a sort of justice. Sometimes he coined money for use within his territories. As lord of the people who settled on his lands, he made political decisions affecting them, resolved disputes among them, and protected them in time of attack. The liberty and privileges of the noble were inheritable, perpetuated by blood and not by wealth alone.

As a vassal a noble was required to fight for his lord or for the king when called on to do so. By the mid-twelfth century, this service was limited in most parts of western Europe to forty days a year. The noble was obliged to attend his lord's court on important occasions when the lord wanted to put on great displays, such as religious holidays or the marriage of a son or daughter.

Originally, most knights focused solely on military skills, but gradually a different ideal of knighthood emerged, usually termed **chivalry.** Chivalry was a code of conduct originally devised by the clergy to transform the crude and brutal behavior of the knightly class. It may have originated in oaths administered to Crusaders in which fighting was declared to have a sacred purpose and knights vowed loyalty to the church as well as to their lords. Other qualities gradually became part of chivalry: bravery, generosity, honor, graciousness, mercy, and eventually gallantry toward women. The chivalric ideal—and it was an ideal, not a standard pattern of behavior—created a new standard of masculinity for nobles, in which loyalty and honor remained the most important qualities, but graceful dancing and intelligent conversation were not considered unmanly.

Until the late thirteenth century, when royal authority intervened, a noble in France or England had great power over the knights and peasants on his estates. He maintained order among them and dispensed justice to them. The quality of life on the manor and its productivity were related in no small way to the temperament and decency of the lord—and his lady.

Women played a large and important role in the functioning of the estate. They were responsible for the practical management of the household's "inner economy"—cooking, brewing, spinning, weaving, caring for yard animals. When the lord was away for long periods, his wife became the sole manager of the family properties. Often the responsibilities of the estate fell permanently to her when she became a widow.

Towns and Cities

The rise of towns and the growth of a new business and commercial class was a central part of Europe's recovery after the disorders of the tenth century. The growth of towns was made possible by several factors: a rise in population; increased agricultural output, which provided an adequate food supply for new town dwellers; and a minimum of peace and political stability, which allowed merchants to transport and sell goods. The development of towns was to lay the foundations for Europe's transformation, centuries later, from a rural agricultural society into an urban industrial society—a change with global implications. In their backgrounds and abilities, townspeople represented diversity and change. Their occupations and their preoccupations were different from those of the feudal nobility and the laboring peasantry. Medieval towns had a few characteristics in common. Walls enclosed the town. (The terms *burgher* and *bourgeois* derive from the Old English and Old German words *burg, burgh, borg,* and *borough* for "a walled or fortified place.") The town had a marketplace. It was likely to have a mint for the coining of money and a court to settle disputes. In each town, many people inhabited a small, cramped area. As population increased, towns rebuilt their walls, expanding the living space to accommodate growing numbers.

The history of towns in the eleventh through thirteenth centuries consists largely of merchants' efforts to acquire liberties. In the Middle Ages *liberties* meant special privileges. For the town dweller, liberties included the privilege of living and trading on the lord's land. The most important privilege a medieval townsperson could gain was personal freedom. It gradually developed that an individual who lived in a town for a year and a day, and was accepted by the townspeople, was free of servile obligations and servile status. More than anything else, perhaps, the personal freedom that came with residence in a town contributed to the emancipation of many serfs in the central Middle Ages. Liberty meant citizenship, and, unlike foreigners and outsiders of any kind, a full citizen of a town did not have to pay taxes and tolls in the market. Obviously, this exemption increased profits.

merchant guilds *Associations of merchants and traders organized to provide greater security and minimize loss in commercial ventures.*

craft guilds *Associations of artisans and craftsmen organized to regulate the quality, quantity, and price of the goods produced as well as the number of affiliated apprentices and journeymen.*

In the acquisition of full rights of self-government, the **merchant guilds** played a large role. Medieval people were long accustomed to communal enterprises. In the late tenth and early eleventh centuries, those who were engaged in foreign trade joined together in merchant guilds; united enterprise provided them greater security and less risk of losses than did individual action. At about the same time, the artisans and craftsmen of particular trades formed their own guilds. These were the butchers, bakers, and candlestick makers. Members of the **craft guilds** determined the quality, quantity, and price of the goods produced and the number of apprentices and journeymen affiliated with the guild. Formal membership in guilds was generally limited to men, but women worked less formally in guild shops.

By the late eleventh century, especially in the towns of the Low Countries (modern Netherlands, Belgium, and Luxembourg) and northern Italy, the leaders of the merchant guilds were rich and powerful. They constituted an oligarchy in their towns, controlling economic life and bargaining with kings and lords for political independence and full rights of self-government.

Medieval cities served, above all else, as markets. In some respects the entire city was a marketplace. The place where a product was made and sold was typically the merchant's residence. Usually the ground floor was the scene of production. A window or

● **Medieval City Street**   This illumination shows a street scene of a medieval town with a barber, cloth merchants, and an apothecary all offering their wares and services on the ground floor of their household-workshops. *(Bibliothèque nationale de France)*

door opened from the main workroom directly onto the street, and passersby could look in and see the goods being produced. The merchant's family lived above the business on the second or third floor. As the business and the family expanded, the merchant built additional stories on top of the house.

Most medieval cities developed haphazardly. There was little town planning. Air and water pollution presented serious problems. Many families raised pigs for household consumption in sties next to their houses. Horses and oxen, the chief means of transportation and power, dropped tons of dung on the streets every year. It was universal practice in the early towns to dump household waste, both animal and human, into the road in front of one's house. The stench must have been abominable. Lack of space, air pollution, and sanitation problems bedeviled urban people in medieval times, as they do today. Still, people wanted to get into medieval cities because they represented opportunities for economic advancement, social mobility, and improvement in legal status.

The Expansion of Long-Distance Trade

The growth of towns went hand-in-hand with a remarkable expansion of trade, as artisans and craftsmen manufactured goods for local and foreign consumption. Most trade centered in towns and was controlled by professional traders. The transportation of goods involved serious risks. Shipwrecks were common. Pirates infested the sea-lanes, and robbers and thieves roamed almost all of the land routes. Since the risks were so great, merchants preferred to share them. A group of people would thus pool some of their capital to finance an expedition to a distant place. When the ship or caravan returned and the goods brought back were sold, the investors would share the profits. If disaster struck the caravan, an investor's loss was limited to the amount of that individual's investment.

The Italian cities, especially Venice, led the West in trade in general and completely dominated the Asian market. In 1082 Venice made an important commercial treaty with the Byzantine Empire, gaining significant trading privileges in Constantinople. The sacking of that city during the Fourth Crusade (see page 364) brought Venice vast trading rights. Venice was ideally located at the northwestern end of the Adriatic Sea, with easy access to the transalpine land routes as well as the Adriatic and Mediterranean sea-lanes. The markets of North Africa, Byzantium, and Russia and the great fairs of Ghent in Flanders and Champagne in France provided commercial opportunities that Venice quickly seized. Venetian ships carried salt from the Venetian lagoon, pepper and other spices from North Africa, and slaves, silk, and purple textiles from the East to northern and western Europe. Wealthy European consumers had greater access to foreign luxuries, and their tastes became more sophisticated.

Merchants from other cities in northern Italy such as Florence and Milan were also important traders, and they developed new business procedures that facilitated the movement of goods and money. The towns of Bruges, Ghent, and Ypres in Flanders were also leaders in long-distance trade and built up a vast industry in the manufacture of cloth. This was made easier by Flanders' geographical situation. Just across the Channel from England, Flanders had easy access to English wool.

Wool was the cornerstone of the English medieval economy. Population growth in the twelfth century and the success of the Flemish and Italian textile industries created foreign demand for English wool. The production of English wool stimulated Flemish manufacturing, and the expansion of the Flemish cloth industry in turn spurred the production of English wool. The availability of raw wool also encouraged the development of domestic cloth manufacture within England, and commercial families in these towns grew fabulously rich.

Hanseatic League *A mercantile association of towns that allowed for mutual protection and security.*

In much of northern Europe, the **Hanseatic League** (known as the Hansa for short), a mercantile association of towns formed to achieve mutual security and exclusive trading rights, controlled trade. During the thirteenth century perhaps two hundred cities from Holland to Poland joined the league, but Lübeck always remained the dominant member. The ships of the Hansa cities carried furs, wax, copper, fish, grain, timber, and wine. These goods were exchanged for finished products, mainly cloth and salt, from western cities. At cities such as Bruges and London, Hanseatic merchants secured special trading concessions exempting them from all tolls and allowing them to trade at local fairs. Hanseatic merchants established foreign trading centers, which they called "factories." The term *factory* was subsequently used in the seventeenth and eighteenth centuries to mean business offices and places in Asia and Africa where goods were stored and slaves held before being shipped to Europe or the Americas. (See Table 9.1 on page 237 for the size of the trans-Saharan slave trade.)

These developments added up to what is often called the **commercial revolution.** In giving the transformation this name, historians point not only to an increase in the sheer volume of trade and in the complexity and sophistication of business procedures, but also to the new attitude toward business and making money. Some even detect a "capitalist spirit" in which making a profit is regarded as a good thing in itself, regardless of the uses to which that profit is put.

commercial revolution *The transformation of the economic structure of Europe, beginning in the eleventh century, from a rural, manorial society to a more complex mercantile society.*

The commercial revolution created a great deal of new wealth, which did not escape the attention of kings and other rulers. Wealth could be taxed, and through taxation kings could create strong and centralized states. In the years to come, alliances with the middle classes were to enable kings to defeat feudal powers and aristocratic interests and to build the states that came to be called "modern."

The commercial revolution also provided the opportunity for thousands of serfs to improve their social position. The slow but steady transformation of European society from almost completely rural and isolated to relatively more sophisticated constituted the greatest effect of the commercial revolution that began in the eleventh century.

THE CULTURE OF THE MIDDLE AGES

What were the primary new cultural institutions and forms developed in medieval Europe?

Just as the first strong secular states emerged in the thirteenth century, so did the first universities. This was no coincidence. The new bureaucratic states and the church needed educated administrators, and universities were a response to this need. This period also gave rise to new styles of architecture and literature.

Universities and Scholasticism

Since the time of the Carolingian Empire, monasteries and cathedral schools had offered the only formal instruction available. Monasteries were located in rural environments and geared to religious concerns. In contrast, schools attached to cathedrals and run by the bishop and his clergy were frequently situated in bustling cities, and in the eleventh century in Bologna and other Italian cities wealthy businessmen established municipal schools. Inhabited by people of many backgrounds and "nationalities," cities stimulated the growth and exchange of ideas. In the course of the twelfth century, cathedral schools in France and municipal schools in Italy developed into universities.

The beginnings of the universities in Europe owe at least one central idea to the Islamic world. As we have seen, features in the structure of Muslim higher education bear striking parallels to later European ones (see page 214). The most significant of these developments was the **college,** which appeared in Europe about a century after its Muslim counterpart, the madrasa, in the Islamic world. First at Paris, then at Oxford in England, universities began as collections of colleges, privately endowed residences for the lodging of poor students. A medieval university was a corporation, an abstract juristic or legal entity with rights and personality. Islamic law accepted only

college *A university was made up of a collection of these privately endowed residences for the lodging of poor students.*

an actual physical person as having a legal personality. Europeans adapted their legal principles to Muslim ideas of the college, and the notion of the university emerged in the West.

The growth of the University of Bologna coincided with a revival of interest in Roman law. The study of Roman law as embodied in Justinian's *Code* had never completely died out in the West, but this sudden burst of interest seems to have been inspired by Irnerius (d. 1125), a great teacher at Bologna. Irnerius not only explained the Roman law of Justinian's *Code* but also applied it to difficult practical situations.

At Salerno, interest in medicine had persisted for centuries. Greek and Muslim physicians there had studied the use of herbs as cures and experimented with surgery. The twelfth century ushered in a new interest in Greek medical texts and in the work of Arab and Greek doctors.

In the first decades of the twelfth century, students converged on Paris. These young men crowded into the cathedral school of Notre Dame and spilled over into the area later called the Latin Quarter—whose name probably reflects the Italian origin of many of the students. The cathedral school's international reputation had already drawn to Paris scholars from all over Europe. One of the most famous of them was Peter Abélard (1079–1142). Fascinated by logic, which he believed could be used to solve most problems, Abélard used a method of systematic doubting in his writing and teaching. As he put it, "By doubting we come to questioning, and by questioning we perceive the truth." Other scholars merely asserted theological principles; Abélard discussed and analyzed them.

In northern Europe—at Paris and later at Oxford and Cambridge in England—associations or guilds of professors organized universities. University faculties grouped themselves according to academic disciplines, or schools—law, medicine, arts, and theology. The professors, known as schoolmen or **Scholastics,** developed a method of thinking, reasoning, and writing in which questions were raised and authorities cited on both sides of a question. The goal of the Scholastic method was to arrive at definitive answers and to provide a rational explanation for what was believed on faith.

Thirteenth-century Scholastics devoted an enormous amount of time to collecting and organizing knowledge on all topics. These collections were published as *summa,* or reference books. There were summa on law, philosophy, vegetation, animal life, and theology. Saint Thomas Aquinas (1225–1274), a professor at Paris, produced the most famous collection, the *Summa Theologica,* which deals with a vast number of theological questions.

At all universities, the standard method of teaching was the *lecture*—that is, a reading. The professor read a passage from the Bible, Justinian's *Code,* or one of Aristotle's treatises. He then explained and interpreted the passage; his interpretation was called a *gloss.* Students wrote down everything. Because books had to be copied by hand, they were extremely expensive, and few students could afford them. Examinations were given after three, four, or five years of study, when the student applied for a degree. Examinations were oral and very difficult. If the candidate passed, he was awarded the first, or bachelor's, degree. Further study, about as long, arduous, and expensive as it is today, enabled the graduate to try for the master's and doctor's degrees. Degrees were technically licenses to teach. Most students, however, did not become teachers. They staffed the expanding royal and papal administrations.

Scholastics *Medieval professors who developed a method of thinking, reasoning, and writing in which questions were raised and authorities cited on both sides of a question.*

Primary Source:
Thomas Aquinas,
From Summa Theologica:
On Free Will

Cathedrals

As we have seen, religious devotion was expressed through daily rituals, holiday ceremonies, and the creation of new institutions such as universities and religious orders. People also wanted permanent visible representations of their piety, and both church and city leaders wanted physical symbols of their wealth and power. These aims found their outlet in the building of tens of thousands of churches, chapels, abbeys, and, most spectacularly, **cathedrals** in the twelfth and thirteenth centuries. A cathedral is the church of a bishop and the administrative headquarters of a diocese, a church district headed by a bishop. The word comes from the Greek word *kathedra,* meaning seat, because the bishop's throne, a symbol of the office, is located in the cathedral.

Between 1180 and 1270 in France alone, eighty cathedrals, about five hundred abbey churches, and tens of thousands of parish churches were constructed. All these churches displayed a new architectural style. Fifteenth-century critics called the new style **Gothic** because they mistakenly believed that the fifth-century Goths invented it. It actually developed partly in reaction to the earlier Romanesque style, which resembled ancient Roman architecture. Cathedrals, abbeys, and village churches testify to the deep religious faith and piety of medieval people.

The inspiration for the Gothic style originated in the brain of Suger, abbot of Saint-Denis, who had decided to reconstruct the old Carolingian church at his monastery. The basic features of Gothic architecture—the pointed arch, the ribbed vault, and the flying buttress—allowed unprecedented interior lightness. From Muslim Spain, Islamic methods of ribbed vaulting seem to have heavily influenced the building of Gothic churches. Since the ceiling of a Gothic church weighed less than that of a

cathedral   *A church, headed by a bishop, which forms the administrative center of a diocese. From the Greek term* kathedra, *meaning "seat," since the cathedral housed the throne of the bishop.*

Gothic   *The term for the architectural and artistic style that prevailed in Europe from the mid-twelfth to the sixteenth century.*

● **Notre Dame Cathedral, Paris (begun 1163), View from the South**   This view offers a fine example of the twin towers (*left*), the spire, the great rose window over the south portal, and the flying buttresses that support the walls and the vaults. Like hundreds of other churches in medieval Europe, it was dedicated to the Virgin. With a nave rising 226 feet, Notre Dame was the tallest building in Europe. *(David R. Frazier/Photo Researchers, Inc.)*

Romanesque church, the walls could be thinner. Stained-glass windows were cut into the stone, so that the interior, Suger exulted, "would shine with the wonderful and uninterrupted light of most sacred windows, pervading the interior beauty."[1]

Cathedrals served secular as well as religious purposes. The sanctuary containing the altar and the bishop's chair belonged to the clergy, but the rest of the church belonged to the people. In addition to marriages, baptisms, and funerals, there were scores of feast days on which the entire town gathered in the cathedral for festivities. Local guilds met in the cathedrals to arrange business deals and to plan recreational events and the support of disabled members. Magistrates and municipal officials held political meetings there. Pilgrims slept there, lovers courted there, and traveling actors staged plays there. First and foremost, however, the cathedral was intended to teach the people the doctrines of Christian faith through visual images. Architecture became the servant of theology.

Troubadour Poetry

troubadours *Medieval poets in southern Europe who wrote and sang lyrical verses devoted to the themes of love, desire, beauty, and gallantry.*

While amateur musicians played for peasant festivities, professional musicians and poets performed and composed at the courts of nobles and rulers in medieval Europe. In southern Europe, especially in the area of southern France known as Provence, poets who called themselves **troubadours** wrote and sang lyric verses celebrating love, desire, beauty, and gallantry. The word *troubadour* comes from the Provençal word *trobar,* which in turn derives from the Arabic *taraba,* meaning "to sing" or "to sing poetry." Troubadour songs had a variety of themes. Men sang about "courtly love," the pure love a knight felt for his lady, whom he sought to win by military prowess and patience; about the love a knight felt for the wife of his feudal lord; or about carnal desires seeking satisfaction. Some poems exalted the married state, and others idealized adulterous relationships; some were earthy and bawdy, and others advised young girls to remain chaste in preparation for marriage.

Troubadours certainly felt Hispano-Arabic influences. In the eleventh century Christians of southern France were in intimate contact with the Arabized world of Andalusia, where reverence for the lady in a "courtly" tradition had long existed. Troubadour poetry represents another facet of the strong Muslim influence on European culture and life.

CRISES OF THE LATER MIDDLE AGES

Why has the late Middle Ages been seen as a time of calamity and crisis?

During the later Middle Ages, the last book of the New Testament, the book of Revelation, inspired thousands of sermons and hundreds of religious tracts. The book of Revelation deals with visions of the end of the world, with disease, war, famine, and death. It is no wonder this part of the Bible was so popular. Between 1300 and 1450 Europeans experienced a frightful series of shocks: climate change, economic dislocation, plague, war, social upheaval, and increased crime and violence. Death and preoccupation with death make the fourteenth century one of the most wrenching periods of history in Europe.

The Great Famine and the Black Death

Economic difficulties originating in the later thirteenth century were fully manifest by the start of the fourteenth. In the first decade, the countries of northern Europe experienced considerable price inflation. The costs of grain, livestock, and dairy products rose sharply. Severe weather, which historical geographers label the Little Ice Age, made a serious situation frightful. An unusual number of storms brought torrential rains, ruining the wheat, oat, and hay crops on which people and animals almost everywhere depended. Population had steadily increased in the twelfth and thirteenth centuries. The amount of food yielded, however, did not match the level of population growth. Bad weather had disastrous results. Poor harvests—one in four was likely to be poor—led to scarcity and starvation. Almost all of northern Europe suffered a terrible famine in the years 1315 to 1322. Famine had dire social consequences: peasants were forced to sell or mortgage their lands for money to buy food; the number of vagabonds, or homeless people, greatly increased, as did petty crime. An undernourished population was ripe for the Grim Reaper, who appeared in 1347 in the form of the **Black Death** (see Map 13.3).

Plague symptoms were first described in 1331 in southwestern China, part of the Mongol Empire. Plague-infested rats accompanied Mongol armies and merchant caravans carrying silk, spices, and gold across central Asia in the 1330s. Then they stowed away on ships, carrying the disease to the ports of the Black Sea by the 1340s. In October 1347 Genoese ships traveling from the Crimea in southern Russia brought the bubonic plague to Messina, from which it spread across Sicily and up into Italy. By late spring of 1348 southern Germany was attacked. Frightened French authorities chased a galley bearing the disease from the port of Marseilles, but not before plague had

Black Death *The bubonic plague that first struck Europe in 1347. It spread either in the bubonic form by flea bites or in the pneumonic form directly from the breath of one person to another. In less virulent forms, the disease reappeared many times until the early eighteenth century.*

MAP 13.3 **The Course of the Black Death in Fourteenth-Century Europe** The bubonic plague followed trade routes as it spread into and across Europe, carried by rats on board ship and in merchants' bags and parcels. A few cities that took strict quarantine measures were spared.

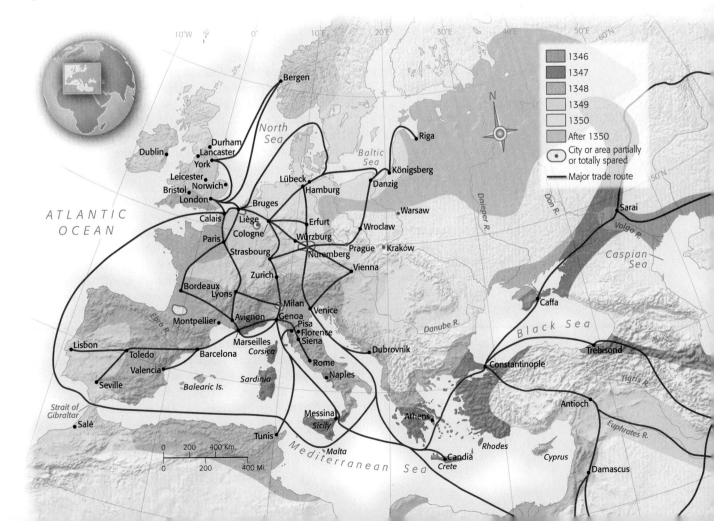

● **Procession of Saint Gregory** According to the *Golden Legend,* a thirteenth-century collection of saints' lives, the bubonic plague ravaged Rome when Gregory I was elected pope (r. 590–604). He immediately ordered special prayers and processions around the city. Here, as people circle the walls, new victims fall (center). The architecture, the cardinals, and the friars all indicate that this painting dates from the fourteenth, not the sixth, century. *(Musée Condé, Chantilly/Art Resource, NY)*

infected the city. In June 1348 two ships entered the Bristol Channel and introduced it into England. All Europe felt the scourge of this horrible disease.

Most historians and almost all microbiologists identify the disease that spread in the fourteenth century as the bubonic plague, caused by the bacillus *Yersinia pestis.* The disease normally afflicts rats. Fleas living on the infected rats drink their blood; the bacteria that cause the plague multiply in the flea's gut; and the flea passes them on to the next rat it bites by throwing up into the bite. Usually the disease is limited to rats and other rodents, but at certain points in history—perhaps when most rats have been killed off—the fleas have jumped from their rodent hosts to humans and other animals. The bacillus could also be transmitted directly from person to person through coughing.

Urban conditions were ideal for the spread of disease. Narrow streets filled with mud, refuse, and human excrement were as much cesspools as thoroughfares. Dead animals and sore-covered beggars greeted the traveler. Houses whose upper stories projected over the lower ones eliminated light and air. And extreme overcrowding was commonplace. Standards of personal hygiene remained frightfully low. Fleas and body lice were universal afflictions: one more bite did not cause much alarm. But if that nibble came from a bacillus-bearing flea, an entire household or area was doomed.

The classic symptom of the bubonic plague was a growth the size of a nut or an apple in the armpit, in the groin, or on the neck. This was the boil, or *bubo,* that gave the disease its name and caused agonizing pain. If the bubo was lanced and the pus thoroughly drained, the victim had a chance of recovery. The secondary stage was the appearance of black spots or blotches caused by bleeding under the skin. Finally, the victim began to cough violently and spit blood. This stage, indicating the presence of thousands of bacilli in the bloodstream, signaled the end, and death followed in two or three days.

Physicians could sometimes ease the pain but had no cure. Most people—lay, scholarly, and medical—believed that the Black Death was caused by some "vicious property in the air" that carried the disease from place to place. When ignorance was joined to fear and ancient bigotry, savage cruelty sometimes resulted. Many people believed that the Jews had poisoned the wells of Christian communities and thereby infected the drinking water. This charge led to the murder of thousands of Jews across Europe.

Because population figures for the period before the arrival of the plague do not exist for most countries and cities, only educated guesses can be made about mortality rates. Of a total English population of perhaps 4.2 million, probably 1.4 million died of the Black Death in its several visits. Densely populated Italian cities endured incredible losses. Florence lost between one-half and two-thirds of its population when the plague visited in 1348. The disease recurred intermittently in the 1360s and 1370s and reappeared many times down to the early 1700s.

Economic historians and demographers sharply dispute the impact of the plague on the economy in the late fourteenth century. The traditional view that the plague had a disastrous effect has been greatly modified. Many parts of Europe suffered from overpopulation in the early fourteenth century. Population decline brought increased demand for labor, which meant greater mobility among peasant and working classes. Wages rose, providing better distribution of income. Per capita wealth among those who survived increased, and some areas experienced economic prosperity as a long-term consequence of the plague.

The psychological consequences of the plague were profound. It is not surprising that some people sought release in orgies and gross sensuality, while others turned to the severest forms of asceticism and frenzied religious fervor. Groups of *flagellants,* men and women who whipped and scourged themselves as penance for their and society's sins, believed that the Black Death was God's punishment for humanity's wickedness.

The Hundred Years' War

The plague ravaged populations in Asia, North Africa, and Europe; in western Europe a long international war added further death and destruction. England and France had engaged in sporadic military hostilities from the time of the Norman Conquest in 1066, and in the middle of the fourteenth century these became more intense. From 1337 to 1453, the two countries intermittently fought one another in what was the longest war in European history, ultimately dubbed the Hundred Years' War though it actually lasted 116 years.

The Hundred Years' War had both distant and immediate causes. The immediate cause of the war was a dispute over who would inherit the French throne. The English claimed Aquitaine as an ancient feudal inheritance. In 1329 England's King Edward III (r. 1327–1377) paid homage to Philip VI (r. 1328–1350) for Aquitaine. French policy, however, was strongly expansionist, and in 1337 Philip, determined to exercise full jurisdiction there, confiscated the duchy. Edward III maintained that the only way he could exercise his rightful sovereignty over Aquitaine was by assuming the title of king of France. As the grandson and eldest surviving male descendant of Philip the Fair, he believed he could rightfully make this claim.

More distant causes included economic factors involving the wool trade and the control of Flemish towns. The wool trade between England and Flanders was the cornerstone of both countries' economies; they were closely interdependent. Flanders was a fief of the French crown, and the Flemish aristocracy was highly sympathetic to

● **Siege of the Castle of Mortagne near Bordeaux (1377)** Medieval warfare usually consisted of small skirmishes and attacks on castles. This miniature of a battle in the Hundred Years' War shows the French besieging an English-held castle, which held out for six months. Most of the soldiers use longbows, although at the left two men shoot primitive muskets above a pair of cannon. Painted in the late fifteenth century, the scene reflects military technology available at the time it was painted, not the time of the actual siege. (© British Library Board. All Rights Reserved. MS royal 14e. iv f.23)

the monarchy in Paris. But the wealth of Flemish merchants and cloth manufacturers depended on English wool, and Flemish burghers strongly supported the claims of Edward III.

The Hundred Years' War was popular because it presented unusual opportunities for wealth and advancement. Poor and unemployed knights were promised regular wages. Great nobles expected to be rewarded with estates. Royal exhortations to the troops before battles repeatedly stressed that, if victorious, the men might keep whatever they seized. The war, fought almost entirely in France and the Low Countries, consisted mainly of a series of random sieges and cavalry raids. During the war's early stages, England was highly successful, using longbows fired by foot soldiers and early cannons against French mounted knights. By 1419 the English had advanced to the walls of Paris. But the French cause was not lost. Though England scored the initial victories, France won the war.

The ultimate French success rests heavily on the actions of an obscure French peasant girl, Joan of Arc, whose vision and work revived French fortunes and led to victory. Born in 1412 to well-to-do peasants, Joan of Arc grew up in a pious household. During adolescence she began to hear voices, which she later said belonged to Saint

Michael, Saint Catherine, and Saint Margaret. In 1428 these voices told her that the dauphin (the uncrowned King Charles VII) had to be crowned and the English expelled from France. Joan went to the French court and secured the support of the dauphin for her relief of the besieged city of Orléans.

Joan arrived before Orléans on April 28, 1429. Seventeen years old, she knew little of warfare and believed that if she could keep the French troops from swearing and frequenting brothels, victory would be theirs. On May 8 the English, weakened by disease and lack of supplies, withdrew from Orléans. Ten days later, Charles VII was crowned king at Reims. These two events marked the turning point in the war.

In 1430 England's allies, the Burgundians, captured Joan and sold her to the English. The French did not intervene. The English wanted Joan eliminated for obvious political reasons, but sorcery (witchcraft) was the charge at her trial. Witch persecution was increasing in the fifteenth century, and Joan's wearing of men's clothes appeared not only aberrant but indicative of contact with the Devil. In 1431 the court condemned her as a heretic, and she was burned at the stake in the marketplace at Rouen. A new trial in 1456 rehabilitated her name. In 1920 she was canonized, and today she is revered as the second patron saint of France.

The relief of Orléans stimulated French pride and rallied French resources. As the war dragged on, loss of life mounted, and money appeared to be flowing into a bottomless pit, demands for an end increased in England. Slowly the French reconquered Normandy and finally ejected the English from Aquitaine. At the war's end in 1453, only the town of Calais remained in English hands.

The long war had a profound impact on the political and cultural lives of the two countries. Most notably, it stimulated the development of the English Parliament. Between 1250 and 1450, representative assemblies from several classes of society flourished in many European countries, but only the English Parliament became a powerful national body. Edward III's constant need for money to pay for the war compelled him to summon it many times, and its representatives slowly built up their powers.

In England and France the war promoted *nationalism*—the feeling of unity and identity that binds together a people who speak the same language, have a common ancestry and customs, and live in the same area. In the fourteenth century nationalism largely took the form of hostility toward foreigners. Both Philip VI and Edward III drummed up support for the war by portraying the enemy as an alien, evil people. Perhaps no one expressed this national consciousness better than Joan of Arc when she exulted that the enemy had been "driven out of *France*."

Challenges to the Church

In times of crisis or disaster, people of all faiths have sought the consolation of religion. While local clergy eased the suffering of many, a dispute over who was the legitimate pope weakened the church as an institution. In 1309, pressure by the French monarchy led the popes to move their court to Avignon in southern France, the location of the papal summer palace. Not surprisingly, all the Avignon popes were French, and they concentrated on bureaucratic and financial matters to the exclusion of spiritual objectives.

In 1376, one of the French popes returned to Rome, and when he died there several years later Roman citizens demanded an Italian pope who would remain in Rome. The cardinals elected Urban VI, but his tactless, arrogant, and bullheaded manner caused them to regret their decision. The cardinals slipped away from Rome and declared Urban's election invalid because it had come about under threats from the Roman mob. They elected a French cardinal, who took the name Clement VII (r. 1378–1394) and set himself up at Avignon in opposition to Urban. There were thus two popes, a situation that was later termed the **Great Schism.**

Great Schism *The period from 1378 to 1417 during which the Western Christian church had two popes, one in Rome and one in Avignon.*

The powers of Europe aligned themselves with Urban or Clement along strictly political lines. France recognized the Frenchman, Clement; England, France's historic enemy, recognized Urban. The scandal provoked horror and vigorous cries for reform. The common people—hard-pressed by inflation, wars, and plague—were thoroughly confused about which pope was legitimate. The schism weakened the religious faith of many Christians.

A first attempt to heal the schism led to a threefold schism, but finally, because of the pressure of the Holy Roman emperor Sigismund, a great council met at Constance (1414–1418). The council eventually deposed the three schismatic popes and elected a new leader, who took the name Martin V (1417–1431). Martin dissolved the council, and the schism was over. Nothing was done about reform, however, though many people hoped the council would address this. In the later fifteenth century the papacy concentrated on Italian problems to the exclusion of universal Christian interests.

Peasant and Urban Revolts

In 1358, when French taxation for the Hundred Years' War fell heavily on the poor, the frustrations of the French peasantry exploded in a massive uprising called the **Jacquerie,** after a supposedly happy agricultural laborer, Jacques Bonhomme (Good Fellow). Recently hit by plague and experiencing famine in some areas, peasants erupted in anger and frustration. Crowds swept through the countryside, slashing the throats of nobles, burning their castles, raping their wives and daughters, and killing or maiming their horses and cattle. Artisans, small merchants, and parish priests joined the peasants. Urban and rural groups committed terrible destruction, and for several weeks the nobles were on the defensive. Then the upper class united to repress the revolt with merciless ferocity. Thousands of the "Jacques," innocent as well as guilty, were cut down.

The Peasants' Revolt in England in 1381, involving perhaps a hundred thousand people, was probably the largest single uprising of the entire Middle Ages. The causes of the rebellion were complex and varied from place to place. In general, though, the thirteenth century had witnessed the steady commutation of labor services for cash rents, and the Black Death had drastically cut the labor supply. As a result, peasants demanded higher wages and fewer manorial obligations. Their lords countered with a law freezing wages and binding workers to their manors. Unable to climb higher, the peasants found release for their economic frustrations in revolt. But economic grievances combined with other factors. The south of England, where the revolt broke out, had been subjected to frequent and destructive French raids. The English government did little to protect the south, and villages grew increasingly scared and insecure. Moreover, decades of aristocratic violence, much of it perpetrated against the weak peasantry, had bred hostility and bitterness.

The straw that broke the camel's back in England was the reimposition of a head tax on all adult males. Beginning with assaults on the tax collectors, the uprising in England followed much the same course as had the Jacquerie in France. Castles and manors were sacked; manorial records were destroyed. Many nobles, including the archbishop of Canterbury, who had ordered the collection of the tax, were murdered. Urban discontent merged with rural violence. Apprentices and journeymen, frustrated because the highest positions in the guilds were closed to them, rioted.

The boy-king Richard II (r. 1377–1399) met the leaders of the revolt, agreed to charters ensuring the peasants' freedom, tricked them with false promises, and then proceeded to crush the uprising with terrible ferocity. Although the nobility tried to restore ancient duties of serfdom, virtually a century of freedom had elapsed, and the commutation of manorial services continued. Rural serfdom had disappeared in England by 1550.

Jacquerie *A massive uprising by French peasants in 1358 protesting heavy taxation.*

Conditions in England and France were not unique. In Florence in 1378 the *ciompi*, or poor propertyless workers, revolted. Serious social trouble occurred in Lübeck, Brunswick, and other German cities. In Spain in 1391 massive uprisings in Seville and Barcelona took the form of vicious attacks on Jewish communities. Rebellions and uprisings everywhere revealed deep peasant and working-class frustration and the general socioeconomic crisis of the time.

Chapter Summary

To assess your mastery of this chapter and read the primary sources listed in the margins, visit **bedfordstmartins.com/mckayworld** or see *Sources of World Societies*.

Key Terms

vassal
fief
feudalism
manorialism
serf
jurors
lay investiture
common law
saints
reconquista
Crusades
chivalry
merchant guilds
craft guilds
Hanseatic League
commercial revolution
college
Scholastics
cathedral
Gothic
troubadours
Black Death
Great Schism
Jacquerie

• How did medieval rulers overcome internal divisions and external threats, and work to create larger and more stable territories?

As Charlemagne's empire broke down, a new form of decentralized government, later known as feudalism, emerged. Local strongmen provided what little security existed. No European political power was strong enough to put up effective resistance to external attack, which came from many directions. Vikings from Scandinavia carried out raids for plunder along the coasts and rivers of Europe and traveled as far as Iceland, Greenland, North America, and Russia. In many places they set up permanent states, as did the Magyars, who came into Europe from the east. The end of the great invasions signaled the beginning of profound changes in European society. As domestic disorder slowly subsided, rulers began to develop new institutions of government and legal codes that enabled them to assert their power over lesser lords and the general population.

• How did the Christian church enhance its power and create new institutions and religious practices?

The eleventh century witnessed the beginnings of a religious revival. Monasteries remodeled themselves, and new religious orders were founded. After a century of corruption and decadence, the papacy reformed itself. The popes worked to clarify church doctrine and codify church law. Religion structured people's daily lives and the yearly calendar. Christianity expanded into Europe's northern and eastern regions, and Christian rulers expanded their holdings in Muslim Spain.

• What were the motives, course, and consequences of the Crusades?

A papal call to retake the holy city of Jerusalem led to the Crusades, nearly two centuries of warfare between Christians and Muslims. The enormous popular response to papal calls for crusading reveals the influence of the reformed papacy and a new sense that war against the church's enemies was a duty of nobles. The Crusades were initially successful, and small Christian states were established in the Middle East. These did not last very long, however, and other effects of the Crusades were disastrous. Jewish communities in Europe were regularly attacked; relations between the Western and Eastern Christian churches were poisoned by the Crusaders' attack on Constantinople; and Christian-Muslim relations became more uniformly hostile than they had been earlier.

• What was life like for the common people of medieval Europe, and how were the lives of nobles and townspeople different?

The performance of agricultural services and the payment of rents preoccupied peasants throughout the Middle Ages. Though peasants led hard lives, the reclamation of wasteland and forestlands, migration to frontier territory, or flight to a town offered a means of social mobility. Nobles were a tiny fraction of the total population, but they exerted great power over all aspects of life. Aristocratic values and attitudes, often described as chivalry, shaded all aspects of medieval culture. Medieval cities recruited people from the countryside with the promise of greater freedom and new possibilities. Cities provided economic opportunity, which, together with the revival of long-distance trade and a new capitalistic spirit, led to greater wealth, a higher standard of living, and upward social mobility for many people. Merchants and artisans formed guilds to protect their means of livelihood. Not everyone in medieval cities shared in the prosperity, however, for many residents lived hand-to-mouth on low wages.

• What were the primary new cultural institutions and forms developed in medieval Europe?

The towns that became centers of trade and production in the High Middle Ages developed into cultural and intellectual centers. Trade brought in new ideas as well as merchandise, and in many cities a new type of educational institution—the university—emerged from cathedral and municipal schools. Universities developed theological, legal, and medical courses of study based on classical models and provided trained officials for the new government bureaucracies. Economic growth meant that merchants, nobles, and guild masters had disposable income they could spend on artistic products and more elaborate consumer goods. They supported the building of churches and cathedrals as visible symbols of their Christian faith and their civic pride; cathedrals in particular grew larger and more sumptuous, with high towers, stained-glass windows, and multiple altars. University education was in Latin and limited to men, but the High Middle Ages also saw the creation of new types of vernacular literature. Poems, songs, and stories were written down in local dialects and celebrated things of concern to ordinary people. In this, the troubadours of southern France led the way, using Arabic models to create romantic stories of heterosexual love.

• Why has the late Middle Ages been seen as a time of calamity and crisis?

In the fourteenth and fifteenth centuries bad weather brought poor harvests, which contributed to the international economic depression and fostered disease. The Black Death caused enormous population losses, with social, psychological, and economic consequences. The Hundred Years' War devastated much of the French countryside and bankrupted England. When peasant frustrations exploded in uprisings, the frightened nobility crushed the revolts. But events had heightened social consciousness among the poor.

Suggested Reading

Bartlett, Robert. *The Making of Europe: Conquest, Colonization and Cultural Change, 950–1350.* 1993. A broad survey of many of the developments traced in this chapter.

Bennett, Judith M. *A Medieval Life: Cecelia Penifader of Brigstock, c. 1297–1344.* 1998. An excellent brief introduction to all aspects of medieval village life from the perspective of one woman, designed for students.

Brooke, Rosalind, and Christopher Brooke. *Popular Religion in the Middle Ages.* 1984. A readable synthesis of material on the beliefs and practices of ordinary Christians.

Glick, Leonard B. *Abraham's Heirs: Jews and Christians in Medieval Europe.* 1999. Provides information on many aspects of Jewish life and Jewish-Christian relations.

Herlihy, David. *The Black Death and the Transformation of the West,* 2d ed. 1997. A fine treatment of the causes and cultural consequences of the disease that remains the best starting point for study of the great epidemic.

Koch, H. W. *Medieval Warfare.* 1978. A beautifully illustrated book covering strategy, tactics, armaments, and costumes of war.

Lawrence, C. H. *Medieval Monasticism: Forms of Religious Life in Western Europe in the Middle Ages.* 1988. Provides a solid introduction to monastic life as it was practiced.

Madden, Thomas. *The New Concise History of the Crusades.* 2005. A highly readable brief survey by the preeminent American scholar of the Crusades.

Sawyer, Peter, ed. *The Oxford Illustrated History of the Vikings.* 1997. Provides a sound account of the Vikings by an international team of scholars.

Shahar, Shulamit. *The Fourth Estate: A History of Women in the Middle Ages,* 2d ed. 2003. Analyzes attitudes toward women and provides information on the lives of women in many situations, including nuns, peasants, noblewomen, and townswomen, in Western Europe between the twelfth and the fifteenth centuries.

Tellenbach, Gerd. *The Church in Western Europe from the Tenth to the Twelfth Century.* 1993. A very good survey by an expert on the investiture controversy.

Tuchman, Barbara. *A Distant Mirror: The Calamitous Fourteenth Century.* 1978. Written for a general audience, the book remains a vivid description of this tumultuous time.

Notes

1. E. Panofsky, trans. and ed., *Abbot Suger on the Abbey Church of St.-Denis and Its Art Treasures* (Princeton, N.J.: Princeton University Press, 1946), p. 101.

Listening to the PAST

An Arab View of the Crusades

The Crusades helped shape the understanding that Arabs and Europeans had of each other and all subsequent relations between the Christian West and the Arab world. To medieval Christians, the Crusades were papally approved military expeditions for the recovery of holy places in Palestine; to the Arabs, these campaigns were "Frankish wars" or "Frankish invasions" for the acquisition of territory.

Early in the thirteenth century, Ibn Al-Athir (1160–1223), a native of Mosul, an important economic and cultural center in northern Mesopotamia (modern Iraq), wrote a history of the First Crusade. He relied on Arab sources for the events he described. Here is his account of the Crusaders' capture of Antioch.

The power of the Franks first became apparent when in the year 478/1085–86* they invaded the territories of Islam and took Toledo and other parts of Andalusia [in Spain]. Then in 484/1091 they attacked and conquered the island of Sicily and turned their attention to the African coast. Certain of their conquests there were won back again but they had other successes, as you will see.

In 490/1097 the Franks attacked Syria. This is how it all began: Baldwin, their King, a kinsman of Roger the Frank who had conquered Sicily, assembled a great army and sent word to Roger saying: "I have assembled a great army and now I am on my way to you, to use your bases for my conquest of the African coast. Thus you and I shall become neighbors."

Roger called together his companions and consulted them about these proposals. "This will be a fine thing for them and for us!" they declared, "for by this means these lands will be converted to the Faith!" At this Roger raised one leg and farted loudly, and swore that it was of more use than their advice. "Why?" "Because if this army comes here it will need quantities of provisions and fleets of ships to transport it to Africa, as well as reinforcements from my own troops. Then,

if the Franks succeed in conquering this territory they will take it over and will need provisioning from Sicily. This will cost me my annual profit from the harvest. If they fail they will return here and be an embarrassment to me here in my own domain." . . .

He summoned Baldwin's messenger and said to him: "If you have decided to make war on the Muslims your best course will be to free Jerusalem from their rule and thereby win great honor. I am bound by certain promises and treaties of allegiance with the ruler of Africa." So the Franks made ready to set out to attack Syria.

Another story is that the Fatimids of Egypt were afraid when they saw the Seljuqids extending their empire through Syria as far as Gaza, until they reached the Egyptian border and Atsiz invaded Egypt itself. They therefore sent to invite the Franks to invade Syria and so protect Egypt from the Muslims.† But God knows best.

When the Franks decided to attack Syria they marched east to Constantinople, so that they could cross the straits and advance into Muslim territory by the easier, land route. When they reached Constantinople, the Emperor of the East refused them permission to pass through his domains. He said: "Unless you first promise me Antioch, I shall not allow you to cross into the Muslim empire." His real intention was to incite them to attack the Muslims, for he was convinced that the Turks, whose invincible control over Asia Minor he had observed, would exterminate every one of them. They accepted his conditions and in 490/1097 they crossed the Bosphorus at Constantinople. . . . They . . . reached Antioch, which they besieged.

When Yaghi Siyan, the ruler of Antioch, heard of their approach, he was not sure how the Christian people of the city would react, so he made the Muslims go outside the city on their own to dig trenches, and the next day sent the Christians out alone to continue the task. When they were ready to return

---

*Muslims traditionally date events from Muhammad's hegira, or emigration, to Medina, which occurred in 622 according to the Christian calendar.

†Although Muslims, Fatimids were related doctrinally to the Shi'ites, but the dominant Sunni Muslims considered the Fatimids heretics.

Miniature showing heavily armored knights fighting Muslims.
(Bibliothèque nationale de France)

home at the end of the day he refused to allow them. "Antioch is yours," he said, "but you will have to leave it to me until I see what happens between us and the Franks." "Who will protect our children and our wives?" they said. "I shall look after them for you." So they resigned themselves to their fate, and lived in the Frankish camp for nine months, while the city was under siege.

Yaghi Siyan showed unparalleled courage and wisdom, strength and judgment. If all the Franks who died had survived they would have overrun all the lands of Islam. He protected the families of the Christians in Antioch and would not allow a hair of their heads to be touched.

After the siege had been going on for a long time the Franks made a deal with . . . a cuirass-maker called Ruzbih whom they bribed with a fortune in money and lands. He worked in the tower that stood over the riverbed, where the river flowed out of the city into the valley. The Franks sealed their pact with the cuirass-maker, God damn him! and made their way to the water-gate. They opened it and entered the city. Another gang of them climbed the tower with their ropes. At dawn, when more than 500 of them were in the city and the defenders were worn out after the night watch, they sounded their trumpets. . . . Panic seized Yaghi Siyan and he opened the city gates and fled in terror, with an escort of thirty pages. His army commander arrived, but when he discovered on

enquiry that Yaghi Siyan had fled, he made his escape by another gate. This was of great help to the Franks, for if he had stood firm for an hour, they would have been wiped out. They entered the city by the gates and sacked it, slaughtering all the Muslims they found there. This happened in jumada I (491/April/May 1098). . . .

It was the discord between the Muslim princes . . . that enabled the Franks to overrun the country.

Questions for Analysis

1. From the Arab perspective, when did the crusade begin?

2. How did Ibn Al-Athir explain the Crusaders' expedition to Syria?

3. Why did Antioch fall to the Crusaders?

4. The use of dialogue in historical narrative is a very old device dating from the Greek historian Thucydides (fifth century B.C.E.). Assess the value of Ibn Al-Athir's dialogues for the modern historian.

Sources: P. J. Geary, ed., *Readings in Medieval History* (Peterborough, Ontario: Broadview Press, 1991), pp. 443–444; E. J. Costello, trans., *Arab Historians of the Crusades* (Berkeley and Los Angeles: University of California Press, 1969).

Index